FAMILIAR
QUOTATIONS

FROM

GREEK AUTHORS

WITH ENGLISH TRANSLATIONS

BY

CRAUFURD TAIT RAMAGE, LL.D.

"This field is so spacious that it were easy for a man to lose himself
in it; and if I should spend all my pilgrimage in this walk, my time
would sooner end than my way."—BISHOP HALL.

LONDON

GEORGE ROUTLEDGE AND SONS, LIMITED

BROADWAY, LUDGATE HILL

MANCHESTER AND NEW YORK

1895

REPUBLISHED BY GALE RESEARCH COMPANY, BOOK TOWER, DETROIT, 1968

This work also appeared under the
title *Beautiful Thoughts from
Greek authors.*

Library of Congress Catalog Card Number 68—22044

PREFACE TO SECOND EDITION.

I AM glad to find my labours continue to be appreciated by the public, as is proved by another edition of my Greek volume being called for. On this new edition I have endeavoured to bring all my previous knowledge to bear, in order that it might be rendered more in keeping with my other works. The poetical translations have been thrown aside, and in every case I have given the passage in prose.

I have illustrated it very fully by reference to my Latin volume, and have taken advantage of Duport's parallelisms from the Holy Scriptures to show the wonderful resemblance that the language of Homer bears more particularly to the sentiments found in the Old Testament. In the other Greek Authors I have also attempted to show the similarity between them and the Sacred Writers.

PREFACE TO SECOND EDITION.

The volume has been nearly doubled by the addition of new passages, and extracts from many writers have been given, which did not appear in the former edition.

PREFACE TO FIRST EDITION.

THE Editor is encouraged by the unexpected favour with which his former work has been received to bring forward a companion volume from " Greek Authors," which he ventures to hope will be found equally inter- esting. While many new topics have been introduced, the reader will here have an opportunity of tracing the original source, from which the master-spirits of Rome derived many of their finest thoughts. So true is the observation of Horace—

> " Græcia capta ferum victorem cepit et artes
> Intulit agresti Latio."

To show how closely the Romans imitated their Greek masters, the Editor has introduced copious illustrations from his former work, and has also taken advantage of Mr Grocott's valuable volume of " Index of Quotations, Ancient and Modern," to point out how much the English classic authors are indebted to the ancients for many of those gems that are scattered so profusely through their writings. Their bold flights of imagination, and the volumes of wisdom compressed into a phrase, are often but loans derived from the classical authors of Greece and Rome. It has been, therefore, an agreeable task to award to those pure and thoughtful spirits of the olden times their due meed of praise, by trying to ascertain the exact contributions which each has made to the intellectual riches of the world.

Another peculiar feature in the present work is the numerous references to the Holy Scriptures for points of resemblance. It is impossible, indeed, to examine the heathen doctrines of religion and ethics without being struck with their wonderful likeness to those which are sometimes considered to be peculiar to Christianity; here may be found many of the moral doctrines and sublime sayings of the Gospel, but there is always something wanting to give them life, and bring them home to the heart and feelings of human beings. Noble truths have always been taught by both Eastern and Western sages; yet they want that clear and perfect ring, which they possess when they are known to issue from Divine lips. The Editor has selected much from the writings of Plato, to show how far this resemblance extends; and, no doubt, he has omitted many passages which would have borne equally strong testimony that it is not without good reason that Plato has been called the " Atticising Moses."

The characteristics of the present work are very much the same as those that distinguished the former.

1. It quotes only from certain specified well-known classical authors.

2. Each passage quoted has a distinct reference to the work of the author, the book, ode, play, and, where it was practicable, the line, so that the passage may be found immediately and without difficulty.

3. To each passage there is appended an English translation by the Editor. The heading to each passage briefly indicates the subject.

4. The Editor has laboured to give a complete and elaborate English Index ; and this he hopes, as in his former volume, will be found a popular feature of the work. While it gives the subject of each passage, it indicates at the same time, with great precision, the leading idea of each quotation. He has not thought that a Greek Index would be of value, as he regrets to think

that the number of Greek scholars, to whom such an Index would be of use, are very few.

5. He has added an Index of the passages from the Holy Scriptures, which are illustrated, and which will be found useful to Biblical scholars.

6. The biographical sketches of each author are slight; but they will be found interesting to those who wish to become acquainted with the period during which the author flourished, and with the few leading facts of his life.

It has been well observed, that nothing can be more useful to young minds having capacity and high aspirations than such selections as the Editor has brought together from the works of great men. Each quotation is a separate bait, a temptation to feel greatly, and to do greatly; and a friend, whose delicate health has obliged him to retire from the busy haunts of men, very beautifully remarks that their charm for the old and infirm is scarcely less : to such " it is nothing short of delightful to have a book at hand which will suit itself either to the exigencies or the deficiencies of the minute with an elastic power of adaptability which no living friend can possess." It was for those of lofty aspirations among the young, and for men of cultivated minds among the old, that the Editor has attempted to make a selection from a treasure that has continued to accumulate from the earliest times, till it now comprehends a brief abstract of the wisdom of all ages. There is not a distinguished name that has not made some small contribution to the great mass of sentential lore; and if the Editor find that his labours continue to be appreciated, he is prepared with another volume from the vast field of literature which the classic authors of France, Italy, Spain, and Germany present.

CRAUFURD TAIT RAMAGE.

INDEX OF AUTHORS.

INDEX OF AUTHORS.

CHRONOLOGICAL INDEX OF AUTHORS.

Homerus, flourished probably about B.C. 1184		
Hesiodus, . . flourished about B.C. 850		
Tyrtæus, ... B.C. 685		
Anacreon, ... B.C. 559–525		
Theognis, ... B.C. 548		
Æschylus, . . . born B.C. 525	. died	. B.C. 456
Pindarus, . . . ,, B.C. 522	. ,,	. B.C. 442
Sophocles, . . . ,, B.C. 484	. ,,	. B.C. 406
Herodotus, . . . ,, B.C. 484	. alive	B.C. 408
Thucydides, . . ,, B.C. 470	. ,,	. B.C. 403
Euripides, . . . ,, B.C. 481	. died	. B.C. 406
Crates, . flourished about B.C. 450		
Aristophon, . . born B.C. 444	. died about B.C. 380	
Xenophon, . . born about B.C. 444	. alive	. B.C. 357
Plato, . . . born B.C. 428	. died	. B.C. 347
Archippus, . . flourished B.C. 415		
Demetrius, . flourished about B.C. 412		
Antiphanes, . born about B.C. 404	. died about B.C. 330	
Philiscus, . flourished about B.C. 400		
Æschines, . . . born B.C. 389	. died	. B.C. 314
Aristoteles, . . ,, B.C. 384	. ,,	. B.C. 322
Demosthenes, . . ,, B.C. 382	. ,,	. B.C. 322
Anaxandrides, . flourished B.C. 376		
Philemon, . . born about B.C. 360	. died	. B.C. 262
Alexis, . . . flourished B.C. 356		
Timocles, . flourished about B.C. 350		
Menander, . . . born B.C. 342	. died	. B.C. 291
Philippides, . flourished B.C. 335		
Amphis, . flourished about B.C. 332		
Nicostratus, . flourished B.C. 330		

Diphilus, . .	flourished B.C.	320
Hipparchus, .	,, B.C.	320
Apollodorus, .	,, B.C.	290
Posidippus, .	,, B.C.	289
Baton, .	flourished about B.C.	280
Bion, . . .	flourished B.C.	280
Callimachus, . .	from B.C. 280 to B.C. 245	
Theocritus, . . .	about B.C.	272
Aratus, . .	flourished B.C.	270
Moschus, .	flourished about B.C.	210
Polybius,	born probably about B.C. 204 . died . B.C. 122	
Dionysius, .	flourished from B.C. 29 to B.C. 7	
Plutarchus, . .	born about A.D. 50 . died about A.D. 120	
Antoninus, . . .	born A.D. 121 . died . A.D. 180	
Arrianus, . .	flourished A.D. 136	
Longinus, . .	born about A.D. 213 . died . A.D. 273	

BEAUTIFUL THOUGHTS

FROM

GREEK AUTHORS.

——◇——

ÆSCHINES.

BORN B.C. 389—DIED B.C. 314.

ÆSCHINES, one of the most celebrated of the Athenian orators, was the son of Tromes, the slave of a schoolmaster, Elpias, and Glaucia, who gained her livelihood by playing and singing at the sacred festivals. His father succeeded to the school of Elpias, and Æschines, in his youth, was employed by his father to clean his schoolroom. When he was somewhat older he assisted his mother in her theatrical performances, being remarkable for a strong and sonorous voice; but in this he does not seem to have been successful, as on one occasion, when he was performing in the character of Œnomäus, he was hissed off the stage. We then find him entering the military service, gaining great distinction at the battle of Mantineia, B.C. 362. It was, however, as an orator that he acquired the reputation which has handed down his name to posterity. At the commencement of his political career he took an active part against Philip of Macedon, though he became convinced, ere long, that nothing but peace with Philip would avert utter ruin from his country. His opponents accused him of having been bribed by the king to support his measures; but there does not appear any reason to believe that he acted treacherously towards his country. He was the opponent of Demosthenes; and though he failed in his attacks, it was to him that we owe the celebrated speech of Demosthenes on the crown,

A

which is considered one of the finest bursts of eloquence which the
world has ever produced. The three great speeches of Æschines
which still remain were called by the ancients the Graces. They
are distinguished by great felicity of diction, wonderful boldness
and vigour of description, so that it is generally allowed that he
was only second to Demosthenes.

DUTIES OF A JUDGE IN A FREE STATE.
Ctesiph. c. 3.

Εὖ γὰρ ἴστε, ὅτι τρεῖς εἰσὶ πολιτεῖαι παρὰ πᾶσιν ἀνθρώποις,
τυραννὶς καὶ ὀλιγαρχία καὶ δημοκρατία, διοικοῦνται δ᾽ αἱ μὲν τυ-
ραννίδες καὶ ὀλιγαρχίαι τοῖς τρόποις τῶν ἐφεστηκότων, αἱ δὲ πόλεις
αἱ δημοκρατούμεναι τοῖς νόμοις τοῖς κειμένοις. Μηδεὶς οὖν ὑμῶν
τοῦτ᾽ ἀγνοείτω, ἀλλὰ σαφῶς ἕκαστος ἐπιστάσθω, ὅτι, ὅταν εἰσίῃ εἰς
δικαστήριον γραφὴν παρανόμων δικάσων, ἐν ταύτῃ τῇ ἡμέρᾳ μέλλει
τὴν ψῆφον φέρειν περὶ τῆς ἑαυτοῦ παρρησίας.

For you ought to be well aware that there are three different
forms of government established in the world—monarchy, oligarchy, and democracy. In the two former the government is
conducted at the will of the ruling powers, while in the latter it
proceeds according to established laws. Let none of you, therefore, be ignorant, but let it be deeply engraven on the minds of
all, that when he enters the tribunal to give judgment on a case
where the law has been violated, he is that day giving sentence
on his own liberties.

See (Lat. Fr.) Judge, Law.

THE PUBLIC AND PRIVATE CHARACTER OF A STATESMAN.
Ctesiph. c. 29.

Ὁ γὰρ μισότεκνος καὶ πατὴρ πονηρὸς οὐκ ἄν ποτε γένοιτο δημαγωγὸς χρηστός, οὐδ᾽ ὁ τὰ φίλτατα καὶ οἰκειότατα σώματα μὴ
στέργων οὐδέποθ᾽ ὑμᾶς περὶ πλείονος ποιήσεται τοὺς ἀλλοτρίους,
οὐδέ γ᾽ ὁ ἰδίᾳ πονηρὸς οὐκ ἄν ποτε γένοιτο δημοσίᾳ χρηστὸς οὐδ᾽
ὅστις ἐστὶν οἴκοι φαῦλος, οὐδέποτ᾽ ἦν ἐν Μακεδονίᾳ καλὸς κἀγαθός·
οὐ γὰρ τὸν τρόπον ἀλλὰ τὸν τόπον μόνον μετήλλαξεν.

He who hates his own children, he who is a bad parent, cannot
be a good leader of the people. He who is insensible to the duties
which he owes to those who are nearest, and who ought to be
dearest, to him, will never feel a higher regard for your welfare,
who are strangers to him. He who acts wickedly in private life
can never be expected to show himself noble in his public conduct.
He who is base at home will not acquit himself with honour when
sent to a foreign country in a public capacity : for it is not the
man, but the place merely, that is changed.

See (Lat.) Statesman.

A Defeat is not the Greatest of Calamities.
Ctesiph. c. 32.

Οὐ γὰρ τὸ δυστυχῆσαι κατὰ πόλεμον μέγιστόν ἐστι κακόν · ἀλλ'
ὅταν τις πρὸς ἀνταγωνιστὰς ἀναξίους ἑαυτοῦ διακινδυνεύων ἀποτύχῃ,
διπλασίαν εἰκὸς εἶναι τὴν συμφοράν.

For a defeat in war is not the greatest of all evils ; but when
the defeat has been inflicted by enemies who are unworthy of you,
then the calamity is doubled.

See (Lat. Fr.) Disgrace.

Character of Boasters.
Ctesiph. c. 34.

Ὁι μὲν γὰρ ἄλλοι ἀλαζόνες ὅταν τι ψεύδωνται, ἀόριστα καὶ
ἀσαφῆ πειρῶνται λέγειν, φοβούμενοι τὸν ἔλεγχον.

For other boasters, when they lie, try not to speak too particularly or plainly, from fear of being disproved afterwards.

See (Lat.) Boaster, Braggart.

Integrity.
Ctesiph. c. 55.

Τήν γ' εὐγνωμοσύνην ἀεὶ προτακτέον τοῦ λόγου.

Integrity is to be preferred to eloquence.

See (Lat.) Eloquence.

A Prodigal.
Ctesiph. c. 57.

Οὐδεὶς γὰρ πώποτε πλοῦτος τρόπου πονηροῦ περιεγένετο.

For no wealth can enrich a vicious prodigal.

Amnesty.
Ctesiph. c. 71.

Τὸ κάλλιστον ἐκ παιδείας ῥῆμα φθεγξάμενοι, μὴ μνησικάκειν.

Amnesty, that noble word, the genuine dictate of wisdom.

A Mere Craftsman of Words.
Ctesiph. c. 83.

Οὗ τὴν γλῶτταν ὥσπερ τῶν αὐλῶν ἐάν τις ἀφέλῃ, τὸ λοιπὸν
οὐδέν ἐστιν.

A fellow, whose tongue is his sole merit, and without it, like a
flute, all that there is of him besides, were good for nothing.

A 2

The Power of a Private Individual in a Republic.

Ctesiph. c. 85.

'Ανὴρ γὰρ ἰδιώτης ἐν πόλει δημοκρατουμένη νόμῳ καὶ ψήφῳ
βασιλεύει· ὅταν δ' ἑτέρῳ ταῦτα παράδῳ, καταλέλυκεν αὐτὸς τὴν
αὐτοῦ δυναστείαν.

For in a republican state every private individual shares regal
power by means of the laws and his vote ; but when he surrenders
these to another, he annuls his own sovereignty.

Vaunting.

Ctesiph. c. 89.

"Οπου, γὰρ τοὺς μὲν ὄντως ἄνδρας ἀγαθούς, οἷς πολλά καὶ καλὰ
σύνισμεν ἔργα, ἐὰν τοὺς καθ' ἑαυτῶν ἐπαίνους λέγωσιν, οὐ φέρομεν.

For men of real merit, and whose noble and glorious deeds we
are ready to acknowledge, are yet not to be endured when they
vaunt their own actions.

                                                    See (Lat.) Bragging.

Education by Example.

Ctesiph. c. 91.

Εὖ γὰρ ἴστε, ὅτι οὐχ αἱ παλαίστραι οὐδὲ τὰ διδασκαλεῖα οὐδ' ἡ
μουσικὴ μόνον παιδεύει τοὺς νεωτέρους, ἀλλὰ πολὺ μᾶλλον τὰ δημόσια
κηρύγματα.

For you are well aware that it is not only by bodily exercises,
by educational institutions, or by lessons in music, that our youth
are trained, but much more effectually by public examples.

                                                    See (Lat. Fr.) Education.

ÆSCHYLUS.

BORN B.C. 525—DIED B.C. 456.

ÆSCHYLUS, the son of Euphorion, a native of Eleusis, in Attica,
was the father of the Athenian drama.   He was present at the
battle of Marathon, B.C. 490, in which he was greatly distinguished
along with his brothers ; and in a picture representing this battle
he was placed in the foreground, and was thus associated in the
honours which were paid to Miltiades.   Six years afterwards, B.C.
484, the same year in which Herodotus was born, Æschylus gained
his first victory as a competitor for the prize of tragedy ; and he

was successful thirteen times during an interval of sixteen years. He visited the court of Hiero, king of Syracuse, who was a distinguished patron of the learned, and who had induced such men as Pindar and Simonides to reside with him. There is a power in the language, a sublimity in the imagery, with which the poet bodies forth the creations of his genius, that makes him rank among the master spirits of the world.

TIES OF KINDRED ARE STRONG.

Prom. 39.

Τὸ συγγενές τοι δεινὸν ἤ θ᾽ ὁμιλία.

Strong are the ties of kindred and long converse.

ALL HAVE THEIR LOT APPOINTED.

Prom. 49.

῎Απαντ᾽ ἐπράχθη πλὴν θεοῖσι κοιρανεῖν.
᾿Ελεύθερος γὰρ οὔτις ἐστὶ πλὴν Διός.

Everything has been accomplished except for the other gods to rule; for no one is free save Jove.

WAVES.

Prom. 89.

Ποντίων τε κυμάτων
ἀνήριθμον γέλασμα.

And countless dimpling of the waves of the deep.

So Milton ("Paradise Lost," iv. 165)—
"Cheered with the grateful smell, old Ocean smiles."

Lord Byron (opening of the "Giaour")—
"There mildly dimpling ocean's cheek
Reflects the tints of many a peak,
Caught by the laughing tides that lave
Those Edens of the eastern wave."

NECESSITY NOT TO BE RESISTED.

Prom. 103.

Τὴν πεπρωμένην δὲ χρὴ
αἶσαν φέρειν ὡς ῥᾷστα, γιγνώσκονθ᾽ ὅτι
τὸ τῆς ἀνάγκης ἐστ᾽ ἀδήριτον σθένος.

But I must endure my doom as easily as may be, knowing, as I do, that the power of necessity is irresistible.

So Shakespeare ("Richard II.," act v. sc. 1)—
"I am sworn brother, sweet,
To grim Necessity; and he and I
Will keep a league till death."

A Tyrant Distrusts.

Prom. 224.

Ἔνεστι γάρ πως τοῦτο τῇ τυραννίδι
νόσημα, τοῖς φίλοισι μὴ πεποιθέναι.

For somehow, there is this disease in tyranny, not to put confidence in friends.

So Shakespeare (" Pericles," act i. sc. 2)—
" Tyrants' fears
Decrease not, but grow faster with their years."

Easy to give Advice to the Afflicted.

Prom. 263.

Ἐλαφρὸν ὅστις πημάτων ἔξω πόδα
ἔχει, παραινεῖν νουθετεῖν τε τὸν κακῶς
πράσσοντ'.

'Tis easy for any man who has his foot unentangled by sufferings both to exhort and to admonish him that is in difficulties.

See (Lat.) The Sick.

Affliction.

Prom. 275.

Ταὐτά τοι πλανωμένη
πρὸς ἄλλοτ' ἄλλον πημονὴ προσιζάνει.

Hence in the same way does affliction, roaming to and fro, settle down on different individuals.

Truth.

Prom. 301.

Γνώσει δὲ τάδ' ὡς ἔτυμ', οὐδὲ μάτην
χαριτογλωσσεῖν ἔνι μοι.

And thou shalt know that these words are sincere, and not the false glozings of a flattering tongue.

To Kick against the Pricks.

Prom. 322.

Οὔκουν ἔμοιγε χρώμενος διδασκάλῳ
πρὸς κέντρα κῶλον ἐκτενεῖς.

If thou takest me for thy instructor, thou wilt not kick against the pricks.

See (Lat.) To Kick. Acts ix. 5.

PETULANT TONGUE.

Prom. 328.

"Η οὐκ οἶσθ' ἀκριβῶς ὤν περισσόφρων ὅτι
γλώσσῃ ματαίᾳ ζημία προστρίβεται.

What! knowest thou not as certain, highly intelligent though
thou art, that punishment is inflicted on a petulant tongue?

See (Lat.) Vituperation

SOFT SPEECH TURNETH AWAY WRATH.

Prom. 377.

ΩΚ. Οὔκουν, Προμηθεῦ, τοῦτο γιγνώσκεις, ὅτι
ὀργῆς ζεούσης εἰσὶν ἰατροὶ λόγοι ;
ΠΡ. 'Εάν τις ἐν καιρῷ γε μαλθάσσῃ κέαρ
καὶ μὴ σφριγῶντα θυμὸν ἰσχναίνῃ βίᾳ.

Oc. Knowest thou not this, then, Prometheus, that words are
the physicians of a distempered mind?
Prom. True, if one soften properly the heart, and do not with
rude violence exasperate the troubled mind.

So Milton ("Samson Agonistes")—
" Apt words have power to suage
The tumours of a troubled mind."

And Proverbs (xv. 1)—" A soft answer turneth away wrath, but grievous
words stir up anger."

THE WISE.

Prom. 384.

'Επεὶ
κέρδιστον εὖ φρονοῦντα μὴ φρονεῖν δοκεῖν.

Since it is of the highest advantage for one that is wise not to
seem to be wise.

See (Lat.) Wisdom

MAN IN A BARBAROUS STATE.

Prom. 442.

Τὰν βροτοῖς δὲ πήματα
ἀκούσαθ', ὡς σφας νηπίους ὄντας τὸ πρὶν
ἔννους ἔθηκα καὶ φρενῶν ἐπηβόλους.
Λέξω δὲ, μέμψιν οὔτιν' ἀνθρώποις ἔχων,
ἀλλ' ὧν δέδωκ' εὔνοιαν ἐξηγούμενος·
οἳ πρῶτα μὲν βλέποντες ἔβλεπον μάτην,
κλύοντες οὐκ ἤκουον, ἀλλ' ὀνειράτων
ἀλίγκιοι μορφαῖσι τὸν μακρὸν βίον
ἔφυρον εἰκῆ πάντα, κοὔτε πλινθυφεῖς
δόμους προσείλους ᾖσαν, οἱ· ξυλουργίαν

κατώρυχες δ' ἔναιον ὥστ' ἀήσυροι
μύρμηκες ἄντρων ἐν μυχοῖς ἀνηλίοις.
῏Ην δ' οὐδὲν αὐτοῖς οὔτε χείματος τέκμαρ
οὔτ' ἀνθεμώδους ἦρος οὔτε καρπίμου
θέρους βέβαιον, ἀλλ' ἄτερ γνώμης τὸ πᾶν
ἔπρασσον, ἔς τε δή σφιν ἀντολὰς ἐγὼ
ἄστρων ἔδειξα τάς τε δυσκρίτους δύσεις.
Καὶ μὴν ἀριθμὸν, ἔξοχον σοφισμάτων,
ἐξηῦρον αὐτοῖς, γραμμάτων τε συνθέσεις,
μνήμης ἁπάντων μουσομήτορ' ἐργάνην.
Κἄζευξα πρῶτος ἐν ζυγοῖσι κνώδαλα
ζεύγλαισι δουλεύοντα σάγμασίν θ', ὅπως
θνητοῖς μεγίστων διάδοχοι μοχθημάτων
γένοινθ', ὑφ' ἅρμα τ' ἤγαγον φιληνίους
ἵππους, ἄγαλμα τῆς ὑπερπλούτου χλιδῆς.
Θαλασσόπλαγκτα δ' οὔτις ἄλλος ἀντ' ἐμοῦ
λινόπτερ' ηὗρε ναυτίλων ὀχήματα.

But as to the ills of men, hear how I made those, who were
before senseless as children, intelligent and possessed of wisdom.
I shall tell you, not with the view of throwing blame upon them,
but to show my kindly feelings from what I gave them ; who at
first seeing, saw not, and hearing, heard not. But like to the
baseless fabric of a dream, for a long time they used to huddle
together all things at random : nought they knew about brick-
built houses, sun-ward, nor the raftered roof ; but, like tiny ants,
they dwelt in the excavated earth, in sunless depths of caves.
They had no certain sign of winter, or flower-perfumed spring, or
fruitful summer ; but they did everything without judgment, till
I instructed them to mark the rising of the stars and their setting,
a harder science yet. And verily I discovered for them numbers,
the most surprising of all inventions, and the union of letters,
and memory, the active mother of all wisdom. I also first taught
the patient steer to bear the yoke ; and in order with their bodies
they might assist mortals in their severest toils, I taught steeds
to whirl cars obedient to the reins, to grace the pride of wealth.
And no one else than I invented the canvas-winged chariots of
mariners that roam over the ocean.

So Matthew (xiii. 14)—"And in them is fulfilled the prophecy of Esaias,
which saith, By hearing ye shall hear, and shall not understand ; and seeing ye shall see, and shall not perceive."

NECESSITY.

Prom. 514.

Τέχνη δ' ἀνάγκης ἀσθενεστέρα μακρῷ.

Necessity is stronger far than art.

See (Lat.) Necessity.

PLEASURES OF HOPE.
Prom. 536.

Ἡδύ τι θαρσαλέαις
τὸν μακρὸν τείνειν βίον ἐλπίσι, φαναῖς
θυμὸν ἀλδαίνουσαν ἐν εὐφροσύναις.

It is pleasant to lengthen out a long life with confident hopes,
making the spirits swell with bright merriment.

FEEBLENESS OF MORTALS.
Prom. 546.

Οὐδ᾽ ἐδέρχθης
ὀλιγοδρανίαν ἄκικυν
ἰσόνειρον, ᾇ τὸ φωτῶν
ἀλαὸν γένος ἐμπεποδισμένον; οὔποτε θνατῶν
τὰν Διὸς ἁρμονίαν ἀνδρῶν παρεξίασι βουλαί.

Sawest thou not the powerless weakness, like a dream, in which
the blind race of men is entangled? Never at any time shall the
plans of mortals get the better of the harmonious system of Jove.
See (Lat.) Man, insignificance of.

REWARD OF SYMPATHY.
Prom. 637.

Ὡς τἀποκλαῦσαι κἀποδύρασθαι τύχας
ἐνταῦθ᾽, ὅπῃ μέλλοι τις οἴσεσθαι δάκρυ
πρὸς τῶν κλυόντων, ἀξίαν τριβὴν ἔχει.

Since to weep and lament over misfortunes, when it draws the
sympathising tear, brings no light recompense.

So Shakespeare (Poems)—
"Companionship in woe, doth woe assuage."
See (Lat.) Man easily affected.

THE SICK.
Prom. 698.

Τοῖς νοσοῦσί τοι γλυκὺ
τὸ λοιπὸν ἄλγος προὐξεπίστασθαι τορῶς.

To the sick, indeed, some gleam of hope flows from a clear
knowledge beforehand of the result of their pains.

MARRY IN YOUR OWN RANK.
Prom. 890.

Ἦ σοφὸς ἦ σοφὸς ὃς
πρῶτος ἐν γνώμᾳ τόδ᾽ ἐβάστασε καὶ γλώσσᾳ διε-
μυθολόγησεν,

A 3

ὡς τὸ κηδεῦσαι καθ᾽ ἑαυτὸν ἀριστεύει μακρῷ,
καὶ μήτε τῶν πλούτῳ διαθρυπτομένων
μήτε τῶν γέννᾳ μεγαλυνομένων
ὄντα χερνήταν ἐραστεῦσαι γάμων.

Wise was the man, ay, wise indeed, who first weighed well this maxim, and with his tongue published it abroad, that to marry in one's own class is best by far, and that a peasant should woo the hand neither of any that have waxed wanton by riches, nor of such as pride themselves in high-traced lineage.

THE WISH IS FATHER TO THE THOUGHT.
Prom. 928.

Σύ θην ἃ χρήζεις, ταῦτ᾽ ἐπιγλωσσᾶ Διός.

Thou indeed art predicting against Jove the things thou wishest.

Shakespeare ("Henry IV.," Pt. ii. act iv. sc. 4) says—
"Thy wish was father, Harry, to that thought."
See Livy, vi. 21 ; Lactant. Inst., vii. 26 ; (Lat.) Wish.

DEAF AS THE BILLOWS.
Prom. 1001.

Οχλεῖς μάτην με κῦμ᾽ ὅπως παρηγορῶν.

Thou troublest me with thy advice as vainly as thou wouldst do the billows.

Shakespeare ("Merchant of Venice," act iv. sc. 1) says—
"You may as well go stand upon the beach,
And bid the main flood bate his usual height."

And Milton ("Samson Agonistes")—
"*Daliiah.* I see thou art implacable, more deaf
To prayers than winds or seas."

OBSTINACY.
Prom. 1012.

Αὐθαδία γὰρ τῷ φρονοῦντι μὴ καλῶς
αὐτὴ καθ᾽ αὑτὴν οὐδενὸς μεῖον σθένει.

For obstinacy in a man that is not gifted with wisdom, itself by itself, is worth less than nothing.

GOD KNOWS NOT TO BE FALSE.
Prom. 1032.

Ψευδηγορεῖν γὰρ οὐκ ἐπίσταται στόμα
τὸ Δῖον, ἀλλὰ πᾶν ἔπος τελεῖ.

The mouth of God knows not to utter falsehood, but brings everything to pass.

So Numbers (xxiii. 19)—"God is not a man, that He should lie; neither the son of man, that He should repent; hath He said, and shall He not do it? or hath He spoken, and shall He not make it good?" And 2 Corinthians (i. 20)—"For all the promises of God in him are yea, and in him Amen, unto the glory of God by us."

THE WISE.
Prom. 1039.

Σοφῷ γὰρ αἰσχρὸν ἐξαμαρτάνειν.

For it is base for the wise to err.

THE LOWLY.
Suppl. 203.

Θρασυστομεῖν γὰρ οὐ πρέπει τοὺς ἥσσονας.

For it is unbecoming in inferiors to assume boldness of speech.

VARIOUS ILLS OF MEN.
Suppl. 327.

Ἄναξ Πελασγῶν, αἰόλ' ἀνθρώπων κακά.
Πόνου δ' ἴδοις ἂν οὐδαμοῦ ταυτὸν πτερόν·

King of the Pelasgians, various are the ills of men : nowhere canst thou behold the same wing of trouble.

GOD REGARDS THE AFFLICTED.
Suppl. 381.

Τὸν ὑψόθεν σκοπὸν ἐπισκόπει,
φύλακα πολυπόνων
βροτῶν, οἳ τοῖς πέλας προσήμενοι
δίκας οὐ τυγχάνουσιν ἐννόμου.
Μένει τοι Ζηνὸς ἱκτίου κότος
δυσπαράθελκτος παθόντος οἴκτοις.

Look up to him that beholds from on high, the protector of suffering mortals, who address their kindred in suppliant tones, but obtain not what justice demands. Therefore the wrath of Jove, guardian of the suppliant, waits on the groans of the sufferers, and is not to be appeased.

See Psalm ix. 12; cxl. 12.

SLANDER.
Suppl. 972.

Πᾶς δ' ἐν μετοίκῳ γλῶσσαν εὔτυκον φέρει
κακήν, τὸ τ' εἰπεῖν εὐπετὲς μύσαγμά πως.

But every one bears a ready evil tongue against a stranger, and to speak slander is an easy thing.

DANGERS OF BEAUTY.

Suppl. 973.

Ὑμᾶς δ᾽ ἐπαινῶ μὴ καταισχύνειν ἐμὲ,
ὥραν ἐχούσας τήνδ᾽ ἐπίστρεπτον βροτοῖς.
Τέρειν᾽ ὀπώρα δ᾽ εὐφύλακτος οὐδαμῶς,
[θῆρες δὲ κηραίνουσι καὶ βροτοί, τί μήν;
καὶ κνώδαλα πτεροῦντα καὶ πεδοστιβῆ.
Καρπώματα στάζοντα κηρύσσει Κύπρις
κἄωρα κωλύουσαν ὡς μένειν ἐρῶ.]
Καὶ παρθένων χλιδαῖσιν εὐμόρφοις ἔπι
πᾶς τις παρελθὼν ὄμματος θελκτήριον
τόξευμ᾽ ἔπεμψεν, ἱμέρου νικώμενος.

But I charge you not to disgrace me, as thou art in the bloom of youth that excitest desire. It is not easy to guard the tender ripe fruit; for beasts and men injure it in some way, and winged insects and four-footed animals. Venus proclaims their opening bloom. I say that rapine is their fate, however much they try to avoid it. And on the fair-formed beauty of virgins every one that passes sends forth a melting dart from his eye, overcome by desire.

A PROSPEROUS STATE.

Sept. c. Theb. 77.

Πόλις γὰρ εὖ πράσσουσα δαίμονας τίει.

For a state that is prosperous honours the gods.

WOMAN.

Sept. c. Theb. 187.

Μήτ᾽ ἐν κακοῖσι μήτ᾽ ἐν εὐεστοῖ φίλῃ
ξύνοικος εἴην τῷ γυναικείῳ γένει.
Κρατοῦσα μὲν γὰρ οὐχ ὁμιλητὸν θράσος,
δείσασα δ᾽ οἴκῳ καὶ πόλει πλέον κακόν.

Neither in adversity nor in the joys of prosperity may I be associated with womankind; for when woman is joyous, her licence is not to be endured; and when she is in terror, she is a still greater plague to her home and city.

OBEDIENCE.

Sept. c. Theb. 224.

Πειθαρχία γάρ ἐστι τῆς εὐπραξίας
μήτηρ, γονῆς σωτῆρος· ὧδ᾽ ἔχει λόγος.

For obedience, woman, is the mother of success, bringing safety; so says the proverb.

DUTIES OF MEN AND WOMEN IN WAR.
Sept. c. Theb. 230.

Ἀνδρῶν τάδ' ἐστὶ, σφάγια καὶ χρηστήρια
θεοῖσιν ἔρδειν, πολεμίων πειρωμένων·
σὸν δ' αὖ τὸ σιγᾶν καὶ μένειν εἴσω δόμων.

It is for men to present victims and offerings to appease the gods, when the enemy are at the gates; 'tis thine, woman, to hold thy peace, and keep within doors.

THE NOBLE AND BRAVE.
Sept. c. Theb. 409.

Μάλ' εὐγενῆ τε καὶ τὸν αἰσχύνης θρόνον
τιμῶντα καὶ στυγοῦνθ' ὑπέρφρονας λόγους.
Αἰσχρῶν γὰρ ἀργὸς, μὴ κακὸς δ' εἶναι φιλεῖ.

Nobly born and honouring the throne of modesty, hating vaunting language—such an one is wont to be slow at base deeds, and no coward.

TO BE, NOT TO SEEM.
Sept. c. Theb. 592.

Οὐ γὰρ δοκεῖν ἄριστος, ἀλλ' εἶναι θέλει,
βαθεῖαν ἄλοκα διὰ φρενὸς καρπούμενος,
ἐξ ἧς τὰ κεδνὰ βλαστάνει βουλεύματα.
Τούτῳ σοφούς τε κἀγαθοὺς ἀντηρέτας
πέμπειν ἐπαινῶ.   δεινὸς ὃς θεοὺς σέβει.

For he does not wish to seem, but to be, the noblest, reaping a rich harvest from a deep furrow in his mind, from which sprout forth excellent counsels. Against such an one I charge thee to send wise and prudent champions. Dreadful is the foe that fears the gods.

See (Lat.) Be what you seem.

IMPIOUS FELLOWSHIP.
Sept. c. Theb. 597.

Φεῦ τοῦ ξυναλλάσσοντος ὄρνιθος βροτοῖς
δίκαιον ἄνδρα τοῖσι δυσσεβεστέροις.
Ἐν παντὶ πράγει δ' ἐσθ' ὁμιλίας κακῆς
κάκιον οὐδὲν καρπὸς ἧς ἀσύμφορος.
ὡς γὰρ ξυνεσβὰς πλοῖον εὐσεβὴς ἀνὴρ
ναύταισι θερμοῖς καὶ πανουργίας πλέῳς
ὄλωλεν ἀνδρῶν σὺν θεοπτύστῳ γένει,

ἢ ξὺν πολίταις ἀνδράσιν δίκαιος ὢν
ἐχθροξένοις τε καὶ θεῶν ἀμνήμοσι
πληγεὶς θεοῦ μάστιγι παγκοίνῳ ᾿δάμη,
ταὐτοῦ κυρήσας ἐκδίκοις ἀγρεύματος·

Alas! it is a bad omen for the just to be associated with the impious. Indeed in everything nought is worse than wicked fellowship, the fruit of which is fraught with death. For whether a good man happens to have embarked with sailors, whose hearts are hot and full of villany, he perishes with the race abhorred of Heaven, or whether, being righteous, he has fixed his seat amidst citizens inhospitably bent and regardless of the gods, he is struck down by the scourge of the Deity, which falls on all alike, having rightly fallen into the same nets with his countrymen.

See (Lat.) The Wicked. 1 Cor. xv. 33.

An Old Head on Young Shoulders.
Sept. c. Theb. 604.

Γέροντα τὸν νοῦν, σάρκα δ᾿ ἡβῶσαν φέρει.

In manhood's vig'rous prime
He bears the providence of age.

The Stars.
Agam. 1.

Θεοὺς μὲν αἰτῶ τῶνδ᾿ ἀπαλλαγὴν πόνων,
φρουρᾶς ἐτείας μῆχος, ἣν κοιμώμενος
στέγαις ᾿Ατρειδῶν ἄγκαθεν, κυνὸς δίκην,
ἄστρων κάτοιδα νυκτέρων ὁμήγυριν,
καὶ τοὺς φέροντας χεῖμα καὶ θέρος βροτοῖς
λαμπροὺς δυνάστας, ἐμπρέποντας αἰθέρι
ἀστέρας, ὅταν φθίνωσιν, ἀντολάς τε τῶν.

I pray the gods that I may be released from these toils, slave of a year-long sentry, during which lying on my elbows on the roofs of the Atridæ, like a dog, I have contemplated the choir of nightly stars, radiant rulers that bring winter and summer, stars shining conspicuously in the firmament, both when they set and when they rise.

What is Fated.
Agam. 67.

῎Εστι δ᾿ ὅπη νῦν
ἔστι· τελεῖται δ᾿ ἐς τὸ πεπρωμένον.

Things are as they are and will be brought to the issue doomed.

Tottering Old Age.

Agam. 71.

'Ημεῖς δ' ἀτίται σαρκὶ παλαιᾷ
τῆς τότ' ἀρωγῆς ὑπολειφθέντες
μίμνομεν ἰσχὺν
ἰσόπαιδα νέμοντες ἐπὶ σκήπτροις.
῝Ο τε γὰρ νεαρὸς μυελὸς στέρνων
ἐντὸς ἀνάσσων
ἰσόπρεσβυς, ῎Αρης δ' οὐκ ἔνι χώρᾳ,
τό θ' ὑπέργηρων φυλλάδος ἤδη
κατακαρφομένης τρίποδας μὲν ὁδοὺς
στείχει, παιδὸς δ' οὐδὲν ἀρείων
ὄναρ ἡμερόφαντον ἀλαίνει.

But wo with our aged frame were left inglorious behind the expedition of those days, propping on staff our steps like children ; for both the marrow of youth, while it is springing up in our breasts, is weak as age, and the vigour for war is not yet attained ; very advanced age, too, when its foliage is withered, totters along its three-footed path, and in no way superior to a child, flits like a day-dream.

God chastens Man for his Good.

Agam. 172.

Ζῆνα δέ τις προφρόνως ἐπινίκια κλάζων
τεύξεται φρενῶν τὸ πᾶν·
τὸν φρονεῖν βροτοὺς ὁδώσαντα, τὸν πάθει μάθος
θέντα κυρίως ἔχειν.
Στάζει δ' ἔν θ' ὕπνῳ πρὸ καρδίας
μνησιπήμων πόνος· καὶ πὰρ ἄκοντας ἦλθε σωφρονεῖν.
Δαιμόνων δέ που χάρις
βιαίως σέλμα σεμνὸν ἡμένων.

The man who cheerfully celebrates Jove in triumphal hymns shall ever be crowned with success—him that guides mortals to wisdom, teaching them by suffering to remain firm. But even in slumber the pangs from the memory of ills keep dripping before the heart, and thus wisdom comes to the unwilling. 'Tis a gracious gift of the gods, compulsory as fate, who sit severely on the awful bench.

See Heb. xii. 6 ; Job iv. 12–16 ; v. 17 ; Rev. iii. 10.

Be not Anxious for the Future.

Agam. 249.

Δίκα δὲ τοῖς μὲν παθοῦσιν μαθεῖν ἐπιρρέπει· τὸ μέλλον δ',
ἐπεὶ γένοιτ' ἂν ἥλυσις, προχαιρέτω·
ἴσον δὲ τῷ προστένειν.
τορὸν γὰρ ἥξει σύνορθρον αὐγαῖς.

To those that suffer justice brings wisdom ; but for futurity, since it will come, farewell to it. 'Tis but the same with sorrowing beforehand ; for the event will come dawning clearly with the morning rays.

This is the Italian proverb, " Che sara, sara."

GOD PUNISHES THE WICKED.

Agam. 367.

Διὸs πλαγὰν ἔχουσιν· εἰπεῖν
πάρεστι τοῦτό κἀξιχνεῦσαι.
Ἔπραξαν ὡs ἔκρανεν. Οὐκ ἔφα τις
θεοὺs βροτῶν ἀξιοῦσθαι μέλειν,
ὅσοιs ἀθίκτων χάρις
πατοῖθ'· ὁ δ' οὐκ εὐσεβήs.
Πέφανται δ' ἐκγόνους
ἀτολμήτων Ἄρη
πνεόντων μεῖζον ἢ δικαίωs,
φλεόντων δωμάτων ὑπέρφευ
ὑπὲρ τὸ βέλτιστον. Ἔστω δ' ἀπήμαντον, ὥστε κἀπαρκεῖν
εὖ πραπίδων λαχόντα.

They feel the stroke of Jove ; we may say this, and trace it out exactly ; they have fared as they deserved. Some one denied that the gods deigned to care for mortals, who trampled on their laws. Not holy was he who said so ; it has come upon the descendants of those who were breathing forth more violently than just a war which they ought not to have dared, while their dwellings were teeming beyond all measure with rich spoils. But may such calm of soul be mine, so as to meet the force of circumstances.

See (Lat.) The Wicked.

THE IMPIOUS SEEN THROUGH THEIR DISGUISE.

Agam. 382.

Οὐ γὰρ ἔστιν ἔπαλξις
πλούτου πρὸs κόρον ἀνδρὶ
λακτίσαντι μέγαν Δίκαs βωμὸν εἰs ἀφάνειαν.
Βιᾶται δ' ἁ τάλαινα πειθὼ,
προβουλόπαις ἄφερτος ἄτας.
Ἄκος δὲ πᾶν μάταιον. Οὐκ ἐκρύφθη,
πρέπει δὲ, φῶς, αἰνολαμπὲs, σίνος·
κακοῦ δὲ χαλκοῦ τρόπον
τρίβῳ τε καὶ προσβολαῖς
μελαμπαγὴs πέλει
δικαιωθεὶs, ἐπεὶ
διώκει παῖs ποτανὸν ὄρνιν,

πόλει πρόστριμμ' ἄφερτον ἐνθείς.
Λιτᾶν δ' ἀκούει μὲν οὔτις θεῶν·
τὸν δ' ἐπίστροφον τῶνδε
φῶτ' ἄδικον καθαιρεῖ.

For riches is no bulwark against destruction to the man who
has wantonly spurned the great altar of Justice; but wretched
Persuasion, preparing intolerable evils for posterity, urges him on,
and there is no remedy. Guilt is never hidden, but is seen through
her disguise, a light of lurid glare; and like adulterated brass,
when proved, is found black by wear and rubbing, fond as a boy
to chase the bird light-flitting round. And not a god lends an
ear to his prayers, but sweeps away the unrighteous that hath
concerned himself with these doings.

The Fate of the Warrior.

Agam. 437.

'Ο χρυσαμοιβὸς δ' Ἄρης σωμάτων
καὶ ταλαντοῦχος ἐν μάχῃ δορὸς
πυρωθὲν ἐξ Ἰλίου
φίλοισι πέμπει βραχὺ
ψῆγμα δυσδάκρυτον ἀντήνορος σποδοῦ γεμίζων
λέβητας εὐθέτου.
Στένουσι δ' εὖ λέγοντες ἄνδρα τὸν μὲν ὡς
μάχης ἴδρις, τὸν δ' ἐν φοναῖς καλῶς πεσόντ'
ἀλλοτρίας διαὶ γυναικός. Τάδε σῖγά τις βαύ-
ζει. Φθονερὸν δ' ὑπ' ἄλγος ἕρπει προδίκοις Ἀτρείδαις.

And Mars, bartering for gold their bodies, and holding the
balance in the tug of war, sends to their friends a small fragment
of scorched dust from Troy, to be wept with many tears, filling
the urns with light ashes instead of the man. And they sigh while
they sing the praises of one as renowned in arms, and another as
having fallen gloriously amid the carnage in defence of another's
wife. Some one mutters these words in silence, and jealous vexation creeps upon the chieftain sons of Atreus.

Murmurs of the People.

Agam. 456.

Βαρεῖα δ' ἀστῶν φάτις ξὺν κότῳ·
δημοκράντου δ' ἀρᾶς τίνει χρέος.

Dreadful are the murmurs of the people if they be accompanied.
with hate; but this is the tribute greatness pays for its exalted
station.

The Oppressor.

Agam. 460.

Τῶν πολυκτόνων γὰρ οὐκ ἄσκοποι θεοι.   Κελαιναὶ δ'
'Ερινύες χρόνῳ
τυχηρὸν ὄντ' ἄνευ δίκας παλιντυχεῖ
τριβᾷ βίου τιθεῖς' ἀμαυρόν, ἐν δ' ἄϊ-
στοις τελέθοντος οὔτις ἀλκά· τὸ δ' ὑπερκότως κλύειν
εὖ βαρύ· βάλλεται γὰρ ὄσσοις Διόθεν κεραυνός.

For the gods are not forgetful of those who cause great slaughter.
The black Furies in one short hour hurl to perdition the man who
is lucky without righteousness by a sad reverse of fortune, nor
does he receive aid from his citizens. For a man to be raised
aloft is dangerous, as the thunderbolt of Jove is sure to be
launched against him.

None but the Gods have Unmixed Happiness.

Agam. 551.

Εὖ γὰρ πέπρακται.   Ταῦτα δ' ἐν πολλῷ χρόνῳ
τὰ μέν τις ἂν λέξειεν εὐπετῶς ἔχειν,
τὰ δ' αὖτε κἀπίμομφα.   Τίς δὲ, πλὴν θεῶν,
ἄπαντ' ἀπήμων τὸν δι' αἰῶνος χρόνον.

Yea, the conflict is well o'er ; in the passage of so long a time
one might say that some things fall out well, while others are
open to complaint ; for who save the gods can claim through life's
whole course an unmixed happiness?

A Fond Wife.

Agam. 601.

Τί γὰρ
γυναικὶ τούτου φέγγος ἥδιον δρακεῖν,
ἀπὸ στρατείας ἀνδρὶ σώσαντος θεοῦ
πύλας ἀνοῖξαι ; ταῦτ' ἀπάγγειλον πόσει·
ἥκειν ὅπως τάχιστ' ἐράσμιον πόλει·
γυναῖκα πιστὴν δ' ἐν δόμοις εὕροι μολὼν
οἵανπερ οὖν ἔλειπε, δωμάτων κύνα
ἐσθλὴν ἐκείνῳ, πολεμίαν τοῖς δύσφροσιν,
καὶ τἄλλ' ὁμοίαν πάντα, σημαντήριον
οὐδὲν διαφθείρασαν ἐν μήκει χρόνου.
Οὐδ' οἶδα τέρψιν οὐδ' ἐπίψογον φάτιν
ἄλλου πρὸς ἀνδρὸς μᾶλλον ἢ χαλκοῦ βαφάs.

For what day is more delightful to woman than that when she
opes the gate to her husband returning gloriously from war, preserved by the gods? Bear this message to my husband, that he
hasten his long-desired return. May he come speedily, where he

will find a faithful wife in his house, such as he left her, a watch-dog of his home, to his enemies irreconcilable, and in all other points alike, not having effaced one single seal in the long course of years. I have known no delight with other men, nor has there been any slanderous report against my character, any more than brass can be tinged with dyes.

So Shakespeare (" Much Ado about Nothing," act iv. sc. 1) says—

> " If I know more of any man alive
> Than that which maiden modesty doth warrant,
> Let all my sins lack mercy."

And "Winter's Tale," (act iii. sc. 2)—

> " If one jot beyond
> The bound of honour, or in act or will
> That way inclining, hardened be the hearts
> Of all that hear me, and my near'st of kin
> Cry, Fie ! upon my grave."

HAPPY ARE THOSE WHO DIE NOT CHILDLESS.

Agam. 750.

Παλαίφατος δ' ἐν βροτοῖς γέρων λόγος
τέτυκται, μέγαν τελεσθέντα φωτὸς ὄλβον
τεκνοῦσθαι μηδ' ἄπαιδα θνήσκειν,
ἐκ δ' ἀγαθᾶς τύχας γένει
βλαστάνειν ἀκόρεστον οἰζύν.

There is among mankind an old adage, uttered in ancient times, " that it is great happiness to see our children rise around us, not dying childless ; but from good fortune often sprouts the bitter fruit of woe to man."

ONE BASE DEED PRODUCES ANOTHER.

Agam. 759.

Τὸ δυσσεβὲς γὰρ ἔργον
μετὰ μὲν πλείονα τίκτει, σφετέρᾳ δ' εἰκότα γέννᾳ.
Οἴκων δ' ἄρ' εὐθυδίκων
Καλλίπαις πότμος ἀεί.

For one base deed engendors more like to its own race ; but to those swayed by unbending justice a beauteous race still flourishes.

Shelley, in his " Hellas," says—

> " Revenge and wrong bring forth their kind,
> The foul cubs like their parents are."

JUSTICE.

Agam. 772.

Δίκα δὲ λάμπει μὲν ἐν δυσκάπνοις δώμασιν,
τὸν δ' ἐναίσιμον τίει βίον.

Τὰ χρυσόπαστα δ' ἔσθλα σὺν πίνῳ χερῶν
παλιντρόποις
ὄμμασι λιποῦσ', ὅσια προσέβαλε δύναμιν οὐ
σέβουσα πλούτου παράσημον αἴνῳ·
πᾶν δ' ἐπὶ τέρμα νωμᾷ.

But justice shines in smoky cottages, and honours the pious.
Leaving with averted eyes the gorgeous glare of gold obtained by
polluted hands, she is wont to draw nigh to holiness, not reverencing wealth when falsely stamped with praise, and assigning
each deed its righteous doom.

THE HYPOCRITE.

Agam. 788.

Πολλοὶ δὲ βροτῶν τὸ δοκεῖν εἶναι
προτίουσι δίκην παραβάντες.
Τῷ δυσπραγοῦντι δ' ἐπιστενάχειν
πᾶς τις ἕτοιμος· δῆγμα δὲ λύπης
οὐδὲν ἐφ' ἧπαρ προσικνεῖται·
καὶ ξυγχαίρουσιν ὁμοιοπρεπεῖς
ἀγέλαστα πρόσωπα βιαζόμενοι.
Ὅστις δ' ἀγαθὸς προβατογνώμων,
οὐκ ἔστι λαθεῖν ὄμματα φωτός,
τὰ δοκοῦντ' εὔφρονος ἐκ διανοίας
ὑδαρεῖ σαίνειν φιλότητι.

Many are desirous to seem good while they do not what is right.
Some are ready to weep with those who weep, though the pang of
sorrow reaches not the heart; others join in the joys of others,
dressing in forced smiles their unwilling face. But when a man
is able to discern character, then it is not possible that the eyes of
a man, that only seem with sympathetic tear to show a kindly
feeling, should deceive him.

ENVY.

Agam. 832.

Παύροις γὰρ ἀνδρῶν ἐστι συγγενὲς τόδε,
φίλον τὸν εὐτυχοῦντ' ἄνευ φθόνου σέβειν.
Δύσφρων γὰρ ἰὸς καρδίαν προσήμενος
ἄχθος διπλοίζει τῷ πεπαμένῳ νόσον,
τοῖς τ' αὐτὸς αὑτοῦ πήμασιν βαρύνεται.
Καὶ τὸν θυραῖον ὄλβον εἰσορῶν στένει·
εἰδὼς λέγοιμ' ἄν, εὖ γὰρ ἐξεπίσταμαι
ὁμιλίας κάτοπτρον, εἴδωλον σκιᾶς,
δοκοῦντας εἶναι κάρτα πρευμενεῖς ἐμοί.

Few men have strength of mind to honour a friend's success
without a touch of envy; for that malignant passion clinging to

the heart doubles the burden of the man infected by it ; he is
weighed down by the weight of his own woes, and sighs to see
the happiness of others. I speak from experience,—for well do I
know, that those who bore in public the semblance of my firmest
friends, were but the looking-glass of friendship, the shadow of a
shade.

THINGS THAT ARE WELCOME.

Agam. 896.

Λέγοιμ ἂν ἄνδρα τόνδε τῶν σταθμῶν κύνα,
σωτῆρα ναὸς πρότονον, ὑψηλῆς στέγης
στύλον ποδήρη, μονογενὲς τέκνον πατρὶ,
καὶ γῆν φανεῖσαν ναυτίλοις παρ᾽ ἐλπίδα,
κάλλιστον ἦμαρ εἰσιδεῖν ἐκ χείματος,
ὁδοιπόρῳ διψῶντι πηγαῖον ῥέος.
Τερπνὸν δὲ τἀναγκαῖον ἐκφυγεῖν ἅπαν.

I would call my husband a watch-dog of the fold, a saving main-
stay of the ship, a foundation pillar of the lofty roof, an only
child to a fond parent, welcome as land to the mariner which he
has descried beyond his hopes, welcome as day after a night of
storms, a gushing rill to a thirsty wayfarer. 'Tis pleasant to
escape from all constraint.

The following beautiful paraphrase is given in the *Quarterly Review :*—

" Faithful—as dog, the lonely shepherd's pride,
True—as the helm, the bark's protecting guide,
Firm—as the shaft that props the towering dome,
Sweet—as to shipwrecked seaman land and home,
Lovely—as child, a parent's sole delight,
Radiant—as morn that breaks a stormy night,
Grateful—as stream that in some deep recess
With rills unhoped the panting traveller bless,
Is he that links with mine his chain of life,
Names himself lord, and deigns to call me wife."

TO BE FREE FROM EVIL THOUGHTS.

Agam. 927.

Καὶ τὸ μὴ κακῶς φρονεῖν
θεοῦ μέγιστον δῶρον. Ὀλβίσαι δὲ χρὴ
βίον τελευτήσαντ᾽ ἐν εὐεστοῖ φίλῃ.

To be without evil thoughts is God's best gift ; but we must
call him happy who has ended life in prosperity.

See " Sirac" (vi 37).

THE POPULAR VOICE.

Agam. 938.

Φήμη γε μέντοι δημόθρους μέγα σθένει.

Yet has the popular voice much potency.

The Unenvied.

Agam. 939.

'Ο δ' ἀφθόνητός γ' οὐκ ἐπίζηλος πέλει.

But the unenvied is not of the happy.

Be not Elated.

Agam. 951.

Τὸν κρατοῦντα μαλθακῶς
θεὸς πρόσωθεν εὐμενῶς προσδέρκεται.
Ἑκὼν γὰρ οὐδεὶς δουλίῳ χρῆται ζυγῷ.

God from afar looks graciously on him that is mild in victory; for no one willingly submits to the yoke of slavery.

Misery is the Lot of Mankind.

Agam. 1000.

Μάλα γάρ τοι τᾶς πολλᾶς ὑγιείας
ἀκόρεστον τέρμα. Νόσος γὰρ
γείτων ὁμότοιχος ἐρείδει,
καὶ πότμος εὐθυπορῶν
ἀνδρὸς ἔπαισεν
ἄφαντον ἔρμα.
Καὶ τὸ μὲν πρὸ χρημάτων
κτησίων ὄκνος βαλὼν
σφενδόνας ἀπ' εὐμέτρου,
οὐκ ἔδυ πρόπας δόμος
πημονᾶς γέμων ἄγαν,
οὐδ' ἐπόντισε σκάφος.
Πολλά τοι δόσις ἐκ Διὸς ἀμφιλαφής τε καὶ
ἐξ ἀλόκων ἐπετειᾶν
νῆστιν ὤλεσεν νόσον.

For there is a limit to the best of health; disease creeps upon it as a close-adjoining neighbour: and a man's destiny holding on a straight course is apt to dash upon a hidden reef. If timidity fling away a part of his wealth with a well-measured cast of the sling, the whole fabric sinks not, though teeming with woe, nor founders the bark beneath the sea. For often, by Jove's gracious goodness, the yearly furrows quell the pangs of hunger.

Who-can Recall Life?

Agam. 1019.

Τὸ δ' ἐπὶ γᾶν πεσὸν ἅπαξ θανάσιμον
προπάροιθ' ἀνδρὸς μέλαν αἷμα τίς ἂν

πάλιν ἀγκαλέσαιτ' ἐπαείδων ;
οὐδὲ τὸν ὀρθοδαῆ
τῶν φθιμένων ἀνάγειν
Ζεύς αὖτ' ἔπαυσ' [ἐπ εὐλαβείᾳ.]
Εἰ δὲ μὴ τεταγμένα
μοῖρα μοῖραν ἐκ θεῶν
εἶργε μὴ πλέον φέρειν,
προφθάσασα καρδία
γλῶσσαν ἂν τάδ' ἐξέχει.

But who can recall by charms man's purple streaming blood,
when it has once fallen on the ground before his feet? Otherwise
Jove would not have put an end to the leech (Œsculapius) who
could raise the dead. And if fate fixed irrevocably by the gods
did not prevent another fate from bringing assistance, I would
bring it, and my heart, outstripping my tongue, would have poured
forth the tale.

Contrast of an Old Family and an Upstart.

Agam. 1042.

Εἰ δ' οὖν ἀνάγκη τῆσδ' ἐπιρρέποι τύχης,
ἀρχαιοπλούτων δεσποτῶν πολλὴ χάρις.
οἳ δ' οὔποτ' ἐλπίσαντες ἤμησαν καλῶς,
ὠμοί τε δούλοις πάντα καὶ παρὰ στάθμην.

If slavery be a man's fate, great is the advantage of having
masters of long-established opulence. For they who have reaped
a rich harvest unexpectedly are harsh to their slaves in all things,
and go beyond the line of right.

Prosperity and Adversity.

Agam. 1327.

'Ιὼ βρότεια πράγματ'· εὐτυχοῦντα μὲν
σκία τις ἂν τρέψειεν· εἰ δὲ δυστυχοῖ,
βολαῖς ὑγρώσσων σπόγγος ὤλεσεν γραφήν.
Καὶ ταῦτ' ἐκείνων μᾶλλον οἰκτείρω πολύ.

Alas for the fate of men! Even in the midst of the highest
prosperity a shadow may overturn them ; but if they be in adverse
fortune, a moistened sponge can blot out the picture.

Prosperous Fortune.

Agam. 1332.

Τὸ μὲν εὖ πράσσειν ἀκόρεστον ἔφυ
πᾶσι βρυτοῖσιν· δακτυλοδεικτῶν δ'
οὔτις ἀπειπὼν εἴργει μελάθρων.
Μηκέτ' εἰσέλθῃς τάδε, φωνῶν.

All men have boundless wishes for prosperous fortune ; none
will banish and keep it from their dwelling, saying, "Enter thou
no more."

To Know and to Conjecture are not the Same.

Agam. 1369.

Τὸ γὰρ τοπάζειν τοῦ σάφ' εἰδέναι δίχα.

To know and to conjecture differ widely.

To Circumvent a Foe under the Form of Friendship.

Agam. 1374.

Πῶς γάρ τις ἐχθροῖς ἐχθρὰ πορσύνων, φίλοις
δοκοῦσιν εἶναι, πημονῆς ἀρκύστατ' ἂν
φάρξειεν, ὕψος κρεῖσσον ἐκπηδήματος.

For how could one, conceiving thoughts of vengeance on a foe,
achieve the deed more surely than to bear the form of friendship,
encircling him with wiles difficult to overleap?

Qualities of Woman.

Agam. 1636.

Τὸ γὰρ δολῶσαι πρὸς γυναικὸς ἦν σαφῶς.

Wiles and deceit are female qualities.

Exiles.

Agam. 1668.

Οἶδ' ἐγὼ φεύγοντας ἄνδρας ἐλπίδας σιτουμένους.

An exile, I well know, feeds on vain hopes.

Success Worshipped as a God.

Choeph. 59.

Τὸ δ' εὐτυχεῖν
τόδ' ἐν βροτοῖς θεός τε καὶ θεοῦ πλέον.

Success ! to thee,
As to a god, men bend the knee.

Justice.

Choeph. 61.

Ροπὴ δ' ἐπισκοπεῖ δίκας
ταχεῖα τοὺς μὲν ἐν φάει,
τὰ δ' ἐν μεταιχμίῳ σκότου
μένει χρονίζοντας ἄχη,
τοὺς δ' ἄκρατος ἔχει νύξ.

The swift stroke of Justice comes down upon some in the noon-day light; pain waits on others slowly in the midst of darkness, and the gloom of night overshadows them.

One Fate alike to Bond and Free.

Choeph. 103.

Τὸ μόρσιμον γὰρ τόν τ' ἐλεύθερον μένει
καὶ τὸν πρὸς ἄλλης δεσποτούμενον χερός.

For destiny awaits alike the free man and him that trembles at the tyrannous hand of a lord.

Doer must Suffer.

Choeph. 306.

'Αλλ' ὦ μεγάλαι Μοῖραι, Διόθεν
τῇδε τελευτᾶν,
ᾗ τὸ δίκαιον μεταβαίνει.
'Αντὶ μὲν ἐχθρᾶς γλώσσης ἐχθρὰ
γλῶσσα τελείσθω· τοὐφειλόμενον
πράσσουσα Δίκη μέγ' ἀϋτεῖ·
ἀντὶ δὲ πληγῆς φονίας φονίαν
πληγὴν τινέτω. Δράσαντι παθεῖν,
τριγέρων μῦθος τάδε φωνεῖ.

But O ye mighty Fates! grant that, by the will of Jove, it may end as justice requires—"In return for a hostile speech, let a hostile speech be paid back," cries Justice, loudly, as she exacts the debt; "and in return for a murderous blow, let him suffer a murderous blow." "Doer must suffer," thus saith the thrice old proverb.

The Soul Lives.

Choeph. 322.

Τέκνον, φρόνημα τοῦ θανόντος οὐ δαμάζει
πυρὸς μαλερὰ γνάθος,
φαίνει δ' ὕστερον ὀργάς·
ὀτοτύζεται δ' ὁ θνήσκων,
ἀναφαίνεται δ' ὁ βλάπτων.

My child, the consuming fire of the funeral pile quells not the spirit of the dead, but in after times he shows his wrath. The dead is bewailed, and he who wronged him is discovered.

Shakespeare ("Hamlet," act i. sc. 2) says—
"Foul deeds will rise,
Though all the earth o'erwhelm them, to men's eyes."

WORDS ARE DAGGERS.

Choeph. 380.

Τοῦτο διαμπερὲς οὖς
ἵκεθ᾽ ἅπερ τι βέλος.

This pierced quite through my ears, like a dart.

Shakespeare ("Hamlet," act iii. sc. 3) says—
" Oh speak to me no more ;
These words like daggers enter in mine ears ;
No more, sweet Hamlet ! "

BLOOD FOR BLOOD.

Choeph. 400.

Ἀλλὰ νόμος μὲν φονίας σταγόνας
χυμένας ἐς πέδον ἄλλο προσαιτεῖν
αἷμα.

But it is a law that drops of gore poured upon the ground call
for other bloodshed in addition.

So Genesis (ix. 6): "Whoso sheddeth man's blood, by man shall his
blood be shed."

WHAT IS FOREDOOMED.

Choeph. 464.

Τὸ μόρσιμον μένει πάλαι,
εὐχομένοις δ᾽ ἂν ἔλθοι.

That which is foredoomed remains from the olden time, and
will come to those who pray for it.

CHILDREN.

Choeph. 505.

Παῖδες γὰρ ἀνδρὶ κληδόνες σωτήριοι
θανόντι· φελλοὶ δ᾽ ὡς ἄγουσι δίκτυον,
τὸν ἐκ βυθοῦ κλωστῆρα σώζοντες λίνον.

For children preserve the fame of the dead with surviving
glory, and are like corks that buoy the net, saving the flaxen line
from sinking to the bottom.

MURDER CANNOT BE EXPIATED.

Choeph. 520.

Τὰ πάντα γάρ τις ἐκχέας ἀνθ᾽ αἵματος
ἑνὸς, μάτην ὁ μόχθος· ὧδ᾽ ἔχει λόγος.

For though one were to pour out every kind of libation for a single murder, vain is the labour ; so runs the proverb.

THE DARING SPIRIT OF MAN.
Choeph. 591.

Πτανά τε καὶ πεδοβάμονα κάνεμοέντων
αἰγίδων φράσαι κότον.
᾿Αλλ᾽ ὑπέρτολμον ἀνδρὸς φρόνημα τίς λέγοι
καὶ γυναικῶν φρεσὶν τλαμόνων
παντόλμους
ἔρωτας ἄταισι συννόμους βροτῶν ;
συζύγους δ᾽ ὁμαυλίας
θηλυκρατὴς ἀπέρωτος ἔρως παρανικᾷ
κνωδάλων τε καὶ βροτῶν.

One may describe creatures that fly and those that crawl, and the fierce rage of hurricanes, but who can describe the arrogant daring of man and of women of hardened spirit, and their loves, leading them to endure everything, even the utmost woes of mortals. Unholy love, lording it in female heart, overcomes the conjugal union of brutes and of men.

MISERY OF MAN.
Choeph. 1018.

Οὔτις μερόπων ἀσινῆ βίοτον
διὰ πάντ᾽ ἄτιμος ἀμείψεται.
᾿Εῆ,
μόχθων δ᾽ ὁ μὲν αὐτίχ, ὁ δ᾽ ἥξει.

None of mortals can hope to live unscathed a life through its whole course, free from misfortunes. Alas! alas! of troubles one is just upon us, and another will come.

FURIES.
Eum. 178.

Ἔξω, κελεύω, τῶνδε δωμάτων τάχος
χωρεῖτ᾽, ἀπαλλάσσεσθε μαντικῶν μυχῶν,
μὴ καὶ λαβοῦσα πτηνὸν ἀργηστὴν ὄφιν,
χρυσηλάτου θώμιγγος ἐξορμώμενον,
ἀνῇς ὑπ᾽ ἄλγους μέλαν᾽ ἀπ᾽ ἀνθρώπων ἀφρὸν,
ἐμοῦσα θρόμβους οὓς ἀφείλκυσας φόνου.
Οὔτοι δόμοισι τοῖυδε χρίμπτεσθαι πρέπει·
ἀλλ᾽ οὗ καρανιστῆρες ὀφθαλμωρύχοι
δίκαι σφαγαί τε σπέρματός τ᾽ ἀποφθοραὶ
παίδων, κακοῦ τε χλοῦνις ἠδ᾽ ἀκρωνία,
λευσμός τε καὶ μύζουσιν οἰκτισμὸν πολὺν

ὑπὸ ῥάχιν παγέντες. Ἄρ ἀκούετε
οἵας ἑορτῆς ἔστ ἀπόπτυστοι θεοῖς
στέργηθρ ἔχουσαι ; πᾶς δ' ὑφηγεῖται τρόπος
μορφῆς. Λέοντος ἄντρον αἱματοῤῥόφου
οἰκεῖν τοιαύτας εἰκὸς, οὐ χρηστηρίοις
ἐν τοῖσδε πλησίοισι τρίβεσθαι μύσος.
Χωρεῖτ ἄνευ βοτῆρος αἰπολούμεναι.
Ποίμνης τοιαύτης δ' οὔτις εὐφιλὴς θεῶν.

Away ! I bid you off with speed from these abodes ; out from the oracular shrines, lest, having received the winged swift snake (arrow) hurled from the golden-twisted string, you disgorge with pain the black gore you sucked from men, vomiting the clots of blood which you have drawn from them. It is in every way unbecoming to enter these abodes of mine ; go where heads are wrenched from the body and eyes are gouged, to revengeful deeds and slaughters, maiming of boys and stonings, and where those impaled by the spine groan with loud yellings. Ye hags abhorred, these are the feasts in which you delight ; your execrable form is proof of this. It is right that such should inhabit the dens of the blood-ravening lion, but not to tarry in these prophetic shrines with impure tread. Of such a herd the gods disdain to take the charge.

The Innocent and the Impious.
Eum. 313.

Τὸν μὲν καθαρὰς χεῖρας προνέμοντ
οὔτις ἐφέρπει μῆνις ἀφ' ἡμῶν,
ἀσινὴς δ' αἰῶνα διοιχνεῖ·
ὅστις δ' ἀλιτὼν ὥσπερ ὅδ' ἀνὴρ
χεῖρας φονίας ἐπικρύπτει,
μάρτυρες ὀρθαὶ τοῖσι θανοῦσιν
παραγιγνόμεναι πράκτορες αἵματος
αὐτῷ τελέως ἐφάνημεν.

No vindictive rage from us (the Furies) comes stealthily on him whose hands are free from guilt, but he passes through life without harm. Whereas whoever, like this man, commits crimes and hides his ruffian hands, we are close at hand as witnesses of the deed, appearing as avengers of blood.

The Murderer.
Eum. 334.

Τοῦτο γὰρ λάχος διανταία
Μοῖρ ἐπέκλωσεν· ἐμπέδως ἔχειν,
θνατῶν τοῖσιν αὐτουργίαι ξυμπέσωσιν μάταιοι,
τοῖς ὁμαρτεῖν, ὄφρ ἂν γᾶν ὑπέλθῃ· θανὼν δ' οὐκ
ἄγαν ἐλεύθερος.

'Επὶ δὲ τῷ τεθυμένῳ τόδε μέλος
παρακοπὰ, παραφορὰ φρενοδαλῆς,
ὕμνος ἐξ 'Ερινύων,
δέσμιος φρενῶν, ἀφόρμικτος, αὐονὰ βροτοῖς.

For avenging Fate has assigned us (the Furies) this office, saying, "Let those guilty of murders without provocation be pursued till they find refuge in the realms below;" even when dead they are not quite free. But over the victims let this be the song, bringing madness, distracting, mind-destroying, the hymn of the Furies, that charms minds without the lyre, causing shrivelling to mortals.

HEAR BOTH PARTIES.
Eum. 428.

Δυοῖν παρόντοιν ἥμισυς λόγος πάρα.

He hears but half that hears one party only.

See (Lat.) Hear the other side.

SORROW.
Eum. 520.

Ξυμφέρει σωφρονεῖν ὑπὸ στένει.

It is good to grow wise under sorrow.

THE INIQUITIES OF THE FATHERS VISITED ON THE CHILDREN.
Eum. 930.

Πάντα γὰρ αὗται τὰ κατ' ἀνθρώπους
ἔλαχον διέπειν.
'Ο δὲ μὴ κύρσας βαρεῶν τούτων
οὐκ οἶδεν ὅθεν πληγαὶ βίοτου.
Τὰ γὰρ ἐκ προτέρων ἀπλακήματά νιν
πρὸς τάσδ' ἀπάγει, σιγῶν ὄλεθρος
καὶ μέγα φωνοῦντ'
ἐχθραῖς ὀργαῖς ἀμαθύνει.

For the Fates have assigned them (the Furies) a despotic sway over men in all things; he who feels their terrors, knows not whence come the ills of life; for the sire's long-passed crimes bring chastening on their sons, and amidst his thoughts of greatness silent ruin with hostile wrath crushes him.

THE MASTER THE EYE OF THE HOUSE.
Pers. 168.

"Ομμα γὰρ δόμων νομίζω δεσπότου παρουσίαν.

For I deem the presence of the master to be the eye of the house.

MEN ARE A SUFFICIENT BULWARK.

Pers. 349.

Ἀνδρῶν γὰρ ὄντων ἕρκος ἐστὶν ἀσφαλές.

For while there are men, there is a sure bulwark.

THE AFFLICTED FEAR ALL THINGS.

Pers. 598.

Φίλοι, κακῶν μὲν ὅστις ἔμπειρος κυρεῖ,
ἐπίσταται βροτοῖσιν ὡς, ὅταν κλύδων
κακῶν ἐπέλθῃ, πάντα δειμαίνειν φιλεῖ.
ὅταν δ' ὁ δαίμων εὐροῇ, πεποιθέναι
τὸν αὐτὸν ἀεὶ δαίμον' οὐριεῖν τύχης.

My friends, whoever has experienced misfortunes knows that
when a mountain-wave of ills comes upon mortals, they are won⁴
to fear all things ; but when the gale of fortune blows smoothly,
they are confident that the same deity will constantly propel their
bark with a favourable breeze.

THE LOT OF MEN MUST BE BORNE.

Pers. 706.

Ἀνθρώπεια δ' ἄν τοι πήματ' ἂν τύχοι βροτοῖς.
Πολλὰ μὲν γὰρ ἐκ θαλάσσης, πολλὰ δ' ἐκ χέρσου κακὰ
γίγνεται θνητοῖς, ὁ μάσσων βίοτος ἢν ταθῇ πρόσω.

Human misfortunes must befal mankind.   For afflictions rise,
many from sea, and many from land, if life be measured through
a lengthened course.

So Job (v. 7)—" Yet man is born to trouble, as the sparks fly upward."

THE DOOMED.

Pers. 742.

Ἀλλ' ὅταν σπεύδῃ τις αὐτὸς, χὡ θεὸς συνάπτεται.

But when a man is rushing on the road to destruction, God
also lends a hand.

OPPRESSION.

Pers. 820.

Ὡς οὐχ ὑπέρφευ θνητὸν ὄντα χρὴ φρονεῖν.
Ὕβρις γὰρ ἐξανθοῦσ' ἐκάρπωσε στάχυν
ἄτης, ὅθεν πάγκλαυτον ἐξαμᾷ θέρος.

How unbecoming it is for one that is mortal to entertain proud aspiring thoughts ; for presumption, when it has put forth the blade, is wont to produce for fruit an all-mournful harvest of woe.

ALEXIS.

FLOURISHED B.C. 356.

ALEXIS, a native of Thurii, in Italy, was the uncle of the celebrated Menander, and one of the principal writers of the middle comedy. He flourished B.C. 356, and continued to exhibit till B.C. 306, being upwards of one hundred years old when he died. He wrote 245 plays, of which Athenæus gives the titles of 113.

SEEK AND WE SHALL FIND.

Fr. Com. Gr. p. 696.

Ἅπαντα τὰ ζητουμεν' ἐξευρίσκεται,
ἂν μὴ προαποστῆς μηδὲ τὸν πόνον φύγῃς·
ὅπου γὰρ εὑρήκασιν ἄνθρωποί τινες
μέρος τι τῶν θείων τοσοῦτο τῷ τόπῳ
ἀπέχοντες, ἄστρων ἐπιτολάς, δύσεις, τροπάς,
ἔκλειψιν ἡλίου, τί τῶν κοινῶν κάτω
καὶ ουγγενικῶν δύναιτ' ἂν ἄνθρωπον φυγεῖν.

All that thou seekest may be found, if thou shrinkest not nor fliest from labour. For since some have discovered things in heaven, though they are far removed, such as the rising and setting of the stars, the solstices and eclipses of the sun, what common things, that are connected with man here below, should be able to escape his search ?

THE CHANGES OF LIFE.

Fr. Com. Gr. p. 697.

Τοιοῦτο τὸ ζῆν ἐστιν ὥσπερ οἱ κύβοι·
οὐ ταῦτ' ἀεὶ πίπτουσιν, οὐδὲ τῷ βίῳ
ταὐτὸν διαμένει σχῆμα, μεταβολὰς δ' ἔχει.

This life is like a game played with dice—the same figures do not always turn up : so, too, life has not always the same shape but is ever changing.

MAN RESEMBLES WINE.

Fr. Com. Gr. p. 700.

Ὁμοιότατος ἄνθρωπος οἴνῳ τὴν φύσιν
τρόπον τίν᾽ ἐστί· καὶ γὰρ οἶνον τὸν νέον
πολλή 'στ᾽ ἀνάγκη καὶ τὸν ἄνδρ᾽ ἀποξέσαι
πρώτιστον ἀφυβρίσαι τ᾽, ἀπανθήσαντα δέ
σκ..ηρὸν γενέσθαι, παρακμάσαντα δ᾽ ὧν λέγω
τούτων ἀπάντων, ἀπαρυθέντα τὴν ἄνω
ταύτην ἄνοιαν ἐπιπολάζουσαν, τότε
πότιμον γενέσθαι καὶ καταστῆναι πάλιν,
ἡδύν θ᾽ ἅπασι τοὐπίλοιπ ον διατελεῖν.

The nature of man is in some respects very much resembling wine. For, like new wine, the youthful mind requires to have its fermentation thrown off, and its roughness skimmed ; but when its excessive violence has abated, and the fury, which swam on the top, has disappeared, then it becomes drinkable, and settles down, continuing pleasant to all future time.

TRUST DEEDS, NOT OATHS.

Fr. Com. Gr. p. 730.

Οὐ τοῖς γὰρ ὀμνύουσι τὸν φρονοῦντα δεῖ,
τοῖς πράγμασιν δ᾽ αὐτοῖσι πιστεύειν ἀεί.

The wise ought not to trust the oaths of men, but always their deeds.

THE EVENING OF LIFE.

Fr. Com. Gr. p. 747.

Ἤδη γὰρ ὁ βίος οὑμὸς ἑσπέραν ἄγει.

For now my life is approaching its evening.

SLEEP.

Fr. Com. Gr. p. 750.

Οὐ θνητὸς οὐδ᾽ ἀθάνατος, ἀλλ᾽ ἔχων τινά
σύγκρασιν, ὥστε μήτ᾽ ἐν ἀνθρώπου μέρει
μήτ᾽ ἐν θεοῦ ζῆν, ἀλλὰ φύεσθαί τ᾽ ἀεί
καινῶς φθίνειν τε τὴν παρουσίαν πάλιν,
ἀόρατος ὄψιν, γνώριμος δ᾽ ἅπασιν ὤν.
B. Ἀεί σὺ χαίρεις ὦ γύναι μ᾽ αἰνίγμασιν.
A. Καὶ μὴν ἁπλᾶ γε καὶ σαφη λέγω μαθεῖν.
B. Τίς οὖν τοσαυτην παῖς ἔχων ἔσται φύσιν.
A. Ὕπνος, βροτείων, ὦ κόρη, παυστὴρ πόνων.

Neither mortal nor immortal, but having a certain composite nature, so as to live neither the life of man nor of the gods, but to be always springing up anew, and again perishing, invisible to the eye, but known to all.—*B.* Thou always lovest, O woman, to speak in riddles.—*A.* Nay, I speak plainly, and in the utmost simplicity.—*B.* Who, then, can this youngster be with such a nature?—*A.* Sleep, my good girl, the soother of the labours of man.

AMPHIS.

FLOURISHED ABOUT B.C. 332.

AMPHIS, a poet of the middle comedy, flourished about B. C. 332. We have the titles of twenty-six of his plays.

ART.

Fr. Com. Gr. p. 645.

Οὐκ ἔστιν οὐδὲν ἀτυχίας ἀνθρωπίνης
παραμύθιον γλυκύτερον ἐν βίῳ τέχνης·
ἐπι τοῦ μαθήματος γὰρ ἐστηκὼς ὁ νοῦς
αὑτοῦ λέληθε παραπλέων τὰς συμφοράς.

There is no sweeter consolation in misfortune than the pursuit of art; for the mind employed in acquiring it sails secretly past its mishaps.

EAT, DRINK, AND BE MERRY.

Fr. Com. Gr. p. 646.

Πῖνε, παῖζε· θνητὸς ὁ βιός, ὀλίγος οὑπὶ γῆ χρόνος·
ἀθάνατος ὁ θάνατός ἐστιν, ἂν ἅπαξ τις ἀποθάνῃ.

Drink, be merry! life is mortal, the time on earth is short; death is immortal when we are once dead.

A MAN IN DISTRESS.

Fr. Com. Gr. p. 653.

Ἄπολλον, ὡς δυσάρεστόν ἐστ᾽ ἀνώμενος
ἄνθρωπος ἐφ᾽ ἅπασίν τε δυσχερῶς ἔχει.

Apollo, how ill to please is man in distress and annoyed by everything.

SILENCE.

Fr. Com. Gr. p. 655.

Οὐκ ἔστι κρεῖττον τοῦ σιωπᾶν οὐδὲ ἕν.

There is nothing more powerful than silence.

B

ANACREON.

FLOURISHED B.C. 559—525.

ANACREON, one of the most celebrated of the Greek lyric poets, was a native of Teos, in Asia Minor, respecting whom we have few facts on which we can depend. He was the contemporary of Cyrus, Cambyses, and Polycrates of Samos, at whose court we find him, B.C. 531, enjoying high favour, and singing the praises of the tyrant. We next hear of him at the court of Hipparchus at Athens, B.C. 525, where he met the poet Simonides. He died at the age of eighty-five, being choked, as the story goes, by a cherry-stone. Except that he was a voluptuary, and spent his time in singing the praises of love, we know little else respecting his private history. There were five books of Anacreon's poems in the time of Suidas, who is supposed to have lived in the eleventh century, but of these only a few extracts have been preserved. We have given a few extracts from his odes, though it is supposed that they may be of a later date than the time of Anacreon.

THE BEAUTY OF WOMEN.

ii.

Φύσις κέρατα ταύροις,
ὁπλὰς δ᾽ ἔδωκεν ἵπποις,
ποδωκίην λαγωοῖς,
λέουσὶ χάσμ᾽ ὀδόντων,
τοῖς ἰχθύσιν τὸ νηκτὸν,
τοῖς ὀρνέοις πέτασθαι,
τοῖς ἀνδράσι φρόνημα·
γυναιξὶν οὐκ ἔτ᾽ εἶχεν.
Τί οὖν δίδωσι; κάλλος,
ἀντ᾽ ἀσπίδων ἀπασῶν,
ἀντ᾽ ἐγχέων ἁπάντων·
νικᾷ δὲ καὶ σίδηρον,
καὶ πῦρ, καλή τις οὖσα.

Nature has given horns to bulls, hoofs to horses, swiftness to hares, the power of swimming to fishes, of flying to birds, understanding to men. She had nothing more for women. What then does she give? Beauty, which can resist shields and spears. She who is beautiful, is stronger than iron and fire.

LIFE PASSES SWIFTLY AWAY.

iv. 7.

Τρόχος ἅρματος γὰρ οἷα
βίοτος τρέχει κυλισθείς,
ὀλίγη δὲ κεισόμεσθα
κόνις, ὀστέων λυθέντων.

For like the chariot's wheel life runs fast away. A little dust
we lie, when our body has sunk in dissolution.

See (Lat.) Life, shortness of.

ENJOY THE PRESENT.

xxiv. 1.

'Επειδὴ βροτὸς τέχθην
τρίβον βιότου ὁδεύειν,
δρόμον ἔγνων, ὃν παρῆλθον,
ὃν ἔχω δραμεῖν δ' οὐκ οἶδα.
Μέθετε δὲ, φροντίδες, με·
μηδὲν ὑμῖν κἀμοὶ ἔστω!
Πρὶν τὸ τέλος φθάσῃ με,
παίξω, γελάσω, χορεύσω
μετὰ τοῦ καλοῦ Λυαίου.

Since I was born a mortal, to pass over the beaten track of life,
the road I have often passed, I know ; what I have to run over,
of that I am unacquainted. Teasing cares, leave me alone ! What
have I to do with you? Before my last hour shall come, I shall
play, I shall laugh, I shall dance with the fair Lyæus.

So Luke (xii. 19)—"Take thine ease, eat, drink, and be merry ;" and
(xv. 23)—" Let us eat and be merry "

See (Lat.) Enjoy the present.

ADVANTAGES OF WINE.

xxv. 1.

'Οταν πίω τὸν οἶνον,
εὕδουσιν αἱ μέριμναι.
Τί πόνων, τί γόων μοι,
τί μοι μέλει μεριμνῶν ;
θανεῖν με δεῖ, κἂν μὴ θέλω·
τί δὲ τὸν βίον πλανῶμαι ;
πίωμεν οὖν τὸν οἶνον,
τὸν τοῦ καλοῦ Λυαίου·
σὺν τῷ δὲ πίνειν ἡμᾶς
εὕδουσιν αἱ μέριμναι.

When I quaff wine, my cares are lulled to rest. What have I
to do with labours, woes, or cares? Die I must, whether I will

B 2

or no. Why should I wander through life? Let us then quaff
the wine of fair Lyœus. With it our cares are forgotten.

GOLD.
xlvi. 10.

Διὰ τοῦτον οὐκ ἀδελφὸs,
διὰ τοῦτον οὐ τοκῆεs,
πόλεμοι, φόνοι δί αὐτόν·
τὸ δὲ χεῖρον, ὀλλύμεσθα
διὰ τοῦτον οἱ φιλοῦντεs.

In consequence of gold there are no brothers, no parents, but
wars and murders arise from it. And, what is worse, for it we
lovers are bought and sold.

See (Lat.) Gold.

ANAXANDRIDES.

FLOURISHED B.C. 376.

ANAXANDRIDES, a writer of the middle comedy, was a native of
the city Camirus, in Rhodes, or, according to others, of Colophon,
in Ionia. He flourished B.C. 376, and was exhibiting his dramatic
pieces till B.C. 347, when he was present at the celebration of the
Olympia at Dium by Philip, king of Macedon. He is said to have
been the first to lay the foundation of a vicious stage by the intro-
duction of love scenes and intrigues. If his play was unsuccessful,
he used to consign it as waste paper to the performers, and never
deigned to retouch it, as other authors were in the habit of doing
(Athen. ix. 374, a.). His death is said to have been caused by the
following circumstance : Euripides had said in one of his tragedies,
"Nature has wished it so, who regards not laws." Anaxandrides
parodied the verse by substituting "the city" instead of "nature."
The Athenians condemned him to die by starvation (Suidas),
Athenæus mentions the names of twenty-two of his comedies.

OLD AGE.
Fr. Com. Gr. p. 589.

Οὗτοι τὸ γῆραs ἐστιν, ὡs οἴει, πάτερ,
τῶν φορτίων μέγιστον, ἀλλ᾽ ὅs ἂν φέρῃ
ἀγνωμόνωs αὔθ᾽, οὗτόs ἐστιν αἴτιοs·
ἂν δ᾽ εὐκόλωs, ἐνίοτε κοιμίζειν ποιεῖ,

μεταλαμβάνων ἐπιδέξι' αὐτοῦ τὸν τρόπον,
λύπην τ' ἀφαιρῶν ἡδονήν τε προστιθείς·
λύπην δὲ ποιῶν, εἴτι δυσκόλως ἔχει.

Old age is not, father, the heaviest of burdens, as thou thinkest ; but whoever bears it unwisely, he is the party who makes it so : if he bears it without grumbling, he sometimes in this way lulls it asleep, dexterously changing its character, taking away pain and substituting pleasure, but making it pain if he is peevish.

A Blabber.

Fr. Com. Gr. p. 590.

Ὅστις λόγους παρακαταθήκην γὰρ λαβὼν
ἐξεῖπεν, ἄδικός ἐστιν ἢ ἀκρατὴς ἄγαν·
ὁ μὲν διὰ κέρδος, ἄδικος· ὁ δὲ τούτου δίχα
ἀκρατής· ἴσον δέ γ' εἰσὶν ἀμφότεροι κακοί.

Whoever receiving a statement in confidence proceeds to repeat it, is a scoundrel, or very leaky. If he does it for personal gain, he is a scoundrel ; and if he does so without a personal object, he is leaky : both characters are equally bad.

Pleasure.

Fr. Com. Gr. p. 591.

Μηδέποτε δοῦλον ἡδονῆς σαυτὸν ποίει·
λάγνης γυναικός ἐστιν οὐκ ἀνδρὸς τόδε.

Don't make thyself a slave to pleasure. That is the act of a lewd woman, not of a man.

Death.

Fr. Com. Gr. p. 593.

Καλόν γ' ἀποθανεῖν πρὶν θανάτου δρᾶν ἄξιον.

It is good to die before a man has done anything worthy of death.

ANTIPHANES.

BORN ABOUT B.C. 404—DIED ABOUT B.C. 330.

ANTIPHANES, the most highly esteemed writer of the middle comedy, of whose personal history we know nothing. We still possess the titles of about 130 of his plays ; but in all they are said to have been 365, or at least 260, as some of the plays ascribed to him were by other writers.

Not Lost, but Gone Before.

Stobœus, Floril. cxxiv. 27.

Πενθεῖν δὲ μετρίως τοὺς προσήκοντας φίλους·
οὐ γὰρ τεθνᾶσιν, ἀλλὰ τὴν αὐτὴν ὁδόν,
ἣν πᾶσιν ἐλθεῖν ἔστ᾽ ἀναγκαίως ἔχον,
προεληλύθασιν. Εἶτα χἠμεῖς ὕστερον
εἰς ταὐτὸ καταγωγεῖον αὐτοῖς ἥξομεν,
κοινῇ τὸν ἄλλον συνδιατρίψοντες χρόνον.

We should lament in moderation the loss of our friends, for
they are not dead, but have gone before the same road which we
must all necessarily pass ; then we also will hereafter come to the
same place with them, spending eternity in their company.

This idea is often referred to by Seneca—

"Indicemas illos abesse, et nosmetipsi fallamus. . . . Dimisimus illos,
immo consecuturi præmisimus" (Con. Marc., 30).—"Let us think that
they are absent, and let us deceive ourselves. . . . We have sent them
away, nay, we have sent them before, about to follow them." Again :
"Quem putas perisse, præmissus est" (Epist 99).—"He has been sent
before, whom those thinkest to have perished." Again : "Erras, &c.
Quid fata defiemas? non reliquit ille nos, sed antecessit" (Con. Polyb. 28).
—"Thou art mistaken, &c. Why do we bemoan what is fated ? He has
not left us, but gone before " Again : "Ex fortasse (si modo sapientium
vera fama est, recipitque nos locus aliquis) quem putamus perisse præmissus est" (Epist. 63).—"And perhaps, if only the idea of the wise is
true, and some place receive us after death, he whom we think to have
perished has been sent before us."

So E. Elliot ("The Excursion")—

"The buried are not lost, but gone before."

"This Night thy Soul shall be required of Thee."

Stobœus, Floril. cxxi. 4.

Οὐδεὶς πώποτε,
ὦ δέσποτ᾽ ἀπέθαν᾽ ἀποθανεῖν πρόθυμος ὤν,
τοὺς γλιχομένους δὲ ζῆν κατασπᾷ τοῦ σκέλους
ἄκοντας ὁ χάρων ἐπὶ τὸ πορθμεῖόν τ᾽ ἄγει
σιτιζομένους καὶ πάντ᾽ ἔχοντας ἀφθόνως.
Ὁ δὲ λιμός εστιν ἀθανασίας φάρμακον.

No one, master, has ever died who was ready to die ; but Charon
draws by the legs to his ferry-boat those who are desirous to live,
and carries them off in the midst of their banquetings, and with
everything around them richly to enjoy. It is hunger that is the
medicine for immortality.

See Luke (xii. 20).

Old Age.

Stobœus, Floril. cxvi. 23.

Ὦ γῆρας, ὡς ἅπασιν ἀνθρώποισιν εἶ
ποθεινόν, ὡς εὐδαιμαινον, εἶθ᾽ ὅταν παρῇς,

ἀχθηρόν, ὡς μοχθηρόν, εὖ λέγει τέ σε
οὐδείς, κακῶς δὲ πᾶς τις ὃς σοφῶς λέγει.

O old age! how desired thou art by all, how happy thou art thought to be ; then, when thou comest, how sad, how full of sorrow ; no one speaks well of thee, every one ill of thee, if he speaks with wisdom.

RICHES AND POVERTY.
Stobæus, Floril. xcvii. 8.

Ὁ πλοῦτός εστι παρακάλυμμα τῶν κακῶν,
ὦ μῆτερ ἥ πενία δὲ περιφανές τε καὶ
ταπεινόν.

Riches are a cloak for ills, O mother; poverty is transparent and abject.

THE UPRIGHT.
Stobæus, Floril. ix. 16.

Ὁ μηδὲν ἀδικῶν ὀυδενὸς δεῖται νόμου.

He who commits no crime requires no law.

UNRIGHTEOUS GAINS.
Stobæus, Floril. xvi. 12.

Τὰ πονηρὰ κέρδη τὰς μὲν ἡδονὰς ἔχει
μικράς, ἔπειτα δ᾽ ὕστερον λύπας μακράς.

Unjust gains give short-lived pleasures, but afterwards lengthened griefs.

So Proverbs (xvi. 8)—"Better is a little with righteousness, than great revenues without right."

THE ACQUISITION OF WEALTH DEADENS THE SENSE OF RIGHT AND WRONG.
Stobæus, Floril. xvi. 12.

Ὡς δυστυχεῖς, ὅσοισι τὸν κέρδους χάριν
ἐν ὑπροσθε ταἰσχρὰ φαίνετ᾽ εἶναι τῶν καλῶν.
Ἐπισκοτεῖ γὰρ τῷ φρονεῖν τὸ λαμβάνειν.

How unhappy thou art, to whom the base appears preferable to the honourable for the sake of gain ; for the acquiring of riches darkens the sense of right and wrong!

MORTALITY OF MAN.
Stobæus, Floril. xxi. 4.

Εἰ θνητὸς εἶ, βέλτιστε, θνητὰ καὶ φρόνει.

My best of friends, if thou art mortal, think of thy mortality.

A Good Conscience.

Stobæus, Floril. xxiv. 7.

Τὸ μὴ συνειδέναι γὰρ αὑτοῦ τῷ βίῳ
ἀδίκημα μηδὲν ἡδονὴν πολλὴν ἔχει.

To be conscious to one's self of having committed no unjust act throughout life is the cause of much pleasure.

Diligence.

Stobæus, Floril. xxix. 51.

Τῆς ἐπιμελείας δοῦλα πάντα γίνεται.

All things are subservient to diligence.

Habits of Honour.

Stobæus, Floril. xxxvii. 13.

Τρόπος δίκαιος κτῆμα τιμιώτατον.

Habits of justice are a most valuable possession.

A Slave.

Stobæus, Floril. lxii. 9.

Δούλῳ γὰρ οἶμαι πατρίδος ἐστερημένῳ
χρηστὸς γενόμενός ἐστι δεσπότης πατρίς.

To a slave deprived of his country, I think a good master is his country.

Pleasures of Love.

Stobæus, Floril. lxiii. 12.

Εἴ φησι τοὺς ἐρῶντας οὐχὶ νοῦν ἔχειν,
ἦ πού τίς ἐστι τοὺς τρόπους ἀβέλτερος.
Εἰ γὰρ ἀφέλοι τις τοῦ βίου τὰς ἡδονάς,
καταλείπετ᾽ οὐδὲν ἕτερον ἢ τεθνηκέναι.

If any one says that those in love have no sense, he is certainly stupid and good for nothing; for if we take away the pleasures of love from life, there is nothing left but to die.

Woman to be Trusted only in One Thing.

Stobæus, Floril. lxxiii. 48.

'Εγὼ γυναικὶ δ᾽ ἕν τι πιστεύω μόνον,
ἐπὰν ἀποθάνῃ μὴ βιώσεσθαι πάλιν,
τὰ δ᾽ ἄλλ᾽ ἀπιστῶ πάνθ᾽ ἕως ἂν ἀποθάνῃ.

One thing only I believe in a woman, that she will not come to life again after she is dead; in everything else I distrust her till she is dead.

Mind and Body.
Stobæus, Floril. lxxiv. 3.

Μὴ χρώμασιν τὸ σῶμα λαμπρύνειν θέλε,
ἔργοις δὲ καθαροῖς καὶ τρόποις τὴν καρδίαν.

Think not about decking thy body with ornaments, but thy heart with pure thoughts and habits.

Honest Poverty and Unjust Gain.
Stobæus, Floril. xcvii. 1.

Καλῶς πένεσθαι μᾶλλον ἢ πλουτεῖν κακῶς·
τὸ μὲν γὰρ ἔλεον, τὸ δ' ἐπιτίμησιν φέρει.

It is better to be poor with honour than to be rich through unjust means ; the one brings pity, the other censure.

Grief.
Stobæus, Floril. xcix. 27.

Λύπη μανίας ὁμότοιχος εἶναι μοι δοκεῖ.

Grief seems to be next neighbour to madness.

Old Age.
Stobæus, Floril. cxvi. 15.

Τὸ γῆρας ὥσπερ βωμός ἐστι τῶν κακῶν·
πάντ' ἐστ' ἰδεῖν εἰς τοῦτο καταπεφευγότα.

Old age is, as it were, the altar of ills ; we may see them all taking refuge in it.

MARCUS ANTONINUS, or AURELIUS.

BORN A.D. 121—DIED A.D. 180.

MARCUS ANTONINUS, or MARCUS AURELIUS, the sixteenth Emperor of Rome in succession from Augustus, was descended from a family which pretended to trace its origin to Numa, and to be connected with a king of the Salentini, in the south of Italy, called Malennius, who had founded the city Lupiæ, now *Lecce.* His more immediate ancestors, however, had come from the small municipal town Succubo, in Spain, and had by their industry and abilities reached the highest dignities in Rome. His father was Annius Verus, the friend of the Emperor Adrian, and his mother was Domitia

B 3

Calvilla, daughter of Calvisius Tullus, who had been twice consul. Marcus Antoninus was born at Rome, 20th April A.D. 121, in the fifth year of Adrian's reign. He was placed by his grandfather under the ablest masters which Rome could supply, and he seems to have been of a disposition which led him to take pleasure in every intellectual pursuit. Philosophy, in all her various ramifications, was his delight from his earliest years; and while he was scarcely twelve years old, he was so earnest in its pursuit that he began to practise some of those foolish austerities which the Stoics were in the habit of recommending. He insisted on being allowed to sleep on the ground; and it required all the authority of his mother to make him forego his boyish freak. He received instruction from Herodes Atticus, Corn. Fronto, Sextus of Chæroneia the grandson of Plutarch, Apollonius, the friend of Antoninus Pius; and even after he had ascended the throne he did not consider it beneath his dignity to attend the public lectures of the philosophers. From the connection of his father with Adrian, he attracted at an early period the attention of the emperor. Adrian adopted Antoninus Pius, A.D. 138, only on condition that he should admit into his family his young friend Annius Verus, and Lucius Verus, the son of that Ælius Verus who had been selected by Adrian to succeed him. He was at this time only eighteen, and seems, by his respectful conduct, soon to have won the heart of his adopted father, who gave him the name of Marcus Aurelius, by which he is generally known in history. As soon as Antoninus succeeded to the throne, he raised Aurelius to the dignity of Cæsar; and though he had been betrothed to the daughter of L. Cejonius Commodus, he prevailed on him to forego his engagement, and marry his youngest daughter, Annia Faustina, who became soon equally profligate as her mother. During the whole of the reign of Antoninus, Aurelius lived in the most complete state of harmony with his father-in-law, and on his deathbed was appointed to succeed him. He ascended the throne, A.D. 161, in the fortieth year of his age. On his accession to the throne his history is merged in that of the Roman Empire, which was then beginning to be attacked on all sides by the neighbouring nations. The Parthians, in the East, first attracted his attention; and no sooner were they compelled to submit, than a still more formidable war broke out on the side of Germany. Though his time was much occupied with state affairs, his greatest pleasure was derived from philosophy and literature. Music, poetry, and painting were not forgotten; and the severer sciences of mathematics and law engaged no small part of his attention. With the exception of a few letters which were found in the recently-discovered remains of Fronto, the only work of Marcus which has come down to us is a volume composed in Greek,—a kind of commonplace book, in which he put down from time to time his thoughts and feelings upon moral and religious subjects, together with remarkable maxims which he had culled from writers distinguished for wisdom and virtue. The greatest blot on his memory is the severity with which he treated the Christians ; and it is the more difficult to understand the reason of his conduct, as it is altogether at variance with his general principles as laid down in his " Meditations."

MAN FORMED OF BODY, SOUL, AND SPIRIT.

ii. 2.

'Οτί ποτε τοῦτό εἰμι, σαρκία ἐστὶ καὶ πνευμάτιον καὶ τὸ ἡγεμονικόν· ἀλλ' ὡς ἤδη ἀποθνήσκων, τῶν μὲν σαρκίων καταφρόνησον.

Whatever I am, I am formed of body, breath, and spirit ; wherefore, as if thou wast now dying, abstain from fleshly lusts.

So 1 Peter (ii. 11)—"Abstain from fleshly lusts, which war against the soul."

THE PRESENT IS THE TIME FOR REFORMATION OF CHARACTER.

ii. 4.

Δεῖ δὲ ἤδη ποτε αἰσθέσθαι, τίνος κόσμου μέρος εἶ, καὶ τίνος διοικοῦντος τὸν κόσμου ἀπόρροια ὑπέστης· καὶ ὅτι ὅρος ἐστί σοι περιγεγραμμένος τοῦ χρόνου, ᾦ ἐὰν εἰς τὸ μὴ ἀπαιθριάσαι χρήσῃ, οἰχήσεται, καὶ οἰχήσῃ, καὶ αὖθις οὐκ ἥξεται.

Thou must now at last perceive of what universe thou formest a part, and of what ruler of the universe thou art an efflux ; and that a term of time is allotted to thee, which if thou dost not use for clearing away the clouds from thy mind, it will go and thou wilt go, and it will not again return.

So 2 Corinthians (vi. 2)—"Behold now is the accepted time, now is the day of salvation."

DO EVERYTHING AS IF IT WERE THE LAST ACT OF THY LIFE.

ii. 5.

Πάσης ὥρας φρόντιζε στιβαρῶς, ὡς Ρωμαῖος, καὶ ἀρρήν, τὸ ἐν χερσὶ μετὰ τῆς ἀκριβοῦς καὶ ἀπλάστου σεμνότητος, καὶ φιλοστοργίας καὶ δικαιότητος πράσσειν· καὶ σχολήν σαυτῷ ἀπὸ πασῶν τῶν ἄλλων φαντασιῶν πορίζειν, πορίεις δὲ ἂν ὡς ἐσχάτην τοῦ βίου, ἑκάστην πρᾶξιν ἐνεργῆς.

See that thou devote thyself zealously, as a Roman and a man of energy, to every work that thou mayest have on hand, with scrupulous and unfeigned dignity of character, with love of the human race,·independence, and a strict adherence to justice, and withdraw thyself from all other thoughts. Thou wilt give thyself relief if thou doest every act of this life as if it were the last.

LIFE THE SAME TO ALL.

ii. 14.

Κἂν τρισχίλια ἔτη βιώσεσθαι μέλλῃς, καὶ τοσαυτάκις μύρια, ὅμως μέμνησο ὅτι οὐδεὶς ἄλλον ἀποβάλλει βίον ἢ τούτον ὃν ζῇ· οὐδ' ἄλλον ζῇ, ἢ ὃν ἀποβάλλει· εἰς ταὐτὸ οὖν καθίσταται τὸ μήκιστον τῷ βραχυτάτῳ, τὸ γὰρ παρὸν πᾶσιν ἴσον καὶ τὸ ἀπολλύμενον· οὔτε γὰρ τὸ παρῳχηκὸς, οὔτε τὸ μέλλον ἀποβάλλοι ἄν τις.

Though thou wert about to live three thousand years, and as many myriads, yet thou oughtest never to forget that no man loses any other portion of life than that which he is living at the moment, nor does he live any other than that which he now loses. Therefore the longest life comes to the same point with the shortest, since the present time is equal to all, and therefore what is lost is equal to all. For a man cannot lose either the past or the future.

EVERYTHING IS MERE OPINION.

ii. 15.

Ὅτι πᾶν ὑπόληψις.

Everything is mere opinion.

This is the motto of Shaftesbury's "Characteristics."

LIFE A WARFARE.

ii. 17.

Συνελόντι δὲ εἰπεῖν, πάντα, τὰ μὲν τοῦ σώματος, ποταμός· τὰ δὲ τῆς ψυχῆς ὄνειρος καὶ τύφος· ὁ δὲ βίος, πόλεμος καὶ ξένου ἐπιδημία· ἡ ὑστεροφημία δὲ, λήθη· τί οὖν τὸ παραπέμψαι δυνάμενον; ἓν καὶ μόνου φιλοσοφία.

And to say everything in the shortest compass, everything which belongs to the body is a stream, and what belongs to the soul is a dream and vapour ; life is a warfare, and a stranger's sojourn, and after-fame is oblivion. What is that, then, which is able to conduct a man ? One thing, and only one, philosophy.

In Seneca (Epist. 96) we have, " Vivere militare est ;" and in Voltaire (Mahomet ii. 3), " Ma vie est un combat."
So James (iv. 14)—" For what is your life? it is even a vapour."

Man should Stand Erect.

iii. 5.

Ἐνέστω δὲ τὸ φαιδρὸν, καὶ τὸ ἀπροσδεὲς τῆς ἔξωθεν ὑπηρεσίας, καὶ τὸ ἀπροσδεὲς ἡσυχίας, ἣν ἄλλοι παρέχουσι· ὀρθὸν οὖν εἶναι χρὴ, οὐχὶ ὀρθούμενον.

Be cheerful also, and seek not external help, nor the tranquillity which others give. A man then must stand erect, not be kept erect by others.

An Upright Man never Unprepared to Leave Life.

iii. 8.

Οὐδὲν ἂν ἐν τῇ διανοίᾳ τοῦ κεκολασμένου καὶ ἐκκεκαθαρμένου πυῶδες, οὐδὲ μὲν μεμολυσμένον, οὐδὲ ὕπουλον εὕροις· οὐδὲ ἀσυντελῆ τὸν βίον αὐτου ἡ πεπρωμένη καταλαμβάνει, ὡς ἂν τις εἴποι τὸν τραγῳδὸν, πρὸ τοῦ τελέσαι καὶ διαδραματίσαι.

In the mind of a man that is chastened and purified thou wilt find nothing foul, impure, or any sore skinned over; nor will fate ever overtake him in a state of being that is imperfect, just as one may say of a tragic actor who leaves the stage before he has finished his part.

The Longest Posthumous Fame is Short.

iii. 10.

Μικρὸν δὲ καὶ ἡ μηκίστη ὑστεροφημία, καὶ αὐτὴ δὴ κατὰ διαδοχὴν ἀνθρωπαρίων τάχιστα τεθνηξομένων, καὶ οὐκ εἰδότων οὐδὲ ἑαυτοὺς οὔτέ γε τὸν πρόπαλαι τεθνηκότα.

Short, too, the longest posthumous fame, and even this only continued by a succession of poor human beings, who will very soon die, and who know not even themselves, much less him who died long ago.

The Vanity of All Things.

iv. 3.

Ἀλλὰ τὸ δοξάριόν σε περισπάσει. Ἄπιδων εἰς τὸ τάχος τῆς πάντων λήθης καὶ τὸ χάος τοῦ ἐφ' ἑκάτερα ἀπείρου αἰῶνος, καὶ τὸ κενὸν τῆς ἀπηχήσεως, καὶ τὸ εὐμετάβολον καὶ ἄκρατον τῶν ἀφ' ἡμῖν δοκούντων καὶ τὸ στενὸν τοῦ τόπου ἐν ᾧ περιγράφεται. Ὅλη τε γὰρ ἡ γῆ στιγμὴ καὶ ταύτης πόσον γωνίδιον ἡ κατοίκησις αὕτη; καὶ ἐνταῦθα πόσοι, καὶ διοί τινες οἱ ἐπαινεσόμενοι.

But perhaps the love of fame may torment thee. Consider how soon all things will be buried in forgetfulness, and what a bottomless chaos exists on both sides of thee; how vain is the applause of the world, how changeable the opinions of the mob of mankind, and how utterly devoid of judgment they are; in short, within how narrow a space this fame, of which thou art so greedy, is circumscribed. For the whole earth is a point, and how small a nook in it is thy dwelling, and how few are there in it, and what kind of people are they who will praise thee?

See Eccles. i. 14.

DEATH AND BIRTH EQUALLY A MYSTERY.

iv. 5.

Ὁ θάνατος τοιοῦτος, οἷον γένεσις, φύσεως μυστήριον, σύγκρισις ἐκ τῶν αὐτῶν στοιχείων (καὶ διάλυσις) εἰς ταὐτά· ὅλως δὲ οὐκ ἐφ' ὧν ἄν τις αἰσχυνθείη· οὐ γὰρ παρὰ τὸ ἑξῆς τῷ νοερῷ ζῴῳ, οὐδὲ παρὰ τὸν λόγον τῆς παρασκευῆς.

Death is something like the birth of man, equally a mystery of nature, a composition out of the same elements, and a decomposition into the same; and nothing at all of which any one need be ashamed, for it is not contrary to the nature of a reasonable animal, and not contrary to the reason of our constitution.

DEATH IS ALWAYS IMPENDING.

iv. 17.

Μὴ ὡς μύρια μέλλων ἔτη ζῆν· τὸ χρεὼν ἐπήρτηται· ἕως ζῆς, ἕως ἔξεστιν, ἀγαθὸς γένου.

Do not act as if thou wert about to live ten thousand years. Death is impending. While thou enjoyest life, and while thou mayest, be good and upright.

See (Lat.) Death.

PREDESTINATION.

iv. 26.

Συμβέβηκέ σοι τι καλῶς; ἐκ τῶν ὅλων ἀπ' ἀρχῆς σοι συγκαθείμαρτο, καὶ συνεκλώθετο πᾶν τὸ συμβαῖνον.

Has any good fortune befallen thee? It has been predestinated to thee from the beginning of the world, and whatever happens has been so fated.

See (Lat.) Predestination.

NOTHING NEW UNDER THE SUN.

iv. 32.

Ἐπινόησον, λόγου χάριν, τοὺς ἐπὶ Οὐεσπασιανοῦ καιρούς, ὄψει ταῦτα πάντα· γαμοῦντας, παιδιοτροφοῦντας, νοσοῦντας, ἀποθνήσκοντας, πολεμοῦντας, ἑορτάζοντας, ἐμπορευομένους, γεωργοῦντας, κολακεύοντας αὐθαδιζομένους, ὑποπτεύοντας, ἐπιβουλεύοντας, ἀποθανεῖν τινας εὐχομένους, γογγύζοντας, ἐπὶ τοῖς παροῦσιν, ἐρῶντας,

Θησαυρίζοντας, ὑπατείας, βασιλείας ἐπιθυμοῦντας· οὐκοῦν ἐκεῖνος μὲν ὁ τούτων βίος, οὐκ ἔτι οὐδαμοῦ.

Consider, for example, and thou wilt find that almost all the transactions in the time of Vespasian differed little from those of the present day. Thou there findest marrying and giving in marriage, educating children, sickness, death, war, joyous holidays, traffic, agriculture, flatterers, insolent pride, suspicions, laying of plots, longing for the death of others, newsmongers, lovers, misers, men canvassing for the consulship and for the kingdom ;—yet all these passed away, and are nowhere.

See (Lat.) Nothing new.

So Ecclesiastes (i. 9)—"The thing that hath been, it is that which shall be ; and that which is done, is that which shall be done ; and there is no new thing under the sun."

What is an Eternal Remembrance ?

iv. 33.

Τί δὲ καὶ ἐστιν ὅλως ἀείμνηστον ; ὅλον κενόν. Τί οὖν ἐστι, περὶ ὃ δεῖ σπουδὴν εἰσφέρεσθαι ; ἓν τοῦτο, διάνοια δικαία, καὶ πράξεις κοινωνικαὶ, καὶ λόγος οἷος μήποτε διαψεύσασθαι, καὶ διάθεσις ἀσπαζομένη πᾶν τὸ συμβαῖνον, ὡς αναγκαῖον, ὡς γνώριμον, ὡς ἀπ᾽ ἀρχῆς τοιαύτης, καὶ πηγῆς ῥέον.

And what is even an eternal remembrance? A mere empty nothing. What is it, then, about which we ought to employ our serious thoughts? This one thing, thoughts just and acts social, words that never are false, a disposition that gladly submits to whatever happens, as necessary, as usual, as flowing from a principle and source of the same kind.

Description of Time.

iv. 43.

Ποταμός τις ἐκ τῶν γινομένων καὶ ῥεῦμα βίαιον, ὁ αἰών· ἅμα τε γὰρ ὤφθη ἕκαστον, τοτὲ παρενήνεκται, καὶ ἄλλο παραφέρεται, τὸ δὲ ἐνεχθήσεται.

Time is like a river, made up of the things which happen, and a torrent ; for as soon as a thing has been seen, then it is carried off and another comes in its place, and this will be carried away also.

Rise Contented from the Feast of Life.

iv. 48.

Πάντα δὲ ἐν βραχεῖ. Τὸ γὰρ ὅλα κατιδεῖν ἀεὶ τὰ ἀνθρώπινα ὡς ἐφήμερα καὶ εὐτελῆ· ἐχθὲς μὲν μυξάριον, αὔριον δὲ τάριχος, ἢ τέφρα· τὸ ἀκαριαῖον οὖν τοῦτο τοῦ χρόνου κατὰ φύσιν διελθεῖν, καὶ ἵλεων καταλῦσαι ὡς ἂν εἰ ἐλαία πέπειρος γενομένη ἔπιπτεν, εὐφημοῦσα τὴν ἐνεγκοῦσαν, καὶ χάριν εἰδυῖα τῷ φύσαντι δένδρῳ.

To conclude, see how ephemeral and worthless human things
are, and what was yesterday a little mucus, to-morrow will be a
mummy or ashes. Pass, then, through this little space of time
suitably to nature, and end thy journey in content, just as an
olive falls off when it is ripe, blessing nature who produced it,
and thanking the tree on which it grew.

So Philippians (iv. 11)—"I have learned, in whatsoever state I am,
therewith to be content."

NOTHING PERISHES UTTERLY.

v. 13.

'Εξ αἰτιώδους καὶ ὑλικοῦ συνέστηκα· οὐδέτερον δὲ τούτων εἰς τὸ
μὴ ὂν φθαρήσεται ὥσπερ οὐδ' ἐκ τοῦ μὴ ὄντος ὑπέστη· οὐκοῦν
καταχθήσεται πᾶν μέρος ἐμὸν κατὰ μεταβολὴν εἰς μέρος τι τοῦ
κόσμου· καὶ πάλιν ἐκεῖνο εἰς ἕτερον μέρος τοῦ κόσμου μεταβαλεῖ.

I consist of figure and matter : neither of these will be annihi-
lated, as neither of them were created from nothing. Therefore,
every part of me, when a change shall take place, will go into
something else in the world, and this again will be changed into
some other thing, and so on *ad infinitum.*

MAN IS AS HIS MIND.

v. 16.

Οἷα ἂν πολλάκις φαντασθῇς, τοιαύτη σοι ἔσται ἡ διάνοια· βάπτεται
γὰρ ὑπὸ τῶν φαντασιῶν ἡ ψυχή.

Such as are thy habitual thoughts, such also will be the character of thy mind ; for the soul is dyed by the thoughts.

THE REAL WORTH OF MAN.

vii. 3.

Παρακολουθεῖν μέντοι, ὅτι τοσούτου ἄξιος ἕκαστός ἐστιν ὅσου ἄξιά
ἐστι ταῦτα περὶ ἃ ἐσπούδακεν.

Be aware, therefore, that every man is worth just so much as
the things are worth about which he busies himself.

OBLIVION OF ALL THINGS.

vii. 21.

'Εγγὺς μὲν ἡ σὴ περὶ πάντων λήθη· ἐγγὺς δὲ ἡ πάντων περὶ σοῦ
λήθη.

The time is at hand when thou wilt forget and be forgotten
by all.

Love your Enemies.
vii. 22.

Ἴδιον ἀνθρώπου φιλεῖν καὶ τοὺς πταίοντας.

It is the duty of men to love even those who injure them.

See Matt. v. 44.

Everything in Change.
vii. 25.

Πάντα ὅσα ὁρᾷς, ὅσον οὔπω μεταβαλεῖ ἡ τὰ ὅλα διοικοῦσα φύσις, καὶ ἄλλα ἐκ τῆς οὐσίας αὐτῶν ποιήσει καὶ πάλιν ἄλλα ἐκ τῆς ἐκείνων οὐσίας, ἵνα ἀεὶ νεαρὸς ᾖ ὁ κόσμος.

Nature, which rules the universe, will soon change all things which thou seest, and out of their substance will make other things, and again other things from the substance of them, that the world may ever be fresh.

Obey God and Love thy Neighbour.
vii. 31.

Φαιδρυνον σεαυτὸν ἁπλότητι καὶ αἰδοῖ καὶ τῇ πρὸς τὸ ἀνὰ μέσον ἀρετῆς καὶ κακίας, ἀδιαφορίᾳ· φίλησον τὸ ἀνθρώπινον γένος· ἀκολούθησον θεῷ.

Be simple and modest in thy deportment, and treat with indifference whatever lies between virtue and vice. Love the human race; obey God.

See Matt. v. 43.

What has Been, will Be.
vii. 49.

Τὰ προγεγονότα ἀναθεωρεῖν· τὰς τοσαύτας τῶν ἡγεμονιῶν μεταβολὰς· ἔξεστι καὶ τὰ ἐσόμενα προεφορᾶν· ὁμοειδῆ γὰρ πάντως ἔσται καὶ οὐχ οἷόν τε ἐκβῆναι τοῦ ῥυθμοῦ τῶν νῦν γενομένων· ὅθεν καὶ ἴσον τὸ τεσσαράκοντα ἔτεσιν ἱστορῆσαι τὸν ἀνθρώπινον βίον, τῷ ἐπὶ ἔτη μύρια· τί γὰρ πλέον ὄψει.

Look at the past—at the innumerable changes of governments. Thou mayest thus conjecture with safety as to the future, for they will be altogether alike, and it will not be possible for them to deviate from the order of the things which are at present. Wherefore, to contemplate human life for forty years is the same as to have contemplated it for ten thousand years. For what more wilt thou see?

God is Merciful.
vii. 70.

Οἱ θεοὶ ἀθάνατοι ὄντες οὐ δυσχεραίνουσιν, ὅτι ἐν τοσούτῳ τῷ αἰῶν.

δεήσει αὐτοὺς πάντως ἀεὶ τοιούτων ὄντων καὶ τόσούτων φαύλων ἀνέχεσθαι· προσέτι δέ καὶ κήδονται αὐτῶν παντοίως.

The gods, being immortal, are not annoyed, because during so long a time they are obliged to endure men such as they are, and so many of them bad ; and, besides this, they also take care of them in all ways.

So Psalm (ciii. 8)—"The Lord is merciful and gracious, slow to anger, and plenteous in mercy."

THE LIAR.

ix. 1.

Ὁ τὸ βούλημα ταύτης παραβαίνων, ἀσεβεῖ δηλονότι εἰς τὴν πρεσβυτάτην τῶν θεῶν· ἡ γὰρ τῶν ὅλων φύσις, ὄντων ἐστὶ φύσις· τὰ δέ γε ὄντα πρὸς τὰ ὑπάρχοντα πάντα οἰκείως ἔχει· ἔτι δὲ καὶ ἀλήθεια αὕτη ὀνομάζεται, καὶ τῶν ἀληθῶν ἀπάντων πρώτη αἰτία ἐστίν· ὁ μὲν οὖν ἐκὼν ψευδόμενος ἀσεβεῖ, καθόσον ἐξαπατῶν ἀδικεῖ· ὁ δὲ ἄκων, καθόσον ἀκοσμεῖ, μαχόμενος τῇ τοῦ κόσμου φύσει· μάχεται γὰρ ὁ ἐπὶ τἀναντία τοῖς ἀλήθεσι φερόμενος παρ' ἑαυτόν· ἀφορμὰς γὰρ προειλήφει παρὰ τῆς φύσεως, ὧν ἀμελήσας οὐχ οἷός τέ ἐστι νῦν διακρίνειν τὰ ψευδῆ ἀπὸ τῶν ἀληθῶν.

He, too, who transgresses her will (*i.e.*, who lies) is clearly guilty of impiety to the eldest of goddesses, for the universal nature is the nature of things that are, and things that are have an intimate relation to all things that come into existence. Moreover, that universal nature is called truth, and is the first cause of all things that are true. He, therefore, who lies intentionally, acts with impiety, inasmuch as he acts unjustly by deceiving, and he also who lies unintentionally, inasmuch as he is at variance with universal nature, fighting against the nature of the universe ; for he fights against it who is borne of himself to that which is contrary to truth, for he had received powers from nature, through the neglect of which he is not able to distinguish falsehood from truth.

DEATH.

ix. 3.

Μὴ καταφρόνει θανάτου, ἀλλὰ εὐαρέστει αὐτῷ, ὡς ἐκ τούτου ἑνὸς ὄντος, ὧν ἡ φύσις ἐθέλει· οἷον γάρ ἐστι τὸ νεάσαι καὶ τὸ γηράσαι, καὶ τὸ αὐξῆσαι, καὶ τὸ ἀκμάσαι, καὶ ὀδόντας, καὶ γένειον, καὶ πολιὰς ἐνεγκεῖν, καὶ σπεῖραι, καὶ κυοφορῆσαι, καὶ ἀποκυῆσαι, καὶ τὰ ἄλλα -ἃ φυσικὰ ἐνεργήματα ὅσα αἱ τοῦ σοῦ βίου ὧραι φέρουσιν, τοιοῦτο καὶ τὸ διαλυθῆναι.

Do not despise death, but receive it with gladness, as one of those things which nature wills. For as it is to be young and to grow old, to increase in size and reach maturity, to have teeth, a beard, and grey hairs, and to beget and to be pregnant, and to bring forth, and all other operations which the seasons of thy life bring, such also is thy dissolution.

DEATH.
ix. 3.

Θᾶττον ἔλθῃς, ὦ θάνατε, μή που καὶ αὐτὸς ἐπιλάθωμαι ἐμαυτοῦ.

O death! mayest thou approach quickly, lest perchance I too should forget myself.

THE WRONG-DOER.
ix. 4.

Ὁ ἁμαρτάνων ἑαυτῷ ἁμαρτάνει· ὁ ἀδικῶν ἑαυτὸν κακοῖ κακὸν ἑαυτὸν ποιῶν.

He who does wrong, does wrong against himself; he, who acts unjustly, acts unjustly to himself, by making himself bad.

So John (viii. 34)—"Whosoever committeth sin is the servant of sin."

FORGIVENESS.
ix. 11.

Εἰ μὲν δύνασαι, μεταδίδασκε, εἰ δὲ μή, μέμνησο, ὅτι πρὸς τοῦτο ἡ εὐμένειά σοι δέδοται· καὶ οἱ θεοὶ δὲ εὐμενεῖς τοῖς τοιούτοις εἰσίν.

If thou art able, correct by teaching those who sin; but if thou art unable, remember that indulgence is given to thee for this purpose; the gods, too, are indulgent to such.

So Matthew (vi. 14)—"For if ye forgive men their trespasses, your heavenly Father will also forgive you."

ALL THINGS ARE THE SAME.
ix. 14.

Πάντα ταῦτα συνήθη μὲν τῇ πείρᾳ· ἐφήμερα δὲ τῷ χρόνῳ· ῥυπαρὰ δὲ τῇ ὕλῃ· πάντα νῦν, οἷα ἐπ᾽ ἐκείνων οὓς κατεθάψαμεν.

All things are the same, familiar in experience, ephemeral in time, and worthless in matter. Everything now is just as it was in the time of those whom we have buried.

ALL THINGS ARE CHANGING.
ix. 19.

Πάντα ἐν μεταβολῇ· καὶ αὐτὸς σὺ ἐν διηνεκεῖ ἀλλοιώσει καὶ κατά τι φθορᾷ· καὶ ὁ κόσμος δὲ ὅλος.

All things are changing; and thou thyself art in continuous mutation, and in a manner in constant wasting away; so also is the whole universe.

Changes come like Wave upon Wave.

ix. 28.

Ἤδη πάντας ἡμᾶς γῆ καλύψει· ἔπειτα καὶ αὐτὴ μεταβαλεῖ· κἀκεῖνα εἰς ἄπειρον μεταβαλεῖ· καὶ πάλιν ἐκεῖνα εἰς ἄπειρον· τὰς γὰρ ἐπικυματώσεις τῶν μεταβολῶν καὶ ἀλλοιώσεων ἐνθυμούμενός τις, καὶ τὸ τάχος, παντὸς θνητοῦ καταφρονήσει.

Soon will the earth cover us all; then, too, the earth will change; and so on things will change for ever and ever; for when a man reflects on the changes and transformations which follow one another, like wave upon wave, and their rapidity, he will despise everything that is mortal.

The Value of a Posthumous Name and Reputation.

ix. 30.

Ἄνωθεν ἐπιθεωρεῖν ἀγέλας μυρίας, καὶ τελετὰς μυρίας, καὶ πλοῦν παντοῖον ἐν χειμῶσι καὶ γαλήναις, καὶ διαφορὰς γινομένων, συγγινομένων, ἀπογινομένων· ἐπινόει δὲ τὸν ὑπ’ ἄλλων πάλαι βεβιωμένον βίον, τὸν μετά σε βιωσησόμενον, καὶ τὸν νῦν ἐν τοῖς βαρβάροις ἔθνεσι βιόμενον· καὶ ὅσοι μὲν οὐδὲ ὄνομά σου γινώσκουσι, ὅσοι δὲ τάχιστα ἐπιλήσονται, ὅσοι δὲ ἐπαινοῦντες ἴσως νῦν σε ταχιστα ψέξουσι· καὶ ὡς οὔτε ἡ μνήμη ἀξιόλογόν γε, οὔτε ἡ δόξα, οὔτε ἄλλό τε τὸ σύμπαν.

Look down from above on the countless herds of men and their countless solemnities, their various voyagings in storms and calms, and the contests among those who are born, who live together and die. And consider also the life lived by others in the olden times, and the life of those who will live after thee, and the life now lived among barbarous nations, and how many know not even thy name, and how many will soon forget it, and how they who are now praising thee will very soon blame thee, and that neither a posthumous name is of any value, nor reputation, nor anything else.

Men Constantly Passing Away.

ix. 33.

Πάντα, ὅσα ὁρᾷς, τάχιστα φθαρήσεται· καὶ οἱ φθειρόμενα αὐτὰ ἐπιδόντες, τάχιστα καὶ αὐτοὶ φθαρήσονται· καὶ ὁ ἐσχατόγηρως ἀποθανὼν εἰς ἴσον καταστήσεται τῷ προώρῳ.

All things which thou seest will soon perish, and those who have looked on them, as they pass away, will themselves soon perish; and he who dies at the extremest old age will be brought into the same condition with him who died prematurely.

What Happens is Prepared from all Eternity.

x. 5.

῞Ο,τι ἄν σοι συμβαίνῃ, τοῦτό σοι ἐξ αἰῶνος προκατεσκευάζετο· καὶ ἡ ἐπιπλοκὴ τῶν αἰτίων συνέκλωθε τήν τε σὴν ὑπόστασιν ἐξ ἀϊδίου, καὶ τὴν τούτου σύμβασιν.

Whatever may happen to thee has been prepared to thee from all eternity; and the concatenation of causes was from eternity spinning the thread of thy being and of that which is incident to it.

What Time is.

x. 17.

Τοῦ ὅλου αἰῶνος, καὶ τῆς ὅλης οὐσίας συνεχῶς φαντασία, καὶ ὅτι πάντα τὰ κατὰ μέρος, ὡς μὲν πρὸς οὐσίαν, κεγχραμίς· ὡς δὲ πρὸς χρόνον, τρυπάνου περιστροφή.

Let the idea of the whole of time and of the whole of substance be constantly before thy thoughts, and thou wilt find that all individual things as to substance are a grain of fig, and as to time, the turning of a gimlet.

What Men are in Reality.

x. 19.

Οἷοί εἰσιν ἐσθίοντες, καθεύδοντες, ὀχεύοντες, ἀποπατοῦντες, τὰ ἄλλα· εἶτα οἷοι ἀνδρονομούμενοι, καὶ γαυρούμενοι, ἢ χαλεπαίνοντες, καὶ ἐξ ὑπεροχῆς ἐπιπλήττοντες· πρὸ ὀλίγου δὲ καὶ οὐ ἐδούλευον πόσοις, καὶ δι᾽ οἷα· καὶ μετ᾽ ὀλίγου ἐν τοιούτοις ἔσονται.

Consider what men are when they are eating, sleeping, generating, easing themselves, and so forth; then what kind of men they are when they bear themselves haughtily, or are angry and scold from their lofty place. And then consider to whom they were slaves a short time ago, and for what things; and then think in what condition they will be after a little time.

The Dramas of Life.

x. 27.

Συνεχῶς ἐπινοεῖν, πῶς πάντα τοιαῦτα ὁποῖα νῦν γίνεται, καὶ πρόσθεν ἐγίνετο· καὶ ἐπινοεῖν γενησόμενα· καὶ ὅλα δράματα καὶ σκήνας ὁμοειδεῖς, ὅσα ἐκ πείρας τῆς σῆς, ἢ τῆς πρεσβυτέρας ἱστορίας ἔγνως πρὸ ὀμμάτων τίθεσθαι· οἷον αὐλὴν ὅλην Ἀδριανοῦ καὶ αὐλὴν ὅλην Ἀντονίνου, καὶ αὐλὴν ὅλην Φιλίππου, Ἀλεξάνδρου, Κροίσου· πάντα γὰρ ἐκεῖνα τοιαῦτα ἦν, μόνον δι᾽ ἑτέρων.

Consider, in a word, how all things, such as they are now, were so formerly, and consider that they will be so again; and place before thy eyes whole dramas and stages of the same kind, whatever thou hast become acquainted with from thy own experience or from the history of olden times—such as the whole court of Hadrian, and the whole court of Antoninus, and the whole court of Philip, Alexander, and Crœsus, for all these were such dramas as we see at present, only with different actors.

The following passages, which speak of the drama of life, may serve as parallels to the sentiments of Antoninus (Demophilus, Similitudines, Moralia, i. 10, Orelli opera):—

Τοῦ βίου, καθάπερ δράματος, πρῶτον μέρος ἐστὶν ἡ νεότης· διὸ πάντες αὐτῇ προσεχουσιν.

"Youth is the first part of life, like that of a drama; wherefore all attach themselves to it."

And again Aristonymus, in Stobœus, cap. cvi. 14 (ed. Meincke, 1855)—

Εδικεν ὁ βίος θεάτρῳ, διὸ πολλάκις χείριστοι τὸν κάλλιστον ἐν αὐτῷ κατέχουσι τόπον.

"Life is like a theatre, for the worst often occupy the best place in it"

And again one of the epigrams of Palladas (Anthol. Græc. x. 72)—

Σκηνὴ πᾶς ὁ βίος, καὶ παίγνιον· ἢ μάθε παίξειν τὴν σπουδὴν μεταμαθείς, ἢ φέρε τὰς ὀδύνας.

"Life is a scene, and we are players; either learn to play, forgetting the labours, or suffer the pain of losing."

This epigram is thus rendered into Latin by Joannes Secundus—

" Vita hominum scena est lususque : aut ludere discas,
Sepositis curis, aut miseranda feras."

Augustus, on his deathbed (Sueton. Aug. c. 99), said—"Ecquid iis videretur mimans vitæ commode transegisse."—"Whether did they think that he had acted the drama of life in a becoming manner."

See (Lat.) World, all.

MEN ARE LIKE LEAVES.

x. 34.

Φυλλάριον δὲ καὶ τὰ τεκνία σου· φυλλάρια δὲ καὶ ταῦτα τὰ ἐπιβοῶντα ἀξιοπίστως καὶ ἐπιφημοῦντα, ἢ ἐκ τῶν ἐναντίων καταρώμενα, ἢ ἡσυχῇ ψέγοντα, καὶ χλεύαζοντα· φυλλάρια δὲ ὁμοίως, καὶ τὰ διαδεξόμενα τὴν ὑστεροφημίαν, πάντα γὰρ ταῦτα εαρος ἐπιγίγνεται ὥρῃ· εἶτα ἄνεμος καταβέβληκεν· ἔπειθ' ἡ ὕλη ἕτερα ἀντὶ τούτων φύει· τὸ δὲ ὀλιγοχρόνιον κοινὸν πᾶσι· ἀλλά σὺ πάντα ὡς αἰώνια ἐσόμενα, φεύγεις, καὶ διώκεις· μικρὸν καὶ καταμύσεις· τὸν δὲ ἐξενεγκόντα σε ἤδη, ἄλλος θρήνησει.

Thy children are like leaves. Leaves, too, are they who bawl out as if they were worthy of credit, and give praise, or, in the opposite way, curse, or secretly find fault and sneer; and leaves, likewise, are those who shall receive and transmit a man's fame to aftertimes. For all such things as these " are produced in the season of spring;" then the wind throws them down; then the forest produces others in their stead. But a brief existence is common to all things, yet thou avoidest and formest all things as if they would be eternal. But a little while and thou shalt close thy eyes, and him who has attended thee to thy grave another soon will lament.

SOME ARE ALWAYS GLAD AT THE DEATH OF ANOTHER.

x. 36.

Οὐδείς ἐστιν οὕτως εὔποτμος, ᾧ ἀποθνήσκοντι οὐ παραστήσονταί τινες ἀσπαζόμενοι τὸ συμβαῖνον κακόν.

There is no one so fortunate to whom at his death there are not some who are pleased at the calamity that has happened.

BE PREPARED TO DIE AT ANY MOMENT.

xi. 3.

Οἵα ἐστὶν ἡ ψυχὴ ἡ ἕτοιμος, ἐὰν ἤδη ἀπολυθῆναι δέῃ τοῦ σώματος, καὶ ἤτοι σβεσθῆναι ἢ σκεδασθῆναι ἢ συμμεῖναι; τὸ δὲ ἕτοιμον τοῦτο, ἵνα ἀπὸ ἰδικῆς κρίσεως ἔρχηται, μὴ κατὰ ψιλὴν παράταξιν, ὡς οἱ χριστιανοί, ἀλλὰ λελογισμένως, καὶ σεμνῶς, καὶ ὥστε καὶ ἄλλον πεῖσαι, ἀτραγῴδως.

What a soul that is which is ready, if at any moment it must be separated from the body, and ready either to be extinguished or dispersed or continue to exist! but so that this readiness comes from a man's own judgment, not from mere obstinacy, as with the Christians, but considerately and with dignity, and in a way to persuade another, without tragic show.

THE VOICE TO BE WRITTEN ON THE FOREHEAD.

xi. 15

Ἐπὶ τοῦ μετώπου γεγράφθαι ὀφείλει εὐθὺς ἡ φωνή· τοιοῦτον ἔχει, εὐθὺς ἐν τοῖς ὄμμασι ἐξέχει· ὡς τῶν ἐραστῶν ἐν τῷ βλέμματι πάντα εὐθὺς γνωρίζει ὁ ἐρώμενος, τοιοῦτον ὅλως δεῖ τὸν ἁπλοῦν καὶ ἀγαθὸν εἶναι, οἷον γράσωνα, ἵνα ὁ παραστὰς, ἅμα τῷ προσελθεῖν, θέλει οὐ θέλει, αἴσθηται· ἐπιτήδευσις δὲ ἁπλότητος υ κάλμη ἐστίν· οὐδέν ἐστιν αἴσχιον λυκοφιλίας· πάντων μάλιστα τοῦτο φεῦγε· ὁ ἀγαθὸς, καὶ ἁπλοῦς καὶ εὐμενὴς, ἐν τοῖς ὄμμασιν ἔχουσιν ταῦτα, καὶ οὐ λανθάνει.

The voice ought to be clearly written on the forehead; according as a man's character is, he shows it forthwith in his eyes, just as he who is beloved reads everything in the eyes of the lover. So, also, ought the upright and good man to be like the strong-smelling goat, so that the bystander, as soon as he comes near, should perceive him, whether he wills it or not. But the affectation of honesty is like a crooked stick. Nothing is more disgraceful than a wolfish friendship. Avoid this most of all. The good, simple, and benevolent, show these feelings in the eyes, and there is no concealment of them.

EVERYTHING LIES NAKED BEFORE GOD.

xii. 2.

'Ο Θεὸς πάντα τὰ ἡγεμονικά, γυμνὰ τῶν ὑλικῶν ἀγγείων καὶ φλοιῶν καὶ καθαρμάτων ὁρᾷ.

God sees the minds of all stripped bare of their bodily coverings and pollutions.

See Heb. iv. 13.

MAN'S SELF-LOVE.

xii. 4.

Πολλάκις ἐθαύμασα, πῶς ἑαυτὸν μὲν ἕκαστος μᾶλλον πάντων φιλεῖ, τὴν δὲ ἑαυτοῦ περὶ αὐτοῦ ὑπόληψιν ἐν ἐλάττονι λόγῳ τίθεται ἢ τὴν τῶν ἄλλων.

I have often wondered how every man loves himself more than all the rest of men, yet sets less value on his own opinion of himself than on the opinion of others.

WHERE ARE NOW MEN OF THE GREATEST FAME?

xii. 27.

Συνεχῶς ἀναπολεῖν, τοὺς ἐπί τινι λίαν ἀγανακτήσαντας, τοὺς ἐν μεγίσταις δόξαις, ἢ συμφοραῖς, ἢ ἔχθραις, ἢ ὁποιαισοῦν τύχαις ἀκμάσαντας· εἶτα ἐφιστάνειν, ποῦ νῦν πάντα ἐκεῖνα; καπνὸς καὶ σποδὸς καὶ μῦθος, ἢ οὐδὲ μῦθος.

Bring always to thy remembrance that those who have made great complaints about anything, those who have been most remarkable by the greatest fame, or misfortunes, or enmities, or fortunes of any kind; then consider, where are they all now? Smoke and ash and a tale, or not even a tale.

APOLLODORUS.

FLOURISHED B.C. 290.

APOLLODORUS, a native of Gela, in Sicily, flourished between B. C. 300–260. He was a celebrated comic poet, of whose poetry some fragments have been preserved.

A PLEASANT LIFE.

Fr. Com. Gr. p. 1108.

Ἀπραγμόνως ζῆν ἡδύ· μακάριος βίος καὶ σεμνός, ἂν ᾖ μεθ' ἑτέρων ἀπραγμόνων·

ἐν θηρίοις δὲ καὶ πιθήκοις ὄντα δεῖ
εἶναι πίθηκον· ὦ ταλαιπώρου βίου.

It is pleasant to lead an idle life ; it is a happy and delightful
life if it be with other idle people : with beasts and apes one
ought to be an ape. O the misery of life!

WHEN NIGHT APPEARS TO BE LONG.

Fr. Com. Gr. p. 1108.

Τοῖς γὰρ μεριμνῶσίν τε καὶ λυπουμένοις
ἅπασα νὺξ ἔοικε φαίνεσθαι μακρά.

For to those overwhelmed in sorrow and grief every night is
sure to appear long.

HOW DEATH APPEARS IN DIFFERENT STAGES OF LIFE.

Fr. Com. Gr. p. 1108.

Ὅτε μειράκιον ἦν, τοὺς ἀώρους ἠλέουν,
νυνὶ δ' ὅταν γέροντος ἐκφορὰν ἴδω,
κλάω· πρὸς ἐμὲ γὰρ ἐστι τοῦτ', ἐκεῖνο δ' οὔ.

When I was a young man, I pitied those who were carried off
prematurely ; but now when I see the funeral of the old, I weep,
for this is my concern, the other was not.

THE HABITS OF THE OLD.

Fr. Com. Gr. p. 1109.

Μὴ καταφρόνει, Φιλῖν' ἐθῶν γεροντικῶν,
οἷς ἔνοχος, εἰς τὸ γῆρας ἂν ἔλθης, ἔσει,
ἀλλὰ μέγα τοῦθ' οἱ πατέρες βλασφημεῖθα
ὑμεῖς μὲν ὠνειδίσατ', εἀν τι μὴ ποιῇ
ὁ πατὴρ προθύμως, οὐ γέγονας αὐτὸς νέος ;
τῷ δὲ πατρὶ πρὸς τὸν υἱόν, ἂν ἀγνωμονῇ,
οὐκ ἔστιν εἰπεῖν, οὐ γέγονας αὐτὸς γέρων ;

Do not despise, Philinus, the habits of the old, to which, if
thou reachest old age, thou wilt be subject. But we, fathers, are
greatly inferior in this. If a father does not act kindly, you
reproach him in some such language as this—"Hast thou never
been young?" And it is not possible for the old to say to his
son, if he acts imprudently, "Hast thou never been old?"

FELLOW-SUFFERERS.

Fr. Com. Gr. p. 1109.

Φυσικόν γε τοῦθ'· ἕκαστος ἐν ταῖς ἀτυχίαις
ἥδιστα πρὸς τοὺς ὁμοπαθεῖς ὀδύρεται.

This is according to nature; every one in misfortune grieves most pleasantly in company with those who are suffering in the same way.

Never Despair.

Fr. Com. Gr. p. 1109.

Οὐδέποτ' ἀθυμεῖν τὸν κακῶς πράττοντα δεῖ,
ἄνδρες, τὰ βελτίω δὲ προσδοκᾶν ἀεί.

Men, it is not right for him who is in misfortune to despair, but always to expect better fortune.

Who is Happy?

Fr. Com. Gr. p. 1110.

Οὐ δεῖ λέγειν γὰρ μακάριον τὸν χρήματα
ἔψοντα πλεῖστα, τὸν δὲ μὴ λυπούμενον.

For it is not right to call the man who possesses much riches happy, but the man who is not in grief.

Fortune.

Fr. Com. Gr. p. 1112.

Χαλεπὸν τύχη 'στὶ πρᾶγμα, χαλεπόν· ἀλλὰ δεῖ
αὐτὴν φέρειν κατὰ τρόπον ὥσπερ φορτίον.

Fortune is a sore, sore thing; but we must bear it in a certain way, as a burden.

Time.

Fr. Com. Gr. p. 1112.

Χρόνον γὰρ εἰς τὰ πράγματ' ἂν λάβῃς,
ἅπαντα λήξει καὶ κατασταλήσεται.

For if thou takest time into thy affairs, it will allay and arrange all things.

ARATUS.

FLOURISHED B.C. 270.

ARATUS, a Greek poet, of Soli, in Cilicia, flourished B.C. 270, in the reign of Ptolemy Philadelphus, and was the contemporary of Theocritus, by whom he is spoken of in honourable terms (vi. 1–45). Aratus spent much of his time at the court of Antigonus Gonatas, B.C. 282–239. He was the author of a work entitled

"Phænomena," which has been preserved, and which is a description of the heavens in hexameter verse. It is a poem of 732 lines, and contains rather a poetical than scientific account of the appearances in the heavens. It seems to have been a great favourite with the Romans, as it was frequently translated into Latin verse. Cicero, in his youth, employed himself in translating it, but it adds little to the reputation of the orator. Another work of Aratus which we possess is entitled "Diosemeia," prognostics of the weather, which was also translated by Cicero.

WE ARE THE OFFSPRING OF GOD.
Phænom. 1.

Ἐκ Διὸς ἀρχώμεσθα, τὸν οὐδέποτ' ἄνδρες ἐῶμεν
ἄρρητον· μεσταὶ δὲ Διὸς πᾶσαι μὲν ἀγυιαί,
πᾶσαι δ' ἀνθρώπων ἀγοραί· μεστὴ δὲ θάλασσα,
καὶ λιμένες· πάντη δὲ Διὸς κεχρήμεθα πάντες·
τοῦ γὰρ καὶ γένος ἐσμέν. Ὁ δ' ἤπιος ἀνθρώποισι
δεξιὰ σημαίνει· λαοὺς δ' ἐπὶ ἔργον ἐγείρει
μιμνήσκων βιότοιο.

Let us begin our song from Jupiter; let us never leave his name unuttered; all paths, all haunts of men are full of Jove, the sea and heavens; we all everywhere require the aid of Jove, for we are his offspring. Benevolent, he warns mankind to good; urges them to toil with hope of food.

See Acts xvii. 28.

GOD PLACED SIGNS IN THE HEAVENS.
Phænom. 10.

Αὐτὸς γὰρ τάδε σήματ' ἐν οὐρανῷ ἐστήριξεν,
ἄστρα διακρίνας.

For God himself placed these signs in the heaven, having set apart the stars.

So Genesis (i. 14) "And God said, Let there be lights in the firmament of heaven, to divide the day from the night, and let them be for signs."

THE GOLDEN AGE.
Phænom. 108.

Οὔπω λευγαλέου τότε νείκεος ἠπίσταντο,
οὐδὲ διακρίσιος περιμεμφέος, οὐδὲ κυδοιμοῦ·
αὔτως δ' ἔζωον· χαλεπὴ δ' ἀπέκειτο θάλασσα,
καὶ βίον οὔπω νῆες ἀπόπροσθεν ἠγίνεεσκον,
ἀλλὰ βόες καὶ ἄροτρα· καὶ αὐτὴ πότνια λαῶν
μυρία πάντα παρεῖχε δίκη δώτειρα δικαίων,
τόφρ' ἦν, ὄφρ' ἔτι γαῖα γένος χρύσειον ἔφερβεν.

They were not then acquainted with miserable strife, nor dissensions, with complaints without end, nor tumults; thus they lived in simplicity. The boisterous sea lay aside, no ships brought food from afar, but oxen and ploughs supplied it; and Justice herself, the bountiful giver of good, furnished boundless gifts to nations; so it was so long as the earth fed a golden race.

ARCHIPPUS.

FLOURISHED B.C. 415.

ARCHIPPUS, an Athenian comic poet of the old comedy, gained a single prize, B.C. 415.

THE SEA.

Fr. Com. Gr. p. 413.

'Ὡς ἡδὺ τὴν θάλατταν ἀπὸ τῆς γῆς ὁρᾶν
ὦ μῆτέρ ἐστι μὴ πλέοντα μηδαμοῦ.

How sweet it is, mother, to see the sea from the land, when we are not sailing!

ARISTOPHANES.

BORN B.C. 444—DIED ABOUT B.C. 380.

ARISTOPHANES, the only writer of the old comedy of whom any entire works are left, was son of Euphorion, an Athenian. Of his private history we know nothing, except that he was fond of pleasure, and spent much of his time in drinking and the society of the witty. There are eleven of his plays still remaining. The period during which he exhibited his plays was one of the most brilliant, and at the same time the most unfortunate, that Athens ever witnessed. It was in the fourth year of the Peloponnesian War, B.C. 427, that he brought on the stage his first play, and for the long period of thirty years he continued to produce a series of caricatures on the leading men of the day, which give us more insight into the private history of the times than we could have got from any other source. The evils of war, the folly of his countrymen in being led by loud-mouthed demagogues, the danger

of an education in which scepticism took the place of religion, and
the excessive love for litigation, to which the Athenians were
addicted, are the subjects against which he inveighs, with a
power and a boldness which show him to have been an honest,
though not always a wise, patriot. Plato called the soul of
Aristophanes a temple for the Graces, and has introduced him
into his "Symposium." His lyrical powers were of a high order,
as may be seen in many of his choruses, where his fancy takes the
widest range : frogs chant choruses, and the grunt of a pig is
formed into an iambic verse. The coarseness and indecency which
are mixed up with some of his finest passages must be referred
more to the age in which he lived than to his own mind.

A ROGUE.

Neph. 443.

Εἴπερ τὰ χρέα διαφευξοῦμαι,
τοῖς ἀνθρώποις τ᾽ εἶναι δόξω
θρασύς, εὔγλωττος, τολμηρός, ἴτης,
βδελυρός, ψευδῶν ξυγκολλητής,
εὑρησιεπής, περίτριμμα δικῶν,
κύρβις, κρόταλον, κίναδος, τρύμη,
μάσθλης, εἴρων, γλοιός, ἀλάζων,
κέντρων, μιαρός, στρόφις, ἀργαλέος, ματιολοιχός,
ταῦτ᾽ εἴ με καλοῦσιν ἀπαντῶντες,
δρώντων ἀτεχνῶς ὅ τι χρῄζουσιν.

If I get clear of my debts, I care not though men call me bold,
glib of tongue, audacious, impudent, shameless, a fabricator of
falsehoods, inventor of words, practised in lawsuits, a law tablet,
a rattle, a fox, a sharper, a slippery knave, a dissembler, a slippery fellow, an impostor, a rogue that deserves the cat-o'-nine-
tails, a blackguard, a twister, a troublesome fellow, a licker-up of
hashes. If they call me all this, when they meet me, they may
do so if they please.

> So that I may but fob my creditors,
> Let the world talk ; I care not though it call me
> A bold-faced, loud-tongued, overbearing bully ;
> A shameless, vile, prevaricating cheat ;
> A tricking, quibbling, double-dealing knave ;
> A prating, pettifogging limb-o'-th'-law ;
> A sly old fox, a perjurer, a hang-dog,
> A ragamuffin made of shreds and patches,
> The leavings of a dunghill. Let 'em rail,
> Yea, marry, let 'em turn my guts to fiddle-strings,
> May my bread be my poison, if I care !

MEMORY OF TWO SORTS.
Neph. 483.

Δύο τρόπω, νὴ τὸν Δία.
Ἢν μὲν γ' ὀφείληταί τί μοι, μνήμων πάνυ·
ἐὰν δ' ὀφείλω, σχέτλιος, ἐπιλήσμων πάνυ.

Oh! as for that,
My memory is of two sorts, long and short :
With them who owe me aught it never fails ;
My creditors, indeed, complain of it
As mainly apt to leak and lose its reckoning.

OLD AGE A SECOND CHILDHOOD.
Neph. 1418.

Eγὼ δέ γ' ἀντείποιμ' ἄν, ὡς δὶς παῖδες οἱ γέροντες.

But I would say, in reply, that old men are boys twice over.

And grant they were, the proverb's in your teeth,
Which says old age is but a second childhood.

WE ARE THE CAUSE OF MISFORTUNES TO OURSELVES.
Neph. 1455.

Aὐτὸς μὲν οὖν σαυτῷ σὺ τούτων αἴτιος,
στρέψας σεαυτὸν ἐς πονηρὰ πράγματα.

Nay, rather, thou art thyself the cause of these things to thyself, having had recourse to wicked courses.

Evil events from evil causes spring,
And what you suffer flows from what you've done.

EVERYTHING SUBSERVIENT TO RICHES.
Plut. 144.

Kαὶ νὴ Δί', εἴ τί γ' ἐστι λαμπρὸν καὶ καλόν,
ἢ χάριεν ἀνθρώποισι, διὰ σὲ γίγνεται.
"Aπαντα τῷ πλουτεῖν γὰρ ἐσθ' ὑπήκοα.

And by Jove, if there be anything grand, beautiful, or pleasing
to men, it is through thee (riches) ; for all things are subservient
to riches.

See (Lat.) Gold, power of.

SELFISHNESS OF MANKIND.
Plut. 340.

"Eστιν δ' ἐμοὶ τοῦτ' αὐτὸ θαυμαστόν γ', ὅπως,
Xρηστόν τι πράττων, τοὺς φίλους μεταπέμπεται.
Oὔκουν ἐπιχώριόν τι πρᾶγμ' ἐργάζεται.

But to me it is a prodigy, that a man, who hath any good luck, should send for his friends to share it. Surely he hath done a very unfashionable thing.

NO MAN RIGHTEOUS.

Plut. 362.

Φεῦ·
ὡς οὐδὲν ἀτεχνῶς ὑγιές ἐστιν οὐδενός,
ἀλλ᾽ εἰσὶ τοῦ κέρδους ἅπαντες ἥττονες.

I know . . . . that there is no man truly honest; we are none of us above the influence of gain.

ADVANTAGE OF POVERTY TO THE HUMAN RACE.

Plut. 509.

Εἰ τοῦτο γένοιθ᾽ ὃ ποθεῖθ᾽ ὑμεῖς, οὔ φημ᾽ ἂν λυσιτελεῖν σφῶν.
Εἰ γὰρ ὁ Πλοῦτος βλέψειε πάλιν, διανείμειέν τ᾽ ἴσον αὑτόν,
οὔτε τέχνην ἂν τῶν ἀνθρώπων, οὔτ᾽ ἂν σοφίαν μελετῴη
οὐδείς· ἀμφοῖν δ᾽ ὑμῖν τούτοιν ἀφανισθέντοιν, ἐθελήσει
τίς χαλκεύειν ἢ ναυπηγεῖν, ἢ ῥάπτειν, ἢ τροχοποιεῖν,
ἢ σκυτοτομεῖν, ἢ πλινθουργεῖν, ἢ πλύνειν ἢ σκυλοδεψεῖν,
ἢ γῆς ἀρότροις ῥήξας δάπεδον, καρπὸν Δηοῦς θερίσασθαι,
ἢν ἐξῇ ζῆν ἀργοῖς ὑμῖν τούτων πάντων ἀμελοῦσι.

Should this which you long for be accomplished, I say it would not be conducive to your happiness; for should Plutus recover his sight, and distribute his favours equally, no man would trouble himself with the theory of any art, nor with the exercise of any craft; and if these two should once disappear, who afterwards will become a brasier, a shipwright, a tailor, a wheelwright, a shoemaker, a brickmaker, a dyer, or a skinner? Or who will plough up the bowels of the earth, in order to reap the fruits of Ceres, if it was once possible for you to live with the neglect of all these things?

POVERTY IS SISTER OF BEGGARY.

Plut. 549.

Οὐκοῦν δήπου τῆς πτωχείας πενίαν φαμὲν εἶναι ἀδελφήν.

Therefore we say, certainly, that poverty is sister of beggary.

THE EFFECT OF POVERTY AND RICHES ON MAN.

Plut. 558.

Οὐ γιγνώσκων, ὅτι τοῦ Πλούτου παρέχω βελτίονας ἄνδρας,
καὶ τὴν γνώμην καὶ τὴν ἰδέαν. Παρὰ τῷ μὲν γὰρ ποδαγρῶντες,
καὶ γαστρώδεις καὶ παχύκνημοι, καὶ πίονές εἰσιν ἀσελγῶς·
παρ᾽ ἐμοὶ δ᾽ ἰσχνοὶ καὶ σφηκώδεις, καὶ τοῖς ἐχθροῖς ἀνιαροί.

And knowing that I (Poverty) furnish men better than Plutus (Riches) both in mind and body ; for with him they are gouty in feet, pot-bellied, thick-legged, and extravagantly fat ; but with me they are thin and wasp-like, and annoying to their enemies.

To Convince against our Will.
Plut. 600.

Οὐ γὰρ πείσεις, οὐδ' ἢν πείσῃς.

For thou shalt not convince me, even if thou shouldst con-vince me.

Gay says—
> " Convince a man against his will,
> He 's of the same opinion still."

A Man's Country where he Lives Best.
Plut. 1151.

Πατρὶς γάρ ἐστι πᾶσ', ἵν' πράττῃ τις εὖ.

That is every man's country, where he lives best.

See (Lat.) Our country.

Elysium.
Ran. 154.

'Εντεῦθεν αὐλῶν τις σὲ περίεισιν πνοή,
ὄψει τε φῶς κάλλιστον, ὥσπερ ἐνθάδε,
καὶ μυρρινῶνας, καὶ θιάσους εὐδαίμονας
ἀνδρῶν, γυναικῶν, καὶ κρότον χειρῶν πολύν.

After that the breath of flutes shall encompass thee, and thou shalt see a most beautiful light, as here, and myrtle groves, and happy bands of men and women, and much clapping of hands.

> Onward the dulcet harmony of flutes
> Shall breathe around thee, while thou shalt behold
> Light's gayest beams, such as we here enjoy,
> And myrtle groves, and troops of either sex
> Moving in mystic choruses, and marking
> With plausive hands their holy ecstasy.

See (Lat.) Elysium.

Debarring the Profane from the Sacred Mysteries.
Ran. 353.

Εὐφημεῖν χρὴ κἀξίστασθαι τοῖς ἡμετέροισι χοροῖσιν,
ὅστις ἄπειρος τοιῶνδε λόγων, ἢ γνώμῃ μὴ καθαρεύει,
ἢ γενναίων ὄργια Μουσῶν μήτ' εἶδεν μήτ' ἐχόρευσε·
μηδὲ Κρατίνου τοῦ ταυροφάγου γλώττης βακχεῖ' ἐτελέσθη,

ἢ βωμολόχοις ἔπεσιν χαίρει, μὴ 'ν καιρῷ τοῦτο ποιεῦσιν,
ἢ στάσιν ἐχθρὰν μὴ καταλύει, μηδ' εὔκολός ἐστι πολίταις,
ἀλλ' ἀνεγείρει καὶ ῥιπίζει, κερδῶν ἰδίων ἐπιθυμῶν·
ἢ τῆς πόλεως χειμαζομένης ἄρχων καταδωροδοκεῖται·
ἢ προδίδωσιν φρούριον ἢ ναῦς, ἢ τἀπόρρητ ἀποπέμπει
ἐξ Αἰγίνης, Θωρυκίων ὤν, εἰκοστολόγος κακοδαίμων,
ἀσκώματα, καὶ λίνα, καὶ πίτταν διαπέμπων ἐς Ἐπίδαυρον·
ἢ χρήματα ταῖς τῶν ἀντιπάλων ναυσὶν παρέχειν τινὰ πείθει.

It is right that he should abstain from ill-omened words, and
retire from our choirs, whoever is unskilled in such words, or is
not pure in mind, and has neither seen nor cultivated with dances
the orgies of the noble Muses, and has not been initiated in the
Bacchanalian orgies of the tongue of Cratinus, the bull-eater, or
takes pleasure in buffoonish verses, exciting buffoonery at an improper time, or does not repress hateful sedition, and is not kind
to the citizens, but, desirous of his private advantage, excites and
blows it up ; or when the commonwealth is tempest-tossed, being
a magistrate, yields to bribes, or betrays a garrison, or ships or
imports from Ægina forbidden goods, being another Thorycion, a
vile collector of tolls, sending across to Epidaurus oar-paddings,
sail-cloth, and pitch, or who persuades any one to supply money
for the ships of the enemy.

> Hushed be each lawless tongue, and, ye profane,
> Ye uninitiated, from our mysteries
> Far off retire!   Whoe'er a bosom boasts not
> Pure and unsullied, nor has ever learned
> To worship at the Muses' hallowed shrine,
> Or lead in sportive dance their votaries,
> Nor in Cratinus' lofty sounding style
> Has formed his tongue to Bacchus' praise ;—whoe'er
> Delights in flattery's unseemly language ;—
> Who strives not to allay the rising storm
> That threats the public weal, nor cultivates
> The sweets of private friendship, but foments
> Intestine discord, blows the rancorous flame
> Of enmity 'twixt man and man, to serve
> Some sordid purpose of his narrow soul ;—
> Whoe'er, intrusted with the government
> Of a divided city, by corruption
> Is led away from th' even path of justice ;—
> Whoe'er betrays the fortress he commands,
> Gives up his ship, or from Ægina sends
> Forbidden stores, as late that vile collector,
> Shameless Thorycio, did to Epidaurus ;—
> Whoe'er persuades another to supply
> The enemy with money for their fleet.

C

TORTURE.

Ran. 618.

Πάντα τρόπον, ἐν κλίμακι
δήσας, κρεμάσας, ὑστριχίδι μαστιγῶν δέρων,
στρεβλῶν, ἔτι δ' εἰς τὰς ῥῖνας ὄξος ἐγχέων,
πλίνθους ἐπιτιθείς, πάντα τἄλλα, πλήν πράσῳ
μὴ τύπτε τοῦτον, μηδὲ γητείῳ νέῳ.

In every way, by tying him to a ladder, by hanging, by scourging
with a whip, by flaying, by racking, and besides by pouring vinegar
nto his nostrils, by heaping bricks upon him, and in every other
vay ; only don't beat him with leek or young onion.

By every method—
Tie him upon the ladder,—hang him up,—
Give him the bristly strap,—flog, torture him,—
Pour vinegar up his nostrils,—t' his feet
Apply the tiles ; question him as thou wilt,
So 'tis not with a rod of leeks and onions.

GOOD FOLKS ARE SCARCE.

Ran. 783.

'Ολίγον τὸ χρηστόν ἐστιν, ὥσπερ ἐνθάδε.

Good folks are scarce ; and so it is with us.

See (Lat.) Best things.

THE AIM OF POETS.

Ran. 1030.

Ταῦτα γὰρ ἄνδρας χρὴ ποιητὰς ἀσκεῖν. Σκέψαι γὰρ ἀπ' ἀρχῆς,
ὡς ὠφέλιμοι τῶν ποιητῶν οἱ γενναῖοι γεγένηνται.
'Ορφεὺς μὲν γὰρ τελετάς θ' ἡμῖν κατέδειξε, φόνων τ' ἀπέχεσθαι,
Μουσαῖος δ' ἐξακέσεις τε νόσων, καὶ χρησμούς· Ἡσίοδος δὲ
γῆς ἐργασίας, καρπῶν ὥρας, ἀρότους· ὁ δὲ θεῖος Ὅμηρος
ἀπὸ τοῦ τιμὴν καὶ κλέος ἔσχεν, πλὴν τοῦδ', ὅτι χρῆστ' ἐδίδαξε,
τάξεις, ἀρετάς, ὁπλίσεις ἀνδρῶν ;

For it becomes poets to practise this. For see how useful noble
poets have been from of old. For Orpheus made known to us
noble mysteries and to abstain from bloodshed ; Musæus, complete
cures of diseases and oracular responses ; Hesiod, agriculture, seed-
time, and harvest; and by what did the divine Homer gain honour
and glory except in this way, that he taught what was useful,
military skill, and all the various use of arms ?

Poets and Schoolmasters.

Ran. 1053.

'Αλλ' ἀποκρύπτειν χρὴ τὸ πονηρὸν τόν γε ποιητήν,
καὶ μὴ παράγειν, μηδὲ διδάσκειν. Τοῖς μὲν γὰρ παιδαρίοισιν
ἔστι διδάσκαλος, ὅστις φράζει· τοῖς ἡβῶσιν δὲ ποιηταί.
Πάνυ δὴ δεῖ χρηστὰ λέγειν ἡμᾶς.

Yet it is right for a poet to throw a veil over evil deeds, not to
bring them unto the light of day, or produce them on the stage;
for he who directs little children is their teacher, while poets are
to those who are grown up. In truth it is our province, above
everything, to instruct men in virtue and truth.

But horrible facts
Should be buried in silence, not bruited abroad,
Nor brought forth on the stage, nor emblazoned in poetry.
Children and boys have a teacher assigned them—
The bard is a master for manhood and youth,
Bound to instruct them in virtue and truth.—Frere.

Noble Thoughts produce Noble Diction.

Ran. 1058.

'Αλλ', ὦ κακόδαιμον, ἀνάγκη
μεγάλων γνωμῶν καὶ διανοιῶν ἴσα καὶ τά γε ῥήματα τίκτειν.
Κἄλλως εἰκὸς τοὺς ἡμιθέους τοῖς ῥήμασι μείζοσι χρῆσθαι.
Καὶ γὰρ τοῖς ἱματίοις ἡμῶν χρῶνται πολὺ σεμνοτέροισιν.

But you, wretch, it is necessary also to produce words that may
correspond with great thoughts and noble sentiments; and besides,
it is natural that demigods should employ language grander than
ours, for they use a more magnificent attire.

Elevated thoughts and noble sentiments,
Of course, produce a correspondent diction;
Heroes, besides, with much propriety,
May use a language raised above the vulgar,
Just as they wear a more superb attire;—
Which, when I showed thee, thou hast done most foully.

Death scorns Gifts.

Ran. 1392.

Μόνος θεῶν γὰρ θάνατος οὐ δώρων ἐρᾷ.

The only power that scorns our gifts is death.

Life is Death.

Ran. 1477.

Τίς οἶδεν, εἰ τὸ ζῆν μέν ἐστι κατθανεῖν,
τὸ πνεῖν δὲ δειπνεῖν, καὶ τὸ καθεύδειν κώδιον;

Who knows but life is death, to breathe a feast,
To sleep nought else but a warm coverlet?

THE NIGHTINGALE.

Aves. 223.

Ὦ Ζεῦ βασιλεῦ, τοῦ φθέγματος τοὐρνθίου·
οἷον κατεμελίτωσε τὴν λόχμην ὅλην.

O King Jove! the voice of the bird! how has it filled with
melody the whole grove!

O Jupiter! the dear, delicious bird!
With what a lovely tone she swells and falls,
Sweetening the wilderness with delicate air.—FRERE.

WE LEARN FROM OUR ENEMIES.

Aves. 374.

Ἀλλ' ἀπ' ἐχθρῶν δῆτα πολλὰ μανθάνουσιν οἱ σοφοί.
Ἡ γὰρ εὐλάβεια σώζει πάντα. Παρὰ μὲν οὖν φίλου
οὐ μάθοις ἂν τοῦθ'· ὁ δ' ἐχθρὸς εὐθὺς ἐξηνάγκασεν.
Αὐτίχ' αἱ πόλεις παρ' ἀνδρῶν ἔμαθον, ἐχθρῶν, κοῦ φίλων,
ἐκπονεῖν θ' ὑψηλὰ τείχη, ναῦς τε κεκτῆσθαι μακράς·
τὸ δὲ μάθημα τοῦτο σώζει παῖδας, οἶκον, χρήματα.

You're mistaken; men of sense often learn from their enemies.
Prudence is the best safeguard. This principle cannot be learned
from a friend, but an enemy extorts it immediately. It is from
their foes, not their friends, that cities learn the lesson of building
high walls and ships of war. And this lesson saves their children,
their homes, and their properties.

See (Lat.) A lesson from an enemy.

"WHAT EYE HATH NOT SEEN NOR EAR HEARD."

Aves. 420.

Λέγει μέγαν τιν' ὄλβον, οὔτε λεκτόν, οὔτε πιστόν· ὡς
σὰ ταῦτα γὰρ δὴ πάντα, καὶ
τὸ τῇδε, καὶ τὸ κεῖσε, καὶ
τὸ δεῦρο, προσβιβᾷ λέγων.

He speaks of a mighty bliss, which cannot be expressed in
words nor believed to be possible; for he will convince you by
arguments that all these things are yours, both what is here and
there and everywhere.

So St Paul (1 Cor. ii. 9)—

Ἀλλὰ καθὼς γέγραπται· (Isa. lxiv. 4) Ἃ ὀφθαλμὸς οὐκ εἶδε, καὶ

οὓς οὐκ ἤκουσε, καὶ ἐπὶ καρδίαν ἀνθρώπου οὐκ ἀνέβη, ἃ ἡτοίμασεν
ὁ Θεὸς τοῖς ἀγαπῶσιν αὐτόν.

"But as it is written, Eye hath not seen, nor ear heard, neither have
entered into the heart of man, the things which God hath prepared for
them that love Him."

SLY AS A FOX.

Aves. 428.

Πυκνότατον κίναδος,
σόφισμα, κύρμα, τρίμμα, παιπάλημ' ὅλον.

He's as sly as a fox; he's contrivance, adroitness, subtilty
itself; he's so cunning that he'd slip through your fingers like
wild-fire.

MORTALS AND IMMORTALS CONTRASTED.

Aves. 684.

Ἄγε δὴ φύσιν ἄνδρες ἀμαυρόβιοι, φύλλων γενεᾷ προσόμοιοι,
ὀλιγοδρανέες, πλάσματα πηλοῦ, σκιοειδέα φῦλ' ἀμενηνά,
ἀπτῆνες ἐφημέριοι, ταλαοὶ βροτοί, ἀνέρες εἰκελόνειροι,
προσέχετε τὸν νοῦν τοῖς ἀθανάτοις ἡμῖν, τοῖς αἰὲν ἐοῦσι,
τοῖς αἰθερίοις, τοῖσιν ἀγήρῳς, τοῖς ἄφθιτα μηδομένοισιν,
ἵν' ἀκούσαντες πάντα παρ' ἡμῶν ὀρθῶς περὶ τῶν μετεώρων,
φύσιν οἰωνῶν, γένεσίν τε θεῶν, ποταμῶν τ', Ἐρέβους τε, Χάους τε,
εἰδότες ὀρθῶς παρ' ἐμοῦ Προδίκῳ κλάειν εἴπητε τὸ λοιπόν.

Mortals, that are condemned to live in darkness—mortals, that
fade like the leaves, emblems of imbecility, images of clay, a race
lightsome and without substance, creatures of a day without
wings—miserable mortals, men that flit away as dreams! give
ear to us who know no decay, to us who live for ever, to us who
dwell on high, who flourish in immortal youth, who harbour
thoughts which perish not; that having received all accurate
information from us on the subject of sublimity, having learnt
correctly the nature of birds, the birth of the gods, of rivers, of
Erebus, and of Chaos, ye may tell Prodicus, with his philosophy,
to go hang.

PEACE BE UPON THIS PLACE.

Aves. 959.

Εὐφημία 'στω.

Peace be upon this place.

So Luke (x. 5)—"Peace be to this house."

THE ADVANTAGES OF WINE.

Equit. 90.

Οἶνον σὺ τολμᾷς εἰς ἐπίνοιαν λοιδορεῖν.
Οἴνου γὰρ εὕροις ἄν τι πρακτικώτερον;

ὁρᾷς; ὅταν πίνωσιν ἄνθρωποι, τότε
πλουτοῦσι, διαπράττουσι, νικῶσιν δίκας,
εὐδαιμονοῦσιν, ὠφελοῦσι τοὺς φίλους.
'Αλλ' ἐξένεγκέ μοι ταχέως οἴνου χόα,
τὸν νοῦν ἵν' ἄρδω, καὶ λέγω τι δεξιόν.

Dost thou dare to find fault with wine as merely giving birth to
ideas? Why, canst thou point out anything more fully engaged
in the practical affairs of life? Consider for a moment: when
men drink, then they are rich, they traffic, are successful in lawsuits, are happy, give aid to their friends. Come, bring out
quickly a stoup of wine, that I may moisten my brain, and say
something clever.

See (Lat.) Wine.

Requisite Qualities for a Demagogue.
Equit. 217.

Τὰ δ' ἄλλα σοι πρόσεστι δημαγωγικά,
φωνὴ μιαρά, γέγονας κακός, ἀγοραῖος εἶ·
ἔχεις ἅπαντα πρὸς πολιτείαν, ἃ δεῖ.

The other qualities requisite for a demagogue are thine—foul-
mouthed, base-born, a low, mean fellow. Thou possessest every
quality necessary to make thy way with the mob.

A Paltry Orator.
Equit. 344.

'Ιδού λέγειν. Καλῶς γ' ἂν οὖν τι πρᾶγμα προσπεσόν σοι
ὠμοσπάρακτον παραλαβών, μεταχειρίσαιο χρηστῶς.
'Αλλ' οἶσθ', ὅ μοι πεπονθέναι δοκεῖς; ὅπερ τὸ πλῆθος.
Εἴ που δικίδιον εἶπας εὖ κατὰ ξένου μετοίκου,
τὴν νύκτα θρυλλῶν, καὶ λαλῶν ἐν ταῖς ὁδοῖς σεαυτῷ,
ὕδωρ τε πίνων, κἀπιδεικνύς, τοὺς φίλους τ' ἀνιῶν,
ᾤου δυνατὸς εἶναι λέγειν. *Ω μῶρε τῆς ἀνοίας.

"To speak," indeed! No doubt thou wouldst cleverly take up
some case that had fallen to thee, and handle it properly, tearing
't in pieces like a piece of raw flesh. But knowest thou in what
way thou seemest to me to be placed? Thou art like the rest of
them. If thou hast anywhere pleaded some paltry suit well
against a resident-alien, babbling the livelong night, and talking
to thyself in the streets, and drinking water, and showing thyself
off, and boring thy friends, thou thoughtst thyself a dab at oratory—thou silly coxcomb!

You're like the rest of 'em—the swarm of paltry, weak pre-
tenders.

You've made your pretty speech, perhaps, and gained a little
law-suit

Against a merchant-foreigner, by dint of water-drinking,
And lying long awake o' nights, composing and repeating,
And studying as you walked the streets, and wearing out the
    patience
Of all your friends and intimates with practising beforehand :
And now you wonder at yourself, elated and delighted
At your own talent for debate—you silly, saucy coxcomb.—FRERE.

" To Build the Lofty Rhyme."
Equit. 529.

Τέκτονες εὐπαλάμων ὕμνων.

Builders of ingenious songs.

Milton, in "Lycidas" (v. 10), says—
    " Who would not sing for Lycidas ? he knew
    Himself to sing, and build the lofty rhyme."

An Aged Bard.
Equit. 531.

Νυνὶ δ᾽ ὑμεῖς αὐτὸν ὁρῶντες παραληροῦντ᾽ οὐκ ἐλεεῖτε,
ἐκπιπτουσῶν τῶν ἠλέκτρων, καὶ τοῦ τόνου οὐκ ἔτ᾽ ἐνόντος,
τῶν θ᾽ ἁρμονιῶν διαχαυκουσῶν.

But now, when you see him in his dotage, you do not pity him,
since the pegs fall out and the tone is no longer there, and the
harmony is dissonant.

Scott, in his "Minstrel," says—
    " His withered cheek and tresses grey
    Seemed to have known a better day."

A Demagogue Fishing in Troubled Waters.
Equit. 864.

Ὅπερ γὰρ οἱ τὰς ἐγχέλεις θηρώμενοι πέπονθας.
Ὅταν μὲν ἡ λίμνη καταστῇ, λαμβάνουσιν οὐδέν·
ἐὰν δ᾽ ἄνω τε καὶ κάτω τὸν βόρβορον κυκῶσιν,
αἱροῦσι. Καὶ σὺ λαμβάνεις, ἢν τὴν πόλιν ταράττῃς.

For thou art like those who fish for eels. When the loch is
tranquil, they catch nothing; but if they stir the mud up and
down, they take. Thou, too, catchest, if thou disturb the city.

Hear Both Sides of a Question.
Vesp. 725.

Ἦπου σοφὸς ἦν, ὅστις ἔφασκεν· πρὶν ἂν ἀμφοῖν μῦθον ἀκούσῃς,
οὐκ ἂν δικάσαις.

Of a truth he was a wise man who said, "Thou shouldst not decide till thou hast heard what both have to say."

The Days that are Gone By.

Vesp. 1060.

Ὦ πάλαι ποτ' ὄντες ἡμεῖς ἄλκιμοι μέν ἐν χοροῖς,
ἄλκιμοι δ' ἐν μάχαις,
καὶ κατ' αὐτὸ τοῦτο δὴ
μόνον ἄνδρες μαχιμώτατοι,
πρίν ποτ' ἦν, πρὶν ταῦτα· νῦν δ'
οἴχεται,
κύκνου τε πολιώτεραι δὴ
αἵδ' ἐπανθοῦσιν τρίχες.

O we! who once in days of old were active in dances, brave in battle, and, on this very account alone, most warlike men. This was of old; but now all that is gone, and these hairs now blossom whiter than the swan.

O we! who once were ardent in the dance,
And brave in fight, of all men most courageous;
But this is of old date—'tis past—and now
These hairs of ours are whiter than the swan.
—Wheelwright.

See Percy's "Reliques," vol. ii. p. 162—

"His reverend locks
In comelye curles did wave;
And on his aged temples grewe
The blossomes of the grave."

The Days that are Gone By.

Vesp. 1091.

Ἆρα δεινὸς ἦ τόθ', ὥστε πάντα μὴ δεδοι-
κέναι· ἀντ.
Καὶ κατεστρεψάμην
τοὺς ἐναντίους, πλέων
ἐκεῖσε ταῖς τριήρεσιν.
Οὐ γὰρ ἦν ἡμῖν ὅπως ῥῆσιν εὖ
λέξειν ἐμέλλομεν τότ', οὐδὲ
συκοφαντήσειν τινὰ
φροντίς, ἀλλ' ὃς ἂν ἐρέτης ἔσοιτ'
ἄριστος.

Truly then I was terrible so as to fear nothing; and I subdued my foes, sailing thither with the triremes; for we thought not how we should speak rightly nor how we should slander any one, but how we should be the best steersman.

Oh the days that are gone by, oh the days that are no more,
When my eye was bold and fearless, and my hand was on the oar!

Merrily then, oh merrily, I beat the brine to lath,
And the sea once crossed, sacked cities were the foot-tracks of my
  path.

> Oh the days that are gone by!
> Then with none was care to find
> Dainty words and speech refined ;
> Reasoning much on taste and tact,—
> Quick of tongue, but slow to act.—MITCHELL.

THE RESULTS OF DRINKING.
Vesp. 1253.

Κακὸν τὸ πίνειν· ἀπὸ γὰρ οἴνου γίγνεται
καὶ θυροκοπῆσαι, καὶ πατάξαι, καὶ βαλεῖν·
κἄπειτ᾽ ἀποτίνειν ἀργύριον ἐκ κραιπάλης.

Drinking is bad ; for it is from wine that spring the breaking
of doors, and the dealing of blows, and the throwing of stones ;
and then the paying of money after your drunken bout.

So Shakespeare ("Othello," act ii. sc. 3)—
  "Every inordinate cup is unblessed, and the ingredient is a devil."

WOMAN'S TIME FOR MARRIAGE IS SHORT.
Lysistr. 595.

Ὁ γὰρ ἥκων μέν, κἂν ᾖ πολιός, ταχὺ παῖδα κόρην γεγάμηκε·
τῆς δὲ γυναικὸς μικρὸς ὁ καιρός· κἂν τούτου μὴ 'πιλάβηται,
οὐδεὶς ἐθέλει γῆμαι ταύτην· ὀττευομένη δὲ κάθηται.

For man, though he be grey-headed when he comes back, soon
gets a young wife. But a woman's time is short within which she
can expect to obtain a husband. If she allows it to slip away, no
one cares to marry her. She sits at home speculating on the pro-
babilities of her marriage.

THE DECEIT OF WOMEN.
Eccles. 236.

Χρήματα πορίζειν εὐπορώτατον γυνή.
Ἄρχουσά τ᾽ οὐκ ἂν ἐξαπατηθείη ποτέ·
αὐταὶ γὰρ εἰσιν ἐξαπατᾶν εἰθισμέναι.

A woman is most ingenious in providing money ; and when she
is at the head of a house, can never be deceived, for they themselves are accustomed to deceive.

> Then, for the ways and means, say who're more skilled
> Than women? They, too, are such arch-deceivers,
> That, when in power, they ne'er will be deceived.—SMITH.

See (Lat.) Woman.

AGRICULTURE.
Fr. Com. Gr. p. 284.

A. Τοῖς πᾶσιν ἀνθρώποισιν Εἰρήνης φίλης
πιστὴ τροφός, ταμία, συνεργός, ἐπίτροπος,
θυγάτηρ, ἀδελφή, πάντα ταῦτ' ἐχρῆτό μοι.
B. Σοὶ δ' ὄνομα δὴ τί εστιν ; A. Ὅτι ; Γεωργία.
B. *Ω ποθεινὴ τοῖς δικαίοις καὶ γεωργοῖς ἡμέρα,
Ἄσμενος σ' ἰδὼν προσειπεῖν βούλομαι τὰς ἀμπέλους.

A. The faithful nurse, housewife, helper, guardian, daughter, sister of beloved, peace to all men, all these epithets are applicable to me.—*B.* But what is your name, pray?—*A.* What, Agriculture.—*B.* O day desired by the just and husbandmen! having seen thee with pleasure, I wish to address the vines.

DEATH.
Fr. Com. Gr. p. 309.

Τὸ γὰρ φοβεῖσθαι τὸν θάνατον λῆρος πολύς·
πᾶσιν γὰρ ἡμῖν τοῦτ' ὀφείλεται παθεῖν.

To fear death is very great folly, for it is fated to all men to die.

ARISTOPHON.

ARISTOPHON, a comic poet, who is supposed to have belonged to the middle comedy, but nothing is known of his life or age. We know the titles of nine of his plays.

POVERTY.
Fr. Com. Gr. p. 675.

Σαφὴς ὁ χειμών ἐστι· τῆς πενίας λύχνος
ἅπαντα φαίνει τὰ κακὰ καὶ τὰ δυσχερῆ.

The storm is evident ; poverty, like a lamp, shows everything bad and annoying.

ARISTOTLE.

BORN B.C. 384—DIED B.C. 322.

ARISTOTLE, the celebrated philosopher, was a native of Stageira, a seaport town of the district of Chalcidice, which became subject to Philip of Macedon. He was son of Nicomachus, physician to Amyntas II., King of Macedon. He lost his father at an early age, and was intrusted to the guardianship of Proxenus of Atarneus in Mysia, who seems to have performed his duties in a way to entitle him to the grateful acknowledgments of his pupil. Aristotle was attracted by his love of learning to Athens, where Plato was in the zenith of his fame, and that master soon discovered the abilities of his ardent disciple. On account of his industry and unwearied efforts in search of the truth, Plato used to call him the "intellect of his school," and say "that he needed a curb, while Xenocrates needed the spur." For twenty years he continued to be on intimate terms with Plato, though he had himself assembled around him a circle of admiring followers; but at the death of Plato, B.C. 347, he left Athens, and joined his former pupil, Hermias, who had become ruler of Atarneus and Assos. When Hermias was destroyed by the Persians, Aristotle fled to Mitylene, and two years after, B.C. 342, we find him invited by Philip, King of Macedon, to undertake the instruction and education of his son, Alexander, then thirteen years of age. The young prince became so strongly attached to him that he valued his instructor above his own father. Aristotle spent seven years in Macedon. In the year B.C. 355, soon after Alexander succeeded to the throne, Aristotle returned to Athens, where he collected a large number of pupils from the cities of Europe and Asia. There he continued for thirteen years to teach his doctrines to those who afterwards became distinguished as philosophers, historians, statesmen, and orators. On the death of Alexander, he was accused of impiety, which was the usual prelude to an unjust condemnation. To deprive the Athenians, as he said, of sinning a second time against philosophy, he left Athens, and spent the remainder of his life at Chalcis, in Euboea, where the Macedonian influence afforded him protection and security. Out of four hundred treatises which he is said to have composed, only forty-eight have been transmitted to the present age.

Happiness.
Ethic. i. 2.

Περὶ δὲ τῆς εὐδαιμονίας, τί ἐστιν, ἀμφισβητοῦσι καὶ οὐχ ὁμοίως οἱ πολλοὶ τοῖς σοφοῖς ἀποδιδόασιν. Οἱ μὲν γὰρ τῶν ἐναργῶν τι καὶ φανερῶν, οἶον ἡδονὴν ἢ πλοῦτον ἢ τιμήν, ἄλλοι δ' ἄλλο, πολλάκις δὲ καὶ ὁ αὐτὸς ἕτερον· νοσήσας μὲν γὰρ ὑγίειαν, πενόμενος δὲ πλοῦτον· συνειδότες δ' ἑαυτοῖς ἄγνοιαν τοὺς μέγα τι καὶ ὑπὲρ αὐτοὺς λέγοντας θαυμάζουσιν.

But concerning happiness, men cannot agree as to its true nature, and the vulgar by no means hold the same opinion respecting it with the educated ; for some are inclined to apply it only to what is distinct and marked in its essence, such as pleasure, wealth, or honour ; each man thinking differently of it from his neighbours, and often the same person entertains different opinions respecting it at different times. For, when he is ill, he thinks it to be health ; when poor, to be riches ; but, being conscious of their own ignorance, men are apt to be struck with admiration at those who say that it is something great and above them.

See (Lat.) Happiness.

One Swallow does not make Spring.
Ethic. i. 6.

Μία γὰρ χελιδὼν ἔαρ οὐ ποιεῖ, οὐδὲ μία ἡμέρα· οὕτω δὲ οὐδὲ μακάριον καὶ εὐδαίμονα μία ἡμέρα οὐδ' ὀλίγος χρόνος.

For one swallow does not make spring, nor yet one fine day ; so, also, neither does one day, nor a short time, make a man blessed and happy.

The Principle Half of the whole Question.
Ethic. i. 7.

Δοκεῖ γὰρ πλεῖον ἢ ἥμισυ παντὸς εἶναι ἡ ἀρχή.

For the principle seems to be more than the half of the whole question.

The Three Qualities included in Happiness.
Ethic. i. 9.

Ἄριστον ἄρα καὶ κάλλιστον καὶ ἥδιστον ἡ εὐδαιμονία, καὶ οὐ διώρισται ταῦτα κατὰ τὸ Δηλιακὸν ἐπίγραμμα·
κάλλιστον τὸ δικαιότατον, λῷστον δ' ὑγιαίνειν·
ἥδιστον δὲ πέφυχ' οὗ τις ἐρᾷ τὸ τυχεῖν.
Ἄπαντα γὰρ ὑπάρχει ταῦτα ταῖς ἀρίσταις ἐνεργείαις· ταύτας δέ, ἢ μίαν τούτων τὴν ἀρίστην, φαμὲν εἶναι τὴν εὐδαιμονίαν.

Happiness is the best, most honourable, and most pleasant of

all things; nor are these qualities to be disjoined, as in the inscription at Delos, where it maintains "that the most just is the
most honourable, that health is what is most to be desired, and
the most pleasant thing is to obtain what we love:" for all these
qualities exist in the best energies, and we say that these, or the
best one of them, is happiness.

HAPPINESS A DIVINE GIFT.
Ethic. i. 10.

*Εἰ μὲν οὖν καὶ ἄλλο τι ἐστὶ θεῶν δώρημα ἀνθρώποις, εὔλογον καὶ
τὴν εὐδαιμονίαν θεόσδοτον εἶναι, καὶ μάλιστα τῶν ἀνθρωπίνων ὅσῳ
βέλτιστον.*

If, then, there is anything that is a gift of the gods to men, it is
surely reasonable to suppose that happiness is a divine gift, and
more than anything else of human things, as it is the best.

IMPORTANCE OF EARLY EDUCATION.
Ethic. ii. 2.

*Διὸ δεῖ ἦχθαί πως εὐθὺς ἐκ νέων, ὡς ὁ Πλάτων φησίν, ὥστε χαί-
ρειν τε καὶ λυπεῖσθαι οἷς δεῖ· ἡ γὰρ ὀρθὴ παιδεία αὕτη ἐστίν.*

Therefore it is necessary to be in a certain degree trained from
our very childhood, as Plato says, to feel pleasure and pain at
what we ought; for this is education in its true sense.

WHAT CONSTITUTES AN ACTION VIRTUOUS.
Ethic. ii. 3.

*Ἔτι οὐδ' ὅμοιόν ἐστιν ἐπὶ τῶν τεχνῶν καὶ τῶν ἀρετῶν· τὰ μὲν γὰρ
ὑπὸ τῶν τεχνῶν γινόμενα τὸ εὖ ἔχει ἐν αὑτοῖς, ἀρκεῖ οὖν ταῦτά πως
ἔχοντα γενέσθαι· τὰ δὲ κατὰ τὰς ἀρετὰς γινόμενα οὐκ ἐὰν αὐτά πως
ἔχῃ, δικαίως ἢ σωφρόνως πράττεται, ἀλλὰ καὶ ἐὰν ὁ πράττων πῶς
ἔχων πράττῃ, πρῶτον μὲν ἐὰν εἰδώς, ἔπειτ' ἐὰν προαιρούμενος, καὶ
προαιρούμενος δι' αὐτά, τὸ δὲ τρίτον καὶ ἐὰν βεβαίως καὶ ἀμετακινή-
τως ἔχων πράττῃ. Ταῦτα δὲ πρὸς μὲν τὸ τὰς ἄλλας τέχνας ἔχειν οὐ
συναριθμεῖται, πλὴν αὐτὸ τὸ εἰδέναι· πρὸς δὲ τὸ τὰς ἀρετὰς τὸ μὲν εἰδέναι μικρὸν ἢ οὐδὲν ἰσχύει, τὰ δ' ἄλλα οὐ μικρὸν ἀλλὰ τὸ πᾶν δύναται,
ἅπερ ἐκ τοῦ πολλάκις πράττειν τὰ δίκαια καὶ σώφρονα περιγίνεται.*

Then, again, it is not the same in regard to the arts and the
virtues, for works of art have their excellence in themselves; it
is sufficient, therefore, that they should themselves possess such
a character. Whereas virtuous deeds are just and temperate, not
if the deeds themselves have this character, but if the agent, who
does them, has in himself this character; first, if he does them
knowingly; then, if with deliberate choice, and deliberate choice
on their own account; thirdly, if he does them on a fixed and

unchangeable principle. Now, with regard to all other arts these ideas are not taken into account, with the exception of knowledge; whereas, with regard to virtues, mere knowledge has little or no weight, while the other qualifications are not of small but of infinite importance, since they spring from the habit of just and temperate actions.

To Hit the Mean is Difficult.
Ethic. ii. 5.

Μεσότης τις ἄρα ἐστὶν ἡ ἀρετή, στοχαστική γε οὖσα τοῦ μέσου. Ἔτι τὸ μὲν ἁμαρτάνειν πολλαχῶς ἔστιν (τὸ γὰρ κακὸν τοῦ ἀπείρου, ὡς οἱ Πυθαγόρειοι εἴκαζον, τὸ δ' ἀγαθὸν τοῦ πεπερασμένου), τὸ δὲ κατορθοῦν μοναχῶς· διὸ καὶ τὸ μὲν ῥάδιον τὸ δὲ χαλεπόν, ῥάδιον μὲν τὸ ἀποτυχεῖν τοῦ σκοποῦ, χαλεπὸν δὲ τὸ ἐπιτυχεῖν. Καὶ διὰ ταῦτ' οὖν τῆς μὲν κακίας ἡ ὑπερβολὴ καὶ ἡ ἔλλειψις, τῆς δ' ἀρετῆς ἡ μεσότης.

Ἐσθλοὶ μὲν γὰρ ἁπλῶς, παντοδαπῶς δὲ κακοί.

Virtue, then, is a kind of mean state, being at least apt to strike the mean. Again, it is possible to go wrong in many ways (for evil, as the Pythagoreans imagined, is of the nature of the infinite, but good of the finite), whereas we can go right only in one way; therefore the former is easy, the latter is difficult; it is easy to miss a mark, difficult to hit it; and for these reasons the excess and defect belong to vice, but the mean to virtue; "for we are good in one way only, but bad in all kinds of ways."

Death is a Limit.
Ethic. iii. 9.

Φοβερώτατον δ' ὁ θάνατος· πέρας γάρ, καὶ οὐδὲν ἔτι τῷ τεθνεῶτι δοκεῖ οὔτ' ἀγαθὸν οὔτε κακὸν εἶναι.

Death is the most terrible of all things; for it is a limit, and it is thought that there is nothing good or bad beyond to the dead.

The Character of the Celtic Race.
Ethic. iii. 10.

Εἰ μηθὲν φοβοῖτο, μήτε σεισμὸν μήτε τὰ κύματα, καθάπερ φασὶ τοὺς Κελτούς.

If he fear nothing, neither earthquake nor the waves, as they say of the Celts.

See (Lat.) Gauls.

Suicide an Act of Cowardice.
Ethic. iii. 11.

Τὸ δ' ἀποθνήσκειν φεύγοντα πενίαν ἢ ἔρωτα ἤ τι λυπηρὸν οὐκ

ἀνδρείου, ἀλλὰ μᾶλλον δειλοῦ· μαλακία γὰρ τὸ φεύγειν τὰ ἐπίπονα, καὶ οὐχ ὅτι καλὸν ὑπομένει, ἀλλὰ φεύγων κακόν.

To die in order to avoid the pains of poverty, love, or anything that is disagreeable, is not the part of a brave man, but of a coward; for it is cowardice to shun the trials and crosses of life, not undergoing death because it is honourable, but to avoid evil.

See (Lat.) Suicide.

THE CONDUCT OF REGULAR TROOPS AND MILITIA CONTRASTED.

Ethic. iii. 11.

Οἱ στρατιῶται δὲ δειλοὶ γίνονται, ὅταν ὑπερτείνῃ ὁ κίνδυνος λείπωνται τοῖς πλήθεσι καὶ ταῖς παρασκευαῖς· πρῶτοι γὰρ φεύγουσι, τὰ δὲ πολιτικὰ μένοντα ἀποθνήσκει, ὅπερ κἀπὶ τῷ Ἑρμαίῳ συνέβη. Τοῖς μὲν γὰρ αἰσχρὸν τὸ φεύγειν καὶ ὁ θάνατος τῆς τοιαύτης σωτηρίας αἱρετώτερυς· οἱ δὲ καὶ ἐξ ἀρχῆς ἐκινδύνευον ὡς κρείττους ὄντες, γνόντες δὲ φεύγουσι, τὸν θάνατον μᾶλλον τοῦ αἰσχροῦ φοβούμενοι· ὁ δ' ἀνδρεῖος οὐ τοιοῦτος.

Regular troops lose their courage when they see the danger greater than they expected, and when they find themselves surpassed in numbers and equipments. For they are the first to turn their backs. But the militia of a country die at their posts, as happened at Hermæum. For in their eyes it is disgraceful to fly, and death is regarded as preferable to safety procured at such a cost. The others only expose themselves to danger while they think themselves superior, but when they find that they are mistaken, they at once run away, fearing death more than dishonour. This certainly is not the character of the brave man.

BELLY-GODS.

Ethic. iii. 13.

Τὸ γὰρ ἐσθίειν τὰ τυχόντα ἢ πίνειν ἕως ἂν ὑπερπλησθῇ ὑπερβάλλειν ἐστὶ τὸ κατὰ φύσιν τῷ πλήθει· ἀναπλήρωσις γὰρ τῆς ἐνδείας ἡ φυσικὴ ἐπιθυμία. Διὸ λέγονται οὗτοι γαστρίμαργοι, ὡς παρὰ τὸ δέον πληροῦντες αὐτήν. Τοιοῦτοι δὲ γίνονται οἱ λίαν ἀνδραποδώδεις.

For to eat or drink till a man is surfeited is going beyond the natural desire in quantity; for the object of natural desire is the satisfying our wants. Therefore these are called belly-gods, as they satisfy their wants more than they ought; people of excessively slavish dispositions are apt to do this.

So Philippians (iii. 19)—"Whose god is their belly, and glory in shame."

THE CHARACTERISTIC OF THE MAGNANIMOUS MAN.
Ethic. iv. 8.

Μεγαλοψύχου δὲ καὶ τὸ μηθενὸς δεῖσθαι ἢ μόγις, ὑπηρετεῖν δὲ προθύμως, καὶ πρὸς μὲν τοὺς ἐν ἀξιώματι καὶ εὐτυχίαις μέγαν εἶναι, πρὸς δὲ τοὺς μέσους μέτριον· τῶν μὲν γὰρ ὑπερέχειν χαλεπὸν καὶ σεμνόν, τῶν δὲ ῥάδιον, καὶ ἐν ἐκείνοις μὲν σεμνύνεσθαι οὐκ ἀγεννές, ἐν δὲ τοῖς ταπεινοῖς φορτικόν, ὥσπερ εἰς τοὺς ἀσθενεῖς ἰσχυρίζεσθαι.

It is the characteristic of a magnanimous man to ask no favour, or scarcely any, but to be ready to do kindness to others, to be haughty in demeanour towards men of rank and fortune, kindly towards those of the middle classes, for to rise superior to the former is difficult and honourable, over the latter it is easy ; among the former there is nothing ungenerous in showing pride, among those of humble rank it is bad taste, just like making a show of strength to the weak.

FLATTERERS.
Ethic. iv. 8.

Καὶ πάντες οἱ κόλακες θητικοὶ καὶ οἱ ταπεινοὶ κόλακες.

All flatterers are mercenary ; and low-minded men are flatterers.

MEN-PLEASERS AND THE CROSS-GRAINED CONTRASTED.
Ethic. iv. 12.

Ἐν δὲ ταῖς ὁμιλίαις καὶ τῷ συζῆν καὶ λόγων καὶ πραγμάτων κοινωνεῖν οἱ μὲν ἄρεσκοι δοκοῦσιν εἶναι, οἱ πάντα πρὸς ἡδονὴν ἐπαινοῦντες καὶ οὐθὲν ἀντιτείνοντες, ἀλλ' οἰόμενοι δεῖν ἄλυποι τοῖς ἐντυγχάνουσιν εἶναι· οἱ δ' ἐξ ἐναντίας τούτοις πρὸς πάντα ἀντιτείνοντες καὶ τοῦ λυπεῖν οὐδ' ὁτιοῦν φροντίζοντες δύσκολοι καὶ δυσέριδες καλοῦνται.

In the intercourse of society and life, in conversation and the affairs of the world, some men appear to be parasites, who praise everything for the sake of giving pleasure, and never contradict an opinion, but think that they ought to give no opinion to those with whom they happen to be ; others, the very opposite characters to these, who oppose everything, and are altogether regardless of the feelings of their neighbour, are called cross-grained and quarrelsome.

TRUTH AND FALSEHOOD.
Ethic. iv. 13.

Τὸ μὲν ψεῦδος φαῦλον καὶ ψεκτόν, τὸ δ' ἀληθὲς καλὸν καὶ ἐπαινετόν.

Falsehood is bad and blameable ; truth honourable and praiseworthy.

The Refined and Gentlemanly Man.
Ethic. iv. 14.

Ὁ δὴ χαρίεις καὶ ἐλευθέριος οὕτως ἕξει, οἷον νόμος ὢν ἑαυτῷ.
Τοιοῦτος μὲν οὖν ὁ μέσος ἐστίν, εἴτ᾽ ἐπιδέξιος εἴτ᾽ εὐτράπελος
λέγεται.

Now the refined and gentlemanly man will so act, being as it
were a law unto himself; and such is he who is in the mean,
whether he be called a man of tact or of graceful wit.

A Ruler is not a Terror to Good Works.
Ethic. v. 10.

Διὸ οὐκ ἐῶμεν ἄρχειν ἄνθρωπον, ἀλλὰ τὸν λόγον, ὅτι ἑαυτῷ τοῦτο
ποιεῖ καὶ γίνεται τύραννος. Ἔστι δ᾽ ὁ ἄρχων φύλαξ τοῦ δικαίου, εἰ
δὲ τοῦ δικαίου, καὶ τοῦ ἴσου.

Wherefore we do not allow man to rule but reason, because
man rules for himself, and becomes a tyrant. A ruler is the protector of the just, and, if of the just, then, also, of what is equitable to all.

See Rom. xiii. 3; 1 Pet. ii. 14.

Rigour of Law.
Ethic. v. 14.

Φανερὸν δ᾽ ἐκ τούτου καὶ ὁ ἐπιεικὴς τίς ἐστιν· ὁ γὰρ τῶν τοιούτων
προαιρετικὸς καὶ πρακτικός, καὶ ὁ μὴ ἀκριβοδίκαιος ἐπὶ τὸ χεῖρον
ἀλλ᾽ ἐλαττωτικός, καίπερ ἔχων τὸν νόμον βοηθόν, ἐπιεικής ἐστι, καὶ
ἡ ἕξις αὕτη ἐπιείκεια, δικαιοσύνη τις οὖσα καὶ οὐχ ἑτέρα τις ἕξις.

From this it is evident what is the character of the equitable
man; for he who is disposed to do such things, and is active in
their performance, who does not assert his rights to the uttermost,
but is willing to take something less, even though he may have
law on his side, is a man of equity: this habit is equity, being a
kind of justice, and not a different habit from justice.

See (Lat.) Rigour of law.

The Past.
Ethic. vi. 2.

Διὸ ὀρθῶς Ἀγάθων.

Μόνου γὰρ αὐτοῦ καὶ θεὸς στερίσκεται,
ἀγένητα ποιεῖν ἅσσ᾽ ἂν ᾖ πεπραγμένα.

Therefore well does Agathon say, "Of this alone is even God
deprived, the power of making that which is past never to have
been."

See (Lat.) The past.

FRIENDSHIP.
Ethic. viii. 1.

Ἐν πενίᾳ τε καὶ ταῖς λοιπαῖς δυστυχίαις μόνην οἴονται καταφυγὴν εἶναι τοὺς φίλους. Καὶ νέοις δὲ πρὸς τὸ ἀναμάρτητον καὶ πρεσβυτέροις πρὸς θεραπείαν καὶ τὸ ἐλλεῖπον τῆς πράξεως δι᾽ ἀσθένειαν βοηθεῖ, τοῖς τ᾽ ἐν ἀκμῇ πρὸς τὰς καλὰς πράξεις.

In poverty and the other misfortunes of life, men think friends to be their only refuge. The young they keep out of mischief, to the old they are a comfort and aid in their weakness, and those in the prime of life they incite to noble deeds.

See (Lat.) Friendship.

FRIENDS.
Ethic. viii. 1.

Καὶ φίλων μὲν ὄντων οὐδὲν δεῖ δικαιοσύνης, δίκαιοι δ᾽ ὄντες προσδέονται φιλίας.

When men are friends, there is no need of justice; but when they are just, they still need friendship.

See Rom. xiii. 10.

FRIENDSHIP REQUIRES TIME.
Ethic. viii. 4.

Κατὰ τὴν παροιμίαν γὰρ οὐκ ἔστιν εἰδῆσαι ἀλλήλους πρὶν τοὺς λεγομένους ἅλας συναναλῶσαι· οὐδ᾽ ἀποδέξασθαι δὴ πρότερον οὐδ᾽ εἶναι φίλους, πρὶν ἂν ἑκάτερος ἑκατέρῳ φανῇ φιλητὸς καὶ πιστευθῇ.

According to the proverb, it is impossible for friends to know each other till they have eaten a certain quantity of salt with each other. Nor can they be on friendly and familiar terms till they appear worthy of each other's friendship and confidence.

THE WICKED.
Ethic. viii. 10.

Οἱ δὲ μοχθηροὶ τὸ μὲν βέβαιον οὐκ ἔχουσιν· οὐδὲ γὰρ αὐτοῖς διαμένουσιν ὅμοιοι ὄντες· ἐπ᾽ ὀλίγον δὲ χρόνον γίνονται φίλοι, χαίροντες τῇ ἀλλήλων μοχθηρίᾳ.

The wicked have no stability, for they do not remain in consistency with themselves; they continue friends only for a short time, rejoicing in each other's wickedness.

TYRANNY.
Ethic. viii. 13.

Παρέκβασις δὲ βασιλείας μὲν τυραννίς· ἄμφω γὰρ μοναρχίαι, διαφέρουσι δὲ πλεῖστον· ὁ μὲν γὰρ τύραννος τὸ ἑαυτῷ συμφέρον σκοπεῖ, ὁ δὲ βασιλεὺς τὸ τῶν ἀρχομένων. Οὐ γάρ ἐστι βασιλεὺς ὁ μὴ αὐτάρκης καὶ πᾶσι τοῖς ἀγαθοῖς ὑπερέχων· ὁ δὲ τοιοῦτος οὐδενὸς προσδεῖται· τὰ ὠφέλιμα οὖν αὐτῷ μὲν οὐκ ἂν σκοποίη, τοῖς δ' ἀρχομένοις.

The deflection of monarchy is tyranny; for both are monarchies, but the difference between them is very marked : for a tyrant thinks only of his own interests, while a king attends to those of his subjects. For he is not a king who is not uncontrolled, and who is not possessed of all kinds of goods, for such a one stands in need of nothing more ; therefore he does not require to be looking after his own interests, but devotes himself to his subjects.

A TYRANT.
Ethic. viii. 12.

Τὸ γὰρ ἑαυτῷ ἀγαθὸν διώκει. · Καὶ φανερώτερον ἐπὶ ταύτης ὅτι χειρίστη· κάκιστον δὲ τὸ ἐναντίον τῷ βελτίστῳ.

For a tyrant pursues his own peculiar good, and it is more manifest for this very reason, that it is the worst form of government, for that is worst which is opposite to the best.

BE JUST BEFORE YOU ARE GENEROUS.
Ethic. ix. 2.

Ὥσπερ δάνειον, ᾧ ὀφείλει ἀποδοτέον μᾶλλον ἢ ἑταίρῳ δοτέον.

We ought rather to pay a debt to a creditor than give to a companion.

GIVE EVERY ONE HIS DUE.
Ethic. ix. 2.

Ἐπεὶ δ' ἕτερα γονεῦσι καὶ ἀδελφοῖς καὶ ἑταίροις καὶ εὐεργέταις, ἑκάστοις τὰ οἰκεῖα καὶ τὰ ἁρμόττοντα ἀπονεμητέον.

But, since we owe different services to parents, brothers, companions, and benefactors, we ought to take care to pay every one his due, and that which is suitable to his character.

See Rom. xiii. 7.

THE INTELLECTUAL PART CONSTITUTES EACH MAN'S SELF.
Ethic. ix. 4.

Οὗτος γὰρ ὁμογνωμονεῖ ἑαυτῷ, καὶ τῶν αὐτῶν ὀρέγεται κατὰ πᾶσαν τὴν ψυχήν, καὶ βούλεται δὴ ἑαυτῷ τἀγαθὰ καὶ τὰ φαινόμενα καὶ πράττει (τοῦ γὰρ ἀγαθοῦ τἀγαθὸν διαπονεῖν) καὶ ἑαυτοῦ ἕνεκα· τοῦ γὰρ διανοητικοῦ χάριν, ὅπερ ἕκαστος εἶναι δοκεῖ.

For the good man agrees in opinion with himself, and desires the same things with all his soul; therefore he wishes what is good for himself, and what appears so, practising it : for it is the part of a good man to labour for what is good, and for his own sake ; for it is for the sake of his intellectual part, which is considered to be a man's own self.

See (Lat.) Mind is the man.

Mind is the Man.
Ethic. ix. 4.

Δόξειε δ' ἂν τὸ νοοῦν ἕκαστος εἶναι, ἢ μάλιστα.

And the thinking principle—or, at least, that rather than any other—must be considered to be each man's self.

A Good Man is without Repentance.
Ethic. ix. 4.

Καὶ θεωρημάτων δ' εὐπορεῖ τῇ διανοίᾳ, συναλγεῖ τε καὶ συνήδεται μάλισθ' ἑαυτῷ· πάντοτε γὰρ ἐστι τὸ αὐτὸ λυπηρόν τε καὶ ἡδύ, καὶ οὐκ ἄλλοτ' ἄλλο· ἀμεταμέλητος γὰρ ὡς εἰπεῖν.

Besides, the good man has abundant subjects for reflection ; he sympathises most with himself in joys and sorrows ; for the same always gives to him the same pain or sorrow, and not sometimes one thing and sometimes another. For he is, if we may be allowed to say so, without repentance.

See 1 Sam. xv. 29 ; Num. xxiii. 19. Cic. Tusc. v. 28.

The Counsels of Good Men.
Ethic. ix. 6.

Τῶν τοιούτων γὰρ μένει τὰ βουλήματα καὶ οὐ μεταρρεῖ ὥσπερ Εὔριπος, βούλονταί τε τὰ δίκαια καὶ τὰ συμφέροντα.

For the counsels of good men remain fixed, and do not ebb and flow like the Euripus ; they desire what is just and proper.

See Isa. lvii. 20.

Why Mothers are Fond of their Children.
Ethic. ix. 7.

Διὰ ταῦτα δὲ καὶ αἱ μητέρες φιλοτεκνότεραι· ἐπιπονωτέρα γὰρ ἡ γέννησις, καὶ μᾶλλον ἴσασιν ὅτι αὐτῶν.

For this reason, also, mothers are more fond of their children than fathers are ; for the bringing them forth is more painful, and they have a more certain knowledge that they are their own.

This is the converse of the Latin proverb—"Sapiens est filius qui novit patrem." See Adagia Erasmi—"Matris ut capra dicitur."

The Masses led by Fear.

Ethic. x. 10.

Τοὺς δὲ πολλοὺς ἀδυνατεῖν πρὸς καλοκαγαθίαν προτρέψασθαι· οὐ
γὰρ πεφύκασιν αἰδοῖ πειθαρχεῖν ἀλλὰ φόβῳ, οὐδ᾽ ἀπέχεσθαι τῶν
φαύλων διὰ τὸ αἰσχρὸν ἀλλὰ διὰ τὰς τιμωρίας· πάθει γὰρ ζῶντες
τὰς οἰκείας ἡδονὰς διώκουσι καὶ δι᾽ ὧν αὗται ἔσονται, φεύγουσι δὲ
τὰς ἀντικειμένας λύπας, τοῦ δὲ καλοῦ καὶ ὡς ἀληθῶς ἡδέος οὐδ᾽
ἔννοιαν ἔχουσιν, ἄγευστοι ὄντες. Τοὺς δὴ τοιούτους τίς ἂν λόγος
μεταρρυθμίσαι ; οὐ γὰρ οἷόν τε ἢ οὐ ῥάδιον τὰ ἐκ παλαιοῦ τοῖς ἤθεσι
κατειλημμένα λόγῳ μεταστῆσαι.

(Treatises) have no power to persuade the multitude to do what
is virtuous and honourable. For the masses are formed by nature
to obey, not a sense of shame, but fear ; nor do they refrain from
vicious things on account of disgrace, but of punishment ; for
they live in obedience to passion, pursuing their own pleasures
and the means of gratifying them ; they fly also from the contrary pains ; but of what is honourable and really delightful, they
have not the slightest idea, inasmuch as they never had a taste
for them. What power of reasoning, then, could bring about a
change on such men as these? For it is not possible, or at least
not easy to change what has been impressed for a long time upon
the moral character.

Education the Duty of the State.

Ethic. x. 10.

Κράτιστον μὲν οὖν τὸ γίνεσθαι κοινὴν ἐπιμέλειαν καὶ ὀρθὴν καὶ
δρᾶν αὐτὸ δύνασθαι· κοινῇ δ᾽ ἐξαμελουμένων ἑκάστῳ δόξειεν ἂ𝑠
προσήκειν τοῖς σφετέροις τέκνοις καὶ φίλοις εἰς ἀρετὴν συμβάλλεσθαι,
ἢ προαιρεῖσθαί γε.

It would therefore be best that the state should pay attention
to education, and on right principles, and that it should have the
power to enforce it ; but if it be neglected as a public measure,
then it would seem to be the duty of every individual to contribute to the virtue of his children and friends, or at least to
make this his deliberate purpose.

Sir Thomas More ("Utopia," page 21) says—"If you suffer your people
to be ill educated, and their manners to be corrupted from their infancy,
and then punish them for those crimes to which their first education dis
posed them,—you first make thieves, and then punish them."

Some Command and Some Obey.

Polit. i. 2.

Ἄρχον δὲ φύσει καὶ ἀρχόμενον διὰ τὴν σωτηρίαν· τὸ μὲν γὰρ
δυνάμενον τῇ διανοίᾳ προορᾶν, ἄρχον φύσει, καὶ δεσπόζον φύσει·
τὸ δὲ δυνάμενον τῷ σώματι ταῦτα ποιεῖν, ἀρχόμενον, καὶ φύσει
δοῦλον. Διὸ δεσπότῃ καὶ δούλῳ ταὐτὸ συμφέρει.

By nature some command and some obey, that all may enjoy safety; for the being that is able to foresee coming events is a ruler of nature's own appointment; whereas he who is only able to assist by bodily service, is a subordinate and natural slave. Hence the interest of master and slave is identical.

THE DOMESTIC TIE IS THE FIRST.

Polit. i. 2.

Καὶ ὀρθῶς Ἡσίοδος εἶπε ποιήσας, "Οἶκον μὲν πρώτιστα, γυναῖκά τε, βοῦν τ' ἀροτῆρα." Ὁ γὰρ βοῦς αντ' οἰκέτου τοῖς πένησίν ἐστιν.

Hesiod is right when he says, "First house, then wife, then oxen for the plough;" for the ox stands in place of slave to the poor.

MAN ALONE HAS PERCEPTION OF GOOD AND EVIL.

Polit. i. 2.

Τοῦτο γὰρ πρὸς τὰ ἄλλα ζῶα τοῖς ἀνθρώποις ἴδιον τὸ μόνον ἀγαθοῦ καὶ κακοῦ καὶ δικαίου καὶ ἀδίκου, καὶ τῶν ἄλλων αἴσθησιν ἔχειν. Ἡ δὲ τούτων κοινωνία ποιεῖ οἰκίαν καὶ πόλιν.

For this is the distinguishing mark between man and the lower animals, that he alone is endowed with the power of knowing good and evil, justice and injustice. It is a participation in these that constitutes a family and a city.

See (Lat.) Man prescient.

THE FREEMAN AND THE SLAVE.

Polit. i. 3.

Τοῖς δὲ παρὰ φύσιν τὸ δεσπόζειν. Νόμῳ γὰρ, τὸν μὲν δοῦλον εἶναι, τὸν δὲ ἐλεύθερον· φύσει δὶ οὐθὲν διαφέρειν. Διόπερ οὐδὲ δίκαιον· βίαιον γάρ.

Some think that the power of one man over another is contrary to nature; for they maintain that it is only human law that makes one man a slave and another a free man. But in nature there is no such distinction; wherefore it is an unjust arrangement, for it is the result of force and compulsion.

See Milton, "Paradise Lost," xii.—

> " But man over men
> He made not lord : such title to Himself
> Reserving—human left from human free."

WORSE SERVED BY MANY SERVANTS THAN BY FEW.

Polit. ii. 2.

Ὥσπερ ἐν ταῖς οἰκετικαῖς διακονίαις οἱ πολλοὶ θεράποντες ἐνίοτε χεῖρον ὑπηρετοῦσι τῶν ἐλαττόνων.

As in a family we are often served worse when we have many
servants than a few.

AFFECTION FOR ONE'S-SELF IS NATURAL.

Polit. ii. 3.

Ἔτι δὲ καὶ πρὸς ἡδονὴν ἀμύθητον, ὅσον διαφέρει τὸ νομίζειν ἴδιόν
τι. Μὴ γὰρ οὐ μάτην τὴν πρὸς αὑτὸν αὐτὸς ἔχει φιλίαν ἕκαστος,
ἀλλ' ἔστι τοῦτο φυσικόν· τὸ δὲ φίλαυτον εἶναι, ψέγεται δικαίως.
Οὐκ ἔστι δὲ τοῦτο τὸ φιλεῖν ἑαυτόν, ἀλλὰ τὸ μᾶλλον ἢ δεῖ φιλεῖν.

And also in regard to pleasure it is not to be expressed what a
difference it makes for a man to think that he has something his
own. For possibly it may not be in vain that each person has an
affection for himself, for this is natural, but selfishness is justly
blamed. This is not merely to love one's-self, but to love one's-
self more than we ought.

MORAL UNITY OF A STATE TO BE PRODUCED BY MORAL MEANS.

Polit. ii. 3.

'Ἀλλὰ δεῖ πλῆθος ὄν, ὥσπερ εἴρηται πρότερον, διὰ τὴν παιδείαν
κοινὴν καὶ μίαν ποιεῖν, καὶ τόν γε μέλλοντα παιδείαν εἰσάγειν, καὶ
νομίζοντα διὰ ταύτης ἔσεσθαι τὴν πόλιν σπουδαίαν, ἄτοπον τοῖς
τοιούτοις οἴεσθαι διορθοῦν, ἀλλὰ μὴ τοῖς ἔθεσι, καὶ τῇ φιλοσοφίᾳ,
καὶ τοῖς νόμοις.

But a state consisting of a multitude of beings, as we have
before said, ought to be brought to unity and community by education; and he who is about to introduce education, and expects
thereby to make the state excellent, will act absurdly if he thinks
to fashion it by any other means than by manners, philosophy,
and laws.

DIFFERENT SPECIES OF MEN.

Polit. ii. 3.

Οὐ γὰρ ὁτὲ μὲν ἄλλοις, ὁτὲ δὲ ἄλλοις μέμικται ταῖς ψυχαῖς ὁ
παρὰ τοῦ θεοῦ χρυσός, ἀλλ' ἀεὶ τοῖς αὐτοῖς. Φησὶ δὲ, τοῖς μὲν εὐθὺ
γινομένοις μῖξαι χρυσὸν, τοῖς δὲ ἄργυρον.

For that golden particle, which God has mixed up in the soul
of man, flies not from one to the other, but always continues with
the same; for he says that some of our species have gold, and
others silver, blended in their composition from the moment of
their birth.

What is the Definition of a Citizen?
Polit. iii. 1.

Πολίτης δ' ἁπλῶς οὐδενὶ τῶν ἄλλων ὀρίζεται μᾶλλον, ἢ τῷ μετέχειν κρίσεως καὶ ἀρχῆς.

The truest definition of a complete citizen that can be given is probably this, that he shares in the judicial and executive part of the government.

To Command and Obey.
Polit. iii. 3.

'Αλλὰ μὴν ἐπαινεῖταί γε τό δύνασθαι ἄρχειν καὶ ἄρχεσθαι· καὶ πολίτου δοκίμου ἡ ἀρετὴ εἶναι τὸ δύνασθαι καὶ ἄρχειν καὶ ἄρχεσθαι καλῶς.

But it is a matter of high commendation to know how to command as well as to obey; to do both these things well is the peculiar quality of a distinguished citizen.

Husband and Wife.
Polit. iii. 3.

'Επεὶ καὶ οἰκονομία ἑτέρα ἀνδρὸς καὶ γυναικός· τοῦ μὲν γὰρ κτᾶσθαι· τῆς δὲ, φυλάττειν ἔργον ἐστίν.

The domestic employment of husband and wife differs in this, that the former tries to acquire subsistence, and the latter to keep it.

When a State is well Governed.
Polit. iii. 5.

'Ανάγκη δ' εἶναι κύριον ἤ ἕνα, ἢ ὀλίγους, ἢ τοὺς πολλούς· ὅταν μὲν ὁ εἷς, ἢ οἱ ὀλίγοι, ἢ οἱ πολλοὶ πρὸς τὸ κοινὸν συμφέρον ἄρχωσι, ταύτας μὲν ὀρθὰς ἀναγκαῖον εἶναι τὰς πολιτείας· τὰς δὲ πρὸς τό ἴδιον, ἢ τοῦ ἑνὸς, ἢ τῶν ὀλίγων, ἢ τοῦ πλήθους, παρεκβάσεις.

The supreme power must necessarily be in the hands of one person, or of a few, or of the many. When the one, the few, or the many direct their whole efforts for the common good, such states must be well governed; but when the advantage of the one, the few, or the many is alone regarded, a change for the worse must be expected.

What Law is a Pledge of.
Polit. iii. 6.

Καὶ ὁ νόμος συνθήκη, καὶ καθάπερ ἔφη Λυκόφρων ὁ σοφιστὴς, ἐγγυητὴς ἀλλήλοις τῶν δικαίων, ἀλλ' οὐχ οἷος ποιεῖν ἀγαθοὺς καὶ δικαίους τοὺς πολίτας.

For the law is an agreement, and, as Lycophron says, a pledge given that citizens will do justice to each other; but yet the law is not able to make all the citizens good and just.

See (Lat.) Law.

WHAT IS A STATE?

Polit. iii. 6.

Φανερὸν τοίνυν ὅτι ἡ πόλις οὐκ ἔστι κοινωνία τόπου, καὶ τοῦ μὴ ἀδικεῖν σφᾶς αὐτοὺς, καὶ τῆς μεταδόσεως χάριν· ἀλλὰ ταῦτα μὲν ἀναγκαῖον ὑπάρχειν, εἴπερ ἔσται πόλις· οὐ μὴν οὐδ' ὑπαρχόντων τούτων ἁπάντων, ἤδη πόλις, ἀλλ' ἡ τοῦ εὖ ζῆν κοινωνία καὶ ταῖς οἰκίαις καὶ τοῖς γένεσι, ζωῆς τελείας χάριν καὶ αὐτάρκους.

Then it is evident that a state is not a mere community of place; nor is it established that men may be safe from injury, and maintain an interchange of good offices. All these things, indeed, must take place where there is a state, and yet they may all exist and there be no state. A state, then, may be defined to be a society of people joining together by their families and children to live happily, enjoying a life of thorough independence.

AN UNION OF THE MANY WITH THE FEW DESIRABLE.

Polit. iii. 7.

Πάντες μὲν γὰρ ἔχουσι συνελθόντες ἱκανὴν αἴσθησιν, καὶ μιγνύμενοι τοῖς βελτίοσι, τὰς πόλεις ὠφελοῦσι, καθάπερ ἡ μὴ καθαρὰ τροφὴ μετὰ τῆς καθαρᾶς τὴν πᾶσαν ποιεῖ χρησιμωτέραν τῆς ὀλίγης· χωρὶς δ' ἕκαστος ἀτελὴς περὶ τὸ κρίνειν ἐστίν.

For the multitude, when they are collected together, have sufficient understanding for this purpose (of electing magistrates), and mingling with those of higher rank, are serviceable to the state; as some kinds of food, which would be poisonous by itself, by being mixed with the wholesome, makes the whole good; in the same way, separately, each individual is unfit to form a judgment by himself.

THE RIGHT MAN IN THE RIGHT PLACE.

Polit. iii. 8.

'Αλλ' ἐξ ὧν πόλις συνέστηκεν, ἐν τούτοις ἀναγκαῖον ποιεῖσθαι τὴν ἀμφισβήτησιν. Διόπερ εὐλόγως ἀντιποιοῦνται τῆς τιμῆς οἱ εὐγενεῖς, καὶ ἐλεύθεροι, καὶ πλούσιοι. Δεῖ γὰρ ἐλευθέρους τ' εἶναι, καὶ τίμημα φέροντας. Οὐ γὰρ ἂν εἴη πόλις ἐξ ἀπόρων πάντων, ὥσπερ οὐδ' ἐκ δούλων. 'Αλλὰ μὴν εἰ δεῖ τούτων, δηλονότι καὶ δικαιοσύνης, καὶ τῆς πολεμικῆς ἀρετῆς· οὐδὲ γὰρ ἄνευ τούτων οἰκεῖσθαι πόλιν δυνατόν· πλὴν ἄνευ μὲν τῶν προτέρων ἀδύνατον εἶναι πόλιν, ἄνευ δὲ τούτων οἰκεῖσθαι καλῶς.

A pretension to offices of state ought to be founded on those qualifications, which are part of itself. And for this reason, men

of birth, independence, and fortune are right in contending with
each other for office ; for those who hold offices of state ought to
be persons of independence and property. A state should no more
consist entirely of poor men than it ought entirely of slaves. But
though such persons are requisite, it is evident that there must
also be justice and military valour ; for without justice and valour
no state can be maintained ; just as without the former class a
state cannot exist, and without the latter it cannot be well
governed.

HONOURABLE DESCENT OF GREAT ESTEEM.

Polit. iii. 8.

Οἱ δ' ἐλεύθεροι καὶ εὐγενεῖς, ὡς ἐγγὺς ἀλλήλων. Πολῖται γὰρ
μᾶλλον οἱ γενναιότεροι, τῶν ἀγεννῶν· ἡ δ' εὐγένεια παρ' ἐκάστοις
οἴκοι τίμιος. Ἔτι διότι βελτίους εἰκὸς τοὺς ἐκ βελτιόνων· εὐγένεια
γάρ ἐστιν ἀρετὴ γένους.

The free-born and men of high birth will dispute the point with
each other as being nearly on an equality ; for citizens that are
well born have a right to more respect than the ignoble. Honourable descent is in all nations greatly esteemed ; besides, it is to be
expected that the children of men of worth will be like their
fathers, for nobility is the virtue of a family.

See Hor. Ode iv. 4, 30.

LAW OUGHT TO BE SUPREME.

Polit. iii. 12.

Ὁ μὲν οὖν τὸν νοῦν κελεύων ἄρχειν, δοκεῖ κελεύειν ἄρχειν τὸν θεὸν
καὶ τοὺς νόμους· ὁ δι' ἄνθρωπον κελεύων, προστίθησι καὶ θηρίον.
Ἥτε γὰρ ἐπιθυμία, τοιοῦτον, καὶ ὁ θυμὸς ἄρχοντας διαστρέφει, καὶ
τοὺς ἀρίστους ἄνδρας. Διόπερ ἄνευ ὀρέξεως νοῦς ὁ νόμος ἐστί.

He, then, who orders the reasoning principle of man to be
supreme, seems to make God and the laws to be supreme ; but he
who gives the power to man gives it to a wild beast. For passion
may be so called, and it is passion that brings ruin on rulers, even
though they be the very best of men : wherefore the law is reason
free from passion.

THE MORAL LAW IS SUPERIOR TO WRITTEN LAW.

Polit. iii. 12.

Ἔτι κυριώτεροι καὶ περὶ κυριωτέρων τῶν κατὰ γράμματα νόμων,
οἱ κατὰ τὰ ἔθη εἰσίν. Ὥστε τῶν κατὰ γράμματα ἄνθρωπος ἄρχων
ἀσφαλέστερος, ἀλλ' οὐ τῶν κατὰ τὸ ἔθος.

The moral law is much superior to the written law, and treats
of matters of greater weight ; for the supreme ruler is more to be
trusted than the written law, though he be inferior to the moral.

What forms a Good Man.
Polit. iii. 12.

Ὥστ᾽ ἔσται καὶ παιδεία καὶ ἔθη ταῦτα σχεδὸν τὰ ποιοῦντα σπουδαῖον ἄνδρα, καὶ τὰ ποιοῦντα πολιτικὸν, καὶ βασιλικόν.

So that education and morals will be found to be almost the whole that goes to make a good man; and the same things will make a good statesman and good king.

The Corruption of the Best is the Worst.
Polit. iv. 2.

Ἀνάγκη γὰρ τὴν μὲν τῆς πρώτης καὶ θειοτάτης (πολιτείας) παρέκβασιν, εἶναι χειρίστην.

The corruption of the best and most divine form of government must be the worst.

This is an illustration of the old proverb, "Corruptio optimi pessima fit." Thomas Aquinas often alludes to this sentiment (Prim. Sec. Quæst. xxxix. art. iv. 1)—"Optimo enim opponitur pessimum, ut dicitur in VIII. Ethic." (Prim. Sec. Qu. cv. art. i. 5)—"Præterea sicut regnum est optimum regimen, ita tyrannis est pessima corruptio regiminis."

See (Lat.) Corruption of opinion.

A Democracy.
Polit. iv. 4.

Ἐν μὲν γὰρ ταῖς κατὰ νόμον δημοκρατουμέναις, οὐ γίνεται δημαγωγός, ἀλλ᾽ οἱ βέλτιστοι τῶν πολιτῶν εἰσιν ἐν προεδρίᾳ. Ὅπου δ᾽ οἱ νόμοι μή εἰσι κύριοι, ἐνταῦθα γίνονται δημαγωγοί. Μόναρχος γὰρ ὁ δῆμος γίνεται, σύνθετος εἷς ἐκ πολλῶν· οἱ γὰρ πολλοὶ κύριοί εἰσιν, οὐχ ὡς ἕκαστος, ἀλλὰ πάντες.

For when a democracy is controlled by fixed laws, a demagogue has no power, but the best citizens fill the offices of state: when the laws are not supreme, there demagogues are found. For the people act like a king, being one body; for the many are supreme, not as individuals, but as a whole.

There is no Free State where the Laws are not Supreme.
Polit. iv. 4.

Ὅπου γὰρ μὴ νόμοι ἄρχουσιν, οὐκ ἔστι πολιτεία. Δεῖ γὰρ τὸν μὲν νόμον ἄρχειν πάντων.

For there is no free state where the laws do not rule supreme; for the law ought to be above all.

PEOPLE LOVE THEIR ANCIENT CUSTOMS.

Polit. iv. 5.

Οὐ γὰρ εὐθὺς μεταβαίνουσιν, ἀλλὰ ἀγαπῶσι τὰ πρῶτα, μικρὰ πλεονεκτοῦντες παρ' ἀλλήλων. ῞Ωσθ' οἱ μὲν νόμοι διαμένουσιν οἱ προυπάρχοντες· κρατοῦσι δ' οἱ μεταβάλλοντες τὴν πολιτείαν.

For people do not change at once, but love their ancient customs, making gradual changes; so that ancient laws remain in force, while the power continues with those who bring about a revolution in the state.

THE MIDDLE STATE TO BE PREFERRED.

Polit. iv. 11.

᾿Εν ἁπάσαις δὴ ταῖς πόλεσίν ἐστι τρία μέρη τῆς πόλεως· οἱ μὲν, εὔποροι σφόδρα, οἱ δὲ, ἄποροι σφόδρα· οἱ δὲ τρίτοι, οἱ μέσοι τούτων. ᾿Επεὶ τοίνυν ὁμολογεῖται τὸ μέτριον ἄριστον, καὶ τὸ μέσον, φανερὸν ὅτι καὶ τῶν εὐτυχημάτων ἡ κτῆσις ἡ μέση, βελτίστη πάντων· ῥᾴστη γὰρ τῷ λόγῳ πειθαρχεῖν. ῾Υπέρκαλον δὲ, ἢ ὑπερίσχυρον, ἢ ὑπερευγενῆ, ἢ ὑπερπλούσιον· ἢ τἀναντία τούτοις, ὑπέρπτωχον, ἢ ὑπερασθενῆ, καὶ σφόδρα ἄτιμον, χαλεπὸν τῷ λόγῳ ἀκολουθεῖν. Γίγνονται γὰρ, οἱ μὲν, ὑβρισταὶ, καὶ μεγαλοπόνηροι μᾶλλον· οἱ δὲ, κακοῦργοι, καὶ μικροπόνηροι λίαν. Τῶν δ' ἀδικημάτων τὰ μὲν γίγνεται δι' ὕβριν, τὰ δὲ διὰ κακουργίαν.

In every state the people are divided into three kinds: the very rich, the very poor, and, thirdly, those who are between them. Since, then, it is universally acknowledged that the mean is best, it is evident that even in respect to fortune, a middle state is to be preferred; for that state is most likely to submit to reason. For those who are very handsome, or very strong, or very noble, or, on the other hand, those who are very poor, or very weak, or very mean, are with difficulty induced to obey reason. And this because the one class is supercilious, and "sin as it were with a cart-rope," the other rascally and mean; and the crimes of each arise respectively from insolence and villainy.

THE BEST STATE WHERE THE MEAN OUTNUMBERS THE EXTREMES.

Polit. iv. 11.

Δῆλον ἄρα ὅτι καὶ ἡ κοινωνία ἡ πολιτικὴ ἀρίστη, ἡ διὰ τῶν μέσων· καὶ τὰς τοιαύτας ἐνδέχεται εὖ πολιτεύεσθαι πόλεις, ἐν αἷς δὴ πολὺ τὸ μέσον, καὶ κρεῖττον, μάλιστα μὲν ἀμφοῖν· εἰ δὲ μὴ, θατέρου μέρους. Προστιθέμενον γὰρ, ποιεῖ ῥοπὴν, καὶ κωλύει γίνεσθαι τὰς ἐναντίας ὑπερβολάς. Διόπερ εὐτυχία μεγίστη τοὺς πολιτευομένους οὐσίαν ἔχειν μέσην καὶ ἱκανήν. ῾Ως ὅπου οἱ μὲν πολλὰ σφόδρα κέκτηνται, οἱ δὲ μηθὲν, ἢ δῆμος ἔσχατος γίγνεται, ἢ ὀλιγαρχία

ἄκρατος, ἢ τυραννὶς, δι' ἀμφοτέρας τὰς ὑπερβολάς. Καὶ γὰρ ἐκ
δημοκρατίας τῆς νεανικωτάτης, καὶ ἐξ ὀλιγαρχίας, γίνεται τυραννίς·
ἐκ δὲ τῶν μέσων καὶ τῶν σύνεγγυς, πολὺ ἧττον.

It is evident, then, that the most perfect political community
is that which is administered by the middle classes, and that those
states are best carried on in which these are the majority and
outweigh both the other classes ; and if that cannot be, at least
when they overbalance each separate. For, being thrown into
the balance, it will prevent either excess from predominating.
Wherefore it is the greatest happiness to possess a moderate and
competent fortune ; since, where some possess too much, and
others nothing at all, the government must be either an extreme
democracy or else a pure oligarchy, or, from the excesses of both,
a tyranny ; for this springs from a headstrong democracy or oligarchy, but far more seldom when the members of the community
are nearly on an equality with each other.

Where the Middle Class is Large Less Sedition.

Polit. iv. 11.

Ὅτι δ' ἡ μέση βελτίστη, φανερόν· μόνη γὰρ ἀστασίαστος· ὅπου
γὰρ πολὺ τὸ διὰ μέσου, ἥκιστα στάσεις, καὶ διαστάσεις γίνονται τῶν
πολιτειῶν. Καὶ αἱ μεγάλαι πόλεις ἀστασιαστότεραι διὰ τὴν αὐτὴν
αἰτίαν, ὅτι πολὺ τὸ μέσον· ἐν δὲ ταῖς μικραῖς, ῥᾴδιόν τε διαλαβεῖν
εἰς δύο πάντας, ὥστε μηθὲν καταλιπεῖν μέσον. Καὶ πάντες σχεδὸν
ἄποροι, ἢ εὔποροί εἰσι.

But it is clear that the state where the middle ranks predominate is the best, for it alone is free from seditious movements.
Where such a state is large, there are fewer seditions and insur-
rections to disturb the peace ; and for this reason extensive states
are more peaceful internally, as the middle ranks are numerous.
In small states it is easy to pass to the two extremes, so as to have
scarcely any middle ranks remaining ; but all are either very poor
or very rich.

The Rule of Husbandmen and Mechanics Contrasted.

Polit. iv. 12.

Οἷον, ἐὰν μὲν τὸ τῶν γεωργῶν ὑπερτείνῃ πλῆθος, τὴν πρώτην
δημοκρατίαν· ἐὰν δὲ τὸ τῶν βαναύσων καὶ μισθαρνούντων, τὴν
τελευταίαν.

Should the number of husbandmen be excessive, it will be of
the best kind ; if of mechanics and those who work for pay, of the
worst.

NOBILITY AND MERIT ARE ONLY AMONGST A FEW.
Polit. v. 1.

Εὐγένεια γὰρ καὶ ἀρετὴ, ἐν ὀλίγοις· ταῦτα δ᾽, ἐν πλείοσιν· εὐ‑
γενεῖς γὰρ καὶ ἀγαθοὶ οὐδαμοῦ ἑκατόν· ἄποροι δὲ πολλοὶ πολλαχοῦ.

For nobility and worth are to be found only amongst a few, but
their opposite amongst the many; for there is not one man of
merit and high spirit in a hundred, while there are many destitute
of both to be found everywhere.

See (Lat.) The good are few.

THE BEGINNING IS THE HALF OF THE BUSINESS.
Polit. v. 4.

᾽Εν ἀρχῇ γὰρ γίγνεται τὸ ἁμάρτημα· ἡ δ᾽ ἀρχὴ λέγεται ἥμισυ
εἶναι παντός.

For the mischief lies in the beginning; for the beginning is said
to be " half of the whole."

WHENCE SEDITIONS ARISE IN A DEMOCRACY.
Polit. v. 5.

Αἱ μὲν οὖν δημοκρατίαι μάλιστα μεταβάλλουσι διὰ τὴν τῶν δημα‑
γωγῶν ἀσέλγειαν. Τὰ μὲν γὰρ, ἰδίᾳ συκοφαντοῦντες τοὺς τὰς οὐσίας
ἔχοντας, συστρέφουσιν αὐτούς· συνάγει γὰρ καὶ τοὺς ἐχθίστους ὁ
κοινὸς φόβος· τὰ δὲ, κοινῇ τὸ πλῆθος ἐπάγοντες.

Democracies are chiefly subject to revolutions from the dishonest
conduct of demagogues.   For partly by lodging informations
against men of property, and partly by rousing the common people
against them, they induce them to unite; for a common fear will
make the greatest enemies to join together.

A HOUSE DIVIDED AGAINST ITSELF.
Polit. v. 6.

᾽Ασθενὲς γὰρ τὸ στασιάζον.

For a government in a constant state of turmoil is weak.

See Matt. xii. 2, 5.

A FIRM STATE.
Polit. v. 7.

Μόνον γὰρ μόνιμον τὸ κατ᾽ ἀξίαν ἴσον, καὶ τὸ ἔχειν τὰ αὐτῶν.

The only stable state is that where every one possesses an
equality in the eye of the law, according to his merit, and enjoys
his own unmolested.

Take Care that Nothing be Done Contrary to Law.
Polit. v. 8.

'Εν μὲν οὖν ταῖς εὖ κεκραμέναις, πολιτείαις, ὥσπερ ἄλλό τι δεῖ
τηρεῖν, ὅπως μηθὲν παρανομῶσι· καὶ μάλιστα τὸ μικρὸν φυλάττειν·
λανθάνει γὰρ ἐπεισδύουσα ἡ παράβασις, ὥσπερ τὰς οὐσίας αἱ μικραὶ
δαπάναι δαπανῶσι, πολλάκις γινόμεναι. Λανθάνει δὲ ἡ μετάβασις,
διὰ τὸ μὴ ἀθρόα γίγνεσθαι.

For in states that are well blended particular care ought, above
all things, to be taken that nothing be done contrary to law; and
this should be chiefly looked to in matters of small moment : for
small violations of law advance by stealthy steps, in the same way
as, in a domestic establishment, trifling expenses, if often repeated,
consume a man's whole estate.

Qualifications of a Statesman.
Polit. v. 9.

Τρία δέ τινα χρὴ ἔχειν τοὺς μέλλοντας ἄρξειν τὰς κυρίας ἀρχάς·
πρῶτον μὲν, φιλίαν πρὸς τὴν καθεστῶσαν πολιτείαν· ἔπειτα, δύναμιν
μεγίστην τῶν ἔργων τῆς ἀρχῆς· τρίτον δ' ἀρετὴν καὶ δικαιοσύνην
ἐν ἑκάστῃ πολιτείᾳ, τὴν πρὸς τὴν πολιτείαν.

There are three qualifications which ought to be possessed by a
man who aspires to fill the high offices of state: first, he must be
well disposed, and prepared to support the established constitution of his country ; next, he ought to have a special aptitude for
the office which he fills ; and, thirdly, he should have the kind of
virtue and love of justice which suits the particular state in which
he lives.

The Good never Flatter.
Polit. v. 11.

Καὶ γὰρ διὰ τοῦτο πονηρόφιλον ἡ τυραννίς· κολακευόμενοι γὰρ
χαίρουσι. Τοῦτο δ' οὐδ' ἂν εἰς ποιήσειε φρόνημα ἔχων ἐλεύθερον·
ἀλλὰ φιλοῦσιν οἱ ἐπιεικεῖς ἢ οὐ κολακεύουσι. Καὶ χρήσιμοι οἱ
πονηροὶ εἰς τὰ πονηρά· ἥλῳ γὰρ ὁ ἧλος, ὥσπερ ἡ παροιμία.

On this account tyrants are fond of bad men ; for they like to
be flattered. No man of high and generous spirit is ever willing
to indulge in this habit : the good may feel affection for others,
but will not flatter them. Besides, bad men assist them in their
evil deeds : "Like to like," as the proverb says.

Tyrants are at Enmity with Men of Merit.
Polit. v. 11.

Διο καὶ τοῖς ἐπιεικέσι πολεμοῦσιν, ὡς βλαβεροῖς πρὸς τὴν ἀρχήν·
οὐ μόνον διὰ τὸ μὴ ἀξιοῦν ἄρχεσθαι δεσποτικῶς, ἀλλὰ καὶ διὰ τὸ

πιστοὺς καὶ ἑαυτοῖς καὶ τοῖς ἄλλοις εἶναι, καὶ μὴ καταγορεύειν μήτε ἑαυτῶν, μήτε τῶν ἄλλων.

For which reason they are always at variance with men of merit as disaffected to their government, not only because they are unwilling to be governed despotically, but because they are faithful to their own principles and to their friends, refusing to inform against themselves or others.

DEFINITION OF DEMOCRACY.

Polit. vi. 2.

Τὰ δημοτικὰ δοκεῖ τἀναντία τούτων εἶναι, ἀγένεια, πενία, βαναυσία.

On the contrary, a democracy is a government in the hands of men of low birth, poverty, and vulgar employments.

ORIGINAL SIN.

Polit. vi. 4.

Ἡ γὰρ ἐξουσία τοῦ πράττειν ὅ, τι ἂν ἐθέλῃ τις, οὐ δύναται φυλάττειν τὸ ἐν ἑκάστῳ τῶν ἀνθρώπων φαῦλον.

For the power of doing whatever a man pleases is not able to check that evil particle which is in every man.

UNIVERSAL SUFFRAGE.

Polit. vi. 4.

Τὴν δὲ τελευταίαν, διὰ τὸ πάντας κοινωνεῖν, οὔτε πάσης ἐστὶ πόλεως φέρειν, οὔτε ῥᾴδιον διαμένειν, μὴ τοῖς νόμοις καὶ τοῖς ἔθεσιν εὖ συγκειμένην.

The last and worst form of democracy is where every citizen has a share in the administration : few states can endure such a form, nor can it exist for any length of time unless it is well supported by laws and purity of manners.

PENALTIES NECESSARY TO KEEP TOGETHER HUMAN SOCIETY.

Polit. vi. 8.

Ὥστ' εἰ μὴ γιγνομένων, κοινωνεῖν ἀδύνατον ἀλλήλοις, καὶ πράξεων μὴ γιγνομένων.

For if human society cannot be carried on without actions at law, it is impossible that it should exist without the infliction of penalties.

HAPPINESS DEPENDS ON VIRTUE AND WISDOM.

Polit. vii. 1.

Ὅτι μὲν οὖν ἑκάστῳ τῆς εὐδαιμονίας ἐπιβάλλει τοσοῦτον, ὅσονπερ ἀρετῆς καὶ φρονήσεως, καὶ τοῦ πράττειν κατὰ ταύτας, ἔστω συνωμολογημένον ἡμῖν, μάρτυρι τῷ θεῷ χρωμένοις· ὃς, εὐδαίμων μὲν ἐστι καὶ μακάριος, δι᾽ οὐθὲν δὲ τῶν ἐξωτερικῶν ἀγαθῶν, ἀλλὰ δι᾽ αὐτὸν αὐτὸς, καὶ τῷ ποῖός τις εἶναι τὴν φύσιν.

Let us be well persuaded that every one of us possesses happiness in proportion to his virtue and wisdom, and according as he acts in obedience to their suggestion, taking God himself as our example, who is completely happy and blessed, not from any external good, but in Himself, and because He is such by nature.

IMPORTANCE OF GOOD WATER.

Polit. vii. 11.

Ἐπεὶ δὲ δεῖ περὶ ὑγιείας φροντίζειν τῶν ἐνοικούντων· τοῦτο δ᾽ ἐστὶν ἐν τῷ κεῖσθαι τὸν τόπον, ἔν τε τοιούτῳ, καὶ πρὸς τοιοῦτον καλῶς· δεύτερον δὲ, ὕδασιν ὑγιεινοῖς χρῆσθαι· καὶ τούτου τὴν ἐπιμέλειαν ἔχειν μὴ παρέργως. Οἷς γὰρ πλείστοις χρώμεθα πρὸς τὸ σῶμα καὶ πλειστάκις, ταῦτα πλεῖστον συμβάλλεται πρὸς τὴν ὑγίειαν. Ἡ δὲ τῶν ὑδάτων καὶ τοῦ πνεύματος δύναμις, τοιαύτην ἔχει τὴν φύσιν. Διόπερ ἐν ταῖς εὖ φρονούσαις δεῖ διωρίσθαι πόλεσιν, ἐὰν μὴ πάνθ᾽ ὅμοια, μήτ᾽ ἀφθονία τούτων ᾖ ναμάτων, χωρὶς τά, τε εἰς τροφὴν ὕδατα, καὶ τὰ πρὸς τὴν ἄλλην χρείαν.

Since every attention should be given to the health of the inhabitants, it is of great importance that the city should have a good situation, and, next, that the inhabitants should have good water to drink ; and this must not be regarded as a matter of secondary moment. For what is used chiefly and in great quantities for the support of the body must, above all, contribute to its health. And this is the influence which the air and the water exercise over the body. Wherefore, in all wise governments the water ought to be apportioned to different purposes, if all is not equally good, and if there is not abundance of both kinds, that for drinking should be separated from that which is used for other purposes.

INFLUENCE OF NATURE, HABIT, AND REASON ON MANKIND.

Polit. vii. 13.

Ἀλλὰ μὴν ἀγαθοί γε καὶ σπουδαῖοι γίγνονται διὰ τριῶν. Τὰ τρία δὲ ταῦτά ἐστι, φύσις, ἔθος, λόγος. Καὶ γὰρ φῦναι δεῖ πρῶτον· οἷον, ἄνθρωπον, ἀλλὰ μὴ τῶν ἄλλων τι ζώων· εἶτα, καὶ ποῖόν τινα τὸ σῶμα καὶ τὴν ψυχήν· ἔνιά τε οὐθὲν ὄφελος φῦναι. Τὰ γὰρ ἔθη

D

μεταβολεῖν ποιεῖ· ἔνια γάρ ἐστι διὰ τῆς φύσεως ἐπαμφοτερίζοντα διὰ τῶν ἐθῶν ἐπὶ τὸ χεῖρον καὶ τὸ βέλτιον. Τὰ μὲν οὖν ἄλλα τῶν ζῴων, μάλιστα μὲν τῇ φύσει ζῇ, μικρὰ δέ ἔνια καὶ τοῖς ἔθεσιν, ἄνθρωπος δὲ καὶ λόγῳ· μόνον γὰρ ἔχει λόγον. Ὥστε δεῖ ταῦτα συμφωνεῖν ἀλλήλοις. Πολλὰ γὰρ παρὰ τοὺς ἐθισμοὺς καὶ τὴν φύσιν πράττουσι διὰ τὸν λόγον, ἐὰν πεισθῶσιν ἄλλως ἔχειν βέλτιον.

Men are made good and honourable in three ways,—by nature, by custom, and by reason. For, in the first place, each individual ought to be a man, and not any other animal ; that is, that he should possess a particular character both of body and soul. In some things, however, it is of no consequence to be born with them, for custom makes great changes, there being some things in nature capable of change either for the better or the worse. Now, other animals live chiefly a life of mere nature, and in very few things according to custom, but man lives also according to reason, with which he alone is endowed, wherefore he ought to make all these accord with each other ; for, if they are persuaded that it is best to follow some other way, men often act contrary to nature and custom.

A MASTER SHOULD SUPERINTEND ALL THINGS.

Œcon. i. 6.

Καὶ τὸ τοῦ Πέρσου, καὶ τὸ Λίβυος ἀπόφθεγμα εὖ ἂν ἔχοι. Ὁ μὲν γὰρ, ἐρωτηθεὶς τί μάλιστα ἵππον πιαίνει, "Ὁ τοῦ δεσπότου ὀφθαλμὸς," ἔφη· ὁ δὲ Λίβυς, ἐρωτηθεὶς ποία κόπρος ἀρίστη, "Τὰ τοῦ δεσπότου ἴχνη," ἔφη.

The saying of the Persian and of the African are both to be highly commended ; for the former being asked what was best for fattening a horse, said, " The eye of the master ;" and the African being asked what was the best manure, answered, " The footsteps of the master."

EARLY TO RISE.

Œcon. i. 6.

Τό τε διανίστασθαι νύκτωρ· τοῦτο γὰρ καὶ πρὸς ὑγίειαν, καὶ οἰκονομίαν, καὶ φιλόσοφον, χρήσιμον.

It is also well to be up before daybreak, for such habits contribute to health, wealth, and wisdom.

A DISCREET WIFE.

Œcon. i. 7.

Ἡ δὲ εὔτακτος γυνὴ, τὰ τοῦ ἀνδρὸς ἤθη παράδειγμα τοῦ ἑαυτῆς βίου, καὶ νόμον αὐτῇ διὰ τῆς συζυγίας τοῦ γάμου τὸ κοινωνίας ἐπικείμενον ὑπὸ θεοῦ νομίσειε δικαίως. Ἐὰν γὰρ ἑαυτὴν πείσῃ τούτων εὐκόλως ἀνέχεσθαι, καὶ τὰ κατὰ τὸν οἶκον ῥᾷστα διοικήσει· ἐὰν δὲ μὴ, χαλεπώτερον.

But the prudent and discreet wife will very properly regard the behaviour of her husband as the pattern which she ought to follow and the law of her life, invested with a divine sanction from the marriage tie : for if she can induce herself to submit patiently to her husband's mode of life, she will have no difficulty to manage her household affairs ; but if not, she will not find it so easy.

PARENTS SHOULD SET A GOOD EXAMPLE TO THEIR CHILDREN.

Œcon. i. 8.

Ἐὰν γὰρ τοῦ βίου παράδειγμα τοῖς υἱοῖς μὴ παραστήσωσιν οἱ γονεῖς, πρόφασιν ἐκείνοις καθ' ἑαυτῶν καταλείψουσιν ἐναργῆ. Καὶ ἔστι τοῦτο δέος μὴ αὐτῶν ὡς μὴ καλῶς βεβιωκότων οἱ υἱοὶ καταφρονήσαντες, ἀπολείψωσιν αὐτοὺς ἐν τῷ γήρᾳ.

For unless parents set a good example to their children, they will furnish a plain reason to be used by them against themselves. And this is to be feared, that, if they have not lived an honourable life, their sons will despise them and abandon them in their old age.

MAN AN IMITATIVE ANIMAL.

Poet. 4.

Τό τε γὰρ μιμεῖσθαι σύμφυτον τοῖς ἀνθρώποις ἐκ παίδων ἐστί, καὶ τούτῳ διαφέρουσι τῶν ἄλλων ζῴων ὅτι μιμητικώτατόν ἐστι καὶ τὰς μαθήσεις ποιεῖται διὰ μιμήσεως τὰς πρώτας, καὶ τὸ χαίρειν τοῖς μιμήμασι πάντας.

For imitation is natural to man from his infancy. Man differs from other animals particularly in this, that he is imitative, and acquires his rudiments of knowledge in this way ; besides, the delight in it is universal.

THE RIDICULOUS.

Poet. 5.

Τὸ γὰρ γελοῖόν ἐστιν ἁμάρτημά τι καὶ αἶσχος ἀνώδυνον καὶ οὐ φθαρτικόν, οἷον εὐθὺς τὸ γελοῖον πρόσωπον αἰσχρόν τι καὶ διεστραμμένον ἄνευ ὀδύνης.

For the ridiculous is produced by any defect that is unattended by pain or by fatal consequences ; thus an ugly and deformed countenance does not fail to cause laughter, if it is not occasioned by pain.

HAPPINESS SPRINGS FROM ACTION.

Poet. 6.

Μέγιστον δὲ τούτων ἐστὶν ἡ τῶν πραγμάτων σύστασις· ἡ γὰρ τραγῳδία μίμησίς ἐστιν οὐκ ἀνθρώπων ἀλλὰ πράξεως καὶ βίου καὶ εὐδαιμονίας καὶ κακοδαιμονίας· καὶ γὰρ ἡ εὐδαιμονία ἐν πράξει ἐστί, καὶ τὸ τέλος πρᾶξίς τις ἐστίν, οὐ ποιότης· εἰσὶ δὲ κατὰ μὲν τὰ ἤθη ποιοί τινες, κατὰ δὲ τὰς πράξεις εὐδαίμονες ἢ τοὐναντίον.

But the principal of these parts is the combination of the incidents ; for tragedy is imitation not of individuals but of actions in general, of human life, of good and bad fortune, for happiness springs from action ; the main purpose of life is action and not quality, and though the manners of men spring from their qualities, their happiness or misery depends on their actions.

No very Small or very Large Animal can be very Beautiful.

Poet. 7.

῎Ετι δ' ἐπεὶ τὸ καλὸν καὶ ζῷον καὶ ἅπαν πρᾶγμα ὃ συνέστηκεν ἐκ τινῶν, οὐ μόνον ταῦτα τεταγμένα δεῖ ἔχειν, ἀλλὰ καὶ μέγεθος ὑπάρχειν μὴ τὸ τυχόν· τὸ γὰρ καλὸν ἐν μεγέθει καὶ τάξει ἐστί, διὸ οὔτε πάμμικρον ἄν τι γένοιτο καλὸν ζῷον (συγχεῖται γὰρ ἡ θεωρία ἐγγὺς τοῦ ἀναισθήτου χρόνου γινομένη) οὔτε παμμέγεθες· οὐ γὰρ ἅμα ἡ θεωρία γίνεται, ἀλλ' οἴχεται τοῖς θεωροῦσι τὸ ἓν καὶ τὸ ὅλον ἐκ τῆς θεωρίας.

Then as to size, an animal, or any other thing that has constituent parts, in order that it may be beautiful, must not only have those justly connected, but should also have a certain proper size ; for beauty depends on size as well as symmetry ; for which reason no very small animal can be beautiful, for the view being made in almost an imperceptible space of time, will be confused ; nor could a very large one, for, as the whole view cannot be taken in at once, the unity and completeness that should result from it will escape the spectator.

Man Easily Affected to Grief or Joy.

Poet. 17.

῞Οσα δὲ δυνατόν, καὶ τοῖς σχήμασι συναπεργαζόμενον. Πιθανώτατοι γὰρ ἀπ' αὐτῆς τῆς φύσεως οἱ ἐν τοῖς πάθεσιν εἰσί, καὶ χειμαίνει ὁ χειμαζόμενος καὶ χαλεπαίνει ὁ ὀργιζόμενος ἀληθινώτατα.

As far as it is possible, the poet should enter into the spirit of the subject while he is composing ; for those who are roused by passions are most likely to express those passions with force ; he who is really agitated storms, and he who is really angry upbraids most naturally.

Moral Character.

Rhet. i. 2.

Σχεδὸν ὡς εἰπεῖν κυριωτάτην ἔχει πίστιν τὸ ἦθος.

Moral character nearly, so to say, carries with it the highest power of causing a thing to be believed.

A DEMOCRACY.
Rhet. i. 4.

Οἶον δημοκρατία οὐ μόνον ἀνιεμένη ἀσθενεστέρα γίνεται ὥστε τέλος ἥξει εἰς ὀλιγαρχίαν, ἀλλὰ καὶ ἐπιτἐινομένη σφόδρα, ὥσπερ καὶ ἡ γρυπότης καὶ ἡ σιμότης οὐ μόνον ἀνιέμενα ἔρχεται εἰς τὸ μέσον, ἀλλὰ καὶ σφόδρα γρυπὰ γινόμενα ἢ σιμὰ οὕτω διατίθεται ὥστε μηδὲ μυκτῆρα δοκεῖν εἶναι.

Thus a democracy, not only when relaxed, but if overstrained, becomes weaker, till at last it will pass into an oligarchy, in the same way as hookedness or flatness of the nose not only when they relax approach the mean, but also when they become excessively hooked or flat dispose the nostrils in such a way as no longer to resemble the nasal organ.

DEFINITION OF HAPPINESS.
Rhet. i. 5.

Ἔστω δὲ εὐδαιμονία εὐπραξία μετ᾽ ἀρετῆς, ἢ αὐτάρκεια ζωῆς, ἢ ὁ βίος ὁ μετα ἀσφαλείας ἥδιστος, ἢ εὐθηνία κτημάτων καὶ σωμάτων μετὰ δυνάμεως φυλακτικῆς τε καὶ πρακτικῆς τούτων· σχεδὸν γὰρ τούτων ἓν ἢ πλείω τὴν εὐδαιμονίαν ὁμολογοῦσιν εἶναι ἅπαντες.

Let happiness be defined to be good fortune in union with virtue—or independency of life—or the life that is most agreeable attended with security—or plenty of property and slaves, with the power to preserve and augment it; for all mankind agree that one or more of these things amount nearly to happiness.

EVILS BRING MEN TOGETHER.
Rhet. i. 6.

Ὅθεν λέγεται ὡς τὰ κακὰ συνάγει τοὺς ἀνθρώπους, ὅταν ᾖ ταὐτὸ βλαβερὸν ἀμφοῖν.

Whence it is said that misery brings men together, when the same thing happens to be hurtful to both.

So Shakespeare ("Tempest," act ii. sc. 2)—
"Misery acquaints a man with strange bedfellows."

"A SOFT ANSWER."
Rhet. ii. 3.

Πρὸς δὲ τοὺς ὁμολογοῦντας δικαίως κολάζεσθαι παυόμεθα θυμούμενοι.

Towards such as acknowledge themselves to be justly punished we cease from our wrath.

So Proverbs (xv. 1)—"A soft answer turneth away wrath."

"No Fear in Love."
Rhet. ii. 4.

Οὐδεὶς γὰρ ὃν φοβεῖται φιλεῖ.

For no one loves the man whom he fears.

So 1 John (iv. 18)—"There is no fear in love ; but perfect love casteth out fear."

Signs of Arrogance.
Rhet. ii. 6.

Καὶ τὸ περὶ αὐτοῦ πάντα λέγειν καὶ ἐπαγγέλεσθαι, καὶ τὸ τἀλλότρια αὐτοῦ φάσκειν. Ἀλαζανείας γάρ.

Again, to talk about one's self, and to be one's own trumpeter, and to assert that to be one's own which belongs to another, these are proofs of arrogance.

All Things Full of God.
De An. i. 5.

Πάντα πλήρη θεῶν.

All things are full of the gods.

So Psalm (lxxii. 19)—"Let the whole earth be full of His glory."

All Men have an Idea of God.
De Cœlo i. 3.

Πάντες ἄνθρωποι περὶ θεῶν ἔχουσιν ὑπόληψιν.

All men have some knowledge of the gods.

So Ephesians (iv. 6)—"One God and Father of all."

The World was Created.
De Cœlo i. 10.

Γενόμενον μὲν οὖν (τὸν κόσμον) ἅπαντες εἶναί φασι.

All say that the world was created.

See Psalm xc. 2.

The Universe.
De Mundo 5.

Τὸν ὅλον οὐρανὸν διεκόσμησε μία ἡ διὰ πάντων διήκουσα δύναμις,

τὰς ἐναντιωτάτας ἐν αὐτῷ φύσεις ἀλλήλαις ἀναγκάσασα ὁμολογῆσαι
καὶ ἐκ τούτων μηχανησαμένη τῷ παντὶ σωτηρίαν.

The Power that extends over everything has arranged the whole
universe, compelling the most opposite natures to harmonise, and
by these ensuring safety to all.

GOD IS A SPIRIT.
De Mundo 6.

Ταῦτα χρὴ καὶ περὶ θεοῦ διανοεῖσθαι, δυνάμει μὲν ὄντως ἰσχυρο-
τάτου, ζωῇ δὲ ἀθανάτου, ἀρετῇ δὲ κρατίστου· διόπερ πάσῃ τῇ θνητῇ
φύσει γενόμενος ἀθεώρητος ἀπ᾽ αὐτῶν τῶν ἔργων θεωρεῖται.

In regard to the Deity we must consider Him as (a spirit) the
most powerful, immortal, and perfection itself ; wherefore, being
invisible to mortal eyes, He is seen by His works.

So 1 Timothy (i. 17)—"Now, unto the King eternal, immortal, invisible,
the only wise God, be honour and glory for ever and ever."

GOD FROM ETERNITY TO ETERNITY.
Aristot. (Stobæus. Eclog. Phys. i. 86.)

Ὁ θεὸς διήκων ἐξ αἰῶνος ἀτέρμονος εἰς ἕτερον αἰῶνα.

God extends from eternity to eternity.

So Psalm (xc. 2)—"Before the mountains were brought forth, or ever
Thou hadst formed the earth and the world, even from everlasting to everlasting, Thou art God."

GOD IS HAPPY AND BLESSED.
De Repub. vii. 1.

Θεὸς εὐδαίμων μέν ἐστι καὶ μακάριος, δι᾽ οὐδὲν δὲ τῶν ἐξωτερικῶν
ἀγαθῶν, ἀλλὰ δι᾽ αὑτὸν αὑτός.

God is happy and blessed from nothing external to Himself, but
Himself from Himself.

So 1 Timothy (vi. 15)—"Who is the blessed and only Potentate, the King
of kings and Lord of lords."

ARRIANUS.

FLOURISHED A.D. 136.

FLAVIUS ARRIANUS, a native of Nicomedia in Bithynia, flourished
in the reign of Adrian, when we find him, A.D. 136, governor of
Cappadocia. He was one of the most celebrated pupils of the

philosopher Epictetus, under whom he studied at Nicopolis in Epirus. The first work which he published was called "Encheiridion" (The Manual), and contains the moral doctrines of his master, being still preserved. He also wrote a work entitled "The Philosophical Disquisitions of Epictetus," of which four books still remain. But the work by which he is best known to us is the "History of Alexander's Campaigns in Asia," in seven books, for which he derived the materials chiefly from the histories of Ptolemy, son of Lagus, and Aristobulus, who both accompanied Alexander. As a continuation to his history, he wrote a little work, still extant, entitled "On India." Another treatise ascribed to him is, "The Periplus of the Erythræan Sea."

The Wish Father to the Thought.
Alex. i. 7.

Οὐ γινώσκοντες τὰ ὄντα, τὰ μάλιστα καθ' ἡδονὴν σφίσιν εἴκαζον.

When men are doubtful of the true state of things, their wishes lead them to believe in what is most agreeable.

A Virtuous Life.
Alex. v. 26.

Καὶ ζῆν τε σὺν ἀρετῇ ἡδύ, καὶ ἀποθνήσκειν κλέος ἀθάνατον ὑπὸ λειπομένους.

To lead a virtuous life is pleasant, and to die is by no means bitter to those who look forward to immortal fame.

The Events of Fortune are Unexpected.
Alex. v. 28.

Τὰ δὲ ἐκ τοῦ δαιμονίου, ἀδόκητά τε καὶ ταύτῃ καὶ ἀφύλακτα τοῖς ἀνθρώποις ἐστί.

The events of fortune are unexpected, and therefore can never be guarded against by men.

AXIONICUS.

Axionicus, an Athenian poet of the middle comedy, of whom some fragments have been preserved.

LENDING MONEY TO THE WICKED.
Fr. Com. Gr. p. 772.

Ὅταν δανείζῃ τις πονηρῷ χρήματα
ἀνὴρ δικαίως τὸν τόκον λύπας ἔχει·

When a man lends money to the wicked, he justly gets pain for
his interest.

BATON,

FLOURISHED ABOUT B.C. 280.

BATON, an Athenian comic poet of the new comedy, flourished
about B.C. 280, of whom we have some fragments.

TO ERR IS HUMAN.
Fr. Com. Gr. p. 1134.

Ἄνθρωπος ὢν ἔπταικας· ἐν δὲ τῷ βίῳ
τέρας ἐστὶν εἴ τις εὐτύχηκε διὰ βίου.

Being a man, thou hast erred; but in life it is a wonder if a
man has been prosperous through life.

BION.

FLOURISHED ABOUT B.C. 280.

BION, a bucolic poet, was born at Phlossæ, on the river Meles, near
Smyrna, but little is known of his history except what is told us
in the third Idyll of Moschus, who laments his untimely death by
poison. Some of his poems are extant entire, but of others we
have only fragments.

"THE KING OF TERRORS."
Idyll. i. 51.

Φεύγεις μακρὸν Ἄδωνι, καὶ ἔρχεαι εἰς Ἀχέροντα
καὶ στυγνὸν βασιληᾶ καὶ ἄγριον· ἁ δὲ τάλαινα
ζώω, καὶ θεὸς ἐμμί, καὶ οὐ δύναμαί σε διώκειν.

Thou fliest far, O Adonis. and comest to Acheron and its gloomy and cruel king, but I live in misery, and am a goddess, and cannot follow thee.

Virgil (Georg. iv. 469) says—
> " Manesque adiit, regemque tremendum
> Nesciaque humanis precibus mansuescere corda."

" And he approached the Manes and their fearful king, hearts not to be softened by the prayers of men."

In Job (xviii. 14) we find—" His confidence shall be rooted out of his tabernacle ; and it shall bring him to the King of Terrors."

Spenser, in his " Faërie Queen," says—
> " O what avails it of immortal seed
> To been ybred, and never born to die ;
> For better I it deem to die with speed,
> Than waste with woe and wailiul miserie."

" HE SHALL FLEE AWAY AS A DREAM."

Idyll. i. 58.

Θνάσκεις ὦ τριπόθατε ; πόθος δὲ μοι ὡς ὄναρ ἔπτη,
χήρη δ᾽ ἁ Κυθέρεια, κενοὶ δ᾽ ἀνὰ δώματ᾽ Ἔρωτες.

Art thou dying, O thrice-regretted? Away my love did fly, even as a dream ; and widowed is Cytherea, and idle are the Loves along my halls.

Thus Job (xx. 8)—" He shall fly away as a dream, and shall not be found ; yea, he shall be chased away as a vision of the night."

A LUXURIOUS LIFE.

Idyll. i. 72.

Κάτθεό νιν μαλακοῖς ἐνὶ φάρεσι, οἷς ἐνίαυεν,
τοῖς μετὰ σεῦ ἀνὰ νύκτα τὸν ἱερὸν ὕπνον ἐμόχθει,
παγχρύσῳ κλιντῆρι· πόθει καὶ στυγνὸν Ἀδωνιν·
βάλλε δ᾽ ἐνὶ στεφάνοισι καὶ ἄνθεσι· πάντα σὺν αὐτῷ,
ὡς τῆνος τέθνακε, καὶ ἄνθεα πάντ᾽ ἐμαράνθη.

Lay him down on those soft vestments, in which he slept the livelong night with thee, on a golden couch. Long thou for Adonis, a sad sight though he be ; and lay him amid chaplets of flowers ; all with him, since he is dead, ay, all flowers have become withered.

In St Luke (vii. 25) we find—" Behold, they which are gorgeously apparelled, and live delicately, are in king's courts."

Milton in his " Comus," near the end, says—
> " Beds of hyacinths and roses
> Where young Adonis oft reposes,
> Waxing well of his deep wound.
> In slumber soft ; and on the ground
> Sadly sits th' Assyrian queen."

Sign of Mourning.
Idyll. i. 79.

Ἀμφὶ δέ μιν κλαίοντες ἀναστέναχουσιν Ἔρωτες,
κειράμενοι χαίτας ἐπ' Ἀδώνιδι· χὼ μὲν ὀϊστὼς,
ὃς δ' ἐπὶ τόξον ἔβαιν', ὃς δ' εὔπτερον ἆγε φαρέτραν.

Around him the weeping Loves set up the wail, having their
locks shorn for Adonis; and one was trampling on his arrows,
another on his bow, and another was breaking his well-feathered
quiver.

In Ezekiel (xxvii. 31) we find the same customs—"They shall make
themselves utterly bald for thee." And in Ovid. (Amor. iii. 9, 7)—

"Ecce puer Veneris fert eversamque pharetram,
Et fractos arcus, et sine luce facem.

"Behold the son of Venus bears his upturned quiver, and broken bow
and quenched torch."

"Dance turned into Mourning."
Idyll. i. 85.

Ἔσβεσε λαμπάδα πᾶσαν ἐπὶ φλιαῖς Ὑμέναιος,
καὶ στέφος ἐξεπέτασσε γαμήλιον· οὐκ ἔτι δ' Ὑμὰν,
Ὑμὰν οὐκ ἔτ' ἀειδόμενον μέλος, ᾄδεται αἲ αἲ,
Αἲ αἲ καὶ τὸν Ἄδωνιν ἔτι πλέον ἢ Ὑμέναιος.

Hymenæus has quenched every torch at the door-posts, shredded
and flung the marriage-wreath away ; and no more is Hymen, no
more is sung Hymen the song, but alas ! alas ! is chanted : alas,
alas ! for Adonis wail the Graces far more than Hymenæus.

In Lamentations (v. 15) we find—"The joy of our heart is ceased ; our
dance is turned into mourning."

The Old.
Idyll. ii. 10.

Αὐτὰρ ὁ πρέσβυς
μειδιόων κίνησε κάρη, καὶ ἀμείβετο παῖδα.

But the old man, smiling, shook his head, and answered the
boy.

In Ecclesiasticus (xii. 18) we find—"He will shake his head and clap his
hands and whisper much and change his countenance."

Briefness of Time.
Idyll. v. 5.

Εἰ μὲν γὰρ βιότω διπλόον χρόνον ἄμμιν ἔδωκεν
ἢ Κρονίδας, ἢ Μοῖρα πολύτροπος ὥστ' ἀνύεσθαι
τὸν μὲν ἐς εὐφροσύναν καὶ χάρματα, τὸν δ' ἐνὶ μόχθῳ,
ἢν τάχα μοχθήσαντι ποθ' ὕστερον ἐσθλὰ δέχεσθαι.

Εἰ δὲ θεοὶ κατένευσαν ἕνα χρόνον ἐς βίον ἐλθεῖν
ἀνθρώποις, καὶ τόνδε βραχὺν καὶ μήονα πάντων,
ἐς πόσον ἃ δειλοὶ καμάτας κ᾿ εἰς ἔργα πονεῦμες ;
ψυχὰν δ᾿ ἄχρι τίνος ποτὶ κέρδεα καὶ ποτὶ τέχνας
βάλλομες, ἱμείροντες ἀεὶ πολὺ πλήονος ὄλβω ;
λαθόμεθ᾿ ἢ ἄρα πάντες ὅτι θνατοὶ γενόμεσθα,
χ᾿ ὡς βραχὺν ἐκ Μοίρας λάχομεν χρόνον.

For if Saturn's son or Fate had assigned us a two-fold lifetime,
so that one portion might be passed in joys and pleasures, and one
in woes, it might be possible that he who had his woes first should
have his joys at last. But since the gods have allotted but one
life to man, and this a brief one—too brief for all we have to do—
why should we, ah! wretched men, toil and moil over never-ending
labours? To what end should we waste our health on gains and
arts, sighing always for more wealth? We surely all forget our
mortal state—how brief the life allotted us by Fate.

Job (xiv. 1) says—"Man that is born of a woman is of few days and full
of trouble." And in the Epistle of James (iv. 13)—"Go to now, ye that
say, To-day or to-morrow we will go into such a city, and continue there a
year, and buy and sell, and get gain ; whereas ye know not what shall be
on the morrow: for what is life? It is even a vapour, that appeareth for a
little time and then vanisheth away."

See (Lat.) Enjoy the present.

The Drop.
Idyll. xi. 1.

Ἐκ θαμινῆς ῥαθάμιγγος, ὅκως λόγος αἰὲν ἰοίσας,
χ᾿ ἁ λίθος ἐς ῥαγμὸν κοιλαίνεται.

From the frequent drop, as the proverb says, ever falling, even
the stone is worn at last into a hollow.

See (Lat.) Drop.

Beauty and Grace.
Idyll. xiv. 1.

Μορφὰ θηλυτέρῃσι πέλει καλόν, ἀνέρι δ᾿ ἀλκά.

Beauty is good for women, firmness for men.

CALLIMACHUS.

FLOURISHED FROM B.C. 260 TO B.C. 240.

CALLIMACHUS was a member of the powerful house at Cyrene,
named from its founder Battus, the Battiadæ. Born probably at

Cyrene, he was a pupil of the grammarian Hermocrates, and flourished in the reign of Ptolemy Philadelphus, dying in that of Euergites, his son and successor. He was chief librarian of the celebrated library at Alexandria, being contemporary of Theocritus and Aratus. Callimachi quæ supersunt recensuit et cum notarum delectu, edidit C. J. Blomfield, Londini, 1815.

"LIFT UP YOUR HEADS, YE GATES."
To Apollo, l. 6.

Αὐτοὶ νῦν κατοχῆες ἀνακλίνεσθε πυλάων,
αὐταὶ δὲ κληῖδες· ὁ γὰρ θεὸς οὐκ ἔτι μακράν.

Now ye bolts of your own accord fall back, and ye bars, for the god is at hand.

So Isaiah (vi. 4)—" And the posts of the door moved at the voice of him that cried, and the house was filled with smoke." And Psalm (xxiv. 7)— " Lift up your heads, O ye gates ; and be ye lift up, ye everlasting doors ; and the King of glory shall come in."

THE GOOD SHALL SEE GOD.
To Apollo, l. 9.

Ἀπόλλων οὐ παντὶ φαείνεται, ἀλλ' ὅ τις ἐσθλός,
ὃς μεν ἴδῃ, μέγας οὗτος· ὃς οὐκ ἴδε, λειτὸς ἐκεῖνος.

Apollo is seen by none except the just; whoso sees him, great is he ; little is the man who hath not seen him.

So Matthew (v. 8)—"Blessed are the pure in heart, for they shall see God."

"HEALING IN HIS WINGS.
To Apollo, l. 38.

Οὐ λίπος Ἀπόλλωνος ἀποστάζουσιν ἔθειραι,
ἀλλ' αὐτὴν πανάκειαν.

The tresses of Apollo drop not mere oil, but healing itself.

So Malachi (iv. 2)—" But unto you that fear my name shall the Sun of righteousness arise with healing in his wings."

CRATES.

FLOURISHED ABOUT B.C. 450.

CRATES, a comic poet of Athens, of the old comedy, flourished B.C. 450, being originally an actor in the plays of Cratinus. He is highly praised by Aristophanes for wit and abilities. He excelled chiefly in mirth and fun.

TIME.

Fr. Com. Gr. p. 85.

Ὁ γὰρ χρόνος μ' ἔκαμψε, τέκτων μὲν σοφός,
ἅπαντα δ' ἐργαζόμενος ἀσθενέστερα.

For time has bent me, a wise workman no doubt, but making all things weaker.

CRATINUS.

BORN B.C. 519—DIED B.C. 422.

CRATINUS, one of the most celebrated of the Athenian poets belonging to the old comedy, was the son of Callimedes. He was born B.C. 519, being six years younger than Æschylus, and died at the age of ninety-seven, B.C. 422 (Lucian. Macrob. 25). He is accused of having been much addicted to wine, and in other respects his private character was by no means reputable (Hor. Ep. i. 20, 21; Sch. Aristoph. Pax. 700). He wrote twenty-one plays, and of these he gained the prize nine times (Suid.). Athenæus gives the titles and some fragments of eighteen plays.

THE FOOL.

Fr. Com. Gr. p. 14.

Ὁ δ' ἠλίθιος ὥσπερ πρόβατον βῆ βῆ λέγων βαδίζει.

The fool goes like the sheep, saying, bah, bah!

DEMOSTHENES.

BORN B.C. 382—DIED B.C. 322.

DEMOSTHENES, the most celebrated of the Greek orators, was a native of Athens, being the son of Demosthenes and of Cleobulë, who was of Scythian extraction. His father died when he was only seven years of age, and left to him a considerable property, which he had amassed by the manufacture of warlike implements.

He tells us (Demosth. Cor. 312–22) that his education was such
as his fortune entitled him to; though Plutarch states that it was
much neglected through the foolish indulgence of his mother. His
property was, at all events, greatly mismanaged by his guardians,
and he found himself obliged, as soon as he had reached the age
of manhood, to call them to account. It is said that he was first
excited to devote himself to the study of eloquence by listening to
the speech of Callistratus in defence of the city Oropus, and by
observing his triumphant reception by the people. He studied
under Isæus the art of oratory, though Isocrates was at this time
the most eminent in his profession. His first attempt was in the
cause against his guardians, B.C. 366; and though he gained it
after some difficulty, he found that his property was so much
diminished that it would be necessary to apply his talents to
business. In the profession which he had chosen he had great
difficulties to surmount; his constitution was weak, his manner
awkward, and he had besides a very defective utterance. In his
first attempts he was repeatedly laughed at; but, by unflinching
perseverance, he completely got the better of all his defects, and
shone forth the most perfect orator the world ever produced. It
was in his twenty-seventh year, B.C. 355, that he made his first
appearance in a political cause. Leptines had got a law passed
forbidding any citizen, except the descendants of Harmodius and
Aristogeiton, to be exempted from certain magistracies which en-
tailed very heavy expenses. Demosthenes attacked the justice of
this law in the case of Ctesippus, who considered the merits of
his father, Chabrias, to confer on him a right of exemption. The
same year he composed the speech against Androtion, which he
did not deliver. It would appear that Demosthenes was in the
habit of writing speeches for citizens, who themselves pronounced
them. In one case he actually composed both the accusation and
the defence. The fierce and impetuous character of Demosthenes
fitted him more peculiarly for the part of an accuser; and it has
been accordingly remarked that, of the numerous speeches that
have come down to us, scarcely any of them are written for the
defendant. In the year B.C. 353 he delivered his speech in favour
of Megalopolis, a colony protected by the Thebans, but which the
Spartans, the allies of Athens, wished to destroy. It is one of
the most striking examples not so much of his eloquence as of his
art, in which he did not less excel. The great leading idea which
seems, from the moment he entered public life, to have directed
his whole conduct, was opposition to Philip and his objects of

aggrandisement. Eleven speeches, delivered within the space of fifteen years, under the name of "Philippics" and "Olynthiacs," show the unwearied spirit with which he maintained what he considered to be the interest of his country. He was one of the ambassadors who proceeded to Macedon to negotiate a peace with Philip; and he was so dissatisfied with the conduct of his colleague, Æschines, that he brought the matter, B.C. 343, before the people in one of his most able and powerful speeches. Æschines defended himself with equal ability, and was so ably supported by the party of Eubulus, that he was acquitted. The battle of Chæronëa followed soon afterwards, B.C. 338, which placed Greece at the mercy of Philip; but though the orator had not distinguished himself by his bravery in the field, he did not despair of the cause of his country. Philip fell by the dagger of an assassin, B.C. 336, and Demosthenes again conceived hopes of the entire independence of his country. The destruction, however, of Thebes by Alexander soon dispelled that illusion, and he found himself one of those ten orators whom that prince required the Athenians to deliver up to him. This demand Athens would have found no means of resisting, if Demades, the friend of Alexander, had not succeeded in procuring its remission. During this period of Grecian servitude the energies of Demosthenes were called forth in his own defence. Even after the fatal battle of Chæronëa the war party at Athens still continued powerful, and it was no doubt of importance to them that they should show it to the public by some decisive act. With this view Ctesiphon, one of the party, proposed the docree for crowning Demosthenes on account of his services; but as these had reference chiefly to the late unsuccessful war, it was in fact an approval of all that had been done. This was felt by Æschines, who was at the head of the opposite party, and finding that the law had not been observed in every particular, he took advantage of this circumstance to bring the matter before the people; but though the suit was commenced against Ctesiphon the same year, it was not till B.C. 330 that it was tried. It was then that Demosthenes made that celebrated speech, περὶ Στεφάνου, which is considered as one of his finest specimens of eloquence. Æschines failed in proving his case, and as a heavy fine would have been the consequence, he preferred to leave his country. When Harpalus fled to Athens with the treasures of Alexander, Demosthenes was accused of accepting a bribe from him, and though he denied the accusation with much vehemence, he was found guilty, and fined fifty talents. He escaped the payment of this fine by retiring to the island Ægina, B.C. 325; but he does not appear to have endured his banishment with the equanimity worthy of his character and high name. On the death of Alexander he was recalled, and proceeded to organise a new league of opposition to the Macedonian power. Antipater, however, soon put an end to it, and the death of Demosthenes was pronounced by his own citizens at the instance of Demades. Demosthenes, with some of his friends who were involved in the same sentence, escaped from Athens by the connivance even of his enemies, and he took refuge in the small island of Calauria in the temple of Neptune. He was followed by some of the friends of Antipater, and, as he saw no means of escape, he placed a poisoned pen in his mouth, and died a short time afterwards.

THE ACTIVE AND INTREPID CONTRASTED WITH THE SLUGGISH.

Philip. i. 5.

Φύσει δ' ὑπάρχει τοῖς παροῦσι τὰ τῶν ἀπόντων καὶ τοῖς ἐθέλουσι πονεῖν καὶ κινδυνεύειν τὰ τῶν ἀμελούντων.

The dominions of the absent belong naturally to those in the field; the property of the lazy and inactive to those who are willing to undergo labour and danger.

MEN WILLING TO UNITE THEMSELVES WITH THE BRAVE.

Philip. i. 6.

Καὶ γὰρ συμμαχεῖν καὶ προσέχειν τὸν νοῦν τούτοις ἐθέλουσιν ἅπαντες οὓς ἂν ὁρῶσι παρεσκευασμένους καὶ πράττειν ἐθέλοντας ἃ χρή.

For all are willing to unite and to take part with those whom they see ready and willing to put forth their strength as they ought.

CURIOSITY OF THE ATHENIANS.

Philip. i. 10.

Ἢ βούλεσθε, εἰπέ μοι, περιϊόντες αὐτοῦ πυνθάνεσθαι κατὰ τὴν ἀγοράν· Λέγεταί τι καινόν;

Or is it your greatest pleasure, tell me, wandering through the public squares to inquire of each other, "What news?"

So Acts (xvii. 21)—"For all the Athenians, and strangers which were there, spent their time in nothing else, but either to tell, or to hear some new thing."

ALLIANCES WITH DESPOTS DANGEROUS TO FREE STATES.

Philip. ii. 21.

Οὐ γὰρ ἀσφαλεῖς ταῖς πολιτείαις αἱ πρὸς τοὺς τυράννους αὗται
λίαν ὁμιλίαι.

For those close and intimate alliances with despots are never
safe to free states.

DISTRUST OF DESPOTS THE GREATEST SECURITY OF FREE STATES.

Philip. ii. 23.

Ἔστι τοίνυν νὴ Δι', ἔφην ἐγώ, παντοδαπὰ εὑρημένα ταῖς πόλεσι
πρὸς φυλακὴν καὶ σωτηρίαν, οἷον χαρακώματα καὶ τείχη καὶ τάφροι
καὶ τἄλλα ὅσα τοιαῦτα. Καὶ ταῦτα μὲν ἐστιν ἅπαντα χειροποίητα,
καὶ δαπάνης προσδεῖται· ἐν δέ τι κοινὸν ἡ φύσις τῶν εὖ φρονούντων ἐν
ἑαυτῇ κέκτηται φυλακτήριον, ὃ πᾶσι μέν ἐστιν ἀγαθὸν καὶ σωτήριον,
μάλιστα δὲ τοῖς πλήθεσι πρὸς τοὺς τυράννους. Τί οὖν ἐστὶ τοῦτο;
ἀπιστία.

Various are the devices for the defence and security of cities, as
palisades, walls, ditches, and other such kinds of fortification, all
which are the result of the labours of the hand, and maintained at
great expense. But there is one common bulwark, which men of
prudence possess within themselves—the protection and guard of
all people, especially of free states, against the attacks of tyrants.
What is this? Distrust.

A TYRANT.

Philip. ii. 25.

Βασιλεὺς γὰρ καὶ τύραννος ἅπας ἐχθρὸς ἐλευθερίᾳ καὶ νόμοις
ἐναντίος.

For every king and tyrant is an enemy to freedom, and an
opposer of equal laws.

THE ADVANTAGES OF SOCIETY SHOULD BE SHARED BY ALL ITS MEMBERS.

Philip. iv. 45.

Δεῖ γὰρ ὦ ἄνδρες Ἀθηναῖοι δικαίως ἀλλήλοις τῆς πολιτείας κοινωνεῖν, τοὺς μὲν εὐπόρους εἰς μὲν τὸν βίον τὸν ἑαυτῶν ἀσφαλῶς ἔχειν
νομίζοντας καὶ ὑπὲρ τούτων μὴ δεδοικότας, εἰς δὲ τοὺς κινδύνους κοινὰ
ὑπὲρ τῆς σωτηρίας τὰ ὄντα τῇ πατρίδι παρέχοντας, τοὺς δὲ λοιποὺς
τὰ μὲν κοινὰ νομίζοντας καὶ μετέχοντας τὸ μέρος, τὰ δὲ ἑκάστου ἴδια
τοῦ κεκτημένου. Οὕτω καὶ μικρὰ πόλις μεγάλη γίγνεται καὶ μεγάλη
σώζεται.

For, Athenians, all ranks of citizens should have an equal share in the advantages of society : the rich ought to feel secure, and have no dread of the confiscation of their property, thus being willing and ready to contribute of their wealth to the defence of their country ; the rest of the citizens should look upon public property to belong to all, and be satisfied with their just share, but all private fortunes as the inalienable right of the possessors. Thus a small state may expect to rise to eminence, and a great one to maintain its high place in the world.

THE BOND THAT UNITES CONFEDERATE POWERS.

Ad Philip. Epist. Orat. vii.

'Ορῶ δὲ ὡς ὅταν μὲν ὑπ' εὐνοίας τὰ πράγματα συνέχηται καὶ πᾶσι ταὐτὰ συμφέρῃ τοῖς μετέχουσι τῶν πολέμων, μένει τὰ συσταθέντα βεβαίως, ὅταν δὲ ἐξ ἐπιβουλῆς καὶ πλεονεξίας ἀπάτῃ καὶ βίᾳ κατέχηται, καθάπερ ὑπὸ τούτου νῦν, μικρὰ πρόφασις καὶ τὸ τυχὸν πταῖσμα ταχέως αὐτὰ διέσεισε καὶ κατέλυσεν.

For I am well convinced that, when confederate powers are united by affection and identical interests, their agreement may be expected to last ; whereas, if the alliance has been formed to carry out fraudulent and rapacious objects, accompanied by deceit and violence (as has been the case on this occasion), any slight pretext or accident will serve to give it a shock, from which it will not easily recover.

SUCCESS VEILS MEN'S EVIL DEEDS.

Ad Philip. Epist. Orat. xiii.

Αἱ γὰρ εὐπραξίαι δειναὶ συγκρύψαι καὶ συσκιάσαι τὰς ἁμαρτίας τῶν ἀνθρώπων εἰσίν.

For success has a great tendency to conceal and throw a veil over the evil deeds of men.

See (Lat.) Might makes right.

RESULT OF A REVERSE OF FORTUNE IN GOVERNMENTS.

Ad Philip. Epist. Orat. xiii.

Συμβαίνει γὰρ ὥσπερ ἐν τοῖς σώμασιν ἡμῶν. "Οταν μὲν ἐρρωμένος ᾖ τις, οὐδὲν ἐπαισθάνεται τῶν καθ' ἕκαστα σαθρῶν, ἐπὰν δὲ ἀρρωστήσῃ, πάντα κινεῖται, κἂν ῥῆγμα κἂν στρέμμα κἂν ἄλλο τι τῶν ὑπαρχόντων ᾖ μὴ τελέως ὑγιεινόν. Οὕτω καὶ τῶν βασιλειῶν καὶ ἁπασῶν τῶν δυναστειῶν, ἕως μὲν ἂν ἐν τοῖς πολέμοις κατορθῶσιν, ἀφανῆ τὰ κακά ἐστι τοῖς πολλοῖς, ἐπὰν δέ τι πταίcωσιν, γίγνεται φανερὰ τὰ δυσχερῆ πάντα τοῖς ἅπασιν.

It happens as in our bodies : when a man is in sound and vigorous health, none of the weak parts of his body are felt ; but when he is laid up by illness, every ailment is made worse, whether

it be a fracture, or a dislocation, or any other member that has
been injured. So in kingdoms and governments : as long as they
are favoured by victory, little notice is paid to the disorders in
the state by the mass of the people ; but when a reverse of fortune
takes place, what is unsound becomes palpable to every eye.

Absolute Monarchies Dangerous to Free States.
Olynth. i. 5.

Καὶ ὅλως ἄπιστον, οἶμαι, ταῖς πολιτείαις ἡ τυραννίς, ἄλλως τε
κἂν ὅμορον χώραν ἔχωσι.

In short, free states, in my opinion, ought to have a wholesome
dread of absolute monarchies, especially if they are situated in
their immediate neighbourhood.

The Ultimate Event determines Man's Judgment.
Olynth. i. 11.

Ἂν μὲν γὰρ, ὅσα ἂν τις λάβῃ, καὶ σώσῃ, μεγάλην ἔχει τῇ τύχῃ
τὴν χάριν, ἂν δ' ἀναλώσας λάθῃ, συνανάλωσε καὶ τὸ μεμνῆσθαι τὴν
χάριν. Καὶ περὶ τῶν πραγμάτων οὕτως οἱ μὴ χρησάμενοι τοῖς καιροῖς
ὀρθῶς, οὐδ' εἰ συνέβη τι παρὰ τῶν θεῶν χρηστόν, μνημονεύουσι· πρὸς
γὰρ τὸ τελευταῖον ἐκβὰν ἕκαστον τῶν πρὶν ὑπαρξάντων κρίνεται.

If a man succeeds in preserving what he has acquired, he is
willing enough to acknowledge the kindness of fortune ; but if he
squanders it foolishly, in parting with it he parts with any feeling
of gratitude. So also in political affairs, those who do not make a
good use of their opportunities forget the favours which they may
have received from the gods. For it is the end which generally
determines man's judgment of what has gone before.

To Find Fault is Easy.
Olynth. i. 16.

Τὸ μὲν οὖν ἐπιτιμᾶν ἴσως φήσαί τις ἂν ῥάδιον καὶ παντὸς εἶναι, τὸ
δ' ὑπὲρ τῶν παρόντων ὅτι δεῖ πράττειν ἀποφαίνεσθαι, τοῦτ' εἶναι
συμβούλου.

To find fault, some one may say, is easy, and in every man's
power ; but to point out the proper course to be pursued in the
present circumstances, that is the proof of a wise counsellor.

Result of Unexpected Success.
Olynth. i. 23.

Τὸ γὰρ εὖ πράττειν παρὰ τὴν ἀξίαν ἀφορμὴ τοῦ κακῶς φρονεῖν
τοῖς ἀνοήτοις γίγνεται.

For great and unexpected successes are often the cause of the
foolish rushing into acts of extravagance.

POWER CANNOT BE FOUNDED UPON INJUSTICE.
Olynth. ii. 10.

Οὐ γὰρ ἔστιν, οὐκ ἔστιν ὦ ἄνδρες Ἀθηναῖοι ἀδικοῦντα καὶ ἐπιορκοῦντα καὶ ψευδόμενον δύναμιν βεβαίαν κτήσασθαι, ἀλλὰ τὰ τοιαῦτα εἰς μὲν ἅπαξ καὶ βραχὺν χρόνον ἀντέχει, καὶ σφόδρα γε ἤνθησεν ἐπὶ ταῖς ἐλπίσιν, ἂν τύχῃ, τῷ χρόνῳ δὲ φωρᾶται καὶ περὶ αὐτὰ καταρρεῖ. Ὥσπερ γὰρ οἰκίας, οἶμαι, καὶ πλοίου καὶ τῶν ἄλλων τῶν τοιούτων τὰ κάτωθεν ἰσχυρότατα εἶναι δεῖ, οὕτω καὶ τῶν πράξεων τὰς ἀρχὰς καὶ τὰς ὑποθέσεις ἀληθεῖς καὶ δικαίας εἶναι προσήκει.

For it is not, O Athenians—it is not, I assure you, possible for lasting power to be founded upon injustice, perjury, and treachery. These may, indeed, succeed for once, and for a short time, putting on the gay and gaudy appearance of hope; but they are at last found out, and bring to ruin all who trust in them. For as in buildings of every kind the foundation ought to be the strongest, so the bases and principles of actions should be true and just. '

THREATS WITHOUT CORRESPONDENT ACTIONS ARE CONTEMPTIBLE.
Olynth. ii. 12.

Ἅπας μὲν λόγος, ἂν ἀπῇ τὰ πράγματα, μάταιόν τι φαίνεται καὶ κενόν.

For words and threats, if they are not accompanied by action, cannot but appear vain and contemptible.

HELP YOURSELF, AND YOUR FRIENDS WILL HELP YOU.
Olynth. ii. 23.

Οὐκ ἔνι δ' αὐτὸν ἀργοῦντα οὐδὲ τοῖς φίλοις ἐπιτάττειν ὑπὲρ αὐτοῦ τι ποιεῖν, μή τί γε δὴ τοῖς θεοῖς.

No man, who will not make an effort for himself, need apply for aid to his friends, and much less to the gods.

MAN IS APT TO BLAME EVERY ONE BUT HIMSELF.
Olynth. iii. 17.

Οὐδὲ γὰρ ἐν τοῖς τοῦ πολέμου κινδύνοις τῶν φυγόντων οὐδεὶς ἑαυτοῦ κατηγορεῖ, ἀλλὰ τοῦ στρατηγοῦ καὶ τῶν πλησίον καὶ πάντων μᾶλλον, ἥττηνται δ' ὅμως διὰ πάντας τοὺς φυγόντας δήπου· μένειν γὰρ ἐξῆν τῷ κατηγοροῦντι τῶν ἄλλων, εἰ δὲ τοῦτ' ἐποίει ἕκαστος, ἐνίκων ἄν.

For in the emergencies of war no one of those who fly ever think of accusing himself; he will rather blame the general, or his fellow-soldiers, or anything else; yet the defeat was certainly occasioned by the cowardice of each individual. For he who accuses others might have maintained his own post, and if each had done so, success must have been the result.

WE READILY BELIEVE WHAT WE WISH.

Olynth. iii. 19.

Διόπερ ῥᾷστον ἀπάντων ἐστὶν αὐτὸν ἐξαπατῆσαι· ὃ γὰρ βούλεται, τοῦθ᾽ ἕκαστος καὶ οἴεται, τὰ δὲ πράγματα πολλάκις οὐχ οὕτω
πέφυκεν.

So that nothing is so easy as to deceive one's self; for what we wish, that we readily believe ; but such expectations are often inconsistent with the real state of things.

We find the same idea in " Achilles Tatius de Leucippes et Clitophontis Amoribus " (lib. vi. 17)—

Λόγος γὰρ ἐλπίδος εἰς τὸ τυχεῖν ἔρωτος ἐς πειθὼ ῥᾴδιος.   Τὸ γὰρ
ἐπιθυμοῦν σύμμαχον, ὃ θέλει λαβών, ἐγείρει τὴν ἐλπίδα.

" For the words which show the hope of obtaining the wished-for object are readily believed ; which arises from this, that the simple desire aiding the wishes excites the hope."

And again, in " Heliodorus " (lib. viii.), we find—

Ἃ γὰρ ἐπιθυμεῖ ψυχή, καὶ πιστεύειν φιλεῖ.

" For what the mind wishes, that it also believes."

See (Lat.) Believe, men.

LOW PURSUITS ENGENDER LOW SENTIMENTS.

Olynth. iii. 31.

Ἔστι δ᾽ οὐδέποτ᾽, οἶμαι, μέγα καὶ νεανικὸν φρόνημα λαβεῖν μικρὰ
καὶ φαῦλα πράττοντας· ὁποῖ᾽ ἄττα γὰρ ἂν τὰ ἐπιτηδεύματα τῶν
ἀνθρώπων ᾖ, τοιοῦτον ἀνάγκη καὶ τὸ φρόνημα ἔχειν.

It is impossible for those who are engaged in low and grovelling pursuits to entertain noble and generous sentiments.   No ; their thoughts must always necessarily be somewhat similar to their employments.

LET THE PROSPEROUS SHOW KINDNESS TO THE UNHAPPY.

Pro Rhod. 21.

Δεῖ γὰρ τοὺς εὐτυχοῦντας περὶ τῶν ἀτυχούντων ἀεὶ φαίνεσθαι τὰ
βέλτιστα βουλευομένους, ἐπειδήπερ ἄδηλον τὸ μέλλον ἅπασιν
ἀνθρώποις.

Those enjoying prosperity should always be ready to assist the unfortunate, for no one can say what the future may bring forth.

In Political Transactions the Powerful prescribe to the Weak.

Pro Rhod. 29.

Τῶν μὲν γὰρ ἰδίων δικαίων τῶν ἐν ταῖς πολιτείαις οἱ νόμοι κοινὴν τὴν μετουσίαν ἔδοσαν καὶ ἴσην καὶ τοῖς ἀσθενέσι καὶ τοῖς ἰσχυροῖς· τῶν δ' Ἑλληνικῶν δικαίων οἱ κρατοῦντες ὁρισταὶ τοῖς ἥττοσι γίγνονται.

For in civil society the rights of individuals, without reference to their power or weakness in the state, are determined by the laws. But in national concerns the powerful always prescribe to the weaker.

The Praising of a Man's Self is Burdensome.

De Cor. 3.

Ἕτερον δ', ὃ φύσει πᾶσιν ἀνθρώποις ὑπάρχει, τῶν μὲν λοιδοριῶν καὶ τῶν κατηγοριῶν ἀκούειν ἡδέως, τοῖς ἐπαινοῦσι δ' αὑτούς ἄχθεσθαι.

It is the natural disposition of all men to listen with pleasure to abuse and slander of their neighbour, and to hear with impatience those who utter praises of themselves.

So Proverbs (xxvii. 2)– "Let another man praise thee, and not thine own mouth ; a stranger, and not thine own lips."

See (Lat.) Bragging.

The True Bond of Friendship.

De Cor. 35.

Οὐ γὰρ τὰ ῥήματα τὰς οἰκειότητας ἔφη βεβαιοῦν, μάλα σεμνῶς ὀνομάζων, ἀλλὰ τὸ ταὐτὰ συμφέρειν.

For it is not words that give strength to friendship, but a similarity of interests.

So Proverbs (xvii. 24)—"A man that hath friends must show himself friendly ; and there is a Friend that sticketh closer than a brother."

See (Lat.) Friendship.

A Traitor.

De Cor. 47.

Οὐδεὶς γάρ, ὦ ἄνδρες 'Αθηναῖοι, τὸ τοῦ προδιδόντος συμφέρον ζητῶν χρήματ' ἀναλίσκει, οὐδ' ἐπειδὰν ὧν ἂν πρίηται κύριος γένηται, τῷ προδότῃ συμβούλῳ περὶ τῶν λοιπῶν ἔτι χρῆται· οὐδὲν γὰρ ἂν ἦν εὐδαιμονέστερον προδότου. 'Αλλ' οὐκ ἔστι ταῦτα· πόθεν ; πολλοῦ γε καὶ δεῖ. 'Αλλ' ἐπειδὰν τῶν πραγμάτων ἐγκρατὴς ὁ ζητῶν ἄρχειν καταστῇ, καὶ τῶν ταῦτα ἀποδομένων δεσπότης ἐστί, τὴν δὲ πονηρίαν εἰδὼς τότε δή, τότε καὶ μισεῖ καὶ ἀπιστεῖ καὶ προπηλακίζει.

It is not the benefit of the traitor that is looked to by the man who bribes him, nor, after he has obtained what he bargained for, is he ever afterwards taken into confidence. If it were so, no one would be happier than a traitor. How should it be so? It is impossible. For when the ambitious man has once succeeded in gaining his object, then knowing the utter baseness of the man, he holds him in detestation, distrusts, and treats him with supreme contempt.

On what Men's Conduct should be Modelled.
De Cor. 95.

Καὶ γὰρ ἄνδρα ἰδίᾳ καὶ πόλιν κοινῇ πρὸς τὰ κάλλιστα τῶν ὑπαρχόντων ἀεὶ δεῖ πειρᾶσθαι τὰ λοιπὰ πράττειν.

Private individuals and public bodies should take as their pattern those actions by which they have acquired their fame.

The Truly Brave.
De Cor. 97

Πέρας μὲν γὰρ ἅπασιν ἀνθρώποις ἐστὶ τοῦ βίου θάνατος, κἂν ἐν οἰκίσκῳ τις αὑτὸν καθείρξας τηρῇ· δεῖ δὲ τοὺς ἀγαθοὺς ἄνδρας ἐγχειρεῖν μὲν ἅπασιν ἀεὶ τοῖς καλοῖς, τὴν ἀγαθὴν προβαλλομένους ἐλπίδα, φέρειν δ' ὅ τι ἂν ὁ θεὸς διδῷ γενναίως.

For death is the inevitable close of every man's life, however much he may try to save it by skulking in some obscure corners ; but the truly brave should not hesitate to draw the sword on all honourable occasions, armed with fair hopes of success, and, whatever may be the result, to bear with resignation the will of Providence.

See (Lat.) The brave.

A Statesman.
De Cor. 122.

Ἔπειτα τοιαῦτα ποιῶν λέγεις ἃ δεῖ προσεῖναι τῷ δημοτικῷ, ὥσπερ ἀνδριάντα ἐκδεδωκὼς κατὰ συγγραφήν, εἶτ' οὐκ ἔχοντα ἃ προσῆκεν ἐκ τῆς συγγραφῆς κομιζόμενος, ἢ λόγῳ τοὺς δημοτικοὺς ἀλλ' οὐ τοῖς πράγμασι καὶ τοῖς πολιτεύμασι γιγνωσκομένους.

And, doing this, you proceed to draw the portrait of a statesman, as if having given a model for a statue, you found that the artist had not attended to your directions, forgetting that the character of a statesman is to be shadowed forth not by words but by actions, and the success of his administration.

See (Lat.) A statesman.

The Sower of Mischief.
De Cor. 159.

Ὁ γὰρ τὸ σπέρμα παρασχών, οὗτος τῶν φύντων αἴτιος.

For the sower of the seed is assuredly the author of the whole harvest of mischief.

So Proverbs (vi. 14)—"Frowardness is in his heart, he deviseth mischief continually ; he soweth discord."

THE TRUE COUNSELLOR AND THE SYCOPHANT.
De Cor. 189.

Ὁ γὰρ σύμβουλος καὶ ὁ συκοφάντης, οὐδὲ τῶν ἄλλων οὐδὲν ἐοικότες, ἐν τούτῳ πλεῖστον ἀλλήλων διαφέρουσιν· ὃ μέν γε πρὸ τῶν πραγμάτων γνώμην ἀποφαίνεται, καὶ δίδωσιν ἑαυτὸν ὑπεύθυνον τοῖς πεισθεῖσι, τῇ τύχῃ, τοῖς καιροῖς, τῷ βουλομένῳ· ὃ δὲ σιγήσας ἡνίκ' ἔδει λέγειν, ἄν τι δύσκολον συμβῇ, τοῦτο βασκαίνει.

For the true counsellor and the flattering sycophant differ from each other particularly in this. The former openly declares his opinion on the proper course to be pursued before the event, and makes himself responsible for his advice to fortune, to the times, and to those whom he has influenced. The latter is silent when he ought to speak ; but if anything unfortunate takes place, he dwells on it with invidious earnestness.

MISFORTUNES.
De Cor. 200.

Νῦν μέν γε ἀποτυχεῖν δοκεῖ τῶν πραγμάτων, ὃ πᾶσι κοινόν ἐστι ἀνθρώποις, ὅταν τῷ θεῷ ταῦτα δοκῇ.

Misfortunes are the lot of all men, whenever it may please Heaven to inflict them.

OUR FATHERLAND COMPREHENDS EVERY ENDEARMENT.
De Cor. 205.

Ἡγεῖτο γὰρ αὐτῶν ἕκαστος οὐχὶ τῷ πατρὶ καὶ τῇ μητρὶ μόνον γεγενῆσθαι, ἀλλὰ καὶ τῇ πατρίδι. Διαφέρει δὲ τί ; ὅτι ὁ μὲν τοῖς γονεῦσι μόνον γεγενῆσθαι νομίζων τὸν τῆς εἱμαρμένης καὶ τὸν αὐτόματον θάνατον περιμένει, ὁ δὲ καὶ τῇ πατρίδι ὑπὲρ τοῦ μὴ ταύτην ἐπιδεῖν δουλεύουσαν ἀποθνήσκειν ἐθελήσει, καὶ φοβερωτέρας ἡγήσεται τὰς ὕβρεις καὶ τὰς ἀτιμίας, ἃς ἐν δουλευούσῃ τῇ πόλει φέρειν ἀνάγκη, τοῦ θανάτου.

Each of them was firmly convinced that a man was born not merely for his parents but also for his country. You may ask what is the difference. It is very clear, for he who thinks himself born only for his parents awaits the fated hour with calm submission, whereas the other will boldly meet his fate that he may not see his country enslaved, and will consider those insults and disgraces which he must endure in a state of slavery as much more to be dreaded than death itself.

See (Lat.) Fatherland

Man Proposes, God Disposes.

De Cor. 209.

Ὁ μὲν γὰρ ἦν ἀνδρῶν ἀγαθῶν ἔργον, ἅπασι πέπρακται, τῇ τύχῃ δὲ, ἣν ὁ δαίμων ἀπένειμεν ἑκάστοις, ταύτῃ κέχρηνται.

Whatever was the duty of brave men, they were all ready to perform, but the sovereign Lord of the universe decided the fate of each.

See (Lat. Fr.) Man proposes.

An Accuser.

De Cor. 242.

Πονηρόν, ὦ ἄνδρες Ἀθηναῖοι, πονηρὸν ὁ συκοφάντης ἀεὶ καὶ πανταχόθεν βάσκανον καὶ φιλαίτιον.

A false accuser is a monster, a dangerous monster, ever and in every way malignant and ready to seek causes of complaint.

A Minister of State.

De Cor. 246.

Τίνα οὖν ἐστι ταῦτα; ἰδεῖν τὰ πράγματα ἀρχόμενα, καὶ προαισθέσθαι, καὶ προειπεῖν τοῖς ἄλλοις. Ταῦτα πέπρακται μοι. Καὶ ἔτι τὰς ἑκασταχοῦ βραδυτῆτας ὄκνους ἀγνοίας φιλονεικίας, ἃ πολιτικὰ ταῖς πόλεσι πρόσεστιν ἁπάσαις καὶ ἀναγκαῖα ἁμαρτήματα, ταῦθ᾽ ὡς εἰς ἐλάχιστον συστεῖλαι, καὶ τοὐναντίον εἰς ὁμόνοιαν καὶ φιλίαν καὶ τοῦ τὰ δέοντα ποιεῖν ὁρμὴν προτρέψαι.

What, then, are the duties of a minister of state?—to watch the rise of every event, to look into the future and forewarn his fellow-citizens of what may happen. This is precisely what I have done. And then, again, to confine within the narrowest limits the fatal results that naturally arise from irresolution, lukewarmness, prejudices, and party spirit; and, on the other hand, to lead men's minds to peace, good understanding, and to rouse them to a vigorous defence of their just rights.

Bribes.

De Cor. 247.

Καὶ μὴν τῷ διαφθαρῆναι χρήμασιν ἢ μὴ κεκράτηκα Φιλίππου· ὥσπερ γὰρ ὁ ὠνούμενος νενίκηκε τὸν λαβόντα, ἐὰν πρίηται, οὕτως ὁ μὴ λαβὼν καὶ διαφθαρεὶς νενίκηκε τὸν ὠνούμενον.

By resisting his bribes, I conquered Philip; for as the purchaser conquers when a man sells himself, so the man who refuses to be sold, and disdains to be corrupted, conquers the purchaser.

WE KNOW NOT WHAT A DAY MAY BRING FORTH.

De Cor. 252.

Ἦν γὰρ ὁ βέλτιστα πράττειν νομίζων καὶ ἀρίστην ἔχειν οἰόμενος
οὐκ οἶδεν εἰ μενεῖ τοιαύτη μέχρι τῆς ἑσπέρας.

The man who is in the highest state of prosperity, and who
thinks his fortune most secure, knows not if it will remain unchanged till the evening.

So Proverbs (xxvii. 1)—"Boast not thyself of to-morrow ; for thou knowest not what a day may bring forth."

See (Lat.) Death.

TO REMIND OF KINDNESS IS TO REPROACH.

De Cor. 269.

Ἐγὼ νομίζω τὸν μὲν εὖ παθόντα δεῖν μεμνῆσθαι πάντα τὸν χρόνον,
τὸν δὲ ποιήσαντα εὐθὺς ἐπιλελῆσθαι, εἰ δεῖ τὸν μὲν χρηστοῦ τὸν δὲ
μὴ μικροψύχου ποιεῖν ἔργον ἀνθρώπου. Τὸ δὲ τὰς ἰδίας εὐεργεσίας
ὑπομιμνήσκειν καὶ λέγειν μικροῦ δεῖν ὅμοιόν ἐστι τῷ ὀνειδίζειν.

For it is in accordance with my principles to believe that he
who receives a favour must retain a recollection of it for all time
to come, but that he who confers should at once forget it, if he is
not to show a sordid and ungenerous spirit. To remind a man of
a kindness conferred on him, and to talk of it, is little different
from reproach.

See (Lat.) Reminding kindnesses.

THE LOYAL STATESMAN.

De Cor. 280.

Ἔστι δ' οὐχ ὁ λόγος τοῦ ῥήτορος Αἰσχίνη τίμιον, οὐδ' ὁ τόνος τῆς
φωνῆς, ἀλλὰ τὸ ταὐτὰ προαιρεῖσθαι τοῖς πολλοῖς καὶ τὸ τοὺς αὐτοὺς
μισεῖν καὶ φιλεῖν οὕσπερ ἂν ἡ πατρίς. Ὁ γὰρ οὕτως ἔχων τὴν ψυχήν,
οὗτος ἐπ' εὐνοίᾳ πάντ' ἐρεῖ· ὁ δ' ἀφ' ὧν ἡ πόλις προορᾶταί τινα κίν-
δυνον ἑαυτῇ, τούτους θεραπεύων οὐκ ἐπὶ τῆς αὐτῆς ὁρμεῖ τοῖς πολλοῖς,
οὔκουν οὐδὲ τῆς ἀσφαλείας τὴν αὐτὴν ἔχει προσδοκίαν.

It is not the language, it is not the tone of voice of a public
speaker that is to be considered, but such an approximation of
feelings and interests with his fellow-citizens, that both his enemies and friends are the same with those of his country. For he
who is thus animated, he it is who will speak his sentiments with
an honest zeal. But he who pays court to those who threaten
danger to the state, is not embarked in the same vessel with his
fellow-citizens, and therefore does not look forward to the same
results for his safety.

THE GODS.
De Cor. 289.

Μηδὲν ἁμαρτεῖν ἐστὶ θεῶν καὶ πάντα κατορθοῦν
ἐν βιοτῇ, μοῖραν δ' οὔ τι φυγεῖν ἔπορεν.

Chance to despise, and fortune to control,
Doth to the immortal gods alone pertain ;
Their joys unchanged, in endless currents roll ;
But mortals combat with their fate in vain.

THE VIRTUOUS CITIZEN.
De Cor. 321.

Δύο δ', ὦ ἄνδρες Ἀθηναῖοι, τὸν φύσει μέτριον πολίτην ἔχειν δεῖ,
ἐν μὲν ταῖς ἐξουσίαις τὴν τοῦ γενναίου καὶ τοῦ πρωτείου τῇ πόλει
προαίρεσιν διαφυλάττειν, ἐν παντὶ δὲ καιρῷ καὶ πράξει τὴν εὔνοιαν·
τούτου γὰρ ἡ φύσις κυρία, τοῦ δύνασθαι δὲ καὶ ἰσχύειν ἕτερα.

There are two qualities which ought always to distinguish a
virtuous citizen : he ought, in the high offices of state, to maintain
the honour and pre-eminence of his country, and in all times and
circumstances to show kindly feelings ; these are dependent upon
nature, but abilities and success are the gifts of another power.

DIONYSIUS HALICARNASSENSIS.

FLOURISHED FROM B.C. 29 TO B.C. 7.

DIONYSIUS, a celebrated writer on Latin antiquities, was a native
of Halicarnassus, and came to Rome about B.C. 29, at the close of
the civil wars. Here he continued for twenty-two years, making
himself acquainted with the customs and transactions of the
Romans. His work is entitled "Roman Antiquities," and goes
back to the origin of the nations of Italy. It closed with the year
B.C. 265, the year before the first Punic war, when the history of
Polybius properly begins. It contains many details on the laws
and customs of Rome, which are valuable, as they are nowhere
else to be found. It was contained in twenty books, of which
eleven only have come down to us, with some fragments of the
others. They bring the history of Rome down to B.C. 440.

The Works of an Author are the Image of his Mind.

i. 1.

'Επεικῶς γὰρ ἅπαντες νομίζουσιν εἰκόνας εἶναι τῆς ἐκάστου ψυχῆς τοὺς λόγους.

For the general observation is strictly correct, that the works of an author may be considered the representation of his mind.

Superiors Govern Inferiors.

i. 5.

Φύσεως γὰρ δὴ νόμος ἅπασι κοινός, ὃν οὐδεὶς καταλύσει χρόνος, ἄρχειν ἀεὶ τῶν ἡττόνων τοὺς κρείττονας.

It is a common law of nature, which no time will ever change, that superiors shall rule their inferiors.

See (Lat.) The weakest go to the wall.

A Nation improved by Sufferings and Difficulties.

i. 9.

'Υπὲρ ταῦτα δὲ πάντα, κόσμῳ τοῦ πολιτεύματος, ὃν ἐκ πολλῶι κατευ̣γ̣υαντο παθημάτων, ἐκ παντὸς καιροῦ λαμβάνοντές τι χρήσιμον.

But, above all these, by their form of government, which they improved by learning wisdom from the various misfortunes which happened to them, always extracting something useful from every occurrence.

So Romans (v. 3)—"Knowing that tribulation worketh patience; and patience, experience; and experience, hope."

See (Lat.) Experience.

Everything Involuntary deserves Forgiveness.

i. 58.

"Απαν δὲ συγγνώμης ἄξιον τὸ ἀκούσιον.

Everything that is involuntary deserves to be forgiven.

God.

i. 77.

Μηδὲν ἂν τοῦ θεοῦ λειτούργημα τῆς ἀφθάρτου καὶ μακαρίας φύσεωι ἀνάξιον ὑπομένοντος.

God is incapable of doing anything which is unworthy of a pure and happy nature.

So Psalm (cxvi. 5)—"Gracious is the Lord, God is merciful."

The Results of Good and Bad National Institutions.

ii. 3.

Μαχητὰs δέ γε καὶ δικαίουs ἄνδραs, καὶ τὰς ἄλλαs ἀρετὰs ἐπιτη-
δεύονταs, τὸ τῆs πολιτείαs σχῆμα ποιεῖν τοῖs φρονίμωs αὐτὸ κατασ-
τησαμένοιs· μαλθακούs τε αὖ καὶ πλεονέκταs, καὶ δούλουs αἰσχρῶν
ἐπιθυμιῶν, τὰ πονηρὰ ἐπιτηδεύματα ἐπιτελεῖν.

The form of government, when it has been prudently established,
produces citizens distinguished for bravery, justice, and every
other good quality ; whereas, on the other hand, bad institutions
render men cowardly, rapacious, and slaves of every foul desire.

See (Fr.) Good laws the foundation of all states.

Causes of Good Government in States.

ii. 18.

Ὅτι τοῦ καλῶs οἰκεῖσθαι τὰs πόλειs αἰτίαs ὑπολαβὼν, ἃs θρυλλοῦσι
μὲν ἅπαντεs οἱ πολιτικοί, κατσακευάζουσι δ' ὀλίγοι· πρώτην μὲι
παρὰ τῶν θεῶν εὔνοιαν, ἧs παρούσηs ἅπαντα τοῖs ἀνθρώποιs ἐπὶ τὰ
κρείττω συμφέρεται· ἔπειτα σωφροσύνην τε καὶ δικαιοσύνην, δι' ἃs
ἧττον ἀλλήλουs βλάπτοντεs μᾶλλον ὁμονοοῦσι, καὶ τὴν εὐδαιμονίαν
οὐ ταῖs αἰσχίσταιs μετροῦσιν ἡδοναῖs ἀλλὰ τῷ καλῷ· τελευταίαν δὲ,
τὴν ἐν πολέμοιs γενναιότητα, τὴν παρασκευάζουσαν εἶναι καὶ τὰs
ἄλλαs ἀρετὰs τοῖs ἔχουσιν ὠφελίμουs.

He was of opinion that the good government of states arose
from causes which are always the subject of praise by politicians,
but are seldom attended to : first, the aid and favour of the gods,
which give success to every human undertaking ; next, attention
to moderation and justice, by love of which citizens are induced to
refrain from injuring each other, and to join in cordial union—
making virtue, not shameful pleasures, the measure of their happiness ; and, lastly, military courage, which renders even the other
virtues to be advantageous to their possessors.

Mercy.

ii. 35.

Ἔλεόν τε κοινῶν κακῶν οὐ μικρὸν ἔρανον εἶναι νομίζοντεs.

Believing that mercy does not in a small degree tend to alleviate
the common evils which flesh is heir to.

So Psalm (xxv. 10)—" All the paths of the Lord are mercy and truth ;"
and (xxxiii. 5)—" The earth is full of the mercy of the Lord ;" and Matthew
(v. 7)—" Blessed are the merciful, for they shall obtain mercy."

So Shakespeare (" Merchant of Venice,' act iv. sc. 1)—

> " The quality of mercy is not strained ;
> It droppeth, as the gentle rain from heaven
> Upon the place beneath ; it is twice blessed ;
> It blesseth him that gives, and him that takes.

'Tis mightiest in the mightiest; it becomes
The thronèd monarch better than his crown:
Ilis sceptre shows the force of temporal power,
The attribute to awe and majesty,
Wherein doth sit the dread and fear of kings:
But mercy is above this sceptred sway;
It is enthronèd in the hearts of kings,
It is an attribute to God himself;
And earthly power doth then show likest God's,
When mercy seasons justice. Therefore, Jew,
Though justice be thy plea, consider this,—
That in the course of justice, none of us
Should see salvation ; we do pray for mercy ;
And that same prayer doth teach us all to render
The deeds of mercy."

CURE FOR ENVY.

iii. 9.

Ἐν γάρ ἐστιν, ὦ Φουφέτιε, λύπης ἀνθρωπίνης ἐπ' ἀλλοτρίοις ἀγαθοῖς γινομένης ἄκος, τοῦ μηκέτι τοὺς φθονοῦντας ἀλλότρια τὰ τῶν φθονουμένων ἀγαθὰ ἡγεῖσθαι.

For the only cure for envy is to look upon the prosperity of the envied person as belonging to one's self.

THE POOR.

iv. 9.

Οὐ γὰρ ἂν γένοιτο φρόνημα εὐγενὲς ἐν ἀνδράσιν ἀπορουμένοις τῶν καθ' ἡμέραν ἀναγκαίων.

For a generous and noble spirit cannot be expected to dwell in the breast of men who are struggling for their daily bread.

LIBERTY.

iv. 83.

Ἔμφυτος πᾶσιν ἀνθρώποις ὁ τῆς ἐλευθερίας πόθος.

The love of liberty is implanted by nature in the breasts of all men.

P. Henry (Speech, March 1775) says—
"Give me liberty or give me death."
See (Lat.) Liberty, that best gift ; what so advantageous.

ENMITIES TO BE GIVEN UP TO FRIENDSHIP.

v. 4.

Ἐνθυμηθέντας ὅτι φρονίμων μὲν ἀνθρώπων ἔργον ἐστὶ ταῖς φιλίαις χαρίζεσθαι τὰς ἔχθρας, ἀνοήτων δὲ καὶ βαρβάρων, τοῖς ἐχθροῖς συναναιρεῖν τοὺς φίλους.

Considering that it is the part of wise men to give up their
enmities to friendships, and that of senseless men and barbarians
to confound friends with enemies.

WE JUDGE OF OTHERS BY OURSELVES.

v. 8.

'Επειδὴ πεφύκασιν ἅπαντες ἀπὸ τῶν οἰκείων τὰ περὶ τῶν ἄλλων
λεγόμενα κρίνειν, καὶ τὸ πιστὸν ἢ ἄπιστον ἐφ' ἑαυτοῖς ποιεῖν.

Since it is the custom of all men to judge of the proceedings of
others by what they would do themselves, and to consider things
credible or incredible by their own experience.

NECESSITY.

v. 64.

Τὰς γὰρ ἀνάγκας κρείττους εἶναι τῆς ἀνθρωπίνης φύσεως.

For necessity is stronger than human nature.

See (Lat.) Necessity.

THE CAUSE OF THE SUBVERSION OF GOVERNMENTS.

v. 66.

'Ενθυμεῖσθαί τ' αὐτοὺς ἠξίου, ὅτι οὐχ ὑπὸ τῶν πενήτων καὶ οὐδεμίαν
ἰσχὺν ἐχόντων αἱ πόλεις ἀπόλλυνται, τὰ δίκαια ποιεῖν ἀναγκαζο-
μένων, ἀλλ' ὑπὸ τῶν εὐπόρων καὶ τὰ πολιτικὰ πράττειν δυναμένων,
ὅταν ὑπὸ τῶν χειρόνων ὑβρίζωνται, καὶ τῶν δικαίων μὴ τυγχάνωσιν.

He requested them to recollect that governments are not put an
end to by the poor, and those who have no power, when they are
compelled to do justice; but by the rich, and those who have a
right by their position to administer public affairs, when they are
insulted by their inferiors, and cannot obtain justice.

THE MOB SHOULD NOT GOVERN.

v. 67.

Ψυχῇ μὲν ἀνδρὸς ἀνάλογον ἐχούσης τι τῆς βουλῆς, σώματι δὲ τοῦ
δήμου. Ἐὰν μὲν οὖν βουλῆς τὸν ἄφρονα δῆμον ἄρχειν ἐῶσιν, ὅμοια
πείσεσθαι αὐτοὺς ἔφη τοῖς ὑποτάττουσι τὴν ψυχὴν τῷ σώματι, καὶ
μὴ κατὰ τὸν λογισμόν, ἀλλὰ κατὰ τὰ πάθη ζῶσιν. Ἐὰν δ' ἄρχεσθαί
τε καὶ ἄγεσθαι τὸν δῆμον συνεθίζωσιν ὑπὸ τῆς βουλῆς, ταὐτὸ ποιή-
σουσι τοῖς ὑποτάττουσι τῇ ψυχῇ τὸ σῶμα, καὶ πρὸς τὸ βέλτιστον,
ἀλλὰ μὴ πρὸς τὸ ἥδιστον τοὺς βίους ἄγουσι.

He said that the commonwealth had in some respects a resemblance to man; for the senate might be considered the soul,
and the people the body. If, then, they allowed the senseless

people to rule the senate, they were doing very much the same thing as if they made the soul subject to the body, and were to live under the influence of their passions and not of their reason. Whereas if they accustomed the people to be governed and directed by the senate, they would act like those who subject the body to the soul, and who lead the best, not the most voluptuous lives.

See (Lat.) Mob ; (Fr.) Multitude.

CHARACTER OF A FOOL.

v. 68.

Εἴωθε γὰρ ἀεί πως τὸ ἀνόητον ἅπαν, ὅταν μέν τις αὐτὸ κολακεύῃ, μεγάλα φρονεῖν· ὅταν δὲ δεδίττηται, σωφρονεῖν.

It is the character of fools to be overbearing when they are flattered, and to yield when they are looked in the face.

So Proverbs (xii. 15)—"The way of a fool is right in his own eyes ;" and (xv. 2)—"The mouth of fools poureth out foolishness "

See (Lat. Fr.) Fools.

THE GRATITUDE OF SOME MEN IS FOR FAVOURS TO COME.

v. 69.

Οὐ γὰρ ὁμοίας εἶναι τὰς διανοίας τῶν ἀνθρώπων δεομένων τε καὶ ἀποπληρωθέντων ὅτου ἂν δεηθῶσιν.

For the feelings of men, when they are looking for a favour, are very different from those of the same men when they have succeeded in obtaining it.

See (Lat. Fr.) Gratitude.

ALL MEN MUST DIE.

vi. 9.

Ἀποθανεῖν μὲν γὰρ πᾶσιν ἀνθρώποις ὀφείλεται, κακοῖς τε καὶ ἀγαθοῖς· καλῶς δὲ καὶ ἐνδόξως μόνοις τοῖς ἀγαθοῖς.

For death is the fate of all men, the coward equally with the brave ; but the brave alone enjoy a noble and glorious death.

So Psalm (xlix. 10)—"For he seeth that wise men die, also the fool."

See (Lat.) Death comes to all.

THE ORIGIN OF A TYRANT.

vi. 60.

Οὐδενὶ γὰρ δὴ ἄδηλον ὅτι πᾶς τύραννος ἐκ δημοκόλακος φύεται· καὶ ταχεῖα ὁδός ἐστι τοῖς καταδουλοῦσθαι τὰς πόλεις βουλομένοις, ἡ διὰ τῶν κακίστων ἄγουσα πολιτῶν ἐπὶ τὰς δυναστείας.

For it is evident to all that a tyrant springs from a flatterer of the people, and that the shortest way for those who desire to enslave their country is to acquire power by the lowest demagogues.

E

CIVIL WAR.

vi. 79.

Πολέμου δὲ πολιτικοῦ, ὡς ἅπαντες ἴσασι, κάκιον χρῆμα οὐδὲν, ἐν
ᾧ τὰ μὲν κρατηθέντα ἀτυχεῖ, τὰ δὲ κρατήσαντα ἀδικεῖ, καὶ περίεστι
τοῖς μὲν ὑπὸ τῶν φιλτάτων ἀπόλλυσθαι, τοῖς δὲ τὰ φίλτατα διο-
λέσαι.

All know that there is nothing more unhappy than a civil war,
in which the conquered are unfortunate and the conquerors are
culpable, and in which the former are destroyed by, and the latter
destroy, their dearest friends.

See (Lat.) Civil war.

REPENTANCE.

vii. 22.

Καὶ ἡ μετάνοια τῶν ὀψὲ ἀρχομένων σωφρονεῖν, ἥττων οὖσα τῆς
προνοίας, καθ' ἕτερον αὖ τρόπον οὐ χείρων οὖσα ἀναφαίνεται, τῇ
κωλύσει τοῦ τέλους ἀφανίζουσα τὸ ἐν τῇ ἀρχῇ ἀγνοηθέν.

The repentance of those who learn wisdom late, though it be an
inferior quality to that of those who are gifted with forethought,
yet if we look at it in another light, it is seen to be not less valuable
from causing the original error to disappear by preventing its consequences.

TIME THE BEST INTERPRETER OF AN AMBIGUOUS LAW.

vii. 52.

Μέγα δὲ τούτου σημεῖόν ἐστιν, ὃ καὶ παντὸς ἀμφισβητουμένου
δικαίου κριτήριον εἶναι δοκεῖ κράτιστον, ὁ χρόνος.

The greatest proof of this is time, which is the best interpreter
of every ambiguous law.

THE MULTITUDE.

vii. 56.

Καὶ γὰρ ἐν ὄχλῳ φιλεῖ γίνεσθαι ἡ τυραννίς.

For the multitude generally give birth to tyranny.

THE GODS ENVIOUS OF EMINENCE.

viii. 25.

Νεμεσᾶταί τε ἅπαντα ὑπὸ θεῶν τὰ ὑπερέχοντα, ὅταν εἰς ἄκρον
ἐπιφανείας ἀφίκηται, καὶ τρέπεται πάλιν εἰς τὸ μηδέν.

The gods take umbrage at the illustrious, when they have
reached the acme of fortune, and turn them again to nothing.

See (Lat.) Gods make sport of men.

Boldness inspired by Dangers.
viii. 26.

Δεινὴ γὰρ ἡ ἀνάγκη, καὶ ὁ περὶ τῶν ἐσχάτων κίνδυνος ἱκανὸς θάρσος ἐνθεῖναι τινι καὶ μὴ προϋπάρχον φύσει.

For necessity is of mighty power; and every man, when his whole fortune is at stake, is inspired with a boldness which nature had previously denied him.

See (Lat.) Boldness best defence.

Love and Hatred.
viii. 34.

Φιλοῦμέν γε ἅπαντες τὰ ὠφελοῦντα, καὶ μισοῦμεν τὰ βλάπτοντα, οὐκ ἀνθρώπων ἡμῖν τινων τόνδε θεμένων τὸν νόμον, οὐδ᾽ ἀνελούντων ποτὲ αὐτὸν, ἐὰν τἀναντία αὐτοῖς δοκῇ· ἀλλ᾽ ὑπὸ τῆς κοινῆς φύσεως ἐξ ἅπαντος τοῦ χρόνου πᾶσι τοῖς αἰσθήσεως μετειληφόσι κείμενον, καὶ εἰς ἀεὶ διαμενοῦντα, παραλαβόντες.

For we all love those who do us good, and hate those who do us harm,—a law which has neither been given to us by man, nor can they annul it when they choose; but it is the universal and eternal law of nature, bestowed upon all who have common sense, and which will ever remain in force.

Compulsory Engagements.
viii. 37.

Τὰς ὁμολογίας τῶν πόλεων, ὡς τῶν γε ὑπ᾽ ἀνάγκης τινὸς, ἢ καιροῦ συγχωρουμένων καὶ ἰδιώταις καὶ πόλεσιν, ἅμα τῷ μεταπεσεῖν τοὺς καιροὺς, ἢ τὰς ἀνάγκας, εὐθὺς διαλυομένων.

Since all engagements, both public and private, that take their rise from necessity or from particular emergencies, soon come to an end, when the conjunctures or necessity ceases.

The Shades below and Elysium.
viii. 52.

Καὶ εἴ τις ἄρα τὰς ἀνθρωπίνας ψυχὰς ἀπολυθείσας τοῦ σώματος ὑποδέξεται τόπος, οὐχ ὁ καταχθόνιος καὶ ἀφεγγὴς ὑποδέξεται τὴν ἐμὴν, ἐν ᾧ φασι τοὺς κακοδαίμονας οἰκεῖν, οὐδὲ τὸ λεγόμενον τῆς Λήθης πεδίον, ἀλλ᾽ ὁ μετέωρος καὶ καθαρὸς αἰθὴρ, ἐν ᾧ τοὺς ἐκ θεῶν φύντας οἰκεῖν λόγος, εὐδαίμονα καὶ μακάριον ἔχοντας βίον.

If there be any place where the souls of men dwell after death, it will not be that subterranean and gloomy place, the abode, as is said, of the wicked, nor the plain of Lethe, as it is called, that will receive mine, but the lofty and pure ether, where, they say, those who are sprung from the gods lead a happy and blessed life.

E 2

Better Late than Never.

ix. 9.

Κρεῖττον γάρ ἐστιν ἄρξασθαι ὀψὲ τὰ δέοντα πράττειν, ἢ μηδί- ποτε.

For it is better to begin late doing our duty than never.

Voluntary Gifts.

ix. 32.

Αἱ γὰρ ἑκούσιοι δωρεαὶ τοῖς τε προεμένοις ἡδίους τῶν ἠναγκασ- μένων εἰσὶ, καὶ τοῖς λαμβάνουσι βεβαιότεραι τῶν μὴ τοιούτων.

For gifts that are bestowed with good will are not only given with greater pleasure by those who grant them than such as are extorted, but are also more lasting to those who receive them.

The Gratification of Wicked Desires.

ix. 52.

Οὐ γὰρ ἐξαιρεῖ τὰς πονηρὰς ἐπιθυμίας ἐκ τῆς ψυχῆς τὸ τυγχάνειν αὐτῶν, ἀλλ' αὔξει, καὶ πονηροτέρας ποιεῖ.

For the gratification of wicked desires does not tend to satiate them, but only inflames them the more, and renders them still more vicious.

DEMETRIUS.

FLOURISHED ABOUT B.C. 412.

DEMETRIUS, an Athenian comic poet of the old comedy, of which there are several fragments remaining.

Wickedness.

Fr. Com. Gr. p. 482.

Σφοδρ' εὐάλωτόν ἐστιν ἡ πονηρία·
εἰς γὰρ τὸ κέρδος μόνον ἀποβλέπουσ' ἀεὶ
ἀφρόνως ἀπαντᾷ καὶ προπετῶς συμπείθεται.

Wickedness is very easily overtaken ; for always looking to gain only, it goes forward foolishly, and is hastily induced to come to a decision.

DIPHILUS.

FLOURISHED B.C. 320.

DIPHILUS, a comic poet, was the contemporary of Menander, and therefore flourished about 320 B.C. He was a native of Sinopë in Asia Minor, and is said to have composed 100 comedies, of which only a few fragments have been preserved. Fabricius cites the titles of 46 of these plays. Both Terence and Plautus derived some of their materials from him.

MAN IS BORN TO TROUBLE.

Fr. Com. Gr. p. 1067.

Ὦ μακάρι', ἀτυχεῖν θνητὸς ὢν ἐπίστασο,
ἵν' αὐτὰ τἀναγκαῖα δυστυχῆς μόνον,
πλείω δὲ διὰ τὴν ἀμαθίαν μὴ προσλάβῃς.

O happy man! being mortal, know that thou art born to trouble, in order that thou mayest suffer only in what is necessary, and not add to it by thy folly.

GOOD FORTUNE IS ONLY FOR A DAY.

Fr. Com. Gr. p. 1078.

Ἀπροσδόκητον οὐδὲν ἀνθρώποις πάθος·
ἐφημέρους γὰρ τὰς τύχας κεκτήμεθα.

No misery is unlooked for by men, for we find good fortune lasting only for a day.

TIME.

Fr. Com. Gr. p. 1087.

Πολὺς τεχνίτης ἐστὶν ὁ χρόνος, ὦ ξένε,
χαίρει μεταπλάττων πάντας ἐπὶ τὰ χείρονα.

My friend, time is the workman of the state; it rejoices to mould all things to the worse.

DEATH RELEASES MAN FROM TROUBLES.

Fr. Com. Gr. p. 1089.

Οὐκ ἔστι βίος ὃς οὐχὶ κέκτηται κακά,
λύπας, μερίμνας, ἁρπαγάς, στρέβλας, νόσους·
τούτων ὁ θάνατος καθάπερ ἰατρὸς φανεὶς
ἀπέλυσε τοὺς ἔχοντας ἀναπαύσας ὕπνῳ.

There is no life that has not evils, griefs, sorrows, annoyances, torments, diseases; death, appearing as the physician of these, proceeds to release those who are thus affected, making them to cease by sleep.

A Sordid Love of Money.

Fr. Com. Gr. p. 1091.

Ἆρ᾽ ἔστιν ἀνοητότατον αἰσχροκερδία·
πρὸς τῷ λαβεῖν γὰρ ὢν ὁ νοῦς τἄλλ᾽ οὐχ ὁρᾷ.

A sordid love of money is certainly a very senseless thing for the mind much occupied with it is blind to everything else.

Conscience.

Fr. Com. Gr. p. 1091.

Ὅστις γὰρ αὐτὸς αὐτὸν οὐκ αἰσχύνεται
συνειδόθ᾽ αὐτῷ φαῦλα διαπεπραγμένῳ,
πῶς τόν γε μηδὲν εἰδότ᾽ αἰσχυνθήσεται.

For whosoever is not ashamed when he is conscious to himself of having committed some base act, how will he be ashamed before him who is ignorant of it?

To Blush.

Fr. Com. Gr. p. 1091.

Ὃς δ᾽ οὔτ᾽ ἐρυθριᾶν οἶδεν οὔτε δεδιέναι,
τὰ πρῶτα πάσης τῆς ἀναιδείας ἔχει.

Whoever does not know to blush or be afraid, has the first principles of every kind of baseness.

Difficult to Gather, Easy to Squander.

Fr. Com. Gr. p. 1092.

Ἔργον συναγαγεῖν σωρὸν ἐν πολλῷ χρόνῳ,
ἐν ἡμέρᾳ δὲ διαφορῆσαι ῥᾴδιον.

It is difficult to gather a heap in a long time, but it is easy to squander the whole in a day.

The Poor.

Fr. Com. Gr. p. 1092.

Πένητος ἀνδρὸς οὐδὲν εὐτυχέστερον·
τὴν ἐπὶ τὸ χεῖρον μεταβολὴν οὐ προσδοκᾷ.

There is no one more happy than the poor man : he expects no change for the worse.

Poverty and Bad Conduct.

Fr. Com. Gr. p. 1092.

Πενία δὲ συγκραθεῖσα δυσσεβεῖ τρόπῳ
ἄρδην ἀνεῖλε καὶ κατέστρεψεν βίον.

Poverty united to bad conduct utterly destroys and upturns the life of man.

Man Born to Trouble.

Fr. Com. Gr. p. 1093.

Ἄνθρωπός εἰμι, τοῦτο δ᾽ αὐτὸ τῷ βίῳ
πρόφασιν μεγίστην εἰς τὸ λυπεῖσθαι φέρει.

I am a mortal; this very thing is the greatest cause of sorrow in life.

The Blessings and Evils of Life.

Fr. Com. Gr. p. 1093.

Ὥσπερ κυαθίζουσ᾽ ἐνίοθ᾽ ἡμῖν ἡ τύχη
ἐν ἀγαθὸν ἐπιχέασα τρί᾽ ἐπαντλεῖ κακά.

As fortune, sometimes, when it is bringing up one blessing for us, in pouring out discharges three evils.

Nothing Fixed in Life.

Fr. Com. Gr. p. 1093.

Βέβαιον οὐδέν ἐστιν ἐν θνητῷ βίῳ,
βιοῖ γὰρ οὐδεὶς ὃν προαιρεῖται τρόπον.

There is nothing fixed in the life of man; for no one lives steadily in the way that he has chosen.

Shamelessness.

Fr. Com. Gr. p. 1093.

Οὐκ ἔστ᾽ ἀναιδοῦς ζῷον εὐθαρσέστερον.

There is no animal more bold than shamelessness.

Man.

Fr. Com. Gr. p. 1093.

Ἂν γνῷς τί ἐστ᾽ ἄνθρωπος, ἡδίων ἔσει.

If thou knowest what man is, thou wilt be more happy.

PRUDENCE.

Fr. Com. Gr. p. 1094.

'Ως μακάριον φρόνησις ἐν χρηστῷ τρόπῳ!

How completely blessed is prudence in a good disposition !

MORTALITY.

Fr. Com. Gr. p. 1094.

Θνητὸς πεφυκὼς μὴ εὐλαβοῦ τεθνηκέναι.
Λύπης δὲ πάσης γίνετ᾽ ἰατρὸς χρόνος.

Being born mortal, be not always watching the approach of death : time is the physician of every sorrow.

LIFE IS EVER CHANGING.

Fr. Com. Gr. p. 1094.

Εὐμετάβολός ἐστιν ἀνθρώπων βίος.

The life of man is ever changing.

EUPHRON.

EUPHRON, an Athenian comic poet of the middle comedy, some fragments of whose works have come down to us.

THE FOOL.

Fr. Com. Gr. p. 1130.

'Ο γὰρ τὸν ἴδιον οἰκονομῶν κακῶς βίον,
πῶς οὗτος ἂν σώσειε τῶν ἔξω τινά ;

For he who manages his own life badly, how is he likely to take proper care of what is external to himself ?

SHORTNESS OF LIFE.

Fr. Com. Gr. p. 1130.

Ὦ Ζεῦ, τί ποθ᾽ ἡμῖν δοὺς χρόνον τοῦ ζῆν βραχύν
πλέκειν ἀλύπως τοῦτον ἡμᾶς οὐκ ἐᾷς ;

Pray, Jupiter, when thou hast granted to us only a short span of life, why dost thou not allow us to pass it without sorrow ?

EURIPIDES.

BORN B.C. 481—DIED B.C. 406.

EURIPIDES, the celebrated tragic writer of Athens, son of Mnesarchus and Cleito, is said to have been born on the very day of the battle of Salamis, to which island his parents had been compelled to fly at the time that Athens was threatened by Xerxes. He was a pupil of Prodicus of Chios, and took lessons from the philosopher Anaxagoras. The persecutions which Anaxagoras underwent warned Euripides of the dangerous path he was pursuing, inducing him to renounce the study of philosophy, and direct his attention to the stage. This took place, it is said, in his eighteenth year, and in 455 B.C. he succeeded in gaining the third prize. Of all the plays which he wrote, only five, according to Varro, were reckoned worthy of being crowned ; but this fact may be explained by the violent spirit of rivalry and jealousy which seems to have prevailed at Athens at this time. In his domestic affairs he was by no means fortunate ; both his wives disgraced him by the irregularity of their lives ; and from this circumstance probably arose his violent hatred of the sex, the weakness of which he took every opportunity of ridiculing and exposing. His private grief became the butt of the comic writers of the day, and Aristophanes more particularly held him up to the ridicule of the public. It was no doubt in consequence of these incessant attacks that Euripides determined to leave Athens. He removed first to Magnesia, and thence to the court of Archelaus, King of Macedonia, who reigned from 413 to 399 B.C., and was then the beneficent patron of literature and science. By him he was received with all that respect to which his distinguished talents entitled him, and some say that he was appointed one of his principal ministers. Here he resided till his death (406 B.C.), which was as full of tragic circumstances as any story ever exhibited upon the stage. As he was strolling through a wood, a pack of the royal hounds attacked the poet, and tore him in pieces. His remains were removed to Pella by the king, and every honour was shown to his memory. The Athenians were now anxious to procure his ashes, but Archelaus refused to gratify those who had neglected the poet in his lifetime.

THE WORDS OF THE WISE.

Bacch. 266.

Ὅταν λάβῃ τις τῶν λόγων ἀνὴρ σοφὸς
καλὰς ἀφορμάς, οὐ μέγ' ἔργον εὖ λέγειν·

E 3

σὺ δ' εὔτροχον μὲν γλῶσσαν ὡς φρονῶν ἔχεις,
ἐν τοῖς λόγοισι δ' οὐκ ἔνεισί σοι φρένες.
Θρασὺς δὲ δυνατὸς καὶ λέγειν οἷός τ' ἀνὴρ
κακὸς πολίτης γίγνεται νοῦν οὐκ ἔχων.

When a wise man chooses a fit subject for his discourse, there is no difficulty in speaking well ; thou hast indeed a fluent tongue ; as if thou wert wisdom itself ; but thy words have not her power. A mighty man, when bold and able to speak, is a bad citizen if he lack discretion.

See (Lat.) Eloquence and loquacity.

The Two best Things among Men.
Bacch. 274.

Δύο γὰρ, ὦ νεανία,
τὰ πρῶτ' ἐν ἀνθρώποισι, Δημήτηρ θεὰ,
γῆ δ' ἐστίν· ὄνομα δ' ὁπότερον βούλει κάλει·
αὕτη μὲν ἐν ξηροῖσιν ἐκτρέφει βροτούς·
ὁ δ' ἦλθεν ἐπὶ τἀντίπαλον, ὁ Σεμέλης γόνος
βότρυος ὑγρὸν πῶμ' εὗρε κεἰσηνέγκατο
θνητοῖς, ὃ παύει τοὺς ταλαιπώρους βροτοὺς
λύπης, ὅταν πλησθῶσιν ἀμπέλου ῥοῆς,
ὕπνον τε, λήθην τῶν καθ' ἡμέραν κακῶν,
δίδωσιν, οὐδ' ἔστ' ἄλλο φάρμακον πόνων.

For, young man, there are two things of prime importance among men. Ceres, the goddess, she is the Earth, call her by what name thou wilt : she nourishes mortals with dry food. But he who is come is a match for her, the son of Semele : he has discovered the liquid drink of the grape, introducing it among mortals, causing the wretched to forget their sorrows, when they are filled with the stream of the vine, giving balmy sleep as an oblivion of the anxieties that beset man day by day, nor is there any other medicine that can cure the troubles of life.

See (Lat. Fr. Ger.) Wine.

Glory not in thy Wisdom.
Bacch. 309.

'Αλλ' ἐμοί, Πενθεῦ, πιθοῦ·
μὴ τὸ κράτος αὔχει δύναμιν ἀνθρώποις ἔχειν,
μηδ', ἢν δοκῇ μέν, ἡ δόξα σου νοσεῖ,
φρονεῖν δόκει τι.

But, Pentheus, be persuaded by me, boast not that thy imperial power has rule over men, nor even, if thou thinkest so, glory not in thy wisdom, for thy glorying is vain.

So Jeremiah (ix. 23 —"Thus saith the Lord, Let not the wise man glory in his wisdom, neither let the mighty man glory in his might, let not the rich man glory in his riches."

The Fool.
Bacch. 369.

Μῶρα γὰρ μῶρος λέγει.

For the fool speaks foolish things.

Pride before a Fall.
Bacch. 385.

'Αχαλίνων στομάτων
ἀνόμου τ' ἀφροσύνας
τὸ τέλος δυστυχία·
ὁ δὲ τᾶς ἡσυχίας
βίοτος καὶ τὸ φρονεῖν
ἀσάλευτόν τε μένει
καὶ συνέχει δώματα· πόρσω γὰρ ὅ,ιως
αἰθέρα ναίοντες ὁρῶ-
σιν τὰ βροτῶν οὐρανίδαι.
Τὸ σοφὸν δ' οὐ σοφία
τό τε μὴ θνητὰ φρονεῖν.
Βραχὺς αἰών· ἐπὶ τούτῳ
δέ τις ἂν μεγάλα διώκων
τὰ παρόντ' οὐχὶ φέροι.
Μαινομένων οἵδε τρόποι
καὶ κακοβούλων παρ' ἔμοιγε φωτῶν.

Misery is the end of unbridled mouths and lawless folly, but a quiet life accompanied by wisdom remains unmoved, and knits together families; for though the heavenly powers dwell in the far distance, inhabiting the air, they behold the deeds of men. But cleverness is not wisdom, nor yet the musing on things that belong not to this world. Life is short, and who pursuing great things in it would not enjoy the present? These are the manners of madmen and of the ill-disposed in my opinion.

So Matthew (v. 9)—"Blessed are the peacemakers: for they shall be called the children of God."

See (Lat.) Pride.

The Ignorant.
Bacch. 480.

Δόξει τις ἀμαθεῖ σοφὰ λέγων οὐκ εὖ φρονεῖν.

A person may seem to the ignorant, even though he speak with wisdom, to be foolish.

Be Angry and Sin not.
Bacch. 641.

Πρὸς σοφοῦ γὰρ ἀνδρὸς ἀσκεῖν σώφρον' εὐοργησίαν.

For it is the part of a wise man to practise moderation in passion. So Ephesians (iv. 26)—" Be ye angry, and sin not: let not the sun go down upon your wrath."

See (Lat.) Anger, control.

WINE AND LOVE.
Bacch. 773.

Οἴνου δὲ μηκέτ' ὄντος οὐκ ἔστιν Κύπρις,
οὐδ' ἄλλο τερπνὸν οὐδὲν ἀνθρώποις ἔτι.

For where there is not wine, love fails, and everything else pleasant to man.

THE DELIGHTS OF LIBERTY.
Bacch. 863.

'Αρ' ἐν παννυχίοις χοροῖς
θήσω ποτὲ λευκὸν
πόδ' ἀναβακχεύουσα, δέραν
εἰς αἰθέρα δροσερὸν
ῥίπτουσ', ὡς νεβρὸς χλοεραῖς
ἐμπαίζουσα λείμακος ἡδοναῖς
ἡνίκ' ἂν φοβερὸν φύγῃ
θήραμ' ἔξω φυλακᾶς
εὐπλέκτων ὑπὲρ ἀρκύων,
θωύσσων δὲ κυναγέτας
συντείνῃ δρόμημα κυνῶν·
μόχθοις τ' ὠκυδρόμοις τ' ἀέλ-
λαις θρώσκει πεδίον
παραποτάμιον, ἡδομένα
βροτῶν ἐρημίαις
σκιαροκόμου τ' ἐν ἔρνεσιν ὕλας.

Shall "I trip it on the light fantastic toe" the livelong night in honour of Bacchus, exposing my neck to the dewy air, frisking like a fawn in the delights of the green meadow, when it has escaped a fearful chase away from the well-woven nets (and the huntsman cheers and hurries on his dogs), and toilfully, like the swift storm, speeds along the plain that skirts the river, rejoicing in the solitude, away from men, and in the thickets of the dark-foliaged wood?

CRIME FOLLOWED BY PUNISHMENT.
Bacch. 882.

'Ορμᾶται μόλις, ἀλλ' ὅμως
πιστὸν τό γε θεῖον

σθένος· ἀπευθύνει δὲ βροτῶν
τούς τ' ἀγνωμοσύναν
τιμῶντας καὶ μὴ τὰ θεῶν
αὔξοντας σὺν μαινομένᾳ δόξᾳ.
Κρυπτεύουσι δὲ ποικίλως
δαρὸν χρόνου πόδα καὶ
θηρῶσιν τὸν ἄσεπτον. Οὐ
γὰρ κρεῖσσόν ποτε τῶν νόμων
γιγνώσκειν χρὴ καὶ μελετᾶν.
Κούφα γὰρ δαπάνα νομί-
ζειν ἰσχὺν τόδ' ἔχειν,
ὅ τι ποτ' ἄρα τὸ δαιμόνιον,
τό τ' ἐν χρόνῳ μακρῷ
νόμιμον ἀεὶ φύσει τε πεφυκός.

The power of the divinity is called forth slowly, but then it is
unerring, chastising those who insanely pay honour to folly, and
show not respect to the gods. The gods cunningly conceal the
long step of time, and hunt after the impious. For it is wrong
to determine or plan anything contrary to their laws. It is surely
a slight matter to regard what is divine as exercising this power,
and that what has been law for a long time is eternal, and the
dictate of nature.

See (Lat.) Crime. Prov. xiv. 29.

The Truly Happy.

Bacch. 902.

Εὐδαίμων μέν, ὃς ἐκ θαλάσσας
ἔφυγε χεῖμα, λιμένα δ' ἔκιχεν·
εὐδαίμων δ', ὃς ὕπερθε μόχθων
ἐγένεθ' ἕτερα δ' ἕτερυς ἕτερον
ὄλβῳ καὶ δυνάμει παρῆλθεν.
Μυρίαι δὲ μυρίοισιν
ἔτ' εἰσὶν ἐλπίδες· αἱ μὲν
τελευτῶσιν ἐν ὄλβῳ
βροτοῖς, αἱ δ' ἀπέβησαν·
τὸ δὲ κατ' ἦμαρ ὅτῳ βίοτος
εὐδαίμων, μακαρίζω.

Happy the man who has escaped the tempest-tossed sea, and
reached the port. Happy he who has got to the end of the
labours of life. Men surpass each other in riches and power.
Myriads of hopes gay-smiling rise before them. Some continue
with them to the close of life, some vanish away. The man who
enjoys the smiles of fortune day by day I pronounce to be happy.

See (Lat.) Happy man.

REVERENCE OF THE GODS.

Bacch. 1149.

Τὸ σωφρονεῖν δὲ καὶ σέβειν τὰ τῶν θεῶν
κάλλιστον· οἶμαί γ᾽ αὐτὸ καὶ σοφώτατον
θνητοῖσιν εἶναι χρῆμα τοῖσι χρωμένοις.

To be modest and pay reverence to the gods, this, I think, to
be the most honourable and wisest thing for mortals.

DIFFERENT FATES OF MEN.

Bacch. 1388.

Πολλαὶ μορφαὶ τῶν δαιμονίων,
πολλὰ δ᾽ ἀέλπτως κραίνουσι θεοί.
Καὶ τὰ δοκηθέντ᾽ οὐκ ἐτελέσθη,
τῶν δ᾽ ἀδοκήτων πόρον εὗρε θεός.
Τοιόνδ᾽ ἀπέβη τόδε πρᾶγμα.

Various are the fates sent by the gods, and much comes to us
that is unexpected; on the one hand, what we looked for is not
accomplished; and on the other, God finds a way to bring about
what we least expected. Such, too, is the end of this awful day.

DIGNITY IN THOSE OF NOBLE BIRTH.

Ion. 238.

Γενναιότης σοι, καὶ τρόπων τεκμήριον
τὸ σχῆμ᾽ ἔχεις τόδ᾽, ἥτις εἶ ποτ᾽, ὦ γύναι.
Γνοίη δ᾽ ἂν ὡς τὰ πολλά γ᾽ ἀνθρώπου πέρι
τὸ σχῆμ᾽ ἰδών τις εἰ πέφυκεν εὐγενής.

Nobleness is thine, and thy form, lady, is the reflection of thy
nature, whoever thou art. For by looking at external appearance
one is generally able to learn whether man is noble by nature.

THINGS AGAINST THE WILL OF THE GODS.

Ion. 378.

Ἂν γὰρ βίᾳ σπεύδωμεν ἀκόντων θεῶν,
ἀνόνητα κεκτήμεσθα τἀγάθ᾽, ὦ γύναι·
ἃ δ᾽ ἂν διδῶσ᾽ ἑκόντες, ὠφελούμεθα.

For such things as we strive after against the will of the gods,
we possess not as real goods, O lady ; but what they give us willingly, by these we are benefited.

EVILS OF LIFE.

Ion. 381.

Πολλαί γε πολλοῖς εἰσι συμφοραὶ βροτοῖς,
μορφαὶ δὲ διαφέρουσιν. *Ἐν δ' ἂν εὐτυχὲς*
μόλις ποτ' ἐξεύροι τις ἀνθρώπων βίῳ.

Countless are the woes of mortals, and various are their forms ;
but one single blessing for a lengthened period one will scarcely
find in the life of men.

See Eccles. i. 14.

A WIFE.

Ion. 398.

Τὰ γὰρ γυναικῶν δυσχερῆ πρὸς ἄρσενας,
κἀν ταῖς κακαῖσιν ἀγαθαὶ μεμιγμέναι
μισούμεθ'· οὕτω δυστυχεῖς πεφύκαμεν.

For woman's condition among men is full of ills ; for the good
women being mixed up with the bad, we are objects of hatred,
so wretched are we by nature.

THE BASE PUNISHED BY THE GODS.

Ion. 440.

Καὶ γὰρ ὅστις ἂν βροτῶν
κακὸς πεφύκῃ, ζημιοῦσιν οἱ θεοί.

For whosoever of mortals is of a base nature, him the gods
chastise.

THE CHILDLESS AND THOSE WITH CHILDREN CONTRASTED.

Ion. 472.

Ὑπερβαλλούσας γὰρ ἔχει
θνατοῖς εὐδαιμονίας
ἀκίνητον ἀφορμάν,
τέκνων οἷς ἂν καρποτρόφοι
λάμπωσιν ἐν θαλάμοις
πατρίοισι νεανίδες ἥβαι,
διαδέκτορα πλοῦτον
ὡς ἔχοντες ἐκ πατέρων
ἑτέροις ἐπὶ τέκνοις·
ἀλκά τε γὰρ ἐν κακοῖς
σύν τ' εὐτυχίαις φίλον,
δορί τε γᾷ πατρίᾳ φέρει
σωτήριον ἀλκάν.
Ἐμοὶ μὲν πλούτου τε πάρος
βασιλικῶν θαλάμων τ' εἶεν
τροφαὶ κήδειοι κεδνῶν τέκνων.

Τὸν ἄπαιδα δ' ἀποστυγῶ
βίον, ᾧ τε δοκεῖ, ψέγω·
μετὰ δὲ κτεάνων μετρίων βιοτὰι
εὔπαιδος ἐχοίμαν.

For there is a constant spring of surpassing happiness to mortals when handsome youths flourish in the paternal hall, with wealth to transmit in succession from sires to children ; for they are an ever-present aid in troubles, a joy in good fortune, and in war they bring help to their country with their spear. May the nurturing care of kind children be mine in preference to riches and alliances with kings. Childless life I abhor, and I blame him who approves of it. But with a competency of this world's goods may I have a noble offspring.

THINGS NEAR APPEAR DIFFERENT FROM THOSE AT A DISTANCE.

Ion. 585.

Οὐ ταὐτὸν εἶδος φαίνεται τῶν πραγμάτων
πρόσωθεν ὄντων ἐγγύθεν θ' ὁρωμένων.

The appearance of things does not appear the same when seen far off and close at hand.

RIVALS IN POLITICAL HONOURS.

Ion. 598.

Ὅσοι δὲ χρηστοὶ δυνάμενοί τ' εἶναι σοφοὶ
σιγῶσι κού σπεύδουσιν εἰς τὰ πράγματα,
γέλωτ' ἐν αὐτοῖς μωρίαν τε λήψομαι
οὐχ ἡσυχάζων ἐν πόλει φόβου πλέα.
Τῶν δ' ἂν λογίων τε χρωμένων τε τῇ πόλει
εἰς ἀξίωμα βὰς πλέον φρουρήσομαι
ψήφοισιν, οὕτω γὰρ τάδ' ὦ πάτερ, φιλεῖ·
οἵ τὰς πόλεις ἔχουσι κάξιώματα,
τοῖς ἀνθαμίλλοις εἰσὶ πολεμιώτατοι.

The good and wise lead a quiet life, and aim not at the honours of the state ; with them I shall incur ridicule, not living tranquilly in the midst of a city full of turmoil. Again, if I aspire to the dignity of those who direct the affairs of the nation, I shall be watched more closely, and subject to hostile votes ; for such is usual, my father ; those who possess influence are most inimical to those who are their rivals.

ROYAL AND HUMBLE LIFE CONTRASTED.

Ion. 621.

Τυραννίδος δὲ τῆς μάτην αἰνουμένης
τὸ μὲν πρόσωπον ἡδύ, τἀν δόμοισι δὲ

λυπηρά· τίς γὰρ μακάριος, τίς εὐτυχής,
ὅστις δεδοικὼς καὶ παραβλέπων βίαν
αἰῶνα τείνει ; δημότης ἂν εὐτυχὴς
ζῆν ἂν θέλοιμι μᾶλλον ἢ τύραννος ὤν,
ᾧ τοὺς πονηροὺς ἡδονὴ φίλους ἔχειν,
ἐσθλοὺς δὲ μισεῖ κατθανεῖν φοβούμενος.
Εἴποις ἂν ὡς ὁ χρυσὸς ἐκνικᾷ τάδε,
πλουτεῖν τε τερπνόν· οὐ φιλῶ ψόγους κλύειν
ἐν χερσὶ σώζων ὄλβον οὐδ' ἔχειν πόνους·
εἴη δ' ἔμοιγε μέτρια μὴ λυπουμένῳ.
Ἃ δ' ἐνθάδ' εἶχον ἀγάθ' ἄκουσόν μου, πάτερ·
τὴν φιλτάτην μὲν πρῶτον ἀνθρώπων σχολὴν
ὄχλον τε μέτριον· οὐδέ μ' ἐξέπληξ' ὁδοῦ
πονηρὸς οὐδείς· κεῖνο δ' οὐκ ἀνασχετὸν
εἴκειν ὁδοῦ χαλῶντα τοῖς κακίοσιν.
Θεῶν δ' ἐν εὐχαῖς ἢ λόγοισιν ἢ βροτῶν,
ὑπηρετῶν χαίρουσιν, οὐ γοωμένοις.
Καὶ τοὺς μὲν ἐξέπεμπον, οἱ δ' ἧκον ξένοι,
ὥσθ' ἡδὺς ἀεὶ καινὸς ὢν καινοῖσιν ἦν.
Ὁ δ' εὐκτὸν ἀνθρώποισι, κἂν ἄκουσιν ᾖ,
δίκαιον εἶναί μ' ὁ νόμος ἡ φύσις θ' ἅμα
παρεῖχε τῷ θεῷ. Ταῦτα συννοούμενος
κρείσσω νομίζω τἀνθάδ' ἢ τἀκεῖ, πάτερ.
Ἔα δ' ἔμ' αὐτοῦ ζῆν· ἴση γὰρ ἡ χάρις,
μεγάλοισι χαίρειν σμικρά θ' ἡδέως ἔχειν.

The outward aspect of vainly-praised sovereignty is indeed delightful, but its inward state is misery. For who can be happy, who can be blessed, dragging on a life full of terrors, and every moment in dread of violence? I would rather live happy in humble life than be a tyrant, forced to choose my friends from the wicked, and hating the good from fear of death. Thou wilt say, no doubt, that gold has sovereign power over such things, and that it is pleasant to be rich. I love not to hear reproach while watching over my riches, and to be subject to toils. What I wish for is a competency, unattended by pains. Now hear, my father, the advantages I have enjoyed in this place. First, indeed, leisure, which is most beloved by men, and no bustling crowd around; nor am I jostled from the path by a knave, for it is intolerable to be obliged to give way to some insolent wretch. I was ever employed in the worship of the gods or in the service of men, who were surrounded by the happy and not by the mourning. Some, indeed, I sent away, while other strangers came in their place, so that I was always joyful, being new with new faces. That which men should pray for, even if it be against their will, to be just before the gods, custom and nature together brought about in me. Taking these things into consideration, my father, I deem my lot better here than there. Suffer me, then, to live here, for there is equal pleasure to be got in humble life as in the palaces of the great.

A Friend.

Ion. 730.

Σὺν τοῖς φίλοις γὰρ ἡδὺ μὲν πράσσειν καλῶς·
ὃ μὴ γένοιτο δ', εἴ τι τυγχάνοι κακόν,
εἰς ὄμματ' εὔνου φωτὸς ἐμβλέψαι γλυκύ.

For it is pleasant to enjoy good fortune with one's friends ; but (avert it, Heaven !) if any ill befall, a friend's kind eye beams comfort.

The Designing and the Simple.

Ion. 832.

Οἴμοι, κακούργους ἄνδρας ὡς ἀεὶ στυγῶ,
οἳ συντιθέντες τἄδικ' εἶτα μηχαναῖς
κοσμοῦσι. Φαῦλον χρηστὸν ἂν λαβεῖν φίλον
θέλοιμι μᾶλλον ἢ κακὸν σοφώτερον.

Alas ! how I always hate ill-designing men, who, devising evil deeds, gild them over with artificial ornament. I would rather have an honest, simple friend, than one whose quicker wit is trained to evil.

The Slave.

Ion. 854.

Ἐν γάρ τι τοῖς δούλοισιν αἰσχύνην φέρει,
τοὔνομα· τὰ δ' ἄλλα πάντα τῶν ἐλευθέρων
οὐδεὶς κακίων δοῦλος, ὅστις ἐσθλὸς ᾖ.

For one thing brings shame to slaves—the name. In everything else the slave is nothing worse than the free-born, if he be virtuous.

A Step-mother.

Ion. 1025.

Ὀρθῶς· φθονεῖν γάρ φασι μητρυιὰς τέκνοις.

Thou hast rightly judged ; for it is a proverb that step-mothers bear hatred to their step-children.

Aid of Heaven.

Ion. 1615.

Ἀεί ποτε
χρόνια μὲν τὰ τῶν θεῶν πως, εἰς τέλος δ' οὐκ ἀσθενῆ.

Slow, indeed, at times, is the aid of the gods, but in the end not weak.

The Good

Ion. 1622.

"Οτῳ δ' ἐλαύνεται
συμφοραῖς οἶκος, σέβοντα δαίμονας θαρσεῖν χρεών
εἰς τέλος γὰρ οἱ μὲν ἐσθλοὶ τυγχάνουσιν ἀξίων,
οἱ κακοὶ δ', ὥσπερ πεφύκασ', οὔποτ' εὖ πράξειαν ἄν.

But him whose house is threatened with calamities it becomes to worship the gods and be of good cheer ; for in the end the good obtain their due, but the wicked, as they are naturally so, will never fare well.

A Step-mother.

Alcest. 309.

'Εχθρὰ γὰρ ἡ 'πιοῦσα μητρυιὰ τέκνοις
τοῖς πρόσθ', ἐχίδνης οὐδὲν ἠπιωιέρα.

For a step-mother is enemy to the children of the former marriage, no milder than a viper.

The Dead.

Alcest. 381.

Χρόνος μαλάξει σ'· οὐδέν ἐσθ' ὁ κατθανών.

Time will soften thy grief ; he that is dead is nothing.

Wisdom in the Good

Alcest. 602.

'Εν τοῖς ἀγαθοῖσι δὲ πάντ' ἔνεστιν σοφίας.

In the good there is all kind of wisdom.

So John (vii. 17)—"If any man will do his will, he shall know of the doctrine, whether it be of God."

The Pious.

Alcest. 604.

Πρὸς δ' ἐμᾷ ψυχᾷ θάρσος ἧσται
θεοσεβῆ φῶτα κεδνὰ πράξειν.

My heart is confident that the man who reveres the gods will fare prosperously.

So Psalm (cxi. 10)—"The fear of the Lord is the beginning of wisdom."

OLD MAN.
Alcest. 668.

Μάτην ἄρ' οἱ γέροντες εὔχονται θανεῖν,
γῆρας ψέγοντες καὶ μακρὸν χρόνον βίου.
Ἦν δ' ἐγγὺς ἔλθῃ θάνατος, οὐδεὶς βούλεται
θνήσκειν, τὸ γῆρας δ' οὐκέτ' ἔστ' αὐτοῖς βαρύ.

It is vain for old men praying for death, complaining of age and
the length of life, since if death come near, not one is willing to
die; then old age is no longer burdensome to them.

TO-MORROW UNCERTAIN.
Alcest. 780.

Τὰ θνητὰ πράγματ' οἶδας ἣν ἔχει φύσιν;
οἶμαι μὲν οὔ· πόθεν γάρ; ἀλλ' ἄκουέ μου.
Βροτοῖς ἅπασι κατθανεῖν ὀφείλεται,
κοὔκ ἔστι θνητῶν ὅστις ἐξεπίσταται
τὴν αὔριον μέλλουσαν εἰ βιώσεται·
τὸ τῆς τύχης γὰρ ἀφανὲς οἷ προβήσεται,
κἄστ' οὐ διδακτὸν οὐδ' ἀλίσκεται τέχνῃ.
Ταῦτ' οὖν ἀκούσας καὶ μαθὼν ἐμοῦ πάρα,
εὔφραινε σαυτόν, πῖνε, τὸν καθ' ἡμέραν
βίον λογίζου σόν, τὰ δ' ἄλλα τῆς τύχης.

Knowest thou of what nature mortal things are? I think not;
how shouldst thou? Death is a debt that all mortals must pay,
and there is not one of them who knows whether he shall see the
coming morrow; for what depends on fortune is uncertain how it
will turn out, and is not to be learned, neither is it to be caught by
art. Having, therefore, heard and learned these things from me,
be merry, drink, and regard the life granted to thee day by day as
thine own, but the rest to be Fortune's.

See (Lat. Gr.) Death; Time, fleetness of.

EFFECT OF WINE.
Alcest. 796.

Καὶ σάφ' οἶδ' ὀθούνεκα
τοῦ νῦν σκυθρωποῦ καὶ ξυνεστῶτος φρενῶν
μεθορμιεῖ σε πίτυλος ἐμπεσὼν σκύφου.
Ὄντας δὲ θνητοὺς θνητὰ καὶ φρονεῖν χρεών,
ὡς τοῖς γε σεμνοῖς καὶ συνωφρυωμένοις
ἅπασίν ἐστιν, ὡς γ' ἐμοὶ χρῆσθαι κριτῇ,
οὐ βίος ἀληθῶς ὁ βίος, ἀλλὰ συμφορά.

And well do I know that the trickling of the cup down thy
throat will change thee from thy present gloomy and pent state

of mind. Being mortals, we should think as mortals ; since to
all those who are morose and of sad countenance, if they take me
as judge at least, life is not truly life, but misery.

HUSBAND AND WIFE.
Med. 15.

Ἧπερ μεγίστη γίγνεται σωτηρία,
ὅταν γυνὴ πρὸς ἄνδρα μὴ διχοστατῇ·
νῦν δ᾽ ἐχθρὰ πάντα καὶ νοσεῖ τὰ φίλτατα.

This is the surest tie of conjugal happiness, when the wife is
not estranged from the husband. But everything here is at
variance, and the dearest ties are weakened.

YOUTH.
Med. 48.

Νέα γὰρ φροντὶς οὐκ ἀλγεῖν φιλεῖ.

For youth holds no society with grief.

EVERY ONE LOVES HIMSELF MORE THAN HIS NEIGHBOUR.
Med. 85.

Ἄρτι γιγνώσκεις τόδε,
ὡς πᾶς τις αὐτὸν τοῦ πέλας μᾶλλον φιλεῖ,
οἱ μὲν δικαίως, οἱ δὲ καὶ κέρδους χάριν.

Dost thou only now know this, that every one loves himself
more than his neighbour, some, indeed, with justice, but others
for the sake of gain?

So Philippians (ii. 21)—" For all seek their own."

See (Lat.) Self-love.

ROYAL AND HUMBLE LIFE.
Med. 105.

Δεινὰ τυράννων λήματα, καί πως
ὀλίγ᾽ ἀρχόμενοι πολλὰ κρατοῦντες
χαλεπῶς ὀργὰς μεταβάλλουσιν.
Τὸ γὰρ εἰθίσθαι ζῆν ἐπ᾽ ἴσοισιν
κρεῖσσον· ἐμοιγ᾽ οὖν, εἰ μὴ μεγάλως,
ὀχυρῶς γ᾽ εἴη καταγηράσκειν.
Τῶν γὰρ μετρίων πρῶτα μὲν εἰπεῖν
τοὔνομα νικᾷ, χρῆσθαί τε μακρῷ
λῷστα βροτοῖσιν· τὰ δ᾽ ὑπερβάλλοντ᾽
οὐδένα καιρὸν δύναται θνατοῖς·
μείζους δ᾽ ἄτας, ὅταν ὀργισθῇ
δαίμων, οἴκοις ἀπέδωκεν.

The acts of tyrants are terrible; being seldom controlled, in most things acting despotically, they lay aside with difficulty their passion. To be accustomed to humble life is far better; may it be my lot then to grow old, not in gorgeous state, but without danger. There is a protection in the very name of moderation, and to enjoy it is far the best for man. Towering greatness remains not long to mortals, and has often brought the greatest woes on families when the Deity is enraged.

MUSIC.
Med. 190.

Σκαιοὺς δὲ λέγων κούδέν τι σοφοὺς
τοὺς πρόσθε βροτοὺς οὐκ ἂν ἁμάρτοις,
οἵτινες ὕμνους ἐπὶ μὲν θαλίαις
ἐπί τ' εἰλαπίναις καὶ παρὰ δείπνοις
εὕροντο βίου τερπνὰς ἀκοάς·
στυγίους δὲ βροτῶν οὐδεὶς λύπας
εὕρετο μούσῃ καὶ πολυχόρδοις
ᾠδαῖς παύειν, ἐξ ὧν θάνατοι
δειναί τε τύχαι σφάλλουσι δόμους.
καίτοι τάδε μὲν κέρδος ἀκεῖσθαι
μολπαῖσι βροτούς· ἵνα δ' εὔδειπνοι
δαῖτες, τί μάτην τείνουσι βοάν;
τὸ παρὸν γὰρ ἔχει τέρψιν ἀφ' αὑτοῦ
δαιτὸς πλήρωμα βροτοῖσιν.

Thou wouldst not err in calling men of the olden time silly and in no way wise who invented songs for festivals, banquets, and suppers, delights that charm the ear; but no one has found out how to soothe with music and sweet symphony those bitter pangs by which death and sad misfortunes destroy families. And yet to assuage such griefs by music were wisdom. For when the banquet is spread, why raise the song? When the table is richly piled, it brings of itself a cheerfulness that wakes the heart to joy.

WOMAN.
Med. 230.

Πάντων δ' ὅσ' ἔστ' ἔμψυχα καὶ γνώμην ἔχει
γυναῖκές ἐσμεν ἀθλιώτατον φυτόν·
ἃς πρῶτα μὲν δεῖ χρημάτων ὑπερβολῇ
πόσιν πρίασθαι δεσπότην τε σώματος
λαβεῖν· κακοῦ γὰρ τοῦτό γ' ἄλγιον κακόν·
κἄν τῷδ' ἀγὼν μέγιστος, ἢ κακὸν λαβεῖν
ἢ χρηστόν. Οὐ γὰρ εὐκλεεῖς ἀπαλλαγαὶ
γυναιξίν, οὐδ' οἷόν τ' ἀνήνασθαι πόσιν.
Εἰς καινὰ δ' ἤθη καὶ νόμους ἀφιγμένην
δεῖ μάντιν εἶναι, μὴ μαθοῦσαν οἴκοθεν.

ὅτῳ μάλιστα χρήσεται συνευνέτῃ.
Κἂν μὲν τάδ' ἡμῖν ἐκπονουμέναισιν εὖ
πόσις ξυνοικῇ μὴ βίᾳ φέρων ζυγόν,
ζηλωτὸς αἰών· εἰ δὲ μή, θανεῖν χρεών.
'Ανὴρ δ' ὅταν τοῖς ἔνδον ἄχθηται ξυνών,
ἔξω μολὼν ἔπαυσε καρδίαν ἄσης,
ἢ πρὸς φίλον τιν' ἢ πρὸς ἥλικας τραπείς·
ἡμῖν δ' ἀνάγκη πρὸς μίαν ψυχὴν βλέπειν.
Λέγουσι δ' ἡμᾶς ὡς ἀκίνδυνον βίον
ζῶμεν κατ' οἴκους, οἱ δὲ μάρνανται δορί·
κακῶς φρονοῦντες· ὡς τρὶς ἂν παρ' ἀσπίδα
στῆναι θέλοιμ' ἂν μᾶλλον ἢ τεκεῖν ἅπαξ.

Of all beings who have life and sense, we women are most wretched. First of all, we must buy a husband with money, and receive in him a lord ; for this is a still greater ill than the former. And then the question is whether we receive a bad or good one. For divorces are not honourable to women, nor is it right to repudiate our husband. For coming to new tempers and new laws, we must be endowed with powers of prophecy if we can know what sort of yoke-fellow we shall have. But should a husband dwell with us, diligently engaged in the performance of our duties, who treats us with kindness, our lot is deserving of envy ; if not, death is to be preferred. If a man find aught unpleasing in his house, going abroad, he seeks relief among his compeers or friends. *We* must look for happiness to one only. Men say of us that we live a life of ease at home, while they are fighting with the spear. Misjudging men! thrice would I engage in fierce conflict than once suffer the pangs of childbirth.

A FIERY IS BETTER THAN A SULLEN SPIRIT.

Med. 319.

Γυνὴ γὰρ ὀξύθυμος, ὡς δ' αὔτως ἀνήρ,
ῥᾴων φυλάσσειν ἢ σιωπηλὸς σοφύς.

For a woman that is quick in anger, and a man too, can be more easily guarded against than one that is crafty and keeps silence.

EXILE.

Med. 462.

Πόλλ' ἐφέλκεται φυγὴ
κακὰ ξὺν αὐτῇ.

Exile draws many evils in its train.

IMPUDENCE.

Med. 472.

Ἡ μεγίστη τῶν ἐν ἀνθρώποις νόσων πασῶν ἀναίδεια.

The worst of all diseases among men is impudence.

THE WICKED.
Med. 516.

*Ω Ζεῦ, τί δὴ χρυσοῦ μὲν ὃς κίβδηλος ᾖ
τεκμήρι' ἀνθρώποισιν ὤπασας σαφῆ,
ἀνδρῶν δ' ὅτῳ χρὴ τὸν κακὸν διειδέναι,
οὐδεὶς χαρακτὴρ ἐμπέφυκε σώματι;

O Jove! why hast thou given us certain proofs to know adulterate gold, but stamped no mark, where it is most needed, on man's base metal?

THE POWER OF THE RHETORICIAN.
Med. 580.

Ἐμοὶ γὰρ ὅστις ἄδικος ὢν σοφὸς λέγειν
πέφυκε, πλείστην ζημίαν ὀφλισκάνει·
γλώσσῃ γὰρ αὐχῶν τἄδικ' εὖ περιστελεῖν,
τολμᾷ πανουργεῖν· ἔστι δ' οὐκ ἄγαν σοφός.

For, in my opinion, the unjust man, whose tongue is full of glozing rhetoric, merits the heaviest punishment. Vaunting that he can with his tongue gloze over injustice, he dares to act wickedly, yet he is not over-wise.

GIFTS OF A BAD MAN.
Med. 618.

Κακοῦ γὰρ ἀνδρὸς δῶρ' ὄνησιν οὐκ ἔχει.

The gifts
Of a bad man can bring no good with them.

TEMPERANCE.
Med. 636.

Σωφροσύνα,
δώρημα κάλλιστον θεῶν.

Temperance, the noblest gift of Heaven.

THE POWER OF GOLD.
Med. 964.

Πείθειν δῶρα καὶ θεοὺς λόγος·
χρυσὸς δὲ κρείσσων μυρίων λόγων βροτοῖς.

The saying is that gifts gain over even the gods; gold has greater power over men than ten thousand arguments.

See (Lat.) Gifts.

The Evils of Life must be Borne.

Med. 1018.

Κούφως φέρειν χρὴ θνητὸν ὄντα συμφοράς.

A mortal must bear calamities with meekness.

So Philippians (i. 23)—"For I am in a strait betwixt two, having a desire to depart, and to be with Christ ; which is far better : nevertheless to abide in the flesh is more needful for you."

"The Evil that I Would not, that I Do.'

Med. 1078.

Καὶ μανθάνω μὲν οἷα τολμήσω κακά·
θυμὸς δὲ κρείσσων τῶν ἐμῶν βουλευμάτων.

I know, indeed, the ills I am about to commit, but my inclination gets the better of me.

So Romans (vii. 14)—"For we know that the law is spiritual ; but I am carnal, sold under sin."

The Bachelor.

Med. 1090.

Καὶ φημι βροτῶν οἵτινές εἰσιν
πάμπαν ἄπειροι μηδ᾿ ἐφύτευσαν
παῖδας, προφέρειν εἰς εὐτυχίαν
τῶν γειναμένων.
οἱ μέν γ᾿ ἄτεκνοι δι᾿ ἀπειροσύνην
εἴθ᾿ ἡδὺ βροτοῖς εἴτ᾿ ἀνιαρὸν
παῖδες τελέθουσ᾿ οὐχὶ τυχόντες
πολλῶν μόχθων ἀπέχονται·
οἷσι δὲ τέκνων ἐστιν ἐν οἴκοις
γλυκερὸν βλάστημ᾿, ἐσορῶ μελέτῃ
κατατρυχομένους τὸν ἅπαντα χρόνον·
πρῶτον μὲν ὅπως θρέψωσι καλῶς,
βίοτόν θ᾿ ὁπόθεν λείψουσι τέκνοις·
ἔτι δ᾿ ἐκ τούτων εἴτ᾿ ἐπὶ φλαύροις
εἴτ᾿ ἐπὶ χρηστοῖς
μοχθοῦσι, τόδ᾿ ἐστὶν ἄδηλον.
Ἓν δὲ τὸ πάντων λοίσθιον ἤδη
πᾶσιν κατερῶ θνητοῖσι κακόν·
καὶ δὴ γὰρ ἅλις βίοτόν θ᾿ εὗρον,
σῶμά τ᾿ ἐς ἥβην ἤλυθε τέκνων
χρηστοί τ᾿ ἐγένοντ᾿· εἰ δὲ κυρήσει
δαίμων οὗτος, φροῦδος ἐς Ἅιδαν
Θάνατος προφέρων σώματα τέκνων,
πῶς οὖν λύει πρὸς τοῖς ἄλλοις

τήνδ' ἔτι λύπην ἀνιαροτάτην
παίδων ἕνεκεν
θνητοῖσι θεοὺς ἐπιβάλλειν ;

I maintain that those entirely free from wedlock, and who claim
no title to a father's name, surpass in happiness those who have
families ; those who are childless, not knowing whether children
give delight or anguish, are relieved of much misery. But those
who have a sweet blooming offspring of children in their house,
I see worn out with care the whole time ; first of all, how they
shall bring them up honourably, and how they shall leave what
may sustain them ; and besides, they know not whether they are
toiling for good or bad children. But one ill to mortals, the
worst of all, I now shall mention. For let us suppose that they
have got together a sufficient fortune, and that their children have
reached manhood, behaving honourably, yet if this should happen,
that death, bearing away their sons, vanishes with them to the
shades of darkness, I ask, why do the gods heap on mortals this
grief in addition, the most bitter of all, to drop the tears on the
lost son's untimely bier?

No Mortal Man is Happy.
Med. 1224.

Τὰ θνητὰ δ' οὐ νῦν πρῶτον ἡγοῦμαι σκιάν,
οὐδ' ἂν τρέσας εἴποιμι τοὺς σοφοὺς βροτῶν
δοκοῦντας εἶναι καὶ μεριμνητὰς λόγων
τούτους μεγίστην ζημίαν ὀφλισκάνειν·
θνητῶν γὰρ οὐδείς ἐστιν εὐδαίμων ἀνήρ·
ὄλβου δ' ἐπιρρυέντος εὐτυχέστερος
ἄλλου γένοιτ' ἂν ἄλλος, εὐδαίμων δ' ἂν οὔ.

But what belongs to mortals I do not now for the first time
deem to be a mere shadow, nor would I fear to say that those who
boast most of their wisdom and acquired knowledge, stray widest
in the paths of folly. No mortal is happy ; if the tide of wealth
flow in upon him, one may be more fortunate than another, more
happy he cannot be.

The Restlessness of the Love-sick.
Hipp. 177.

Ὦ κακὰ θνητῶν στυγεραί τε νόσοι·
Τί σ' ἐγὼ δράσω ; τί δὲ μὴ δράσω ;
τόδε σοι φέγγος, λαμπρὸς ὅδ' αἰθήρ·
ἔξω δὲ δόμων ἤδη νοσερᾶς
δέμνια κοίτης.
δεῦρο γὰρ ἐλθεῖν πᾶν ἔπος ἦν σοι·
τάχα δ' εἰς θαλάμους σπεύσεις τὸ πάλιν.

Ταχὺ γὰρ σφάλλει κοὐδενὶ χαίρεις,
οὐδέ σ' ἀρέσκει τὸ παρόν, τὸ δ' ἀπὸν
φίλτερον ἡγεῖ.
Κρεῖσσον δὲ νοσεῖν ἢ θεραπεύειν·
τὸ μὲν ἐστιν ἁπλοῦν, τῷ δὲ συνάπτει
λύπη τε φρενῶν χερσίν τε πόνος.
Πᾶς δ' ὀδυνηρὸς βίος ἀνθρώπων,
κοὐκ ἔστι πόνων ἀνάπαυσις·
ἀλλ' ὅ τι τοῦ ζῆν φίλτερον ἄλλο
σκότος ἀμπίσχων κρύπτει νεφέλαις.
δυσέρωτες δὴ φαινόμεθ' ὄντες
τοῦδ', ὅτι τοῦτο στίλβει κατὰ γῆν,
δι' ἀπειροσύνην ἄλλου βιότου
κοὐκ ἀπόδειξιν τῶν ὑπὸ γαίας·
μύθοις δ' ἄλλως φερόμεσθα.

Alas! the evils of mortals and their hateful diseases! What shall I do for thee? what not? Here *is* the bright light of day, here the clear air; and now thy couch on which thou liest sick is out of the house; for every word thou spokest was to bring thee hither; but soon thou wilt be in a hurry to return back to thy chamber; thou art soon changed, and rejoice in nothing; nothing present pleases, thou reckonest what is not present as more agreeable. It is better to be sick than to tend the sick: the one is a simple ill, but with the other is joined both pain of mind and toil of body. The whole life of men is full of pain and trouble, knows no rest. But whatever else there is more precious than life, darkness hangs round it, concealing it in clouds; hence we appear to dote on this present state, because it gilds the earth, for we know nothing of our future life, and cannot discover aught of the realms below; but all is wrapped in perplexing fables.

A plague on the whimsies of sickly folk:
　　What am I to do? what not?
　　Why, here's the fair sky,
　　And here you lie,
　　With your couch in a sunny spot.
For this you were puling, whenever you spoke,
　　Craving to lie outside,
　　And now you'll be sure not to bide;
You won't be here for an hour—
You'll want to be back to your bower;
Longing and never enjoying,
　　Shifting from yea to nay;
For all that you taste is cloying,
　　And sweet is the far away.
'Tis bad to be sick, but worse
To have to sit by and nurse;
For that is single, but this is double,—
The mind in pain, and the hands in trouble.

The life men live is a weary coil ;
There is no rest from woe and toil :
And if there's aught, elsewhere, more dear
Than drawing breath as we do here,
That darkness holds
In black inextricable folds.
Love-sick it seems are we
Of this, whate'er it be,
That gleams upon the earth,
Because that second birth,
That other life, no man hath tried ;
What lies below
No god will show,
And we, because the truth's denied,
Drift upon idle fables to and fro.
—From THACKERAY'S "Anthologia Græc., Fr. 9."

See (Lat. Gr.) Future.

SICKNESS OF THE HEART.
Hipp. 261.

Βιότου δ' ἀτρεκεῖς ἐπιτηδεύσεις
φασὶ σφάλλειν πλέον ἢ τέρπειν
τῇ θ' ὑγιείᾳ μᾶλλον πολεμεῖν.
Οὕτω τὸ λίαν ἧσσον ἐπαινῶ
τοῦ μηδὲν ἄγαν·
καὶ ξυμφήσουσι σοφοί μοι.

The cares of life, they say, if carried too far, bring more of pain
than pleasure, and war against the health. Thus I praise less
what is in extreme than the sentiment of "Nothing in excess,"
and the wise will agree with me.

See (Lat.) Excess.

PURE HANDS BUT IMPURE THOUGHTS.
Hipp. 317.

Χεῖρες μὲν ἀγναί, φρὴν δ' ἔχει μίασμά τι.

My hands are clean, but my heart has somewhat of impurity,
So Romans (xiii. 9)—" Thou shalt not covet."

WE KNOW THE GOOD BUT DO IT NOT.
Hipp. 379.

Τὰ χρήστ' ἐπιστάμεσθα καὶ γιγνώσκομεν,
οὐκ ἐκπονοῦμεν δ' οἱ μὲν ἀργίας ὕπο,
οἱ δ' ἡδονὴν προθέντες ἀντὶ τοῦ καλοῦ
ἄλλην τιν'. Εἰσὶ δ' ἡδοναὶ πολλαὶ βίου,

μακραί τε λέσχαι καὶ σχολή, τερπνὸν κακόν,
αἰδώς τε. Δισσαὶ δ' εἰσίν· ἡ μὲν οὐ κακή,
ἡ δ' ἄχθος εἴκων. Εἰ δ' ὁ καιρὸς ἦν σαφής,
οὐκ ἂν δύ' ἤστην ταῦτ' ἔχοντε γράμματα.

What is good we understand and know, but practise not, some from sloth, and others preferring some other pleasure to what is right. For there are many pleasures in life—lengthened hours of frivolous conversation, indolence, a pleasing ill, and shame; but there are two, the one indeed not base, but the other, the weight that pulls down houses; but if the occasion in which each is used were clear, the two things would not have the same letters.

See (Lat.) Evil that I would not. Rom. vii. 19.

The Influence of High Rank.

Hipp. 411.

Ὅταν γὰρ αἰσχρὰ τοῖσιν ἐσθλοῖσιν δοκῇ,
ἦ κάρτα δόξει τοῖς κακοῖς εἶναι καλά.

For when base deeds appear right to those of highest rank, all below them esteem them as objects of honest imitation.

A Parent's Misdeeds.

Hipp. 424.

Δουλοῖ γὰρ ἄνδρα, κἂν θρασύσπλαγχνός τις ᾖ,
ὅταν ξυνειδῇ μητρὸς ἢ πατρὸς κακά.
Μόνον δὲ τοῦτό φασ' ἁμιλλᾶσθαι βίῳ,
γνώμην δικαίαν κἀγαθήν, ὅτῳ παρῇ.
Κακοὺς δὲ θνητῶν ἐξέφην', ὅταν τύχῃ,
προθεὶς κάτοπτρον ὥστε παρθένῳ νέᾳ
χρόνος. Παρ' οἷσι μήποτ' ὀφθείην ἐγώ.

For it enslaves a man, though he be valiant-hearted, when he is conscious of a mother's or a father's misdeeds. This alone, an honest and good name, to whomsoever it belongs, possesses a worth excelling life; it is time, when it so chances, that shows the bad, as a mirror reflects a virgin's fair face; never among such may I be seen.

Pride.

Hipp. 474.

Οὐ γὰρ ἄλλο πλὴν ὕβρις
τάδ' ἐστί, κρείσσω δαιμόνων εἶναι θέλειν.

For this is nothing else than pride to wish to be superior, to be gods.

So Proverbs (xvi. 3)—"Every one that is proud in heart is an abomination to the Lord."

FLATTERY.

Hipp. 486.

Τοῦτ᾽ ἔσθ᾽ ὃ θνητῶν εὖ πόλεις οἰκουμένας
δόμους τ᾽ ἀπόλλυσ᾽, οἱ καλοὶ λίαν λόγοι.
Οὐ γάρ τι τοῖσιν ὠσὶ τερπνὰ χρὴ λέγειν,
ἀλλ᾽ ἐξ ὅτου τις εὐκλεὴς γενήσεται.

It is this that ruins many a well-built city and houses—thin
glozing speech. We want not words that charm the ear, but what
excites to virtuous deeds.

DECEIT RECOMMENDED.

Hipp. 612.

Ἡ γλῶσσ᾽ ὀμώμοχ᾽, ἡ δὲ φρὴν ἀνώμοτος.

My tongue indeed hath sworn, but not my mind.

WOMAN.

Hipp. 627.

Τούτῳ δὲ δῆλον ὡς γυνὴ κακὸν μέγα·
προσθεὶς γὰρ ὁ σπείρας τε κἀκθρέψας πατὴρ
φερνὰς ἀπώκισ᾽, ὡς ἀπαλλαχθῇ κακοῦ·
ὁ δ᾽ αὖ λαβὼν ἀτηρὸν εἰς δόμους φυτὸν
γέγηθε κόσμον προστιθεὶς ἀγάλματι
καλὸν κακίστῳ καὶ πέπλοισιν ἐκπονεῖ
δύστηνος, ὄλβον δωμάτων ὑπεξελών.
Ἔχει δ᾽ ἀνάγκην, ὥστε κηδεύσας καλοῖς
γαμβροῖσι χαίρων σώζεται πικρὸν λέχος,
ἢ χρηστὰ λέκτρα, πενθεροὺς δ᾽ ἀνωφελεῖς
λαβὼν πιέζει τἀγαθῷ τὸ δυστυχές.
Ῥᾷστον δ᾽, ὅτῳ τὸ μηδέν, ἀλλ᾽ ἀνωφελὴς
εὐηθίᾳ κατ᾽ οἶκον ἵδρυται γυνή.
Σοφὴν δὲ μισῶ· μὴ γὰρ ἔν γ᾽ ἐμοῖς δόμοις
εἴη φρονοῦσα πλεῖον ἢ γυναῖκα χρή.
Τὸ γὰρ κακοῦργον μᾶλλον ἐντίκτει Κύπρις
ἐν ταῖς σοφαῖσιν· ἡ δ᾽ ἀμήχανος γυνὴ
γνώμῃ βραχείᾳ μωρίαν ἀφῃρέθη.

By this, too, it is evident that woman is a great evil; for the
father, who begot and brought her up, gives her a dowry and
sends her away, to be rid of the evil. But the husband, on the
other hand, when he has received the bane into his house, rejoices,
and puts splendid ornaments on the vile image, tricking her out
with robes, unhappy man! exhausting all the riches of his house
upon her. But he makes a virtue of necessity, for, having allied
himself to noble kinsmen, he retains with seeming joy his uneasy
bed, or, if he has received a good bride, but worthless parents-in-

law, he forgets the evil in consideration of the good. Happier is he who leads to his house a plain, gentle-hearted, simple wife. I hate the knowing dame ; may there not be in my house one more wise than woman ought to be. For Venus with ease engenders wiles in these knowing dames ; but a woman of simple capacity, by reason of her small understanding, is removed from folly.

WE JUDGE BY THE EVENT.

Hipp. 700.

Εἰ δ' εὖ γ' ἔπραξα, κάρτ' ἂν ἐν σοφοῖσιν ἦν·
πρὸς τὰς τύχας γὰρ τὰς φρένας κεκτήμεθα.

If I had been successful, I would have assuredly been ranked among the wise ; for our reputation for wisdom depends much on our success.

THE FOOL.

Hipp. 916.

Ὦ πόλλ' ἁμαρτάνοντες ἄνθρωποι μάτην,
τί δὴ τέχνας μὲν μυρίας διδάσκετε
καὶ πάντα μηχανᾶσθε κἀξευρίσκετε,
ἓν δ' οὐκ ἐπίστασθ' οὐδ' ἐθηράσασθέ πω,
φρονεῖν διδάσκειν οἷσιν οὐκ ἔνεστι νοῦς ;

O men erring in many things ! why do ye teach ten thousand arts, contriving and inventing everything? but one thing you know not, nor yet have searched out, to teach that man wisdom who is void of sense.

THE DEMAGOGUE.

Hipp. 988.

Οἱ γὰρ ἐν σοφοῖς
φαῦλοι παρ' ὄχλῳ μουσικώτεροι λέγειν.

For those who are worthless among the wise are best fitted to charm the rabble.

EXILE.

Hipp. 1047.

Ταχὺς γὰρ Ἅιδης ῥᾷστος ἀνδρὶ δυστυχεῖ,
ἀλλ' ἐκ πατρῴας φυγὰς ἀλητεύων χθονὸς
ξένην ἐπ' αἶαν λυπρὸν ἀντλήσεις βίον·
μισθὸς γὰρ οὗτός ἐστιν ἀνδρὶ δυσσεβεῖ.

For a speedy death is best to the wretched ; but wandering an exile from thy fatherland, thou shalt drag out a life of bitterness; for this is the reward for the impious.

THE RIGHTEOUS AND THE GUILTY.

Hipp. 1339.

Τοὺς γὰρ εὐσεβεῖς θεοὶ
θνῄσκοντας οὐ χαίρουσι· τούς γε μὲν κακοὺς
αὐτοῖς τέκνοισι καὶ δόμοις ἐξόλλυμεν.

For gods rejoice not when the pious die ; the wicked, however, with their children and houses, we utterly destroy.

THE GREAT.

Hipp. 1465.

Τῶν γὰρ μεγάλων ἀξιοπενθεῖς
φῆμαι μᾶλλον κατέχουσιν.

For the sad stories of the great make a deep impression.

THE ENMITY OF RELATIONS IS DREADFUL.

Phœn. 374.

Ὡς δεινὸν ἔχθρα, μῆτερ, οἰκείων φίλων
καὶ δυσλύτους ἔχουσα τὰς διαλλαγάς.

How dreadful, mother, is the enmity of relations, and how difficult a reconciliation.

BEAR WITH PATIENCE THE CALAMITIES OF LIFE.

Phœn. 382.

Δεῖ φέρειν τὰ τῶν θεῶν.

We ought to submit to the inflictions of the gods.

So 2 Corinthians (vi. 4)—" But in all things approving ourselves as the ministers of God, in much patience."

RICH HAVINGS WIN RESPECT.

Phœn. 438.

Πάλαι μὲν οὖν ὑμνηθέν, ἀλλ' ὅμως ἐρῶ·
τὰ χρήματ' ἀνθρώποισι τιμιώτατα
δύναμίν τε πλείστην τῶν ἐν ἀνθρώποις ἔχει.

It is a proverb long ago sung, but which I shall nevertheless repeat, " Wealth is most honoured among men, and brings to them the greatest power."

PRECIPITATE HASTE.

Phœn. 452.

Οὔτοι τὸ ταχὺ τὴν δίκην ἔχει·
βραδεῖς δὲ μῦθοι πλεῖστον ἀνύουσιν σοφόν.

Precipitate haste leads to injustice, but slowly-matured counsels
bring forth deeds of wisdom.

How a Reconciliation ought to be Brought about.

Phœn. 461.

Ὅταν φίλος τις ἀνδρὶ θυμωθεὶς φίλῳ,
εἰς ἓν συνελθὼν ὄμματ' ὄμμασιν διδῷ,
ἐφ' οἷσιν ἥκει, ταῦτα χρὴ μόνον σκοπεῖν,
κακῶν δὲ τῶν πρὶν μηδενὸς μνείαν ἔχειν.

When a friend is angry with his friend, let him meet him face
to face, and fix his eyes on his friend's eyes, remembering only the
object for which he is come, and forgetting all former grievances.

If all Judged alike, there would be no Disputes.

Phœn. 499.

Εἰ πᾶσι ταὐτὸν καλὸν ἔφυ σοφόν θ' ἅμα,
οὐκ ἦν ἂν ἀμφίλεκτος ἀνθρώποις ἔρις·
νῦν δ' οὔθ' ὅμοιον οὐδὲν οὔτ' ἴσον βροτοῖς,
πλὴν ὀνομάσαι, τὸ δ' ἔργον οὐκ ἔστιν τόδε.

If the same thing were judged honourable alike by all, and also
wise, no contest or debate would arise among men ; but now
nothing is the same or like except the names ; each gives his own
meaning to them.

Ambition.

Phœn. 531.

Τί τῆς κακίστης δαιμόνων ἐφίεσαι
φιλοτιμίας, παῖ ; μὴ σύ γ'· ἄδικος ἡ θεός·
πολλοὺς δ' ἐς οἴκους καὶ πόλεις εὐδαίμονας
εἰσῆλθε κἀξῆλθ' ἐπ' ὀλέθρῳ τῶν χρωμένων·
ἐφ' ᾗ σὺ μαίνει· κεῖνο κάλλιον, τέκνον,
ἰσότητα τιμᾶν, ἢ φίλους ἀεὶ φίλοις
πόλεις τε πόλεσι συμμάχους τε συμμάχοις
συνδεῖ· τὸ γὰρ ἴσον νόμιμον ἀνθρώποις ἔφυ,
τῷ πλέονι δ' ἀεὶ πολέμιον καθίσταται
τοὐλασσον ἐχθρᾶς θ' ἡμέρας κατάρχεται.
Καὶ γὰρ μέτρ' ἀνθρώποισι καὶ μέρη σταθμῶν
ἰσότης ἔταξε κἀριθμὸν διώρισε,
νυκτός τ' ἀφεγγὲς βλέφαρον ἡλίου τε φῶς
ἴσον βαδίζει τὸν ἐνιαύσιον κύκλον,
κοὐδέτερον αὐτοῖν φθόνον ἔχει νικώμενον.
εἶθ' ἥλιος μὲν νύξ τε δουλεύει βροτοῖς,
σὺ δ' οὐκ ἀνέξει δωμάτων ἔχων ἴσον,
καὶ τῷδ' ἀπονέμειν ; κᾆτα ποῦ 'στιν ἡ δίκη ;

F

τί τὴν τυραννίδ᾽, ἀδικίαν εὐδαίμονα,
τιμᾷς ὑπέρφευ καὶ μέγ᾽ ἥγησαι τόδε ;
περιβλέπεσθαι τίμιον ; κενὸν μὲν οὖν.
῞Η πολλὰ μοχθεῖν πόλλ᾽ ἔχων ἐν δώμασι
βούλει ; τί δ᾽ ἔστι τὸ πλέον ; ὄνομ᾽ ἔχει μόνον
ἐπεὶ τά γ᾽ ἀρκοῦνθ᾽ ἱκανὰ τοῖς γε σώφροσιν.
Οὗτοι τὰ χρήματ᾽ ἴδια κέκτηνται βροτοί,
τὰ τῶν θεῶν δ᾽ ἔχοντες ἐπιμελούμεθα·
ὅταν δὲ χρῄζωσ᾽, αὖτ᾽ ἀφαιροῦνται πάλιν.

Why, my child, dost thou court ambition, the most baneful of deities? Do it not, she is an unjust goddess. For often hath she entered into houses and flourishing cities, and issued forth again, bringing destruction on those who welcomed her. Of such an one thou art madly enamoured. My child, it is nobler to pay honour to equality, which ever knits friends to friends, states to states, and allies to allies ; for equality is sanctioned both by nature and by human laws. Whereas the less is always at enmity with the greater, and hence springs the day of hatred. For it was equality that established measures among men, and weights and numbers. The dark eye of night and the light of the sun equally walk their yearly round, and neither of them being inferior, envies the other. Thus the sun and the night equally serve mortals, and wilt thou not brook equality and give up his share to him ? Then, where is justice? Why dost thou honour so extravagantly the royal state —a prosperous injustice—and think so highly of her ? To be conspicuous?—a mere empty glory. Or wouldst thou labour to have thy house full of riches? And what is this abundance? 'tis nothing but a name, since what is sufficient is abundance to the wise. Man enjoys his stores, not as his own, but as the gifts of the gods, who, when they choose, again resume them.

So Proverbs (xxiii. 5)—"Wilt thou set thine eyes upon that which is not ? for riches certainly make themselves wings ; they fly away as an eagle toward heaven."

The Necessity of Fate.
Phœn. 1763.

Τὰς γὰρ ἐκ θεῶν ἀνάγκας θνητὸν ὄντα δεῖ φέρειν.

For a mortal must endure the necessity of fate proceeding from the gods.

The Rich and the Poor
Supp. 176.

Σοφὸν δὲ πενίαν τ᾽ εἰσορᾶν τὸν ὄλβιον,
πένητά τ᾽ εἰς τοὺς πλουσίους ἀποβλέπειν
ζηλοῦνθ᾽, ἵν᾽ αὐτὸν χρημάτων ἔρως ἔχῃ,
τά τ᾽ οἰκτρὰ τοὺς μὴ δυστυχεῖς δεδορκέναι.

It is good for the prosperous to cast their eye on the poor, and
for the poor to look upward to the rich with a feeling of rivalry,
that the desire of wealth may spur on the one, and the high fortune of the other may fear a sad change.

THE BENEFICENCE OF THE DEITY.

Supp. 195.

"Αλλοισι δὴ 'πόνησ' ἀμιλληθεὶς λόγῳ
τοῖφδ'. "Ελεξε γάρ τις ὡς τὰ χείρονα
πλείω βροτοῖσίν ἐστι τῶν ἀμεινόνων.
'Εγὼ δὲ τούτοις ἀντίαν γνώμην ἔχω,
πλείω τὰ χρηστὰ τῶν κακῶν εἶναι βροτοῖς.
εἰ μὴ γὰρ ἦν τόδ', οὐκ ἂν ἦμεν ἐν φάει.
Αἰνῶ δ' ὃς ἡμῖν βίοτον ἐκ πεφυρμένου
καὶ θηριώδους θεῶν διεσταθμήσατο,
πρῶτον μὲν ἐνθεὶς σύνεσιν, εἶτα δ' ἄγγελον
γλῶσσαν λόγων δούς, ὡς γεγωνίσκειν ὅπ♠,
τροφήν τε καρποῦ τῇ τροφῇ τ' ἀπ' οὐρανοῦ
σταγόνας ὑδρηλάς, ὡς τά γ' ἐκ γαίας τρέφῃ
ἄρδῃ τε νηδύν· πρὸς δὲ τοῖσδε χείματος
προβλήματ', αἶθόν τ' ἐξαμύνασθαι θεοῦ,
πόντου τε ναυστολήμαθ', ὡς διαλλαγὰς
ἔχοιμεν ἀλλήλοισιν ὧν πένοιτο γῆ.

With others, indeed, I have disputed the question : for some
assert that the ills of life outweigh the good to man. But my
opinion is the opposite, I believe that blessings are more abundant ; for, if it were not so, we should not enjoy the light of life.
The Being who called us forth from foul and savage life I thank,
enduing us with reason, and then giving us the tongue as the
messenger of words, so as to distinguish speech ; the growth of
fruits he gave, and for that growth the heaven-descending rain,
that it might nourish the fruits of the earth and sustain the
stomach ; besides, he invented coverings against the cold of winter, and to ward off the burning heat of the sun, and the sailing
over the sea, that we might exchange with each other the fruits
which each wants.

See St Paul's speech at Lystra (Acts xiv. 17)—" He left not Himself without witness, in that He did good, and gave us rain from heaven, and fruitful
seasons, filling our hearts with food and gladness." See also Psalm (civ.)
throughout.

THE INNOCENT INVOLVED WITH THE GUILTY.

Supp. 226.

Κοινὰς γὰρ ὁ θεὸς τὰς τύχας ἡγούμενος
τοῖς τοῦ νοσοῦντος πήμασιν διώλεσε
τὸν οὐ νοσοῦντα κοὐδὲν ἠδικηκότα.

For the Deity, deeming fortune the same to all, is wont to involve with him that is guilty the man that is innocent and has done no evil.

THERE ARE THREE CLASSES IN EACH STATE.

Supp. 238.

Τρεῖς γὰρ πολιτῶν μερίδες· οἱ μὲν ὄλβιοι
ἀνωφελεῖς τε πλειόνων τ' ἐρῶσ' ἀεί.
οἱ δ' οὐκ ἔχοντες καὶ σπανίζοντες βίου
δεινοί, νέμοντες τῷ φθόνῳ πλεῖον μέρος,
εἰς τοὺς ἔχοντας κέντρ' ἀφιᾶσιν κακά,
γλώσσαις πονηρῶν προστατῶν φηλούμενοι·
τριῶν δὲ μοιρῶν ἡ 'ν μέσῳ σώζει πόλεις,
κόσμον φυλάσσουσ' ὅντιν' ἂν τάξῃ πόλις.

There are three classes of citizens ; some are rich, listless, and yet ever craving for more ; others, having nothing, and short of the means of life, are clamorous, much addicted to envy, aiming their bitter shafts against the rich, and led away by the tongues of evil leaders.   Betwixt these extremes there are those who save the state, guarding the laws which the state may appoint.

NO ONE HAPPY TO THE END OF LIFE.

Supp. 271.

Τῶν γὰρ ἐν βροτοῖς
οὐκ ἔστιν οὐδὲν διὰ τέλους εὐδαιμονοῦν.

For in regard to the affairs of mortals, there is nothing happy throughout.

THE DUTY OF A SON TO HIS PARENTS.

Supp. 361.

Τοῖς τεκοῦσι γὰρ
δύστηνος, ὅστις μὴ ἀντιδουλεύει τέκνων,
κάλλιστον ἔρανον· δοὺς γὰρ ἀντιλάξυται
παίδων παρ' αὑτοῦ τοιάδ', ἂν τοκεῦσι δῷ.

Unhappy the child who does not help his parents, a most honourable service ; for he receives back from his children what he has bestowed on his parents.

THE DEMAGOGUE.

Supp. 410.

Οὐδ' ἔστιν αὐτὴν ὅστις ἐκχαυνῶν λόγοις
πρὸς κέρδος ἴδιον ἄλλος ἄλλοσε στρέφει.

Ο δ' αὐτίχ' ἡδύς καὶ διδοὺς πολλὴν χάριν
εἰσαῦθις ἔβλαψ', εἶτα διαβολαῖς νέαις
κλέψας τὰ πρόσθε σφάλματ' ἐξέδυ δίκης.
*Ἄλλως τε πῶς ἄν μὴ διορθεύων λόγους
ὀρθῶς δύναιτ' ἄν δῆμος εὐθύνειν πόλιν ;
ὁ γὰρ χρόνος μάθησιν ἀντὶ τοῦ τάχους
κρείσσω δίδωσι, γαπόνος δ' ἀνὴρ πένης
εἰ καὶ γένοιτο μὴ ἀμαθής, ἔργων ὕπο
οὐκ ἄν δύναιτο πρὸς τὰ κοίν' ἀποβλέπειν.
Ἡ δὴ νοσῶδες τοῦτο τοῖς ἀμείνοσιν,
ὅταν πονηρὸς ἀξίωμ' ἀνὴρ ἔχῃ
γλώσσῃ κατασχὼν δῆμον, οὐδὲν ὤν τὸ πρίν.

We have not there the inflated demagogue, who, puffing the people up with words, turns them as interest prompts him. For he that is pleasant, and winds himself into their hearts to-day, offends to-morrow ; then, with fresh calumnies cloaking his former errors, he escapes from justice. And then how can a people rightly guide the city who do not examine minutely the reasons that are brought forward ? For time gives wisdom superior to imprudent haste. But a poor labourer of the soil, even if he were not unschooled in knowledge, cannot, from his very employment, be able to look to the common weal. Surely ill fares it with the better ranks when those of low degree hold dignity, "wielding at will the fierce democracy," rising from base obscurity.

See (Lat.) Demagogues ; multitude.

"The Land where, girt with Friends or Foes, A Man may Speak the Thing he Will."

Supp. 429.

Οὐδὲν τυράννου δυσμενέστερον πόλει,
ὅπου τὸ μὲν πρώτιστον οὐκ εἰσὶν νόμοι
κοινοί, κρατεῖ δ' εἷς τὸν νόμον κεκτημένος
αὐτὸς παρ' αὐτῷ, καὶ τόδ' οὐκέτ' ἔστ' ἴσον.
Γεγραμμένων δὲ τῶν νόμων ὅ τ' ἀσθενὴς
ὁ πλούσιός τε τὴν δίκην ἴσην ἔχει,
ἔστιν δ' ἐνισπεῖν τοῖσιν ἀσθενεστέροις
τὸν εὐτυχοῦντα ταῦθ', ὅταν κλύῃ κακῶς,
νικᾷ δ' ὁ μείων τὸν μέγαν δίκαι' ἔχων.
Τοὐλεύθερον δ' ἐκεῖνο· τίς θέλει πόλει
χρηστόν τι βούλευμ' εἰς μέσον φέρειν ἔχων ;
καὶ ταῦθ' ὁ χρῄζων λαμπρός ἐσθ', ὁ μὴ θέλων
σιγᾷ. Τί τούτων ἔστ' ἰσαίτερον πόλει ;
καὶ μὴν ὅπου γε δῆμος αὐθέντης χθονός,
ὑποῦσιν ἀστοῖς ἤδεται νεανίαις·
ἀνὴρ δὲ βασιλεὺς ἐχθρὸν ἡγεῖται τόδε
καὶ τοὺς ἀρίστους, οὓς ἄν ἡγῆται φρονεῖν,

κτείνει, δεδοικὼς τῆς τυραννίδος πέρι.
Πῶς οὖν ἔτ᾽ ἂν γένοιτ᾽ ἂν ἰσχυρὰ πόλις,
ὅταν τις ὡς λειμῶνος ἠρινοῦ στάχυν
τόλμας ἀφαιρῇ κἀπολωτίζῃ νέους ;

There is no greater evil to a state than a tyrant, when in the
first and chiefest place the laws hold not one common tenor, but
one man, lording it over the laws, keeps it to himself ; here is no
equality. Where the laws are written, the weak and powerful
have equal justice, and the lower ranks, when wronged, can
answer the higher in bold words ; the weaker, with justice on its
side, triumphs over the great. This is to be free. Is there a man
fraught with good counsel, useful to the state? He speaks it,
and becomes illustrious : else, if he chooses, he holds his peace.
What can there be more just thán this? And then, when the
people are sovereigns of the land, it glories in its valiant youth ;
while a tyrant hates such a state of things, and slays the best
men, who he thinks are wise, fearing for his power. How, then,
can a state become strong, when ruthless power cuts off each
brave spirit, and mows down each opening floweret, like the crops
in the vernal meadow?

Discretion is Valour.

Supp. 506.

Φιλεῖν μὲν οὖν χρὴ τοὺς σοφοὺς πρῶτον τέκνα,
ἔπειτα τοκέας πατρίδα θ᾽, ἣν αὔξειν χρεὼν
καὶ μὴ κατᾶξαι. Σφαλερὸν ἡγεμὼν θρασὺς
νεώς τε ναύτης· ἥσυχος καιρῷ σοφός.
Καὶ τοῦτό τοι τἀνδρεῖον, ἡ προμηθία.

A wise man's love streams first to his children, then to his
parents and country, which he should desire to raise to glory and
not to crush. Dangerous is a daring pilot and sailor in a ship ;
wise is he who knows his time to moor it in safety. To my mind
discretion is valour.

Shakespeare makes Falstaff ("King Henry IV." part i. act v. scene 4)
say—
　　　　" The better part of valour is discretion."

And "Othello" (act ii. scene 3)—
　　　　" Let's teach ourselves that honourable stop,
　　　　Not to out-sport discretion."

War not with the Dead.

Supp. 524.

Νεκροὺς δὲ τοὺς θανόντας, οὐ βλάπτων πόλιν
οὐδ᾽ ἀνδροκμῆτας προσφέρων ἀγωνίας,
θάψαι δικαιῶ, τὸν Πανελλήνων νόμον
σῴζων. Τί τούτων ἐστὶν οὐ καλῶς ἔχον ;

εἰ γάρ τι καὶ πεπόνθατ' Ἀργείων ὕπο,
τεθνᾶσιν, ἠμύνασθε πολεμίους καλῶς,
αἰσχρῶς δ' ἐκείνοις, χἠ δίκη διοίχεται.
Ἐάσατ' ἤδη γῇ καλυφθῆναι νεκρούς.
Ὅθεν δ' ἕκαστον εἰς τὸ σῶμ' ἀφίκετο,
ἐνταῦθ' ἀπῆλθε, πνεῦμα μὲν πρὸς αἰθέρα,
τὸ σῶμα δ' εἰς γῆν· οὔτε γὰρ κεκτήμεθα
ἡμέτερον αὐτὸ πλὴν ἐνοικῆσαι βίον,
κἄπειτα τὴν θρέψασαν αὐτὸ δεῖ λαβεῖν.
Δοκεῖς κακουργεῖν Ἄργος οὐ θάπτων νεκρούς;
ἥκιστα· πάσης Ἑλλάδος κοινὸν τόδε,
εἰ τοὺς θανόντας νοσφίσας ὧν χρῆν λαχεῖν
ἀτάφους τις ἕξει· δειλίαν γὰρ εἰσφέρει
τοῖς ἀλκίμοισιν, οὗτος ἦν τεθῇ νόμος.

1 deem it right to bury the dead, from no desire to injure the
city or bring on man-slaying contests, but preserving the common
law of Greece. What is there wrong in this? For suppose you
have suffered from the Argives, they are now dead ; ye have
driven them away with credit to yourselves and disgrace to them,
and thus justice has been done. Allow the dead to be entombed
in the earth ; for each part that forms the frame of man, must
return whence it came, the soul to the ethereal sky, the body to
the earth. For we do not possess this body as our own save to
dwell in during this breathing space of life, and then we must
give it back to the earth that sustained it. Dost thou think to
do injury to Argos only by not burying the dead? By no means ;
this is a question common to all Greece, if any deprive the dead
of their right, keeping them unburied ; for it would be a disgrace
to the brave if such a law were allowed to hold good.

See (Lat. Gr.) Soul.

LIFE IS A STRUGGLE.

Supp. 549.

Ἀλλ', ὦ μάταιοι, γνῶτε τἀνθρώπων κακά·
παλαίσμαθ' ἡμῶν ὁ βίος, εὐτυχοῦσι δὲ
οἱ μὲν τάχ, οἱ δ' ἐσαῦθις, οἱ δ' ἤδη βροτῶν.
Τρυφᾷ δ' ὁ δαίμων· πρός τε γὰρ τοῦ δυστυχοῦς,
ὡς εὐτυχὴς ᾖ, τίμιος γεραίρεται,
ὁ δ' ὄλβιός νιν πνεῦμα δειμαίνων λιπεῖν
ὑψηλὸν αἴρει.

But, ye silly men, learn the state of man : our life is a struggle ;
some gain the prize early, some hereafter, some now ; for fortune
plays the wanton. By the wretched she is greatly honoured, that
she may favour him, while the prosperous hold her in high honour,
dreading the veering gale.

See (Lat.) Life is a warfare.

COURAGE VAIN.

Supp. 596.

'Αρετὴ δ' οὐδὲν φέρει
βροτοῖσιν, ἢν μὴ τὸν θεὸν χρῄζοντ' ἔχῃ.

Courage profits men nought, if God denies His aid.

VANITY OF MEN.

Supp. 744.

*Ὦ κενοὶ βροτῶν,
οἳ τόξον ἐντείνοντες ὡς καιροῦ πέρα,
καὶ πρὸς δίκης γε πολλὰ πάσχοντες κακά,
φίλοις μὲν οὐ πείθεσθε, τοῖς δὲ πράγμασι.

Vain mortals! stretching the bow beyond what is fitting, and
justly suffering many ills, ye yield not to the advice of friends,
but learn only from circumstances.

THE BRAVE MAN.

Supp. 910.

Τὸ γὰρ τραφῆναι μὴ κακῶς αἰδῶ φέρει·
αἰσχύνεται δὲ τάγάθ' ἀσκήσας ἀνὴρ
κακὸς κεκλῆσθαι πᾶς τις. Ἡ δ' εὐανδρία
διδακτόν, εἴπερ καὶ βρέφος διδάσκεται
λέγειν ἀκούειν θ' ὧν μάθησιν οὐκ ἔχει.
Ἅ δ' ἂν μάθῃ τις, ταῦτα σώζεσθαι φιλεῖ
πρὸς γῆρας. Οὕτω παῖδας εὖ παιδεύετε.

For when a man is brought up honourably, he feels ashamed to
act basely ; every one trained to noble deeds blushes to be found
recreant ; valour may be taught, as we teach a child to speak, to
hear those things which he knows not ; such love as the child
learns he retains with fondness to old age—strong incitements to
train your children well.

TO BE TWICE YOUNG.

Supp. 1080.

Οἴμοι· τί δή βροτοῖσιν οὐκ ἔστιν τόδε,
νέους δὶς εἶναι καὶ γέροντας αὖ πάλιν ;
ἀλλ' ἐν δόμοις μὲν ἤν τι μὴ καλῶς ἔχῃ,
γνώμαισιν ὑστέραισιν ἐξορθούμεθα,
αἰῶνα δ' οὐκ ἔξεπτιν. Εἰ δ' ἦμεν νέοι
δὶς καὶ γέροντες, εἴ τις ἐξημάρτανε,
διπλοῦ βίου λαχόντες ἐξωρθούμεθ' ἄν.

Alas! why is it not permitted to mortals twice to be young, and thence return once more to old age? For in our domestic affairs, if aught be ill-conducted, we put it right by after thoughts, but we have not this power over life. If we could be twice young, twice old, when we made a mistake, having this twofold life, we could correct it.

MOURNING FOR THE DEATH OF A DAUGHTER.

Supp. 1094.

Εἶεν. Τί δὴ χρὴ τὸν ταλαίπωρόν με δρᾶν;
στείχειν πρὸς οἴκους; κᾆτ' ἐρημίαν ἴδω
πολλὴν μελάθρων ἀπορίαν τ' ἐμῷ βίῳ;
ἢ πρὸς μέλαθρα τοῦδε Καπανέως μόλω;
ἥδιστα πρίν γε δῆθ', ὅτ' ἦν παῖς ἥδε μοι.
'Αλλ' οὐκέτ' ἔστιν· ἥ γ' ἐμὴν γενειάδα
προσῆγετ' ἀεὶ στόματι καὶ κάρα τόδε
κατεῖχε χειρί· πατρὶ δ' οὐδὲν ἥδιον
γέροντι θυγατρός· ἀρσένων δὲ μείζονες
ψυχαί, γλυκεῖαι δ' ἦσσον εἰς θωπεύματα.
Οὐχ ὡς τάχιστα δῆτά μ' ἄξετ' εἰς δόμους,
σκότῳ τε δώσετ'; ἔνθ' ἀσιτίαις ἐμὸν
δέμας γεραιὸν συντακεὶς ἀποφθερῶ.
Τί μ' ὠφελήσει παιδὸς ὀστέων θιγεῖν;
ὦ δυσπάλαιστον γῆρας, ὡς μισῶ σ' ἔχων,
μισῶ δ' ὅσοι χρῄζουσιν ἐκτείνειν βίον,
βρωτοῖσι καὶ ποιοῖσι καὶ μαγεύμασι
παρεκτρέποντες ὀχετὸν ὥστε μὴ θανεῖν·
οὓς χρῆν, ἐπειδὰν μηδὲν ὠφελῶσι γῆν,
θανόντας ἔρρειν κἀκποδὼν εἶναι νέοις.

Be it so. What must I, wretched, do? Go home, and there see the sad desolation of my home, and loneliness of my life? Or shall I go to the dwelling of this Capaneus? Most pleasant, indeed, it was to me before, when my daughter was yet living, but she lives no longer; then she used to caress my beard and stroke this head with her hand. Nothing is dearer to an aged sire than a daughter; sons have spirits of higher pitch, but are less inclined to endearing fondness. Will you not speedily lead me to my house, and give me up to darkness, when I may perish, wasting away my aged frame with fastings? What will it avail me to touch the bones of my child? O age! difficult to be contended with, how I hate thee when I have reached thee, and hate all who are anxious to lengthen out existence with food, drink, and spells, turning aside the stream of life so as not to die! It is more fitting for thee, nought but a useless burden upon earth, to pass away in death, and make room for the young.

Affliction for Death of Children.

Supp. 1122.

Τί γὰρ ἀν μεῖζον τοῦδ' ἐπὶ θνατοῖς
Παθὸς ἐξεύροις,
Ἢ τέκνα θανόντ' ἐσιδέσθαι.

For what greater grief canst thou find out for mortals than to
see their children dead?

Hope Always.

Her. Fur. 105.

Οὗτος δ' ἀνὴρ ἄριστος ὅστις ἐλπίσι
πέποιθεν ἀεί· τὸ δ' ἀπορεῖν ἀνδρὸς κακοῦ.

That is the noble man, who is full of confident hopes; the abject
soul despairs.

The Good.

Her. Fur. 235.

Ἆρ οὐκ ἀφορμὰς τοῖς λόγοισιν ἀγαθοὶ
θνητῶν ἔχουσι, κἂν βραδύς τίς ᾗ λέγειν;

Are not the good, though slow to speak, oft provoked to give
vent to their feelings?

Sedition.

Her. Fur. 272.

Οὐ γὰρ εὖ φρονεῖ πόλις
στάσει νοσοῦσα καὶ κακοῖς βουλεύμασιν.

For a city does not prosper that shakes with sedition and is rent
by evil counsels.

Fate.

Her. Fur. 309.

Τὰς τῶν θεῶν γὰρ ὅστις ἐκμοχθεῖν τύχας
πρόθυμός ἐστιν, ἡ προθυμία δ' ἄφρων·
ὃ χρὴ γὰρ οὐδεὶς μὴ χρεὼν θήσει ποτέ.

For whosoever strives against heaven-sent calamities, his
striving is folly. What must be, no one will ever make so that
it be not.

See (Lat.) Fate.

Inconstancy of Human Things.

Her. Fur. 502.

Ἀλλ', ὦ γέροντες, μικρὰ μὲν τὰ τοῦ βίου·
τοῦτον δ' ὅπως ἥδιστα διαπεράσετε,

ἐξ ἡμέρας εἰς νύκτα μὴ λυπούμενοι.
ὡς ἐλπίδας μὲν ὁ χρόνος οὐκ ἐπίσταται
σώζειν, τὸ δ' αὑτοῦ σπουδάσας διέπτατο.

But ye old men, brief is the space of life allotted to you ; pass it as pleasantly as ye can, not grieving from morn till eve. Since time knows not how to preserve our hopes, but, attentive to its own concerns, flies away.

See (Lat.) Fortune, fickleness of.

YOUTH AND AGE.

Her. Fur. 637.

Ἀ νεότας μοι φίλον· ἄχθος δὲ τὸ γῆρας ἀεὶ
βαρύτερον Αἴτνας σκοπέλων ἐπὶ κρατὶ κεῖται,
βλεφάρων σκοτεινὸν φάος ἐπικαλύψαν.
Μή μοι μήτ' Ἀσιήτιδος
τυραννίδος ὄλβος εἴη.
μὴ χρυσοῦ δώματα πλήρη
τᾶς ἥβας ἀντιλαβεῖν,
ἃ καλλίστα μὲν ἐν ὄλβῳ,
κάλλιστα δ' ἐν πενίᾳ.
Τὸ δὲ λυγρὸν φόνιόν τε γῆρας μισῶ· κατὰ κυμάτων δ'
ἔρροι μηδέ ποτ' ὤφελεν
θνατῶν δώματα καὶ πόλεις
ἐλθεῖν, ἀλλὰ κατ' αἰθέρ' ἀ-
εὶ πτεροῖσι φορείσθω.
Εἰ δὲ θεοῖς ἦν ξύνεσις καὶ σοφία κατ' ἄνδρας,
δίδυμον ἂν ἥβαν ἔφερον, φανερὸν χαρακτῆρ',
ἀρετῆς, ὅσοισιν μέτα, κατθανόντες τ'
εἰς αὐγὰς πάλιν ἀλίου
δισσοὺς ἂν ἔβαν διαύλους,
ἁ δυσγένεια δ' ἁπλᾶν ἂν
εἶχε ζωᾶς βιοτάν,
καὶ τῷδ' ἦν τούς τε κακοὺς ἂν
γνῶναι καὶ τοὺς ἀγαθούς,
ἴσον ἄτ' ἐν νεφέλαισιν ἄ-
στρων ναύταις ἀριθμὸς πέλει.
Νῦν δ' οὐδεὶς ὅρος ἐκ θεῶν
χρηστοῖς οὐδὲ κακοῖς σαφής,
ἀλλ' εἱλισσόμενός τις αἰ-
ὼν πλοῦτον μόνον αὔξει.

Youth is dear to me, but age ever lies upon my head a heavier burden than the rocks of Ætna, dimming mine eyelids with sober veil. I would not have the riches of Asia's throne, nor that my house should shine with gold, in preference to youth, which is fairest in wealth and fairest in poverty. Sad and funereal age I

abhor. Hence may it perish in the billows, and never enter the
houses and cities of men, but be borne on wings through the air.
But if the gods had understood and been wise in the affairs of men,
they would have bestowed a twofold youth, as an undoubted mark
of virtue, upon such as shared it ; and after death they would have
returned a second time to the light of the sun, whereas baseness
would have had a single term of life, and in this way would the
bad and good have been distinguished, in the same way as amidst
the clouds the stars are a guide to the sailors. Whereas now
there is no certain mark given by the gods to distinguish the good
and bad, but time, as it revolves, is studious of wealth alone.

DESCRIPTION OF MADNESS.

Her. Fur. 857.

ἸΡΙΣ.

Οὐχὶ σωφρονεῖν γ᾽ ἔπεμψε δεῦρό σ᾽ ἡ Διὸς δάμαρ.

ΛΥΤΤΑ.

Ἥλιον μαρτυρόμεσθα δρῶσ᾽ ἃ δρᾶν οὐ βούλομαι.
εἰ δὲ δή μ᾽ Ἥρᾳ θ᾽ ὑπουργεῖν σοί τ᾽ ἀναγκαίως ἔχει
τάχος ἐπιρροίβδην θ᾽ ὁμαρτεῖν ὡς κυνηγέτῃ κύνας,
εἶμι γ᾽· οὔτε πόντος οὕτω κύμασι στένων λάβρος,
οὔτε γῆς σεισμὸς κεραυνοῦ τ᾽ οἶστρος ὠδῖνας πνέων,
οἷ᾽ ἐγὼ σταδιοδραμοῦμαι στέρνον εἰς Ἡρακλέους
καὶ καταρρήξω μέλαθρα καὶ δόμους ἐπεμβαλῶ,
τέκν᾽ ἀποκτείνασα πρῶτον· ὁ δὲ κανὼν οὐκ εἴσεται
παῖδας οὓς ἔτικτ᾽ ἐναίρων, πρὶν ἂν ἐμῆς λύσσης ὑφῇ.
Ἢν ἰδοὺ καὶ δὴ τινάσσει κρᾶτα βαλβίδων ἄπο
καὶ διαστρόφους ἑλίσσει σῖγα γοργωποὺς κόρας.
Ἀμπνοὰς δ᾽ οὐ σωφρονίζει, ταῦρος ὣς ἐς ἐμβολήν,
δεινὰ μυκᾶται δὲ Κῆρας ἀνακαλῶν τὰς Ταρτάρου.
Τάχα σ᾽ ἐγὼ μᾶλλον χορεύσω καὶ καταυλήσω φόβῳ.
Στεῖχ᾽ ἐς Οὔλυμπον πεδαίρουσ᾽, Ἶρι, γενναῖον πόδα·
εἰς δόμους δ᾽ ἡμεῖς ἄφαντοι δυσόμεσθ᾽ Ἡρακλέους.

Iris. The wife of Jove did not surely send thee hither to show
thy wisdom.

Madness. I swear by the sun that I am doing what I desire not
to do. But if I must needs be subservient to Juno and thee, I
must follow swiftly and with a rush, as dogs follow the huntsman.
On I go; not the sea raging with billows, nor the rocking earthquake, nor the thunder's rage inflicting pangs, is so furious as I
when I rush with racing speed against the breast of Hercules.
And I shall break down these walls and desolate his house, having
first caused him to slay his children ; but he that kills them shall
not know that they are his sons who fall beneath his hands, till
he has respite from my madness. See even now he shakes his
head, standing at the barriers, and rolls in silence his distorted

gorgon eyes. And he has no command over his breathing ; like a bull prepared for the onslaught, he bellows dreadfully, invoking the Furies from Tartarus. Quickly shall I rouse thee to the dance, and give forth music rife with terror. Away, Iris, to Olympus, raising thy noble foot ; but we shall enter unseen the abode of Hercules.

INGRATITUDE.
Her. Fur. 1223.

Χάριν δὲ γηράσκουσαν ἐχθαίρω φίλων
καὶ τῶν καλῶν μὲν ὅστις ἀπολαύειν θέλει,
συμπλεῖν δὲ τοῖς φίλοισι δυστυχοῦσιν οὔ.

I abhor the gratitude of friends that grows old, and those, too, who wish to share the prosperous gale, but forsake the bark in adverse storms.

GOD IS ALL-SUFFICIENT.
Her. Fur. 1345.

Δεῖται γὰρ ὁ θεός, εἴπερ ἔστ' ὄντως θεός,
οὐδενός· ἀοιδῶν οἵδε δύστηνοι λόγοι.

For God, if he be really God, wants nothing. These are but the miserable tales of poets.

So Sirac (xlii. 22).

THE VIRTUOUS.
Heracl. 201.

Ἡ γὰρ αἰσχύνη πάρος
τοῦ ζῆν παρ' ἐσθλοῖς ἀνδράσιν νομίζεται.

For among the virtuous disgrace is considered before life.

So Revelation (ii. 10)—"Be thou faithful unto death, and I will give thee a crown of life."

TWO TO ONE IS ODDS.
Heracl. 275.

Μιᾶς γὰρ χειρὸς ἀσθενὴς μάχη.

Weak the conflict of one hand.

WOMAN.
Heracl. 476.

Γυναικὶ γὰρ σιγή τε καὶ τὸ σωφρονεῖν
κάλλιστον, εἴσω θ' ἥσυχον μένειν δόμων.

For silence and modesty are the best ornaments of a woman, and to remain quietly within the house.

So 1 Corinthians (xiv. 34)—" Let your women keep silence in the churches: for it is not permitted unto them to speak."

See (Lat.) Woman.

No One Happy before his Death.

Heracl. 863.

Τῇ δὲ νῦν τύχῃ
βροτοῖς ἅπασι λαμπρὰ κηρύσσει μαθεῖν,
τὸν εὐτυχεῖν δοκοῦντα μὴ ζηλοῦν, πρὶν ἂν
θανόντ᾽ ἴδῃ τις· ὡς ἐφήμεροι τύχαι.

By his present fortune he proclaims aloud to all this truth, not to envy the man who seems prosperous, ere we see his death, as fortune is but for a day.

See (Lat.) Blessed, no one, before death.

The High-born ought to be Truthful.

Heracl. 890.

'Εν δὲ τοῖς τοιοῖσδε χρὴ
ἀψευδὲς εἶναι τοῖσι γενναίοις στόμα.

In such noble people as you the mouth ought to be truthful.

High and Humble Life.

Iphig. in Aul. 18.

Ζηλῶ δ᾽ ἀνδρῶν ὃς ἀκίνδυνον
βίον ἐξεπέρασ᾽ ἀγνώς, ἀκλεής·
τοὺς δ᾽ ἐν τιμαῖς ἧσσον ἐπαινῶ.

I envy the man who has passed through life without danger, to the world, to fame unknown, not those raised to greatness.

The Wily Tongue.

Iphig. in Aul. 333.

Πονηρὸν γλῶσσ᾽ ἐπὶ φθόνον σοφή.

The tongue cunning to excite envy is an evil.

The Waverer.

Iphig. in Aul. 334.

Νοῦς δέ γ᾽ οὐ βέβαιος ἄδικον κτῆμα κοὐ σαφὲς φίλοις.

The wavering mind is a base possession, not to be trusted by friends.

THE CUNNING CANDIDATE FOR POWER.
Iphig. in Aul. 337.

Οἶσθ' ὅτ' ἐσπούδαζες ἄρχειν Δαναΐδαις πρὸς Ἴλιον,
τῷ δοκεῖν μὲν οὐχὶ χρῄζων, τῷ δὲ βούλεσθαι θέλων,
ὡς ταπεινὸς ἦσθα, πάσης δεξιᾶς προσθιγγάνων
καὶ θύρας ἔχων ἀκλήστους τῷ θέλοντι δημοτῶν,
καὶ διδοὺς πρόσρησιν ἑξῆς πᾶσι, κεἰ μή τις θέλοι,
τοῖς τρόποις ζητῶν πρίασθαι τὸ φιλότιμον ἐκ μέσου ;
κᾆτ' ἐπεὶ κατέσχες ἀρχάς, μεταβαλὼν ἄλλους τρόπους
τοῖς φίλοισιν οὐκέτ' ἦσθα τοῖς πρὶν ὡς πρόσθεν φίλος,
δυσπρόσιτος ἔσω τε κλήθρων σπάνιος. Ἄνδρα δ' οὐ χρεὼι
τὸν ἀγαθὸν πράσσοντα μεγάλα τοὺς τρόπους μεθιστάναι,
ἀλλὰ καὶ βέβαιον εἶναι τότε μάλιστα τοῖς φίλοις
ἡνίκ' ὠφελεῖν μάλιστα δυνατός ἐστιν εὐτυχῶν.

Thou knowest when thou wast striving to gain the leadership
of the Greeks against Troy—in appearance careless of the honour,
but secretly desirous of it—how humble thou wast, shaking every
one by the hand, and keeping open door to all who wished to
enter ; giving audience to all in turn, even if he wished it not,
seeking by affability to buy popularity among the multitude.
And then when thou wert successful, changing thy mode of acting,
thou wast no longer the same to thy old friends, difficult of access,
and seldom within doors. Ill does it become an honest man when
prosperous to change his manners, but rather then to be staunch
to his friends, when by his changed position he can serve them.

THE RULER OF A STATE.
Iphig. in Aul. 373.

Μηδέν' οὖ χρέους ἕκατι προστάτην θείμην χθονός,
μηδ' ὅπλων ἄρχοντα· νοῦν χρὴ τὸν στρατηλάτην ἔχειν.
πόλεος ὡς ἄρχων ἀνὴρ πᾶς, ξύνεσιν ἢν ἔχων τύχῃ.

I would not make any one ruler of a state or general of an army
on account of his wealth : the leader should have wisdom : every
man sago in counsel is a leader.

THE NOBLE AND IGNOBLE.
Iphig. in Aul. 446.

Ἡ δυσγένεια δ' ὡς ἔχει τι χρήσιμον.
Καὶ γὰρ δακρῦσαι ῥᾳδίως αὐτοῖς ἔχει,
ἅπαντά τ' εἰπεῖν. Τῷ δὲ γενναίῳ φύσιν
ἄνολβα ταῦτα. Προστάτην δὲ τοῦ βίου
τὸν ὄγκον ἔχομεν τῷ τ' ὄχλῳ δουλεύομεν.

What advantages attend ignoble birth ! Such persons are at

liberty to weep and bemoan themselves, but to the noble this is denied. We have pride as the guide of our life, and are slaves to the people.

Ennius, quoted by St Jerome (in Epith. Nepotiani), thus imitates this passage :—

" Plebes in hoc regi antestat loco, licet
Lacrumare plebi, regi honesta non licet."

LOVE.

Iphig. in Aul. 543.

Μάκαρες οἱ μετρίας θεοῦ
μετά τε σωφροσύνας μετέ-
σχον λέκτρων Ἀφροδίτας,
γαλανείᾳ χρησάμενοι
μαινομένων οἴστρων, ὅθι δὴ
δίδυμ' Ἔρως ὁ χρυσοκόμας
τόξ' ἐντείνεται χαρίτων,
τὸ μὲν ἐπ' εὐαίωνι πότμῳ,
τὸ δ' ἐπὶ συγχύσει βιοτᾶς.
Ἀπενέπω νιν ἀμετέρων,
Κύπρι καλλίστα, θαλάμων.
Εἴη δέ μοι μετρία μὲν
χάρις, πόθοι δ' ὅσιοι,
καὶ μετέχοιμι τᾶς Ἀφροδί-
τας, πολλὰν δ' ἀποθείμαν.

Blest are they who enjoy the nuptial couch of Aphrodite, the temperate and modest goddess, obtaining a calm from those maddening stings, when Love with golden locks bends both his bows of graces, one for a prosperous fate, the other for life's wild tumult. I deprecate, O fairest Venus, the latter; but mine be love's temperate grace, the holy flame of chaste desire; mine be mild Venus and not ungoverned passion.

See Ovid, Met. i. 468.

THE POWERFUL.

Iphig. in Aul. 596.

Θεοί τοι κρείσσους οἵ τ' ὀλβοφόροι
τοῖς οὐκ εὐδαίμοσι θνατῶν.

To th' inferior ranks of life
The powerful and the wealthy are as gods.

A DAUGHTER.

Iphig. in Aul. 688.

Ἀποστολαὶ γὰρ μακάριαι μὲν, ἀλλ' ὅμως
δάκνουσι τοὺς τεκόντας, ὅταν ἄλλοις δόμοις
παῖδας παραδιδῷ πολλὰ μοχθήσας πατήμ

It is good that a daughter leave her home, but yet it pains a father's heart when he delivers a child to another house, the object of his tender care.

A WIFE.

Iphig. in Aul. 749.

Χρὴ δ' ἐν δόμοισιν ἄνδρα τὸν σοφὸν τρέφειν
γυναῖκα χρηστὴν κἀγαθήν, ἢ μὴ τρέφειν.

A wise man should have a useful and good wife in his house, or not marry at all.

A MOTHER.

Iphig. in Aul. 917.

Δεινὸν τὸ τίκτειν καὶ φέρει φίλτρον μέγα
πᾶσίν τε κοινὸν ὥσθ' ὑπερκάμνειν τέκνων.

Childbirth is painful, and yet a child is a matter of great endearment; 'tis common to the whole human race to toil on behalf of children.

LEAN NOT TO YOUR OWN UNDERSTANDING.

Iphig. in Aul. 924.

Ἔστιν μὲν οὖν ἵν' ἡδὺ μὴ λίαν φρονεῖν,
ἔστιν δὲ χὥπου χρήσιμον γνώμην ἔχειν.

There is a time when it is pleasant not to build too much on our own wisdom; but then, again, there is a time when it is useful to exert our judgment.

So Proverbs (iii. 5)—"Trust in the Lord with all thine heart; and lean not unto thine own understanding."

TO TOUCH WITH THE TIP OF THE FINGER.

Iphig. in. Aul. 950.

Οὐχ ἅψεται σῆς θυγατρὸς Ἀγαμέμνων ἄναξ,
οὐδ' εἰς ἄκραν χεῖρ', ὥστε προσβαλεῖν πέπλοις.

King Agamemnon will not touch thy daughter even with the tip of his finger, so as to lay hold of her garment.

Our Saviour (Luke xi. 46) says of the Pharisees, that they "will not touch with one of their fingers" the burthens which they lay on others; and Cicero (pro Cœl. 12) says—"Extremis, ut dicitur, digitis attingere,"—"To touch, so to speak, with the finger-tips"

EXCESS OF PRAISE.

Iphig. in Aul. 979.

Αἰνούμενοι γὰρ ἀγαθοὶ τρόπον τινὰ
μισοῦσι τοὺς αἰνοῦντας, ἢν αἰνῶσ' ἄγαν.

The noble, if praised, hate in a certain degree those who praise them, if they praise too much.

THE DISTRESSED.

Iphig. in Aul. 984.

Ἀλλ' οὖν ἔχει τοι σχῆμα, κἂν ἄπωθεν ᾖ
ἀνὴρ ὁ χρηστός, δυστυχοῦντας ὠφελεῖν.

But, in fact, the good man, even though he be a stranger, has good reason to assist the distressed.

So Burns ("Winter Night")—
"Affliction's sons are brothers in distress;
A brother to relieve, how exquisite the bliss."

SILENCE GIVES CONSENT.

Iphig. in Aul. 1142.

Αὐτὸ δὲ τὸ σιγᾶν ὁμολογοῦντός ἐστί σου.

E'en thy silence and thy sighs
Confess it.

DUTY OF A WIFE.

Iphig. in Aul. 1157.

Οὗ σοι καταλλαχθεῖσα περὶ σὲ καὶ δόμους
συμμαρτυρήσεις ὡς ἄμεμπτος ἦν γυνή,
εἴς τ' Ἀφροδίτην σωφρονοῦσα καὶ τὸ σὸν
μέλαθρον αὔξουσ', ὥστε σ' εἰσιόντα τε
χαίρειν θύραξέ τ' ἐξιόντ' εὐδαιμονεῖν.
σπάνιον δὲ θήρευμ' ἀνδρὶ τοιαύτην λαβεῖν
δάμαρτα· φλαύραν δ' οὐ σπάνις γυναῖκ' ἔχειν.

When I was reconciled to thee and thy house, thou wilt thyself bear witness how irreproachable a wife I was, modest and adding to the splendour of thy house, so that both going in and going out thou wast blest. A wife like this is a rare prize; the worthless are not rare.

LIFE.

Iphig. in Aul. 1250.

Τὸ φῶς τόδ' ἀνθρώποισιν ἥδιστον βλέπειν,
τὰ νέρθε δ' οὐδέν· μαίνεται δ' ὃς εὔχεται
θανεῖν. Κακῶς ζῆν κρεῖσσον ἢ καλῶς θανεῖν.

To enjoy the light of heaven is most sweet to mortals; things below are nothing; mad is he who prays for death; to live in misery is better than anything there is of good in death.

The Multitude.

Iphig. in Aul. 1558.

Τὸ πολὺ γὰρ δεινὸν κακόν.

The many are, indeed,
A dreadful ill.

The Gods save whom they love.

Iphig. in Aul. 1610.

Ἀπροσδόκητα δὲ βροτοῖς τὰ τῶν θεῶν,
σώζουσί θ' οὕς φιλοῦσιν.

The gods dispense to men what is unlooked for, and those whom they love they save.

Endure Death with Patience.

Iphig. in Taur. 484.

Οὗτοι νομίζω σοφόν, ὃς ἂν μέλλων κτανεῖν
οἴκτῳ τὸ δεῖμα τοὐλέθρου νικᾶν θέλῃ·
οὐδ' ὅστις Ἅιδην ἐγγὺς ὄντ' οἰκτίζεται,
σωτηρίας ἄνελπις· ὡς δύ' ἐξ ἑνὸς
κακὼ συνάπτει, μωρίαν τ' ὀφλισκάνει
θνήσκει θ' ὁμοίως· τὴν τύχην δ' ἐᾶν χρεών.

I esteem not him to be wise who, when he sees death near, tries to overcome its terrors with wailings, being without hope of safety, since he thus has two ills instead of one, and makes his folly known, dying none the less. But one must needs let fortune have its way.

Woman quick to form Devices.

Iphig. in Taur. 1032.

Δειναὶ γὰρ αἱ γυναῖκες εὑρίσκειν τέχνας.

To form devices quick is woman's wit.

Women a Faithless Race.

Iphig. in Taur. 1298.

Ὁρᾶτ', ἄπιστον ὡς γυναικεῖον γένος,
μέτεστί θ' ὑμῖν τῶν πεπραγμένων μέρος.

See how faithless is the female race! and ye are partners in what has been done.

To Fight against the Gods.

Iphig. in Taur. 1478.

Πρὸς τοὺς σθένοντας θεοὺς ἀμιλλᾶσθαι καλόν ;

What benefit is there to fight against the powerful gods?

The Coward is Valiant in the Dark.

Rhes. 69.

Ἐν ὄρφνῃ δραπέτης μέγα σθένει.

In darkness a runaway has mighty strength.

Men have Different Natures.

Rhes. 106.

Ἀλλ' οὐ γὰρ αὐτὸς πάντ' ἐπίστασθαι βροτῶν
πέφυκεν· ἄλλῳ δ' ἄλλο πρόσκειται γέρας,
σὲ μὲν μάχεσθαι, τοὺς δὲ βουλεύειν καλῶς.

Nature grants to none to know all things ; one gift belongs to
one, another to another ; to thee, indeed, to fight,—but to others,
to give good counsel.

A Glorious Death.

Rhes. 758.

Θανεῖν γὰρ εὐκλεῶς μέν, εἰ θανεῖν χρεών,
λυπρὸν μὲν οἶμαι τῷ θανόντι· πῶς γὰρ οὔ ;
τοῖς ζῶσι δ' ὄγκος καὶ δόμων εὐδοξία.

To die, if a man must die, is no doubt painful to him that dies :
for how should it not be so? but if with glory to the living, it is a
pride and renown for one's family.

A State in Adversity.

Troad. 26.

Ἐρημία γὰρ πόλιν ὅταν λάβῃ κακή,
νοσεῖ τὰ τῶν θεῶν οὐδὲ τιμᾶσθαι θέλει.

For when sad calamity befalls a state the gods are neglected
and there is no desire to honour them.

Affliction.

Troad. 470.

Ὅμως δ' ἔχει τι σχῆμα κικλήσκειν θεούς,
ὅταν τις ἡμῶν δυστυχῇ λάβῃ τύχην.

Yet there is good reason to invoke the gods when we fall into affliction.

THE DEAD.
Troad. 602.

'Ο θανὼν δ' ἐπι-
λάθεται ἀλγέων ἀδάκρυτος.

The tearless dead forgets his sorrows.

See Eccles. ix. 5.

TEARS.
Troad. 605.

'Ως ἡδὺ δάκρυα τοῖς κακῶς πεπραγόσι
θρήνων τ' ὀδυρμοὶ μοῦσά θ', ἢ λύπας ἔχει.

How sweet are tears to those who have fared ill, and strains of lamentation and the Muse, who tunes her notes to woe!

See (Lat.) Tears.

THE DEAD.
Troad. 623.

Οὐ ταὐτὸν, ὦ παῖ τῷ βλέπειν τὸ κατθανεῖν·
τὸ μὲν γὰρ οὐδέν, τῷ δ' ἔνεισιν ἐλπίδες.

My child, to die is not the same as to behold the light of day; for the one is nothing, while in the other there are hopes.

TO FALL FROM HIGH FORTUNE.
Troad. 627.

Τὸ μὴ γενέσθαι τῷ θανεῖν ἴσον λέγω,
τοῦ ζῆν δὲ λυπρῶς κρεῖσσόν ἐστι κατθανεῖν.
'Αλγεῖ γὰρ οὐδὲν τῶν κακῶν ᾐσθημένος·
ὁ δ' εὐτυχήσας εἰς τὸ δυστυχὲς πεσὼν
ψυχὴν ἀλᾶται τῆς πάροιθ' εὐπραξίας.

Not to be born and to die I deem to be the same; but to die is far better than to live in misery, for he knows no grief who does not feel his misery. But to fall from high fortune to abject wretchedness distracts the soul with the feeling of former happiness.

A WIFE.
Troad. 649.

Γλώσσης τε σιγὴν ὄμμα θ' ἥσυχον πόσει
παρεῖχον· ᾔδειν δ' ἃ μὲ χρῆν νικᾶν πόσιν,
κείνῳ τε νίκην ὧν ἐχρῆν παριέναι.

With silence of the tongue and cheerfulness of look I entertained my husband. I knew in what things I ought to command my husband, and how to yield obedience in what it behoved me.

A Second Marriage.

Troad. 660.

Καίτοι λέγουσιν ὡς μι' εὐφρόνη χαλᾷ
τὸ δυσμενὲς γυναικὸς εἰς ἀνδρὸς λέχος·
ἀπέπτυσ' αὐτήν, ἥτις ἄνδρα τὸν πάρος
καινοῖσι λέκτροις ἀποβαλοῦσ' ἄλλον φιλεῖ.
Ἀλλ' οὐδὲ πῶλος ἥτις ἂν διαζυγῇ
τῆς συντραφείσης, ῥᾳδίως ἕλξει ζυγόν.
Καίτοι τὸ θηριῶδες ἄφθογγόν τ' ἔφυ
ξυνέσει τ' ἄχρηστον τῇ φύσει τε λείπεται.

And yet they say that short time changes a woman's unwillingness to a new love. I abhor her who, discarding from her thoughts a former husband, loves another. For not even the mare, which has been separated from its fellow, will easily draw the yoke ; and yet the race of beasts is without articulate voice, and fails in reason, being less excellent by nature.

God rules with Justice.

Troad. 884.

Ὦ γῆς ὄχημα κἀπὶ γῆς ἔχων ἕδραν,
ὅστις ποτ' εἶ σύ, δυστόπαστος εἰδέναι,
Ζεύς, εἴτ' ἀνάγκη φύσεος εἴτε νοῦς βροτῶν,
προσευξάμην σε· πάντα γὰρ δι' ἀψόφου
βαίνων κελεύθου κατὰ δίκην τὰ θνήτ' ἄγεις.

O Jove, who rulest this revolving globe, and hast thy throne above it, whoever thou art, hard to be known even by conjecture, whether the necessity of nature or the ruling mind, I adore thee ; for, proceeding by a noiseless track, thou guidest with justice all mortal affairs.

So Psalm (cxlv. 17)—"The Lord is righteous in all His ways, and holy in all His works."

Lament of Hecuba over Astyanax.

Troad. 1173.

Δύστηνε, κρατὸς ὥς σ' ἔκειρεν ἀθλίως
τείχη πατρῷα, Λοξίου πυργώματα,
ὃν πόλλ' ἐκήπευσ' ἡ τεκοῦσα βόστρυχον
φιλήμασίν τ' ἔδωκεν, ἔνθεν ἐκγελᾷ
ὀστέων ῥαγέντων φόνος, ἵν' αἰσχρὰ μὴ λέγω.
ὦ χεῖρες, ὡς εἰκοὺς μὲν ἡδείας πατρὸς
κέκτησθ', ἐν ἄρθροις δ' ἔκλυτοι πρόκεισθέ μοι.

Ὦ πολλὰ κόμπους ἐκβαλὸν φίλον στόμα,
ὄλωλας, ἐψεύσω μ' ὅτ' εἰσπίπτων λέχος,
ὦ μῆτερ, ηὔδας, ἦ πολύν σοι βοστρύχων
πλόκαμον κεροῦμαι, πρὸς τάφον θ' ὁμηλίκων
κώμους ἀπάξω, φίλα διδοὺς προσφθέγματα.
Σὺ δ' οὐκ ἔμ', ἀλλ' ἐγὼ σὲ τὸν νεώτερον,
γραῦς, ἄπολις, ἄτεκνος, ἄθλιον θάπτω νεκρόν.
Οἴμοι, τὰ πόλλ' ἀσπάσμαθ' αἵ τ' ἐμαὶ τροφαὶ
ὕπνοι τ' ἐκεῖνοι φροῦδά μοι.   Τί καί ποτε
γράψειεν ἄν σε μουσοποιὸς ἐν τάφῳ ;
τὸν παῖδα τόνδ ἔκτειναν Ἀργεῖοί ποτε
δείσαντες ; αἰσχρὸν τοὐπίγραμμά γ' Ἑλλάδι.

O wretched one! how miserably have thy ancestral walls, the towers by Phœbus raised, rent the crisped ringlets from thy head, which thy mother fondly cherished with kisses, whence, amidst the crushed bones, murder grins out, to abstain from words more shocking! O hands! which once bore the dear image of thy father's, but now lie with loosened joints. O thou dear mouth! which utteredst many a pleasantry, thou hast perished; thou hast deceived me, when, flinging thyself on my couch, thou wouldst exclaim, "O mother! I shall cut off these clustering locks for thee, and to thy tomb shall lead bands of compeers, hailing thee with dear address." Thou dost not bury me, but I, old, reft of my children, of my country, bury thee, dead in thy early bloom, a wretched corse. Alas! those fond embraces, those nursing cares, those lullabies, have all vanished. And on thy tomb what verse shall the bard inscribe?—"This boy who lies here the Greeks once slew, for they feared him,"—a verse recording the disgrace of Greece.

FORTUNE.

Troad. 1203.

Θνητῶν δὲ μῶρος ὅστις εὖ πράσσειν δοκῶν
βέβαια χαίρει· τοῖς τρόποις γὰρ αἱ τύχαι
ἔμπληκτος ὡς ἄνθρωπος, ἄλλοτ' ἄλλοσε
πηδῶσι, κοὐδεὶς αὐτὸς εὐτυχεῖ ποτε.

Foolish I deem him who, thinking that his state is blest, rejoices in security ; for fortune, like a man distempered in his senses, leaps now this way, now that, and no man is always fortunate.

THE DEAD.

Troad. 1248.

Δοκῶ δὲ τοῖς θανοῦσι διαφέρειν βραχύ,
εἰ πλουσίων τις τεύξεται κτερισμάτων.
Κενὸν δὲ γαύρωμ' ἐστὶ τῶν ζώντων τόδε.

I deem that it is of little importance to the dead whether he obtain costly obsequies; this is the vain affectation of the living.

To Die is Better.
Hec. 214.

'Αλλὰ θανεῖν μοι
ξυντυχία κρείσσων ἐκύρησεν.

But death, a better fate, has befallen me.
So Philippians (i. 21)—" To die is gain."

The Demagogue.
Hec. 254.

'Αχάριστον ὑμῶν σπέρμ', ὅσοι δημηγόρους
ζηλοῦτε τιμάς· μηδὲ γιγνώσκοισθέ μοι,
οἳ τοὺς φίλους βλάπτοντες οὐ φροντίζετε,
ἢν τοῖσι πολλοῖς πρὸς χάριν λέγητέ τι.

A thankless race you are, who try to gain honour from the mob by oratory; would that you were not known to me, who reck not of injuries done to friends if your fine speech wins you favour with the people.

Weight of Counsel.
Hec. 294.

Λόγος γὰρ ἔκ τ' ἀδοξούντων ἰὼν
κἀκ τῶν δοκούντων αὐτὸς οὐ ταὐτὸν σθένει.

It is not the counsel but the speaker's worth that gives weight to his eloquence.

See (Lat.) Tumult.

Nobility.
Hec. 379.

Δεινὸς χαρακτὴρ κἀπίσημος ἐν βροτοῖς
ἐσθλῶν γενέσθαι, κἀπὶ μεῖζον ἔρχεται
τῆς εὐγενείας ὄνομα τοῖσιν ἀξίοις.

To be born of noble parents is a great and distinguishing badge among men, and the name of nobility among the illustrious advances from great to greater still.

The Good and the Bad.
Hec. 595.

"Ανθρωποι δ' ἀεὶ
ὁ μὲν πονηρὸς οὐδὲν ἄλλο πλὴν κακός,

ὁ δ᾽ ἐσθλὸς ἐσθλός, οὐδὲ συμφορᾶς ὕπο
φύσιν διέφθειρ᾽, ἀλλὰ χρηστός ἐστ᾽ ἀεί ;
ἆρ᾽ οἱ τεκόντες διαφέρουσιν ἢ τροφαί ;
ἔχει γε μέντοι καὶ τὸ θρεφθῆναι καλῶς
δίδαξιν ἐσθλοῦ· τοῦτο δ᾽ ἤν τις εὖ μάθῃ,
οἶδεν τό γ᾽ αἰσχρὸν κανόνι τοῦ καλοῦ μαθών.

To all eternity the bad can never be but bad, the good but good ;
nor in misfortune does man degenerate from his nature, but he is
always good. Is this difference from parents or from education ?
To be brought up well instils, indeed, the principles of honour ;
and he that is thus taught knows, by the law of honour, what is
base.

THE SAILOR.

Hec. 606.

Ἔν τοι μυρίῳ στρατεύματι
ἀκόλαστος ὄχλος ναυτική τ᾽ ἐναρχία
κρείσσων πυρός, κακὸς δ᾽ ὁ μή τι δρῶν κακόν.

In a large army the rabble are riotous, and the sailors' insolence
runs like wildfire ; not to join in wickedness is a crime.

THE GODS.

Hec. 799.

Ἀλλ᾽ οἱ θεοὶ σθένουσι χὠ κείνων κρατῶν
νόμος· νόμῳ γὰρ τοὺς θεοὺς ἡγούμεθα
καὶ ζῶμεν ἄδικα καὶ δίκαι᾽ ὡρισμένοι.

The gods are strong, and powerful is their law ; for by the law
we judge that there are gods, and form our lives, having right and
wrong strictly defined.

PERSUASION.

Hec. 813.

Ὦ τάλαιν᾽ ἐγώ.

Τί δῆτα θνητοὶ τἄλλα μὲν μαθήματα
μοχθοῦμεν ὡς χρὴ πάντα καὶ μαστεύομεν,
πειθὼ δὲ τὴν τύμιννυν ἀνθρώποις μόνην,
οὐδέν τι μᾶλλον εἰς τέλος σπουδάζομεν
μισθοὺς διδόντες μανθάνειν, ἵν᾽ ἦν ποτε
πείθειν ἅ τις βούλοιτο τυγχάνειν θ᾽ ἅμα ;

Wretch that I am, why should we poor mortals strive after
sciences of all kinds as matter of duty, diving into them, while we
slight, as nothing worth, Persuasion, the sole mistress o'er the
minds of men, refusing to pay money for that by which we might
persuade and gain what we wish ?

THE EVENTS OF LIFE.
Hec. 846.

Δεινόν γε, θνητοῖς ὡς ἄπαντα συμπίτνει,
καὶ τὰς ἀνάγκας οἱ νόμοι διώρισαν,
φίλους τιθέντες τούς γε πολεμιωτάτους,
ἐχθρούς τε τοὺς πρὶν εὐμενεῖς ποιούμενοι.

How strange the events of human life! laws control even the
Fates, changing the sternest foe to a kind friend, and making
enemies of those who before were on good terms.

THE BOASTED LIBERTY OF MAN.
Hec. 864.

Οὐκ ἔστι θνητῶν ὅστις ἔστ᾽ ἐλεύθερος·
ἢ χρημάτων γὰρ δοῦλός ἐστιν ἢ τύχης,
ἢ πλῆθος αὐτὸν πόλεος ἢ νόμων γραφαὶ
εἴργουσι χρῆσθαι μὴ κατὰ γνώμην τρόποις.

There is no man free ; for he is a slave either to wealth or fortune, or else the populace of the city or the laws prevent him from
acting according to the dictates of his will.

THE WICKED.
Hec. 902.

Πᾶσι γὰρ κοινὸν τόδε,
ἰδίᾳ θ᾽ ἑκάστῳ καὶ πόλει, τὸν μὲν κακὸν
κακόν τι πάσχειν, τὸν δὲ χρηστὸν εὐτυχεῖν.

For this is for the general good of all—individuals and states,
that punishment should overtake the wicked, and that the virtuous should enjoy happiness.

WOMEN.
Hec. 1177.

Ὡς δὲ μὴ μακροὺς τείνω λόγους,
εἴ τις γυναῖκας τῶν πρὶν εἴρηκεν κακῶς,
ἢ νῦν λέγων τίς ἐστιν ἢ μέλλει λέγειν,
ἅπαντα ταῦτα συντεμὼν ἐγὼ φράσω·
γένος γὰρ οὔτε πόντος οὔτε γῆ τρέφει
τοιόνδ᾽· ὁ δ᾽ ἀεὶ ξυντυχὼν ἐπίσταται.

To be brief, if any one in past times has reviled women, if any
one now does, or hereafter shall revile them, in one brief sentence
I shall comprise the whole: it is a breed which neither sea nor
earth produces the like ; he who is always with them knows them
best.

FRIENDSHIP.
Hec. 1226.

’Εν τοῖς κακοῖς γὰρ ἀγαθοὶ σαφέστατοι
φίλοι· τὰ χρηστὰ δ’ αὔθ’ ἔκαστ’ ἔχει φίλους.

In adversity the friendship of the good shines most clearly;
prosperity never fails in friends.

MAN’S EVIL MANNERS.
Hel. 264.

Καὶ τὰς τύχας μὲν τὰς κακάς, ἃς νῦν ἔχω,
Ἕλληνες ἐπελάθοντο, τὰς δὲ μὴ κακὰς
ἔσωζον ὥσπερ τὰς κακὰς σώζουσί μου.

Would that the Greeks had forgotten the evil fortune which I
now endure, but preserved the good in memory as they preserve
my bad.
Shakespeare (“Henry VIII.,” act iv. sc. 4) says—
“ Men's evil manners live in brass ; their virtues
We write in water.”

A RUDE HUSBAND.
Hel. 296.

’Αλλ’ ὅταν πόσις πικρὸς
ξυνῇ γυναικί, καὶ τὸ σῶν ἐστιν πικρόν
θανεῖν κράτιστον.

When a husband treats a woman roughly, it is better to die.

NOTHING STRONGER THAN NECESSITY.
Hel. 513.

Λόγος γάρ ἐστιν οὐκ ἐμός, σοφῶν δ’ ἔπος,
δεινῆς ἀνάγκης οὐδὲν ἰσχύειν πλέον.

Not mine
This saying, but the sentence of the sage,
Nothing is stronger than necessity.

DIFFERENT FORTUNES TO DIFFERENT MEN.
Hel. 710.

Ὦ θύγατερ, ὁ θεὸς ὡς ἔφυ τι ποικίλον
καὶ δυστέκμαρτον. Εὖ δέ πως ἀναστρέφει
ἐκεῖσι κἀκεῖσ’ ἀναφέρων· ὁ μὲν πονεῖ,
ὁ δ’ οὐ πονήσας αὖθις ὄλλυται κακῶς,
βέβαιον οὐδὲν τῆς ἀεὶ τύχης ἔχων.

My daughter, how God assigns to different men fortunes different and inscrutable! But well I ween He turns affairs upside down, bearing them hither and thither: one toils, another knows not toil, but ruin overwhelms him, having no firm hold on fortune.

PRUDENCE.

Hel. 756.

Κοὐδεὶς ἐπλούτησ᾽ ἐμπύροισιν ἀργὸς ὤν·
γνώμη δ᾽ ἀρίστη μάντις ἥ τ᾽ εὐβουλία.

No one ever grew rich on hallowed flames by idly gazing: discernment and prudence are the best of prophets.

LIGHT LIES THE EARTH ON THE BRAVE.

Hel. 851.

Εἰ γάρ εἰσιν οἱ θεοὶ σοφοί,
εὔψυχον ἄνδρα πολεμίων θανόνθ᾽ ὕπο
κούφῃ καταμπίσχουσιν ἐν τύμβῳ χθονί,
κακοὺς δ᾽ ἐφ᾽ ἕρμα στερεὸν ἐκβάλλουσι γῆς.

For, if the gods be wise, they will lay the earth lightly on the grave of the brave, but cast the craven beneath a hard mound of earth.

THE UNRIGHTEOUS.

Hel. 1030.

Οὐδεὶς ποτ᾽ εὐτύχησεν ἔκδικος γεγώς,
ἐν τῷ δικαίῳ δ᾽ ἐλπίδες σωτηρίας.

No one that is unrighteous has ever prospered, but hopes of safety never forsake the just.

"WHO HATH KNOWN THE MIND OF THE LORD?"

Hel. 1137.

Ὅ τι θεὸς ἢ μὴ θεὸς ἢ τὸ μέσον,
τίς φύσιν ἐρευνήσας βροτῶν·
μακρότατον πέρας εὗρεν.

Whether it was a god, or not a god, or something between, who of mortals by searching to the end can find out?

See Romans xi. 34.

THE LABOURER.

Elect. 75.

Εἰσιόντι δ᾽ ἐργάτῃ
θύραθεν ἡδὺ τἄνδον εὑρίσκειν καλῶς.

It is pleasant for a labourer returning from a distance to find things in his house aright.

The Noble to be Judged by Manners and by Deeds.

Elect. 368.

Οὐκ ἔστ' ἀκριβὲς οὐδὲν εἰς εὐανδρίαν·
ἔχουσι γὰρ ταραγμὸν αἱ φύσεις βροτῶν.
Ἤδη γὰρ εἶδον ἄνδρα γενναίου πατρὸς
τὸ μηδὲν ὄντα, χρηστά τ' ἐκ κακῶν τέκνα,
λιμόν τ' ἐν ἀνδρὸς πλουσίου φρονήματι,
γνώμην τε μεγάλην ἐν πένητι σώματι.
Πῶς οὖν τις αὐτὰ διαλαβὼν ὀρθῶς κρινεῖ;
πλούτῳ; πονηρῷ γ' ἆρα χρήσεται κριτῇ·
ἢ τοῖς ἔχουσι μηδέν; ἀλλ' ἔχει νόσον
πενία, διδάσκει δ' ἄνδρα τῇ χρείᾳ κακόν.
Ἀλλ' εἰς ὅπλ' ἔλθω; τίς δὲ πρὸς λόγχην βλέπων
μάρτυς γένοιτ' ἂν ὅστις ἐστὶν ἀγαθός;
κράτιστον εἰκῇ ταῦτ' ἐᾶν ἀφειμένα.
Οὗτος γὰρ ἀνὴρ οὔτ' ἐν Ἀργείοις μέγας
οὔτ' αὖ δοκήσει δωμάτων ὠγκωμένος,
ἐν τοῖς τε πολλοῖς ὢν ἄριστος εὑρέθη.
Οὐ μὴ φρονήσηθ', οἳ κενῶν δοξασμάτων
πλήρεις πλανᾶσθε· τῇ δ' ὁμιλίᾳ βροτοὺς
κρινεῖτε καὶ τοῖς ἤθεσιν τοὺς εὐγενεῖς.
Οἱ γὰρ τοιοίδε τὰς πόλεις οἰκοῦσιν εὖ
καὶ δώμαθ', αἱ δὲ σάρκες αἱ κεναὶ φρενῶν
ἀγάλματ' ἀγορᾶς εἰσιν. Οὐδὲ γὰρ δόρυ
μᾶλλον βραχίων σθεναρὸς ἀσθενοῦς μένει·
ἐν τῇ φύσει δὲ τοῦτο κἀν εὐψυχίᾳ.

There is no outward mark to note the noble, for the inward qualities of man are never clearly to be distinguished. I have often seen a man of no worth spring from a noble sire, and worthy children arise from vile parents, meanness grovelling in the rich man's mind and generous feelings in the poor. How, then, shall we discern and judge aright? By wealth? we shall make use of a bad criterion. By poverty? poverty has this disadvantage: it prompts a man to evil deeds. Shall it be by arms? But who, by looking to the spear, could thereby discern the dauntless heart? It is best to leave these things to be decided as they may. For this man, neither great among the Argives nor puffed up by the honours of his house, being plebeian, has proved his nobility by nature. Will ye not, then, learn wisdom, ye who wander in the paths of vanity? Will ye not learn to judge the noble by manners and by deeds? For such men as these discharge their duties with honour to the state and to their house. Mere flesh without a spirit is nothing more than statues in the Forum. For the strong arm does not abide the shock of battle better than the weak : this depends on nature and an intrepid mind.

See (Lat.) Mind is the man.

JUDGE NOT BY OUTWARD APPEARANCE.

Elect. 550.

'Αλλ' εὐγενεῖς μέν, ἐν δὲ κιβδήλῳ τόδε·
πολλοὶ γὰρ ὄντες εὐγενεῖς εἰσιν κακοί.

They are noble in appearance, but this is mere outside; for many noble-born are base.

MARRY YOUR EQUAL.

Elect. 930.

Πᾶσιν δ' ἐν Ἀργείοισιν ἤκουες τάδε·
ὁ τῆς γυναικός, οὐχὶ τἀνδρὸς ἡ γυνη.
Καίτοι τόδ' αἰσχρόν, προστατεῖν γε δωμάτων
γυναῖκα, μὴ τὸν ἄνδρα· κἀκείνους στυγῶ
τοὺς παῖδας, ὅστις τοῦ μὲν ἄρσενος πατρὸς
οὐκ ὠνόμασται, τῆς δὲ μητρὸς ἐν πόλει.
Ἐπίσημα γὰρ γήμαντι καὶ μείζω λέχη
τἀνδρὸς μὲν οὐδείς, τῶν δὲ θηλειῶν λόγος.

And among all the Argives thou didst hear such words as these—
"The man obeys the wife, and not the wife her husband." This is shameful for the woman, that the man should not rule the household; and I hate those children who are spoken of as sprung from the mother, not the father. For he who weds a wife of higher rank and nobler blood sinks into nothing, lost in her superior splendour.

UNJUST WEALTH.

Elect. 941.

Ἡ γὰρ φύσις βέβαιος,' οὐ τὰ χρήματα.
Ἡ μὲν γὰρ ἀεὶ παραμένουσ' αἴρει κάρα·
ὁ δ' ὄλβος ἄδικος καὶ μετὰ σκαιῶν ξυνὼν
ἐξέπτατ' οἴκων, σμικρὸν ἀνθήσας χρόνον.

Nature is immovable, not riches; she remains for ever and uplifts her head: but wealth unjustly acquired, and in the possession of the base, is wont to flit from the house, having flourished for some short space.

See Proverbs xxiii. 5.

A WOMAN.

Elect. 1013.

Δόξ' ὅταν λάβῃ κακὴ
γυναῖκα, γλώσσῃ πικρότης ἔνεστί τις.

When a wrong idea possesses a woman, much bitterness flows from her tongue.

WOMAN.
Elect. 1071.

Γυνὴ δ' ἀπόντος ἀνδρὸς ἥτις ἐκ δόμων
εἰς κάλλος ἀσκεῖ, διάγραφ' ὡς οὖσαν κακήν.
Οὐδὲν γὰρ αὐτὴν δεῖ θύρασιν εὐπρεπὲς
φαίνειν πρόσωπον, ἤν τι μὴ ζητῇ κακόν.

The woman who, in her husband's absence, seeks to set her
beauty forth, mark her as a wanton; she would not adorn her
person to appear abroad unless she was inclined to ill.

VICE HOLDS A MIRROR TO THE GOOD.
Elect. 1084.

Τὰ γὰρ κακὰ
παράδειγμα τοῖς ἐσθλοῖσιν εἴσοψίν τ' ἔχει.

Evil deeds hold up an example and mirror to the good.

WED NOT A VICIOUS WOMAN.
Elect. 1097.

Ὅστις δὲ πλοῦτον ἢ εὐγένειαν εἰσιδὼν
γαμεῖ πονηράν, μῶρός ἐστι· μικρὰ γὰρ
μεγάλων ἀμείνω σώφρον' ἐν δόμοις λέχη.

Whoever, allured by riches or high rank, marries a vicious
woman, is a fool; for an humble yet modest partner is better in
our house than a noble one.

WOMAN.
Elect. 1100.

Τύχη γυναικῶν εἰς γάμους. Τὰ μὲν γὰρ εὖ,
τὰ δ' οὐ καλῶς πίπτοντα δέρκομαι βροτῶν.

Fortune rules in nuptials; for some I see to be a source of joy
to mortals, others turn out badly.

THE HAPPY.
Elect. 1357.

Χαίρειν δ' ὅστις δύναται
καὶ ξυντυχίᾳ μή τινι κάμνει
θνητῶν, εὐδαίμονα πράσσει.

Whoever is able to pass through life calmly, and labours not
under affliction, we deem to be blest.

AN UNBRIDLED TONGUE.

Orest. 10.

'Ακόλαστον ἔσχε γλῶσσαν, αἰσχίστην νόσον.

He had an unbridled tongue, the worst of diseases.

NATURE.

Orest. 126.

Ὦ φύσις, ἐν ἀνθρώποισιν ὡς μέγ' εἶ κακόν,
σωτήριόν τε τοῖς καλῶς κεκτημένοις.

O nature, how great an ill thou art among the bad, but in the virtuous a safeguard.

SLEEP.

Orest. 211.

Ὦ φίλον ὕπνου θέλγητρον, ἐπίκουρον νόσου,
ὡς ἡδύ μοι προσῆλθες ἐν δέοντί τε.
ὦ πότνια λήθη τῶν κακῶν, ὡς εἶ σοφὴ
καὶ τοῖσι δυστυχοῦσιν εὐκταία θεός.

O precious balm of sleep, thou that soothest disease, how pleasant thou camest to me in the time of need! O divine oblivion of my sufferings, how wise thou art, and a goddess to be invited by all in distress!

Shakespeare ("Henry IV.," part ii. act iii. sc. 1)—

> "O sleep, O gentle sleep!
> Nature's soft nurse, how have I frighted thee,
> That thou no more wilt weigh my eyelids down,
> And steep my senses in forgetfulness."
>
> See (Lat. Gr.) Sleep.

MAN THAT IS FORTUNATE IN HIS CHILDREN.

Orest. 541.

Ζηλωτὸς ὅστις εὐτύχησεν εἰς τέκνα,
καὶ μὴ 'πισήμους συμφορὰς ἐκτήσατο.

Happy the man who is blest in his children, and hath not in them experienced grievous calamities.

A HAPPY MARRIAGE.

Orest. 602.

Γάμοι δ' ὅσοις μὲν εὖ καθεστᾶσιν βροτῶν,
μακάριος αἰών· οἷς δὲ μὴ πίπτουσιν εὖ,
τά τ' ἔνδον εἰσὶ τά τε θύραξε δυστυχεῖς.

Life is blest to those whose connubial state is well arranged ;
but to those to whom it falls not out well, their affairs are unfortunate at home and abroad.

A Friend in Need.

Orest. 666.

Τοὺς φίλους
ἐν τοῖς κακοῖς χρὴ τοῖς φίλοισιν ὠφελεῖν·
ὅταν δ᾽ ὁ δαίμων εὖ διδῷ, τί δεῖ φίλων ;
ἀρκεῖ γὰρ αὐτὸς ὁ θεὸς ὠφελεῖν θέλων.

Friends should assist friends in misfortunes ; when fortune
smiles, what need of friends? For God himself sufficeth, being
willing to assist.

An Excited Mob.

Orest. 695.

Ὅταν γὰρ ἡβᾷ δῆμος εἰς ὀργὴν πεσών,
ὅμοιον ὥστε πῦρ κατασβέσαι λάβρον·
εἰ δ᾽ ἡσύχως τις αὐτὸς ἐντείνοντι μὲν
χαλκῶν ὑπείκοι καιρὸν εὐλαβούμενος,
ἴσως ἂν ἐκπνεύσει· ὅταν δ᾽ ἀνῇ πνοάς,
τύχοις ἂν αὐτοῦ ῥᾳδίως ὅσον θέλεις.
Ἔνεστι δ᾽ οἶκτος, ἔνι δὲ καὶ θυμὸς μέγας,
καραδοκοῦντι κτῆμα τιμιώτατον.

When the excited populace is in full fury, it is as difficult to
control them as it is to extinguish a rolling flame ; but if we yield
to their violence as it is spreading, watching our opportunity,
they may perhaps exhaust their rage, and, as their fury abates,
thou may then turn them as thou pleasest. Their passions vary,
now melting to pity, now rough with rage, affording an excellent
advantage to one who watches carefully his opportunity.

A Friend in Need.

Orest. 727.

Πιστὸς ἐν κακοῖς ἀνὴρ
κρείσσων γαλήνης ναυτίλοισιν εἰσορᾶν.

In distress a friend comes like a calm to the tempest-tossed
mariner.

Sympathy.

Orest. 805.

Ὡς ἀνήρ, ὅστις τρόποισι συντακῇ, θυραῖος ὢν
μυρίων κρείσσων ὁμαίμων ἀνδρὶ κεκτῆσθαι φίλος.

G

Since the man who melts with social sympathy, though not
allied in blood, is more valuable as a friend than ten thousand
kinsmen.

THE SMOOTH TONGUE.

Orest. 903.

Ἀνήρ τις ἀθυρόγλωσσος, ἰσχύων θράσει,
Ἀργεῖος οὐκ Ἀργεῖος, ἠναγκασμένος,
θορύβῳ τε πίσυνος κἀμαθεῖ παρρησίᾳ,
πιθανὸς ἔτ᾽ αὐτοὺς περιβαλεῖν κακῷ τινι.
Ὅταν γὰρ ἡδὺς τοῖς λόγοις φρονῶν κακῶς
πείθῃ τὸ πλῆθος, τῇ πόλει κακὸν μέγα·
ὅσοι δὲ σὺν νῷ χρηστὰ βουλεύουσ᾽ ἀεί,
κἂν μὴ παραυτίκ᾽, αὖθίς εἰσι χρήσιμοι
πόλει.   Θεᾶσθαι δ᾽ ὧδε χρὴ τὸν προστάτην
ἰδόνθ᾽.

After him rises up a man of licentious tongue, intemperate, an
Argive, yet not an Argive, forced upon us, trusting to thoughtless
tumult, and prompt to lead with empty words the populace to
mischief. For the smooth tongue that charms to ill brings great
evil on the city. Whereas those who give good advice with forethought, though not immediately, yet eventually are of use to the
state ; but the far-seeing ruler ought to look to this.

THE MAN OF INTEGRITY AND PRUDENCE.

Orest. 917.

Ἄλλος δ᾽ ἀναστὰς ἔλεγε τῷδ᾽ ἐναντία,
μορφῇ μὲν οὐκ εὐωπός, ἀνδρεῖος δ᾽ ἀνήρ,
ὀλιγάκις ἄστυ κἀγορᾶς χραίνων κύκλον,
αὐτουργός, οἵπερ καὶ μόνοι σώζουσι γῆν,
ξυνετὸς δὲ χωρεῖν ὁμόσε τοῖς λόγοις θέλων
ἀκέραιος, ἀνεπίληπτον ἠσκηκὼς βίον.

But another rose altogether different, not made to please the
eye, but of manly form, one who rarely joined the city circles, a
yeoman, which class of men alone preserve the country, prudent,
wishing his conduct to be in harmony with his words, passing a
pure and blameless life.

THE WISE FRIEND.

Orest. 1155.

Οὐκ ἔστιν οὐδὲν κρεῖσσον ἢ φίλος σαφής,
οὐ πλοῦτος, οὐ τυραννίς· ἀλόγιστον δέ τι
τὸ πλῆθος ἀντάλλαγμα γενναίου φίλου.

There is no blessing like a prudent friend, neither riches nor the power of monarchs : popular applause is of little value in exchange for a generous friend.

LIFE IS SWEET.

Orest. 1523.

Πᾶς ἀνήρ, κἂν δοῦλος ᾖ τις, ἥδεται τὸ φῶς ὁρῶν.

To every man, even though he be a slave, the light of heaven is sweet.

WOMEN.

Androm. 93.

Ἐμπέφυκε γὰρ
γυναιξὶ τέρψις τῶν παρεστώτων κακῶν
ἀνὰ στόμ' ἀεὶ καὶ διὰ γλώσσης ἔχειν.

For women are formed by nature to feel some consolation in present troubles, by having them always in their mouth and on their tongue.

WOMAN BROOKS NOT A RIVAL.

Androm. 181.

Ἐπίφθονόν τι χρῆμα θηλειῶν ἔφυ
καὶ ξυγγάμοισι δυσμενὲς μάλιστ' ἀεί.

Woman is prone by nature to jealousy, and brooks not a rival in the nuptial bed.

THE HIGH-BORN.

Androm. 189.

Οἱ γὰρ πνέοντες μεγάλα τοὺς κρείσσους λόγους
πικρῶς φέρουσι τῶν ἐλασσόνων ὕπο.

For those who are puffed up with pride ill brook the speech of their inferiors, though urged with reason.

A BAD WOMAN.

Androm. 269.

Δεινὸν δ' ἑρπετῶν μὲν ἀγρίων
ἄκη βροτοῖσι θεῶν καταστῆσαί τινα,
ἃ δ' ἔστ' ἐχίδνης καὶ πυρὸς περαιτέρω,
οὐδεὶς γυναικὸς φάρμακ' ἐξεύρηκέ πω
κακῆς· τοσοῦτόν ἐσμεν ἀνθρώποις κακόν.

Strange that one of the gods should have given healing medicines against the venom of savage serpents, yet none have found a cure against a bad woman, more noxious than the viper or fire itself : so pestilent an ill are we to men.

GLORY.

Androm. 319.

*Ὦ δόξα δόξα, μυρίοισι δὴ βροτῶν
οὐδὲν γεγῶσι βίοτον ὤγκωσας μέγαν.
Εὔκλεια δ' οἷς μέν ἐστ' ἀληθείας ὕπο,
εὐδαιμονίζω· τοὺς δ' ὑπὸ ψευδῶν ἔχειν
οὐκ ἀξιώσω πλὴν τύχῃ φρονεῖν δοκεῖν.

Glory, O glory! thou hast uplifted high in life countless mortals who were nought: those I deem to be happy who have acquired glory truthfully; but those who have it falsely I consider to have it not; it is the mere wantonness of fortune that has given it to them.

THE SEMBLANCE OF POWER.

Androm. 330.

*Ἔξωθέν εἰσιν οἱ δοκοῦντες εὖ φρονεῖν
λαμπροί, τὰ δ' ἔνδον πᾶσιν ἀνθρώποις ἴσοι,
πλὴν εἴ τι πλούτῳ· τοῦτο δ' ἰσχύει μέγα.

Those who only wear the semblance of worth have splendid outsides, but within are found like other men, unless they gain some eminence for wealth; this, indeed, hath mighty power.

THE DAUGHTER OF A BAD MOTHER.

Androm. 619.

Κἀγὼ μὲν ηὔδων τῷ γαμοῦντι μήτε σοι
κῆδος ξυνάψαι μήτε δώμασιν λαβεῖν
κακῆς γυναικὸς πῶλον· ἐκφέρουσι γὰρ
μητρῷ' ὀνείδη. Τοῦτο κἀι σκοπεῖτέ μοι,
μνηστῆρες, ἐσθλῆς θυγατέρ' ἐκ μητρὸς λαβεῖν.

Before his nuptials, I warned my son not to form alliance with thee, nor receive within his house the foal of a bad mother, for such bring with them their mother's faults; wherefore.remember this, ye wooers, make your brides daughters of a virtuous mother.

THE TONGUE.

Androm. 642.

Σμικρᾶς ἀπ' ἀρχῆς νεῖκος ἀνθρώποις μέγα
γλῶσσ' ἐκπορίζει· τοῦτο δ' οἱ σοφοὶ βροτῶι
ἐξευλαβοῦνται, μὴ φίλοις τεύχειν ἔριν.

From a small beginning the tongue excites mighty strife among men; but the prudent guard against contention with their friends.

See James iii. 5–8.

SOCIAL INTERCOURSE.

Androm. 683.

'Η δ' ὁμιλία
πάντων βροτοῖσι γίγνεται διδάσκαλος.

Social intercourse is the teacher of all things to mortals.

OLD AGE.

Androm. 727.

'Ανειμένον τι χρῆμα πρεσβυτῶν ἔφυ
καὶ δυσφύλακτον ὀξυθυμίας ὕπο.

The race of old men is by nature hasty and impatient of control, through choler.

THE PASSIONATE.

Androm. 732.

Θυμούμενος δὲ τεύξεται θυμουμένων,
ἔργοισι δ' ἔργα διάδοχ' ἀντιλήψεται.

If he be passionate, he will meet with passion, and shall receive deeds in return for deeds.

So Matt. (v. 21)—"Ye have heard that it was said by them of old time, Thou shalt not kill; and whosoever shall kill shall be in danger of the judgment: but I say unto you, that whosoever is angry with his brother without a cause shall be in danger of the judgment."

A VOICE AND NOTHING MORE.

Androm. 744.

Τοὺς σοὺς δὲ μύθους ῥᾳδίως ἐγὼ φέρω·
σκιᾷ γὰρ ἀντίστοιχος ὢν Φωνὴν ἔχεις,
ἀδύνατος οὐδὲν ἄλλο πλὴν λέγειν μόνον.

What thou sayest I bear unmoved; for thou hast a voice void of power, like a shadow: thou can'st do nought but talk.

See (Lat.) Mind is the man.

CALAMITIES SOONER OR LATER.

Androm. 852.

Συμφοραὶ θεήλατοι
πᾶσιν βροτοῖσιν ἢ τότ' ἦλθον ἢ τότε.

Calamities sent by the gods come to all mortals sooner or later.

So Proverbs (xvi. 33)—"The lot is cast into the lap; but the whole disposing thereof is of the Lord."

FEMALE BUSYBODIES.

Androm. 943.

'Αλλ' οὔποτ' οὔποτ', οὐ γὰρ εἰσάπαξ ἐρῶ,
χρὴ τούς γε νοῦν ἔχοντας, οἷς ἔστιν γυνή,
πρὸς τὴν ἐν οἴκοις ἄλοχον εἰσφοιτᾶν ἐᾶν
γυναῖκας· αὗται γὰρ διδάσκαλοι κακῶν·
ἡ μέν τι κερδαίνουσα συμφθείρει λέχος,
ἡ δ' ἀμπλακοῦσα συννοσεῖν αὐτῇ θέλει,
πολλαὶ δὲ μαργότητι. Κἀντεῦθεν δόμοι
νοσοῦσιν ἀνδρῶν. Πρὸς τάδ' εὖ φυλάσσετε
κλείθροισι καὶ μοχλοῖσι δωμάτων πύλας·
ὑγιὲς γὰρ οὐδὲν αἱ θύραθεν εἴσοδοι
δρῶσιν γυναικῶν, ἀλλὰ πολλὰ καὶ κακά.

But never, never (for I shall repeat it more than once), should
the wise allow females to frequent their house ; they are in-
structors to evil deeds. One corrupts the wife to make gain by
it ; another, who has fallen from virtue, wishes to make her vile
like herself ; and many do this from mere wantonness ; hence the
homes of men are ruined. Against such let him guard well his
gates with bolts and bars ; for these visits of women from without
do no good, but abundant ill.

FATES OF MEN.

Frag. Androm. (*Stob.*)

Τὸ δαιμόνιον οὐχ ὁρᾷς ὅπη μοίρας
διεξέρχεται, στρέφει δ' ἄλλους ἄλλως
εἰς ἀμέραν.

See'st thou not what various fates the Divinity makes man to
pass through, changing and turning them from day to day.

TIME.

Frag. Æol. (*Stob.*)

'Ο χρόνος ἅπαντα τοῖσιν ὕστερον φράσει.
Λάλος ἐστὶν οὗτος, οὐκ ἐρωτῶσιν λέγει.

Time will discover everything to posterity : it is a babbler, and
speaks even when no question is put.

See (Lat.) Time.

FATHERLAND.

Frag. Œg. (*Stob.*)

Τί γὰρ πατρῴας ἀνδρὶ φίλτερον χθονός ;

What is more dear to a man than his fatherland ?

See (Lat.) Fatherland.

DEATH.

Frag. Œg. (Stob.)

Κατθανεῖν δ' ὀφείλεται
καὶ τῷ κατ' οἴκους ἐκτὸς ἡμένῳ πόνων.

The debt of nature must be paid, even by the man who remains at home, away from all dangers.

See (Lat. Gr.) Death.

VIRTUOUS LIFE.

Frag. Œg. (Stob.)

*Ἦ που κρεῖσσον τῆς εὐγενίας
τὸ καλῶς πράσσειν.

Virtuous and noble deeds are better than high descent.

See (Lat.) Virtue.

THE TONGUE.

Frag. Œg. (Stob.)

Εἰ μὴ καθέξεις γλῶσσαν, ἔσται σοι κακά.

If thou wilt not restrain thy tongue, it will bring evil upon thee.

See James iii. 5–8.

RICH AND POOR.

Frag. Æol. (Stob.)

Δοκεῖτ' ἂν οἰκεῖν γαῖαν, εἰ πένης ἅπας
λαὸς πολιτεύοιτο πλουσίων ἄτερ ;
οὐκ ἂν γένοιτο χωρὶς ἐσθλὰ καὶ κακά,
ἀλλ' ἔστι τις σύγκρασις ὥστ' ἔχειν καλῶς,
ἃ μὴ γὰρ ἐστι τῷ πένηθ', ὁ πλούσιος
δίδωσ' ὁ δ' οἱ πλουτοῦντες οὐ κεκτήμεθα,
τοῖσιν πένησι χρώμενοι θηρώμεθα.

Do you think that a land can prosper where the whole government is in the hand of the poor, without any admixture of the rich ? The rich and poor should not be separate ; but there should be a mixture, that the country may prosper. For the rich supply what the poor have not ; and what we rich men do not possess, we can obtain by employing the poor.

WICKED ACTIONS OF MEN.

Frag. Melanip. (Stob.)

Δοκεῖτε πηδᾶν τ' ἀδικήματ' εἰς θεοὺς
πτεροῖσι, κἄπειτ' ἐν Διὸς δέλτου πτυχαῖς
γράφειν τιν' αὐτά, Ζῆνα δ' εἰσορῶντα νιν

θνητοῖς δικάζειν ; Οὐδ' ὁ πᾶς οὖν οὐρανὸς
Διὸς γράφοντας τὰς βροτῶν ἁμαρτίας
ἐξαρκέσειεν, οὐδ' ἐκεῖνος αὖ σκοπῶν
πέμπειν ἑκάστῳ ζημίαν· ἀλλ' ἡ Δίκη
ἐνταῦθα πού 'στιν ἐγγὺς, εἰ βούλεσθ' ὁρᾷν.
Ταύτας μὲν ἀνθρώποισιν, ὦ γύναι, θεοὶ
τίσεις διδοῦσιν, οὓς ἂν ἐχθαίρωσ', ἐπεὶ
οὐ σφιν πονηρόν ἐστι δήποτ' ἂν φίλον.

Do you think that the evil deeds of men fly on wings to heaven,
and are there registered in the books of Jove, and that he, examining each, inflicts punishment on men? If it were so, the whole
expanse of heaven would not be sufficient to contain the sins of
mankind, nor could Jove have time to read and punish each.
Yet Vengeance, if we only carefully watch, dwells always near us.
O woman, the gods send this to take vengeance on those men
whom they hate, for no bad man is beloved by them.

Vengeance overtakes the Wicked.

Frag. Phryx. (Stob.)

Ὅστις δὲ θνητῶν οἴεται τοὐφ' ἡμέραν
κακόν τι πράσσων τοὺς θεοὺς λεληθέναι,
δοκεῖ πονηρά, καὶ δοκῶν ἁλίσκεται
ὅτ' ἂν σχόλην ἄγουσα τυγχάνει Δίκη,
τιμωρίαν τ' ἔτισεν ὧν ἦρξεν κακῶν.

Whoever thinks that he can go on committing sin without the
knowledge of the gods, acts foolishly ; he will be overtaken, when
Vengeance finds leisure, and will suffer for all his former misdeeds.

See (Lat.) Wicked, the.

Vengeance Slow of Foot.

Frag. ex. Stob.

Οὔτοι προσελθοῦσ' ἡ Δίκη σε πώποτε
παίσει πρὸς ἧπαρ, οὐδὲ τῶν ἄλλων βροτῶν.
Τὸν ἄδικον, ἀλλὰ σῖγα, καὶ βραδεῖ ποδὶ
στείχουσα, μάρπτει τοὺς κακοὺς ἀεὶ βροτῶν.

Vengeance comes not openly, either upon you or any wicked
man, but steals silently and imperceptibly, placing his foot on the
bad.

See (Lat.) Punishment of, slow pace.

Fortune attends on the Wise.

Frag. Pel. (Stob.)

Ὁ πρῶτος εἰπὼν, οὐκ ἀγυμνάστῳ φρενὶ
ἔῤῥιψεν, ὅστις τόνδ' ἐκαίνισεν λόγον,
ὡς τοῖσιν εὐφρονοῦσι συμμαχεῖ Τύχη.

Experience has shown that whoever first uttered the proverb was right when he said "that Fortune is the constant attendant on the wise and prudent."

VARIOUS INCLINATIONS OF MEN.

Frag. Rhadam. (Stob.)

Ἔρωτες εἰσὶν ἡμῖν παντοῖοι βίου·
ὁ μὲν γὰρ εὐγένειαν ἱμείρει λαβεῖν,
τῷ δ᾽ οὐχὶ τοῦτο φροντίς, ἀλλὰ χρημάτων
πολλῶν κεκλῆσθαι βούλεται πατὴρ δόμοις.
Ἄλλῳ δ᾽ ἀρέσκει μηδὲν ὑγιὲς ἐκ φρενῶν
λεγόντι πείθειν τούς πέλας τόλμῃ κακῇ·
οἱ δ᾽ αἰσχρὰ κέρδη πρόσθε τοῦ καλοῦ βροτῶν
ζητοῦσιν· οὕτω βίος ἀνθρώπων πλάνη.
Ἐγὼ δὲ τούτων οὐδενὸς χρῄζω τυχεῖν,
δόξαν δ᾽ ἐβουλοίμην ἂν εὐκλείας ἔχειν.

Various are the inclinations of man : one desires to be considered noble ; another cares nothing for high birth, but wishes to be possessed of much wealth. Others long for eloquence to persuade their audience to anything, however audacious. Others, again, prefer gain to honour ; so dissimilar are men. For my own part, I care for none of these, but pray for a good name and reputation.

A BAD BEGINNING BRINGS A BAD ENDING.

Frag. Æol. (Stob.)

Κακῆς ἀπ᾽ ἀρχῆς γίγνεται τέλος κακόν.

A bad ending follows a bad beginning.

DEATH THE FATE OF ALL.

Frag. Alex. (Stob.)

Πάντων τὸ θανεῖν· τὸ δὲ κοινὸν ἄχος
μετρίως ἀλγεῖν σοφία μελετᾷ.

All must die ; it is wisdom to submit with patience to the common lot.

See (Lat.) Death

CHILDREN LIKE THEIR FATHER.

Frag. Alcm. (Stob.)

Ὦ παῖ Κρέοντος, ὡς ἀληθὲς ἦν ἄρα
ἐσθλῶν ἀπ᾽ ἀνδρῶν ἐσθλὰ γίγνεσθαι τέκνα,
κακῶν δ᾽ ὅμοια τῇ φύσει τῇ τοῦ πατρός.

Son of Creon, how true is the observation, that noble children spring from noble fathers ; and that the children of the bad are like in nature to their parents.

NEVER DESPAIR.

Fragm. xviii.

'Εν ἐλπίσιν χρὴ τοὺς σοφοὺς ἔχειν βίον.

The wise should possess their lives in hope.

See (Lat.) Despair, never.

GOD DEPRIVES OF REASON HIM WHOM HE WISHES TO DESTROY.

Fragm.

"Οταν δὲ Δαίμων ἀνδρὶ πορσύνη κακά,
τὸν νοῦν ἔβλαψε πρῶτον.

When God is contriving misfortunes for man, He first deprives him of his reason.

See (Lat.) Jupiter.

PLEASANT TO REMEMBER PAST LABOURS.

Fragm. x. 2.

'Ως ἡδὺ τὸν σωθέντα μεμνῆσθαι πόνου.

How pleasant it is for him who is saved to remember his danger.

A FATHER'S ADVICE TO HIS SON.

Fragm. Erechtheus.

Πρῶτον φρένας μὲν ἠπίους ἔχειν χρεών,
τῷ πλουσίῳ τε τῷ τε μὴ διδοὺς μέρος
ἴσον σεαυτὸν εὐσεβεῖν πᾶσιν δίδου·
δυοῖν παρόντοιν πραγμάτοιν πρὸς θάτερον
γνώμην προσάπτων τὴν ἐναντίαν μέθες,
ἀδίκως δὲ μὴ κτῶ χρήματ' ἢν βούλη πολὺν
χρόνον μελάθροις ἐμμένειν· τὰ γὰρ κακῶς
οἴκους ἐσελθόντ' οὐκ ἔχει σωτηρίαν·
ἔχειν δὲ πειρῶ. τοῦτο γὰρ τό τ' εὐγενὲς
καὶ τοὺς γάμους δίδωσι τοὺς πρώτους ἔχειν.
'Εν τῷ πένεσθαι δ' ἐστὶν ἥ τ' ἀδοξία,
κἂν ᾖ σοφός τις, ἥ τ' ἀτιμία βίου,
φίλους δὲ τοὺς μὲν μὴ χαλῶντας ἐν λόγοις
κέκτησο, τοὺς δὲ πρὸς χάριν σὺν ἡδονῇ
τῇ σῇ πονηροὺς κλεῖθρον εἰργέτω στέγης,

ὁμιλίας τε τὰς γεραιτέρας φίλει,
ἀκόλαστα δ' ἤθη, λαμπρὰ συγγελᾶν μόνον,
μίσει· βραχεῖα τέρψις ἡδονῆς κακῆς.

In the first place, thou must have a gentle disposition : pay respect to all, giving the rich not more than an equal portion : be not opinionative when one of two things must be determined : get not riches by unjust means, if thou wishest them to continue in thy family, for riches unjustly acquired quickly vanish ; yet try to get them, for riches and high descent enable a man to marry well : in poverty there is dishonour, even though a man be wise, and also disgrace : get friends who are not willing to yield to thy wishes, and shut the bars of thy doors against the wicked, who are anxious to gratify thy desires : love the conversation of those who are older than thyself, and hate those of intemperate habits, only pleasant to joke with ; the enjoyment of unholy pleasure is of short duration.

ENVY.

Fragm. Ino. (Stob.)

Τίς ἆρα μήτηρ ἢ πατὴρ κάκον μέγα
βροτοῖς ἔφυσε τὸν δυσώνυμον φθόνον;
ποῦ καί ποτ' οἰκεῖ σώματος λαχὼν μέρος ;
ἐν χερσὶν, ἢ σπλάγχνοισιν, ἢ παρ' ὄμματα
ἐσθ' ἡμιν ; ὡς ἦν μόχθος ἰατροῖς μέγας
τομαῖς ἀφαιρεῖν ἢ ποτοῖς ἢ φαρμάκοις
πασῶν μεγίστην τῶν ἐν ἀνθρώποις νόσων.

Who was the mother or father that produced ill-omened envy, such a great ill to mortals? Where does she dwell, and in what part of the body? Is she in our hands, or heart, or eyes? What a dreadful labour for physicians to remove this greatest of all diseases in men, whether by the knife, by potions, or drugs !

PEACE.

Fragm. Cresphontes (Stob.)

Εἰρήνα, βαθύπλουτε καὶ
καλλίστα μακάρων θεῶν,
ζῆλός μοι σέθεν, ὡς χρονίζεις.
Δέδοικα δὲ, μὴ πρὶν πόνοις
ὑπερβάλῃ με γῆρας,
πρὶν σὰν χαρίεσσαν προσιδεῖν ὥραν
καὶ καλλιχόρους ἀοιδὰς
φιλοστεφάνους τε κώμους,
ἴθι μοι, πότνια, πόλιν·
τὰν δ' ἐχθρὰν στάσιν εἴργ' ἀπ' οἴκων τὰν μαινομέναν τ' ἔριν,
θηκτῷ τερπομέναν σιδάρῳ.

Peace, thou richest and most beautiful of the happy gods, the
envy of all, why dost thou loiter? I fear lest old age overtake
me with its ailments before I behold thy delightful produce,
songs with the dance and garland-crowned revellings. Thou
benignant goddess, visit my city, and drive off from my house
bloody sedition and frantic contention, delighting in the sharp-
pointed sword.

GOD HELPS THEM THAT HELP THEMSELVES.

Fragm. Temenid. (Stob.)

Αὐτός τι νῦν δρᾶ, χοὔτω δαίμονας κάλει·
τῷ γὰρ πονοῦντι χὠ θεὸς συλλαμβάνει.

Call in self-help, then ask the gods to aid,
For the gods aid the man who helps himself.

So the French—"Aide-toi et Dieu t'aidera."
This is the Greek proverb (Zenob. v. 93)—"Σὺν 'Αθηνᾷ καὶ χεῖρα κίνει;"
and the Spanish—"A dios vezando y con el mazo dando."

HERODOTUS.

BORN B.C. 484—WAS ALIVE B.C. 408.

HERODOTUS, the father of history, was a native of Halicarnassus,
a town of Caria, in Asia Minor. Of his private history very little
information, on which reliance can be put, has come down to us.
He was the son of Lyxes and Dryo, being descended from a family
not less distinguished for its wealth and political influence than
for its love of literature. His uncle, Panyasis, was highly esteemed
as an epic poet. The tyranny of Lygdamis drove him from his
native town, and though he assisted in delivering his country, the
disputes among the citizens after their liberation were so little to
his taste that he withdrew again, and settled at Thurii, in the
south of Italy, where he spent the remainder of his life, and
wrote, according to Pliny, his work in his old age. According to
Lucian, Herodotus read his work to the assembled Greeks at
Olympia, B.C. 456, with the great applause of the audience, in
consequence of which the nine books of the work have been
honoured with the name of the Nine Muses. He also states that
Thucydides, then about fifteen or sixteen years of age, was present
at this recitation, and was moved to tears. To this work we are
indebted for our knowledge of the origin and progress of the Persian monarchy; of that of the Medes and Assyrians.

Seeing better than Hearing.

i. 8.

Ὦτα γὰρ τυγχάνει ἀνθρώποισι ἐόντα ἀπιστότερα ὀφθαλμῶν.

1 am satisfied that we are less convinced by what we hear than by what we see.

See (Lat.) Seeing is believing.

Attend to our own Affairs.

i. 8.

Παλαι δὲ τὰ καλὰ ἀνθρώποισι ἐξεύρηται, ἐκ τῶν μανθάνειν δεῖ· ἐν τοῖσι ἐν τόδε ἐστὶ, σκοπέειν τινὰ τὰ ἑωυτοῦ.

Many are the precepts recorded by the sages for our instruction, but we ought to listen to none with more attention than that, "It becomes a man to give heed to those things only which regard himself."

See (Lat.) Our own.

Life is nothing but Misery.

i. 32.

Οὕτω ὦν, ὦ Κροῖσε, πᾶν ἐστι ἄνθρωπος συμφορή.

Thus, Crœsus, does our nature appear an uninterrupted series of misfortunes.

So Ecclesiastes (i. 14)—"I have seen all the works that are done under the sun ; and, behold, all is vanity and vexation of spirit."

The Rich Man and the Poor contrasted.

i. 82.

Οὐ γάρ τοι ὁ μέγα πλούσιος μᾶλλον τοῦ ἐπ' ἡμέρην ἔχοντος ὀλβιώτερός ἐστι, εἰ μή οἱ τύχη ἐπίσποιτο πάντα καλὰ ἔχοντα τελευτῆσαι εὖ τὸν βίον. Πολλοὶ μὲν γὰρ ξἀπλουτοι ἀνθρώπων, ἀνόλβιοί εἰσι· πολλοὶ δὲ μετρίως ἔχοντες βίου, εὐτυχέες.

The man of affluence is not, in fact, more happy than the possessor of a bare competency ; unless, in addition to his wealth, the end of his life be fortunate. We often see misery dwelling in the midst of splendour, whilst real happiness is found in humbler stations.

See (Lat.) Safety of an humble life ; The happy man.

The Happy Man.

i. 32.

Ὁ μὲν, ἐπιθυμίην ἐκτελέσαι, καὶ ἄτην μεγάλην προσπεσοῦσαν ἐνεῖκαι δυνατώτερος. Ὁ δὲ, τοισίδε προέχει ἐκείνου· ἄτην μὲν κα᾽

ἐπιθυμίην οὐκ ὁμοίως δυνατὸς ἐκείνῳ ἐνεῖκαι, ταῦτα δὲ ἡ εὐτυχίη οἱ
ἀπερύκει· ἄπηρος δὲ ἐστί, ἄνουσος, ἀπαθὴς κακῶν, εὔπαις, εὐειδής.
Εἰ δὲ πρὸς τούτοισι ἔτι τελευτήσει τὸν βίον εὖ, οὗτος ἐκεῖνος τὸν σὺ
ζητεῖς, ὄλβιος κεκλῆσθαι ἄξιός ἐστι.　Πρὶν δ᾽ ἂν τελευτήσῃ, ἐπισ-
χέειν, μηδὲ καλέειν κω ὄλβιον, ἀλλ᾽ εὐτυχέα.

The rich man, indeed, is better able to indulge his passions,
and to bear up against any harm that may befall him.　The poor
man's condition prevents him from enjoying such advantages ;
but then, as a set-off, he may possess strength of body, freedom
from disease, a mind relieved from many of the ills of life, is
blessed in his children, and active in his limbs.　If he shall,
besides, end his life well, then, O Crœsus, this is the happy man,
about whom thou art curiously inquiring.　Call no man happy
till thou knowest the end of his life ; up till that moment he can
only be called fortunate.

Look to the Event.

i. 32.

Σκοπέειν δὲ χρὴ παντὸς χρήματος τὴν τελευτὴν κῇ ἀποβήσεται.
Πολλοῖσι γὰρ δὴ ὑποδέξας ὄλβον ὁ θεὸς, προρρίζους ἀνέτρεψε.

It is the part of wisdom to wait to see the final result of things,
for God often tears up by the roots the prosperous, and overwhelms with misery those who have reached the highest pinnacle
of worldly happiness.

Heavy Punishments for Great Crimes.

ii. 120.

Τῶν μεγάλων ἀδικημάτων μεγάλαι εἰσὶ καὶ αἱ τιμωρίαι παρὰ τῶν
θεῶν.

The gods inflict heavy punishment on great crimes.

So Psalm (xlv. 18)—"Come, behold the works of the Lord, what desola-
tions He hath made in the earth.　He maketh wars to cease unto the end
of the earth ; He breaketh the bow, and cutteth the spear in sunder ; He
burneth the chariot in the fire.　Be still, and know that I am God."

All Work and no Play makes Jack a Dull Boy.

ii. 173.

Τὰ τόξα οἱ κεκτημένοι. ἐπεὰν μὲν δέωνται χρᾶσθαι, ἐντανύουσι·
ἐπεὰν δὲ χρήσωνται, ἐκλύουσι.　Εἰ γὰρ δὴ τὸν πάντα χρόνον ἐντετα-
μένα εἴη, ἐκραγείη ἄν· ὥστε ἐς τὸ δέον οὐκ ἂν ἔχοιεν αὐτοῖσι χρῆσθαι.
Οὕτω δὴ καὶ ἀνθρώπου κατάστασις· εἰ ἐθέλοι κατεσπουδάσθαι αἰεὶ,
μηδὲ ἐς παιγνίην τὸ μέρος ἑωυτὸν ἀνιέναι, λάθοι ἂν ἤτοι μανεὶς, ἢ
ὅγε ἀπόπληκτος γενόμενος.　Τὰ ἐγὼ ἐπιστάμενος μέρος ἑκατέρῳ
νέμω.

They who are skilled in archery bend their bow only when they are preparing to use it; when they do not require it, they allow it to remain unbent, for otherwise it would be unserviceable when the time for using it arrived. So it is with man. If he were to devote himself unceasingly to a dull round of business, without breaking the monotony by cheerful amusements, he would fall imperceptibly into idiocy, or be struck by paralysis. It is the conviction of this truth that leads to the proper division of my time.

See (Lat.) Relaxation.

CUSTOM.

iii. 38.

Οὕτω μὲν νῦν ταῦτα νενόμισται· καὶ ὀρθῶς μοι δοκέει Πίνδαρος ποιῆσαι, νόμον πάντων βασιλέα φήσας εἶναι.

Such is the force of custom; and Pindar seems to me to have spoken with peculiar propriety when he observed that custom was the universal sovereign.

See (Lat.) Custom.

UPS AND DOWNS OF LIFE.

iii. 40.

'Ηδὺ μὲν πυνθάνεσθαι ἄνδρα φίλον καὶ ξεῖνον εὖ πρήσσοντα· ἐμοὶ δὲ αἱ σαὶ μεγάλαι εὐτυχίαι οὐκ ἀρέσκουσι τὸ θεῖον ἐπισταμένῳ ὡς ἔστι φθονερόν. Καὶ κως βούλομαι καὶ αὐτὸς καὶ τῶν ἂν κήδωμαι τὸ μέν τι εὐτυχέειν τῶν πρηγμάτων, τὸ δὲ προσπταίειν· καὶ οὕτω δια-φέρειν τὸν αἰῶνα ἐναλλὰξ πρήσσων ἢ εὐτυχέειν ιὰ ηάντα. Οὐδένα γάρ κω λόγῳ οἶδα ἀκούσας, ὅστις ἐς τέλος οὐ κακῶς ἐτελεύτησε πρόῤῥιζος εὐτυχέων τὰ πάντα. Σὺ ὦν νῦν ἐμοὶ πειθόμενος ποίησον πρὸς τὰς εὐτυχίας τοιάδε· φροντίσας τὸ ἂν εὕρῃς ἐόν τοι πλείστου ἄξιον καὶ ἐπ' ᾧ σὺ ἀπολομένῳ μάλιστα τὴν ψυχὴν ἀλγήσεις, τοῦτο ἀπόβαλε οὕτω, ὅκως μηκέτι ἥξει ἐς ἀνθρώπους. ῍Ην τε μὴ ἐναλλάξ ἤδη τὠπὸ τούτου αἱ εὐτυχίαι τοι αὐταῖσι πάθαισι προσπίπτωσι, τρόπῳ τῷ ἐξ ἐμεῦ ὑποκειμένῳ ἀκέο.

It is no doubt pleasant to hear of the prosperity of a friend and ally; but, as I know the envious nature of Fortune, and how jealous she is of our success, thou must not be surprised that I feel some apprehensions respecting thee. In fact, if I could be allowed to choose for myself, and for those dear to me, I should prefer that the gale blew sometimes favourable and sometimes adverse. I would rather that my life was chequered with good and evil than that I should enjoy an uninterrupted course of good fortune. I do not remember of having ever heard of a man remarkable for a long run of good luck who did not in the end close his life with some extraordinary calamity. If, then, thou wilt attend to my advice, thou wilt provide the following remedy

against the excess of thy prosperity. Consider in thy own mind
on what thou placest the highest value, and the loss of which
thou wouldst most deplore ; cast this from thee, so that there
may be no possibility of its return. If thy good fortune still continue, thou wilt do well to repeat the remedy.

See (Lat.) Fortune.

BETTER TO BE ENVIED THAN PITIED.

iii. 52.

Σὺ δὲ μαθὼν ὅσῳ φθονέεσθαι κρέσσον ἐστὶ ἢ οἰκτείρεσθαι

Thou hast learned by experience how much better it is to be
envied than pitied.

POWER IS PRECARIOUS.

iii. 53.

Τυραννὶς χρῆμα.

Power, which many so assiduously court, is in its nature precarious.

See (Lat.) Power.

CHARACTER OF TYRANTS.

iii. 80.

Ἐγγίνεται μὲν γάρ οἱ ὕβρις ὑπὸ τῶν παρεόντων ἀγαθῶν, φθόνος δέ
ἀρχῆθεν ἐμφύεται ἀνθρώπῳ. Δύο δ᾽ ἔχων ταῦτα ἔχει πᾶσαν κακό-
τητα· τὰ μὲν γὰρ ὕβρι κεκορημένος ἔρδει πολλὰ καὶ ἀτάσθαλα· τὰ
δε φθόνῳ. Καίτοι ἄνδρα γε τύραννον ἄφθονον ἔδει εἶναι ἔχοντά γε
πάντα τὰ ἀγαθά· τὸ δ᾽ ὑπεναντίον τούτου ἐς τοὺς πολιήτας πέφυκε.
Φθονέει γὰρ τοῖσι ἀρίστοισι περιεοῦσί τε καὶ ζώουσι, χαίρει δὲ τοῖσι
κακίστοισι τῶν ἀστῶν, διαβολὰς δὲ ἄριστος ἐνδέκεσθαι. Ἀναρμοστό-
τατον δὲ πάντων· ἤν τε γὰρ αὐτὸν μετρίως θωυμάζῃς, ἄχθεται ὅτι οὐ
κάρτα θεραπεύεται· ἤν τε θεραπεύῃ τις κάρτα, ἄχθεται ἅτε θωπί.

For insolence is the natural result of great prosperity, while
envy and jealousy are innate qualities in the mind of man. When
these two vices are combined, they lead to the most enormous
crimes : some atrocities are committed from insolence, and others
from envy. Princes ought to be superior to all such feelings ;
but, alas ! we know that this is not the case. The noble and the
worthiest are the object of their jealousy, merely because they
feel that their lives are a reproach to them ; with the most abandoned they rejoice to spend their time. Calumny they drink in
with greedy ears. But what is the most paradoxical of all, if
thou showest them merely respectful homage, they take umbrage
because thou art not sufficiently humble ; whereas, if thou bend
the knee with the most submissive looks, thou art kicked away as
a flatterer.

See (Lat.) Tyrant

ENVY.

iii. 80.

Φθόνος ἀρχῆθεν ἐμφύεται ἀνθρώπῳ.

Envy is implanted by nature in man.

So Proverbs (xiv. 30)—"Envy is the rottenness of the bones."

FORCE OF LITTLE AVAIL.

iii. 127.

Ἔνθα γὰρ σοφίης δέει, βίης ἔργον οὐδέν.

For where wisdom is required, force is of little avail.

See (Lat.) The violent.

POWERS OF MIND STRENGTHEN AND GROW WEAK WITH THE BODY.

iii. 134.

Αὐξανομένῳ γὰρ τῷ σώματι συναύξονται καὶ αἱ φρένες· γηράσκοντι δὲ συγγηράσκουσι, καὶ ἐς τὰ πρήγματα πάντα ἀπαμβλύνονται.

For the powers of the mind gather strength with those of the body ; and in the same way, as old age creeps on, they get weaker and weaker, till they are finally insensible to everything.

BENEFITS OF DISCUSSION.

vii. 10.

Ὦ βασιλεῦ, μὴ λεχθεισέων μὲν γνωμέων ἀντιέων ἀλλήλῃσι, οὐκ ἔστι τὴν ἀμείνω αἱρεόμενον ἑλέσθαι, ἀλλὰ δεῖ τῇ εἰρημένῃ χρῆσθαι· λεχθεισέων δὲ, ἔστι· ὥσπερ τὸν χρυσὸν τὸν ἀκήρατον, αὐτὸν μὲν ἐπ᾿ ἑωυτοῦ οὐ διαγινώσκομεν, ἐπεὰν δὲ παρατρίψωμεν ἄλλῳ χρυσῷ, διαγινώσκομεν τὸν ἀμείνω.

Unless a variety of opinions are laid before us, we have no opportunity of selection, but are bound of necessity to adopt the particular view which may have been brought forward. The purity of gold cannot be ascertained by a single specimen ; but when we have carefully compared it with others, we are able to fix upon the finest ore.

So Thomson ("Liberty," Part ii.)—

" Friendly free discussion calling forth
From the fair jewel Truth its latent ray.

DELIBERATION AND FORETHOUGHT.

vii. 10.

Τὸ γὰρ εὖ βουλεύεσθαι κέρδος μέγιστον εὑρίσκω ἐόν. Εἰ γὰρ καὶ ἐναντιωθῆναί τι θέλει, βεβούλευται μὲν οὐδὲν ἧσσον εὖ, ἕσσωται δὲ ὑπὸ τῆς τύχης τὸ βούλευμα· ὁ δὲ βουλευσάμενος αἰσχρῶς, εἴ οἱ ἡ τύχη ἐπίσποιτο, εὕρημα εὕρηκε, ἧσσον δὲ οὐδέν οἱ κακῶς βεβούλευται. Ὁρᾷς τὰ ὑπερέχοντα ζῷα ὡς κεραυνοῖ ὁ θεὸς, οὐδὲ ἐᾷ φαντάζεσθαι, τὰ δὲ σμικρὰ οὐδέν μιν κνίζει ; ὁρᾷς δὲ ὡς ἐς οἰκήματα τὰ μέγιστα αἰεὶ, καὶ δένδρεα τὰ τοιαῦτα, ἀποσκήπτει τὰ βέλεα ; φιλέει γὰρ ὁ θεὸς τὰ ὑπερέχοντα πάντα κολούειν. Οὕτω δὴ καὶ στρατὸς πολλὸς ὑπὸ ὀλίγου διαφθείρεται κατὰ τοιόνδε. Ἐπεάν σφι ὁ θεὸς φθονήσας φόβον ἐμβάλῃ, ἢ βροντὴν, δι᾽ ὧν ἐφθάρησαν ἀναξίως ἑωυτῶν· οὐ γὰρ ἐᾷ φρονέειν μέγα ὁ θεὸς ἄλλον ἢ ἑωυτόν.

For my own part, I have found from experience that the greatest good is to be got from forethought and deliberation ; even if the result is not such as we expected, at all events we have the feeling that we have done all in our power to merit success, and therefore the blame must be attached to fortune alone. The man who is foolish and inconsiderate, even when fortune shines upon him, is not the less to be censured for his want of sense. Dost thou not see how the thunderbolts of heaven lay prostrate the mightiest animals, while they pass over the weak and insignificant ? The most splendid palaces and the loftiest trees fall before these weapons of the gods. For God loves to humble the mighty. So also we often see a powerful army melt away before the more contemptible force. For when God in His wrath sends His terrors among them, they perish in a way that is little worthy of their former glory. The Supreme Being allows no one to be infinite in wisdom but Himself.

So Psalm (cxlvii. 5, 6)—"Great is our Lord, and of great power: His understanding is infinite. The Lord lifteth up the meek : He casteth the wicked down to the ground." And Mark (x. 27)—"With God all things are possible."

CALUMNY.

vii. 10.

Διαβολὴ γάρ ἐστι δεινότατον· ἐν τῇ δύο μέν εἰσι οἱ ἀδικέοντες, εἷς δὲ ὁ ἀδικεόμενος. Ὁ μὲν γὰρ διαβάλλων ἀδικέει οὐ παρεόντος κατηγορέων· ὁ δὲ ἀδικέει ἀναπειθόμενος πρὶν ἢ ἀτρεκέως ἐκμάθῃ. Ὁ δὲ δὴ ἀπεὼν τοῦ λόγου τάδε ἐν αὐτοῖσι ἀδικέεται, διαβληθείς τε ὑπὸ τοῦ ἑτέρου, καὶ νομισθεὶς πρὸς τοῦ ἑτέρου κακὸς εἶναι.

Calumny is a monstrous vice ; for, where parties indulge in it, there are always two that are actively engaged in doing wrong, and one who is subject to injury. The calumniator inflicts wrong by slandering the absent : he who gives credit to the calumny, before he has investigated the truth, is equally implicated. The person traduced is doubly injured—first by him who propagates, and secondly by him who credits, the calumny.

See (Lat.) Calumny.

DREAMS.

vii. 16.

Πεπλανῆσθαι αὗται μάλιστα ἐώθασι αἱ ὄψιες τῶν ὀνειράτων, τά τις ἡμέρης φροντίζει.

Dreams, in general, take their rise from those incidents which have most occupied the thoughts during the day.

DEATH IS THE REFUGE OF THE UNFORTUNATE.

vii. 46.

Ἐν γὰρ οὕτω βραχέϊ βίῳ οὐδεὶς οὕτω ἄνθρωπος ἐὼν εὐδαίμων πέφυκε, οὔτε τουτέων, οὔτε τῶν ἄλλων, τῷ οὐ παραστήσεται πολλάκις, καὶ οὐκὶ ἅπαξ, τεθνάναι βούλεσθαι μᾶλλον ἢ ζώειν. Αἵ τε γὰρ συμφοραὶ προσπίπτουσαι, καὶ αἱ νοῦσοι συμταράσσουσαι, καὶ βραχὺν ἐόντα μακρὸν δοκέειν εἶναι ποιεῦσι τὸν βίον. Οὕτω ὁ μὲν θάνατος, μοχθηρῆς ἐούσης τῆς ζόης, καταφυγὴ αἱρετωτάτη τῷ ἀνθρώπῳ γέγονε· ὁ δὲ θεὸς γλυκὺν γεύσας τὸν αἰῶνα φθονερὸς ἐν αὐτῷ εὑρίσκεται ἐών.

Brief as this life is, there is no one in the multitude, nor yet in the whole universe, that has been so happy at all times as not repeatedly to have prayed for death rather than life. Heavy trials in worldly affairs, the pangs of disease, render the short span of life of too long duration. Thus death, when life becomes a burden, is a delightful hiding-place for wearied man; and the Divinity, by giving us pleasures, and thereby inducing us to wish for length of days, may in reality be considered as doing us an injury.

CIRCUMSTANCES COMMAND MEN.

vii. 49.

Μάθε ὅτι αἱ συμφοραὶ τῶν ἀνθρώπων ἄρχουσι, καὶ οὐκὶ ἄνθρωποι τῶν συμφορέων.

Remember that men are dependent on circumstances, and not circumstances on men.

See (Lat.) Independence.

GREAT RESULTS FROM GREAT DANGERS.

vii. 50.

Μεγάλα πρήγματα μεγάλοισι κινδύνοισι ἐθέλει καταιρέεσθαι.

Great results usually arise from great dangers.

So Acts (xiv. 22)—"That we must through much tribulation enter into the kingdom of God."

"We Know in Part."

vii. 50.

Εἰδέναι δὲ ἄνθρωπον ἐόντα, ὅκως χρὴ, τὸ βέβαιον; δοκέω μὲν οὐδαμῶς.

Can one who is mortal be infallible? I believe that he cannot.

So 1 Corinthians (xiii. 9)—"For we know in part, and we prophesy in part."

Inactivity condemned.

vii. 50.

Κρέσσον δὲ πάντα θαρσέοντα ἥμισυ τῶν δεινῶν πάσχειν μᾶλλον, ἢ πᾶν χρῆμα προδειμαίνοντα μηδαμᾶ μηδὲν παθεῖν.

It is better by a noble boldness to run the risk of being subject to half of the evils which we anticipate, than to remain in cowardly listlessness for fear of what may happen.

So 1 Thessalonians (i. 6)—"Having received the Word in much affliction, with joy of the Holy Ghost."

A Wise Man receives a Kindness.

vii. 104.

Οὔκων οἰκός ἐστι ἄνδρα τὸν σώφρονα εὐνοίην φαινομένην διωθέεσθαι, ἀλλὰ στέργειν μάλιστα.

Wherefore it is not to be supposed that a wise man should refuse a kindness that is offered to him, but rather be anxious to embrace it.

So Luke (vi. 33)—"And if ye do good to them which do good to you, what thank have ye? for sinners also do ever the same."

Envy.

vii. 237.

Ὅτι πολιήτης μὲν πολιήτῃ εὖ πρήσσοντι φθονέει, καὶ ἐστι δυσμενὴς τῇ σιγῇ· οὐδ' ἂν, συμβουλευομένου τοῦ ἀστοῦ, πολιήτης ἀνὴρ τὰ ἄριστά οἱ δοκέοντα εἶναι ὑποθέοιτο, εἰ μὴ πρόσω ἀρετῆς ἀνήκοι· σπάνιοι δ' εἰσὶ οἱ τοιοῦτοι. Ξεῖνος δὲ ξείνῳ εὖ πρήσσοντί ἐστι εὐμενέστατον πάντων, συμβουλευομένου τε ἂν συμβουλεύσειε τὰ ἄριστα.

One man envies the success in life of another, and hates him in secret; nor is he willing to give him good advice when he is consulted, except it be by some wonderful effort of good feeling, and there are, alas! few such men in the world. A real friend, on the other hand, exults in his friend's happiness, rejoices in all his joys, and is ready to afford him his best advice.

So James (iii. 16)—"Where envying is, there is confusion, and every evil work."

See (Lat.) Envy.

PRUDENCE AND RASHNESS.

viii. 60.

Οἰκότα μέν νυν βουλευομένοισι ἀνθρώποισι ὡς τὸ ἐπίπαν ἐθέλει γίνεσθαι· μὴ δὲ οἰκότα βουλευομένοισι οὐκ ἐθέλει οὐδὲ ὁ θεὸς προσχωρέειν πρὸς τὰς ἀνθρωπηΐας γνώμας.

Those who are guided by reason are generally successful in their plans ; those who are rash and precipitate seldom enjoy the favour of the gods.

So Ecclesiastes (v. 2)—" Be not rash with thy mouth, and let not thine heart be hasty to utter anything before God : for God is in heaven, and thou upon earth ; therefore let thy words be few."

See (Lat.) Prudence ; Rashness.

KINGS HAVE LONG ARMS.

viii. 140.

Καὶ γὰρ δύναμις ὑπὲρ ἄνθρωπον ἡ βασιλῆός ἐστι, καὶ χεὶρ ὑπερμήκης.

For the power of a king is superhuman, and his hand is very long.

See (Lat.) King, wrath of, do not excite.

THE WILL OF PROVIDENCE CANNOT BE RESISTED.

ix. 16.

Ξεῖνε, ὅ τι δεῖ γενέσθαι ἐκ τοῦ θεοῦ, ἀμήχανον ἀποτρέψαι ἀνθρώπῳ· οὐδὲ γὰρ πιστὰ λέγουσι ἐθέλει πείθεοθαι οὐδείς. Ταῦτα δὲ Περσέων συχνοὶ ἐπιστάμενοι ἑπόμεθα ἀναγκαίῃ ἐνδεδεμένοι. Ἐχθίστη δὲ ὀδύνη ἐστὶ τῶν ἐν ἀνθρώποισι αὕτη, πολλὰ φρονέοντα μηδενὸς κρατέειν.

My friend, it is vain for man to contend with the will of Providence ; though the words of the wise are seldom listened to. Many of the Persians think as I do, but, forced by necessity, they yield to what they find it impossible to avoid. This is one of the saddest evils to which mankind is subject, that the advice of the wise is little attended to.

So Hebrews (xii. 5)—"My son despise not thou the chastening of the Lord, nor faint when thou art rebuked of him."

CHARACTER OF MEN DEPENDS ON THE NATURE AND CLIMATE OF THE COUNTRY.

ix. 122.

Φιλέειν γὰρ ἐκ τῶν μαλακῶν χώρων μαλακοὺς ἄνδρας γίνεσθαι· οὐ γάρ τοι τῆς αὐτῆς γῆς εἶναι, καρπόν τε θωμαστὸν φύειν καὶ ἄνδρας ἀγαθοὺς τὰ πολέμια.

It is a law of Nature that faint-hearted men should be the fruit of luxurious countries, for we never find that the same soil produces delicacies and heroes.

HESIODUS

FLOURISHED PROBABLY ABOUT B.C. 850.

HESIODUS, a celebrated poet, was a native of Ascra, in Bœotia, whither his father had emigrated from the Æolian Cuma, in Asia Minor. The early years of the poet were spent in the mountains of Bœotia, in the humble capacity of a shepherd ; but his circumstances seem to have improved, as we find him engaged, on the death of his father, in a lawsuit with his brothers, respecting the property left by his father. The judges of Ascra gave judgment against him, and in consequence of this he left his native city, and retired to Orchomenos, where he spent the remainder of his life. The ancients attributed to Hesiod a variety of works, but few of them have come down to us. The " Works and Days " is considered the most valuable, not so much from its own intrinsic worth as for having suggested to Virgil the idea of the Georgics. Its style is plain and homely, without much poetical imagery or ornament ; but it must be looked upon as the most ancient specimen of didactic poetry.

WISE KING.
Theog. 85.

Οἱ δέ νυ λαοὶ
πάντες ἐς αὐτὸν ὁρῶσι διακρίνοντα θέμιστας
ἰθείῃσι δίκῃσιν· ὁ δ᾽ ἀσφαλέως ἀγορεύων
αἶψά τε καὶ μέγα νεῖκος ἐπισταμένως κατέπαυσε.
Τούνεκα γὰρ βασιλῆες ἐχέφρονες, οὕνεκα λαοῖς
βλαπτομένοις ἀγορῆφι μετάτροπα ἔργα τελεῦσι
ῥηϊδίως, μαλακοῖσι παραιφάμενοι ἐπέεσσιν.
Ἐρχόμενον δ᾽ ἀνὰ ἄστυ θεὸν ὣς ἱλάσκονται
αἰδοῖ μειλιχίῃ, μετὰ δὲ πρέπει ἀγρομένοισι.

The people all look up to him as he administers justice with impartial judgment ; with wise words quickly he calms even the wildest tumult, for kings are endued with wisdom that they may easily quell factious deeds when the people are misled by dema-

gogues, soothing them with soft words ; as he goes through the
city all hail him as a god, with gentlest awe, and he stands conspicuous midst the assembled council.

See (Lat.) A tumult.

THE BARD.

Theog. 96.

'Ο δ' ὄλβιος, ὅντινα Μοῦσαι
φίλωνται· Γλυκερή οἱ ἀπὸ στόματος ῥέει αὐδή.
Εἰ γάρ τις καὶ πένθος ἔχων νεοκηδέϊ θυμῷ
ἄζηται κραδίην ἀκαχήμενος, αὐτὰρ ἀοιδὸς
Μουσάων θεράπων κλεῖα προτέρων ἀνθρώπων
ὑμνήσῃ, μάκαράς τε θεούς, οἳ Ὄλυμπον ἔχουσιν,
αἶψ' ὅγε δυσφρονέων ἐπιλήθεται, οὐδέ τι κηδέων
μέμνηται· ταχέως δὲ παρέτραπε δῶρα θεάων.

Blessed is he whom the Muses love! sweetly do his words flow
from his lips. Is there one afflicted with fresh sorrow, pining
away with deep grief? then if the minstrel, servant of the Muses,
sings the glorious deeds of men of yore, the praise of the blessed
gods who dwell in Olympus, quickly does he forget his sorrows,
nor remembers aught of all his griefs ; for the gifts of these goddesses swiftly turn his woes away.

THE DRONES.

Theog. 594.

Ὡς δ' ὁπότ' ἐν σίμβλοισι κατηρεφέεσσι μέλισσαι
κηφῆνας βόσκουσι, κακῶν ξυνήονας ἔργων,
αἱ μέν τε πρόπαν ἦμαρ ἐς ἠέλιον καταδύντα
ἠμάτιαι σπεύδουσι, τιθεῖσί τε κηρία λευκά,
οἱ δ' ἔντοσθε μένοντες ἐπηρεφέας κατὰ σίμβλους,
ἀλλότριον κάματον σφετέρην ἐς γαστέρ' ἀμῶνται.

As when bees in close-roofed hives feed the drones, partners in
evil deeds, the former all day long, to the setting sun, their murmuring labours ply, filling the pure combs ; while the drones, remaining within, reap the labours of others for their own maws.

SLEEP AND DEATH.

Theog. 758.

Ἔνθα δὲ Νυκτὸς παῖδες ἐρεμνῆς οἰκί' ἔχουσιν,
Ὕπνος καὶ Θάνατος, δεινοὶ θεοί· οὐδέ ποτ' αὐτοὺς
Ἠέλιος φαέθων ἐπιδέρκεται ἐκτίνεσσιν
οὐρανὸν εἰσανιὼν οὐδ' οὐρανόθεν καταβαίνων.
Τῶν ἕτερος μὲν γῆν τε καὶ εὐρέα νῶτα θαλάσσης
ἥσυχος ἀναστρέφεται καὶ μείλιχος ἀνθρώποισι,

τοῦ δὲ σιδηρέη μὲν κραδίη, χάλκεον δὲ οἱ ἦτορ
νηλεὲς ἐν στήθεσσιν· ἔχει δ᾽ ὃν πρῶτα λάβῃσιν
ἀνθρώπων· ἐχθρὸς δὲ καὶ ἀθανάτοισι θεοῖσιν.

There dwell Sleep and Death, dread gods, the progeny of gloomy Night; the sun never looks upon them with its bright rays, neither when he mounts the vault of heaven nor when he descends; the former in silence passes over the earth and the wide expanse of sea, giving pleasure to mortals; of the other, iron is the heart, and his brazen breast is merciless; whomsoever of men he first seizes he holds, and is hostile even to the immortal gods.

FATE OF MAN DETERMINED BY GOD.

Works, 3.

Ὅν τε διὰ βροτοὶ ἄνδρες ὁμῶς ἄφατοί τε φατοί τε,
ῥητοί τ᾽ ἄῤῥητοί τε, Διὸς μεγάλοιο ἕκητι.
Ῥέα μὲν γὰρ βριάει, ῥέα δὲ βριάοντα χαλέπτει,
ῥεῖα δ᾽ ἀρίζηλον μινύθει καὶ ἄδηλον ἀέξει,
ῥεῖα δέ τ᾽ ἰθύνει σκολιὸν καὶ ἀγήνορα κάρφει
Ζεὺς ὕψι βρεμέτης, ὃς ὑπέρτατα δώματα ναίει.

By whom mortal men are raised to fame or live obscurely, noble or ignoble, by the will of Jove; with ease he lifts or brings low, with ease he dims the brightest name and ennobles the meanest; with ease high-thundering Jove, who dwells on high, makes the crooked straight and unnerves the strong.

So 1 Samuel (ii. 7, 8)—"The Lord maketh poor, and maketh rich : He bringeth low, and lifteth up. He raiseth up the poor out of the dust, and lifteth up the beggar from the dunghill, to set them among princes, and to make them inherit the throne of glory : for the pillars of the earth are the Lord's, and He hath set the world upon them." And Psalm (cxiii. 7, 8)— "He raiseth up the poor out of the dust, and lifteth the needy out of the dunghill ; that He may set him with princes, even with the princes of His people." And Luke (i. 51–53)—"He hath showed strength with His arm : He hath scattered the proud in the imagination of their hearts. He hath put down the mighty from their seats, and exalted them of low degree. He hath filled the hungry with good things ; and the rich He hath sent empty away."

See (Lat.) Life, changes of ; The gods.

EMULATION IS GOOD.

Works, 24.

Ἀγαθὴ δ᾽ Ἔρις ἥδε βροτοῖσιν.

Emulation is good for mankind.

THE ENVIOUS.

Works, 25.

Καὶ κεραμεὺς κεραμεῖ κοτέει καὶ τέκτονι τέκτων,
καὶ πτωχὸς πτωχῷ φθονέει καὶ ἀοιδὸς ἀοιδῷ.

The potter envies the potter, the carpenter the carpenter, the
poor is jealous of the poor, and the bard of the bard.

HALF BETTER THAN THE WHOLE.

Works, 40.

Νήπιοι, οὐδὲ ἴσασιν ὅσῳ πλέον ἥμισυ παντός,
οὐδ' ὅσον ἐν μαλάχῃ τε καὶ ἀσφοδέλῳ μέγ' ὄνειαρ.

Fools that they are, they know not how much the half is better
than the whole, nor how great pleasure there is in wholesome
herbs—the mallow and the asphodel.

See (Lat.) Frugality, Temperance, Half better.

GOD LAUGHS AT VAIN DESIGNS.

Works, 59.

Ὣς ἔφατ'· ἐκ δ' ἐγέλασσε πατὴρ ἀνδρῶν τε θεῶν τε.

Thus he spoke; and the sire of men and gods out-laughed.

So Psalm (ii. 4)—" He that sitteth in the heavens shall laugh : the Lord
shall have them in derision." And Milton, "Paradise Lost " (Bk. v. 735)—
" Mighty Father, thou my foes
Justly hast in derision, and secure,
Laugh'st at their vain designs and tumults vain."

THE WORLD FULL OF ILLS.

Works, 101.

Πλείη μὲν γὰρ γαῖα κακῶν, πλείη δὲ θάλασσα·
νοῦσοι δ' ἀνθρώποισιν ἐφ' ἡμέρῃ ἠδ' ἐπὶ νυκτὶ
αὐτόματοι φοιτῶσι κακὰ θνητοῖσι φέρουσαι
σιγῇ, ἐπεὶ φωνὴν ἐξείλετο μητίετα Ζεύς.
Οὕτως οὔτι πῃ ἔστι Διὸς νόον ἐξαλέασθαι.

For the earth is full of woes, and also the sea ; diseases go about
noiselessly, bearing of themselves sorrows to mortals night and
day, since Jove has taken from them the power of speech ; so impossible is it to avoid the will of Jove.

EASY DEATH.

Works, 116.

Θνῆσκον δ' ὡς ὕπνῳ δεδμημένοι.

They died as if overcome with sleep.

Guardian Spirits.

Works, 121.

Τοὶ μὲν δαίμονές εἰσι Διὸς μεγάλου διὰ βουλὰς
ἐσθλοί, ἐπιχθόνιοι, φύλακες θνητῶν ἀνθρώπων·
οἵ ῥα φυλάσσουσίν τε δίκας καὶ σχέτλια ἔργα,
ἠέρα ἑσσάμενοι πάντῃ φοιτῶντες ἐπ᾽ αἶαν,
πλουτοδόται· καὶ τοῦτο γέρας βασιλήϊον ἔσχον.

These are the aërial spirits of great Jove, beneficent, walking over the earth, guardians of mankind ; they watch our actions, good and bad, passing everywhere over the earth, invisible to mortal eyes ; such royal privilege they possess.

Macrobius (Cic. Som. Scip. i. 9) thus translates this passage—
" Indigetes divi fato summi Jovis hi sunt
Quondam homines, modo cum superis humana tuentes,
Largi ac munifici, rerum jus nunc quoque nacti."

So Psalm (xci. 11)—"For He shall give His angels charge over thee, to keep thee in all thy ways."

See (Lat.) Register of good and evil deeds.

Justice and Right prevail.

Works, 212.

Ὕβρις γάρ τε κακὴ δειλῷ βροτῷ· οὐδὲ μὲν ἐσθλὸς
ῥηϊδίως φερέμεν δύναται, βαρύθει δέ θ᾽ ὑπ᾽ αὐτῆς
ἐγκύρσας ἄτῃσιν· ὁδὸς δ᾽ ἑτέρηφι παρελθεῖν
κρείσσων ἐς τὰ δίκαια· δίκη δ᾽ ὑπὲρ ὕβριος ἴσχει
ἐς τέλος ἐξελθοῦσα· παθὼν δέ τε νήπιος ἔγνω.

For insolence is unsuited to wretched mortals, often even the high and powerful allow themselves to be carried away by arrogance, and, yielding to this feeling, subject themselves to misery and losses. On the other hand, the road leading to justice is the safer ; justice at last gets the better over wrong: this truth even the fool knows by experience.

The Upright Governor.

Works, 223.

Οἳ δὲ δίκας ξείνοισι καὶ ἐνδήμοισι διδοῦσιν
ἰθείας καὶ μή τι παρεκβαίνουσι δικαίου,
τοῖσι τέθηλε πόλις, λαοὶ δ᾽ ἀνθεῦσιν ἐν αὐτῇ·
εἰρήνη δ᾽ ἀνὰ γῆν κουροτρόφος, οὐδέ ποτ᾽ αὐτοῖς
ἀργαλέον πόλεμον τεκμαίρεται εὐρύοπα Ζεύς.

Those who administer the laws with justice to strangers and natives, never transgressing what is right, by these the city flourishes in peace, and the people prosper. Peace is a good nursing-mother to the land, nor does far-seeing Jove send among them troublous war.

A SINNER.

Works, 238.

Πολλάκι καὶ ξύμπασα πόλις κακοῦ ἀνδρὸς ἀπηύρα,
ὅστις ἀλιτραίνει καὶ ἀτάσθαλα μηχανάαται.
Τοῖσιν δ' οὐρανόθεν μέγ' ἐπήγαγε πῆμα Κρονίων,
λιμὸν ὁμοῦ καὶ λοιμόν· ἀποφθινύθουσι δὲ λαοί.

Oft a whole state suffers for the acts of a bad man, who breaks the laws of heaven and devises evil. On them Jove brings great calamity, both famine and pestilence, and the people perish.

THE WICKED BRING EVIL ON THEMSELVES.

Works, 263.

Οἳ αὐτῷ κακὰ τεύχει ἀνὴρ ἄλλῳ κακὰ τεύχων,
Ἡ δὲ κακὴ βουλὴ τῷ βουλεύσαντι κακίστη.
Πάντα ἰδὼν Διὸς ὀφθαλμὸς καὶ πάντα νοήσας
Καὶ νυ τάδ' αἴκ' ἐθέλησ' ἐπιδέρκεται οὐδέ ἑ λήθει
Οἵην δὴ καὶ τήνδε δίκην πόλις ἐντὸς εέργει.

What calamities does a man contriving evil for his neighbour bring upon himself! An evil design is worst for the contriver. The eye of Jove, that sees and knows all things, looks upon these things, if he wills it, nor is it concealed from him what kind of justice a state administers.

A. Gellius (iv. 5) says—"Malum consilium consultori pessimum."

ROAD TO WICKEDNESS EASILY FOUND.

Works, 285.

Τὴν μέν τοι κακότητα καὶ ἰλαδὸν ἔστιν ἑλέσθαι
ῥηϊδίως· λείη μὲν ὁδός, μάλα δ' ἐγγύθι ναίει.
Τῆς δ' ἀρετῆς ἱδρῶτα θεοὶ προπάροιθεν ἔθηκαν
ἀθάνατοι· μακρὸς δὲ καὶ ὄρθιος οἶμος ἐπ' αὐτὴν
καὶ τρηχὺς τὸ πρῶτον· ἐπὴν δ' εἰς ἄκρον ἵκηαι,
ῥηϊδίη δὴ ἔπειτα πέλει, χαλεπή περ ἐοῦσα.
Οὗτος μὲν πανάριστος, ὃς αὐτὸς πάντα νοήσῃ,
[φρασσάμενος τά κ' ἔπειτα καὶ ἐς τέλος ᾖσιν ἀμείνω·]
ἐσθλὸς δ' αὖ κάκεῖνος, ὃς εὖ εἰπόντι πίθηται·
ὃς δέ κε μήτ' αὐτὸς νοέῃ μήτ' ἄλλου ἀκούων
ἐν θυμῷ βάλληται, ὁ δ' αὖτ' ἀχρήϊος ἀνήρ.

It is easy for thee to get associates in wickedness; the road is smooth, and the dwellers are all around thee. But the immortal gods have placed the sweat of the brow before virtue : long and steep is the path that leads to it, and rough at first ; but when the summit is reached, then it is easy, however difficult it may have been. That man is by far the wisest who is able of himself to determine what is best both for the present moment and for the future ; next, he is wise who yields to good advice ; but he that is not wise himself, nor can hearken to wisdom, is a good-for-nothiug man.

Milton, in his "Essay on Education," seems to have imitated this passage—"I shall detain you now no longer in the demonstration of what we should not do, but straight conduct you to a hill-side, where I will point you out the right path of a virtuous and noble education ; laborious indeed at the first ascent, but also so smooth, so green, so full of goodly prospect and melodious sounds on every side, that the harp of Orpheus was not more charming."

See (Lat.) The fool; Wise man. Matt. vii. 13.

THE SLUGGARD.

Works, 300.

Τῷ δέ θεοὶ νεμεσῶσι καὶ ἀνέρες, ὅς κεν ἀεργὸς
ζώῃ, κηφήνεσσι κοθούροις εἴκελος ὀργήν,
οἵ τε μελισσάων κάματον τρύχουσιν ἀεργοὶ
ἔσθοντες.

Both gods and men are indignant with him who lives a slug gard's life like to the stingless drones, who lazily consume the labours of the bees.

See (Lat.) Idleness, result of.

LABOUR NO DISGRACE.

Works, 311.

Ἔργον δ' οὐδὲν ὄνειδος, ἀεργίη δέ τ' ὄνειδος.

Work is no disgrace, but idleness is a disgrace.

See Xenophon (Memorab. i. 2).

SHAME.

Works, 315.

Αἰδώς δ' οὐκ ἀγαθὴ κεχρημένον ἄνδρα κομίζει
αἰδώς, ἥτ' ἄνδρας μέγα σίνεται ἠδ' ὀνίνησιν.
Αἰδώς τοι πρὸς ἀνολβίῃ, θάρσος δὲ πρὸς ὄλβῳ.
Χρήματα δ' οὐχ' ἁρπακτά· θεόσδοτα πολλὸν ἀμείνω.

It is not well for false shame to accompany the needy, shame that both injures greatly and aids mankind ; false shame leads to poverty, but confidence to wealth ; wealth should not be got by plunder : what is given by God is far better.

So Ecclesiasticus (iv. 21)—"For there is a shame that bringeth sin ; and there is a shame which is glory and grace."

See Hom. Od. xvii. 347 ; Il. xxiv. 44.

A Bad Neighbour.

Works, 346.

Πῆμα κακὸς γείτων ὅσσον τ᾽ ἀγαθὸς μέγ᾽ ὄνειαρ.

A bad neighbour is as great a misfortune as a good one is a blessing.

Return Love for Love.

Works, 351.

Τὸν φιλέοντα φιλεῖν, καὶ τῷ προσιόντι προσεῖναι·
καὶ δόμεν ὅς κεν δῷ, καὶ μὴ δόμεν ὅς κεν μὴ δῷ.

Return love for love, and assist him who assists thee ; give to him who gives to thee, and give not to him who gives not.

Evil Gains equal to a Loss.

Works, 352.

Μὴ κακὰ κερδαίνειν· κακὰ κέρδεα ἶσ᾽ ἄτῃσιν.

Do not make unjust gains ; they are equal to a loss.

Every Little adds to the Heap.

Works, 359.

Εἰ γάρ κεν καὶ σμικρὸν ἐπὶ σμικρῷ καταθεῖο,
καὶ θαμὰ τοῦτ᾽ ἔρδοις, τάχα κεν μέγα καὶ τὸ γένοιτο
ὅς δ᾽ ἐπ᾽ ἐόντι φέρει, ὁ δ᾽ ἀλύξεται αἴθοπα λιμόν.

For if thou addest little to little, and doest so often, soon it will become a great heap to him who gathers, and he will thus keep off keen hunger.

"One Soweth and another Reapeth.

Works, 495.

Ἀλλότριων κάματον σφετέρην ἐς γαστέρ᾽ ἀμωνται.

They reap the labours of others for their own belly.

Callimachus, the poet of Alexandria (circ. 200 B.C.), has a line in his "Hymn to Ceres" (137)—

"And those who ploughed the field shall reap the corn."

Thomas Fuller, an excellent quoter of and commentator on proverbs, better than any moralist we know, purveys an antidote to bitterness at seeing others reap what we ourselves have sown, in his "Holy State." "The preacher of the Word," he says, "is in some places like the planting of woods, where, though no profit is received for twenty years together, it comes afterwards. And grant that God honoureth not *thee* to build His temple in *thy* parish, yet thou mayest with David provide metals and materials for Solomon thy successor to build it with."

Money is Life.

Works, 686.

Χρήματα γὰρ ψυχὴ πέλεται δειλοῖσι βροτοῖσι.

Money is life to us wretched mortals.

How to Choose a Wife.

Works, i. 693.

'Ωραῖος δὲ γυναῖκα τεὸν ποτὶ οἶκον ἄγεσθαι,
μήτε τριηκόντων ἐτέων μάλα πόλλ' ἀπολείπων
μήτ' ἐπιθεὶς μάλα πολλά· γάμος δέ τοι ὥριος οὗτος,
ἡ δὲ γυνὴ τέτορ' ἡβώοι, πέμπτῳ δὲ γαμοῖτο.
Παρθενικὴν δὲ γαμεῖν, ἵνα ἤθεα κεδνὰ διδάξῃς.
Τὴν δὲ μάλιστα γαμεῖν ἥτις σέθεν ἐγγύθι ναίει,
πάντα μάλ' ἀμφὶς ἰδὼν μὴ γείτοσι χάρματα γήμῃς.
οὐ μὲν γάρ τι γυναικὸς ἀνὴρ ληΐζετ' ἄμεινον
τῆς ἀγαθῆς, τῆς δ' αὖτε κακῆς οὐ ῥίγιον ἄλλο,
δειπνολόχης· ἥτ' ἄνδρα καὶ ἴφθιμόν περ ἐόντα
εὕει ἄτερ δαλοῦ καὶ ὠμῷ γήραϊ δῶκεν.

In the spring-time of life, neither much above nor below thirty lead home thy wife. Marriage at this age is seasonable. Thy wife should be in her nineteenth year. Marry a virgin, that thou mayest teach her discreet manners, and be sure to marry thy neighbour's daughter, acting with all prudence, lest thou marry one who may prove a source of pleasure to thy neighbours. For there is nothing better than a good wife, and nothing worse than a bad one, who is fond of gadding about. Such a one roasts her husband, stout-hearted though he may be, without a fire, and hands him over to a premature old age.

A Sparing Tongue.

Works, 717.

Γλώσσης τοι θησαυρὸς ἐν ἀνθρώποισιν ἄριστος
φειδωλῆς, πλείστη δὲ χάρις κατὰ μέτρον ἰούσης.

The best treasure among men is a frugal tongue, and that which moves measurably is hung with most grace.

So Proverbs (**xv.** 23)—" A word spoken in due season, how good is it!"

An Evil Report.

Works, 760.

Φήμη γάρ τε κακὴ πέλεται· κούφη, μὲν ἀεῖραι
'Ρεῖα μάλ', ἀργαλέη δε φέρειν, χαλεπὴ δ' ἀποτιθέσθαι.

There is also an evil report; light, indeed, and easy to raise, but difficult to bear, and still more difficult to get rid of.

HIPPARCHUS.

FLOURISHED ABOUT B.C. 320.

HIPPARCHUS, an Athenian comic poet of the new comedy, was a contemporary of Diphilus and Menander.

SKILL.

Fr. Com. Gr. p. 1097.

Πολὺ γ' ἐστὶ πάντων κτῆμα τιμιώτατον
ἅπασι ἀνθρώποισιν εἰς τὸ ζῆν τέχνη.
Τὰ μὲν ἄλλα καὶ πόλεμος καὶ μεταβολαὶ
τύχης ἀνήλωσ', ἡ τέχνη δὲ σώζεται.

By far the most valuable possession of all to all men for life is skill. Both war and the chances of fortune destroy other things, but skill is preserved.

HOMERUS.

HOMER, the greatest epic poet of Greece, lived at so remote a period that his existence is considered by some as a myth. At all events, he lived beyond what may be regarded the strictly historical epoch of Greek literature, the date of the period when he flourished varying no less than 500 years (from B.C. 1184–684). Many towns claimed to be his birthplace, but Smyrna seems to have established the best claim : he is said to have died at Ios, one of the Cyclades.

ANGER.

Il. i. 1.

Μῆνιν ἄειδε, θεά, Πηληϊάδεω Ἀχιλῆος,
οὐλομένην, ἣ μυρί' Ἀχαιοῖς ἄλγε' ἔθηκεν,
πολλὰς δ' ἰφθίμους ψυχὰς Ἄϊδι προΐαψεν
ἡρώων.

O goddess ! sing of the deadly wrath of Achilles, son of Peleus, which brought unnumbered woes upon the Greeks, and hurled untimely many valiant heroes to the viewless shades.

So Proverbs (xxvii. 4)—"Wrath is cruel, and anger is outrageous."

"The Counsel of the Lord."
Il. i. 6.

Διὸς δ' ἐτελείετο βουλή.

And yet the will of Jove was being accomplished.

So Psalm (xxxiii. 11)— "The counsel of the Lord standeth for ever, the thoughts of His heart to all generations."

A Pestilence.
Il. i. 9.

'Ο γὰρ βασιλῆϊ χολωθεὶς
νοῦσον ἀνὰ στρατὸν ὦρσε κακήν, ὀλέκοντο δὲ λαοί.

For Apollo, enraged at the king, sent throughout the host a deadly pestilence, and the people died.

So 2 Samuel (xxiv. 15)— "So the Lord sent a pestilence upon Israel, from the morning even to the time appointed, and there died of the people, from Dan even to Beersheba, seventy thousand men "
See (Lat.) Subjects suffer when kings dispute.

A Dream.
Il. i. 63.

'Αλλ' ἄγε δή τινα μάντιν ἐρείομεν, ἢ ἱερῆα,
ἢ καὶ ὀνειροπόλον—καὶ γάρ τ' ὄναρ ἐκ Διός ἐστιν.

Come now let us consult some prophet or priest, or some vision-seer, since even visions are from Jove.

So Numbers (xii. 6)—"And He said, Hear now my words : if there be a prophet among you, I the Lord will make myself known unto him in a vision, and will speak unto him in a dream."

To Know the Past, the Present, and Future.
Il. i. 70.

'Ος ᾔδη τά τ' ἐόντα τά τ' ἐσσόμενα πρό τ' ἐόντα.

Who knew the present, the future, and the past.

In Isaiah (xli. 23) we have—"Shew the things that are to come hereafter, that we may know that ye are gods."

The Anger of a King.
Il. i. 80.

Κρείσσων γὰρ βασιλεύς, ὅτε χώσεται ἀνδρὶ χέρηϊ·
εἴπερ γάρ τε χόλον γε καὶ αὐτῆμαρ καταπέψῃ,
ἀλλά τε καὶ μετόπισθεν ἔχει κότον, ὄφρα τελέσσῃ,
ἐν στήθεσσιν ἑοῖσι.

For a king is the more powerful of the two when he is enraged with a man of low degree; for though he may veil his wrath for a while, yet in his heart it still is nursed till the time arrive for his revenge.

A Prophet of Ill.

Il. i. 106.

Μάντι κακῶν, οὐ πώποτέ μοι τὸ κρήγυον εἶπας.
Αἰεί τοι τὰ κάκ' ἐστὶ φίλα φρεσὶ μαντεύεσθαι.

Thou prophet of ill, thou never speakest what is pleasing; ever dost thou take delight to augur ill.

So also in 1 Kings (xxii. 8)—"And the King of Israel said unto Jehoshaphat, There is yet one man, Micaiah the son of Imlah, by whom we may inquire of the Lord : but I hate him; for he doth not prophesy good concerning me, but evil."

"No Pleasure in the Death of the Wicked."

Il. i. 117.

Βούλομ' ἐγὼ λαὸν σῶν ἔμμεναι ἢ ἀπολέσθαι.

I wish rather my people's safety, than that they should perish.

So Ezekiel (xxxiii. 11)—"Say unto them, As I live, saith the Lord God, I have no pleasure in the death of the wicked ; but that the wicked turn from his way and live ;" and 2 Peter (iii. 9)—"The Lord is not slack con cerning His promise, as some men count slackness ; but is long-suffering to us-ward, not willing that any should perish, but that all should come to repentance ;" and 1 Timothy (ii. 4)—"Who will have all men to be saved, and to come to the knowledge of the truth."

"Glory not in thy Wisdom."

Il. i. 178.

Εἰ μάλα καρτερός ἐσσι, θεός που σοὶ τόγ' ἔδωκεν.

If thou art stronger, some deity, I believe, has bestowed this gift on thee.

The idea is found in Jeremiah (ix. 23)—"Thus saith the Lord, Let not the wise man glory in his wisdom, neither let the mighty man glory in his might, let not the rich man glory in his riches ;" and in 1 Corinthians (iv. 7)—"For who maketh thee to differ from another? and what hast thou that thou didst not receive? now if thou didst receive it, why dost thou glory, as if thou hadst not received it ?"

The Gods.

Il. i. 218.

Ὅς κε θεοῖς ἐπιπείθηται, μάλα τ' ἔκλυον αὐτοῦ

Those who revere the gods, the gods will bless.

So Proverbs (xv. 29)—"The Lord is far from the wicked : but He heareth the prayer of the righteous ;" and John (ix. 31)—"Now we know that God heareth not sinners ; but if any man be a worshipper of God, and doeth His will, him He heareth."

H

The Sceptre of the King.

Il. i. 234.

Ναὶ μὰ τόδε σκῆπτρον, τὸ μὲν οὔποτε φύλλα καὶ ὄζους
φύσει, ἐπειδὴ πρῶτα τομὴν ἐν ὄρεσσι λέλοιπεν,
οὐδ' ἀναθηλήσει· περὶ γάρ ῥά ἑ χαλκὸς ἔλεψεν
φύλλα τε καὶ φλοιόν· νῦν αὖτέ μιν υἷες Ἀχαιῶν
ἐν παλάμῃς φορέουσι δικασπόλοι, οἵτε θέμιστας
πρὸς Διὸς εἰρύαται.

Yea, by this sceptre, which shall never again put forth leaves
and branches, since first it left its parent trunk upon the mountain-side, nor will it blossom more, since all around, in very truth,
has the axe lopped both leaf and bark ; and now 'tis borne emblem
of justice by the sons of the Greeks, those who watch over the
laws received from Jove.

See (Lat.) Sceptre, royal.

Words sweeter than Honey.

Il. i. 249.

Τοῦ καὶ ἀπὸ γλώσσης μέλιτος γλυκίων ῥέεν αὐδή.

From whose tongue, also, flowed the stream of speech sweeter
than honey.

So Psalm (cxix. 103)—"How sweet are thy words unto my taste! yea,
sweeter than honey to my mouth!"

Thine Enemies will Rejoice.

Il. i. 255.

Ἦ κεν γηθήσαι Πρίαμος Πριάμοιό τε παῖδες,
ἄλλοι τε Τρῶες μέγα κεν κεχαροίατο θυμῷ,
εἰ σφῶϊν τάδε πάντα πυθοίατο μαρναμένοιιν.

In very truth, what joy for Priam and the sons of Priam, and
what exultation for the men of Troy, if they should hear of feuds
between you !

So Psalm (lxxxix. 42)—"Thou hast set up the right hand of his adver-
saries ; thou hast made all his enemies to rejoice ;" and 2 Samuel (i. 20)—
"Publish it not in the streets of Askelon ; lest the daughters of the Philistines rejoice, lest the daughters of the uncircumcised triumph."

" Ye Younger, submit yourselves to the Elder."

Il. i. 259.

Ἀλλὰ πίθεσθ'· ἄμφω δὲ νεωτέρω ἐστὸν ἐμεῖο.

But obey, for ye are both younger than I am.

So 1 Peter (v. 5)—"Likewise, ye younger, submit yourselves unto the
elder."

SUBMIT TO THE KING.

Il. i. 277.

Μήτε σὺ, Πηλείδη, θέλ' ἐριζέμεναι βασιλῆϊ
ἀντιβίην, ἐπεὶ οὔποθ' ὁμοίης ἔμμορε τιμῆς
σκηπτοῦχος βασιλεύς, ᾧτε Ζεὺς κῦδος ἔδωκεν.

Do not, son of Peleus, feel inclined to fight with the monarch,
since never to sceptred king has Jove given such glory as to
Atrides.

So 1 Peter (ii. 13)—" Submit yourselves to every ordinance of man for
the Lord's sake ; whether it be to the king, as supreme."

NOD OF JUPITER.

Il. i. 528.

Ἦ, καὶ κυανέῃσιν ἐπ' ὀφρύσι νεῦσε Κρονίων·
ἀμβρόσιαι δ' ἄρα χαῖται ἐπερρώσαντο ἄνακτος
κρατὸς ἀπ' ἀθανάτοιο· μέγαν δ' ἐλέλιξεν Ὄλυμπον.

The son of Saturn spoke, and nodded with his dark eyebrows ;
thereupon the ambrosial locks streamed down from the head of
the immortal king, and he caused the mighty Olympus to tremble
to its base.

See (Lat.) God, all-subduing power of.

GOD NOT TO BE RESISTED.

Il. i. 589.

Ἀργαλέος γὰρ Ὀλύμπιος ἀντιφέρεσθαι.

For the Olympian king is difficult to be opposed.

So Romans (ix. 19)—"Thou wilt then say unto me, Why doth He yet
find fault ? For who hath resisted His will ?"—and 1 Corinthians (x. 22 —
"Do we provoke the Lord to jealousy ? are we stronger than He ?"

THE LEADER OUGHT TO BE AWAKE.

Il. ii. 24.

Οὐ χρὴ παννύχιον εὕδειν βουληφόρον ἄνδρα,
ᾧ λαοί τ' ἐπιτετράφαται καὶ τόσσα μέμηλεν.

It is not right for a statesman to sleep to whom nations are
intrusted, and the public weal.

" THE POOR MAN'S WISDOM IS DESPISED."

Il. ii. 80.

Εἰ μέν τις τὸν ὄνειρον Ἀχαιῶν ἄλλος ἔνισπεν,
ψεῦδός κεν φαῖμεν καὶ νοσφιζοίμεθα μᾶλλον·
νῦν δ' ἴδεν ὃς μέγ' ἄριστος Ἀχαιῶν εὔχεται εἶναι.

H 2

If any other of the Greeks had related to us this vision, we should in all likelihood have deemed it false, and laughed to scorn the idle tale ; but now he who is the noblest of the Greeks has seen it.

So Ecclesiastes (ix. 16)—"Then said I, Wisdom is better than strength ; nevertheless the poor man's wisdom is despised, and his words are not heard."

BEES.
Il. ii. 87.

Ἠΰτε ἔθνεα εἰσι μελισσάων ἀδινάων,
Πέτρης ἐκ γλαφυρῆς αἰεὶ νέον ἐρχομενάων·
βοτρυδὸν δὲ πέτονται ἐπ᾽ ἄνθεσιν εἰαρινοῖσιν·
αἱ μέν τ᾽ ἔνθα ἅλις πεποτήαται, αἱ δέ τε ἔνθα.

Even as go swarms of closely-thronging bees, always issuing in fresh numbers from the hollow rock : they fly in clusters to the vernal flowers ; some have sped their flight in crowds here, others there.

See (Lat.) Bees.

THE POWER OF GOD.
Il. ii. 116.

Οὕτω που Διὶ μέλλει ὑπερμενέϊ φίλον εἶναι,
ὃς δὴ πολλάων πολίων κατέλυσε κάρηνα
ἠδ᾽ ἔτι καὶ λύσει· τοῦ γὰρ κράτος ἐστὶ μέγιστον.

Such, I suppose, now appears the sovereign will of Jove, who oft has destroyed, and again will pull down, lofty cities ; for his power is omnipotent.

So Ezekiel (xxxv. 4)—"I will lay thy cities waste, and thou shalt be desolate ; and thou shalt know that I am the Lord."

THE WRATH OF A KING.
Il. ii. 196.

Θυμὸς δὲ μέγας ἐστὶ διοτρεφέος βασιλῆος,
Τιμὴ δ᾽ ἐκ Διός ἐστι· φιλεῖ δὲ ἑ μητίετα Ζεύς.

Great is the wrath of a king under the protection of Jove ; his high office, too, is from Jove, and counselling Jove loves him.

So Proverbs (xvi. 14)—"The wrath of a king is as messengers of death : but a wise man will pacify it ;" and (viii. 15)—"By me kings reign and princes decree justice ;" and Daniel (ii. 21)—"And He changeth the times and the seasons : He removeth kings and setteth up kings : He giveth wisdom unto the wise, and knowledge to them that know understanding ;" and Romans (xiii. 1)—"Let every soul be subject unto the higher powers. For there is no power but of God : the powers that be are ordained of God."

See (Lat.) God.

The Mob.

Il. ii. 204.

Οὐκ ἀγαθὸν πολυκοιρανίη· εἶς κοίρανος ἔστω,
εἶς βασιλεὺς, ᾧ ἔδωκε Κρόνου παῖς ἀγκυλομήτεω,
[Σκῆπτρόν τ᾽ ἠδὲ θέμιστας, ἵνα σφίσι βασιλεύῃ.]

The government of the multitude is not good : let there be one lord, one sole monarch, to whom wise Saturn's son commits the sway and ministry of law, in token of sovereign power.

So Judges (ix. 12)—"Then said the trees unto the vine, Come thou and reign over us ;" and 1 Samuel (viii. 5)—"Now make us a king to judge us like all the nations ;" and Proverbs (xxviii. 2)—"For the transgression of a land many are the princes thereof ; but by a man of understanding and knowledge the state thereof shall be prolonged ;" and James (iii. 1)—"My brethren, be not many masters, knowing that we shall receive the greater condemnation."

See (Lat.) Mob.

Character of a Demagogue.

Il. ii. 212.

Θερσίτης δ᾽ ἔτι μοῦνος ἀμετροεπὴς ἐκολῴα,
ὃς ῥ᾽ ἔπεα φρεσὶν ᾗσιν ἄκοσμά τε πολλά τε ᾔδη,
μὰψ, ἀτὰρ οὐ κατὰ κόσμον, ἐριζέμεναι βασιλεῦσιν,
ἀλλ᾽ ὅ τι οἱ εἴσαιτο γελοίϊον Ἀργείοισιν
ἔμμεναι. Αἴσχιστος δὲ ἀνὴρ ὑπὸ Ἴλιον ἦλθεν·
φολκὸς ἔην, χωλὸς δ᾽ ἕτερον πόδα· τὼ δέ οἱ ὤμω
κυρτὼ, ἐπὶ στῆθος συνοχωκότε· αὐτὰρ ὕπερθεν
φοξὸς ἔην κεφαλὴν, ψεδνὴ δ᾽ ἐπενήνοθε λάχνη.
Ἔχθιστος δ᾽ Ἀχιλῆϊ μάλιστ᾽ ἦν ἠδ᾽ Ὀδυσῆϊ·
τὼ γὰρ νεικείεσκε.

But Thersites alone, with unmeasured words, kept still clamouring among the throng, for he had store of them, to rate the chiefs ; not over-seemly, controlled by no respect, but, with witty malice, uttering what might move the Greeks to laughter. He was, moreover, the ugliest man that came beneath the walls of Troy : bandy-legged, and lame in one foot ; shoulders crooked, and drawn together towards his breast ; his head pointed upwards, while thin woolly hair bestrewed it ; he was specially hateful to Achilles and Ulysses, for he was ever reviling them

See (Lat.) Demagogues.

"The Prince that wanteth Understanding."

Il. ii. 233.

Οὐ μὲν ἔοικεν
ἀρχὸν ἐόντα κακῶν ἐπιβασκέμεν υἷας Ἀχαιῶν.

It is not proper for a ruler to bring evils on the sons of the Greeks.

So Proverbs (xxviii. 16)—" The prince that wanteth understanding is also a great oppressor."

" Be wise, O ye Kings ! "
Il. ii. 368.

'Αλλά, ἄναξ, αὐτός τ' εὖ μήδεο πείθεό τ' ἄλλῳ.

But, O king, be well-advised thyself, and yield to wholesome advice.

So Psalm (ii. 10)—" Be wise now, therefore, O ye kings : be instructed, ye judges of the earth."

" Whatsoever thy Hand findeth to do."
Il. ii. 435.

Μηκέτι νῦν δήθ' αὖθι λεγώμεθα, μηδ' ἔτι δηρὸν
ἀμβαλλώμεθα ἔργον, ὃ δὴ θεὸς ἐγγυαλίζει.

No longer let us be talking here, nor put off the work which God has trusted to our hands.

So Ecclesiastes (ix. 10)—" Whatsoever thy hand findeth to do, do it with thy might ; for there is no work, nor device, nor knowledge, nor wisdom in the grave, whither thou goest."

Flocks of Birds.
Il. ii. 459.

Τῶν δ', ὥστ' ὀρνίθων πετεηνῶν ἔθνεα πολλά,
χηνῶν ἢ γεράνων ἢ κύκνων δουλιχοδείρων,
'Ασίῳ ἐν λειμῶνι, Καϋστρίου ἀμφὶ ῥέεθρα,
ἔνθα καὶ ἔνθα ποτῶνται ἀγαλλόμενα πτερύγεσσιν,
κλαγγηδὸν προκαθιζόντων, σμαραγεῖ δέ τε λειμών.

Just as a numerous flock of winged fowl—of geese, or cranes, or long-necked swans—in the Asian mead, beside the streams of the Cayster, fly about, making a loud flapping with their wings, then settle down with clamorous noise, while all the mead resounds.

Insects.
Il. ii. 469.

'Ηΰτε μυιάων ἀδινάων ἔθνεα πολλά.
αἵτε κατὰ σταθμὸν ποιμνήϊον ἠλάσκουσιν
ὥρῃ ἐν εἰαρινῇ, ὅτε τε γλάγος ἄγγεα δεύει.

As the thickly-swarming flies which gather round some shepherd's pen in spring-tide, while the milk is frothing in the pails.

DIVERSITY OF TONGUES.
Il. ii. 804.

Ἄλλη δ' ἄλλων γλῶσσα πολυσπερέων ἀνθρώπων.

The widespread nations spoke a variety of languages.

So Genesis (xi. 9)—"Therefore is the name of it called Babel ; because the Lord did there confound the language of all the earth ;" and Acts (ii. 4) —"They began to speak with other tongues, as the Spirit gave them utterance."

A SON SLAIN FOR DISOBEDIENCE TO HIS FATHER.
Il. ii. 831.

Ὑῖε δύω Μέροπος Περκωσίου, ὃς περὶ πάντων
ᾔδεε μαντοσύνας, οὐδὲ οὓς παῖδας ἔασκεν
στείχειν ἐς πόλεμον φθισήνορα.   Τὼ δέ οἱ οὔτι
πειθέσθην· κῆρες γὰρ ἄγον μέλανος θανάτοιο.

The two sons of the Percosean Merops, who was skilled above all in prophetic lore, nor would give permission to his sons to be present in the life-destroying war ; but they refused to listen to him, for fate led them on to gloomy death.

So 1 Samuel (ii. 25)—"Notwithstanding they hearkened not unto the voice of their father, because the Lord would slay them."

PROPHETIC LORE SAVES NOT A MAN.
Il. ii. 859.

Ἀλλ' οὐκ οἰωνοῖσιν ἐρύσσατο κῆρα μέλαιναν.

But he did not ward off black death by his knowledge of future events.

So Isaiah (xlvii. 13)—"Let now the astrologers, the stargazers, the monthly prognosticators, stand up and save thee from these things that shall come upon thee."

THE THIEF IN THE NIGHT.
Il. iii. 10.

Εὖτ' ὄρεος κορυφῇσι Νότος κατέχευεν ὀμίχλην,
ποιμέσιν οὔτι φίλην, κλέπτῃ δέ τε νυκτὸς ἀμείνω.

As when the south wind spreads a mist on the tops of the mountain, in no way a friend to the shepherd, but better to the thief than even the night.

So Job (xxiv. 14)—"The murderer rising with the light killeth the poor and needy, and in the night is as a thief ;" and 1 Thessalonians (v. 2)— "For yourselves know perfectly that the day of the Lord so cometh as a thief in the night."

THE GIFTS OF GOD NOT TO BE DESPISED.
Il. iii. 65.

Οὔτοι ἀπόβλητ᾽ ἐστὶ θεῶν ἐρικυδέα δῶρα,
ὅσσα κεν αὐτοὶ δῶσιν, ἑκὼν δ᾽ οὐκ ἄν τις ἕλοιτο.

The glorious gifts of the gods are not to be despised which they may have bestowed on thee, for we cannot select them ourselves.

So Ecclesiastes (iii. 13)—" And also that every man should eat and drink and enjoy the fruit of all his labour ; it is the gift of God ;" and 1 Timothy (iv. 4)—" For every creature of God is good, and nothing to be refused, if it be received with thanksgiving."

SWEAR NOT FALSELY.
Il. iii. 107.

Μή τις ὑπερβασίῃ Διὸς ὅρκια δηλήσηται.

Let no one violate what is ratified by oath by wanton violence.

So Leviticus (xix. 12) —"And ye shall not swear by my name falsely, neither shalt profane the name of thy God : I am the Lord ;" and Matthew (v. 33)—" Again, ye have heard that it hath been said by them of old time, Thou shalt not forswear thyself, but shalt perform unto the Lord thine oaths."

THE AGED.
Il. iii. 108.

Αἰεὶ δ᾽ ὁπλοτέρων ἀνδρῶν φρένες ἠερέθονται·
οἷς δ᾽ ὁ γέρων μετέῃσιν, ἅμα πρόσσω καὶ ὀπίσσω
λεύσσει, ὅπως ὄχ᾽ ἄριστα μετ᾽ ἀμφοτέροισι γένηται.

For the spirits of the young are too quickly stirred ; but in what things the old take a part, he looks before and after, that due provision be made for all interests.

So Ecclesiastes (xi. 10)—" Therefore remove sorrow from thy heart, and put away evil from thy flesh : for childhood and youth are vanity ;" and Titus (ii. 6)—" Young men likewise exhort to be sober-minded."

A MAN OF FEW WORDS.
Il. iii. 214.

Παῦρα μὲν, ἀλλὰ μάλα λιγέως, ἐπεὶ οὐ πολύμυθος
οὐδ᾽ ἀφαμαρτοεπὴς, ἢ καὶ γένει ὕστερος ἦεν.

Few words, but in very clear and musical tones, since he was not a babbler nor a random talker, though young in years.

So Proverbs (x. 19)—" In the multitude of words there wanteth not sin ; but he that refraineth his lips is wise."

THE SUN.
Il. iii. 277.

Ἥλιός θ', ὃς πάντ' ἐφορᾷς καὶ πάντ' ἐπακούεις.

And thou, O sun ! thou seest all things and hearest all things
in thy daily course.

So Psalm (xix. 6)—"His going forth is from the end of the heaven, and
his circuit unto the ends of it; and there is nothing hid from the heat
thereof."

YIELDING PACIFIETH GREAT OFFENCES.
Il. iv. 62.

Ἀλλ' ἤτοι μὲν ταῦθ' ὑποείξομεν ἀλλήλοισιν,
σοὶ μὲν ἐγώ, σὺ δ' ἐμοί· ἐπὶ δ' ἕψονται θεοὶ ἄλλοι
ἀθάνατοι.

But we shall give way to each other in these matters, I to thee
and thou to me ; and the other immortal gods will follow us.

So Ecclesiastes (x. 4)—"If the spirit of the ruler rise up against thee,
leave not thy place ; for yielding pacifieth great offences."

A METEOR.
Il. iv. 75.

Οἷον δ' ἀστέρα ἧκε Κρόνου παῖς ἀγκυλομήτεω,
ἢ ναύτῃσι τέρας ἠὲ στρατῷ εὐρέϊ λαῶν,
λαμπρόν· τοῦ δέ τε πολλοὶ ἀπὸ σπινθῆρες ἵενται.

Like to a bright meteor which the son of deep-designing Saturn
sends, a portent to sailors or the broad army of the people, scat-
tering fiery sparks around.

Shakespeare ("Henry VI.," part i., act i., sc. 1) says—

"Hung be the heavens with black, yield day to night !
Comets, importing change of times and states,
Brandish your crystal tresses in the sky ;
And with them scourge the bad revolting stars,
That have consented unto Henry's death."

"THE BATTLE IS THE LORD'S."
Il. iv. 84.

Ζεὺς, ὅστ' ἀνθρώπων ταμίης πολέμοιο τέτυκται.

Jove, who dispenses peace and war to men.

So 1 Samuel (xvii. 47)—"And all this assembly shall know that the Lord
saveth not with sword and spear ; for the battle is the Lord's, and he will
give you into our hands ;" and Proverbs (xxi. 31)—"The horse is prepared
against the day of battle : but safety is of the Lord."

"God shall Avenge."

Il. iv. 160.

Εἴπερ γάρ τε καὶ αὐτίκ' Ὀλύμπιος οὐκ ἐτέλεσσεν,
ἔκ τε καὶ ὀψὲ τελεῖ, σύν τε μεγάλῳ ἀπέτισαν,
σὺν σφῇσιν κεφαλῇσι γυναιξί τε καὶ τεκέεσσιν.

For though Clympian Jove does not avenge at once, he will avenge, though it may be after many days, and that severely, —with their own lives, and the lives of their wives and children.

So Habakkuk (i. 3)—" Why dost thou show me iniquity, and cause me to behold grievance? for spoiling and violence are before me : and there are that raise up strife and contention ;" and Luke (xviii. 7)—" And shall not God avenge His own elect, which cry day and night unto Him, though He bear long with them? I tell you that He will avenge them speedily. Nevertheless when the Son of man cometh, shall He find faith on the earth ?"

The Liar.

Il. iv. 235.

Οὐ γὰρ ἐπὶ ψευδέσσι πατὴρ Ζεὺς ἔσσετ' ἀρωγὸς.

For Jove shall not assist the liar.

So Proverbs (xix. 9)—" False witness shall not be unpunished ; and he that speaketh lies shall perish."

"Years teach Wisdom."

Il. iv. 322.

Ἀλλὰ καὶ ὡς ἱππεῦσι μετέσσομαι ἠδὲ κελεύσω
βουλῇ καὶ μύθοισι· τὸ γὰρ γέρας ἐστὶ γερόντων.
Αἰχμὰς δ' αἰχμάσσουσι νεώτεροι.

But I shall still go forth with the chariots and give counsel and commands, for this is the privilege of the old, while the younger shall fight in the ranks.

So Job (xxxii. 7)—" I said, Days should speak, and multitude of years should teach wisdom."

Lying.

Il. iv. 390.

Ἀτρείδη, ποῖόν σε ἔπος φύγεν ἕρκος ὀδόντων.

Son of Atreus, what kind of words has escaped from thy lips?

So Colossians (iii. 9)—" Lie not one to another, seeing that ye have put off the old man with his deeds."

The Roar of the Sea.

Il. iv. 422.

Ὡς δ᾽ ὅτ᾽ ἐν αἰγιαλῷ πολυηχέϊ κῦμα θαλάσσης
ὅρνυτ᾽ ἐπασσύτερον Ζεφύρου ὕπο κινήσαντος·
πόντῳ μὲν τὰ πρῶτα κορύσσεται, αὐτὰρ ἔπειτα
χέρσῳ ῥηγνύμενον μεγάλα βρέμει, ἀμφὶ δέ τ᾽ ἄκρας
κυρτὸν ἐὸν κορυφοῦται, ἀποπτύει δ᾽ ἁλὸς ἄχνην.

As when the ocean waves dash forward on the far-resounding
shore, driven by the west wind, wave upon wave ; first it curls
with whitening crests ; but anon it breaks upon the beach with
thundering roar, and, recoiling, flings in great curves its head
aloft, and tosses high the spray of the sea.

Silent March of an Army.

Il. iv. 429.

Οἱ δ᾽ ἄλλοι ἀκὴν ἴσαν—οὐδέ κε φαίης
τόσσον λαὸν ἕπεσθαι ἔχοντ᾽ ἐν στήθεσιν αὐδήν.
σιγῇ δειδιότες σημάντορας· ἀμφὶ δὲ πᾶσιν
τεύχεα ποικίλ᾽ ἔλαμπε, τὰ εἱμένοι ἐστιχόωντο.

The rest in s ence marched, nor couldst thou have said that all
that moving host had voice in their breast : awe for their leaders
wrought silence deep ; while round all flashed the varied armour
with which hey were girt.

Discord.

Il. iv. 440.

Ἔρις, ἄμοτον μεμαυῖα,
Ἄρεος ἀνδροφόνοιο κασιγνήτη ἑτάρη τε,
ἥτ᾽ ὀλίγη μὲν πρῶτα κορύσσεται, αὐτὰρ ἔπειτα
οὐρανῷ ἐστήριξε κάρη καὶ ἐπὶ χθονὶ βαίνει.
Ἥ σφιν καὶ τότε νεῖκος ὁμοίϊον ἔμβαλε μέσσῳ
ἐρχομένη καθ᾽ ὅμιλον, ὀφέλλουσα στόνον ἀνδρῶν.

Discord, restless without ceasing, sister and companion of man-
slaying Mars, small at her birth, but afterwards with her head
reachir g heaven, while she stalks upon earth ; then she rouses
dire fury, rushing into the midst of the crowd, adding woe to
mortals.

o Proverbs (xvii. 4)—"A wicked doer giveth heed to false lips ; and a
liar giveth ear to a naughty tongue ;" and James (iii. 5)—"Even so the
tongue is a little member, and boasteth great things. Behold how great a
matter a little fire kindleth !"

Mountain Torrent.
Il. iv. 452.

'Ὡς δ' ὅτε χείμαρροι ποταμοὶ κατ' ὄρεσφι ῥέοντες
ἐς μισγάγκειαν συμβάλλετον ὄβριμον ὕδωρ
κρουνῶν ἐκ μεγάλων, κοίλης ἔντοσθε χαράδρης·
τῶν δέ τε τηλόσε δοῦπον ἐν οὔρεσιν ἔκλυε ποιμήν.

As when wintry torrents rushing down the mountains join together their furious waters from mighty springs within some deep ravine, while from afar the shepherd hears the roar on the far mountain's top.

An Unstable Man.
Il. v. 85.

Τυδείδην δ' οὐκ ἂν γνοίης ποτέροισι μετείη.

As for Diomede, thou couldst not know on which side he was.

So James (i. 8)—"A double-minded man is unstable in all his ways."

"Let us not Fight against God."
Il. v. 130.

Μήτι σύγ' ἀθανάτοισι θεοῖς ἀντικρὺ μάχεσθαι
τοῖς ἄλλοις.

Fight not against the other immortal gods.

So Acts (xxiii. 9)—"And there arose a great cry : and the scribes that were of the Pharisees' part arose, and strove, saying, We find no evil in this man ; but if a spirit or an angel hath spoken to Him, let us not fight against God."

The Wrath of God.
Il. v. 178.

Χαλεπὴ δὲ θεοῦ ἔπι μῆνις.

The wrath of God is difficult to be withstood.

So Psalm (ii. 12)—"Kiss the Son, lest He be angry, and ye perish from the way, when His wrath is kindled but a little. Blessed are all they that put their trust in Him ;" and (xc. 11)—"Who knoweth the power of thine anger? even according to thy fear, so is thy wrath ;" and Revelations (vi. 17)—"For the great day of His wrath is come; and who shall be able to stand ?"

Blood of the Gods.
Il. v. 339.

'Ρέε δ' ἄμβροτον αἷμα θεοῖο,
ἰχώρ, οἷός πέρ τε ῥέει μακάρεσσι θεοῖσιν.

οὐ γὰρ σῖτον ἔδουσ', οὐ πίνουσ' αἴθοπα οἶνον,
τοὔνεκ' ἀναίμονές εἰσι καὶ ἀθάνατοι καλέονται.

An immortal stream flowed from the god, ichor, such as flows
from the blessed gods ; for they do not feed on bread nor drink
sparkling wine, therefore they are bloodless, and become immortal.

AFFLICTION AT THE DEATH OF A FATHER.
Il. v. 408.

Οὐδέ τι μιν παῖδες ποτὶ γούνασι παππάζουσι
'Ελθόντ' ἐκ πολέμοιο καὶ αἰνῆς δηϊοτῆτος.

No children shall any longer, clinging to his knees, call him
sire, returning safe from the war and fields of death.

See Gray's "Elegy in Churchyard," st. 6.

CONTEND NOT WITH THE GODS.
Il. v. 440.

Φράζεο, Τυδείδη, καὶ χάζεο, μηδὲ θεοῖσιν
ἶσ' ἔθελε φρονέειν, ἐπεὶ οὔποτε φῦλον ὁμοῖον
ἀθανάτων τε θεῶν χαμαὶ ἐρχομένων τ' ἀνθρώπων.

Be advised, son of Tydeus ; retire, and esteem not thyself a
god, since not alike is the race of immortal gods and men, mere
reptiles of the earth.

So Isaiah (xlvi. 3)—" Hearken unto me, O house of Jacob, and all the
remnant of the house of Israel, which are borne by me from the belly, which
are carried from the womb ; " and Acts (v. 39)—" But if it be of God, ye cannot overthrow it, lest haply ye be found even to fight against God."

THE HOURS.
Il. v. 749.

Αὐτόμαται δὲ πύλαι μύκον οὐρανοῦ, ἃς ἔχον Ὧραι,
τῆς ἐπιτέτραπται μέγας οὐρανὸς Οὔλυμπός τε,
ἠμὲν ἀνακλῖναι πυκινὸν νέφος ἠδ' ἐπιθεῖναι.

Heaven's gates spontaneous open, guarded by the Hours, to
whom great heaven and Olympus is given in charge, either to roll
aside or draw the veil of thick clouds.

STENTORIAN VOICE.
Il. v. 785.

Στέντορι εἰσαμένη μεγαλήτορι, χαλκεοφώνῳ,
ὃς τόσον αὐδήσασχ' ὅσον ἄλλοι πεντήκοντα.

Likening herself to strong Stentor, endued with brazen lungs,
whose shout surpassed the force of fifty tongues.

Quit you like Men.
Il. vi. 112.

Ἀνέρες ἔστε, φίλοι, μνήσασθε δὲ θούριδος ἀλκῆς.

My friends, quit ye like men, and be firm in the battle.

So 1 Samuel (iv. 9)—"Be strong, and quit yourselves like men, O ye Philistines! that ye be not servants unto the Hebrews, as they have been to you : quit yourselves like men, and fight ;" and 1 Corinthians (xvi. 13) —"Watch ye, stand fast in the faith, quit you like men, be strong."

Race succeeds Race like Leaves.
Il. vi. 146.

Οἵη περ φύλλων γενεὴ, τοίη δὲ καὶ ἀνδρῶ .
Φύλλα τὰ μέν τ' ἄνεμος χαμάδις χέει, ἄλλα δὲ θ' ὕλη
τηλεθόωσα φύει, ἔαρος δ' ἐπιγίγνεται ὥρη·
ὡς ἀνδρῶν γενεὴ ἡ μὲν φύει, ἡ δ' ἀπολήγει.

As is the race of leaves, such is man : the wind scatters some on the ground, others the wood budding puts forth, and the season of spring brings out ; so also the race of men, one generation flourishes, another decays.

So Sirach (xiv. 18, 19) ; and Ecclesiastes (i. 4)—"One generation passeth away, and another generation cometh : but the earth abideth for ever."

First in Worth as in Command.
Il. vi. 207.

Πέμπε δέ μ' ἐς Τροίην. καί μοι μάλα πόλλ' ἐπέτελλεν,
αἰὲν ἀριστεύειν καὶ ὑπείροχον ἔμμεναι ἄλλων,
μηδὲ γένος πατέρων αἰσχυνέμεν, οἳ μέγ' ἄριστοι
ἔν τ' Ἐφύρῃ ἐγένοντο καὶ ἐν Λυκίῃ εὐρείῃ.

He sent me to Troy, and enjoined me oft to stand the first in worth as in command, nor bring discredit on my fathers' race, who had always held the foremost rank in Ephyre and Lycia's wide domain.

So 1 Corinthians (xii. 31)—"But covet earnestly the best gifts : and yet show I unto you a more excellent way ;" and (xiv. 12)—"Even so ye, forasmuch as ye are zealous of spiritual gifts, seek that ye may excel to the edifying of the Church."

The Advantage of Wine.
Il. vi. 261.

Ἀνδρὶ δὲ κεκμηῶτι μένος μέγα οἶνος ἀέξει.

Wine gives much strength to wearied man.

So 1 Timothy (v. 23)—"Drink no longer water, but use a little wine for thy stomach's sake, and thine often infirmities."

WINE.
Il. vi. 264.

Μή μοι οἶνον ἄειρε μελίφρονα, πότνια μῆτερ,
μή μ' ἀπογυιώσῃς, μένεος δ' ἀλκῆς τε λάθωμαι.

Mine honoured mother, bring me not luscious wine, lest thou
unnerve my limbs, and make me lose my wonted prowess and
strength.

TO OFFER SACRIFICES WITH POLLUTED HANDS.
Il. vi. 266.

Χερσὶ δ' ἀνίπτοισιν Διὶ λείβειν αἴθοπα οἶνον
ἄζομαι.

I fear to offer a libation of rosy wine with unwashen hands.

So Isaiah (i. 15)—"And when ye spread forth your hands, I will hide
mine eyes from you ; yea, when ye make many prayers, I will not hear :
your hands are full of blood ;" and Psalm (xxvi. 6)—"I will wash mine
hands in innocency : so will I compass thine altar, O Lord."

MAN PROPOSES, GOD DISPOSES.
Il. vi. 339.

Νίκη δ' ἐπαμείβεται ἄνδρας.

Victory changes oft her side.

See (Lat.) Man proposes.

AN EXAMPLE OF A LOVING WIFE.
Il. vi. 429.

Ἕκτορ, ἀτὰρ σύ μοί ἐσσι πατὴρ καὶ πότνια μήτηρ
ἠδὲ κασίγνητος, σὺ δέ μοι θαλερὸς παρακοίτης.

Hector, thou art my father and honoured mother, and brother ;
thou, too, my blooming husband.

Lord Derby thus translates it :—
> "But, Hector, thou to me art all in one,
> Sire, mother, brethren ; thou, my wedded love !"

FRIGHTENED CHILD.
Il. vi. 467.

Ἂψ δ' ὁ πάϊς πρὸς κόλπον ἐϋζώνοιο τιθήνης
ἐκλίνθη ἰάχων, πατρὸς φίλου ὄψιν ἀτυχθείς,
ταρβήσας χαλκόν τε ἰδὲ λόφον ἱππιοχαίτην,
δεινὸν ἀπ' ἀκροτάτης κόρυθος νεύοντα νοήσας.
Ἐκ δ' ἐγέλασσε πατήρ τε φίλος καὶ πότνια μήτηρ.

The babe clung crying to his nurse's breast, scared at the sight of his father, startled by the brazen helm and horse-hair plume, seeing it nodding fearfully on the warrior's crest; but his affectionate father and honoured mother laughed fondly.

THE FATE OF ALL IS FIXED.

Il. vi. 487.

Οὐ γάρ τίς μ' ὑπὲρ αἶσαν ἀνὴρ ῎Αϊδι προϊάψει·
μοῖραν δ' οὔτινά φημι πεφυγμένον ἔμμεναι ἀνδρῶν,
οὐ κακὸν, οὐδὲ μὲν ἐσθλὸν, ἐπὴν τὰ πρῶτα γένηται.

For no man can antedate my doom ; though I am aware that no one can escape his fate, neither the coward nor the brave, as it has been determined at his birth.

So John (vii. 30)—"Then they sought to take Him : but no man laid hands on Him, because His hour was not yet come."

See (Lat.) Death.

A LADY'S WORK.

Il. vi. 490.

'Αλλ' εἰς οἶκον ἰοῦσα τὰ σ' αὐτῆς ἔργα κόμιζε,
ἱστόν τ' ἠλακάτην τε, καὶ ἀμφιπόλοισι κέλευε
ἔργον ἐποίχεσθαι·

But, going to thy house, attend to thy household cares, thy web and thy spindle, and assign thy maidens their several tasks.

So Proverbs (xxxi. 19)—" She layeth her hands to the spindle, and her hands hold the distaff."

MAN IN THE HANDS OF GOD.

Il. vii. 101.

Αὐτὰρ ὕπερθεν
νίκης πείρατ' ἔχονται ἐν ἀθανάτοισι θεοῖσιν.

But the decision of the victory is placed in the hands of the immortal gods.

So Proverbs (xxi. 30)—" There is no wisdom, nor understanding, nor counsel, against the Lord ; " and 1 Corinthians (xv. 57)—" But thanks be to God, which giveth us the victory, through our Lord Jesus Christ."

See (Lat.) Man proposes.

THE BRAVE MAN.

Il. vii. 111.

Μηδ' ἔθελ' ἐξ ἔριδος σεῦ ἀμείνονι φωτὶ μάχεσθαι.

And think not to contend with a man mightier than thou.

So Ecclesiastes (vi. 10)—"That which hath been is named already, and it is known that it is man : neither may he contend with him that is mightier than he."

Night Approacheth.

Il. vii. 282.

Νὺξ δ' ἤδη τελέθει· ἀγαθὸν καὶ νυκτὶ πιθέσθαι.

Now the night is at hand ; it is wise to obey the night.

So Judges (xix. 9)—"Behold, now the day draweth toward evening, I pray you tarry all night : behold, the day groweth to an end ; lodge here, that thine heart may be merry ; and to-morrow get you early on your way, that thou mayest go home ;" and Luke (xxiv. 29)—"But they constrained Him, saying, Abide with us ; for it is toward evening, and the day is far spent. And He went in to tarry with them."

The Wisdom of the Gods.

Il. vii. 446.

Ζεῦ πάτερ, ἦ ῥά τίς ἐστι βροτῶν ἐπ' ἀπείρονα γαῖαν
ὅστις ἔτ' ἀθανάτοισι νόον καὶ μῆτιν ἐνίψει ;

Father Jove, is there any of mortals on the wide-spread earth who will rival us in wisdom and understanding?

So Isaiah (xl. 13)—"Who hath directed the Spirit of the Lord, or, being His counsellor, hath taught Him ?"—and Romans (xi. 34)—"For who hath known the mind of the Lord? or who hath been His counsellor ?"

Gloomy Tartarus.

Il. viii. 13.

Ἦ μιν ἑλὼν ῥίψω ἐς Τάρταρον ἠερόεντα,
τῆλε μάλ', ἧχι βάθιστον ὑπὸ χθονός ἐστι βέρεθρον,
ἔνθα σιδήρειαί τε πύλαι καὶ χάλκεος οὐδός,
τόσσον ἔνερθ' Ἀΐδεω ὅσον οὐρανός ἐστ' ἀπὸ γαίης.

Be assured that I shall seize and hurl him into gloomy Tartarus deep down, where is the lowest abyss beneath the earth, where are iron gates and brazen floors, as far below Hades as heaven is from the earth.

So 2 Peter (ii. 4)—"For if God spared not the angels that sinned, but cast them down to hell, and delivered them into chains of darkness, to be reserved unto judgment."

The Golden Chain.

Il. viii. 19.

Σειρὴν χρυσείην ἐξ οὐρανόθεν κρεμάσαντες
πάντες δ' ἐξάπτεσθε θεοὶ πᾶσαί τε θέαιναι·
ἀλλ' οὐκ ἂν ἐρύσαιτ' ἐξ οὐρανόθεν πεδίονδε
Ζῆν', ὕπατον μήστωρ', οὐδ' εἰ μάλα πολλὰ κάμοιτε.

Having suspended a golden chain from heaven, do you, gods and goddesses, all of you lay hold of it: yet would you fail to

drag the mighty and all-wise Jove from heaven to earth, strive as
you may.

So Isaiah (xl. 15)—"Behold, the nations are as a drop of a bucket, and
are counted as the small dust of the balance: behold, He taketh up the
isles as a very little thing."

Strength of God Irresistible.
Il. viii. 30.

Ὦ πάτερ ἡμέτερε Κρονίδη, ὕπατε κρειόντων,
εὖ νυ καὶ ἡμεῖς ἴδμεν ὅ τοι σθένος οὐκ ἐπιεικτόν.

Our father, son of Saturn, mightiest of kings, we all know well
that thy strength is not to be resisted.

So Job (xlii. 2)—"I know that Thou canst do everything, and that no
thought can be withholden from Thee."

"God weighs Actions."
Il. viii. 69.

Καὶ τότε δὴ χρύσεια πατὴρ ἐτίταινε τάλαντα.

And then the father of heaven hung out his golden scales.

So 1 Samuel (ii. 3)—"By Him acticns are weighed;" and Proverbs (xvi.
2)—"But the Lord weigheth the spirits;" and Isaiah (xl. 12—"Who hath
measured the waters in the hollow of His hand, and meted out heaven with
the span, and comprehended the dust of the earth in a measure, and
weighed the mountains in scales, and the hills in a balance?"

The Irresistible Power of God.
Il. viii. 143.

Ἀνὴρ δέ κεν οὔτι Διὸς νόον εἰρύσσαιτο
οὐδὲ μάλ' ἴφθιμος, ἐπειὴ πολὺ φέρτερός ἐστιν.

No man can withstand the will of Jove, however powerful he
be, for he is much mightier.

So Job (ix. 12)—"Behold, He taketh away, who can hinder Him? who
will say unto Him, What doest Thou?"—and 1 Corinthians (i. 25)—"Because
the foolishness of God is wiser than men; and the weakness of God is
stronger than men."

The Fixedness of Fate.
Il. viii. 477.

Ὡς γὰρ θέσφατόν ἐστι· σέθεν δ' ἐγὼ οὐκ ἀλεγίζω
χωομένης, οὐδ' εἴ κε τὰ νείατα πείραθ' ἵκηαι
γαίης καὶ πόντοιο, ἵν' Ἰαπετός τε Κρόνος τε
ἥμενοι οὔτ' αὐγῆς Ὑπερίονος Ἠελίοιο

τέρπον τ᾽ οὔτ᾽ ἀνέμοισι, βαθὺς δέ τε Τάρταρος ἀμφίς.
Οὐδ᾽ ἢν ἔνθ᾽ ἀφίκηαι ἀλωμένη, οὐ σεῦ ἔγωγε
σκυζομένης ἀλέγω, ἐπεὶ οὐ σέο κύντερον ἄλλο.

For such is the unalterable decree of fate ; but I reck not of thy
wrath, nor should I care even though thou wert thrust beneath
the lowest depths of earth and sea, where Jäpetus and Saturn
dwell, uncheered by rays of sun and fanned by no cool breeze,
encompassed by the profound abyss of Tartarus,—not even, I say,
though thou wert there consigned to banishment, do I care, but
hear thy reproaches unheeded, since nothing is more vile than
thou.

LOVELY NIGHT.
Il. viii. 555.

Ὡς δ᾽ ὅτ᾽ ἐν οὐρανῷ ἄστρα φαεινὴν ἀμφὶ σελήνην
φαίνετ᾽ ἀριπρεπέα, ὅτε τ᾽ ἔπλετο νήνεμος αἰθήρ·
[ἔκ τ᾽ ἔφανεν πᾶσαι σκοπιαὶ καὶ πρώονες ἄκροι
καὶ νάπαι· οὐρανόθεν δ᾽ ἄρ᾽ ὑπερράγη ἄσπετος αἰθήρ,]
πάντα δέ τ᾽ εἴδεται ἄστρα, γέγηθε δέ τε φρένα ποιμήν.

As when in heaven the stars around the glittering moon beam
loveliest amid the breathless air, and in clear outline appear every
hill, sharp peak, and woody dell ; deep upon deep the sky breaks
open, and each star shines forth, while joy fills the shepherd's
heart.

A KING DESTITUTE OF BRAVERY.
Il. ix. 37.

Σοὶ δὲ διάνδιχα δῶκε Κρόνου παῖς ἀγκυλομήτεω·
σκήπτρῳ μέν τοι δῶκε τετιμῆσθαι περὶ πάντων,
ἀλκὴν δ᾽ οὔτοι δῶκεν, ὅ τε κράτος ἐστὶ μέγιστον.

The son of deep-designing Saturn bestows his gifts in differing
measure : he has granted to thee to be honoured for thy royal
command, but valour he has not granted thee, which is the noblest
boon of heaven.

THE MAN DELIGHTING IN WAR.
Il. ix. 63.

Ἀφρήτωρ ἀθέμιστος ἀνέστιός ἐστιν ἐκεῖνος
ὃς πολέμου ἔραται ἐπιδημίου ὀκρυόεντος.

That man is bound by no social, religious, and domestic tie who
would court civil war with all its horrors.

See (Lat.) Peace.

The Man Favoured by God.
Il. ix. 117.

'Αντί νυ πολλῶν
λαῶν ἐστὶν ἀνὴρ ὅντε Ζεὺς κῆρι φιλήσῃ.

The man whom Jove loves is a match for many.

So Joshua (xxiii. 10)—"One man of you shall chase a thousand: for the Lord your God, He it is that fighteth for you, as He hath promised you;" and 2 Samuel (xviii. 3)—"But now thou art worth ten thousand of us."

Pluto.
Il. ix. 158.

'Αΐδης τοι ἀμείλιχος ἠδ᾽ ἀδάμαστος.
Τοὔνεκα καί τε βροτοῖσι θεῶν ἔχθιστος ἀπάντων.

Pluto, the merciless and inexorable, and therefore the most hateful of all the gods to mortals.

No Remedy to an Evil once Endured.
Il. ix. 249.

Αὐτῷ σοὶ μετόπισθ᾽ ἄχος ἔσσεται, οὐδέ τι μῆχος
ῥεχθέντος κακοῦ ἔστ᾽ ἄκος εὑρεῖν.

There will be grief to thee thyself hereafter, nor will there be found a remedy to the evil that is done.

Restrain thy Passion.
Il. ix. 255.

Σὺ δὲ μεγαλήτορα θυμὸν
ἴσχειν ἐν στήθεσσι· φιλοφροσύνη γὰρ ἀμείνων.

Do thou restrain thy haughty spirit in thy breast, for better far is gentle courtesy.

So Proverbs (xvi. 32)—"He that is slow to anger is better than the mighty: and he that ruleth his spirit than he that taketh a city.'

"Leave off from Contention."
Il. ix. 257.

Ληγέμεναι δ᾽ ἔριδος κακομηχάνου.

And cease from angry strife.

So Proverbs (xvii. 14)—"The beginning of strife is as when one letteth out water; therefore leave off contention, before it be meddled with."

The Hypocrite.

Il. ix. 312.

'Εχθρὸς γάρ μοι κεῖνος ὁμῶς 'Αΐδαο πύλῃσιν
ὅς χ' ἕτερον μὲν κεύθῃ ἐνὶ φρεσὶν, ἄλλο δὲ εἴπῃ.

For that man is detested by me as the gates of hell whose outward words conceal his inmost thoughts.

So Psalm (lv. 21)—" The words of his mouth were smoother than butter, but war was in his heart : his words were softer than oil, yet were they drawn swords ;" and (cxix. 163)—" I hate and abhor lying."

See (Lat.) Ambition.

The Brave and the Coward die alike.

Il. ix. 318.

'Ίση μοῖρα μένοντι, καὶ εἰ μάλα τις πολεμίζοι·
ἐν δὲ ἰῇ τιμῇ ἠμὲν κακὸς ἠδὲ καὶ ἐσθλός·
κάτθαν' ὁμῶς ὅ τ' ἀεργὸς ἀνὴρ ὅ τε πολλὰ ἐοργώς.

The same fate awaits him that fights or fights not. The coward and the brave are held in equal honour. The man who yields ignobly and he who exerts himself die alike.

So Ecclesiastes (ix. 2)—" All things come alike to all : there is one event to the righteous, and to the wicked ; to the good, and to the clean, and to the unclean ; to him that sacrificeth, and to him that sacrificeth not : as is the good, so is the sinner ; and he that sweareth, as he that feareth an oath."

Seneca (Ep. 91) says :—" Œquat omnes cinis : impares nascimur, pares morimur." " The dust levels all ; we are born in unequal conditions, but die equal."

What Advantage have I by Exposing myself to Danger?

Il. ix. 321.

Οὐδέ τί μοι περίκειται, ἐπεὶ πάθον ἄλγεα θυμῷ,
αἰὲν ἐμὴν ψυχὴν παραβαλλόμενος πολεμίζειν.

There is no profit to me after all my labours, though I am always setting my life at stake.

So Job (xxxv. 3)—" For thou saidst, What advantage will it be unto thee ? and, What profit shall I have if I be cleansed from my sin ?"—and Psalm (lxxiii. 13)—" Verily I have cleansed my heart in vain, and washed my hands in innocency ;" and Ecclesiastes (vi. 8)—" For what hath the wise more than the fool ?"

A Wife.

Il. ix. 341.

'Επεὶ ὅστις ἀνὴρ ἀγαθὸς καὶ ἐχέφρων,

τὴν αὐτοῦ φιλέει καὶ κήδεται, ὡς καὶ ἐγὼ τὴν
ἐκ θυμοῦ φίλεον, δουρικτητήν περ ἐοῦσαν.

Every wise and sensible man loves the wife of his choice ; so I too loved her in my heart's core, slave though she was, taken by my spear.

So Colossians (iii. 19)—"Wives, submit yourselves unto your own husbands, as it is fit in the Lord."

LIFE NOT TO BE BOUGHT.

Il. ix. 401.

Οὐ γὰρ ἐμοὶ ψυχῆς ἀντάξιον οὐδ᾽ ὅσα φασὶν
Ἴλιον ἐκτῆσθαι, εὐναιόμενον πτολίεθρον,
τὸ πρὶν ἐπ᾽ εἰρήνης, πρὶν ἐλθεῖν υἷας Ἀχαιῶν,
οὐδ᾽ ὅσα λάϊνος οὐδὸς ἀφήτορος ἐντὸς ἐέργει,
Φοίβου Ἀπόλλωνος, Πυθοῖ ἔνι πετρηέσσῃ.
Ληϊστοὶ μὲν γάρ τε βόες καὶ ἴφια μῆλα,
κτητοὶ δὲ τρίποδές τε καὶ ἵππων ξανθὰ κάρηνα·
ἀνδρὸς δὲ ψυχὴ πάλιν ἐλθεῖν οὔτε λεϊστὴ
οὔθ᾽ ἑλετή, ἐπεὶ ἄρ κεν ἀμείψεται ἕρκος ὀδόντων.

Life is not to be weighed against all the treasures which they say Troy, that well-inhabited city, possessed formerly in peaceful times, ere the sons of the Greeks came, nor yet by all that is contained within the stone-built temple of the archer Apollo in rocky Pytho. For oxen and goodly sheep may be provided by successful forays, tripods and chestnut mares ; but the soul of man can never more be recalled when the spark of life has passed his lips.

So Job (ii. 4)—"Skin for skin, yea, all that a man hath will he give for his life;" and Matthew (xvi. 26)—"For what is a man profited, if he shall gain the whole world, and lose his own soul? or what shall a man give in exchange for his soul?"—and Job (xiv. 12)—"So man lieth down, and riseth not : till the heavens be no more, they shall not awake, nor be raised out of their sleep. If a man die, shall he live again? All the days of my appointed time will I wait, till my change come."

"THEY SAY, AND DO NOT."

Il. ix. 443.

Μύθων τε ῥητῆρ᾽ ἔμεναι πρηκτῆρά τε ἔργων.

To be a speaker of words, and also a doer of deeds.

So Matthew (vii. 21)—"Not every one that saith unto me, Lord, Lord, shall enter into the kingdom of heaven ; but he that doeth the will of my Father which is in heaven ;" and (xxiii. 3)—"For they say, and do not;" and 2 Corinthians (x. 11)—"Let such an one think this, that such as we are in word by letters when we are absent, such will we be also in deed when we are present."

Prayers are Daughters of Heaven.

Il. ix. 496.

'Αλλ' 'Αχιλεῦ, δάμασον θυμὸν μέγαν· οὐδέ τί σε χρὴ
νηλεὲς ἦτορ ἔχειν· στρεπτοὶ δέ τε καὶ θεοὶ αὐτοί,
τῶνπερ καὶ μείζων ἀρετὴ τιμή τε βίη τε.
Καὶ μὲν τοὺς θυέεσσι καὶ εὐχωλῆς ἀγανῆσιν
λοιβῇ τε κνίσῃ τε παρατρωπῶσ' ἄνθρωποι
λισσόμενοι, ὅτε κέν τις ὑπερβήῃ καὶ ἁμάρτῃ.
Καὶ γάρ τε Λιταί εἰσι Διὸς κοῦραι μεγάλοιο,
χωλαί τε ῥυσαί τε παραβλῶπές τ' ὀφθαλμὼ,
αἵ ῥά τε καὶ μετόπισθ' "Ατης ἀλέγουσι κιοῦσαι.
'Η δ' "Ατη σθεναρή τε καὶ ἀρτίπος, οὕνεκα πάσας
πολλὸν ὑπεκπροθέει, φθάνει δέ τε πᾶσαν ἐπ' αἶαν
βλάπτουσ' ἀνθρώπους· αἱ δ' ἐξακέονται ὀπίσσω.
*Ος μέν τ' αἰδέσεται κούρας Διὸς ἆσσον ἰούσας,
τὸν δὲ μέγ' ὤνησαν καὶ τ' ἔκλυον εὐχομένοιο·
ὃς δέ κ' ἀνήνηται καὶ τε στερεῶς ἀποείπῃ,
λίσσονται δ' ἄρα ταίγε Δία Κρονίωνα κιοῦσαι
τῷ "Ατην ἄμ' ἔπεσθαι, ἵνα βλαφθεὶς ἀποτίσῃ.

But, Achilles, curb thy furious rage : thou shouldst not cherish
an implacable heart, for the gods themselves, excelling in virtue,
honour, and strength, may yet be mollified, for they may be
soothed by incense, humble suit, libations, and sacrifices, when
they may have transgressed and gone astray. For Prayers are the
daughters of mighty Jove,—lame, indeed, of foot, looking askance,
—who, coming after the Temptress, are heedful of their course. But
the Temptress is bold, swift of foot, for she far outruns them, and
gets before them over all the earth, bringing sad disaster on mankind. But Prayers behind her heal the wrongs she has done to
him who bows in reverence to these daughters of Jove as they
approach : such an one they greatly aid, and listen to his entreaties ;
but whosoever rejects, and boldly refuses their assistance, Prayers,
approaching their father Jupiter, beg that the Temptress may
follow him, that he may suffer and pay a due penalty.

So Genesis (viii. 21)—" And Noah offered burnt-offerings on the altar ;
and the Lord smelled a sweet savour ;" and 1 Kings (viii. 38, 39)—" What
prayer and supplication soever be made by any man, or by all Thy people
Israel, which shall know every man the plague of his own heart, and spread
forth his hands toward this house : then hear Thou in heaven Thy dwelling-
place, and forgive, and do, and give to every man according to his ways,
whose heart Thou knowest ; (for Thou, even Thou only, knowest the hearts
of all the children of men)."

A Friend.

Il. ix. 615.

Καλόν τοι σὺν ἐμοὶ τὸν κήδειν ὅς κ' ἐμὲ κήδῃ.

It is right that my friend should honour him who honours me.

PRUDENT COUNSEL.
Il. x. 44.

Χρεὼ βουλῆς ἐμὲ καὶ σὲ, διοτρεφὲς ὦ Μενέλαε,
κερδαλέης, ἥτις κεν ἐρύσσεται ἠδὲ σαώσει.

Godlike Menelaus, both I and you have need of sagest counsels
to guard and protect us.

So Proverbs (xx. 18)—"Every purpose is established by counsel ; and
with good advice make war ;" and (xxiv. 6)—"For by wise counsel thou
shalt make war : and in multitude of counsellors there is safety."

WATCH CAREFULLY.
Il. x. 193.

Οὕτω νῦν, φίλα τέκνα, φυλάσσετε, μηδέ τιν' ὕπνος
Αἱρείτω, μὴ χάρμα γενώμεθα δυσμενέεσσι.

Dear children, now guard carefully ; let not sleep come upon
you, lest we be a laughing-stock to our enemies.

So Nehemiah (vii. 3)—"Appoint watches . . . every one in his watch
and every one to be over against his house ;" and Jeremiah (li. 12)—"Make
the watch strong, set up the watchmen ;" and Mark (xiii. 37)—"And what
I say unto you I say unto all, Watch."

HOW GREAT DEEDS ARE DONE.
Il. x. 224.

Σύν τε δύ' ἐρχομένω, καί τε πρὸ ὅ τοῦ ἐνόησεν,
ὅππως κέρδος ἔῃ· μοῦνος δ' εἴπερ τε νοήσῃ,
ἀλλά τέ οἱ βράσσων τε νόος, λεπτὴ δέ τε μῆτις.

When two go together, the one may perceive before the other how
an enterprise may be best accomplished ; and even though a man
by himself discover the better course, yet his judgment is slower,
and his resolution less firm.

So Genesis (ii. 18)—"It is not good that the man should be alone ;" and
Ecclesiastes (iv. 9, 10)—"Two are better than one ; because they have a
good reward for their labour. For if they fall, the one will lift up his fellow :
but woe to him that is alone when he falleth ; for he hath not another to
help him up."

THE ADVANTAGES OF PRUDENCE.
Il. x. 246.

Τούτου γ' ἐσπομένοιο καὶ ἐκ πυρὸς αἰθομένοιο
ἄμφω νοστήσαιμεν, ἐπεὶ περίοιδε νοῆσαι.

Should he attend us, we shall both return safe even from the
midst of burning fire, since he is wonderfully wise.

So Psalm (lxvi. 12)—"We went through fire and through water ; but Thou
broughtest us out into a wealthy place ;" and Isaiah (xliii. 2)—"When thou

passest through the waters, I will be with thee; and through the rivers,
they shall not overflow thee: when thou walkest through the fire, thou
shalt not be burnt; neither shall the flame kindle upon thee."

Visiting the Iniquity of the Fathers upon the Children.

Il. xi. 142.

Νῦν μὲν δὴ τοῦ πατρὸς ἀεικέα τίσετε λώβην.

Now in truth you shall pay for the heavy sins of your father.

So Exodus (xx. 5)—"I the Lord thy God am a jealous God, visiting the
iniquity of the fathers upon the children ;" and Ezekiel (xviii. 2)—"The
fathers have eaten sour grapes and the children's teeth are set on edge."

God shall Protect thee.

Il. xi. 163.

Ἕκτορα δ' ἐκ βελέων ὕπαγε Ζεὺς ἔκ τε κονίης
ἔκ τ' ἀνδροκτασίης ἔκ θ' αἵματος ἔκ τε κυδοιμοῦ.

Jove withdrew Hector from darts, dust, slaughter, blood, and
turmoil.

So Psalm (xci. 7)—"A thousand shall fall at thy side, and ten thousand
at thy right hand ; but it shall not come nigh thee."

"The Lord shall Deliver thee into my Hand."

Il. xi. 365.

Η θήν σ' ἐξανύω γε καὶ ὕστερον ἀντιβολήσας,
εἴ πού τις καὶ ἔμοιγε θεῶν ἐπιτάρρόθός ἐστιν.

Assuredly I shall end thee if I shall hereafter meet thee, at
least if any of the gods assist me.

So 1 Samuel (xvii. 46)—"This day will the Lord deliver thee into mine
hand, and I will smite thee, and take thine head from thee."

The Coward and the Brave.

Il. ix. 390.

Κωφὸν γὰρ βέλος ἀνδρὸς ἀνάλκιδος οὐτιδανοῖο.
Ἦ τ' ἄλλως ὑπ' ἐμεῖο, καὶ εἴ κ' ὀλίγον περ ἐπαύρῃ,
ὀξὺ βέλος πέλεται, καὶ ἀκήριον αἶψα τίθησιν·
τοῦ δὲ γυναικὸς μέν τ' ἀμφίδρυφοί εἰσι παρειαί,
παῖδες δ' ὀρφανικοί· ὁ δέ θ' αἵματι γαῖαν ἐρεύθων
πύθεται, οἰωνοὶ δὲ περὶ πλέες ἠὲ γυναῖκες.

A worthless coward's weapon has no point: that from my hand
is not so, even if it slightly touch ; it is sharp, and when it strikes

it slays; his widow's cheeks are disfigured with scars of grief, and his children orphans; but he, reddening the ground with blood, rots, while his funeral rites are paid by carrion birds, and not by women.

So Judges (viii. 21)—"For as the man is, so is the strength."

THE BRAVE MAN.

Il. xi. 408.

Οἶδα γὰρ ὅττι κακοὶ μὲν ἀποίχονται πολέμοιο,
ὅς δέ κ' ἀριστεύῃσι μάχῃ ἔνι, τὸν δὲ μάλα χρεὼ
ἑστάμεναι κρατερῶς, ἤτ' ἔβλητ' ἤτ' ἔβαλ' ἄλλον.

For I know that cowards fly from battle; but the warrior distinguished in fight must, above all, stand undaunted, wounded or wounding.

A WOUNDED STAG.

Il. xi. 474.

'Ωσεί τε δαφοινοὶ θῶες ὄρεσφιν
ἀμφ' ἔλαφον κεραὸν βεβλημένον, ὅντ' ἔβαλ' ἀνὴρ
ἰῷ ἀπὸ νευρῆς· τὸν μέν τ' ἤλυξε πόδεσσιν
φεύγων, ὄφρ' αἷμα λιαρὸν καὶ γούνατ' ὀρώρῃ·
αὐτὰρ ἐπειδὴ τόνγε δαμάσσεται ὠκὺς ὀϊστός,
ὠμοφάγοι μιν θῶες ἐν οὔρεσι δαρδάπτουσιν
ἐν νέμεϊ σκιερῷ· ἐπί τε λῖν ἤγαγε δαίμων
σίντην· θῶες μέν τε διέτρεσαν, αὐτὰρ ὁ δάπτει.

As spotted lynxes pursue in the mountains a wounded stag with bushy antlers, whom a hunter has wounded with an arrow from his bow; flying, it has escaped by its swiftness, while its blood ran warm and its limbs yet served. But when the swift arrow has drained its strength, the ravenous lynxes, tearing, devour it in the shady wood, till chance brings a furious lion; then the lynxes fly in terror, while the lion feeds on the prey.

AN INUNDATION.

Il. xi. 492.

'Ως δ' ὁπότε πλήθων ποταμὸς πεδίονδε κάτεισιν
χειμάρρους κατ' ὄρεσφιν, ὀπαζόμενος Διὸς ὄμβρῳ,
πολλὰς δὲ δρῦς ἀζαλέας, πολλὰς δέ τε πεύκας
ἐσφέρεται, πολλὸν δέ τ' ἀφυσγετὸν εἰς ἅλα βάλλει.

As when an overflowing river descends to the plain, rushing from the mountains, swollen by the storms of heaven, it carries off many blighted oaks and many pines, throwing much mud into the ocean.

The Lion.
Il. xi. 547.

'Ὡς δ' αἴθωνα λέοντα βοῶν ἀπὸ μεσσαύλοιο
ἐσσεύαντο κύνες τε καὶ ἀνέρες ἀγροιῶται,
οἵτε μιν οὐκ εἰῶσι βοῶν ἐκ πῖαρ ἑλέσθαι
πάννυχοι ἐγρήσσοντες· ὁ δὲ κρειῶν ἐρατίζων
ἰθύει, ἀλλ' οὔτι πρήσσει· θαμέες γὰρ ἄκοντες
ἀντίον ἀΐσσουσι θρασειάων ἀπὸ χειρῶν,
καιόμεναί τε δεταί, τάστε τρεῖ ἐσσύμενός περ·
ἠῶθεν δ' ἀπονόσφιν ἔβη τετιηότι θυμῷ.

As a furious lion is driven from the cattle-fold by dogs and rustics, who, watching all night, balk him of his prey. Eager for food, he renews the attempt ; but still in vain, for numerous darts are hurled from vigorous hands, and blazing torches, from which he retires, though maddened. In the morning he slinks off with saddened heart.

The Ass.
Il. xi. 558.

'Ὡς δ' ὅτ' ὄνος παρ' ἄρουραν ἰὼν ἐβιήσατο παῖδας
νωθής, ᾧ δὴ πολλὰ περὶ ῥόπαλ' ἀμφὶς ἐάγη,
κείρει τ' εἰσελθὼν βαθὺ λήϊον· οἱ δέ τε παῖδες
τύπτουσιν ῥοπάλοισι· βίη δέ τε νηπίη αὐτῶν·
σπουδῇ δ' ἐξήλασσαν, ἐπεί τ' ἐκορέσσατο φορβῆς.

As when a stubborn ass entering the corn-field overpowers the boys, on whose back many clubs are broken : going in, it crops the rich corn, while the boys ply their cudgels ; but their strength is puny, yet they drive him out with ease when he is satisfied with food.

The Advice of a Friend.
Il. xi. 793.

'Αγαθὴ δὲ παραίφασίς ἐστιν ἑταίρου.

The advice of a friend is good.

So Proverbs (xxvii. 9)—"Ointment and perfume rejoice the heart: so doth the sweetness of a man's friend by hearty counsel."

"Shall the Sword devour for ever?"
Il. xi. 801.

'Ολίγη δέ τ' ἀνάπνευσις πολέμοιο.

A slight breathing-time from war is pleasant.

So 2 Samuel (ii. 26)—"Shall the sword devour for ever?"

"Physician, heal thyself."
Il. xi. 834.

'Οἴομαι ἕλκος ἔχοντα
χρηΐζοντα καὶ αὐτὸν ἀμύμονος ἰητῆρος.

I think that a physician, being wounded, also requires a leech's aid.

So Luke (iv. 23)—"Physician, heal thyself."

Against the Will of God.
Il. xii. 8.

Θεῶν δ' ἀέκητι τέτυκτο
ἀθανάτων· τὸ καὶ οὔτι πολὺν χρόνον ἔμπεδον ἦεν.

It was done against the will of the immortal gods; wherefore it did not long endure.

So Acts (v. 38)—"And now I say unto you, Refrain from these men, and let them alone: for if this counsel or this work be of men, it will come to nought."

Oaks.
Il. xii. 132.

Ἕστασαν ὡς ὅτε τε δρύες οὔρεσιν ὑψικάρηνοι,
αἵτ' ἄνεμον μίμνουσι καὶ ὑετὸν ἤματα πάντα,
ῥίζῃσιν μεγάλῃσι διηνεκέεσσ' ἀραρυῖαι.

They stood as oaks raise their high heads on the mountain-side, which many a day have borne the wind and rain, firm rifted by their strong, far-extending roots.

Let us Obey God.
Il. xii. 241.

Ἡμεῖς δὲ μεγάλοιο Διὸς πειθώμεθα βουλῇ,
ὃς πᾶσι θνητοῖσι καὶ ἀθανάτοισιν ἀνάσσει.

Let us obey the will of mighty Jove, who rules over mortals and immortals.

So Acts (v. 29)—"We ought to obey God rather than men."

The Brave.
Il. xii. 243.

Εἷς οἰωνὸς ἄριστος, ἀμύνεσθαι περὶ πάτρης.

Let the best omen be our country's cause.

So 2 Samuel (x. 12)—" Be of good courage, and let us play the men for our people, and for the cities of our God : and the Lord do that which seemeth Him good."

ALL ARE NECESSARY.
Il. xii. 269.

Ὦ φίλοι, Ἀργείων ὅς τ' ἔξοχος ὅς τε μεσήεις
ὅς τε χερειότερος, ἐπεὶ οὔπω πάντες ὁμοῖοι
ἀνέρες ἐν πολέμῳ, νῦν ἔπλετο ἔργον ἅπασιν.

My friends, whoever of the Greeks is of noble spirit, of moderate or inferior strength, since all men are not with equal powers, here is work for all.

So 1 Corinthians (xii. 21, 22)—"And the eye cannot say unto the hand, I have no need of thee; nor again the head to the feet, I have no need of you. Nay, much more those members of the body, which seem to be more feeble, are necessary."

THE SNOW-STORM.
Il. xii. 278.

Ὥστε νιφάδες χιόνος πίπτωσι θαμειαὶ
ἤματι χειμερίῳ, ὅτε τ' ὤρετο μητίετα Ζεὺς
νιφέμεν, ἀνθρώποισι πιφαυσκόμενος τὰ ἅ κῆλα·
κοιμήσας δ' ἀνέμους χέει ἔμπεδον, ὄφρα καλύψῃ
ὑψηλῶν ὀρέων κορυφὰς καὶ πρώονας ἄκρους
καὶ πεδία λωτεῦντα καὶ ἀνδρῶν πίονα ἔργα,
καί τ' ἐφ' ἁλὸς πολιῆς κέχυται λιμέσιν τε καὶ ἀκταῖς,
κῦμα δέ μιν προσπλάζον ἐρύκεται· ἄλλα τε πάντα
εἰλύαται καθύπερθ', ἥτ' ἐπιβρίσῃ Διὸς ὄμβρος.

As thick as the snow-flakes on a winter's day, when all-wise Jove has begun to snow, showing his power to mortals. Stilling the winds, he pours snow down on the ground, so that the tops of the lofty mountains, the sharp peaks, the lotus-plains, and man's productive labours are buried deep. It is scattered over the hoary sea, lakes, and shores; but the wave, as it approaches, controls it : everything else is wrapped up beneath, when the storm of Jove rages with fury.

THE FORCE OF UNION.
Il. xii. 412.

Πλεόνων δέ τοι ἔργον ἄμεινον.

The force of powerful union conquers all.

See (Lat.) Concord.

God is easily Known.

Il. xiii. 72.

'Ἀρίγνωτοι δὲ θεοί περ.

'Tis easy to discern the outward signs of a god.

So Psalm (ix. 16)—"The Lord is known by the judgment which He executeth;" and (lxxvi. 1)—"In Judah is God known."

The Inclinations of the Good.

Il. xiii. 115.

'Ἀκεσταί τοι φρένες ἐσθλῶν.

A brave man's spirit its vigour soon regains.

So Proverbs (xxi. 11)—"When the scorner is punished, the simple is made wise;" and (xxiv. 16)—"For a just man falleth seven times and riseth up again."

"To whom much is given."

Il. xiii. 116.

Ὑμεῖς δ' οὐκέτι καλὰ μεθίετε θούριδος ἀλκῆς
πάντες ἄριστοι ἐόντες ἀνὰ στρατόν. Οὐδ' ἂν ἔγωγε
ἀνδρὶ μαχησαίμην ὅστις πολέμοιο μεθείη
λυγρὸς ἐών· ὑμῖν δὲ νεμεσσῶμαι περὶ κῆρι.

All who are the best and bravest of the host should not desist from the battle : I might not blame them, if meaner men should shrink ; but I am highly indignant with you.

So Matthew (xxv. 15)—"And unto one he gave five talents, to another two, and to another one ; to every man according to his several ability ;" and Luke (xii. 48)—"For unto whomsoever much is given, of him shall be much required."

Slothfulness.

Il. xiii. 120.

Ὦ πέπονες, τάχα δή τι κακὸν ποιήσετε μεῖζον
τῆδε μεθημοσύνῃ· ἀλλ' ἐν φρεσὶ θέσθε ἕκαστος
αἰδῶ καὶ νέμεσιν.

Dear friends, you will certainly sustain some heavier misfortune by this dastardly remissness : let each of you reflect on the shame of your conduct and feel keen remorse.

So Ecclesiastes (x. 18)—"By much slothfulness the building decayeth ; and through idleness of the hands the house droppeth through."

A Huge Boulder.

Il. xiii. 137.

'Ολοοίτροχος ὡς ἀπὸ πέτρης,
ὅντε κατὰ στεφάνης ποταμὸς χειμάρροος ὤσῃ,
ῥήξας ἀσπέτῳ ὄμβρῳ ἀναιδέος ἔχματα πέτρης·
ὕψι δ' ἀναθρώσκων πέτεται, κτυπέει δέ θ' ὑπ' αὐτοῦ
ὕλη· ὁ δ' ἀσφαλέως θέει ἔμπεδον, εἷος ἵκηται
ἰσόπεδον, τότε δ' οὔτι κυλίνδεται ἐσσύμενός περ.

As some huge boulder detached from a rock, which the wintry torrent has hurled down the cliff's steep face, having undermined the firm hold of the massive rock by constant rains : with giant bounds it flies, and the wood crashes beneath it ; still it hurries on, until it reaches the level plain, and then it no longer rolls, however much impelled.

United Strength.

Il. xiii. 237.

Συμφερτὴ δ' ἀρετὴ πέλει ἀνδρῶν καὶ μάλα λυγρῶν.

The strength even of weak men when united avails much.

So Ecclesiastes (iv. 12)—" And if one prevail against him, two shall withstand him ; and a threefold cord is not quickly broken."

A Daughter who Excels all.

Il. xiii. 430.

Τὴν περὶ κῆρι φίλησε πατὴρ καὶ πότνια μήτηρ
ἐν μεγάρῳ· πᾶσαν γὰρ ὁμηλικίην ἐκέκαστο
κάλλεϊ καὶ ἔργοισιν ἰδὲ φρεσί· τοὔνεκα καί μιν
γῆμεν ἀνὴρ ὥριστος ἐνὶ Τροίῃ εὐρείῃ.

The father and revered mother loved her with deep affection ; for she surpassed all of her own age in beauty, in skill, and mind : therefore the noblest man of wide Troy married her.

So Proverbs (xxxi. 20)—"Many daughters have done virtuously, but thou excellest them all."

Satiety of Everything.

Il. xiii. 636.

Πάντων μὲν κόρος ἐστί, καὶ ὕπνου καὶ φιλότητος
μολπῆς τε γλυκερῆς καὶ ἀμύμονος ὀρχηθμοῖο,
τῶν πέρ τις καὶ μᾶλλον ἐέλδεται ἐξ ἔρον εἶναι
ἢ πολέμου· Τρῶες δὲ μάχης ἀκόρητοι ἔασιν.

With everything men are sated : sleep, love, sweet singing, and

the joyous dance—of all these man gets sooner tired than of war ;
the Trojans are insatiable in fight.

So Proverbs (xxv. 16)—"Hast thou found honey? eat so much as is
sufficient for thee, lest thou be filled therewith, and vomit it."

MEN HAVE DIFFERENT TALENTS.

Il. xiii. 729.

'Αλλ' οὔπως ἅμα πάντα δυνήσεαι αὐτὸς ἐλέσθαι.
"Αλλῳ μὲν γὰρ ἔδωκε θεὸς πολεμήϊα ἔργα·
[ἄλλῳ δ' ὀρχηστὺν, ἑτέρῳ κίθαριν καὶ ἀοιδήν·]
ἄλλῳ δ' ἐν στήθεσσι τιθεῖ νόον εὐρύοπα Ζεὺς
ἐσθλόν, τοῦ δέ τε πολλοὶ ἐπαυρίσκοντ' ἄνθρωποι,
καί τε πολέας ἐσάωσε, μάλιστα δέ κ' αὐτὸς ἀνέγνω.

But thou alone canst not engross all gifts of heaven : to one man
God has granted the knowledge of what belongs to the affairs of
war, to another the power of dancing, to another song and music ;
but in the breast of another loud-thundering Jove places the spirit
of wisdom, of which many enjoy the fruit, for by him cities are
preserved, and he himself specially feels the value of the precious
gift.

So 1 Corinthians (xii. 4-6)—"Now there are diversities of gifts, but the
same Spirit. And there are differences of administrations, but the same
Lord. And there are diversities of operations, but it is the same God which
worketh all in all ;" and (vii. 7)—"But every man hath his proper gift of
God, one after this manner, and another after that."

See (Lat.) Statesman.

ACCORDING TO THAT A MAN HATH.

Il. xiii. 787.

Πὰρ δύναμιν δ' οὐκ ἔστι, καὶ ἐσσύμενον, πολεμίζειν.

Beyond his power the bravest cannot fight.

So 2 Corinthians (viii. 12)—"For if there be first a willing mind, it is
accepted according to that a man hath, and not according to that he hath
not."

AVOID EVILS.

Il. xiv. 80.

Οὐ γάρ τις νέμεσις φυγέειν κακὸν, οὐδ' ἀνὰ νύκτα.
Βέλτερον ὃς φεύγων προφύγῃ κακὸν ἠὲ ἁλώῃ.

For a man is not to be blamed if he flies from an impending evil,
though by night ; he will act more wisely who by flying escapes,
than he who is overtaken by the threatened danger.

So Butler (" Hudibras," Part iii., c. 3, l. 243) says :—
"For those that fly may fight again,
Which he can never do that 's slain."

So Matthew (x. 23)—"But when they persecute you in this city, flee ye
into another."

What is thy Petition ?
Il. xiv. 195.

Αὖδα ὅ τι φρονέεις· τελέσαι δέ με θυμὸς ἄνωγεν,
εἰ δύναμαι τελέσαι γε, καὶ εἰ τετελεσμένον ἐστί.

Tell me thy wish; my inclination urges me to grant it if my
power may aught avail, and if it can be done.

So Esther (v. 6)—"And the king said unto Esther at the banquet of wine,
What is thy petition? and it shall be granted thee: and what is thy request?
even to the half of the kingdom it shall be performed."

The Charms of Love.
Il. xiv. 214.

*Η καὶ ἀπὸ στήθεσφιν ἐλύσατο κεστὸν ἱμάντα
ποικίλον, ἔνθα τέ οἱ θελκτήρια πάντα τέτυκτο·
ἔνθ' ἔνι μὲν φιλότης, ἐν δ' ἵμερος, ἐν δ' ὀαριστὺς
πάρφασις, ἥτ' ἔκλεψε νόον πύκα περ φρονεόντων.

She said, and unloosed from her breast her zone embroidered
with various colours, wrought with every charm to win the heart;
there dwelt love, amorous desire, fond discourse, persuasion,
which often steals away the senses even of wisest men.

So Proverbs (vii. 21)—"With her much fair speech she caused him to
yield, with the flattering of her lips she forced him."

Sleep the Brother of Death.
Il. xiv. 231.

Ενθ' Ὕπνῳ ξύμβλητο, κασιγνήτῳ Θανάτοιο.

There he met with Sleep, twin-born with Death.

So John (xi. 11-13)—"Our friend Lazarus sleepeth; but I go, that I may
awake him out of sleep. Then said His disciples, Lord, if he sleep, he shall
do well. Howbeit Jesus spake of his death: but they thought that He had
spoken of taking of rest in sleep."

Love seized Him.
Il. xiv. 296.

'Ως δ' ἴδεν, ὥς μιν ἔρως πυκινὰς φρένας ἀμφεκάλυψεν.

When he saw her, suddenly love overshadowed his mind.

So Genesis (iii. 6)—"And when the woman saw that the tree was good
for food, and that it was pleasant to the eyes, and a tree to be desired to
make one wise, she took of the fruit thereof and did eat;" and (vi. 1)—
"The sons of men saw the daughters of men that they were fair, and they
took them wives of all which they chose."

I

Wine maketh Merry.

Il. xiv. 325.

Ἡ δὲ Διώνυσον Σεμέλη τέκε, χάρμα βροτοῖσιν.

and Semele brought forth Bacchus, causing joy to mortals.

So Judges (ix. 13)—" Should I leave my wine, which cheereth God and man ?"—and Psalm (civ. 15)—" And wine that maketh glad the heart of man ; " and Ecclesiastes (x. 19)—" And wine maketh merry."

Dreadful to Fall into the Hands of the Living God.

Il. xiv. 417.

Χαλεπὸς δὲ Διὸς μεγάλοιο κεραυνός.

The lightning of mighty Jove is fearful.

So Hebrews (x. 31)—" It is a fearful thing to fall into the hands of the living God."

The Power of Recollection.

Il. xv. 80.

Ὡς δ᾽ ὅτ᾽ ἂν ἀΐξῃ νόος ἀνέρος, ὅστ᾽ ἐπὶ πολλὴν
γαῖαν ἐληλουθὼς φρεσὶ πευκαλίμῃσι νοήσῃ
"Ἔνθ᾽ εἴην, ἢ ἔνθα," μενοινήῃσί τε πολλά.

As when the mind of man wanders in thought over the many lands which he hath traversed, and thinks " Here was I such a day, or here," thinking of his numerous adventures.

" They have Ears, but Hear not."

Il. xv. 128.

Μαινόμενε, φρένας ἠλέ, διέφθορας. Ἦ νύ τοι αὔτως
οὔατ᾽ ἀκούεμεν ἐστί, νόος δ᾽ ἀπόλωλε καὶ αἰδώς.

Madman, void of reason, thou art lost ; surely thou hast ears in vain, thy mind and sense of reverence are utterly destroyed.

So Psalm (cxv. 6)—" They have ears, but they hear not ; " and Matthew (xi. 15)—" He that hath ears to hear, let him hear."

" A Faithful Ambassador."

Il. xv. 159.

Πάντα τάδ᾽ ἀγγεῖλαι, μηδὲ ψευδάγγελος εἶναι.

Tell all these things, and be not a false messenger.

So Proverbs (xiii. 17)—" A faithful messenger is health ; " and Acts (xx. 20)—" And how I kept back nothing . . . but have shown you ; " and (xx. 27)—" For I have not shunned to declare unto you all the counsel of God."

ALL THINGS DIVIDED INTO THREE.

Il. xv. 189.

Τριχθὰ δὲ πάντα δέδασται, ἕκαστος δ' ἔμμορε τιμῆς.

Threefold was our partition, and each enjoys his meed of honour.

So 1 John (v. 7)—"For there are three that bear record in heaven, the Father, the Word, and the Holy Ghost: and these three are one."

THE NOBLE.

Il. xv. 203.

Στρεπταὶ μέν τε φρένες ἐσθλῶν.

Noblest minds are easiest bent.

So Psalm (xlv. 19)—"They have no changes, therefore they fear not God;" and Ezekiel (xxxiii. 11)—"Turn ye, turn ye from your evil ways; for why will ye die?"

HONOUR THE HOARY HEAD.

Il. xv. 204.

Οἶσθ' ὡς πρεσβυτέροισιν 'Ερινύες αἰὲν ἕπονται.

Thou knowest that the Furies always watch to avenge the aged.

So Leviticus (xix. 32)—"Thou shalt rise up before the hoary head, and honour the face of the old man."

THE STALL-FED HORSE.

Il. xv. 263.

Ὡς δ' ὅτε τις σιατὸς ἵππος, ἀκοστήσας ἐπὶ φάτνῃ,
δεσμὸν ἀπορρήξας θείη πεδίοιο κροαίνων,
εἰωθὼς λούεσθαι ἐϋρρεῖος ποταμοῖο,
κυδιόων· ὑψοῦ δὲ κάρη ἔχει, ἀμφὶ δὲ χαῖται
ὤμοις ἀΐσσονται· ὁ δ' ἀγλαΐηφι πεποιθὼς,
ῥίμφα ἑ γοῦνα φέρει μετά τ' ἤθεα καὶ νομὸν ἵππων.

As when a stall-fed horse, fattened on barley, having broken his halter, scours the plain, stamping with his feet, accustomed to bathe in the beautiful-flowing stream, exulting; he tosses his head aloft, while his mane streams o'er his shoulders; in conscious pride, his limbs bear him with ease to the accustomed pastures of the mares.

See Virgil, Æn. xi. 492.

A CHILD PLAYING ON THE SEA-SHORE.

Il. xv. 362.

Ὡς ὅτε τις ψάμαθον παῖς ἄγχι θαλάσσης,
ὅστ' ἐπεὶ οὖν ποιήσῃ ἀθύρματα νηπιέῃσιν,
ἂψ αὖτις συνέχευε ποσὶν καὶ χερσὶν ἀθύρων.

I 2

As when a child heaps up sand near the sea, making playthings
with infantine folly ; again in wanton play he scatters it with
hands and feet.

To Die for One's Country.

Il. xv. 496.

Οὔ οἱ ἀεικὲς ἀμυνομένῳ περὶ πάτρης
τεθνάμεν· ἀλλ' ἄλοχός τε σόη καὶ παῖδες ὀπίσσω,
καὶ οἶκος καὶ κλῆρος ἀκήρατος.

A glorious death is his who dies fighting for his country, while
his wife is safe, children and home and heritage unimpaired.

So 2 Samuel (x. 12)—"Be of good courage, and let us play the men for our
people, . . . and the Lord do that which seemeth Him good."

The Coward.

Il. xv. 563.

Αἰδομένων δ' ἀνδρῶν πλέονες σόοι ἠὲ πέφανται·
φευγόντων δ' οὔτ' ἂρ κλέος ὄρνυται οὔτε τις ἀλκή.

For more of the brave are saved than die ; but to the coward
there is neither glory nor safety.

Storm at Sea.

Il. xv. 624.

'Ως ὅτε κῦμα θοῇ ἐν νηῒ πέσῃσιν
λάβρον ὑπὸ νεφέων ἀνεμοτρεφές· ἡ δέ τε πᾶσα
ἄχνῃ ὑπεκρύφθη, ἀνέμοιο δὲ δεινὸς ἀήτης
ἱστίῳ ἐμβρέμεται, τρομέουσι δέ τε φρένα ναῦται
δειδιότες· τυτθὸν γὰρ ὑπὲκ θανάτοιο φέρονται.

As when a wave descends heavily on the swift ship, raised
rapidly by the wind bursting from the clouds ; the deck is
drenched with spray, while the fierce blast howls in the shrouds ;
the affrighted sailors tremble, but little way removed from death.

So Jonah (i. 5)—"Then the mariners were afraid, and cried every man
unto his god, and cast forth the wares that were in the ship into the sea,
to lighten it of them : but Jonah was gone down into the sides of the ship."

A Good Son from a Wicked Father.

Il. xv. 642.

Τοῦ γένετ' ἐκ πατρὸς πολὺ χείρονος υἱὸς ἀμείνων
παντοίας ἀρετὰς.

A son distinguished for his many virtues was born from a wicked father.

So Ezekiel (xviii. 14, 17)—" Lo, if he beget a son, that seeth all his father's sins which he hath done, and doeth not such like, . . . he shall not die for the iniquity of his father, he shall surely live."

A Skilful Rider.

Il. xv. 679.

'Ὡς δ' ὅτ' ἀνὴρ ἵπποισι κελητίζειν εὖ εἰδὼς,
ὅστ' ἐπεὶ ἐκ πολέων πίσυρας συναείρεται ἵππους,
σεύας ἐκ πεδίοιο μέγα προτὶ ἄστυ δίηται
λαοφόρον καθ' ὁδόν· πολέες τέ ἑ θηήσαντο
ἀνέρες ἠδὲ γυναῖκες· ὁ δ' ἔμπεδον ἀσφαλὲς αἰεὶ
θρώσκων ἄλλοτ' ἐπ' ἄλλον ἀμείβεται, οἱ δὲ πέτονται.

As a man skilled in feats of horsemanship, having selected four from a troop of horses, drives swiftly from the plains to the great city, along the public road, while many men and women gaze in wonder at him : leaping always without missing, he springs from horse to horse as on they fly.

On what Victory depends.

Il. xv. 741.

Τῷ ἐν χερσὶ φόως, οὐ μειλιχίῃ πολέμοιο.

There is safety in vigour of hand and not in giving way in the battle.

So Isaiah (ix. 15)—" For every battle of the warrior is with confused noise, and garments rolled in blood."

One Calamity upon another.

Il. xvi. 111.

Πάντη δὲ κακὸν κακῷ ἐστήρικτο.

Everywhere one calamity is heaped upon another.

So Job (i. 17, &c.)—" While he was yet speaking, there came also another," &c. ; and Isaiah (xxx. 1)—" That they may add sin to sin ; " and Job (v. 19) —" He shall deliver thee in six troubles : yea, in seven there shall no evil touch thee."

Riches, but no Enjoyment.

Il. xvi. 250.

Τῷ δ' ἕτερον μὲν ἔδωκε πατήρ, ἕτερον δ' ἀνένευσεν.

Father Jove has granted half his prayer, and half denied.

So Ecclesiastes (vi. 1)—" There is an evil which I have seen under the sun, and it is common among men : a man to whom God hath given riches.

wealth, and honour, so that he wanteth nothing for his soul of all that he
desireth, yet God giveth him not power to eat thereof, but a stranger eateth
it : this is vanity, and it is an evil disease."

A Pillar in Honour of the Dead.

Il. xvi. 457.

Τύμβῳ τε στήλῃ τε· τὸ γὰρ γέρας ἐστὶ θανόντων.

A tomb and a pillar: the fitting tribute to the mighty dead.

So 2 Samuel (xviii. 18)—" Absalom had reared up for himself a pillar, for
he had said, This shall be a memorial of my name."

Deeds and not Words.

Il. xvi. 630.

'Εν γὰρ χερσὶ τέλος πολέμου, ἐπέων δ' ἐνὶ βουλῇ·
τῷ οὔτι χρὴ μῦθον ὀφέλλειν, ἀλλὰ μάχεσθαι.

Hands are meet for battle, but words for council; wherefore
now we must use not words, but fight.

Sleep and Death.

Il. xvi. 672.

Ὕπνῳ καὶ Θανάτῳ διδυμάοσιν.

Sleep and death twin-born.

So Matthew (ix. 24)—" The maid is not dead, but sleepeth."

The Power of Jove.

Il. xvi. 688.

'Αλλ' αἰεί τε Διὸς κρείσσων νόος ἠέπερ ἀνδρῶν·
[ὅστε καὶ ἄλκιμον ἄνδρα φοβεῖ καὶ ἀφείλετο νίκην
ῥηϊδίως, ὅτε δ' αὐτὸς ἐποτρύνῃσι μάχεσθαι.]

But Jove's will is always mightier than the will of man : who
strikes panic into the bravest, and easily robs him of victory, and
anon urges to battle.

So Ecclesiastes (ix. 11)—"I returned, and saw under the sun, that the
race is not to the swift, nor the battle to the strong, neither yet bread to the
wise, nor yet riches to men of understanding, nor yet favour to men of skill ;
but time and chance happeneth to them all."

"This Night thy Soul shall be Required of thee."

Il. xvi. 852.

Οὔ θην οὐδ' αὐτὸς δηρὸν βέῃ, ἀλλά τοι ἤδη
ἄγχι παρέστηκεν θάνατος καὶ μοῖρα κραταιή.

Thou shalt not long survive me, but death and irresistible doom now hang over thee.

So Luke (xii. 20)—"Thou fool, this night thy soul shall be required of thee: then whose shall those things be which thou hast provided?"—and 2 Timothy (iv. 6)—"The time of my departure is at hand."

Why Boastest thou Thyself?
Il. xvii. 19.

Οὐ μὲν καλὸν ὑπέρβιον εὐχετάασθαι.

It ill beseems a man to vaunt arrogantly.

So Psalm (lii. 1)—"Why boastest thou thyself?"—and Romans (xi. 18)— "Boast not against the branches;" and 1 Corinthians (v. 6)—"Your glorying is not good;" and James (iv. 16)—"All such rejoicing is evil."

Fools.
Il. xvii. 32.

Ρεχθὲν δέ τε νήπιος ἔγνω.

Even the fool is wise after the event.

So Proverbs (xxii. 3)—"A prudent man foreseeth the evil, and hideth himself: but the simple pass on, and are punished."

The Lion.
Il. xvii. 61.

Ὡς δ' ὅτε τίς τε λέων ὀρεσίτροφος, ἀλκὶ πεποιθὼς,
βοσκομένης ἀγέλης βοῦν ἁρπάσῃ, ἥτις ἀρίστη·
τῆϛ δ' ἐξ αὐχέν' ἔαξε λαβὼν κρατεροῖσιν ὀδοῦσιν
πρῶτον, ἔπειτα δέ θ' αἷμα καὶ ἔγκατα πάντα λαφύσσει
δῃῶν· ἀμφὶ δὲ τόνγε κύνες τ' ἄνδρες τε νομῆες
πολλὰ μάλ' ἰύζουσιν ἀπόπροθεν οὐδ' ἐθέλουσιν
ἀντίον ἐλθέμεναι· μάλα γὰρ χλωρὸν δέος αἱρεῖ.

As when a lion, bred in the mountains, in pride of strength, has carried off a heifer amid the pasturing herd—the choicest; he breaks her neck, first seizing her with strong teeth, then gorging on her entrails, laps the blood; though dogs and shepherds roar loudly from afar, yet none venture to come near, but pale fear seizes them.

"He that hath Laboured for the Wind."
Il. xvii. 75.

Νῦν σὺ μὲν ὧδε θέεις, ἀκίχητα διώκων.

Thou indeed so runnest, pursuing what cannot be reached.

So Ecclesiastes (v. 16)—"And what profit hath he that hath laboured for the wind?"—and Galatians (ii. 2)—"Lest by any means I should run, or had run, in vain."

To Fight against a Man honoured by God.

Il. xvii. 98.

'Οππότ' ἀνὴρ ἐθέλει πρὸς δαίμονα φωτὶ μάχεσθαι,
ὅν κε θεὸς τιμᾷ, τάχα οἱ μέγα πῆμα κυλίσθη.

When a man strives, against the Divine will, with one beloved
of heaven, a bitter doom comes quickly upon him.

So Exodus (xiv. 25)—"The Egyptians said, Let us flee from the face of
Israel, for the Lord fighteth for them against the Egyptians;" and Isaiah
(xli. 11-13)—"Behold, all they that were incensed against thee shall be
ashamed and confounded : they shall be as nothing ; and they that strive with
thee shall perish. Thou shalt seek them, and shalt not find them, even them
that contended with thee : they that war against thee shall be as nothing,
and as a thing of nought. For I the Lord thy God will hold thy right
hand, saying unto thee, Fear not ; I will help thee."

Of Evils this is the Least.

Il. xvii. 105.

Κακῶν δέ κε φέρτατον εἴη.

Of evils this would be the best to be chosen.

So 2 Samuel (xxiv. 14)—"And David said unto Gad, I am in a great
strait ; let us fall now into the hand of the Lord (for His mercies are great),
and let me not fall into the hand of man."

God Omnipotent.

Il. xvii. 176.

'Αλλ' αἰεί τε Διὸς κρείσσων νόος αἰγιόχοιο,
ὅστε καὶ ἄλκιμον ἄνδρα φοβεῖ καὶ ἀφείλετο νίκην
ῥηϊδίως, ὁτὲ δ' αὐτὸς ἐποτρύνει μαχέσασθαι.

But the will of ægis-bearing Jove is uncontrolled, who confounds
the strong, and easily robs him of victory, and anon excites to
war.

"The Sword devoureth One as well as Another."

Il. xvii. 227.

Τῷ τις νῦν ἰθὺς τετραμμένος ἢ ἀπολέσθω,
ἠὲ σαωθήτω· ἡ γὰρ πολέμου ὀαριστύς.

Wherefore let each, rushing boldly onward, either perish or
escape safe ; for such is the chance of war.

So 2 Samuel (xi. 25)— "For the sword devoureth one as well as another."

"HONOUR THY PARENTS."

Il. xvii. 301.

Οὐδὲ τοκεῦσιν
θρέπτρα φίλοις ἀπέδωκε, μινυνθάδιος δέ οἱ αἰὼν
ἔπλεθ᾽.

Neither had he an opportunity of paying back their early care to his dear parents, for short was his term of life.

So Exodus (xx. 12)—"Honour thy father and thy mother;" and 1 Timothy (v. 4)—"Let them learn to show piety at home, and to requite their parents."

KIND WORDS AND THREATS.

Il. xvii. 431.

Πολλὰ δὲ μειλιχίοισι προσηύδα, πολλὰ δ᾽ ἀρετῇ.

He addressed many honeyed words and many curses.

So Deuteronomy (xxx. 19)—"I have set before you life and death, blessing and cursing."

NOTHING MORE WRETCHED THAN MAN.

Il. xvii. 446.

Οὐ μὲν γάρ τί τού ἐστιν ὀϊζυρώτερον ἀνδρὸς
πάντων, ὅσσα τε γαῖαν ἔπι πνείει τε καὶ ἕρπει.

For there is nought of all that breathe and creep upon the earth more wretched than man.

So Job (xiv. 1)—"Man that is born of a woman is of few days, and full of trouble;" and (xxv. 6)—"How much less man, that is a worm; and the son of man, which is a worm?"

MAN PROPOSES, GOD DISPOSES.

Il. xvii. 515.

Ήσω γὰρ καὶ ἐγώ, τὰ δέ κεν Διὶ πάντα μελήσει.

For I shall hurl the spear, but Jove directs the blow.

So James (iv. 15)—"Ye ought to say, If the Lord will, we shall live, and do this and that;" and 1 Kings (xxii. 34)—"And a certain man drew a bow at a venture, and smote the King of Israel between the joints of the harness."

SAD NEWS.

Il. xviii. 18.

Η μάλα λυγρῆς
πεύσεαι ἀγγελίης, ἣ μὴ ὤφελλε γενέσθαι.
Κεῖται Πάτροκλος.

I 3

Assuredly thou shalt hear woful tidings, which, would to Heaven, I had not to impart : Patroclus lies in death.

Pliny (Ep iv. 11) says—"Loquutus est pro absente Liciniano Herennius Senecio tale quiddam, quale est illud. ' Κεῖται Πάτροκλος.' "—" Herennius Senecio said, in defence of the absent Licinianus, some such thing as, ' Patroclus is gone.' "
So 1 Kings (xiv. 6)—" I am sent to thee with heavy tidings."

"A FOOL'S MOUTH."
Il. xviii. 95.

Ὠκύμορος δή μοι, τέκος, ἔσσεαι, οἶ᾽ ἀγορεύεις·

In sooth, my son, thou wilt be short-lived if thou talkest thus.

So Proverbs (xviii. 7)—"A fool's mouth is his destruction, and his lips are the snare of his soul."

STRIFE AND RAGE.
Il. xviii. 107.

'Ὡς ἔρις ἔκ τε θεῶν ἔκ τ᾽ ἀνθρώπων ἀπόλοιτο,
καὶ χόλος, ὅστ᾽ ἐφέηκε πολύφρονά περ χαλεπῆναι,
ὅστε πολὺ γλυκίων μέλιτος καταλειβομένοιο
ἀνδρῶν ἐν στήθεσσιν ἀέξεται ἠΰτε καπνός.

Would that strife were far removed from gods and men, and anger, which impels even the wisest to violence, which mounts in the breast of man like smoke, and is sweeter to the taste than honey.

So Romans (xiii. 13)—"Not in strife and envying ;" and Philippians (ii. 3)—" Let nothing be done through strife or vain-glory ; " and Ecclesiastes (vii. 9)—" Be not hasty in thy spirit to be angry ; for anger resteth in the bosom of fools."

DEATH WHEN GOD WILLS IT.
Il. xviii. 115.

Κῆρα δ᾽ ἐγὼ τότε δέξομαι, ὁππότε κεν δὴ
Ζεὺς ἐθέλῃ τελέσαι ἠδ᾽ ἀθάνατοι θεοὶ ἄλλοι.

I shall then meet death when it is the will of Jove and the other gods.

So Job (xiv. 14)—" All the days of my appointed time will I wait, till my change come."

DEATH.
Il. xviii. 121.

Κείσομ᾽, ἐπεί κε θάνω· νῦν δὲ κλέος ἐσθλὸν ἀροίμην.

I shall lie a senseless clod when I die ; but now is the time to win glory.

So Ecclesiastes (ix. 10)—"Whatsoever thy hand findeth to do, do it with thy might ; for there is no work, nor device, nor knowledge, nor wisdom, in the grave, whither thou goest."

FATE OF MAN IN WAR.
Il. xviii. 309.

Ξυνὸς 'Ευυάλιος, καί τε κτανέοντα κατέκτα.

The fortune of war is common to all, and oft slays the slayer.

So 2 Samuel (xi. 25)—" For the sword devoureth one as well as another."

DESIGNS OF MAN CUT SHORT.
Il. xviii. 328.

Αλλ' οὐ Ζεὺς ἄνδρεσσι νοήματα πάντα τελευτᾷ.

But Jove does not accomplish all that man designs.

ANGER.
Il. xix. 68.

Νῦν δ' ἤτοι μὲν ἐγὼ παύω χόλον, οὐδέ τί με χρὴ
ἀσκελέως αἰεὶ μενεαινέμεν.

Now indeed I here abjure my wrath, for it is not right that it should burn for ever unappeased.

So Jeremiah (iii. 12)—" I will not keep mine anger for ever ;" and Ephesians (iv. 26)—" Let not the sun go down upon your wrath."

A NOISY MEETING.
Il. xix. 79.

Εσταότος μὲν καλὸν ἀκούειν, οὐδὲ ἔοικεν
ὑββάλλειν· χαλεπὸν γὰρ, ἐπισταμένῳ περ ἐόντι
'Ανδρῶν δ' ἐν πολλῷ ὑμάδῳ πως κέν τις ἀκούσαι
Ἢ εἴποι; βλάβεται δὲ λιγὺς περ ἐὼν ἀγορητής.

'Tis meet to listen in silence without interruption, for it is difficult for a man even skilled in speaking to deliver his sentiments amidst interruptions. In a great tumult who can hear or speak? Even the best of orators is injured in such a case.

So 1 Corinthians (xiv. 31-33)—" If any thing be revealed to another that sitteth by, let the first hold his peace. For ye may all prophesy one by one, that all may learn, and all may be comforted. And the spirits of the prophets are subject to the prophets For God is not the author of confusion, but of peace, as in all churches of the saints."

" WHY DO YOU STAND HERE ALL THE DAY IDLE ?"
Il. xix. 149.

Οὐ γὰρ χρὴ κλυτοπεύειν ἐνθάδ' ἐόντας
οὐδὲ διατρίβειν· ἔτι γὰρ μέγα ἔργον ἄρεκτον.

For it is not meet to stand here wasting our time, or idly loitering, for there is still a great work to be done.

So Matthew (xx. 6)—"Why stand ye here all the day idle?"

FOOD NECESSARY FOR THE WARRIOR.

Il. xix. 162.

Οὐ γὰρ ἀνὴρ πρόπαν ἦμαρ ἐς ἠέλιον καταδύντα
ἄκμηνος σίτοιο δυνήσεται ἄντα μάχεσθαι·
εἴπερ γὰρ θυμῷ γε μενοινάᾳ πολεμίζειν,
ἀλλά τε λάθρῃ γυῖα βαρύνεται, ἠδὲ κιχάνει
δίψα τε καὶ λιμός, βλάβεται δέ τε γούνατ᾽ ἰόντι.
Ὃς δέ κ᾽ ἀνὴρ οἴνοιο κορεσσάμενος καὶ ἐδωδῆς
ἀνδράσι δυσμενέεσσι πανημέριος πολεμίζῃ,
θαρσαλέον νύ οἱ ἦτορ ἐνὶ φρεσὶν, οὐδέ τι γυῖα
πρὶν κάμνει, πρὶν πάντας ἐρωῆσαι πολέμοιο.

For no man all day till set of sun may fight without food. Even though his spirit may prompt him to fight, yet his limbs by degrees sink under him ; worn out by thirst and hunger, his knees shake as he advances. But the man satiated with wine and food all day maintains the combat with his enemy ; his spirit remains unbroken, and his limbs are unwearied, till both armies quit the field of battle.

So Psalm (civ. 15)—"Bread which strengtheneth man's heart ;" and 1 Samuel (xiv. 28)—"Cursed be the man that eateth any food this day. And the people were faint. Then said Jonathan, Mine eyes have been enlightened, because I tasted a little of this honey; how much more, if haply the people had eaten freely to-day, for had not there been now a much greater slaughter among the Philistines."

NO SOONER SAID THAN DONE.

Il. xix. 242.

Αὐτίκ᾽ ἔπειθ᾽ ἅμα μῦθος ἔην, τετέλεστο δὲ ἔργον.

Then, soon as the word was uttered, the work was done.

So Genesis (i. 3)—"And God said, Let there be light : and there was light ;" and Psalm (xxxiii. 9)—"For He spake, and it was done : He commanded, and it stood fast."

THE PERJURED.

Il. xix. 259.

Ἐρινύες, αἵθ᾽ ὑπὸ γαῖαν
ἀνθρώπους τίνυνται, ὅτις κ᾽ ἐπίορκον ὀμόσσῃ.

The Furies, ye who wreak vengeance beneath the earth on souls of men forsworn.

So Exodus (xx. 7)—"The Lord will not hold him guiltless that taketh

His name in vain ; " and Zechariah (v. 4)—" And it shall enter into the house of the thief and into the house of him that sweareth falsely by my name."

GOD CAUSES GRIEFS TO MAN.

Il. xix. 270.

Ζεῦ πάτερ, ἦ μεγάλας ἄτας ἀνδρεσσι διδοῖσθα.

Father Jove, thou certainly bringest sad woes on men.

So Job (xxi. 17)—God distributeth sorrows in His anger ; " and Isaiah (xlv. 7)—" I form the light, and create darkness ; I make peace, and create evil. I the Lord do all these things ; " and Amos (iii. 6)—" Shall there be evil in a city, and the Lord hath not done it ? "

WHAT IS FATED TO MAN.

Il. xx. 127.

"Ὕστερον αὖτε τὰ πείσεται ἄσσα οἱ Αἶσα
γεινομένῳ ἐπένησε λίνῳ, ὅτε μιν τέκε μήτηρ.

The time shall come when he shall meet the doom which Fate has spun with its thread at his birth.

So Job (xxiii. 14)—" He performeth the thing that is appointed for me."

THE GODS.

Il. xx. 131.

Χαλεποὶ δὲ θεοὶ φαίνεσθαι ἐναργεῖς.

The gods are terrible to be seen.

So Exodus (xxxiii. 22)—" There shall no man see me and live ; " and Job (xxxvii. 22)—" With God is terrible majesty."

COURAGE.

Il. xx. 241.

Ζεὺς δ' ἀρετὴν ἄνδρεσσιν ὀφέλλει τε μινύθει τε,
ὅππως κεν ἐθέλῃσιν· ὁ γὰρ κάρτιστος ἁπάντων.

It is Jove that at will gives and takes courage from men ; for he is lord of all.

So 1 Corinthians (xii. 11)—" Dividing to every man severally as He will ; " and Ephesians (iv. 2)—" Unto every one of us is given grace according to the measure of the gift of Christ."

A WAR OF WORDS.

Il. xx. 244.

'Αλλ' ἄγε μηκέτι ταῦτα λεγώμεθα νηπύτιοι ὥς,
ἑσταότ' ἐν μέσσῃ ὑσμίνῃ δηϊοτῆτος.

Ἐστι γὰρ ἀμφοτέροισιν ὀνείδεα μυθήσασθαι
πολλὰ μάλ'· οὐδ' ἂν νηῦς ἑκατόζυγος ἄχθος ἄροιτο.
Στρεπτὴ δὲ γλῶσσ' ἐστὶ βροτῶν, πολέες δ' ἔνι μῦθοι
παντοῖοι, ἐπέων δὲ πολὺς νομὸς ἔνθα καὶ ἔνθα.
Ὁπποῖόν κ' εἴπησθα ἔπος, τοῖόν κ' ἐπακούσαις.
Ἀλλὰ τίη ἔριδας καὶ νείκεα νῶϊν ἀνάγκη
νεικεῖν ἀλλήλοισιν ἐναντίον, ὥστε γυναῖκας,
αἵτε χολωσάμεναι ἔριδος πέρι θυμοβόροιο
νεικεῦσ' ἀλλήλῃσι μέσην ἐς ἄγυιαν ἰοῦσαι,
πόλλ' ἐτεά τε καὶ οὐκί· χόλος δέ τε καὶ τὰ κελεύει.

But come, let us not talk to each other like babbling fools,
standing in the midst of the battlefield. For we might both find
terms of reproach enough to sink a hundred-oared galley; so
voluble is the tongue of man, glibly giving words without end of
all kinds ; wide is the range of language ; such words shalt thou
hear as thou speakest ; but why should we rail and fight like
women, who, arrayed in fierce contest, jar in the streets with
wordy war, using opprobrious terms, some true, some false, for so
their rage suggests.

So Job (xviii. 6)—" A fool's lips enter into contention, and his mouth
calleth for strokes ;" and James (iii. 5, &c.)—" And the tongue is a fire, a
world of iniquity ; so is the tongue among our members, that it defileth the
whole body, and setteth on fire the course of nature ; and it is set on fire of
hell : the tongue can no man tame : it is an unruly evil, full of deadly
poison ;" and Matthew (vii. 2)—" With what measure ye mete, it shall be
measured to you again ;" and 2 Timothy (ii. 23)—" The servant of the Lord
must not strive ;" and Proverbs (xxx. 33)—" The forcing of wrath bringeth
forth strife."

EVEN THE STRONGEST CANNOT ACCOMPLISH ALL THINGS.

Il. xx. 369.

Οὐδ' Ἀχιλεὺς πάντεσσι τέλος μύθοις ἐπιθήσει,
ἀλλὰ τὸ μὲν τελέει, τὸ δὲ καὶ μεσσηγὺ κολούει.

Nor will Achilles be able to make all his words good: some
things he will fulfil, and in others he will fail.

So Psalm (xxi. 11)—" They imagined a mischievous device, which they
are not able to perform."

" YOUR FATHERS, WHERE ARE THEY ? "

Il. xxi. 106.

Ἀλλά, φίλος, θάνε καὶ σύ· τίη ὀλοφύρεαι οὕτως ;
κάτθανε καὶ Πάτροκλος, ὅπερ σέο πολλὸν ἀμείνων.

But, my friend, thou, too, must die : why vainly wail ? Patroclus, too, is dead, thy better far.

So Zechariah (i. 5)—" Your fathers, where are they ? and the prophets, do
they live for ever ?"—and John (viii. 52)—" Art Thou greater than our
father Abraham, which is dead ? and the prophets are dead : whom makest
Thou thyself ? "

DEATH COMES AT ALL TIMES.

Il. xxi. 109.

Οὐχ ὁρᾳς οἷος καὶ ἐγὼ καλός τε μέγας τε ;
πατρὸς δ' εἴμ' ἀγαθοῖο, θεὰ δέ με γείνατο μήτηρ·
ἀλλ' ἔπι τοι καὶ ἐμοὶ θάνατος καὶ μοῖρα κραταιή
ἔσσεται ἢ ἠὼς ἢ δείλη ἢ μέσον ἦμαρ.

Seest thou not how fair and stalwart I am? I am the son of
noble sire, and goddess-mother born; but death and stubborn fate
will come upon thee and me at morn, or eve, or mid-day.

So Ecclesiastes (iii. 2)—"A time to die ;" and Hebrews (ix. 27)—"It is
appointed unto men once to die ;" and Mark (xiii. 35)—"Watch ye therefore ; for ye know not when the master of the house cometh, at even, or at
midnight, or at the cock-crowing, or in the morning."

And Shakespeare ("Hamlet," act. i. sc. 2)—
"All that lives must die,
Passing through nature to eternity."

THE GODS MORE POWERFUL THAN MEN.

Il. xxi. 264.

Θεοὶ δέ τε φέρτεροι ἀνδρῶν.

The gods are more powerful than men.

So 1 Corinthians (i. 25)—"Because the foolishness of God is wiser than
men ; and the weakness of God is stronger than men."

LIFE OF MEN.

Il. xxi. 463.

Εἰ δὴ σοίγε βροτῶν ἕνεκα πτολεμίζω
δειλῶν, οἱ φύλλοισιν ἐοικότες ἄλλοτε μέν τε
ζαφλεγέες τελέθουσιν, ἀρούρης καρπὸν ἔδοντες,
ἄλλοτε δὲ φθινύθουσιν ἀκήριοι.

If indeed I should fight for the sake of wretched mortals, who,
like leaves, sometimes flourish in beauty, and eat the fruits of
earth, and then again wither on the ground.

So Isaiah (lxiv. 6)—"We all do fade as a leaf." See Sirach (xiv. 18).

"GOD'S WAYS ARE PAST FINDING OUT."

Il. xxii. 9.

Τίπτε με, Πηλέος υἱὲ, ποσὶν ταχέεσσι διώκεις,
αὐτὸς θνητὸς ἐὼν θεὸν ἄμβροτον; οὐδέ νύ πώ με
ἔγνως ὡς θεός εἰμι.

Why, son of Peleus, pursuest thou me with swift feet, who am an immortal, while thou art a mortal? Hast thou not yet discovered my godhead?

So Psalm (lxxvii. 19)—"Thy footsteps are not known;" and Acts (ix. 4) —"Why persecutest thou me?"—and Romans (xi. 33)—"His ways are past finding out."

To Die in Youth.
Il. xxii. 71.

Νέῳ δέ τε πάντ' ἐπέοικεν,
ἀρηῒ κταμένῳ, δεδαϊγμένῳ ὀξέϊ χαλκῷ
κεῖσθαι· πάντα δὲ καλὰ θανόντι περ, ὅττι φανήῃ·
ἀλλ' ὅτε δὴ πολιόν τε κάρη πολιόν τε γένειον,
αἰδῶ τ' αἰσχύνωσι κύνες κταμένοιο γέροντος,
τοῦτο δὴ οἴκτιστον πέλεται δειλοῖσι βροτοῖσιν.

It is honourable for youth to die in battle, struck with the sharp spear; all things are becoming to him in death; but when dogs disfigure the hoary head and hoary beard of the old man lying in death, this is misery the last and worst to mortals.

Familiar Talk.
Il. xxii. 126.

Οὐ μέν πως νῦν ἔστιν ἀπὸ δρυὸς οὐδ' ἀπὸ πέτρης
τῷ ὀαριζέμεναι, ἅτε παρθένος ἠΐθεός τε,
παρθένος ἠΐθεός τ' ὀαρίζετον ἀλλήλοιιν.

This is not the time to hold light talk, like youth and maid under the shade of oak or rock, as youth and maid might hold.

The Balance in which Man's Fate is Weighed.
Il. xxii. 209.

Καὶ τότε δὴ χρύσεια πατὴρ ἐτίταινε τάλαντα,
ἐν δ' ἐτίθει δύο κῆρε τανηλεγέος θανάτοιο,
τὴν μὲν Ἀχιλλῆος, τὴν δ' Ἕκτορος ἱπποδάμοιο,
ἕλκε δὲ μέσσα λαβών· ῥέπε δ' Ἕκτορος αἴσιμον ἦμαρ,
ᾤχετο δ' εἰς Ἀΐδαο λίπεν δέ ἑ Φοῖβος Ἀπόλλων.

And then the father of gods hung out the golden scales, and put in each the lots of doom,—the one of Achilles, the other of horse-taming Hector,—and weighs with equal hands their destinies; down sank the scale, weighted with Hector's death, down to Pluto; and then even Apollo abandons him to his fate.

Milton (Paradise Lost, iv. 999) says:—

"First He weighed
The pendulous round earth, with balanced air
In counterpoise; now ponders all events,
Battles and realms: in these He puts two weights,
The sequel each of parting and of fight;
The latter quick flew and kicked the beam."

THE WOLF AND THE LAMB.
Il. xxii. 262.

'Ὡς οὐκ ἔστι λέουσι καὶ ἀνδράσιν ὅρκια πιστά,
οὐδὲ λύκοι τε καὶ ἄρνες ὁμόφρονα θυμὸν ἔχουσιν,
ἀλλὰ κακὰ φρονέουσι διαμπερὲς ἀλλήλοισιν.

As no firm concord can exist between lions and men, nor do wolves and lambs unite in harmony, but ceaseless enmity dwells between them.

So Isaiah (lxv. 25)—"The wolf and the lamb shall feed together;" and Luke (x. 3)—"I send you forth as lambs among wolves."

EVERY KIND OF VIRTUE.
Il. xxii. 268.

παντοίης ἀρετῆς μιμνήσκεο.

Be mindful of every kind of virtue.

So 2 Peter (i. 5–7)—"And besides this, giving all diligence, add to your faith, virtue; and to virtue, knowledge; and to knowledge, temperance; and to temperance, patience; and to patience, godliness; and to godliness, brotherly kindness; and to brotherly kindness, charity."

THE SOUL.
Il. xxiii. 103.

'Ὢ πόποι, ἦ ῥά τίς ἐστι καὶ εἰν 'Αΐδαο δόμοισιν
ψυχὴ καὶ εἴδωλον, ἀτὰρ φρένες οὐκ ἔνι πάμπαν.

Strange, but true, that there are souls and spectres in the abodes of Hades, but corporeal materials there are none at all.

So Ecclesiastes (ix. 5)—"For the living know that they shall die: but the dead know not anything, neither have they any more a reward; for the memory of them is forgotten."

See (Lat.) Soul.

GRIEF.
Il. xxiii. 157.

Γόοιο μὲν ἔστι καὶ ἆσαι.

There is also a satiety of grief.

So 1 Samuel (xvi. 1)—"How long wilt thou mourn?"—also Sirach (xxxviii. 17).

NOT STRENGTH BUT SKILL OBTAINS THE PRIZE.
Il. xxiii. 315.

Μήτι τοι δρυτόμος μέγ' ἀμείνων ἠὲ βίηφιν·
μήτι δ' αὖτε κυβερνήτης ἐνὶ οἴνοπι πόντῳ

νῆα θοὴν ἰθύνει ἐρεχθομένην ἀνέμοισιν·
μήτι δ’ ἡνίοχος περιγίγνεται ἡνιόχοιο.

The woodman is superior by knowledge of his art rather than
by strength ; the pilot guides the swift ship in the dark-blue sea
by skill, when it is tempest-tossed ; the charioteer is superior to
his rival by his skill.

So Ecclesiastes (ix. 16)—" Wisdom is better than strength ; " and (x. 10)
—" If the iron be blunt, and he do not whet the edge, then must he put to
more strength ; but wisdom is profitable to direct."
See (Lat.) Mind is the man.

BE CAUTIOUS.
Il. xxiii. 340.

Λίθου δ’ ἀλέασθαι ἐπαυρεῖν,
χάρμα δὲ τοῖς ἄλλοισιν, ἐλεγχείη δὲ σοὶ αὐτῷ
ἔσσεται. Ἀλλὰ, φίλος, φρονέων πεφυλαγμένος εἶναι.

Beware of striking thy foot against a stone, a source of joy to
others, a shame to thyself; but, my friend, be cautious and
guarded.

So Psalm (xci. 12)—" Lest thou dash thy foot against a stone."

JUDGE IMPARTIALLY.
Il. xxiii. 574.

Ἐς μέσον ἀμφοτέροισι δικάσσατε, μηδ’ ἐπ’ ἀρωγῷ.

Decide between both justly, and not with favour.

So Deuteronomy (i. 17)—" Ye shall not respect persons in judgment, but
ye shall hear the small as well as the great ; " and Proverbs (xviii. 5)—" It
is not good to accept the person of the wicked, to overthrow the righteous
in judgment."

THE FOLLIES OF YOUTH.
Il. xxiii. 589.

Οἶσθ’ οἷαι νέου ἀνδρὸς ὑπερβασίαι τελέθουσιν·
κραιπνότερος μὲν γάρ τε νόος, λεπτὴ δέ τε μῆτις.

Thou knowest the over-eager vehemence of youth ; quick in
temper, but weak in judgment.

So Job (xviii. 5)—"Thou makest me to possess the iniquities of my
youth ;" and Psalm (xxv. 7)—" Remember not the sins of my youth."

THE FAILING OF OLD AGE.
Il. xxiii. 621.

Οὐ γὰρ πύξ γε μαχήσεαι, οὐδὲ παλαίσεις,
οὐδέ τ’ ἀκοντιστὺν ἐσδύσεαι, οὐδὲ πόδεσσιν
θεύσεαι· ἤδη γὰρ χαλεπὸν κατὰ γῆρας ἐπείγει.

For thou no more canst box or wrestle, or throw the javelin in
sportive strife, or race with flying feet in running ; for now the
heavy hand of age rests upon thee.

So John (xxi. 18)—"When thou wast young, thou girdedest thyself, and
walkedest whither thou wouldest : but when thou shalt be old, thou shalt
stretch forth thy hands, and others shall gird thee, and carry thee whither
thou wouldest not."

MAN DOOMED TO LOSE FRIENDS.

Il. xxiv. 46.

Μέλλει μέν πού τις καὶ φίλτερον ἄλλον ὀλέσσαι,
ἠὲ κασίγνητον ὁμογάστριον ἠὲ καὶ υἱόν·
ἀλλ' ἤτοι κλαύσας καὶ ὀδυράμενος μεθέηκεν·
τλητὸν γὰρ Μοῖραι θυμὸν θέσαν ἀνθρώποισιν.

For some may have lost a friend dearer than brother or son ;
but after having wept and lamented, he dismisses his care, for the
Fates have bestowed a patient mind on man.

So Job (v. 7)—"Yet man is born unto trouble, as the sparks fly upward."

GRIEF.

Il. xxiv. 128.

Τέκνον ἐμὸν, τέο μέχρις ὀδυρόμενος καὶ ἀχεύων
σὴν ἔδεαι κραδίην, μεμνημένος οὔτε τι σίτου
οὔτ' εὐνῆς.

My son, why, weeping and grieving, dost thou wear away thy
soul, forgetful both of food and sleep?

So 1 Samuel (i. 8)—"Why weepest thou? and why eatest thou not? and
why is thy heart grieved?"—and Proverbs (xi. 10)—"By sorrow of the
heart the spirit is broken."

LOSS OF CHILDREN.

Il. xxiv. 255.

Ὤ μοι ἐγὼ πανάποτμος, ἐπεὶ τέκον υἷας ἀρίστους
τῶν δ' οὔτινά φημι λελεῖφθαι.

Unhappy that I am, since I had the noblest children, and now
I have none of them left.

So Genesis (xlii. 36)—"Me have ye bereaved of my children : Joseph is
not, and Simeon is not, and ye will take Benjamin away," and Jeremiah
(xxxi. 15)—"A voice was heard in Ramah, lamentation. and bitter weeping, Rachel weeping for her children, refused to be comforted for her children, because they were not."

TWO URNS CONTAINING GOOD AND EVIL.

Il. xxiv. 524.

Οὐ γάρ τις πρῆξις πέλεται κρυεροῖο γόοιο.
Ὡς γὰρ ἐπεκλώσαντο θεοὶ δειλοῖσι βροτοῖσιν.

ζώειν ἀχνυμένοις· αὐτοὶ δέ τ' ἀκηδέες εἰσίν.
Δοιοὶ γάρ τε πίθοι κατακείαται ἐν Διὸς οὔδει
δώρων οἷα δίδωσι, κακῶν, ἕτερος δὲ ἑάων·
ᾧ μέν κ' ἀμμίξας δοίη Ζεὺς τερπικέραυνος,
ἄλλοτε μέν τε κακῷ ὅγε κύρεται, ἄλλοτε δ' ἐσθλῷ·
ᾧ δέ κε τῶν λυγρῶν δοίη, λωβητὸν ἔθηκεν·
καί ἑ κακὴ βούβρωστις ἐπὶ χθόνα δῖαν ἐλαύνει,
φοιτᾷ δ' οὔτε θεοῖσι τετιμένος οὔτε βροτοῖσιν.

For there is no advantage to be gained from woful lamentation: the gods have spun the thread for wretched mortals that they should live in sorrow, while they themselves are free from cares. Two urns lie beside the door of Jove, one full of evil gifts, and one of good, from which thundering Jove, mingling, gives portions, now of the bad and now of the good. To whomsoever he gives of the bad, he makes him wretched indeed ; grinding misery drives him an outcast over the earth ; he wanders abroad, honoured neither by gods nor men.

So Job (ii. 10)—"What! shall we receive good at the hand of God, and shall we not receive evil?"—and Psalm (lxxv. 8)—"In the hand of the Lord there is a cup; it is full of mixture;" and Isaiah (xlv. 7)—"I form the light, and create darkness ; I make peace, and create evil."

FOOLS PERISH BY THEIR OWN FOLLY.

Odyss. i. 7.

Αὐτῶν γὰρ σφετέρῃσιν ἀτασθαλίῃσιν ὄλοντο
νήπιοι.

Fools! they perished in their mad arrogance.

So 1 Chronicles (x. 13)—"So Saul died for his transgressions;" and Proverbs (xi. 5)—"The wicked shall fall by his own wickedness;" and (xiii. 6)—"Wickedness overthroweth the sinners;" and Hosea (xiii. 9)—"Thou hast destroyed thyself."

MAN THE CAUSE OF HIS OWN ILLS.

Odyss. i. 32.

Ὦ πόποι, οἷον δή νυ θεοὺς βροτοὶ αἰτιόωνται.
Ἐξ ἡμέων γάρ φασι κάκ' ἔμμεναι· οἱ δὲ καὶ αὐτοὶ
σφῇσιν ἀτασθαλίῃσιν ὑπέρμορον ἄλγε' ἔχουσιν.

Strange that men should blame the gods, laying all their woes on us, while it is they themselves that bring, by their own senseless acts, pangs which fate had never decreed.

So Lamentations (iii. 33)—"For He doth not afflict willingly, nor grieve the children of men. Wherefore doth a living man complain, a man for the punishment of his sins?" and Ezekiel (xviii. 24)—"In his trespass that he hath trespassed, and in his sin that he hath sinned, in them shall he die. Yet ye say, The way of the Lord is not equal. Hear now, O house of Israel, Is not my way equal? are not your ways unequal?"

IT IS A WISE SON WHO KNOWS HIS OWN FATHER.

Odyss. i. 215.

Μήτηρ μέν τ' ἐμέ φησι τοῦ ἔμμεναι, αὐτὰρ ἔγωγε
οὐκ οἶδ'· οὐ γάρ πώ τις ἐὸν γόνον αὐτὸς ἀνέγνω.

My mother says in sooth that I am sprung from him, but I
myself do not know, for no one can by himself by any means
know his own father.

AFFLUENCE.

Odyss. i. 217.

Ὡς δὴ ἔγωγ' ὄφελον μάκαρός νύ τευ ἔμμεναι υἱὸς
ἀνέρος, ὃν κτεάτεσσιν ἑοῖς ἔπι γῆρας ἔτετμεν.

Would that I were the happy son of some blest man whom old
age has overtaken in full enjoyment of his wealth.

REMEMBER THAT THOU ART NO LONGER A CHILD.

Odyss. i. 296.

Οὐδέ τί σε χρὴ
νηπιάας ὀχέειν, ἐπεὶ οὐκέτι τηλίκος ἐσσί.

Thou shouldst not follow after childish things, since thou art
no longer a child.

So 1 Corinthians (xiii. 11)—"When I was a child, I spake as a child, I
understood as a child, I thought as a child ; but when I became a man, I
put away childish things."

FEW SONS RIVAL THEIR BRAVE SIRES.

Odyss. ii. 276.

Παῦροι γάρ τοι παῖδες ὁμοῖοι πατρὶ πέλονται,
οἱ πλέονες κακίους, παῦροι δέ τε πατρὸς ἀρείους.

For few sons are equal to their sires ; most of them are less
worthy ; only a few are superior to their father.

So Ecclesiastes (ii. 18)—"Yea, I hated all my labour which I had taken
under the sun ; because I should leave it unto the man that shall be
after me. And who knoweth whether he shall be a wise man or a fool?"

WALK NOT IN THE WAYS OF THE UNGODLY.

Odyss. ii. 281.

Ἔα βουλήν τε νόον τε
ἀφραδέων, ἐπεὶ οὔτι νοήμονες οὐδὲ δίκαιοι·
οὐδέ τι ἴσασιν θάνατον καὶ κῆρα μέλαιναν,
ὃς δή σφι σχεδόν ἐστιν.

Fly the advice and ways of fools, since they are neither sensible nor just; they know not that death and gloomy fate are close by.

So Psalm (l. 1)—"Blessed is the man that walketh not in the counsel of the ungodly;" and Ecclesiastes (ix. 12)—"For man also knoweth not his time: as the fishes that are taken in an evil net, and as the birds that are caught in the snare; so are the sons of men snared in an evil time, when it falleth suddenly upon them."

Enjoy the Present.

Odyss. ii. 303.

Μήτι τοι ἄλλο
ἐν στήθεσσι κακὸν μελέτω ἔργον τε ἔπος τε,
ἀλλά μοι ἐσθιέμεν καὶ πινέμεν, ὡς τὸ πάρος περ.

Let no thoughts of outrage, let no rough words, hanker in thy bosom, but eat and drink as of old.

This is not without the Will of God.

Odyss. ii. 372.

Θάρσει, μαῖ', ἐπεὶ οὔτοι ἄνευ θεοῦ ἥδε γε βουλή.

Be of good cheer, my nurse, since this counsel is of heaven.

So 2 Kings (xviii. 25)—"Am I now come up without the Lord against this place to destroy it?"—and Acts (xxvii. 22)—"And now I exhort you to be of good cheer; for there stood by me this night the angel of God."

Modesty.

Odyss. iii. 24.

Αἰδὼς δ' αὖ νέον ἄνδρα γεραίτερον ἐξερέεσθαι. ·

It is a shame for a young man to question men of riper years.

So Job (xxxii. 6)—"I am young, and ye are very old; wherefore I was afraid, and durst not show you mine opinion."

God will Suggest some Things.

Odyss. iii. 27.

Ἄλλα μὲν αὐτὸς ἐνὶ φρεσὶ σῇσι νοήσεις,
ἄλλα δὲ καὶ δαίμων ὑποθήσεται.

Thou thyself wilt imagine some things in thine own inmost breast, and a god will suggest others.

So Luke (xii. 12)—"For the Holy Ghost shall teach you in the same hour what ye ought to say."

ALL REQUIRE THE AID OF GOD.
Odyss. iii. 48.

Εὔχεσθαι· πάντες δὲ θεῶν χατέουσ' ἄνθρωποι.

Pray, for all mankind require the assistance of the gods.

So Acts (xvii. 25)—"As though God needed anything, seeing He giveth to all life and breath and all things ; that they should seek the Lord, if haply they might feel after Him and find Him ; for in Him we live, and move, and have our being ;" and James (i. 5)—"If any of you lack wisdom, let him ask of God ;" and 1 Timothy (ii. 4)—"Who will have all men to be saved, and to come unto the knowledge of the truth."

THE MIND OF GOD IS UNCHANGEABLE.
Odyss. iii. 147.

Οὐ γάρ τ' αἶψα θεῶν τρέπεται νόος αἰὲν ἐόντων.

For the mind of the ever-existing gods is not lightly changed.

So Malachi (iii. 6)—"For I am the Lord ; I change not ;" and James (i. 17)—"With whom is no variableness, neither shadow of turning."

GOD OMNIPOTENT.
Odyss. iii. 231.

'Ρεῖα θεός γ' ἐθέλων καὶ τηλόθεν ἄνδρα σαώσαι.

God can easily, if He wills, save man even from the most remote part of space.

So Jeremiah (xxiii. 23)—"Am I a God at hand, and not a God afar off?"

DEATH.
Odyss. iii. 236.

'Αλλ' ἤτοι θάνατον μὲν ὁμοίϊον οὐδὲ θεοί περ
καὶ φίλῳ ἀνδρὶ δύνανται ἀλαλκέμεν, ὁππότε κεν δὴ
μοῖρ' ὀλοὴ καθέλῃσι τανηλεγέος θανάτοιο.

But death is the common lot of all ; nor are the gods able to ward it off even from their favourites when the destroying fate which is to lay him out at length has come upon him.

So Psalm (xlix. 10)—"For he seeth that wise men die, likewise the fool and the brutish person perish, and leave their wealth to others."

A LITTLE STONE.
Odyss. iii. 296.

Μικρὸς δὲ λίθος μέγα κῦμ' ἀποέργει.

A rock, however small, may keep back a great wave.

So James (iii. 4)—"Behold also the ships, which, though they be so great, and are driven of fierce winds, yet are they turned about with a very small helm, whithersoever the governor listeth."

Wander not Far from your Home.
Odyss. iii. 313.

Καὶ σὺ, φίλος, μὴ δηθὰ δόμων ἄπο τῆλ᾿ ἀλάλησο.

And thou, my friend, be not long at a distance from thy home.

So Proverbs (xxvii. 8)—"As a bird that wandereth from her nest; so is a man that wandereth from his place."

No one can Contend with Jove.
Odyss. iv. 78.

Ἤτοι Ζηνὶ βροτῶν οὐκ ἄν τις ἐρίζοι.

Assuredly no one mortal-born would think to vie with Jove.

So Isaiah (xlv. 9)—"Woe unto him that striveth with his Maker."

Mourning for the Dead.
Odyss. iv. 195.

Νεμεσσῶμαί γε μὲν οὐδὲν
κλαίειν ὅς κε θάνῃσι βροτῶν καὶ πότμον ἐπίσπῃ.
τοῦτό νυ καὶ γέρας οἶον ὀϊζυροῖσι βροτοῖσιν,
κείρασθαί τε κόμην βαλέειν τ᾿ ἀπὸ δάκρυ παρειῶν.

I do not deem it improper to shed tears over him who has died and met a gloomy fate : the rites of woe are all that the living can bestow, to shear the graceful curl and let fall the tender tear down the cheek.

So Ecclesiastes (xii. 5)—"Man goeth to his long home, and the mourners go about the streets;" and Sirach (xxxviii. 16).

Wisdom of Silence.
Odyss. iv. 204.

Τόσα εἶπες ὅσ᾿ ἂν πεπνυμένος ἀνὴρ.

Thou hast spoken as much as a prudent man ought.

See Proverbs (x. 19); and Ecclesiastes (v. 2)—"Let thy words be few."

A Mirth-inspiring Bowl.
Odyss. iv. 220.

Αὐτίκ᾿ ἄρ᾿ εἰσ οἶνον βάλε φάρμακον, ἔνθεν ἔπινον,
νηπενθές τ᾿ ἄχολόν τε, κακῶν ἐπίληθον ἁπάντων.

Ὅς τὸ καταβρόξειεν, ἐπὲν κρητῆρι μιγείη,
οὔ κεν ἐφημέριός γε βάλοι κατὰ δάκρυ παρειῶν,
οὐδ' εἴ οἱ κατατεθναίη μήτηρ τε πατήρ τε,
οὐδ' εἴ οἱ προπάροιθεν ἀδελφεὸν ἢ φίλον υἱὸν
Χαλκῷ δηϊόωεν, ὁ δ' ὀφθαλμοῖσιν ὁρῷτο.

Forthwith Helen mixed a mirth-inspiring bowl, from which they drank, assuager of sorrow and wrath, that makes man forgetful of all the ills of life. Whoever swallows the draught, when it has been mixed in the bowl, will not let fall a tear for one whole day adown his cheek, not even though his father and mother were lying in the throes of death, not even though a man should slay before his eyes a brother or a son; no, not even though his own eyes beheld it.

So Proverbs (xxxi. 6)—"Give strong drink unto him that is ready to perish, and wine unto those that be of heavy hearts. Let him drink, and forget his poverty, and remember his misery no more."

REMEMBER THE COMMANDS OF GOD.
Odyss. iv. 353.

Οἱ δ' αἰεὶ βούλοντο θεοὶ μεμνῆσθαι ἐφετμέων.

The gods have always wished men to be mindful of their precepts.

So Numbers (xv. 38)—"Let them make fringes, that he may look upon them, and remember all the commandments of the Lord."

PUT A GUARD ON THY TONGUE.
Odyss. iv. 502.

Καί νύ κεν ἔκφυγε κῆρα, καὶ ἐχθόμενός περ Ἀθήνῃ,
εἰ μὴ ὑπερφίαλον ἔπος ἔκβαλε καὶ μέγ' ἀάσθη.

And he would have escaped death, even though hated by Minerva, if he had not uttered arrogant words, and thus fallen into great crime.

So Proverbs (xii. 13)—"The wicked is snared by the transgression of his lips;" and (xiii. 3)—"He that keepeth his mouth keepeth his life: but he that openeth wide his lips shall have destruction;" and (xviii. 7)—"A fool's mouth is his destruction, and his lips are the snare of his soul."

ELYSIUM.
Odyss. iv. 563.

Ἀλλά σ' ἐς Ἠλύσιον πεδίον καὶ πείρατα γαίης
ἀθάνατοι πέμψουσιν, ὅθι ξανθὸς Ῥαδάμανθυς,
τῇπερ ῥηΐστη βιοτὴ πέλει ἀνθρώποισιν·
οὐ νιφετός, οὔτ' ἄρ χειμὼν πολὺς οὔτε ποτ' ὄμβρος,
ἀλλ' αἰεὶ Ζεφύροιο λιγὺ πνείοντας ἀήτας
Ὠκεανὸς ἀνίησιν ἀναψύχειν ἀνθρώπους.

But the immortal gods shall send thee to the plains of Elysium, and the utmost bounds of earth, where dwells Rhadamanthus with auburn hair : there man's whole existence is a state of ease : no snow is there, nor violent storms, nor rain ; but Oceanus ever sends the gently-blowing western gales to refresh wearied men.

Tennyson (" Morte d'Arthur ") says—
" Where falls nor hail or rain or any snow,
Nor ever wind blows loudly."
Swinbourne (" Atalanta in Calydon ") says—
" Lands undiscoverable in the unheard-of west,
Round which the strong stream of a sacred sea
Rolls without wind for ever, and the sun
There shows not her white wings and windy feet,
Nor thunder, nor swift rain saith anything,
Nor the sun burns,—but all things rest and thrive."

To Speak to the Air.

Odyss. iv. 837.

Κακὸν δ' ἀνεμώλια βάζειν.

It is base to speak vain words.

So Job (xv. 2)—" Should a wise man utter vain words, and fill his belly with the east wind ?"—and (xvi. 3) - " Shall vain words have an end ? "

A Sylvan Scene.

Odyss. v. 63

῞Υλη δὲ σπέος ἀμφὶ πεφύκει·τηλεθόωσα,
κλήθρη τ' αἴγειρός τε καὶ εὐώδης κυπάρισσος
ἔνθα δέ τ' ὄρνιθες τανυσίπτεροι εὐνάζοντο,
σκῶπές τ' ἴρηκές τε τανύγλωσσοί τε κορῶναι
εἰνάλιαι, τῇσίντε θαλάσσια ἔργα μέμηλεν.
῾Η δ' αὐτοῦ τετάνυστο περὶ σπείους γλαφυροῖο
ἡμερὶς ἡβώωσα, τεθήλει δὲ σταφυλῇσιν·
κρῆναι δ' ἑξείης πίσυρες ῥέον ὕδατι λευκῷ,
πλησίαι ἀλλήλων τετραμμέναι ἄλλυδις ἄλλη.
᾿Αμφὶ δὲ λειμῶνες μαλακοὶ ἴου ἠδὲ σελίνου
θήλεον· ἔνθα κ' ἔπειτα καὶ ἀθάνατός περ ἐπελθὼν
θηήσαιτο ἰδὼν καὶ τερφθείη φρεσὶν ᾗσιν.

Around the cave trees grew in utmost beauty—alders and poplars and fragrant-scented cypresses, in which all birds of ample wing had nests—owls, hawks, and long-tongued water-fowl, that plunge into the sea-waves. The cave in front was spread with a green vine, clustering with ripe grapes ; four springs ran with limpid water near to each other, flowing here and there ; around, a meadowy ground was seen, covered with violets and green parsley : such a spot even a god might well admire and wander over with delight.

THE WILL OF GOD.

Odyss. v. 103.

'Αλλὰ μάλ' οὔπως ἔστι Διὸς νόον αἰγιόχοιο
οὔτε παρεξελθεῖν ἄλλον θεὸν οὔθ' ἀλιῶσαι.

But assuredly it is by no means possible that any other god should dare to disobey the will of Jove, or render it null.

So Job (xxiii. 13)—" But He is in one mind, and who can turn Him ; " and Proverbs (xix. 21)— " There are many devices in a man s heart ; nevertheless the counsel of the Lord, that shall stand."

BEWARE OF THE ANGER OF GOD.

Odyss. v. 146.

Διὸς δ' ἐποπίζεο μῆνιν,
μήπως τοι μετόπισθε κοτεσσάμενος χαλεπήνῃ.

Beware of the wrath of Jove, lest at some future period he wreak his anger upon thee.

So Psalm (ii. 12)—" Kiss the Son, lest He be angry, and ye perish from the way, when His wrath is kindled but a little."

THE OMNISCIENCE OF GOD.

Odyss. v. 169.

Αἴ κε θεοὶ γ' ἐθέλωσι, τοὶ οὐρανὸν εὐρὺν ἔχουσιν,
οἵ μευ φέρτεροί εἰσι νοῆσαί τε κρῆναί τε.

The gods, who dwell in the broad heaven, superior to me in knowledge and understanding.

So Psalm (xciv. 10)—" He that teacheth man knowledge, shall He not know ? "—and 1 Corinthians (i. 25)—" Because the foolishness of God is wiser than men ; and the weakness of God is stronger than men."

A MERCIFUL DISPOSITION.

Odyss. v. 190.

Καὶ γὰρ ἐμοὶ νόος ἐστὶν ἐναίσιμος, οὐδέ μοι αὐτῇ
θυμὸς ἐνὶ στήθεσσι σιδήρεος, ἀλλ' ἐλεήμων.

For I have a kind disposition, nor am I iron-hearted, but pitiful

So Psalm (xxxvii. 26)—" A good man is ever merciful ; " and (cxii. 4)—" He is gracious and full of compassion ; a good man showeth favour."

DIANA.

Odyss. vi. 102.

Οἵη δ' Ἄρτεμις εἶσι κατ' οὔρεος ἰοχέαιρα,
ἢ κατὰ Τηΰγετον περιμήκετον ἢ Ἐρύμανθον,

τερπομένη κάπροισι καὶ ὠκείης ἐλάφοισιν·
τῇ δέ θ' ἅμα νύμφαι, κοῦραι Διὸς αἰγιόχοιο,
ἀγρονόμοι παίζουσι· γέγηθε δέ τε φρένα Λητώ·
πασάων δ' ὑπὲρ ἥγε κάρη ἔχει ἠδὲ μέτωπα,
ῥεῖά τ' ἀριγνώτη πέλεται, καλαὶ δέ τε πᾶσαι·
ὣς ἥγ' ἀμφιπόλοισι μετέπρεπε παρθένος ἀδμής.

Like the huntress Diana, whose delight is set on her arrows, in
the mountains, either on lofty Taygetus or Erymanthus, delighting in boars and swift stags; with her the rural nymphs, daughters
of ægis-bearing Jove, sport in playful games, while her mother,
Latona, is glad at heart; in head and shoulders she overtops
them all, but is easily distinguished, even where all are lovely.
So also did the virgin excel all her maidens.

So Proverbs (xxxi. 28)—" Her children arise up and call her blessed ; her
husband also, and he praiseth her."

See Virg. Æn. i. 498.

DESCRIPTION OF THE HAPPY LIFE OF WOMAN.
Odyss. vi. 180.

Σοὶ δὲ θεοὶ τόσα δοῖεν ὅσα φρεσὶ σῇσι μενοινᾷς,
ἄνδρα τε καὶ οἶκον καὶ ὁμοφροσύνην ὀπάσειαν
ἐσθλήν· οὐ μὲν γὰρ τοῦγε κρεῖσσον καὶ ἄρειον
ἢ ὅθ' ὁμοφρονέοντε νοήμασιν οἶκον ἔχητον
ἀνὴρ ἠδὲ γυνή· πόλλ' ἄλγεα δυσμενέεσσιν,
χάρματα δ' εὐμενέτῃσι· μάλιστα δέ τ' ἔκλυον αὐτοί.

May the gods grant to thee all thy heart's desire, a husband,
and home, and firm union of soul with thy partner ; for there is
nothing more delightful than when husband and wife manage
their affairs in close union, exciting envy in their foes and joy to
all who wish them well ; they themselves feel and enjoy their
happy state.

So Ecclesiastes (ix. 9)—" Live joyfully with the wife whom thou lovest
all the days of the life of thy vanity, which He hath given thee under the
sun, all the days of thy vanity : for that is thy portion in this life, and in
thy labour which thou takest under the sun."

HAPPINESS.
Odyss. vi. 188.

Ζεὺς δ' αὐτὸς νέμει ὄλβον Ὀλύμπιος ἀνθρώποισιν,
ἐσθλοῖς ἠδὲ κακοῖσιν, ὅπως ἐθέλῃσιν, ἑκάστῳ.

God himself metes out happiness to men, to the good and bad,
to each as to Him seems best.

So 1 Chronicles (xxix. 12)—" Both riches and honour come of Thee, and
Thou reignest over all ; and in Thine hand is power and might ; and in
Thine hand it is to make great, and to give strength unto all ; " and Eccle-

siastes (ix. 1)—" No man moveth either love or hatred by all that is before them ; all things are alike to all, there is one event to the righteous and to the wicked."

What we Give to the Poor we Lend to God.

Odyss. vi. 207.

Πρὸς γὰρ Διός εἰσιν ἅπαντες
ξεῖνοί τε πτωχοί τε, δόσις δ' ὀλίγη τε φίλη τε.

For strangers and poor are all sent by Jove ; a gift, however little, is grateful to them.

So Proverbs (xix. 17)—" He that hath pity upon the poor lendeth unto the Lord ; and that which he hath given will He pay him again."

Rugged Mariners.

Odyss. vii. 32.

Οὐ γὰρ ξείνους οἵδε μάλ ἀνθρώπους ἀνέχονται,
οὐδ' ἀγαπαζόμενοι φιλέουσ' ὅς κ' ἄλλοθεν ἔλθῃ.
νηυσὶ θοῇσιν τοίγε πεποιθότες ὠκείῃσιν
λαῖτμα μέγ' ἐκπερόωσιν, ἐπεί σφισι δῶκ' ἐνοσίχθων·
τῶν νέες ὠκεῖαι ὡσεὶ πτερὸν ἠὲ νόημα.

For they do not endure foreigners, nor do they care for those who come from other lands. Trusting in their swift-sailing ships, they make their way over the mighty deep, since the Ruler of the sea has given it to them ; their ships are swift as winged bird, or even thought.

So Job (ix. 26)—" My days are passed away as the swift ships ; " and Psalm (xc. 9)—" We spend our years as a tale that is told."

Manly Firmness.

Odyss. vii. 50.

Μηδέ τι θυμῷ
τάρβει· θαρσαλέος γὰρ ἀνὴρ ἐν πᾶσιν ἀμείνων
ἔργοισιν τελέθει, εἰ καί ποθεν ἄλλοθεν ἔλθοι.

Let not thy spirit fail thee, for the undaunted does best in every enterprise, even though he come from realms unknown.

So Deuteronomy (xxxi. 8)—" Fear not, neither be dismayed."

He Destroys and is Destroyed.

Odyss. vii. 60.

Ἀλλ' ὁ μὲν ὤλεσε λαὸν ἀτάσθαλον, ὤλετο δ' αὐτός.

He extirpated the godless race, but perished in their ruin.

So Proverbs (xxix. 2)—" But when the wicked beareth rule, the people mourn."

A Beloved Queen.

Odyss. vii. 69.

Ὣς κείνη περὶ κῆρι τετίμηταί τε καὶ ἔστιν
ἔκ τε φίλων παίδων ἔκ τ᾽ αὐτοῦ Ἀλκινόοιο
καὶ λαῶν, οἵ μίν ῥα θεὸν ὣς εἰσορόωντες
δειδέχαται μύθοισιν, ὅτε στείχῃσ᾽ ἀνὰ ἄστυ.
Οὐ μὲν γάρ τι νόου γε καὶ αὐτὴ δεύεται ἐσθλοῦ·
οἷσίν τ᾽ εὖ φρονέῃσι καὶ ἀνδράσι νείκεα λύει.

Thus she was honoured from the heart, and is so both by dear
children, by Alcinous and people, in whose eyes she is as it were
a goddess, as she passes through the city; for she lacks nothing in
sound sense and judgment, healing the strife among those whom
she loves.

A Garden.

Odyss. vii. 112.

Ἔκτοσθεν δ᾽ αὐλῆς μέγας ὄρχατος ἄγχι θυράων
τετράγυος· περὶ δ᾽ ἕρκος ἐλήλαται ἀμφοτέρωθεν.
Ἔνθα δὲ δένδρεα μακρὰ πεφύκει τηλεθόωντα,
ὄγχναι καὶ ῥοιαὶ καὶ μηλέαι ἀγλαόκαρποι
συκέαι τε γλυκεραὶ καὶ ἐλαῖαι τηλεθόωσαι.
Τάων οὔποτε καρπὸς ἀπόλλυται οὐδ᾽ ἀπολείπει
χείματος οὐδὲ θέρους, ἐπετήσιος· ἀλλὰ μάλ᾽ αἰεὶ
Ζεφυρίη πνείουσα τὰ μὲν φύει, ἄλλα δὲ πέσσει.
Ὄγχνη ἐπ᾽ ὄγχνῃ γηράσκει, μῆλον δ᾽ ἐπὶ μήλῳ,
αὐτὰρ ἐπὶ σταφυλῇ σταφυλή, σῦκον δ᾽ ἐπὶ σύκῳ.

Outside the palace, near the door, a spacious garden lies, four
acres in extent; round it a fence on all sides; tall trees spring
in abundance, pears, pomegranates, apple-trees with fair fruit,
luscious fig-trees and luxuriant olives; their fruit is always there,
nor fails all the year round, winter and summer, but ever the
western breeze causes some to bud and others to ripen; each
dropping pear another pear supplies, on apples apples, grapes on
grapes, figs on figs arise.

The Fate of Man.

Odyss. vii. 196.

Ἔνθα δ᾽ ἔπειτα
πείσεται ἅσσα οἱ Αἶσα κατὰ Κλῶθές τε βαρεῖαι
γεινομένῳ νήσαντο λίνῳ, ὅτε μιν τέκε μήτηρ.

There shall he suffer whatever destiny and the dread Fates
have spun for him with their thread of doom when his mother
gave him birth.

Hunger.

Odyss. vii. 216.

Οὐ γάρ τι στυγερῇ ἐπὶ γαστέρι κύντερον ἄλλο
ἔπλετο, ἥτ᾽ ἐκέλευσεν ἕο μνήσασθαι ἀνάγκῃ
καὶ μάλα τειρόμενον καὶ ἐνὶ φρεσὶ πένθος ἔχοντα.

For there is nothing more importunate than a hungry stomach,
which will not allow a man to forget it, whatever be his cares and
sorrows.

So Ecclesiastes (vi. 7)—"All the labour of man is for his mouth, and yet
the appetite is not filled;" and Proverbs (xvi 26)—"He that laboureth,
laboureth for himself; for his mouth craveth it of him."

Men a Jealous Race.

Odyss. vii. 307.

Δύσζηλοι γάρ τ᾽ εἰμὲν ἐπὶ χθονὶ φῦλ᾽ ἀνθρώπων.

For we, the race of men, are jealous in temper.

So Numbers (v. 14)—"If the spirit of jealousy come upon a man."

Drinking according to the Pleasure of Each.

Odyss. viii. 70.

Πὰρ δὲ δέπας οἴνοιο, πιεῖν ὅτε θυμὸς ἀνώγοι.

And beside him a cup of wine to drink at his pleasure.

So Esther (i. 8)—"And the drinking was according to the law, that they
should do according to every man's pleasure."

God Gives Different Talents to Different Men.

Odyss. viii. 167.

Οὕτως οὐ πάντεσσι θεοὶ χαρίεντα διδοῦσιν
ἀνδράσιν, οὔτε φυὴν οὔτ᾽ ἆρ φρένας οὔτ᾽ ἀγορητύν,
ἄλλος μὲν γάρ τ᾽ εἶδος ἀκιδνότερος πέλει ἀνήρ,
ἀλλὰ θεὸς μορφὴν ἔπεσι στέφει, οἱ δέ τ᾽ ἐς αὐτὸν
τερπόμενοι λεύσσουσιν· ὁ δ᾽ ἀσφαλέως ἀγορεύει
αἰδοῖ μειλιχίῃ, μετὰ δὲ πρέπει ἀγρομένοισιν,
ἐρχόμενον δ᾽ ἀνὰ ἄστυ θεὸν ὣς εἰσορόωσιν.
Ἄλλος δ᾽ αὖ εἶδος μὲν ἀλίγκιος ἀθανάτοισιν,
ἀλλ᾽ οὔ οἱ χάρις ἀμφιπεριστέφεται ἐπέεσσιν.

God gives not noble gifts to all men, neither nature's charms,
nor intellect, nor eloquence, for one man is inferior in outward form, while God makes up for this defect by eloquence, and
thus he is admired by all; he speaks sweeter than honey, and
with modesty steals away our souls, distinguished amidst the

surrounding multitude ; in public he appears a god ; while another is fair as the ethereal beings in form, but " round his words grace sits not like a coronet."

So Psalm (xlv. 4)—"Grace is poured into thy lips ;" and Song of Solomon (iv. 3)—" Thy speech is comely ;" and 1 Corinthians (xii. 4)—" Now there are diversities of gifts, but the same Spirit ;" and Matthew (xxv. 15)—" And unto one he gave five talents, to another two, and to another one ; to every man according to his several ability."

Women should Remain in their Homes.

Odyss. viii. 324.

Θηλύτεραι δὲ θεαὶ μένον αἰδοῖ οἴκοι ἑκάστη.

The goddesses remained each modestly at home.

So Titus (ii. 5)—" Discreet, chaste, keepers at home."

The Gods Givers of Blessings.

Odyss. viii. 325.

Θεοὶ, δωτῆρες ἑάων.

The gods, givers of what is good.

So Matthew (vii. 11)—" God will give good things to them that ask Him ;" and James (i. 17)—" Every good gift and every perfect gift is from above, and cometh down from the Father of lights, with whom is no variableness, neither shadow of turning."

Evil Deeds.

Odyss. viii. 329.

Οὐκ ἀρετᾷ κακὰ ἔργα.

Evil deeds prosper never.

So Proverbs (xi. 21)—" Though hand join in hand, the wicked shall not be unpunished ;" and (xxix. 6)—" In the transgression of an evil man there is a snare."

Surety for the Unjust.

Odyss. viii. 351.

Δειλαί τοι δειλῶν γε καὶ ἐγγύαι ἐγγυάασθαι

He suffers who gives surety for the unjust.

So Proverbs (vi. 1)—" If thou be surety for thy friend, thou art snared with the words of thy mouth ;" and (xi. 15)—" He that is surety for a stranger shall smart for it ; and he that hateth suretyship is sure."

The Poet.

Odyss. viii. 479.

Πᾶσι γὰρ ἀνθρώποισιν ἐπιχθονίοισιν ἀοιδοὶ
τιμῆς ἔμμοροί εἰσι καὶ αἰδοῦς, οὕνεκ' ἄρα σφέας
οἴμας Μοῦσ' ἐδίδαξε, φίλησε δὲ φῦλον ἀοιδῶν.

Poets are worthy of honour and respect from all men upon the earth, because the Muse has taught them to sing lays, and loves the harmonious race.

See (Lat.) Poet.

A Feast.

Odyss. viii. 542.

Ὁμῶς τερπώμεθα πάντες
ξεινοδόκοι καὶ ξεῖνος, ἐπεὶ πολὺ κάλλιον οὕτως.

Let us all rejoice together, hosts and guests, since it is best so.

So Ecclesiastes (viii. 15)—" Then I commended mirth, because a man hath no better thing under the sun than to eat, and to drink, and to be merry;" and (x. 19)—"A feast is made for laughter."

The Will of the Lord be Done.

Odyss. viii. 570.

Τὰ δέ κεν θεὸς ἢ τελέσειεν,
ἤ κ' ἀτέλεστ' εἴη, ὥς οἱ φίλον ἔπλετο θυμῷ.

Some things God will bring to pass, and others will be un-accomplished, according to His will.

So Acts (xxi. 14)—" The will of the Lord be done;" and James (iv. 15)— " If the Lord will, we shall do this or that."

The Calamity is from God.

Odyss. viii. 579.

Τὸν δὲ θεοὶ μὲν τεῦξαν, ἐπεκλώσαντο δ' ὄλεθρον
ἀνθρώποις, ἵνα ᾖσι καὶ ἐσσομένοισιν ἀοιδή.

The gods have contrived this misfortune, and destined it for men, that it might be a theme of future song.

So 2 Kings (vi. 33)—"This evil is of the Lord;" and Amos (iii. 6)— "Shall there be evil in the city, and the Lord hath not done it?"

An Equal Division.

Odyss. ix. 41.

Κτήματα πολλὰ λαβόντες
δασσάμεθ', ὡς μὴ τίς μοι ἀτεμβόμενος κίοι ἴσης.

K

We have divided the many possessions which we received, so that no one has gone away deprived of his share.

So 1 Samuel (xxx. 24)—" As his part is that goeth down to the battle, so shall his part be that tarrieth by the stuff : they shall part alike."

All Grow Spontaneously.

Odyss. ix. 108.

Οὔτε φυτεύουσιν χερσὶν φυτὸν οὔτ' ἀρόωσιν,
ἀλλὰ τάγ' ἄσπαρτα καὶ ἀνήροτα πάντα φύονται,
πυροὶ καὶ κριθαὶ ἠδ' ἄμπελοι.

They neither plant nor sow, but all things grow without plough- ing or sowing, wheat, barley, and vines.

See 2 Kings (xix. 29)—" Ye shall eat this year things that grow of them- selves."

Thou canst not Escape the Disease sent by God.

Odyss. ix. 411.

Νοῦσόν γ' οὔπως ἔστι Διὸς μεγάλου ἀλέασθαι.

Thou canst by no means escape the disease sent by mighty Jove.

So 1 Samuel (iv. 8)—" Who shall deliver us out of the hand of these mighty Gods ? these are the Gods that smote the Egyptians ;" and 1 Peter (v. 6)—" Humble yourselves therefore under the mighty hand of God."

Do not Irritate the Irascible.

Odyss. ix. 494.

Σχέτλιε, τίπτ' ἐθέλεις ἐρεθιζέμεν ἄγριον ἄνδρα.

Unhappy man, why dost thou exasperate a savage wretch?

So Judges (xviii. 25)—" Let not thy voice be heard among us, lest angry fellows run upon thee, and thou lose thy life, with the lives of thy house- hold."

Folly.

Odyss. x. 27.

Αὐτῶν γὰρ ἀπωλόμεθ' ἀφραδίῃσιν.

For we perished by our own folly.

So Proverbs (i. 32)—" The turning away of the simple shall slay them ;" and (xi. 3)—" The perverseness of transgressors shall destroy them ;" and Hosea (xiii. 9)—" Thou hast destroyed thyself "

THE ADVICE OF BAD COMPANIONS.

Odyss. x. 46.

Βουλὴ δὲ κακὴ νίκησεν ἑταίρων.

The bad counsel of my companions got the better of me.

So 2 Samuel (xvii. 14)—"And Absalom and all the men of Israel said, The counsel of Hushai the Archite is better than the counsel of Ahithophel : for the Lord had appointed to defeat the good counsel of Ahithophel. to the intent that the Lord might bring evil upon Absalom ; " and 1 Kings (xii. 13)—"And the king answered the people roughly, and forsook the old men's counsel that they gave him ; and spake to them after the counsel of the young men, saying, My father made your yoke heavy, I will add to your yoke : my father also chastised you with whips, but I will chastise you with scorpions."

BAD COMPANIONS.

Odyss. x. 68.

Ἄασάν μ' ἕταροί τε κακοὶ πρὸς τοῖσί τε ὕπνος
σχέτλιος.

Bad companions have ruined me, and in addition to these, excessive sleep.

So Proverbs (xxiii. 20)—"Be not among the wine-bibbers ; among riotous eaters of flesh ; for the drunkard and the glutton shall come to poverty, and drowsiness shall clothe a man with rags."

"LOVE NOT SLEEP."

Odyss. x. 84.

Ἄϋπνος ἀνὴρ δοιοὺς ἐξήρατο μισθούς.

A man who does not sleep has a double reward.

So Proverbs (xx. 13)—"Love not sleep, lest thou come to poverty : open thine eyes, and thou shalt be satisfied with bread."

TEARS VAIN IN MISERY.

Odyss. x. 202.

Ἀλλ' οὐ γάρ τις πρῆξις ἐγίγνετο μυρομένοισιν.

But tears in mortal miseries are vain.

See (Lat.) Tears.

A MIND NOT TO BE CHARMED.

Odyss. x. 329.

Σοὶ δέ τις ἐν στήθεσσιν ἀκήλητος νόος ἐστίν.

In thy breast there is a mind that cannot be gained over by charming.

So Psalm (lviii. 5)—"Which will not hearken to the voice of charmers, charming never so wisely."

K 2

Why dost thou Sit like a Dumb Man ?
Odyss. x. 378.

Τίφθ' οὕτως, 'Οδυσεῦ, κατ' ἄρ' ἕζεαι ἶσος ἀναύδῳ,
θυμὸν ἔδων, βρώμης δ' οὐχ ἅπτεαι οὐδὲ ποτῆτος;

Why, Ulysses, dost thou sit thus like a man bereft of speech,
wasting away thy heart, and touching neither bread nor drink?

See 1 Samuel (i. 8) ; and 1 Kings (xxi. 5)—" Why is thy spirit so sad, that
thou eatest no bread ? "

A Wild Scamp.
Odyss. x. 552.

Ἐλπήνωρ δέ τις ἔσκε νεώτατος, οὔτε τι λίην
ἄλκιμος ἐν πολέμῳ οὔτε φρεσὶν ᾖσιν ἀρηρὼς,
ὅς μοι ἄνευθ' ἑτάρων ἱεροῖς ἐν δώμασι Κίρκης,
ψύχεος ἱμείρων, κατελέξατο οἰνοβαρείων.

Elpenor was the youngest, neither famed in war nor for sense,
who, away from his companions in the sacred hall of Circe, delighting in a cool recess, slept, overcome with wine.

Who can see God ?
Odyss. x. 573.

Τίς ἂν θεὸν οὐκ ἐθέλοντα
ὀφθαλμοῖσιν ἴδοιτ' ἢ ἔνθ' ἢ ἔνθα κιόντα ;

Who can see God with his eyes if He wills not, going hither and
thither?

So Isaiah (xlv. 15)—" Verily Thou art a God that hidest Thyself ; " and
John (i. 18)—" No man hath seen God at any time ; " and 1 Timothy (vi.
16)—" Whom no man hath seen, nor can see."

Visionary Ghosts.
Odyss. xi. 36.

Αἱ δ'·ἀγέροντο
ψυχαὶ ὑπὲξ Ἐρέβευς νεκύων κατατεθνηώτων.
[νύμφαι τ' ἠΐθεοί τε πολύτλητοί τε γέροντες
παρθενικαί τ' ἀταλαὶ νεοπενθέα θυμὸν ἔχουσαι·
πολλοὶ δ' οὐτάμενοι χαλκήρεσιν ἐγχείῃσιν,
ἄνδρες ἀρηΐφατοι βεβροτωμένα τεύχε' ἔχοντες·
οἱ πολλοὶ περὶ βόθρον ἐφοίτων ἄλλοθεν ἄλλος
θεσπεσίῃ ἰαχῇ· ἐμὲ δὲ χλωρὸν δέος ᾕρει.]

The shades of the dead came thronging forth from Erebus—
virgins, youths, and old men who in their day had endured much,
and tender little maidens overwhelmed with recent grief ; many

a man, too, wounded by the brazen spear, slain in the battlefield in mail, and all blood-stained, who flitted by in numbers beside the trench, here and there, with loud wailings ; pale, I trembled with fear.

The Evils of Drunkenness.

Odyss. xi. 61.

Ἀσέ με δαίμονος αἶσα κακὴ καὶ ἀθέσφατος οἶνος.

I have been ruined by an evil fate and excess in wine.

So Proverbs (xxiii. 30 —"Who hath woe? who hath sorrow? They that tarry long at the wine ; they that go to seek mixed wine."

The Dead.

Odyss. xi. 218.

'Αλλ' αὕτη δίκη ἐστὶ βροτῶν, ὅτε κέν τε θάνωσιν·
οὐ γὰρ ἔτι σάρκας τε καὶ ὀστέα ἶνες ἔχουσιν,
ἀλλὰ τὰ μέν τε πυρὸς κρατερὸν μένος αἰθομένοιο
δαμνᾷ, ἐπεί κε πρῶτα λίπῃ λεύκ' ὀστέα θυμός,
ψυχὴ δ' ἠΰτ' ὄνειρος ἀποπταμένη πεπότηται.

But this is the law of mortals when they die : their muscles hold no longer flesh and bones, but the strong force of flaming fire destroys these parts, after the spirit has first left the white bones, while the soul wings its flight, vanishing like a dream.

So Luke (xxiv. 39)—"A spirit hath not flesh and bones."

Lying Vagrants.

Odyss. xi. 363.

Ὦ 'Οδυσεῦ, τὸ μὲν οὔτι σ' ἐΐσκομεν εἰσορόωντες
ἠπεροπῆά τ' ἔμεν καὶ ἐπίκλοπον, οἷά τε πολλοὺς
βόσκει γαῖα μέλαινα πολυσπερέας ἀνθρώπους
ψεύδεά τ' ἀρτύνοντας, ὅθεν κέ τις οὐδὲ ἴδοιτο·
σοὶ δ' ἔπι μὲν μορφὴ ἐπέων, ἔνι δὲ φρένες ἐσθλαί,
μῦθον δ' ὡς ὅτ' ἀοιδὸς ἐπισταμένως κατέλεξας,
πάνκων τ' 'Αργείων σέο τ' αὐτοῦ κήδεα λυγρά.

Ulysses, we do not suspect in looking at thee that thou art capable of guile and tricky frauds, though such the earth produces in numbers, vagrants, artful to deceive, so as to elude detection ; to thee there is a grace of language, and gifts of mind ; thou hast told thy story skilfully, like some bard the sad woes of all the Greeks and of thyself.

So Titus (i. 10)—"There are many unruly and vain talkers and deceivers ;" and 2 John (7)—"For many deceivers are entered into the world."

A Time for Everything.
Odyss. xi. 378.

Ὥρη μὲν πολέων μύθων, ὥρη δὲ καὶ ὕπνου.

A time for talking, however prolonged ; a time, too, for sleep.

So Ecclesiastes (iii. 7)—"A time to keep silence, and a time to speak."

Women.
Odyss. xi. 427.

Ὡς οὐκ αἰνότερον καὶ κύντερον ἄλλο γυναικός
[ἥτις δὴ τοιαῦτα μετὰ φρεσὶν ἔργα βάληται.]

Than woman there is no fouler and viler fiend, when her mind
is bent to ill.

See Sirach (xxv. 19).

Trust not a Secret to a Woman.
Odyss. xi. 441.

Τῷ νῦν μήποτε καὶ σὺ γυναικί περ ἤπιος εἶναι·
μή οἱ μῦθον ἄπαντα πιφαυσκέμεν, ὅν κ᾽ εὖ εἰδῇς,
ἀλλὰ τὸ μὲν φάσθαι, τὸ δὲ καὶ κεκρυμμένον εἶναι.

Though thou lovest thy wife, tell not everything which thou
knowest to her ; but unfold some trifle, while thou concealest the
rest.

So Micah (vii. 5)—" Keep the doors of thy mouth from her that lieth
in thy bosom."

Think all Women False.
Odyss. xi. 456.

Ἐπεὶ οὐκέτι πιστὰ γυναιξίν.

There is no trust to be placed in women.

Rather be a Slave on Earth than Reign in Hell.
Odyss. xi. 489.

Βουλοίμην κ᾽ ἐπάρουρος ἐὼν θητευέμεν ἄλλῳ,
ἀνδρὶ παρ᾽ ἀκλήρῳ, ᾧ μὴ βίοτος πολὺς εἴη,
ἢ πᾶσιν νεκύεσσι καταφθιμένοισιν ἀνάσσειν.

I would rather be a peasant and slave to some poor hind of
slenderest means, than reign over the dead who have passed from
life.

Milton ("Paradise Lost," i. 252) says the reverse of this—
" Better to reign in hell than serve in heaven !"

"To go down Alive into the Pit."

Odyss. xii. 21.

Σχέτλιοι, οἳ ζώοντες ὑπήλθετε δῶμ᾽ Ἀΐδαο,
δισθανέες, ὅτε τ᾽ ἄλλοι ἅπαξ θνήσκουσ᾽ ἄνθρωποι.

Unhappy wretches, who alive go down into the pit of Hades,
dying twice, while other men die only once.

So Numbers (xvi. 33—" They went down alive into the pit;" and Psalm
(lv. 15)—" Let them go down into hell;" and Hebrews (ix. 27)—" And it is
appointed unto men once to die."

We are not Ignorant of Misfortunes.

Odyss. xii. 208.

Ὦ φίλοι, οὐ γάρ πώ τι κακῶν ἀδαήμονές εἰμεν.

O friends! we have by no means been unacquainted with woes.

So Romans (v. 4)—"Patience worketh experience;" and 2 Corinthians
(ii. 11)—"We are not ignorant of his devices."

Death by Hunger.

Odyss. xii. 341.

Πάντες μὲν στυγεροὶ θάνατοι δειλοῖσι βροτοῖσιν,
λιμῷ δ᾽ οἴκτιστον θανέειν καὶ πότμον ἐπισπεῖν.

Death in all shapes is hateful to unhappy man, but the most
dreadful is to die and meet our fate by hunger.

See (Lat.) Famine.

A Twice-told Tale.

Odyss. xii. 451.

Ἐχθρὸν δέ μοί ἐστιν
αὖτις ἀριζήλως εἰρημένα μυθολογεύειν.

And what so tedious as a twice-told tale?

So Matthew (vi. 7)—"Use not vain repetitions."

Honour to the Old.

Odyss. xiii. 141.

Χαλεπὸν δέ κεν εἴη
πρεσβύτατον καὶ ἄριστον ἀτιμίῃσιν ἰάλλειν.

It would be improper to afflict with disgrace the oldest and
worthiest.

So Proverbs (xvi. 31)—" The hoary head is a crown of glory, if it be found
in the way of righteousness."

The Oppressed are Cared for by God.

Odyss. xiii. 213.

Ζεὺς σφέας τίσαιτο ἱκετήσιος, ὅστε καὶ ἄλλους
ἀνθρώπους ἐφορᾷ καὶ τίνυται ὅστις ἁμάρτῃ.

May they be punished by Jove, the protector of suppliants, who
watches over men, and makes those who commit wrong pay a
due penalty.

So Psalm (x. 14)—"Thou beholdest mischief and spite, to requite it with
Thy hand."

Endure what Happens from Necessity.

Odyss. xiii. 306.

Ὅσσα τοι αἶσα δόμοις ἔνι ποιηταῖσιν
κήδε' ἀνασχέσθαι· σὺ δὲ τετλάμεναι καὶ ἀνάγκῃ.

Whatsoever sorrows may be thy doom, bear them with patience
if necessity entail them.

So Hebrews (xii. 1)—"Let us run with patience the race that is set before us;" and James (i. 4)—"Let patience have her perfect work."

Endure.

Odyss. xiii. 309.

Σιωπῇ
πάσχειν ἄλγεα πολλά, βίας ὑποδέγμενος ἀνδρῶν.

Submit in silence to many ills, enduring the violence of men.

So Isaiah (liii. 7)—"He was oppressed and He was afflicted, yet He opened
not His mouth."

I cannot Leave Thee.

Odyss. xiii. 331.

Τῷ σε καὶ οὐ δύναμαι προλιπεῖν δύστηνον ἐόντα.

Wherefore I am not able to leave thee, since thou art unfortunate.

So Psalm (xxxvii. 28)—"The Lord forsaketh not His saints."

"If God be for us."

Odyss. xiii. 389.

Αἴ κέ μοι ὣς μεμαυῖα παρασταίης, γλαυκῶπι,
καί κε τριηκοσίοισιν ἐγὼν ἄνδρεσσι μαχοίμην
σὺν σοί, πότνα θεά, ὅτε μοι πρόφρασσ' ἐπαρήγοις.

Would that thou wouldst stand by me and encourage me, thou

blue-eyed goddess ; with thee on my side would I be willing to encounter three hundred men.

So Psalm (iii 6)—"I will not be afraid of ten thousands of people that have set themselves against me round about ;" and Romans (viii. 31)—"If God be for us, who can be against us?"

THE TORMENT OF A GUILTY CONSCIENCE.

Odyss. xiv. 83.

Οὐ μὲν σχέτλια ἔργα θεοὶ μάκαρες φιλέουσιν,
ἀλλὰ δίκην τίουσι καὶ αἴσιμα ἔργ᾽ ἀνθρώπων.
Καὶ μὲν δυσμενέες καὶ ἀνάρσιοι, οἵτ᾽ ἐπὶ γαίης
ἀλλοτρίης βῶσιν καί σφι Ζεὺς ληΐδα δώῃ,
πλησάμενοι δέ τε νῆας ἔβαν οἶκόνδε νέεσθαι,
καὶ μὲν τοῖς ὄπιδος κρατερὸν δέος ἐν φρεσὶ πίπτει.

The blessed gods love not impious acts, but honour justice and the pious deeds of men ; the foes of peace and scourges of mankind, who overrun the lands of others, given to them by Jove as a prey, filling their vessels with ill-got spoil, proceed homeward, yet great fear of divine vengeance falls upon them.

So Psalm (v. 5)—"Thou art not a God that hath pleasure in wickedness ; neither shall evil dwell with Thee ; Thou hatest all workers of iniquity ;" and (xxxiii. 5)—"Thou lovest righteousness and judgment."

A WIFE LONGING FOR HER LOST HUSBAND.

Odyss. xiv. 122.

Ὦ γέρον, οὔτις κεῖνον ἀνὴρ ἀλαλήμενος ἐλθὼν
ἀγγέλλων πείσειε γυναῖκά τε καὶ φίλον υἱὸν,
ἀλλ᾽ ἄλλως κομιδῆς κεχρημένοι ἄνδρες ἀλῆται
ψεύδοντ᾽, οὐδ᾽ ἐθέλουσιν ἀληθέα μυθήσασθαι.
Ὃς δέ κ᾽ ἀλητεύων Ἰθάκης ἐς δῆμον ἵκηται,
ἐλθὼν ἐς δέσποιναν ἐμὴν ἀπατήλια βάζει·
ἡ δ᾽ εὖ δεξαμένη φιλέει καὶ ἕκαστα μεταλλᾷ,
καί οἱ ὀδυρομένη βλεφάρων ἄπο δάκρυα πίπτει,
ἣ θέμις ἐστὶ γυναικὸς, ἐπὴν πόσις ἄλλοθ᾽ ὄληται.

Old man, it is not every vagrant that coming with his stories can persuade the wife and son ; for needy strangers, that they may have a kind reception, are prone to manufacture stories ; nor do they care to speak the truth. Every vagrant who comes to Ithaca goes to my mistress with his falsehoods. She receives them kindly, inquiring each particular, while tears drop from her eyelids, like a woman who has lost her husband in some foreign land.

K 3

You can Guess the Grain from the Stubble.

Odyss. xiv. 214.

Ἀλλ' ἔμπης καλάμην γέ σ' ὀΐομαι εἰσορόωντα
γιγνώσκειν.

I think that, looking at the stubble, thou mayest guess the
grain.

The Various Employments of Men.

Odyss. xiv. 227.

Αὐτὰρ ἐμοὶ τὰ φίλ' ἔσκε τά που θεὸς ἐν φρεσὶ θῆκεν·
ἄλλος γάρ τ' ἄλλοισιν ἀνὴρ ἐπιτέρπεται ἔργοις.

The things which God suggested were agreeable to me ; for men
take delight in various employments.

So Genesis (iv. 2)—"Abel was a keeper of sheep, and Cain was a tiller
of the ground ;" and Matthew (xxii. 5)—"And went their ways, one to his
farm, another to his merchandise."

"Lie not One to Another."

Odyss. xiv. 364.

Τί σε χρὴ τοῖον ἐόντα
μαψιδίως ψεύδεσθαι ;

Why shouldst thou, being such as thou art, lie rashly ?

So Colossians (iii. 9)—"Lie not one to another."

Enjoy the Present.

Odyss. xiv. 443.

Τέρπεο τοῖσδε,
οἷα πάρεστι· θεὸς δὲ τὸ μὲν δώσει, τὸ δ' ἐάσει.

Enjoy such things as thou hast; for God will give one thing
and one withhold.

So Philippians (iv. 11)—"I have learned, in whatsoever state I am, therewith to be content ;" and Hebrews (xiii. 5)—"Be content with such thingc
as ye have."

Powers of Wine.

Odyss. xiv. 463.

Οἶνος γὰρ ἀνώγει
ἠλεός, ὅστ' ἐφέηκε πολύφρονά περ μάλ' ἀεῖσαι
καί θ' ἁπαλὸν γελάσαι, καί τ' ὀρχήσασθαι ἀνῆκεν,
καί τι ἔπος προέηκεν ὅπερ τ' ἄρρητον ἄμεινον.

For wine leads to folly, making even the wise to laugh immoderately, to dance, and to utter what had better have been kept silent.

So Proverbs (**xx.** 1)—" Wine is a mocker, strong drink is raging ; and whosoever is deceived thereby is not wise ; " and Isaiah (xxviii. 7)—" They have erred through wine, and through strong drink are out of the way."

Woman Married a Second Time.
Odyss. xv. 20.

Οἶσθα γὰρ οἶος θυμὸς ἐνὶ στήθεσσι γυναικός·
κείνου βούλεται οἶκον ὀφέλλειν ὅς κεν ὀπυίῃ,
παίδων δὲ προτέρων καὶ κουριδίοιο φίλοιο
οὐκέτι μέμνηται τεθνηότος οὐδὲ μεταλλᾷ.

For thou knowest the dispositions of women ; whoever marries a second time wishes her family to prosper, forgetting her former children and dead husband, never thinking of them.

So 1 Timothy (v. 9)—"A widow having been the wife of one man ; but the younger widows refuse ; for when they have begun to wax wanton against Christ, they will marry."

" Welcome the Coming, speed the Parting Guest."
Odyss. xv. 70.

Ὃς κ' ἔξοχα μὲν φιλέῃσιν,
ἔξοχα δ' ἐχθαίρῃσιν· ἀμείνω δ' αἴσιμα πάντα.
Ἴσόν τοι κακόν ἐσθ', ὅς τ' οὐκ ἐθέλοντα νέεσθαι
ξεῖνον ἐποτρύνει καὶ ὃς ἐσσύμενον κατερύκει.
[Χρὴ ξεῖνον παρεόντα φιλεῖν, ἐθέλοντα δὲ πέμπειν.]

Who loves too much hates in the same extreme ; the golden mean is to be preferred. It is equally wrong to urge the unwilling to come back and to detain him who desires to depart. True friendship's rule is "to welcome the coming, to speed the parting guest."

So Ecclesiastes (iii. 8)—"A time to love, and a time to hate ; a time of war. and a time of peace ; " and Romans (xii. 13)—"Given to hospitality ; " and Hebrews (xiii. 2.)—" Be not forgetful to entertain strangers ; " and 1 Peter (iv. 9)—" Use hospitality one to another without grudging ; " and Genesis (xviii. 16)—" And Abraham went with them, to bring them on the way ; " and Romans (xv. 24)—" For I trust to see you in my journey, and to be brought on my way thitherward by you ; " and 3 John (6)—" Whom if thou bring forward on their journey, thou shalt do well."

Men of Mean Estate.
Odyss. xv. 319.

Ἑρμείαο ἕκητι διακτόρου, ὅς ῥά τε πάντων
ἀνθρώπων ἔργοισι χάριν καὶ κῦδος ὀπάζει,

δρηστοσύνη οὐκ ἄν μοι ἐρίσσειε βροτὸς ἄλλος,
πῦρ τ᾽ εὖ νηῆσαι διά τε ξύλα δανὰ κεάσσαι,
δαιτρεῦσαί τε καὶ ὀπτῆσαι καὶ οἰνοχοῆσαι,
οἷά τε τοῖς ἀγαθοῖσι παραδρώωσι χέρηες.

With the good-will of the messenger Mercury, who imparts grace and honour to the works of men, few could with me cope in dexterous service, to pile the fire, to split the dry wood, to cut up the carcase, roast the flesh, pour out the wine, offices in which the humble wait upon the rich.

The Emigrant.
Odyss. xv. 342.

Πλαγκτοσύνης δ᾽ οὐκ ἔστι κακώτερον ἄλλο βροτοῖσιν.

There is nothing worse for mortals than a vagabond life.

So Proverbs (xxvii. 8)—" As a bird that wandereth from her nest ; so is a man that wandereth from his place."

Too much Rest.
Odyss. xv. 394.

᾽Ανίη καὶ πολὺς ὕπνος.

For too much rest itself becomes a pain.

So Proverbs vi. 9)—"How long wilt thou sleep, O sluggard ? when wilt thou arise out of thy sleep ? Yet a little sleep, a little slumber, a little folding of the hands to sleep."

The Return of an Only Son.
Odyss. xvi. 17.

Πατὴρ ὃν παῖδα φίλα φρονέων ἀγαπάζει
ἐλθόντ᾽ ἐξ ἀπίης γαίης δεκάτῳ ἐνιαυτῷ,
μοῦνον τηλύγετον, τῷ ἔπ᾽ ἄλγεα πολλὰ μογήσῃ.

The father receiving his only son, the child of his old age, embraces him affectionately, as he returns from some far distant land after an absence of ten years, for whom he has suffered many a bitter pang of anxious care.

So Luke (xv. 20)—" And when he was yet a great way off, his father saw him, and had compassion, and ran and fell on his neck and kissed him."

I Know and Understand.
Odyss. xvi. 136.

Γιγνώσκω, φρονέω· τάγε δὴ νοέοντι κελεύεις.

I know, I understand; thou art giving directions to one who is acquainted with these things.

So Job (xiii. 1)—" Lo, mine eye hath seen all this, mine ear hath heard and understood it. What ye know, the same do I know also : I am not inferior unto you."

GOD INVISIBLE.
Odyss. xvi. 161.

Οὐ γάρ πω πάντεσσι θεοὶ φαίνονται ἐναργεῖς.

For the gods do not make themselves visible to all.

So Exodus (xxxiii. 20)—" Thou canst not see my face : for there shall no man see me and live ; " and 1 Timothy (vi. 16)—" Whom no man hath seen, nor can see."

I AM NOT A GOD.
Odyss. xvi. 187.

Οὔτις τοι θεός εἰμι· τί μ' ἀθανάτοισιν ἐΐσκεις ;

I am no god ; why dost thou liken me to the immortals?

See 2 Kings (v. 7)—" Am I God ? "—and Psalm (lxxxix. 6)—" Who in the heaven can be compared unto the Lord ? "—and Isaiah (xlvi. 5)—" To whom will ye liken me, and make me equal and compare me, that we may be like ? "

THE POWER OF GOD.
Odyss. xvi. 212.

'Ρηΐδιον δὲ θεοῖσι, τοὶ οὐρανὸν εὐρὺν ἔχουσι,
'Η μὲν κυδῆναι θνητὸν βροτὸν, ἠδὲ κακῶσαι.

It is easy for the gods, who inhabit the wide heaven, to raise or cast down mortal man.

See 1 Samuel (ii. 7) ; and 2 Chronicles (xxv. 8)—" God hath power to help and cast down ; " and Psalm (lxxv. 7)—" God is the judge ; He putteth down one and setteth up another ; " and Luke (i. 52)—" He hath put down the mighty from their seats, and exalted them of low degree."

READY SWORDS OFT CAUSE BLOODSHED.
Odyss. xvi. 294.

Αὐτὸς γὰρ ἐφέλκεται ἄνδρα σίδηρος.

The steel blade itself oft incites to deeds of violence.

CONTRIVE NOT EVIL AGAINST ONE ANOTHER.
Odyss. xvi. 423.

Οὐδ' ὅσιη κακὰ ῥάπτειν ἀλλήλοισιν.

Men ought not to devise evils against one another.

So Proverbs (iii. 29)—"Devise not evil against thy neighbour;" and (xxiv. 8)—"He that deviseth to do evil shall be called a mischievous person."

One Rogue is Usher to Another.
Odyss. xvii. 217.

Νῦν μὲν δὴ μάλα πάγχυ κακὸς κακὸν ἡγηλάζει,
ὡς αἰεὶ τὸν ὁμοῖον ἄγει θεὸς ὡς τὸν ὁμοῖον.

Here sure one rogue leads on another ; thus it is that God for evermore links like with like.

So Matthew (xv. 14)—"Blind leaders of the blind."

The Idle.
Odyss. xvii. 226.

Ἀλλ' ἐπεὶ οὖν δὴ ἔργα κάκ' ἔμμαθεν, οὐκ ἐθελήσει
ἔργον ἐποίχεσθαι, ἀλλὰ πτώσσων κατὰ δῆμον
βούλεται αἰτίζων βόσκειν ἣν γαστέρ' ἄναλτον.

Since he has learned evil deeds he will not be willing to turn to labour ; but at the people's heels for ever cowering, he wishes to feed his insatiable belly by begging.

So Proverbs (xix. 24)—"A slothful man hideth his hand in his bosom, and will not so much as bring it to his mouth again."

Bad Shepherds.
Odyss. xvii. 246.

Μῆλα κακοὶ φθείρουσι νομῆες.

Bad shepherds destroy their sheep.

So Ezekiel (xxxiv. 2)—"Woe be to the shepherds, ye eat the fat, and ye clothe you with the wool, ye kill them that are fed, but ye feed not the flock ;" and John (x. 12)—"But he that is an hireling, and not the shepherd, whose own the sheep are not, seeth the wolf coming, and leaveth the sheep, and fleeth ; and the wolf catcheth them, and scattereth the sheep."

Want.
Odyss. xvii. 286.

Γαστέρα δ' οὔπως ἔστιν ἀποκρύψαι μεμαυῖαν,
οὐλομένην, ἢ πολλὰ κάκ' ἀνθρώποισι δίδωσιν,
τῆς ἕνεκεν καὶ νῆες ἐΰζυγοι ὁπλίζονται
πόντον ἐπ' ἀτρυγετον, κακὰ δυσμενέεσσι φέρουσαι.

It is not possible for the hungry belly to conceal her wants, causing unnumbered woes to mortals, for which well-benched galleys are equipped for the barren sea, bearing ills to the enemy.

So Ecclesiastes (vi. 7)—" All the labour of man is for his mouth, and yet the appetite is not filled."

PLAYTHINGS OF THE GREAT.
Odyss. xvii. 306.

Εὔμαι', ἦ μάλα θαῦμα, κύων ὅδε κεῖτ' ἐνὶ κόπρῳ.
Καλὸς μὲν δέμας ἐστὶν, ἀτὰρ τόδε γ' οὐ σάφα οἶδα,
εἰ δὴ καὶ ταχὺς ἔσκε θέειν ἐπὶ εἴδεϊ τῷδε, '
ἢ αὔτως οἷοί τε τραπεζῆες κύνες ἀνδρῶν
γίγνοντ'· ἀγλαΐης δ' ἕνεκεν κομέουσιν ἄνακτες.

Eumœus, surely this is very wonderful, this dog lies in the dirt, beauteous in form, but I do not know whether or not he was swift in running as he is handsome, or like those lap-dogs which the rich keep for their beauty.

A SLAVE.
Odyss. xvii. 322.

Ἥμισυ γάρ τ' ἀρετῆς ἀποαίνυται εὐρύοπα Ζεὺς
ἀνέρος, εὖτ' ἄν μιν κατὰ δούλιον ἦμαρ ἕλῃσιν.

For loud-thundering Jove takes away half the worth of a man when he has made him a slave.

So Proverbs (xxix. 19)—" A servant will not be corrected by words; for though he understand, he will not answer."

THE BEGGAR.
Odyss. xvii. 347.

Αἰδὼς δ' οὐκ ἀγαθὴ κεχρημένῳ ἀνδρὶ παρεῖναι.

Modesty is not good for a needy beggar.

So Luke (xi. 8)—" Though he will not rise and give him, because he is his friend, yet because of his importunity, he will rise and give him as many as he needeth."
See Sirach (xl. 30).

PRUDENCE NOT EQUAL TO BEAUTY.
Odyss. xvii. 454.

Ὦ πόποι, οὐκ ἄρα σοίγ' ἐπὶ εἴδεϊ καὶ φρένες ἦσαν.

My good friend, thy wisdom is not equal to thy good looks.

So Proverbs (xi. 22)—" As a jewel of gold in a swine's snout, so is a fair woman which is without discretion."

GOD PROTECTS THE POOR.

Odyss. xvii. 475.

Πτωχῶν γε θεοὶ καὶ Ἐρινύες εἰσίν.

The gods and avenging Furies are the protectors of the poor.

So Psalm (xii. 5)—" For the oppression of the poor, for the sighing of the needy, now will I arise, saith the Lord ;" and (lix. 33)—" For the Lord heareth the poor."

GOD WATCHES THE INJUSTICE OF MEN.

Odyss. xvii. 485.

Καὶ τοὶ θεοὶ ξείνοισιν ἐοικότες ἀλλοδαποῖσιν
παντοῖοι τελέθοντες, ἐπιστρωφῶσι πόληας,
ἀνθρώπων ὕβριν τε καὶ εὐνομίην ἐφορῶντες.

The gods, like strangers from some foreign land, assuming different forms, wander through cities, watching the injustice and justice of men.

So Proverbs (xv. 3)—" The eyes of the Lord are in every place, beholding the evil and the good ; " and Acts (xiv. 11)—" The gods are come down to us in the likeness of men."

ENVY NOT THY NEIGHBOUR'S PROPERTY.

Odyss. xviii. 17.

Οὐδέ τί σε χρὴ
ἀλλοτρίων φθονέειν.

Thou oughtest not to envy the wealth of thy neighbour.

So Matthew (xx. 15)—" Is it not lawful for me to do what I will with mine own ? Is thine eye evil, because I am good ? "

MAN SUBJECT TO VICISSITUDES.

Odyss. xviii. 130.

Οὐδὲν ἀκιδνότερον γαῖα τρέφει ἀνθρώποιο,
πάντων ὅσσα τε γαῖαν ἔπι πνείει τε καὶ ἔρπει.
Οὐ μὲν γάρ ποτέ φησι κακὸν πείσεσθαι ὀπίσσω,
ὄφρ' ἀρετὴν παρέχωσι θευὶ καὶ γούνατ' ὀρώρῃ·
ἀλλ' ὅτε δὴ καὶ λυγρὰ θεοὶ μάκαρες τελέσωσιν,
καὶ τὰ φέρει ἀεκαζόμενος τετληότι θυμῷ.
Τοῖος γὰρ νόος ἐστὶν ἐπιχθονίων ἀνθρώπων
οἷον ἐπ' ἦμαρ ἄγῃσι πατὴρ ἀνδρῶν τε θεῶν τε.

The earth produces nothing feebler than man, of all that breathes or creeps on earth ; for he thinks himself exempt from evil in years to come, while the gods give him strength and his knees are able to support him. But when the blest gods bring sorrow, he is unwilling to bear it with patience. For men are such as the Father of men and gods wills it.

So Job (xxv. 6); and Psalm (xxxix. 5)—"Verily every man at his best state is altogether vanity;" and (xc. 5) — "Thou carriest them away as with a flood; they are as a sleep: in the morning they are like grass which groweth up. In the morning it flourisheth, and groweth up; in the evening it is cut down, and withereth;" and (xxx. 6)—"And in my prosperity I said, I shal. never be moved;" and Psalm (xxxi. 15)—"My times are in Thy hand;" and Ecclesiastes (vii. 14)—"In the day of prosperity be joyful. but in the day of adversity consider: God also hath set the one over against the other, to the end that man should find nothing after Him."

To Sorrow without Ceasing.

Odyss. xviii. 174.

Κάκιον πενθήμεναι ἄκριτον αἰεί.

It is wrong to sorrow without ceasing.

So 2 Corinthians (ii. 7)—"Lest perhaps such an one should be swallowed up with overmuch sorrow;" and (vii. 10)—"The sorrow of the world worketh death."

"I Thought as a Child."

Odyss. xviii. 228.

Αὐτὰρ ἐγὼ θυμῷ νοέω καὶ οἶδα ἕκαστα,
ἐσθλά τε καὶ τὰ χέρηα· πάρος δ' ἔτι νήπιος ἦα.
'Αλλὰ τοι οὐ δύναμαι πεπνυμένα πάντα νοῆυαι.

But I know and understand everything, good and bad : in days gone by I was a mere child, yet I am not able to perceive what is prudent in all circumstances.

So 1 Corinthians (xiii. 11)—"When I was a child, I spake as a child, I understood as a child I thought as a child: but when I became a man, I put away childish things;" and (xiii. 9)—"We know in part."

A Hypocrite.

Odyss. xviii. 282.

Θέλγε δὲ θυμὸν
μειλιχίοις ἐπέεσσι, νόος δέ οἱ ἄλλα μενοίνα.

He soothed him with honeyed words, but his intentions were far otherwise.

So Psalm (xxviii. 3)—"Which speak peace to their neighbours, but mischief is in their hearts;" and Jeremiah (ix. 8)—"One speaketh peaceably to his neighbours with his mouth, but in heart he layeth his wait."

To Reject a Gift.
Odyss. xviii. 287.

Οὐ γὰρ καλὸν ἀνήνασθαι δόσιν ἐστίν.

It is not good to refuse a gift.

So 1 Timothy (iv. 4)—" For every creature of God is good, and nothing to be refused, if it be received with thanksgiving."

Effects of Wine.
Odyss. xviii. 331.

Ἦ ῥά σε οἶνος ἔχει φρένας, ἤ νύ τοι αἰεὶ
τοιοῦτος νόος ἐστίν· ὁ καὶ μεταμώνια βάζεις.

Surely wine possesses thy senses, or else thou art always such as to speak in a foolish way.

So Isaiah (xxviii. 7)—" They also have erred through wine, and through strong drink are out of the way;" and Acts (ii. 13)—" Others mocking said, These men are full of new wine."

Attend to your Household Affairs.
Odyss. xix. 21.

Αἲ γὰρ δή ποτε, τέκνον, ἐπιφροσύνας ἀνέλοιο
οἴκου κήδεσθαι καὶ κτήματα πάντα φυλάσσειν.

I wish, my son, that thou wouldst look with care after thy household, and guard all thy possessions.

So Proverbs (xxvii. 23)—" Be thou diligent to know the state of thy flocks, and look well to thy herds;" and 1 Timothy (iii. 4)—"One that ruleth well his own house."

The Idle.
Odyss. xix. 27.

Οὐ γὰρ ἀεργὸν ἀνέξομαι ὅς κεν ἐμῆς γε
Χοίνικος ἅπτηται, καὶ τηλόθεν εἰληλουθώς.

I shall not allow any one to be idle who lives at my expense, though he has come from far.

So Genesis (iii. 19)—" In the sweat of thy face shalt thou eat bread ;" and Proverbs (xx. 4)—" The sluggard will not plow by reason of the cold ; therefore shall he beg in harvest, and have nothing;" and 2 Thessalonians (iii. 10)—" If any would not work, neither should he eat."

Confusion of Tongues.
Odyss. xix. 175.

Ἄλλη δ' ἄλλων γλῶσσα μεμιγμένη.

There was a great confusion of tongues.

So Genesis (xi. 9)—" There the Lord did confound the language of all the earth ; " and Acts (ii. 4)—" They began to speak with other tongues."

SHORTNESS OF LIFE.

Odyss. xix. 328.

Ἀνθρωποι δὲ μινυνθάδιοι τελέθουσιν.

Mortals have a short span of life.

So Job (viii. 9)—" For we are but of yesterday, and know nothing, because our days upon earth are a shadow ; " and xiv. 1); and Psalm (xxxix. 5)— " Behold, thou hast made my days as an hand-breadth, and mine age is as nothing before Thee : verily every man at his best state is altogether vanity ; " and (xc. 10)—" The days of our years are threescore years and ten ; and if by reason of strength they be fourscore years, yet is their strength labour and sorrow : for it is soon cut off, and we fly away."

BE PATIENT.

Odyss. xx. 18.

Τέτλαθι δή, κραδίη· καὶ κύντερον ἄλλο ποτ' ἔτλης.

Be patient, my soul ; thou hast at another time suffered something still worse than this.

So Psalm (xlii. 5)—" Why art thou cast down, O my soul? and why art thou disquieted in me ? " and Romans (v. 4,—" And patience worketh experience : and experience, hope."

GOD KNOWS ALL THINGS.

Odyss. xx. 75.

'Ο γάρ τ' εὖ οἶδεν ἅπαντα,
μοῖράν τ' ἀμμορίην τε καταθνητῶν ἀνθρώπων.

For God knows all things well, the evil and good that befalls men.

So Psalm (cxxxix. 1-4)—" O Lord, Thou hast searched me, and known me. Thou knowest my down-sitting and mine up-rising : Thou understandest my thought afar off. Thou compassest my path, and my lying down, and art acquainted with all my ways. For there is not a word in my tongue, but, lo, O Lord, Thou knowest it altogether."

EVEN KINGS SUFFER CALAMITIES.

Odyss. xx. 195.

'Αλλὰ θεοὶ δυόωσι πολυπλάγκτους ἀνθρώπους,
ὑππότε καὶ βασιλεῦσιν ἐπικλώσωνται ὀϊζύν.

The gods overwhelm those men with misfortunes who ramble about, when even on kings they impose toil.

So Job (v. 6)—"Although affliction cometh not forth of the dust, neither doth trouble spring out of the ground."

They Smiled against their Inclination.

Odyss. xx. 347.

Οἱ δ' ἤδη γναθμοῖσι γελοίων ἀλλοτρίοισιν.

They smiled with the jaws of another.

So Proverbs (xiv. 13)—"Even in laughter the heart is sorrowful, and the end of that mirth is heaviness."

Do not Put off by Pretexts.

Odyss. xxi. 111.

'Αλλ' ἄγε μὴ μύνῃσι παρέλκετε.

But come, do not put off under false pretexts.

So Proverbs (iii. 28)—"Say not unto thy neighbour, Go, and come again, and to-morrow I will give ; when thou hast it by thee."

Better to Die than to Live.

Odyss. xxi. 154.

Πολὺ φέρτερόν ἐστιν
τεθνάμεν ἢ ζώοντας ἁμαρτεῖν, οὔθ' ἔνεκ' αἰεὶ
ἐνθάδ' ὁμιλέομεν, ποτιδέγμενοι ἤματα πάντα.

It is much better to die than to live, being baulked in our objects about which we are always employed, living in hope every day.

So 1 Corinthians (ix 15)—"It were better for me to die, than that any man should make my glorying void."

To Perish by our own Folly.

Odyss. xxi. 301.

'Ο δὲ φρεσὶν ᾗσιν ἀασθεὶς
ᾔεν ἣν ἄτην ὀχέων ἀεσίφρονι θυμῷ.

He proceeded on, destroyed by his own folly, bearing his own evils in his arrogant mind.

So Galatians (vi. 5)—"Every man shall bear his own burden."

Thou shalt Suffer what thou Intendest for Another.

Odyss. xxii. 218.

Οἶα μενοινᾶς
ἔρδειν ἐν μεγάροις· σῷ δ' αὐτοῦ κράτι τίσεις.

What thou thoughtest to perpetrate, that thou shalt suffer in thy own person.

So Psalm (vii. 16)—" His mischief shall return upon his own head ;" and 1 Kings (ii. 44)—" The Lord shall return thy wickedness upon thine own head."

To Bring Death by Wicked Conduct.

Odyss. xxii. 317.

'Αλλά μοι οὐ πείθοντο κακῶν ἄπο χεῖρας ἔχεσθαι·
τῷ καὶ ἀτασθαλίῃσιν ἀεικέα πότμον ἐπέσπον.

But they did not obey me to keep their hands from evil, therefore they met a shameful death for their folly.

So Proverbs (xi. 3)—" The perverseness of transgressors shall destroy them ;" and (xiii. 6)—" Wickedness overthroweth the sinner."

Insult not the Dead.

Odyss. xxii. 412.

Οὐχ ὁσίη κταμένοισιν ἐπ' ἀνδράσιν εὐχετάασθαι.

It is impious to insult the dead.

So Proverbs (xxiv. 17)—" Rejoice not when thine enemy falleth, and let not thine heart be glad when he stumbleth."

A Stony Heart.

Odyss. xxiii. 103.

Σοὶ δ' αἰεὶ κραδίη στερεωτέρη ἐστὶ λίθοιο.

Thy heart is always harder than stone.

So Ezekiel (xi. 19)—" I will take the stony heart out of their flesh."

The Poor Man is Despised.

Odyss. xxiii. 115.

Νῦν δ' ὅττι ῥυπόω, κακὰ δὲ χροῒ εἵματα εἷμαι,
τοὔνεκ ἀτιμάζει με καὶ οὔπω φησὶ τὸν εἶναι.

Now. because I am in squalor, and clothed in rags, he despises me, and says that I am not the person I assume to be.

So James (ii. 2)—"For if there come unto your assembly a man with a gold ring, in goodly apparel, and there come in also a poor man in vile raiment ; and ye have respect to him that weareth the gay clothing, and say unto him, Sit thou here in a good place ; and say to the poor, Stand thou there, or Sit here under my footstool."

His Fame shall never Perish.

Odyss. xxiv. 195.

Τῷ οἱ κλέος οὔποτ' ὀλεῖται
ἧς ἀρετῆς, τεύξουσι δ' ἐπιχθονίοισιν ἀοιδὴν
ἀθάνατοι χαρίεσσαν ἐχέφρονι Πηνελοπείῃ.

The fame of his virtuous deeds shall never be forgotten, while the gods will in beauteous song preserve the name of wise Penelope.

So Psalm (cxii. 6)—"The righteous shall be in everlasting remembrance ;" and Proverbs (x. 7)—" The memory of the just is blessed."

A Wise Son.

Odyss. xxiv. 514.

Τίς νύ μοι ἡμέρη ἥδε, θεοὶ φίλοι; ἦ μάλα χαίρω·
υἱός δ' υἱωνός τ' ἀρετῆς πέρι δῆριν ἔχουσιν.

What a joyful day is this, ye friendly gods ! I am in the height of joy : my son and grandson are contending for the prize of merit.

So Proverbs (x. 1)—"A wise son maketh a glad father."

LONGINUS.

BORN ABOUT A.D. 213—DIED A.D. 273.

LONGINUS, a distinguished Greek philosopher of the third century of our era, is believed to have been born at Athens, where he was educated by his uncle, Phronto, and on his death he inherited his fortune. He had travelled through various countries with his parents, and got acquainted with all the principal philosophers of his time, of whom the most distinguished were Ammonius Saccas,

Origen, Plotinus, and Amelius. He then settled at Athens, where he collected a large number of pupils, to whose instruction he devoted himself with such zeal that he had little time for the composition of any literary production. Towards the end of his life he travelled to the East, and was induced to remain at Palmyra in the service of Queen Zenobia. He encouraged her to assert her independence, and is said to have dictated a spirited letter to the Emperor Aurelian, renouncing the allegiance of the Romans. When Aurelian took the city of Palmyra, A.D. 273, Longinus was given up to the Romans, who ordered him to be executed, a fate to which he submitted with the utmost firmness. Of all his works, which were numerous, all that has come down to us consists of a considerable part of his work "On the Sublime."

In what does Man most Resemble the Gods ?
De Subl. i.

Ἐν γὰρ δὴ ὁ ἀποποφηνάμενος τί θεοῖς ὅμοιον ἔχομεν, " Εὐεργεσίαν, εἶπε, καὶ ἀλήθειαν."

For well did Pythagoras answer the question, " In what do we most resemble the gods? " when he replied, " In doing good and speaking truth."

So Proverbs (xiv. 22)—"Mercy and truth be to them that devise good ;" and Ephesians (vi. 14)—"Stand, having your loins girt about with truth ;" and Psalm (xcviii. 3)—" He hath remembered His mercy and His truth."

The Sublime.
De Subl. i.

Ὕψος δέ που καιρίως ἐξενεχθὲν τά τε πράγματα δίκην σκηπτοῦ πάντα διεφόρησεν, καὶ τὴν τοῦ ῥήτορος εὐθὺς ἀθρόαν ἐνεδείξατο δύναμιν.

But the sublime, when it is introduced at a seasonable moment, has often carried all before it with the rapidity of lightning, and shown at a glance the mighty power of genius.

[This sentence, in the original, has always been regarded as a fine specimen in itself of the sublime, and has often been quoted to show what power the very position of words has to give beauty. The structure of the words at the close of the sentence is admirable. They trip along hurriedly, from the concourse of short vowels This represents, in an admirable manner, the rapid motion either of lighting or of the sublime.]

See (**Fr.**) Sublime.

Genius.
De Subl. ii.

Δεῖ γὰρ αὐτοῖς, ὡς κέντρον πολλάκις, οὕτω δὴ καὶ χαλινοῦ.

Genius may at times want the spur, but it stands as often in need of the curb.

From the Sublime to the Ridiculous.
De Subl. iii.

Ἐκ τοῦ φοβεροῦ κατ᾽ ὀλίγον ὑπονοστεῖ πρὸς τὸ εὐκαταφρόνητον.

Little by little we depart from the terrible and reach the ridiculous.

[Napoleon adopted this idea when he said, "Du sublime au ridicule il n'y a qu'un pas."]

See (Fr.) Napoleon I.

Great Attempts.
De Subl. iii.

Πειθόμενοι τῷ, Μεγάλων ἀπολισθαίνειν ὅμως εὐγενὲς ἁμάρτημα.

They call to remembrance the maxim, that "In great attempts 'tis glorious e'en to fall."

See (Lat.) Great undertakings.

Puerility.
De Subl. iii.

Τί ποτ᾽ οὖν τὸ μειρακιῶδές ἐστιν; ἢ δῆλον, ὡς σχολαστικὴ νόησις, ὑπὸ περιεργασίας λήγουσα εἰς ψυχρότητα. Ὀλισθαίνουσι δ᾽ εἰς τοῦτο τὸ γένος ὀρεγόμενοι μὲν τοῦ περιττοῦ καὶ πεποιημένου, δὲ μάλιστα τοῦ ἡδέος, ὑποκέλλοντες δὲ εἰς ῥωπικὸν καὶ κακόζηλον.

What is the idea implied in puerility? Why, it is certainly nothing more than the expressions and ideas that naturally occur to a schoolboy, and which become flat and insipid from being over-wrought. And those persons are apt to fail in this particular who, aiming at an over-subtle, accurate, and, above all, a sweet style, imperceptibly degenerate into vulgar language and frothy affectation.

What is Really Sublime?
De Subl. vii.

Τοῦτο γὰρ τῷ ὄντι μέγα, οὗ πολλὴ μὲν ἡ ἀναθεώρησις, δύσκολος δέ, μᾶλλον δ᾽ ἀδύνατος ἡ κατεξανάστασις· ἰσχυρὰ δ᾽ ἡ μνήμη καὶ δυσεξάλειπτος. Ὅλως καὶ καλὰ νόμιζε ὕψη τὰ ἀληθινὰ τὰ διαπαντὸς ἀρέσκοντα καὶ πᾶσιν· ὅταν γὰρ τοῖς ἀπὸ διαφόρων ἐπιτηδευμάτων, βίων, ζήλων, ἡλικιῶν, λόγων, ἕν τι καὶ ταυτὸν ἅμα περὶ τῶν αὐτῶν δοκῇ, τόθ᾽ ἡ ἐξ ἀσυμφώνων ὡς κρίσις καὶ συγκατάθεσις τὴν ἐπὶ τῷ θαυμαζομένῳ πίστιν ἰσχυρὰν λαμβάνει καὶ ἀναμφίλεκτον.

That is really grand and sublime which, the more we consider, the more difficult, nay, I would say impossible, it is to withstand; the impression of which sinks so deep, and is so engraven on the mind, that it cannot be effaced. In a word, you may pronounce that to be truly and really sublime which pleases at all times, and delights all kinds of men. For when men of different pursuits, modes of life, inclinations, ages, and reasoning powers, all unite in admiration of a particular work, then this united assent, and combination of so many different judgments, stamps a high and unequivocal value on that work which meets with such admiration.

GREATEST THOUGHTS UTTERED BY THE GREATEST SOULS.
De Subl. ix.

Οὐδὲ γὰρ οἷόν τε μικρὰ καὶ δουλοπρεπῆ φρονοῦντας καὶ ἐπιτηδεύοντας παρὰ ὅλον τὸν βίον θαυμαστόν τι καὶ τοῦ παντὸς αἰῶνος ἐξενεγκεῖν ἄξιον· μεγάλοι δὲ οἱ λόγοι τούτων κατὰ τὸ εἰκός, ὧν ἂν ἐμβριθεῖς ὦσιν αἱ ἔννοιαι.

For it is impossible for those who have low, mean, and grovelling ideas, and who have spent their lives in mercenary employments, to produce anything worthy of admiration, or to be a possession for all times. Grand and dignified expressions must be looked for from those, and those alone, whose thoughts are ever employed on glorious and noble objects.

LET THERE BE LIGHT.
De Subl. ix.

Ταύτῃ καὶ ὁ τῶν Ἰουδαίων θεσμοθέτης, οὐχ ὁ τυχὼν ἀνήρ, ἐπειδὴ τὴν τοῦ θείου δύναμιν κατὰ τὴν ἀξίαν ἐχώρησε, κᾀξέφηνεν, εὐθὺς ἐν τῇ εἰσβολῇ γράψας τῶν νόμων, " Εἶπεν ὁ θεὸς " φησί· τί; " γενέσθω φῶς καὶ ἐγένετο· γενέσθω γῆ καὶ ἐγένετο."

In the same way the Jewish lawgiver, a man of no ordinary genius, when he had conceived in his mind a just idea of the grandeur of the Supreme Being, has given expression to it in noble language, in the beginning of his work containing His laws:— " And God said," " What?" " Let there be light : and there was light. Let the earth be : and the earth was."

So Genesis (i. 3)—"And God said, Let there be light : and there was light."

HOMER.
De Subl. ix.

Ὅθεν ἐν τῇ Ὀδυσσείᾳ παραεικάσαι τις ἂν καταδυομένῳ τὸν Ὅμηρον ἡλίῳ, οὗ δίχα τῆς σφοδρότητος παραμένει τὸ μέγεθος.

So that, in the Odyssey, we may liken Homer with justice to

the setting sun, whose glory, indeed, still remains, though the excessive heat of his beams has abated.

See (Lat.) Homer sometimes nods.

SUBLIME SPIRIT OF THE ANCIENTS.

De Subl. xiii.

Οὕτως ἀπὸ τῆς τῶν ἀρχαίων μεγαλοφυΐας εἰς τὰς τῶν ζηλούντων ἐκείνους ψυχὰς, ὡς ἀπὸ ἱερῶν στομίων, ἀπόρροιαί τινες φέρονται, ὑφ' ὧν ἐπ πνεόμενοι, καὶ οἱ μὴ λίαν φοιβαστικοὶ, τῷ ἑτέρων συνενθουσιῶσι μεγέθει.

In like manner, from the sublime and lofty spirit of the ancients there flow certain emanations, like vapours from the sacred vents, which penetrate imperceptibly into the breasts of imitators, inspiring those who are not distinguished for genius with the fire and vigour of others.

FEELINGS OF AN AUTHOR RESPECTING HIS WORK.

De Subl. xiv.

Εἰ δέ τις αὐτόθεν φοβοῖτο, μὴ τοῦ ἰδίου βίου καὶ χρόνου οὐ φθέγξαιτό τι ὑπερήμερον, ἀνάγκη καὶ τὰ συλλαμβανόμενα ὑπὸ τῆς τούτου ψυχῆς ἀτελῆ καὶ τυφλὰ ὥσπερ ἀμβλοῦσθαι, πρὸς τὸν τῆς ὑστεροφημίας, ὅλης μὴ τελεσφορούμενα χρόνον.

For if any man, at the very moment he is composing a work, should be filled with dread lest he should be producing what will not live beyond his own life and time, it must necessarily be that the labours of such a man, who feels so little confidence in himself that he cannot look forward to the esteem and applause of succeeding ages, should be imperfect and abortive.

FANCY IN ORATORY.

De Subl. xv.

Τί οὖν ἡ ῥητορικὴ φαντασία δύναται; πολλὰ μεν ἴσως καὶ ἄλλα τοῖς λόγοις ἐναγώνια καὶ ἐμπαθῆ προσεισφέρειν.

What, then, is the use of allowing full play to the fancy in oratory? It is, perhaps, that it enables us to make our speeches impassioned and full of vigour.

IT IS AN ART TO CONCEAL ART.

De Subl. xxii.

Τότε γὰρ ἡ τέχνη τέλειος, ἡνίκ' ἂν φύσις εἶναι δοκῇ, ἡ δ' αὖ φύσις ἐπιτυχὴς. ὅταν λανθάνουσαν περιέχῃ τὴν τέχνην.

For art may then be termed perfect and complete, when it seems to be nature ; and nature then is most successful, when she conceals what aid she receives from art.

What Nature designed Man for.
De Subl. xxxv.

Ἡ φύσις οὐ ταπεινὸν ἡμᾶς ζῷον, οὐδ' ἀγενὲς ἔκρινε τὸν ἄνθρωπον, ἀλλ' ὡς εἰς μεγάλην τινὰ πανήγυριν, εἰς τὸν βίον καὶ εἰς τὸν σύμπαντα κόσμον ἐπάγουσα, θεατάς τινας τῶν ὅλων αὐτῆς ἐσομένους καὶ φιλοτιμωτάτους ἀγωνιστάς, εὐθὺς ἄμαχον ἔρωτα ἐνέφυσεν ἡμῖν ταῖς ψυχαῖς παντὸς ἀεὶ τοῦ μεγάλου καὶ ὡς πρὸς ἡμᾶς δαιμονιωτέρου.

Nature never meant man to be a low, grovelling creature ; but, placing him in the world, as in a wide and crowded theatre, intended that he should be the spectator of her mighty works, giving him an eager desire for every honourable pursuit. From the first moment of his birth, she implanted in his soul an inextinguishable love for all that is good and noble, and a constant longing to approach nearer to the Divine nature.

Free Government the Nurse of Genius.
De Subl. xliv.

Ἦ, νὴ Δία, πιστευτέον ἐκείνῳ τῷ θρυλλουμένῳ, ὡς ἡ δημοκρατία τῶν μεγάλων ἀγαθὴ τιθηνὸς, ᾗ μόνῃ σχεδὸν καὶ συνήκμασαν οἱ περὶ λόγους δεινοὶ καὶ συναπέθανον ; Θρέψαι τε γὰρ, φησὶν, ἱκανὴ τὰ φρονήματα τῶν μεγαλοφρόνων ἡ ἐλευθερία τὸ ἐφελκύσαι, καὶ ἅμα διωθεῖν τὸ πρόθυμον τῆς πρὸς ἀλλήλους ἔριδος καὶ τῆς περὶ τὰ πρωτεῖα φιλοτιμίας. Ἔτι γε μὴν διὰ τὰ προκείμενα ἐν ταῖς πολιτείαις ἔπαθλα ἑκάστοτε τὰ ψυχικὰ προτερήματα τῶν ῥητόρων μελετώμενα ἀκονᾶται, καὶ οἷον ἐκτρίβεται, καὶ τοῖς πράγμασι κατὰ τὸ εἰκὸς ἐλεύθερα συνεκλάμπει.

Must we at last give credit to that common observation so highly praised, that free government is the true nurse of genius, and that in such a state alone do perfect orators flourish, and with it decline or die? For Liberty, it is said, is alone fitted to bring out the noble thoughts of men of genius, filling them with hopes of success, with a generous emulation and desire for victory. And above all, as the labours of orators are nobly rewarded in free states, it brings into full play the innate powers of their mind, which are sharpened and polished by constant practice ; and the freedom of their thoughts, as might be expected, shines forth clearly in the liberty of their debates.

See (Lat.) Liberty.

SLAVERY.
De Subl. xliv.

Οὕτως ἅπασαν δουλείαν, κἄν ᾖ δικαιοτάτη, ψυχῆς γλωττόκομον
καὶ κοινὸν δή τις ἀποφήναιτο δεσμωτήριον.

Slavery, however easy may be its chains, cannot be altogether
divested of its bitterness, and can only be regarded as a prison of
the soul, and a public dungeon.

See (Lat.) Death to be preferred to slavery.

LOVE OF MONEY AND LOVE OF PLEASURE.
De Subl. xliv.

Φιλαργυρία μὲν νόσημα μικροποιὸν, φιληδονία δ' ἀγεννέστατον.

For love of money is the disease which renders us most pitiful
and grovelling, and love of pleasure is that which renders us most
despicable.

See (Lat.) Money.

MENANDER.

BORN B.C. 342—DIED B.C. 291.

MENANDER, the most celebrated poet of the new comedy, was a
native of Athens, son of Diopeithes and Hegesistrate, flourishing
in the time of the successors of Alexander. He was born the same
year his father commanded the Athenian forces on the Hellespont,
against Philip of Macedon. He was educated under the eye of his
paternal uncle, Alexis, the comic poet, and received instruction
from Theophrastus, the philosopher. He was the intimate friend
of Epicurus, enjoyed the friendship of Demetrius Phalereus, and
was greatly admired by the first Greek king of Egypt, Ptolemy,
the son of Lagus. He is said to have been drowned while he was
swimming in the harbour of Peiræeus, near which he had an
estate. Notwithstanding his fame as a poet, his public dramatic
career, during his lifetime, was not particularly successful; for,
though he composed upwards of a hundred comedies, he only
gained the prize eight times.

[Fragmenta Comicorum Græcorum, collegit et disposuit Augustus
Meineke, Berohn. 1847.]

The Bachelor is Happy.

Adelph. 1.

Ὦ μακάριόν μ' ὅστις γυναῖκ' οὐ λαμβάνω.

Happy am I, who have no wife.

So Terence ("Adelph." i. 1, 18)—

" Quod fortunatum isti putant,
Uxorem nunquam habui."

Children to be Bound to you by Gentleness.

Adelph. 2.

Οὐ λυποῦντα δεῖ
παιδάριον ὀρθοῦν, ἀλλὰ καὶ πείθοντά τι.

We ought to lead our child to the right path, not by severity,
but by persuasion.

See (Lat.) Children.

The Relatives of the Poor.

Adelph. 7.

Ἔργον εὑρεῖν συγγενῆ
πένητὸς ἐστιν. Οὐδεὶς γὰρ ὁμολογεῖ
αὐτῷ προσήκειν τὸν βοηθείας τινὸς
δεόμενον. Αἰτεῖσθαι γὰρ ἅμα τι προσδοκᾷ.

It is difficult to discover the relatives of a poor man, for no one
likes to acknowledge his relationship with one who is in want, lest
he should be asked for assistance.

The Poor.

Adelph. 9.

Πρὸς ἅπαντα δειλὸς ὁ πενής ἐστι πράγματα,
καὶ πάντας αὐτοῦ καταφρονεῖν ὑπολαμβάνει.
Ὁ δὲ μετρίως πράττων περισκελέστερον
ἅπαντα τ' ἀνιαρὰ, Λαμπρία, φέρει.

The poor man is full of fears, and imagines himself despised by
all mankind. The man who enjoys only a moderate fortune is apt
to look on the dark side of life.

See (Lat.) The poor are suspicious of neglect.

THE POOR.
Piscat. 5.

Πρῶτος εὑρὼν διατροφὴν πτωχῷ τέχνην,
πολλοὺς ἐποίησεν ἀθλίους. Ἁπλοῦν γὰρ ἦν
τὸν μὴ δυνάμενον ζῆν ἀλύπως, ἀποθανεῖν.

Whoever first discovered the means to support the poor increased the number of the miserable; for it would have been more simple for the man who could not live happily to die.

A DAUGHTER.
Piscat. 6.

Χαλεπόν γε θυγάτηρ κτῆμα, καὶ δυσδιάθετον.

A daughter is an embarrassing and ticklish possession.

So Sheridan ("The Duenna," act i. sc. 3)—
  "If a daughter you have, she's the plague of your life,
  No peace shall you know, though you've buried your wife!
  At twenty she mocks at the duty you taught her—
  Oh, what a plague is an obstinate daughter!"

HAIL, FATHERLAND!
Piscat. 8.

Χαῖρ' ὦ φίλη γῆ, διὰ χρόνου πολλοῦ σ' ἰδών
ἀσπάζομαι· τουτὶ γὰρ οὐ πᾶσαν ποιῶ
τὴν γῆν, ὅταν δὲ τοὐμὸν ἐσίδω χωρίον·
τὸ γὰρ τρέφον με τοῦτ' ἐγὼ κρίνω θεόν.

Hail, beloved land! I embrace thee, seeing thee after a long time; for it is not every land I so address, but only when I see my own; for what supports me with food, that I regard as a god.

So Scott ("Lay of the Last Minstrel," can. vi. st. 1)—
  "Breathes there the man with soul so dead,
  Who never to himself has said—
  This is my own, my native land?"

LOVE.
Andria. i.

      Τὸ ἐρᾶν ἐπισκοτεῖ
ἅπασιν, ὡς ἔοικε, καὶ τοῖς εὐλόγως,
καὶ τοῖς κακῶς ἔχουσι.

Love blinds all men, both those who act reasonably and those who act foolishly.

See (Lat.) Love blinds mankind.

Habits.
Androg. 3.

Τὸ γὰρ σύνηθες οὐδαμοῦ παροπτέον.

For habits are never to be neglected.

See (Lat.) Habit.

The Events of Life.
Androg. 4.

Τὰ προσπεσόντα προσδοκᾶν ἄπαντα δεῖ
ἄνθρωπον ὄντα. Παραμένει γὰρ οὐδὲ ἔν.

Man must be prepared for every event of life, for there is
nothing that is durable.

See (Lat.) Life, changes of.

Son and Daughter.
Consob. 2.

Εὐδαιμονίας τοῦτ᾽ ἔστιν υἱὸς νοῦν ἔχων·
ἀλλὰ θυγάτηρ κτῆμ᾽ ἐστὶν ἐργῶδες πατρί.

A wise son is a delight to his father, while a daughter is a
troublesome possession.

So Proverbs (x. 1)—" A wise son maketh a glad father; but a foolish son
is the heaviness of his mother."

God.
Arreph. 6.

Πάντ᾽ ἐστὶ τῷ καλῷ λόγῳ
ἱερόν· ὁ νοῦς γὰρ ἐστιν ὁ λαλήσων Θεῷ.

All places are the temple of God, for it is the mind which prays
to God.

So Acts (vii. 48)—Howbeit the most High dwelleth not in temples made
with hands ; as saith the prophet, Heaven is my throne, and earth is my
footstool : what house will ye build me ? saith the Lord ; or what is the
place of my rest ? Hath not my hand made all these things ? "
See (Lat.) The world is the temple of God : God is in us.

How the Character of Man is Known.
Arreph. 8.

Ανδρὸς χαρακτὴρ ἐκ λόγου γνωρίζεται.

The character of man is known from his conversation.

See (Lat.) Like speech, like life. Terent. Heaut. ii. 4, 4.

The Wish is Father to the Thought.

Clyp. 4.

'Ο βούλεται γὰρ μόνον ὁρῶν καὶ προσδοκῶν.
'Αλόγιστός ἐστι τῆς ἀληθείας κριτής.

He who sees and expects only what he wishes is a foolish judge of what is true.

So Shakespeare ("King Henry IV.," part iii., act iv., sc. 4)—
"Thy wish was father, Harry, to that thought."
See (Lat.) Wish.

Riches.

Ex Se ipsum lugente, i.

'Ο δὲ πλοῦτος τυφλὸν,
Τυφλοὺς δ' ἐς αὐτὸν ἐμβλέποντας δεικνύει.

Riches are blind, and render men blind who set their affections upon them.

Annoyances of Life.

Bœot. 2.

Πολλὰ δύσκολα
ἐν τοῖς πᾶσιν εὕροις πράγμασ'· ἀλλ' εἰ πλείονα
τὰ συμφέροντ' ἔνεστι, τοῦτο δεῖ σκοπεῖν.

In everything thou wilt find annoyances, but thou oughtest to consider whether the advantages do not predominate.

To Die Young.

Ex bis fallente, 4.

'Ον οἱ Θεοὶ φιλοῦσιν, ἀποθνῄσκει νέος.

He whom the gods love dies young.
See (Lat.) Death in youth.

Every Difficulty is Overcome by Labour.

E Moroso, 5.

Οὐδενὸς χρὴ πράγματος
τὸν εὖ πονοῦνθ' ὅλως ἀπογνῶναι ποτέ.
'Αλωτὰ γίγνετ' ἐπιμελείᾳ καὶ πόνῳ
ἅπαντα.

He who labours diligently need never despair. We can accomplish everything by diligence and labour.
See (Lat.) Industry

What is Unexpected.

Pug. 1.

Οὐχ ὅθεν ἂν ᾤμην ἠτύχηκα· πάντα δὲ
τὰ μηδὲ προσδοκῶμεν ἔκστασιν φέρει.

I have not been unfortunate, whence I might have expected;
but all things that are unexpected cause surprise.

A Modest Assurance Necessary.

Spons. 1.

Τὸ σὸν ταπεινὸν, ἄν συ σεμνύνῃ, καλὸν
ἔξω φανεῖται, φὶλ' ἄνερ· ἂν δ' αὐτὸς ποιῇς
ταπεινὸν αὐτὸ καὶ τιθῇς ἐν μηδενί,
Οἰκεῖος οὗτος καταγέλως νομίζεται.

Thy modesty, if thou art of grave demeanour, will appear suitable in the eyes of the world, my friend ; if thou humblest thyself,
and makest little of thyself, this is thought a just despising of
thyself.

Fight not against God.

Eunuch. 2.

Μὴ θεομάχει, μηδὲ προσάγου τῷ πράγματι
χειμῶνας ἑτέρους, τοὺς ἀναγκαίους φέρε.

Fight not against the decrees of God, nor add other annoyances
to the occurrences of life ; bear patiently whatever happens.

So Acts (v. 29)—" We ought to obey God rather than man."

The Ills of Fortune.

Auriga. 4.

῟Ων δὲ μὴ τρόπος αἴτιος,
τὰ Τύχης φέρειν δεῖ γνησίως τὸν εὐγενῆ.

The noble ought to bear with patience the evils of life which
Fortune brings upon them, when they have not themselves to
blame.

Evil Communications.

Thais. 2.

Φθείρουσιν ἤθη χρησθ' ὁμιλίαι κακαί.

Evil communications corrupt good manners.

See 1 Cor. xv. 33.

L

A Prophet.

Ex Adflata. i.

'Ο πλεῖστον νοῦν ἔχων
μάντις ἄριστός ἐστι, σύμβουλός θ' ἅμα.

The wisest man is the best prophet and counsellor.

See (Lat.) A prophet.

Prudence.

Ex Adflata. 3.

Αρ ἔστιν ἀγαθῶν πανταπλείστων αἰτία
ἡ σύνεσις, ἂν ᾖ πρὸς τὰ βελτίω σοφή.

Prudence and forethought are the origin of much that is good,
if they be applied to a proper object.

Imprudence.

Thessala, 1.

Μικρά γε πρόφασίς ἐστι τοῦ πρᾶξαι κακῶς.

It requires little exertion on our part to bring misfortune upon
ourselves.

Know Thyself.

Thrasyleon, 1.

Κατὰ πόλλ' ἂν ἐστιν οὐ καλῶς εἰρημένον
τὸ γνῶθι σεαυτόν· χρησιμώτερον γὰρ ἦν,
τὸ γνῶθι τοὺς ἄλλους.

In many things thou dost not well to say, "Know thyself ;" for
it would be better to say, "Know others."

See (Lat.) Know thyself.

The Sluggard.

Thrasyleon, 4.

Ο πανταμέλλων, σιτόκουρος, ἄθλιος,
ἄχρηστος εἰς γῆν, παρατρέφεσθ' ὁμολογῶν.

A procrastinator, born merely to consume the fruits of the
earth ; a miserable wretch ; a useless being on earth, acknow-
ledging that he has been brought up in vain.

See (Lat.) The vulgar horde.

INDUSTRY.

E Canistriferis, 1.

Τίς γὰρ προθύμως μὴ πονῆσαν εὐτυχεῖ;

Who can be happy without strenuous labour?

See (Lat.) Industry

FOLLY.

E Canistriferis, 2.

Ἀλογίστου τρόπου
ἀτύχημα φεύγειν ἐστὶν οὐκ αὐθαίρετον.

It is not in the power of a foolish person to escape misfortune.

So Proverbs (x. 10)—"A prating fool shall fall;" and (xxvii. 22)—
"Though thou shouldest bray a fool in a mortar."

GOOD RESULTS.

E. Carthaginiense, p. 96.

Τὸ καλῶς ἔχον που κρεῖττόν ἐστι καὶ νόμου.

That which turns out well is better than any law.

CHANCE.

Cnid. 2.

Ταὐτόματόν ἐστιν, ὡς ἔοικέ του Θεὸς,
σώζει τε πολλὰ τῶν ἀοράτων πραγμάτων.

Chance is, as it seems, a kind of god, for it preserves many
things which we do not observe.

THE JUST.

Adsentator, 6.

Οὐδεὶς ἐπλούτησε ταχέως δίκαιος ὤν.

No just man has ever become suddenly rich.

See (Lat.) Rich.

ADVERSITY.

Luctat. 1.

Ὥστε μηδεὶς πρὸς Θεῶν
πράττων κακῶς λίαν ἀθυμήσῃ ποτέ.
ἴσως γὰρ ἀγαθοῦ τοῦτο πρόφασις γίνεται.

L 2

No one ought ever to despond in adverse circumstances, for they may turn out to be the cause of good to us.

So Job (v. 17)—"Behold, happy is the man whom God correcteth ; therefore despise not thou the chastening of the Almighty ;" and Hebrews (xii. 6)—"For whom the Lord loveth He chasteneth, and scourgeth.every son whom He receiveth."

So Shakespeare ("As You Like It," act ii., sc. 1)—

"Sweet are the uses of adversity ;
Which, like the toad, ugly and venomous,
Wears yet a precious jewel in his head."

And "Measure for Measure," (act. iv., sc. 6)—

"'Tis a physic
That's bitter to sweet end."

KNOW THYSELF.

Luctat. 2.

Τὸ γνῶθι σαυτόν ἐστιν, ἂν τὰ πράγματα
ἴδῃς τὰ σαυτοῦ, καὶ τί σοι ποιητέον.

That saying, "Know thyself," has this meaning, that thou get acquainted with thy own abilities, and with what thou art able to accomplish.

THE POOR.

Ex Leucadia, p. 112.

Ἀεὶ νομίζονθ' οἱ πένητες τῶν Θεῶν.

The poor are always considered to be under the peculiar care of the gods.

So Psalm (lxix. 33)—"For the Lord heareth the poor, and despiseth not His prisoners."

THE CONTINGENCIES OF FORTUNE.

Xenolog. 1.

Οὐκ ἔστιν εἰπεῖν ζῶντα, τοῦτ' οὐ πείσομαι. .

It does not become any living man to say, "This will not happen to me."

THE GOOD ARE KNOWN BY A BLUSH.

E Germanis, p. 134.

Ἅπας ἐρυθριῶν χρηστὸς εἶναι μοι δοκεῖ.

Whoever blushes seems to be good.

So Young (Night vii., l. 496.)—

"The man that blushes is not quite a brute."

See (Lat.) A blush, all's safe.

The Honourable.
E Germanis, 2.

Χρηστοὺς νομιζομένους ἐφόδιον ἀσφαλές
εἰς πάντα καιρὸν, καὶ Τύχης πᾶσαν ῥοπήν.

A good and honourable character is a safe provision for every
event and every turn of fortune.

God.
Ex Pellice, 1.

'Αλλὰ τῶν
χρηστῶν ἔχει τιν' ἐπιμέλειαν καὶ Θεός.

God takes particular care of the good.

Country Life.
E Plocio, 7.

"Αρ' ἐστὶν ἀρετῆς καὶ βίου διδάσκαλος
ἐλευθέρου, τοῖς πᾶσιν ἀνθρώποις, ἀγρός.

Men are taught virtue and a love of independence by living in
the country.

See (Lat.) Country life.

Pleasure and Pain closely United.
E Plocio, 8.

'Ω Παρμένων οὐκ ἔστιν ἀγαθὸν τῷ βίῳ
φυόμενον ὥσπερ δένδρον ἐκ ῥίζης μιᾶς.
'Αλλ' ἐγγὺς ἀγαθοῦ παραπέφυκε καὶ κακόν,
ἐκ τοῦ κακοῦ τ' ἤνεγκεν ἀγαθὸν ἡ φύσις.

There is no pleasure of life, sprouting like a tree from one root,
but there is some pain closely joined to it; and, again, nature
brings good out of evil.

The Pains of Life.
E Plocio, 9.

'Αεὶ τὸ λυποῦν ἀποδίωκε τοῦ βίου,
μικρόν τι τὸν βίου καὶ στενὸν ζῶμεν χρόνον.

If thou expungest from life all that part which thou passest
unhappily, it reduces life to a small infinitesimal fragment.

See (Lat.) Shortness of life.

A Servant.

Ex Præaccusante, 1.

Τὸ δὲ κελευόμενόν ἐστιν ἀσφαλέστατον
δούλῳ ποιεῖν, ὥς φασιν.

It is safest for a servant to do what he is ordered, as the proverb
says.

Pleasant at Times to Play the Fool.

Ex Vendito, 2.

Οὐ πανταχοῦ τὸ φρόνιμον ἁρμόττει παρόν,
καὶ συμμανῆναι δ᾽ ἔνια δεῖ.

It is not always suitable to be wise ; to play the fool in some
things is proper.

So Ecclesiastes (iii. 4)—"A time to mourn and a time to dance."
See (Lat.) Enjoy the present.

Truth.

Ex Verberatâ, 3.

Ἔρχεται
τ᾽ ἀληθὲς εἰς φῶς ἐνίοτ᾽ οὐ ζητούμενον.

Truth, when not sought after, sometimes come to light.

Man.

E Supposititio, 2.

Τοῦτον εὐτυχέστατον λέγω,
ὅστις θεωρήσας ἀλύπως, Παρμένων,
τὰ σεμνὰ ταῦτ᾽ ἀπῆλθεν, ὅθεν ἦλθεν ταχύ,
τὸν ἥλιον τὸν κοινὸν ἀστέρ᾽, ὕδωρ, νέφη,
πῦρ. Ταὐτὰ, κἂν ἑκατὸν ἔτη βιώσεται,
ὄψει παρόντα, κἂν ἐνιαυτοὺς σφόδρ᾽ ὀλίγους.
Σεμνότερα τούτων ἕτερα οὐκ ὄψει ποτέ.
Πανήγυριν νόμισόν τιν᾽ εἶναι τὸν χρόνον,
ὃν φημὶ, τοῦτον, κἀπιδημίαν βροτῶν.
Ὄχλος, ἀγορὰ, κλέπται, κυβεῖαι, διατριβαί.
Ἂν πρῶτος ἀπέλθῃς, καταλύσεις σὺ βελτίον,
ἐφόδι᾽ ἔχων ἀπῆλθες, ἐχθρὸς οὐδενί.
Ὁ προσδιατρίβων δὲ, κοπιάσας ἀπώλεσε·
κακῶς τε γηρῶν, ἐνδεής του γίνεται,
ῥεμβόμενος ἐχθροὺς εὗρ᾽, ἐπεβουλεύθη πόθεν.
Οὐκ εὐθανάτως ἀπῆλθεν ἐλθὼν εἰς χρόνον.

I maintain that he is most happy who, after contemplating at his ease those beautiful objects of nature, the sun, stars, water, clouds, fire, has departed speedily to the home whence he came. Whether he live a hundred years or a few, he will always have the same objects before him. Consider, therefore, the time of which I speak to be merely the place of meeting and sojourning for men, where we meet together, traffic, are cheated, gamble, and amuse ourselves. If thou departest early, thou wilt enjoy the better fate ; thou hast gone furnished with provisions for the way, hated by no one. He who remains a longer time in the world, after all his labours, at last comes to an end, and, reaching a miserable old age, finds himself in want of everything. Roaming about, he finds enemies, who lay snares for him : having at last come to an end, the spirit parts from the body with great difficulty.

Lean not on Your own Understanding.
E Supposititio, 3.

Παύσασθε νοῦν ἔχοντες· οὐδὲν γὰρ πλέον
ἀνθρώπινος νοῦς ἐστιν, ἀλλ' ὁ τῆς Τύχης,
εἴτ' ἔστι τὸ πνεῦμα θεῖον, εἴτε νοῦς.
Τοῦτ' ἔστι πάντα καὶ κυβερνῶν καὶ στρέφον,
καὶ σῶζον· ἡ πρόνοια δ' ἡ θνητὴ καπνὸς,
καὶ φλήναφος, πείθεσθε κ' οὐ μέμψεσθέ με.
Ἅπαντα δ' δσα νοοῦμεν, ἤγουν πράττομεν,
τύχη 'στιν, ἡμεῖς δ' ἐσμὲν ἐπιγεγραμμένοι.
Τύχη κυβερνᾷ πάντα· ταύτην καὶ φρένας
Δεῖ καὶ πρόνοιαν τὴν Θεὸν καλεῖν μόνην,
εἰ μή τις ἄλλως ὀνόμασιν χαίρει κενοῖς.

Cease to lean on your own understanding, for the wisdom of man is nothing else but the dictates of chance, whether that be considered Divine inspiration or pure intellect. It is this that rules, turns, and preserves all things, while the wisdom of man is mere smoke and idle talk : believe what I say, and you will not have cause to blame me. All things that we do or meditate are the results of chance, though we ascribe them to our own wisdom. Chance directs all things: we ought to call this, whether intellect or forethought, as the only goddess, unless we foolishly take pleasure in vain appellations.

So Proverbs (iii. 5)—"Lean not unto thine own understanding."

Truth.
E Supposititio, 7.

Ἀεὶ κράτιστόν ἐστι τ' ἀληθῆ λέγειν
ἐν παντὶ καιρῷ. Τοῦτ' ἐγὼ παρεγγυῶ
εἰς ἀσφάλειαν τῷ βίῳ πλεῖστον μέρος.

To speak the truth is always the best policy ; this I maintain to be the safest course in life.

Woman.

E Supposititio, 8.

Πολλῶν κατὰ γῆν καὶ κατὰ θάλατταν θηρίων
ὄντων, μέγιστόν ἐστι θηρίον γυνή.

Of all wild beasts on earth or in sea, the greatest is a woman.

Social Life.

Ex Fratrum Amante, 5.

'Ως ἡδὺ τὸ ζῆν, εἰ μεθ' ὧν κρίνει τὶς ἂν
Τοῦτ' ἔστι τὸ ζῆν, οὐχ ἑαυτῷ ζῆν μόνον.

How pleasant is life if you live with those with whom you think
you should live, and not merely for yourself!

[The following are from the edition of Menander: " Menandri et Phile-
monis Reliquiæ, quotquot reperiri potuerunt, Græce et Latine cum notis
Hugonis Grotii," &c. Amstelodami, 1709.]

The Wicked.

Ex Fratrib. p. 2.

Εἴπερ τὸν ἀδικοῦντ' ἀσμένως ἠμύνετο
ἕκαστος ἡμῶν, καὶ συνηγωνίσατο,
ἴσως νομίζων ἴδιον εἶναι τὸ γεγονὸς
ἀδίκημα, καὶ συνέπραττον ἀλλήλοις πικρῶς,
οὐκ ἂν ἐπὶ πλεῖον τὸ κακὸν ἡμῖν ηὔξατο
τὸ τῶν πονηρῶν, ἀλλὰ παρατηρούμενοι
καὶ τυγχάνοντες ἧς ἔδεε τιμωρίας,
ἤτοι σπάνιοι σφόδρ' ἂν ἦσαν, ἢ πεπαυμένοι.

If we were all eager to resist the man who inflicted injury, and
were ready to bring aid, regarding any injury done as done to ourselves, and if we were prepared to assist each other, there would
be less mischief done by the bad ; for when these men found that
they were watched and properly punished, they would either be
few in number, or would disappear altogether.

Friends.

Ex Fratrib. p. 4.

Τὰ τῶν φίλων κοιν' οὐ μόνον τὰ χρήματα,
καὶ νοῦ δὲ καὶ φρονήσεως κοινωνία.

Not only are the riches of friends common property, but their
wisdom and forethought also ought to be so.

HEIGHT OF IMPUDENCE.
Ex Fratrib. p. 6.

'Ος δ' οὔτ', ἐρυθριᾷν οἶδ', οὐδὲ δεδοικέναι,
τὰ πρῶτα πάσης τῆς ἀναιδείας ἔχει.

The man who cannot blush, and who has no feelings of fear, has
reached the acme of impudence.

See (Lat.) A blush.

IGNORANCE.
Ex Fratrib. p. 6.

Οὐκ ἐστ' ἀνοίας οὐδὲν τολμηρώτερον.

There is nothing more daring than ignorance.

UNFORESEEN MISFORTUNE.
Ex Fratrib. p. 6.

Οἴ μοι, τὸ γὰρ ἄφνω δυστυχεῖν μανίαν ποιεῖ.

Ah me! unforeseen misfortune is apt to bring on madness.

GOOD HEALTH.
Ex Andr. p. 16.

'Υγιὴς νοσοῦντα ῥᾷστα πᾶς τις νουθετεῖ.

In good health we are ready to give advice to the sick.

See (Lat.) The sick.

LOVERS.
Ex Andr. p. 16.

'Οργὴ φιλούντων ὀλίγον ἰσχύει χρόνον.

The wrath of lovers lasts only a short time.

See (Lat.) Lovers

LAW.
Ex Legislatore, p. 130.

Νόμος ὁ φυλαχθεὶς οὐδέν ἐστιν, ἢ νόμος,
ὁ μὴ φυλαχθεὶς καὶ νόμος καὶ δήμιος.

Law when kept is nothing else but law; whereas law broken is
both law and executioner.

L 3

LAW.
Ex Legislatore, p. 132.

Νόμον φοβηθεὶς μὴ ταραχθήσῃ νόμῳ.

If thou respect the law, thou wilt not be terrified by the law.

LAW.
Ex Legislatore, p. 132.

Μὴ πάσχε πρῶτον τὸν νόμον καὶ μάνθανε,
πρὸ τοῦ παθεῖν σε τῷ φόβῳ προλαμβάνου.

Do not first suffer the punishment of the law, and then learn its nature; but, before thou suffer, anticipate it by thy respect for it.

FALSEHOOD AND TRUTH.
Ex Incert. Comœd. p. 108.

Κρεῖττον δ' ἑλέσθαι ψεῦδος, ἢ ἀληθὲς κακόν.

It is better to prefer falsehood to truth when it is injurious.

MUTUAL ASSISTANCE.
Ex Incert. Comœd. p. 202.

Εἰ πάντες ἐβοηθοῦμεν ἀλλήλοις ἀεὶ,
οὐδεὶς ἂν ὢν ἄνθρωπος ἐδεήθη Τύχης.

If we gave assistance to each other, no one would be in want of fortune.

WICKEDNESS.
Ex Incert. Comœd. p. 202.

Ἀσυλλόγιστόν ἐστιν ἡ πονηρία.

Wickedness does not act according to reason.

See (Lat.) Wickedness.

ABUSING THE GOOD THINGS OF LIFE.
Ex Incert. Comœd. p. 206.

Ο μὴ φέρων γὰρ εὖ τι τῶν ἐν τῷ βίῳ
ἀγαθῶν, ἀσυλλόγιστός ἐστ', οὐ μακάριος.

For he who abuses the good things of life is a senseless being and not happy.

Injure no Man.

Ex Incert. Comœd. p. 206.

Τὸ μηδὲν ἀδικεῖν πᾶσιν ἀνθρώποις πρέπει.

Do injury to no man.

The Plausible.

Ex Incert. Comœd. p. 208.

Τὸ πιθανὸν ἰσχὺν τῆς ἀληθείας ἔχει
ἐνίοτε μείζω, καὶ πιθανοτέραν ὄχλῳ.

The plausible has sometimes greater power than the truth, and more influence over the multitude.

A Lie.

Ex Incert. Comœd. p. 208.

Ψεῦδος δὲ μισεῖ πᾶς σοφὸς καὶ χρήσιμος.

Every wise and honourable man hates a lie.

So Proverbs (xiii. 5)—"A righteous man hateth lying."

A Liar.

Ex Incert. Comœd. p. 208.

Ψευδόμενος οὐδεὶς λανθάνει πολὺν χρόνον.

No liar long escapes discovery.

So Proverbs (xix. 5)—"He that speaketh lies shall not escape."

The Purse-proud.

Ex Incert. Comœd. p. 212.

Ὅταν δ' ἴδῃς πρὸς ὕψος ἡρμένον τινὰ,
λαμπρῶς τε πλούτῳ καὶ γένει γαυρούμενον,
ὀφρῦν τε μείζω τῆς Τύχης ἐπηρκότα,
τούτου ταχεῖαν νέμεσιν εὐθὺς προσδόκα,
ἐπαίρεται γὰρ μεῖζον, ἵνα μεῖζον πέσῃ.

When thou seest a man elated with pride glorying in his riches and high descent, rising even above fortune, look out for his speedy punishment, for he is only raised the higher that he may fall with a heavier crash.

See (Lat.) Pride.

Who Knows the Future.
Ex Incert. Comœd. p. 212.

Οἱ τὰς ὀφρῦς αἴροντες ὡς ἀβέλτεροι,
καὶ σκέψομαι, λέγοντες. Ἄνθρωπος γὰρ ὢν
σκέψῃ σὺ περί του, δυστυχὴς κἂν εὐτυχῇ ;
αὐτόματα γὰρ τὰ πράγματ᾽ ἐπὶ τὸ συμφέρον
ῥεῖ, κἂν καθευδήσῃς, πάλιν τἀναντία.

The proud and supercilious are like fools when they say, " I
shall think of it by and by ; " for since thou art mortal, how dost
thou know that thou wilt have time to consider anything, miserable even in the midst of prosperity?   For thy fortune, of its own
accord, even while thou sleepest, sometimes is improving, and
again goes to wreck,

See Luke xii. 20.

The Mote in our Brother's Eye.
Ex. Incert. Comœd. p. 216.

Οὐθεὶς ἐφ᾽ αὑτοῦ τὰ κακὰ συνορᾷ, Πάμφιλε,
Σαφῶς, ἑτέρου δ᾽ ἀσχημονοῦντος ὄψεται.

No one sees his own faults, but is lynx-eyed to those of his
neighbour.

So Luke (vi. 41)—"And why beholdest thou the mote that is in thy
brother's eye, but perceivest not the beam that is in thine own eye?"

See (Lat.) Mote.

Conscience.
Ex Incert. Comœd. p. 216.

Ὁ συνιστορῶν αὑτῷ τι, κἂν ᾖ θρασύτατος,
ἡ σύνεσις αὐτὸν δειλότατον εἶναι ποιεῖ.

The man who is conscious to himself of crime, even though he
be of the boldest nature, becomes a coward.

So Shakespeare ("Hamlet," act iii., sc. 1)—
"Thus conscience does make cowards of us all."

See (Lat.) Conscience.

Silence.
Ex Incert. Comœd. p. 216

Οὐθὲν σιωπῆς ἔστι χρησιμώτερον.

Nothing is more useful to man than silence.

See (Lat.) The silent.

A Word Spoken.

Ex Incert. Comœd. p. 216.

Οὔτ' ἐκ χερὸς μεθέντα καρτερὸν λίθον
ῥᾷον κατασχεῖν, οὔτ' ἀπὸ γλώσσης λόγον.

It is as easy to draw back a stone thrown with force from the
hand as to recall a word once spoken.

See (Lat.) The inquisitive.

Goodness of Disposition.

Ex Incert. Comœd. p. 216.

Ὡς ἡδὺ συνέσει χρηστότης κεκραμένη.

How sweet is goodness of disposition when tempered with
wisdom!

Goodness of Disposition.

Ex Incert. Comœd. p. 216.

Νὴ τὴν Ἀθηνᾶν, μακάριον γ' ὁ χρηστότης
πρὸς πάντα, καὶ θαυμαστὸν ἐφόδιον βίῳ.
Τούτῳ λαλήσας ἡμέρας μικρὸν μέρος,
εὔνους ἐγὼ νῦν εἰμί· πιστικὸν λόγος,
πρὸς τοῦτ' ἂν εἴποι τις, μάλιστα τῶν σοφῶν.
Τί οὖν ἑτέρους λαλοῦντας εὖ βδελύττομαι;
τρόπος ἐσθ' ὁ πείθων τοῦ λέγοντος, οὐ λόγος.

By Minerva, goodness of disposition and honesty of character
are happy possessions and a wonderful provision for life. Conversing with such a man, even for a short time, I become well
inclined to him. Some will say, in opposition to this, that it is
eloquence, particularly of the wise, that inspires confidence. Why,
then, do I curse others who are equally eloquent? It is not so,
but it is the character of the speaker, and not merely his words,
that persuades us to feel confidence in what is said.

The Envious.

Ex Incert. Comœd. p. 218.

Ὁ φθονερὸς αὑτῷ πολέμιος καθίσταται,
αὐθαίρετος γὰρ συνέχεται λύπαις ἀεί.

The envious man is an enemy to himself, for his mind is always
spontaneously occupied with its own unhappy thoughts.

ENVY.

Ex Incert. Comœd. p. 218.

Μειράκιον, οὔ μοι κατανοεῖν δοκεῖς ὅτι
Ὑπὸ τῆς ἰδίας ἕκαστα κακίας σήπεται.
καὶ πάντα τὰ λυμαινόμεν' ἔνεστιν ἔνδοθεν·
οἷον ὁ μὲν ἰὸς τὸν σίδηρον, ἂν σκοπῇς,
τὸ δ' ἱμάτιον οἱ σῆπες, ἡ δὲ θρὶψ ξύλον.
Ὁ δὲ τὸ κάκιστον τῶν κακῶν πάντων φθόνος,
Φθισικὸν πεποίηκε, καὶ ποιήσει, καὶ ποιεῖ,
Ψυχῆς πονηρᾶς δυσσεβὴς παραστάτης.

O young man, thou dost not seem to me to be aware that everything is deteriorated by its own imperfections, and that what
hurts comes from within. Thus rust corrodes iron, if thou rightly
consider the matter; the moth eats away the garment; the worm
gnaws the wood. But of all the ills of life, the worst is envy,
which has done, will do, and does, most mischief,—the base
attendant of an impious soul.

See (Lat.) Envy.

SLANDER.

Ex Incert. Comœd. p. 220.

Ὅστις δὲ διαβολαῖσι πείθηται ταχὺ
ἤτοι πονηρὸς αὐτός ἐστι τοὺς τρόπους,
ἢ παντάπασι παιδαρίου γνώμην ἔχει.

Whosoever lends a greedy ear to a slanderous report is either
himself of a radically bad disposition, or a mere child in sense.

See (Lat.) Calumny.

SILENCE.

Ex Incert. Comœd. p. 220.

Ὦ παῖ σιώπα, πόλλ' ἔχει σιωπὴ καλά.

O boy, hold thy tongue, silence has many advantages.

COUNTRY LIFE.

Ex Incert. Comœd. p. 221.

Ὁ τῶν γεωργῶν ἡδονὴν ἔχει βίος,
ταῖς ἐλπίσιν τ' ἀλγεινὰ παραμυθούμενος.

The life of those who live in the country possesses pleasures,
comforting the sorrows and annoyances of man with hope.

See (Lat.) Country life.

LISTEN BEFORE DECIDING.
Ex Incert. Comœd. p. 222.

'Ο προκαταγινώσκων δὲ πρὶν ἀκοῦσαι σαφῶς,
αὐτὸς πονηρός ἐστι, πιστεύσας κακῶς.

He who condemns before he has heard clearly the case is himself
a bad man, ready to believe ill of his neighbour.

IMPUDENCE.
Ex Incert. Comœd. p. 222.

Οὐκ ἔστι τόλμης ἐφόδιον μεῖζον βίῳ.

There is no better provision for life than impudence and a
brazen face.

WISDOM COMES NOT FROM YEARS.
Ex Incert. Comœd. p. 224.

Οὐχ αἱ τρίχες ποιοῦσιν αἱ λευκαὶ φρονεῖν,
ἀλλ' ὁ τρόπος ἐνίων ἐστὶ τῇ φύσει γέρων.

It is not hoary hairs that bring wisdom ; but some have an old
head on young shoulders.

PEACE AND WAR.
Ex Incert. Comœd. p. 224.

Εἰρήνη γεωργὸν κἂν πέτραις
τρέφει καλῶς· πόλεμος δὲ κἂν πεδίῳ κακός.

Peace gives food to the husbandman, even in the midst of rocks ;
war brings misery to him, even in the most fertile plains.

See (Lat.) Peace.

A BARREN COUNTRY.
Ex Incert. Comœd. p. 224.

Τὰ κακῶς τρέφοντα χωρί' ἀνδρείους ποιεῖ.

The country which is cultivated with difficulty produces brave
men.

WOMAN.
Ex Incert. Comœd. p. 224.

Ὅπου γυναῖκές εἰσι, πάντ' ἐκεῖ κακά.

Where are women, there are all kinds of mischief.

An Attached Servant.

Ex Incert. Comœd. p. 226.

῞Οταν τύχῃ τὶς εὐνοοῦντος οἰκέτου,
οὐκ ἔστιν οὐδὲν κτῆμα καλλίον βίῳ.

When one has got an attached servant, there is no nobler possession on earth.

Wife and Children.

Ex Incert. Comœd. p. 228.

Τὸ γυναῖκ᾽ ἔχειν, εἶναι τε παίδων, Παρμένων,
πατέρα, μερίμνας τῷ βίῳ πολλὰς φέρει.

To have a wife, and to be the father of children, brings many anxieties to life.

A Wife is a Necessary Evil.

Ex Incert. Comœd. p. 230.

Τὸ γαμεῖν, ἐάν τις τὴν ἀλήθειαν σκοπῇ,
κακὸν μέν ἐστιν, ἀλλ᾽ ἀναγκαῖον κακόν.

To marry a wife, if we regard the truth, is an evil, but it is a necessary evil.

A House without an Heir.

Ex Incert. Comœd. p. 236.

᾽Οδύνηρόν ἐστιν εὐτυχοῦντα τῷ βίῳ
ἔχειν ἔρημον διαδόχου τὴν οἰκίαν.

The man who has abundance of this world's riches, and is without an heir to inherit them, is to be pitied.

A Father.

Ex Incert. Comœd. p. 238.

Μηδὲν δ᾽ ἀδύνατον πατέρα γινώσκειν, ὅτι
ὁ μέγιστ᾽ ἀγαπῶν καὶ δι᾽ ἐλάχιστ᾽ ὀργίζεται.

It is not difficult to know a father, for he loves much; is also irritated at the smallest faults in those he loves.

A Father.

Ex Incert. Comœd. p. 240.

῝Ως ἡδὺ πρᾷος, καὶ νεάζων τῷ τρόπῳ
πατήρ.

How delightful is a father, gentle and cheerful in his manners!

BROTHERS.

Ex Incert. Comœd. p. 240.

'Ὠs ἡδύ γ' ἐν ἀδέλφοισιν ὁμονοίας ἔρως.

How pleasant a thing it is for brothers to dwell together in unity!

So Psalm (cxxxiii. 1)—"Behold, how good and how pleasant it is for brethren to dwell together in unity!"

FOLLY OF PRIDING ONE'S-SELF ON HIGH BIRTH.

Ex Incert. Comœd. p. 240.

'Απολεῖ με τὸ γένος· μὴ λέγ', εἰ φιλεῖς ἐμέ,
μῆτερ, ἐφ' ἑκάστῳ τὸ γένος. Οἷς ἂν τῇ φύσει
ἀγαθὸν ὑπάρχει μηδὲν οἰκεῖον προσὸν,
ἐκεῖσε καταφεύγουσιν, εἰς τὰ μνήματα,
καὶ τὸ γένος, ἀριθμοῦσί τε τοὺς πάππους ὅσοι.
Οὐδ' ἕνα δ' ἔχοις ἰδεῖν ἄν, οὐδ' εἰπεῖν, ὅτῳ
οὐκ εἰσὶ πάπποι· πῶς γὰρ ἐγένοντ' ἄν ποτε;
οἱ μὴ λέγειν δ' ἔχουσι τοῦτο, διά τινα
τόπου μεταβολὴν, ἢ φίλων ἐρημίαν,
τί τῶν λεγόντων εἰσὶ δυσγενέστεροι;
ὃς ἂν εὖ γεγονὼς ᾖ τῇ φύσει πρὸς τ ἀγαθά,
κἂν Αἰθίοψ ᾖ, μῆτερ, ἐστὶν εὐγενής.
Σκύθης τίς ὄλεθρος; ὁ δ' 'Ανάχαρσις οὐ Σκύθης.

My high birth suffocates me. If thou love me, mother, thou wilt not on all occasions quote my high rank; it is those only who have no peculiar good in their own nature who have recourse to splendid monuments and their noble birth, and who count up all their ancestors who have preceded them. But thou canst not see nor name a man who has not had ancestors. For how otherwise could they have come into existence? Those who are not able to name them, from change of country or want of friends, why are they less noble than those who can enumerate them? He who is by nature good and virtuous, though he be a blackamoor, is noble-born. Is some Scythian a rascal? Yet was not Anacharsis a Scythian?

See (Lat.) Ancestors.

THE WELL-BORN IN ADVERSITY.

Ex Incert. Comœd. p. 240.

Τοὺς εὖ γεγονότας καὶ τετραμμένους καλῶς,
κἂν τοῖς κακοῖς δεῖ λόγον ἔχειν εὐφημίας.

Those who have been well born, and honourably brought up, though they have fallen into adversity, ought to pay regard to the world's opinion.

TRUE RICHES.
Ex Incert. Comœd. p. 242.

Ψυχὴν ἔχειν δεῖ πλουσίαν· τὰ δὲ χρήματα
ταῦτ' ἐστὶν ὄψις, παραπέτασμα τοῦ βίου.

It is the mind that ought to be rich ; for the riches of this world
only feed the eyes, and serve merely as a veil to cover the realities
of life.

THE WIFE OUGHT TO GIVE WAY TO THE HUSBAND.
Ex Incert. Comœd. p. 244.

Τὰ δευτερεῖα τὴν γυναῖκα δεῖ λέγειν,
τὴν δ' ἡγεμονίαν τῶν ὅλων τὸν ἄνδρ' ἔχειν.
Ἡ δ' οἰκία ἐν ᾗ πάντα πρωτεύει γυνὴ,
οὐκ ἔστιν ἥτις πώποτ' οὐκ ἀπώλετο.

The wife ought to play the second part, the husband ruling in
everything ; for there is no family in which the wife has had the
upper hand that has not gone to ruin.

HAPPINESS AND PAIN EQUALLY DISTRIBUTED.
Ex Incert. Comœd. p. 248.

Ἔξωθεν εἰσὶν οἱ δοκοῦντες εὐτυχεῖν,
τὰ δ' ἔνδον εἰσὶ πᾶσιν ἀνθρώποις ἴσοι.

There are men who seem to the world around to be happy ; but
inwardly, men are very much alike.

AN OLD WOMAN.
Ex Incert. Comœd. p. 258.

Πολὺ χεῖρόν ἐστιν ἐρεθίσαι γραῦν, ἢ κύνα.

It is much worse to irritate an old woman than a dog.

SANITARY LAWS.
Ex Incert. Comœd. p. 264.

Εἰς τ' ἀκάθαρτα λοιμὸς ἐσοικίζεται.

The plague dwells where the sanitary laws are neglected.

THE MALICIOUS.
Ex Incert. Comœd. p. 264.

Πρᾷον κακοῦργος σχῆμ' ἐπεισελθὼν ἀνὴρ
κεκρυμμένη παγὶς πρόκειται τοῖς πέλας.

When a malicious man puts on a kind and agreeable manner. it is a mere trap set for his neighbour.

See (Lat.) The malevolent.

TITTLE-TATTLE.

Ex Incert. Comæd. p. 266.

Οὐδὲν γὰρ οὕτως ἡδὺ ἀνθρώποις ἔφυ
ὡς τὸ λαλέειν τ' ἀλλότρια.

There is nothing so pleasant to men as to talk of the affairs of their neighbours.

THE DIVINE NATURE.

Ex Incert. Comæd. p. 272.

Τίς ἐστιν ὁ Θεὸς, οὐ θέλῃς σὺ μανθάνειν,
ἀσεβεῖς τὸν οὐ θέλοντα μανθάνειν θέλων.

Do not search into the essence of the Divine nature ; for thou art impious, wishing to know what God has not revealed.

GOD IS TO BE PROPITIATED BY A PURE HEART.

Ex Incert. Comæd. p. 268.

Εἴτις δὲ θυσίαν προσφέρων, ὦ Πάμφιλε,
ταύρων τε πλῆθος ἢ ἐρίφων, ἢ, νὴ Δία,
ἑτέρων τοιούτων, ἢ κατασκευάσματα
χρυσᾶς ποιήσας χλαμύδος ἤτοι πορφυρᾶς,
ἢ δι' ἐλέφαντος, ἢ σμαράγδου ζώδια,
εὔνουν νομίζει τὸν Θεὸν καθιστάναι,
πλανᾶτ' ἐκεῖνος καὶ φρένας κούφας ἔχει.
Δεῖ γὰρ τὸν ἄνδρα χρήσιμον πεφυκέναι,
μὴ παρθένους φθείροντα, μὴ μοιχώμενον,
κλέπτοντα καὶ σφάττοντα χρημάτων χάριν.
Μηδὲ βελόνης ἔναμμ' ἐπιθυμῇς, Πάμφιλε,
ὁ γὰρ Θεὸς βλέπει σε πλησίον παρών.

If any one, offering sacrifices of numerous bulls and of goats, or, by Jupiter, of any such things, or making presents of gold or purple robes, or images of ivory or emerald, think thereby to propitiate God, he errs, and shows himself to be of a silly understanding ; for he ought to be a virtuous and upright man, committing no crimes for the sake of gain. Thou shouldest not even covet a needle, Pamphilus ; for God, standing near thee, sees whatever thou doest.

See (Lat.) God looks to pure hands.

340   *MOSCHUS.*

A Friend Tried by Adversity.

Ex Incert. Comœd. p. 272.

Χρυσὸς μὲν οἶδεν ἐξελέγχεσθαι πυρί,
ἡ δ' ἐν φίλοις εὔνοια καιρῷ κρίνεται.

Gold is tried by fire ; so also the affections of a friend is proved
by time.

Dust we Are, and to Dust we Return.

Ex Incert. Comœd. p. 276.

'Όταν εἰδέναι θέλῃς σεαυτὸν ὅστις εἶ,
ἔμβλεψον εἰς τὰ μνήμαθ', ὡς ὁδοιπορεῖς·
ἐνταῦθ' ἔνεστιν ὀστέα καὶ κούφη κόνις
ἀνδρῶν βασιλέων καὶ τυράννων καὶ σοφῶν,
καὶ μέγα φρονούντων ἐπὶ γένει καὶ χρήμασιν,
αὐτῶν τε δόξῃ, τῷ τε κάλλει σωμάτων·
καὶ οὐδὲν αὐτῶν τῶνδ' ἐπήρκεσεν χρόνον,
κοινὸν τὸν ᾅδην ἔσχον οἱ πάντες βροτοί.
Πρὸς ταῦθ' ὁρῶν γίνωσκε σαυτὸν ὅστις εἶ.

If thou wishest to know what thou art, look at the monuments
of the dead as thou passest along the road ; there thou wilt find
the bones and light dust of kings, and tyrants, and wise men, and
of those who prided themselves on their blood and riches, on their
glorious deeds, and the beauty of their person ; but none of these
things could resist the power of time.   All men have a common
grave.   Looking at these things, thou mayest understand what
thou art.

So Genesis (iii. 19)—"For dust thou art, and unto dust shalt thou
return."

MOSCHUS.

FLOURISHED ABOUT B.C. 210.

Moschus, a bucolic poet of Syracuse, lived about the close of the
third century B.C., of whose personal history we know little more
than that he was a pupil of Bion, and was acquainted with the
grammarian Aristarchus.   Theocritus was his model; but he is
far inferior to that poet in simplicity.

The Deceitfulness of Love.

Idyll. i.

Οὐ γὰρ ἴσον νοέει καὶ φθέγγεται· ὡς μέλι φωνά·
ἢν δὲ χολᾷ, νόος ἐστὶν ἀνάμερος, ἠπεροπευτὰς,
οὐδὲν ἀλαθεύων, δόλιον βρέφος, ἄγρια παίσδει.

For he does not speak the same as he thinks ; his word is honey;
but, if he be enraged, he is ruthless, deceitful, never telling the
truth. Wily child! he laughs at the beguiled.

See (Lat.) The heart steeped in vinegar.

The Great, the Brave, and the Learned Lie Forgotten.

Idyll. iii. 106.

Αἲ αι, ταὶ μαλάχαι μὲν ἐπὰν κατὰ κᾶπον ὄλωνται,
ἢ τὰ χλωρὰ σέλινα, τό, τ' εὐθαλὲς οὖλον ἄνηθον,
ὑστέρον αὖ ζώαντι, καὶ εἰς ἔτος ἄλλο φύοντι·
ἄμμες δ', οἱ μεγάλοι καὶ καρτεροὶ ἢ σοφοὶ ἄνδρες,
ὁππότε πρῶτα θάνωμες, ἀνάκοοι ἐν χθονὶ κοίλᾳ
εὕδομες εὖ μάλα μακρὸν ἀτέρμονα νήγρετον ὕπνον.
Καὶ σὺ μὲν εν σιγᾷ πεπυκασμένος ἔσσεαι ἐν γᾷ,
ταῖς νύμφαισι δ' ἔδοξεν ἀεὶ τὸν βάτραχον ᾄδειν,
τῷ δ' ἐγώ οὐ φθονέοιμι· τὸ γὰρ μέλος οὐ καλὸν ᾄδει.

Alas, alas! when the mallows have died in a garden, or the
green parsley, or blooming crisp dill, they revive and bloom
another year. But we, the great, the brave, the learned, soon as
the hand of death has closed our eyes, unheard of, in hollow tombs
sleep a right long and endless slumber, to wake no more. Thou
too in the earth wilt be buried with the silent dead ; but it has
appeared good to the nymphs that the frog should croak for ever.
Yet I do not envy him : for 'tis no pretty song he sings.

In Job (xiv. 7) we find—"There is hope of a tree, if it be cut down, that
it will sprout again, and that the tender branch thereof will not cease.
Though the root thereof wax old in the earth, and the stock thereof die in
the ground ; yet through the scent of water it will bud and bring forth boughs
like a plant. But man dieth and wasteth away : yea, man giveth up the
ghost, and where is he?"

Spenser says—

> "Whence is it that the flow'ret of the field doth fade
> And lyeth buried long in winter's vale ?
> Yet soon as spring his mantle hath displayed,
> It flow'reth fresh, as it should never fail,
> But thing on earth that is of most avail,
> As virtue's branch and beauty's bud,
> Reliven not for any good."

See (Lat.) One eternal night for all.

A Bird over her Young.
Idyll. iv. 21.

Ὡς δὲ τ' ὀδύρεται ὄρνις ἐπὶ σφετέροισι νεοσσοῖς
ὀλλυμένοις, οὕς τ' αἰνὸς ὄφις, ἔτι νηπιάχοντας,
θάμνοις ἐν πυκινοῖσι κατεσθίει· ἡ δὲ κατ' αὐτοὺς
πωτᾶται κλάζουσα μάλα λιγὺ πότνια μήτηρ·
οὐδ' ἄρ' ἔχει τέκνοισιν ἐπαρκέσαι· ἦ γὰρ οἱ αὐτῇ
ἆσσον ἴμεν μέγα τάρβος ἀμειλίκτοιο πελώρου.

As when a bird bewails her callow brood as they perish, which, still young, a fierce snake devours in the thick bushes, while she, kind mother, hovers over them, shrieking wildly, yet is not able, I ween, to aid her children ; for she, in truth, herself is in great dread to come nearer to the cruel monster.

Virgil (Georg. iv., 512) has imitated this very closely—
" Qualis populeâ mœrens Philomela sub umbrâ
Amissos queritur fœtus, quos durus arator
Observans nido implumes, detraxit ; at illa
Flet noctem, ramoque sedens miserabile carmen
Integrat et mœstis late loca questibus implet."
" As the sad nightingale under the shade of the poplar bewails the loss of her young, which a hard-hearted ploughman has found unfledged in her nest and carried off, while she laments the night long, and, sitting on the branch, renews her piteous song, and fills far and wide the woods with her mournful complaints."

Weeping.
Idyll. iv. 45.

Σὺ δ' ἠΰτε λείβεαι ὕδωρ,
νύκτας τε κλαίουσα καὶ ἐκ Διὸς ἤμαθ' ὁπόσσα.

But thou meltest away like water, weeping both at night and as many days as are given by Jove.

Thus in Joshua (vii. 5) we find—" Wherefore the hearts of the people melted and became as water ; " and in Psalm (xxii. 14)—" I am poured out like water ; my heart also in the midst of my body is like melting wax ; " and Psalm (lviii. 7)—" Let them melt away as waters which run continually."

NICOSTRATUS.

FLOURISHED ABOUT B.C. 380.

NICOSTRATUS, the youngest of the three sons of Aristophanes, was also a comic poet ; the titles of nineteen of his plays have come down to us.

A Chatterer.

Fr. Com. Gr. p. 638.

Εἰ τὸ συνεχῶς καὶ πολλὰ καὶ ταχέως λαλεῖν
ἦν τοῦ φρονεῖν παράσημον, αἱ χελιδόνες
ἐλέγοντ' ἂν ἡμῶν σωφρονέστεραι πολύ.

If to speak without ceasing, and much and quickly, were the
sign of sense, the swallows would be regarded much wiser than
we are.

No Man Happy in every Respect.

Fr. Com. Gr. p. 639.

" Οὐκ ἔστιν ὅστις πάντ' ἀνὴρ εὐδαιμονεῖ."
Νὴ τὴν Ἀθηνᾶν συντόμως γε, φίλτατε
Εὐριπίδη, τὸν βίον ἔθηκας εἰς στίχον.

"No man is happy in every way." By Minerva, beloved Euripides, thou hast described human life in one verse.

Old Things become New again.

Fr. Com. Gr. p. 639.

Πάλιν χρόνῳ τἀρχαῖα καινὰ γίνεται.
Οὐκ ἔστι δυσαρεστότερον οὐδὲ ἐν χρόνου·
οὐδεπότ' ἀρέσκει ταὐτὰ τούτῳ τῷ θεῷ.

Old things become new again in course of time. There is
nothing more difficult to please than Time. The same things
never continue to please this god.

Poverty.

Fr. Com. Gr. p. 639.

Ἆρ' οἶσθ' ὅτι τὸ τῆς πενίας ὅπλον
παρρησία; ταύτην ἔαν τις ἀπολέσῃ,
τὴν ἀσπίδ' ἀποβέβληκεν οὗτος τοῦ βίου.

Dost thou know that freedom of speech is the arms of
poverty? If any one lose that, he has thrown away the shield
of life.

PHILEMON.

BORN ABOUT B.C. 360—DIED B.C. 262.

PHILEMON, a Greek dramatist, who stands next to Menander among the poets of the new comedy, was the son of Damon, and a native of Soli, in Cilicia. He flourished in the reign of Alexander, a little earlier than Menander, whom, however, he long survived, and spent his life at Athens. His career seems to have been singularly prosperous. Though inferior to Menander, he was a greater favourite with the Athenians, and often conquered his rival in the dramatic contests. He continued to write till he had produced ninety-seven comedies. He died, it is said, from excessive laughter at a ludicrous incident.

[Fragmenta Comicorum Græcorum collegit et disposuit Augustus Meineke, Berol. 1847.]

NATURE OF MAN.

E Rustico i.

Ὦ τῶς πονηρόν ἐστιν ἀνθρώπου φύσις
τὸ σύνολον, οὐ γὰρ ἄν ποτ᾽ ἐδεήθη νόμου.
Οἴει τι τῶν ἄλλων διαφέρειν θηρίων;
διαφέρει οὐδὲ μικρὸν, ἀλλὰ σχήματι,
πλάγι᾽ ἐστὶ τ᾽ ἄλλα, τοῦτο δ᾽ ὀρθὸν θηρίον.

How radically bad is the nature of man! for otherwise he would stand in need of no laws to restrain him. Dost thou think that he differs in any respect from other animals? In nothing, certainly, but in figure. Other animals are bent; but man is a wild beast upright in form.

OUR EVILS FOUND LIGHT WHEN COMPARED WITH THOSE OF OTHERS.

E Corinthia i.

Εἰ τὰ παρὰ τοῖς ἄλλοισιν εἰδοίης κακὰ,
ἄσμενος ἔχοις ἂν, Νικωφῶν, ἃ νῦν ἔχεις.

If thou only knewest the evils which others suffer, thou wouldst willingly submit to those which thou now bearest.

See (Lat.) None miserable but by comparison.

How seldom Man Obtains his Wishes.

E Mendica, p. 3.

Εἰ πάντες ἀποθανοίμεθ᾽, οἷς μὴ γίγνεται
ἃ βουλόμεσθα, πάντες ἀποθανοίμεθα.

If we were all to perish who did not succeed in obtaining what we wished, all mankind would die.

Tears.

Ex Sardio i.

Α. Εἰ τὰ δάκρυ᾽ ἡμῶν τῶν κακῶν ἦν φάρμακον,
ἀεὶ θ᾽ ὁ κλαύσας τοῦ πονεῖν ἐπαύετο,
ἠλλαττόμεσθ᾽ ἂν δάκρυα, δόντες χρυσίον.
νῦν δ᾽ οὐ προσέχει τὰ πράγματ᾽, οὐδ᾽ ἀποβλέπει,
εἰς ταῦτα, δέσποτ᾽, ἀλλὰ τὴν αὐτὴν ὁδὸν,
ἐάν τε κλαίῃς, ἐάν τε μὴ, πορεύεται.
Τί δὴ ποιεῖς; Β. Πλέον οὐδέν· ἡ λύπη δ᾽ ἔχει,
ὥσπερ τὸ δένδρον τοῦτο καρπὸν, τὸ δάκρυον.

A. If tears proved a remedy for our misfortunes, and if he who wept always ceased to grieve, we would buy tears with gold. But, alas! our affairs are in no way influenced by tears, pursuing their own course whether we weep or not. What wilt thou do, then? *B.* 1 am in no way influenced by such thoughts; for grief, like a tree, has tears for its fruit.

Advice.

E Sicilico i.

Ανθρωπον ὄντα ῥᾴδιον παραινέσαι
ἐστὶν, πειῆσαι δ᾽ αὐτὸν οὐχὶ ῥᾴδιον.
τεκμήριον δὲ τοὺς ἰατροὺς οἶδ᾽ ἐγώ,
ὑπὲρ ἐγκρατείας τοῖς νοσοῦσιν εὖ σφόδρα
πάντας λαλοῦντας· εἶτ᾽ ἐπὰν πταισωσί τι,
αὐτοὺς ποιοῦντας πάνθ᾽, ὅσ᾽ οὐκ εἴων τότε.
Ἑτέρων, τό, τ᾽ ἀλγεῖν καὶ θεωρεῖν ἔστ᾽ ἴσως.

It is easy for a man to give advice to his neighbour; but to follow it one's-self is not so easy. As a proof of this, I have known physicians lecturing their patients most eloquently on the benefits of abstinence; then, if they are themselves overtaken by disease, doing the very same things which they would not allow their patients to do. Theory and practice are very different.

See (Lat.) The sick.

The Husbandman.

E Supposititio i.

'Aεὶ γεωργὸς εἰς νέωτα πλούσιος.

The husbandman is always to be rich the next year.

Man and other Animals Contrasted.

Ex Incert. Comœd. 3.

Τί ποθ' ὁ Προμηθεὺς, ὃν λέγουσ' ἡμᾶς πλάσαι,
καὶ τ' ἄλλα πάντα ζῶα, τοῖς μὲν θηρίοις
ἔδωχ' ἑκάστῳ κατὰ γένος μίαν φύσιν;
ἅπαντες οἱ λέοντες εἰσὶν ἄλκμιοι,
δειλοὶ πάλιν ἑξῆς πάντες εἰσὶν οἱ λαγοί.
Οὐκ ἔστ' ἀλώπηξ, ἡ μὲν εἴρων τὴν φύσει,
ἡ δ' αὐθέκαστος· ἀλλ' ἐὰν τρισμυρίας
ἀλώπεκάς τις συναγάγοι, μίαν φύσιν
ἀπαξαπάσαις ὄψεται, τρόπον θ' ἕνα.
Ἡμῶν δ' ὅσα καὶ τὰ σώματ' ἐστὶ τὸν ἀριθμὸν
καθενὸς, τοσούτους ἐστὶ καὶ τρόπους ἰδεῖν.

Why, pray, did Prometheus, who, they say, formed us and all other animals, give to each of the beasts his own peculiar nature? All lions are brave, whereas all hares are timid. Then, as to the foxes, one is not cunning and another simple in its nature ; but if thou wert to collect three myriads of foxes, they would all have the same nature and the same habits. With man it is different ; whatever number of persons there are, the same will be found the number of minds and of characters.

See (Lat.) Differences of opinion.

The Just Man.

Ex Incert. Comœd. 10.

'Ανὴρ δίκαιος ἐστιν, οὐχ ὁ μὴ ἀδικῶν,
ἀλλ' ὅστις ἀδικεῖν δυνάμενος μὴ βούλεται.
Οὐδ' ὃς τὰ μικρὰ λαμβάνειν ἀπέσχετο,
ἀλλ' ὃς τὰ μεγάλα καρτερεῖ μὴ λαμβάνων,
ἔχειν δυνάμενος καὶ κρατεῖν ἀζημίως.
Οὐδ' ὅς γε ταῦτα πάντα διατηρεῖ μόνον,
ἀλλ' ὅστις ἄδολον γνησίαν τ' ἔχων φύσιν,
εἶναι δίκαιος κ' οὐ δοκεῖν εἶναι θέλει.

The just man is not he who does no man an injury, but he who, being able to inflict it, does not wish to do so ; nor yet is it the man who has abstained from seizing petty gains, but who determines not to lay hold of great possessions, when he might do so, and might hold them with impunity ; nor is it the man who observes all these things, but who, endued with a noble and ingenuous disposition, wishes to be just, and not merely to seem so.

See (Lat.) The just man.

The Fool and the Wise Man.
Ex Incert. Comœd. 11.

Τὸν μὴ λέγοντα τῶν δεόντων μηδὲ ἕν
μακρὸν νόμιζε, κἂν δύ' εἴπη συλλαβάς.
Τὸν δ' εὖ λέγοντα, μὴ νόμιζ' εἶναι μακρὸν,
μηδ' ἃ σφόδρ' εἴπη πολλὰ, καὶ πολὺν χρόνον·
Τεκμήριον δὲ τοῦδε τὸν Ὅμηρον λάβε,
οὗτος γὰρ ἡμῖν μυριάδας ἐπῶν γράφει,
ἀλλ' οὐδὲ εἷς Ὅμηρον εἴρηκεν μακρόν.

The man who never utters a word of sense consider to be tedious, even though he only give forth two syllables. The man who speaks with prudence, do not think him to be tedious, though he speak much and long. Take Homer as a proof of this : he writes myriads of words, yet no one ever called Homer tedious.

The Snail.
Ex Incert. Comœd. 19.

Ὡς εὐφυὲς ζῷον ὁ κοχλίας, νὴ τὸν Θεὸν,
ὅταν πονηρῷ περιπέσῃ τῷ γείτονι,
τὸν οἶκον ἄρας εἰς ἕτερον πορεύεται.
Νέμεται δ' ἀμέριμνος τοὺς κακοὺς φεύγων ἀεί.

How ingenious an animal is a snail, by God ! When it falls in with a bad neighbour, it takes up its house, and moves off ; for it dwells without anxiety, always flying the bad.

The Divine Nature.
Ex Incert. Comœd. 25.

Θεὸν νόμιζε καὶ σέβου, ζήτει δὲ μὴ,
πλεῖον γὰρ οὐδὲν ἄλλο ἢ ζητεῖν ἔχεις.
Εἴ τ' ἐστιν, εἴ τ' οὐκ ἔστι μὴ βούλου μαθεῖν,
ὡς ὄντα τοῦτον καὶ παρόντ' ἀεὶ σέβου.

Believe that there is a God, worship Him, but do not inquire too curiously into His essence ; for thou wilt have nothing for thy trouble except the labour of inquiry. Do not care to know whether He exists or not ; worship Him as if He existed, and were present.

A Slave.

Ex Incert. Comœd. 39.

Κ ᾂν δοῦλός ἐστι, σάρκα τὴν αὐτὴν ἔχει·
φύσει γὰρ οὐδεὶς δοῦλος ἐγενήθη ποτέ.
Ἡ δ᾽ αὖ Τύχη τὸ σῶμα κατεδουλεύσατο.

Though a man be a slave, he is the same flesh as thyself ; for no one has ever been born a slave by nature ; but Fortune subjected his body to servitude.

Anger.

Ex Incert. Comœd. 59.

Μαινόμεθα πάντες, ὁπόταν ὀργίζομεθα.
Τὸ γὰρ κατασχεῖν ἐστὶ τὴν ὀργὴν πόνος.

We are all mad when we are in a passion ; for it is a difficult task to restrain anger.

See (Lat.) Anger.

Bygone Evils.

Ex Incert. Comœd. 61.

Ὡς ἡδέως μοι γέγονε τὰ πρότερα κακά·
εἰ μὴ τότ᾽ ἐπόνουν, νῦν ἂν οὐκ εὐφραινόμην.

How pleasant it is to think of former evils ! for if I had not then been in difficulties, I would not now be in joy.

The Differences of Men.

Ex Incert. Comœd. 67.

Ἐνταῦθ᾽ ἀνὴρ γάρ ἐστιν ἀνδρὸς διάφορος,
ἐν τῷ τό, τε κακὸν εὖ φέρειν καὶ τ᾽ ἀγαθόν.

In this thing one man is superior to another, that he is better able to bear adversity and prosperity.

What we Ought to Pray for.

Ex Incert. Comœd. 68.

Αἰτῶ δ᾽ ὑγείαν πρῶτον, εἶτ᾽ εὐπραξίαν,
τρίτον δὲ χαίρειν, εἶτ᾽ ὀφείλειν μηδενί.

I pray, first, for good health ; then, for prosperity; thirdly, for happiness ; and, lastly, to owe no man anything.

So Romans (xiii. 8)—" Owe no man anything."

ANTICIPATION OF EVIL.
Ex Incert. Comœd. 71.

'Αγαθὴ γὰρ ἡ λύπη καθ' αὐτῆς ἀναπλάσαι
ἀτεχνῶς διπλάσια τῆς ἀληθείας κακά.

Grief is apt to imagine to itself evils more than double the reality.

See (Lat.) Foreboding of evil.

A GIFT OF AFFECTION.
Ex Incert. Comœd. 75.

"Απαν διδόμενον δῶρον, εἰ καὶ μίκρον ᾖ,
μέγιστόν ἐστιν, εἰ μετ' εὐνοίας διδῷς.

Every gift which is given, even though it be small, is in reality great if it be given with affection.

See (Lat.) A gift.

HONOUR YOUR FATHER AND MOTHER.
Ex Incert. Comœd. 107.

Βούλου γονεῖς πρὸ παντὸς ἐν τιμαῖς ἔχειν.

Before all things, pay respect to thy parents.

So Exodus (xx. 12)—"Honour thy father and mother."

AN AFFECTIONATE FATHER.
Ex Incert. Comœd. 108.

'Ηδύ γε πατὴρ τέκνοισιν, εἰ στοργὴν ἔχοι.

A father is dear if he treat affectionately his children.

[The two following are regarded to be doubtful.]

THE SWALLOW.
Ex Incert. Comœd. 114.

'Η μὲν χελιδὼν αὐτὸ θέρος, ὦ γύναι, λαλεῖ.

O woman! it is the swallow which announces the spring.

GOD.
Ex Incert. Comœd. 360.

A. Θεὸν δὲ ποῖον εἰπέ μοι νοητέον;
B. Τὸν πάνθ' ὁρῶντα κ' αὐτὸν οὐχ ὁρώμενον.

A. Tell me what thou understandest by God. *B.* The Being who sees all things, and yet is seen by none.

See (Lat.) God.

THE DEAD.

Ex Incert. Comæd. 360.

Οἴει σὺ τοὺς θανόντας, ᾧ Νικήρατε,
τρυφῆς ἀπάσης μεταλαβόντας ἐν βίῳ
πεφευγέναι τὸ Θεῖον ὡς λεληθότας ;
ἔστιν Δίκης ὀφθαλμὸς, ὃς τὰ πάνθ' ὁρᾷ·
καὶ γὰρ καθ' ᾅδην δύο τρίβους νομίζομεν,
μίαν δικαίων, χἀτέραν ἀσεβῶν ὁδόν.
Εἰ γὰρ δίκαιος κἀσεβὴς ἕξουσιν ἕν,
ἡ γῆ δὲ καλύψει τοὺς δύο τῷ παντὶ χρόνῳ,
ἅρπαζ' ἀπελθὼν, κλέπτ', ἀποστέρει, κύκα·
μηδὲν πλανηθῇς· ἔστι κἂν ᾅδου κρίσις,
ἥνπερ ποιήσει Θεὸς ὁ πάντων δεσπότης.
οὗ τ' ὄνομα φοβερὸν, οὐδ' ἂν ὀνομάσαιμ' ἐγώ,
ὃς τοῖς ἁμαρτάνουσι πρὸς μῆκος βίον
δίδωσι.

Dost thou think that the dead who have enjoyed the good things of this life have escaped the notice of the Divinity, as if they were forgotten? Nay, there is an eye of Justice which sees all things; for we believe that there are two roads to the lower regions, one for the just and one for the impious. For if the just and the impious are to have one and the same road, and if the grave covers them both for ever, then thou mayest rob, steal, plunder, and do every mischief thou choosest. Yet do not be mistaken, for there is a place of judgment below, which God the Lord of all shall occupy, whose name is terrible, and which I dare not utter, who gives a long licence to sinners.

PHILIPPIDES.

FLOURISHED B.C. 335.

PHILIPPIDES, one of the principal writers of the new comedy, who flourished B.C. 335, and is said to have written forty-five comedies. He is said to have died at an advanced age from excessive joy at having conquered unexpectedly in a contest with other poets.

To Commit a Fault.

Fr. Com. Gr. p. 1118.

Ὅταν δ᾽ ἁμαρτάνῃς τι, χαῖρ᾽ ἡττώμενος·
μάλιστα γὰρ οὕτω σώζεται τὸ συμφέρον.

When thou hast committed some fault, be glad that thou hast
failed, for it is chiefly in this way that the becoming is preserved.

Difference between Saying and Doing.

Fr. Com. Gr. p. 1119.

Οὐ χαλεπόν ἐστι τῷ κακῶς διακειμένῳ
εἰπεῖν τιν᾽ ἐσθίοντα " Μὴ κακῶς ἔχε,"
πύκτῃ τ᾽ ἐπιτιμᾶν οὐδὲν ἔργον μαχομένῳ,
αὐτὸν μάχεσθαι δ᾽ οὐκ ἔτ᾽ ἐστὶ ῥᾴδιον,
ἕτερόν τι τὸ λέγειν ἐστὶ τοῦ πεπονθέναι.

It is not difficult for one feasting to say to another in a sorry
plight, " Don't be miserable : " it is not hard to find fault with a
boxer fighting, but it is no easy matter to fight : there is a great
difference between saying and doing.

Man is Born to Trouble.

Fr. Com. Gr. p. 1128.

Ὅταν ἀτυχεῖν σοι συμπέσῃ τι, δέσποτα,
Εὐριπίδου μνήσθητι, καὶ ῥᾴων ἔσει.
" Οὐκ ἔστιν ὅστις πάντ᾽ ἀνὴρ εὐδαιμονεῖ."
Εἶναι δ᾽ ὑπόλαβε καὶ σὲ τῶν πολλῶν ἕνα.

When it has happened to thee to be unfortunate, master,
remember the saying of Euripides, and thou wilt be more easy—
" There is no man who is happy in every way." Then imagine
thyself to be one of the great crowd of mankind.

Time.

Fr. Com. Gr. p. 1129.

Ὁ κοινὸς ἰατρός σε θεραπεύσει χρόνος.

Time, the common physician, will heal thee.

PHILISCUS.

FLOURISHED ABOUT B.C. 400.

PHILISCUS, an Athenian comic poet of the middle comedy, of whom little is known.

THE BED.
Fr. Com. Gr. p. 793.

Εἰς τὸ μεταπεῖσαι ῥᾳδίως ἃ βούλεται
πιθανοὺς ἔχειν εἴωθεν ἡ κλίνη λόγους.

The bed usually possesses powerful reasons of persuasion to obtain what one wishes.

NOT EASY TO GAIN WITHOUT LABOUR.
Fr. Com. Gr. p. 794.

Οὐκ ἔστιν ὦ μάταιε σὺν ῥαθυμίᾳ
τὰ τῶν πονούντων μὴ πονήσαντας λαβεῖν.

O fool! it is not with ease that one can get without exertion the possessions of those who exert themselves.

PINDARUS.

BORN B.C. 522—DIED B.C. 442.

PINDAR, the greatest lyric poet of Greece, was a native of Bœotia, born either at Thebes, the capital of that country, or at Cynoscephalæ, a village in the territory of Thebes. We know very little of his private history, but he belonged to one of the noblest families of his country. He was sent by his father to Athens, where, under the celebrated dithyrambist, Lasos of Hermione, he learned music, dancing, and all the mysteries of the chorus requisite for his training as a lyric poet. He also attended the school of Agathocles and Apollodorus. Between the age of twenty and twenty-two Pindar began his professional career as a poet, but in the great events that took place in Greece during his time, Pindar seems to have taken no share.

WATER AND GOLD.

Olymp. i. 1.

Ἄριστον μὲν ὕδωρ· ὁ δὲ
χρυσὸς αἰθόμενον πῦρ
ἄτε διαπρέπει νυ-
κτὶ μεγάνορος ἔξοχα πλούτου.

Water is the best of all things : gold, like a blazing fire that gleams conspicuous from afar in the night, shines prominently amidst lordly riches.

POETICAL FICTIONS.

Olymp. i. 43.

Ἦ θαύματα πολλά·
καὶ πού τι καὶ βροτῶν φρένας
ὑπὲρ τὸν ἀληθῆ λόγον
δεδαιδαλμένοι ψεύδεσι ποικίλοις
ἐξαπατῶντι μῦθοι.
Χάρις δ᾽, ἅπερ ἅπαντα τεύχει τὰ μείλιχα θνατοῖς,
ἐπιφέροισα τιμάν,
καὶ ἄπιστον ἐμήσατο πιστὸν
ἔμμεναι τὸ πολλάκις.
Ἀμέραι δ᾽ ἐπίλοιποι
μάρτυρες σοφώτατοι.
Ἔστι δ᾽ ἀνδρὶ φάμεν
ἐοικὸς ἀμφὶ δαιμόνων κα-
λά· μείων γὰρ αἰτία.

Truly many things are wonderful : and it is not unlikely that in some cases fables decked out in cunning fictions beyond the truth give false accounts of the traditions of man. But Poesy, that smooth enchantress of mankind, by causing credit to be given to these myths, ofttimes makes the incredible to appear credible : the rolling years, however, are the surest test of truth. Now it is wise for man to speak nothing unseemly of the gods, and thus he will be free from guilt.

SLANDERERS.

Olymp. i. 84.

Ἀκέρδεια λέλογχεν θαμινὰ κακαγόρως.

Ofttimes slanderers get no good for their pains.

M

God is not to be Deceived.
Olymp. i. 102.

Εἰ δὲ θεὸν
ἀνήρ τις ἔλπεταί τι λασέ-
μεν ἔρδων, ἁμαρτάνει.

If a man expects that his deeds will escape the all-seeing eyes
of God, he is mistaken.

See Psalm xliv. 21.

Life not to be Passed Ingloriously.
Olymp. i. 129.

Ὁ μέγας δὲ κίνδυ-
νος ἄναλκιν οὐ φῶ-
τα λαμβάνει. Θανεῖν δ᾽ οἷσιν ἀνάγκα,
τί κέ τις ἀνώνυμον γῆρας ἐν σκότῳ
καθέμενος ἕψοι μάταν, ἁπάντων
καμῶν ἄμμορος.

A danger that is great does not allow man to be a coward.
Since death is the fate of all men, why should we sit in the dark,
and spend to no purpose a nameless life, taking no part in any
glorious deeds?

Differences in Mankind.
Olymp. i. 181.

Ἐπ᾽ ἄλλοι-
σι δ᾽ ἄλλοι μεγάλοι· τὸ δ᾽ ἔσχατον κορυφοῦται βασιλεῦσι.

Some are great in this, others in that; but the highest point of
glory is reached in kings.

What is Done cannot be Undone.
Olymp. ii. 29.

Τῶν δὲ πεπραγμένων,
ἐν δίκᾳ τε καὶ παρὰ δίκαν,
ἀποίητον οὐδ᾽ ἂν
χρόνος, ὁ πάντων πατὴρ,
δύναιτο θέμεν ἔργων τέλος.
Λάθα δὲ πότμῳ σὺν εὐδαίμονι γένοιτ᾽ ἄν.
Ἐσλῶν γὰρ ὑπὸ χαρμάτων,
πῆμα θνάσκει παλίγκοτον δαμασθὲν.
Ὅταν θεοῦ μοῖρα πέμπη
ἀνεκὰς ὄλβον ὑψηλόν.

O: deeds that have been done, whether rightly or wrongly, not even Time, the sire of all things, can annul their accomplishment; yet oblivion may come with prosperity. For by success a rankling sore is got the better of and put an end to, when kind Heaven causes happiness to spread from far.

See (Lat.) The past.

OUR FUTURE LOT UNKNOWN.

Olymp. ii. 55.

᾽Ητοι
βροτῶν κέκριται
πεῖρας οὔ τι θανάτου,
οὐδ᾽, ἀσύχιμον ᾽Αμέραν
ὁπότε, παῖδ᾽ ᾽Αλίου,
ἀτειρεῖ σὺν ἀγαθῷ
τελευτάσομεν.
Ροαὶ δ᾽ ἄλλοτ᾽ ἄλλαι
εὐθυμιᾶν τε μέτα καὶ
πόνων ἐς ἄνδρας ἔβαν.

There is no appointed term to men for their death; nor do we know when we shall pass through a quiet day, the child of the sun, with never-failing good; for currents run now this way, now that, bringing both pleasures and sorrows to mortals.

WEALTH WITH VIRTUE.

Olymp. ii. 96.

῾Ο μὰν πλοῦτος ἀρεταῖς
δεδαιδαλμένος
φέρει τῶν τε καὶ τῶν
καιρὸν, βαθεῖαν ὑπέχων
μέριμναν ἀγροτέραν,
ἀστὴρ ἀρίζηλος, ἀλαθινὸν
ἀνδρὶ φέγγος.

It is wealth, when adorned by virtues, that brings the attainment of our different aims, suggesting to the mind a deep care for them, a conspicuous star, the brightest lamp to men.

THE WICKED PUNISHED IN THE INFERNAL REGIONS.

Olymp. ii. 107.

Εἰ δέ μιν ἔχει
τις, ἴδεν τὸ μέλλον,
ὅτι θανόντων μὲν ἐν-
θάδ᾽ αὐτίκ᾽ ἀπάλαμνοι φρένες

M 2

ποινὰς ἔτισαν. Τὰ δ' ἐν τᾷδε Διὸς ἀρχᾷ
ἀλιτρὰ, κατὰ γᾶς δικά-
ζει τις, ἐχθρᾷ λόγον φράσαις ἀνάγκᾳ.

But he who possesses wealth is well aware of what is in store
for him,—that the guilty souls of those who die here have to dree
their penance in another life,—for there is one beneath the earth
who judges the crimes committed in this empire of Zeus, passing
sentence by a hateful constraint.

The Good in Elysium.

Olymp. ii. 109.

Ἴσον δὲ νύκτεσσιν αἰεὶ,
ἴσα δ' ἐν ἀμέραις, ἄλι-
ον ἔχοντες, ἀπονέστερον
ἐσθλοὶ νέμονται βίο-
τον, οὐ χθόνα ταράσσον-
τες ἀλκᾷ χερῶν,
οὐδὲ πόντιον ὕδωρ,
κεινὰν παρὰ δίαιταν· ἀλ-
λὰ παρὰ μὲν τιμίοις
θεῶν, οἵτινες ἔχαι
ρον εὐορκίαις,
ἄδακρυν νέμονται
αἰῶνα. Τοὶ δ' ἀπροσόρα-
τον ὀκχέοντι πόνον.

But the good, enjoying eternal sunshine night and day, pass a
life free from labour, never stirring the earth by strength of hand,
nor yet the waters of the sea in that blessed abode, but with the
honoured of the gods, all such as took pleasure in keeping their
plighted faith, spend a tearless existence, while the impious have
to endure woes too horrible to look upon.

The Man of Genius.

Olymp. ii. 154.

Σοφὸς ὁ πολ-
λὰ εἰδὼς φυᾷ·
μαθόντες δὲ, λάβροι
παγγλωσσίᾳ, κόρακες ὣς,
ἄκραντα γαρυέμεν,
διὸς πρὸς ὄρνιχα θεῖον.

That man is a true poet who knows much by inherent genius ,
while those who have acquired their knowledge, loquacious, like
crows, chatter vainly against the divine bird of Zeus.

DEEDS OF VALOUR WITHOUT RISK.

Olymp. vi. 14.

'Ακίνδυνοι δ' ἀρεταὶ
οὔτε παρ' ἀνδράσιν, οὔτ' ἐν ναυσὶ κοίλαις
τίμιαι· πολλοὶ δὲ μέ-
μναται, καλὸν εἴ τι πονάθῃ

Deeds of valour without risk are unhonoured either among men or in hollow ships ; whereas many speak of it if a noble action has been done with labour.

UNCERTAINTY OF HUMAN LIFE.

Olymp. vii. 43.

'Αμφὶ δ' ἀνθρώ-
πων φρεσὶν ἀμπλακίαι
ἀναρίθματοι κρέμανται.
Τοῦτο δ' ἀμάχανον εὑρεῖν,
ὅ τι νῦν, καὶ ἐν τελευ-
τᾷ φέρτατον ἀνδρὶ τυχεῖν.

Countless mistakes hang about the minds of men ; and it is a difficult thing to discover what now and also in the end is best to happen to a man.

MAN TURNED FROM HIS PURPOSE.

Olymp. vii. 79.

'Εν δ' ἀρετὰν
ἔβαλεν καὶ χάρματ' ἀνθρώ-
ποισι προμαθέος αἰδώς.
'Επὶ μὰν βαίνει τι καὶ
λάθας ἀτέκμαρτα νέφος,
καὶ παρέλκει πραγμάτων ὀρ-
θὰν ὁδὸν γ' ἔξω φρενῶν.

Now it is respectful obedience arising from forethought on which the merit and success of men depend ; but it sometimes happens, in an incomprehensible way, that a cloud of forgetfulness comes over the mind, and causes the right way of doing things to be unattended to, and to pass from the memory.

THE UPS AND DOWNS OF LIFE.

Olymp. vii. 173.

'Εν
δὲ μιᾷ μοίρᾳ χρόνου,
ἄλλοτ' ἀλλοῖαι διαιθύσσουσιν αὖραι.

But at one and the same point of time different breezes go rapidly in different directions.

VARIOUS FORTUNES OF MEN.

Olymp. viii. 16.

"Ἄλλα δ' ἐπ' ἄλλον ἔβαν
ἀγαθῶν, πολλαὶ δ' ὁδοὶ
σὺν θεοῖς εὐπραξίας.

Still different blessings come to different people, and many are the roads to fortune by the favour of the gods.

TO REPROACH THE GODS IS WISDOM MISAPPLIED.

Olymp. ix. 56.

Λοιδορῆσαι
Θεοὺς, ἐχθρὰ σοφία.

To reproach the gods is wisdom misapplied.

WHAT COMES BY NATURE IS THE BEST.

Olymp. ix. 152.

Τὸ δὲ φυᾷ, κράτιστον ἅπαν,
πολλοὶ δὲ διδακταῖς
ἀνθρώπων ἀρεταῖς κλέος
ὤρουσαν ἑλέσθαι.
"Ἄνευ δὲ θεοῦ, σεσιγα-
μένον γ' οὐ σκαιότερον χρῆ-
μ' ἕκαστον. Ἐντὶ γὰρ ἄλλαι.
Ὁδῶν ὁδοὶ περαίτεραι,
μία δ' οὐχ ἅπαντας ἄμμε θρέψει
μελέτα, σοφίαι μὰν αἰπειναί.

That which comes by nature is in all cases the best, though many men have tried to gain glory by taking lessons in valour. Whatsoever is done without the aid of the god had better be kept quiet. For there are different roads to glory, one better than another, yet one training will not lead us all alike. Perfect skill is difficult to attain.

NATURE REMAINS EVER THE SAME.

Olymp. xi. 19.

Τὸ γὰρ
ἐμφυὲς οὔτ' αἴθων ἀλώπηξ
οὔτ' ἐρίβρομοι λέοντες
διαλλάξαιντο ἦθος.

For their inborn character neither tawny fox nor roaring lions
are likely to change.

FUTURITY UNKNOWN TO MAN.
Olymp. xii. 11.

Σύμβολον δ' οὔ πώ τις ἐπιχθονίων
πιστὸν ἀμφὶ πράξιος ἐσ-
σομένας εὗρεν θεόθεν·
τῶν δὲ μελλόντων τετύφλωνται φράδαι.
Πολλὰ δ' ἀνθρώποις παρὰ γνώμαν ἔπεσεν,
ἔμπαλιν μὲν τέρψιος· οἱ δ', ἀνιαραῖς
ἀντικύρσαντες ζάλαις,
ἐσλὸν βαθὺ πήματος ἐν μι-
κρῷ πεδάμειψαν χρόνῳ.

No man on earth has ever yet found any sure presage from
Heaven about his future success. For the indications of coming
events are impervious to mortals. Many things befall men contrary to expectations, often against their wishes; while others,
meeting the stormy waves of woe, have in the twinkling of an eye
exchanged their deep sorrow for some substantial good.

MAN PROPOSES, GOD DISPOSES.
Olymp. xiii. 149.

Νῦν δ' ἔλπομαι μεν. Ἐν θεῷ γε μὰν
τέλος

At present I live in hope, but the issue is in the hand of the
gods.

ERUPTION OF ÆTNA.
Pyth. i. 40.

Τᾶς ἐρεύγονται μὲν ἀπλά-
του πυρὸς ἀγνόταται
ἐκ μυχῶν παγαί· ποταμοὶ
δ' ἀμέραισιν μὲν προχέοντι ῥόον καπνοῦ
αἴθων· ἀλλ' ἐν ὀρφναισιν πέτρας
φοίνισσα κυλινδομένα φλὸξ ἐς βαθεῖαν φέρει πόντου πλάκα σὺν πατάγῳ.

From it are belched out of its abysses the purest jets of un-
approachable fire. By day the streams of lava pour forth a lurid
torrent of smoke; but in the dark the ruddy flame, rolling in
volumes, carries rocks into the deep, level sea with a fearful roar.

Joy of Mariners returning Home.

Pyth. i. 64.

Ναυσιφορήτοις
δ' ἀνδράσι πρῶτα χάρις
ἐς πλόον, ἐρχομένοις πομ-
παῖον ἐλθεῖν οὖρον· ἐοικότα γὰρ
κᾀν τελευτᾷ φερτέρου νό-
στου τυχεῖν.

And to seafaring men, what first cheers them on their departure
is a favourable breeze for the voyage; for it is expected, too, in the
end, that they will obtain a better passage home.

Everything Proceeds from the Gods.

Pyth. i. 79.

'Εκ θεῶν γὰρ μαχαναὶ πᾶ-
σαι βροτέαις ἀρεταῖς,
καὶ σοφοὶ καὶ χερσὶ βια-
ταὶ περίγλωσσοί τ' ἔφυν.

For all the means of mortal valour come from the gods; they
make men to be wise, mighty in deeds, and eloquent in language.

Envy.

Pyth. i. 160.

'Απὸ γὰρ κόρος ἀμβλύνει
αἰανὴς ταχείας ἀπάδις.
'Αστῶν δ' ἀκοὰ κρύφιον θυμὸν βαρύ-
νει μάλιστ' ἐσλοῖσιν ἐπ' ἀλλοτρίοις.

For the mind is offended by hearing the constant praise of an
individual; and the gossip of the citizens gives secret pain to the
mind chiefly when the merit of others is the theme.

Envied rather than Pitied.

Pyth. i. 164.

Κρέσσων γὰρ οἰκτιρμῶν φθόνος.

To be envied is a nobler fate
Than to be pitied.

Truth.

Pyth. i. 167.

'Αψευδεῖ δὲ πρὸς ἄκμονι
χάλκευε γλῶσσαν.

Point thy tongue on the anvil of truth.

The Posthumous Verdict of Public Opinion.

Pyth. i. 179.

'Οπιθόμβροτον άν-
χημα δόξας
οἶον ἀποιχομένων ἀν-
δρῶν δίαιταν μανύει
καὶ λογίοις καὶ ἀοιδοῖς.

The posthumous verdict of public opinion alone shows the life of the dead to historians and poets.

What is to be Desired in Life.

Pyth. i. 191.

Τὸ δὲ παθεῖν εὖ, πρῶτον ἄθλων·
εὖ δ' ἀκούειν, δευτέρα μοῖ-
ρ'. 'Αμφοτέροισι δ' ἀνὴρ
ὅς ἂν ἐγκύρσῃ καὶ ἕλῃ,
στέφανον ὕψιστον δέδεκται.

The enjoyment of prosperity is what is first to be desired; to be well-spoken is the next best thing in life; but he who has enjoyed both, and really felt them, has received the highest crown of all.

A Benefactor should be Repaid.

Pyth. ii. 39.

Θεῶν δ' ἐφετμαῖς
Ἰξίονα φαντὶ ταῦτα
βροτοῖς λέγειν ἐν πτερόεντι τροχῷ
παντᾷ κυλινδόμενον·
τὸν εὐεργέταν ἀγαναῖς ἀμοιβαῖς
ἐποιχομένους τίνεσθαι.

It is by the express direction of the gods, as the story goes, that Ixion warns mortals, as he writhes and sprawls on the revolving wheel, "to pay back to one's benefactor, requiting him by kindly returns."

A Straightforward, Plain-speaking Man.

Pyth. ii. 157.

'Εν πάντα δὲ νομὸν εὐθύγλωσ-
σος ἀνὴρ προφέρει,
παρὰ τυραννίδι, χὠπόταν ὁ
λάβρος στρατός, χὠ̈ταν πόλιν οἱ σοφοὶ
τηρέωντι.

M 3

In every form of government a straightforward, plain-speaking man is most respected, whether it be a despotism, or tumultuous democracy, or where the educated few hold the sway.

WE MUST NOT FIGHT AGAINST GOD.

Pyth. ii. 162.

Χρὴ δὲ πρὸς
θεὸν οὐκ ἐρίζειν.

We should not fight against God.

FOOLS.

Pyth. iii. 36.

Ἔστι δὲ φῦλον ἐν ἀν-
θρώποισι ματαιότατον,
ὅστις, αἰσχύνων ἐπιχώ-
ρια, παπταίνει τὰ πόρσω,
μεταμώνια θη-
ρεύων ἀκράντοις ἐλπίσιν.

But that set of men is the most foolish of all who despise things at home, and feel pleasure at what is far off, pursuing vain objects with silly hopes.

SELF-INTEREST GETS THE BETTER OF WISDOM.

Pyth. iii. 96.

Ἀλλὰ κέρδει καὶ σοφία δέδεται.

For even wisdom is got the better of by self-interest.

ASK OF THE GODS WHAT IS REASONABLE.

Pyth. iii. 106.

Χρὴ τὰ ἐοικότα πὰρ
δαιμόνων μασευέμεν θναταῖς φρεσί,
γνόντα τὸ πὰρ ποδὸς, οἵας εἰμὲν αἴσας.
Μὴ, φίλα ψυχὰ, βίον ἀθάνατον
σπεῦδε· τὰν δ' ἔμπρακτον ἄντλει μα-
χανάν.

It is right to ask of the gods what is suitable to reason, recollecting what is before our feet, and of what nature we are. Do not, my soul, be anxious for an immortal life, but draw only on what is practicable.

GOOD AND EVIL.
Pyth. iii. 145.

Ἕν παρ' ἐσλὸν, πήματα σὺν
δύο δαίονται βροτοῖς
ἀθάνατοι. Τὰ μὲν ὦν
οὐ δύνανται νήπιοι κόσμῳ φέρειν,
ἀλλ' ἀγαθοὶ, τὰ καλὰ τρέψαντες ἔξω.

The immortals award to mortals a couple of woes with every good. These woes the silly cannot submit to with patience, but only the well-born, who turn the fair side outwards (as we do old clothes).

WISDOM AND FORTUNE NECESSARY TO BE JOINED.
Pyth. iii. 182.

Εἰ
δὲ νόῳ τις ἔχει
θνατῶν ἀλαθείας ὁδὸν,
χρὴ πρὸς μακάρων
τυγχάνοντ' εὖ πασχέμεν. Ἄλλοτε δ' ἀλλοῖαι πνοαὶ
ὑψιπετᾶν ἀνέμων.
Ὄλβος οὐκ ἐς μακρὸν ἀνδρῶν ἔρχεται,
ὃς πολὺς εὖτ' ἂν ἐπιβρίσαις ἄπηται.

But if any one has found the way of truth by his understanding, his prosperity he must obtain from the gods. Yet there are different currents of violent winds at different times. Man's happiness does not continue long if it be excessive.

"THERE IS A TIDE IN THE AFFAIRS OF MEN."
Pyth. iv. 509.

Ὁ γὰρ
καιρὸς πρὸς ἀνθρώπων βραχὺ μέτρον ἔχει.

For the right time of action has a brief limit for men.

WEALTH GIVES INFLUENCE.
Pyth. v. 1.

Ὁ πλοῦτος εὐρυσθενὴς,
ὅταν τὶς ἀρετᾷ κεκρα-
μένον καθαρᾷ βροτήσιος ἀνὴρ,
πότμου παραδόντος, αὐτὸν ἀνάγῃ
πολύφιλον ἐπέταν.

'Tis their wealth that gives men their influence, when they have received it from fortune combined with disinterested virtue, and take it to their house as an attendant that finds him many friends.

EXCUSE.
Pyth. v. 35.

Ὃς οὐ τὰν Ἐπιμαθέος
ἄγων ὀψινόου θυγατέρα πρό-
φασιν.

In that he did not take with him Excuse, the child of late-minded Afterthought.

WE ARE CREATURES OF A DAY.
Pyth. viii. 135.

Ἐπάμεροι. Τί δέ τις ; τί δ' οὔ τις ;
σκιᾶς ὄναρ, ἄνθρωποι. Ἀλλ', ὅταν αἴγλα
διόσδοτὸς ἔλθῃ,
λαμπρὸν φέγγος ἔπεσιν ἀνδρῶν
καὶ μείλιχος αἰών.

We are creatures of a day ; what man is no one can say. Man is but a shadowy dream ; and yet, when glory comes to them from Heaven, a bright light shines around them, and a pleasant life attends them.

VARIOUS PARTS TO VARIOUS MEN.
Nem. i. 36.

Τέχναι δ' ἑτέρων ἕτεραι.
Χρὴ δ' ἐν εὐθείαις ὁδοῖς
στείχοντα μάρνασθαι φυᾷ.
Πράσσει γὰρ ἔργῳ μὲν σθένος,
βουλαῖσι δὲ φρήν, ἐσσόμενον προϊδεῖν,
συγγενὲς οἷς ἔπεται.

Various parts are assigned to various men, but every one should proceed in a straightforward path, and contend with his understanding. For strength succeeds in action, but mind in counsel in those who naturally foresee the future.

THE MISER.
Nem. i. 44.

Οὐκ ἔραμαι πολὺν ἐν μεγάρῳ πλοῦ-
τον κατακρύψαις ἔχειν·

ἀλλ' ἐόντων, εὖ τε παθεῖν καὶ ἀκοῦ-
σαι, φίλοις ἐξαρκέων.
Κοιναὶ γὰρ ἔρχοντ' ἐλπίδες
Πολυπόνων ἀνδρῶν.

I care not to keep buried in my hall great wealth, but I would
rather enjoy what I have, and be regarded as liberal to my friends,
for the hopes of much-toiling men proceed on common interests.

OUR OWN SORROWS.

Nem. i. 82.

Τὸ γὰρ οἰκεῖον πιέζει
πάνθ' ὁμῶς· εὐθὺς δ' ἀπήμων κραδία
κᾶδος ἀμφ' ἀλλότριον.

For a family trouble seizes on every one alike, though for
another's woes the heart soon ceases to grieve.

INBORN MERIT.

Nem. iii. 69.

Συγγενεῖ δέ τις
εὐδοξίᾳ μέγα βρίθει.
Ὃς δὲ διδάκτ' ἔχει, ψεφηνὸς ἀνὴρ,
ἄλλοτ' ἄλλα πνέων, οὔποτ' ἀτρεκεῖ·
κατέβα ποδί, μυριᾶν
δ' ἀρετᾶν ἀτελεῖ νόῳ γεύεται.

'Tis by inborn merit that a man acquires pre-eminence; whereas
he who acts by precepts is a man of nought, swaying from this side
to that, never setting down a firm, well-directed foot; much he
attempts, but to little purpose.

MIRTH THE BEST PHYSICIAN FOR MAN'S TOILS.

Nem. iv. 1.

Ἄριστος εὐφροσύνα
πόνων κεκριμένων
ἰατρός· αἱ δὲ σοφαὶ
μοισᾶν θυγατέρες ἀοιδαὶ
θέλξαν νιν ἀπτόμεναι.
Οὐδὲ θερμὸν ὕδωρ τόσον
γε μαλθακὰ τεύχει
γυῖα, τόσσον εὐλογία φόρ-
μιγγι συνάορος.
Ῥῆμα δ' ἐργμάτων χρονιώ-
τερον βιοτεύει,
ὅ, τι κε σὺν Χαρίτων τύχᾳ
γλῶσσα φρενὸς ἐξέλοι βαθείας.

Mirth is the best physician for man's toils, when brought to a close. Songs, the wise daughters of the Muses, soothe him by their gentle approach. Nor does the warm water of the bath so soften the limbs as pleasing words set to the music of the harp relieve toil. A poem lives longer than deeds, when by the aid of the Graces the tongue draws it forth from the depth of the heart.

TRUTH NOT ALWAYS TO BE TOLD.

Nem. v. 30.

Οὔ τοι ἅπασα κερδίων
φαίνοισα πρόσωπον ἀλάθει' ἀτρεκής.
Καὶ τὸ σιγᾷν, πολλάκις ἔστι σαφώ-
τατον ἀνθρώπων νοῆσαι.

Truth is not always the best thing to show its face; silence is often the wisest thing for man to observe.

DESTINY DECIDES MAN'S ACTIONS.

Nem. v. 73.

Πότμος δὲ κρίνει
συγγενὴς ἔργων πέρι
πάντων.

It is the destiny that is born with man which determines all his actions.

THE RACE OF GODS AND MEN.

Nem. vi. 1.

Ἐν ἀνδρῶν, ἓν θεῶν γένος· ἐκ
μιᾶς δὲ πνέομεν
ματρὸς ἀμφότεροι.
Διείργει δὲ πᾶσα κεκριμένα
δύναμις, ὡς τὸ μὲν οὐδέν,
ὁ δὲ χάλκεος ἀσφαλὲς αἰεὶ ἔδος
μένει οὐρανός. Ἀλλά τι προσφέρομεν
ἔμπαν, ἢ μέγαν νόον, ἤ-
τοι φύσιν, ἀθανάτοις·
καί περ ἐφαμερίαν
οὐκ εἰδότες οὐδὲ μετὰ
νύκτας ἄμμε πότμος ἀν-
τιν' ἔγραψε δραμεῖν ποτὶ στάθμαν.

There is one and the same race of gods and men; it is from the same mother that we draw the breath of life; but powers wholly distinct separate us, for the one race is nought, while the brazen vault of heaven remains for all time a secure abode to the others. Yet we are in some respects like to the immortals both in mighty intellect and in form ; though we are ignorant of the goal that fate has marked out for us to run to, both by night and by day.

PUSILLANIMITY.

Nem. xi. 37.

'Αλλὰ βροτῶν
τὸν μὲν κενεόφρονες αὔχαι
ἐξ ἀγαθῶν ἔβαλον·
τὸν δ' αὖ, καταμεμφθέντ' ἄγαν
ἰσχὺν, οἰκείων παρέσφαλεν καλῶν,
χειρὸς ἕλκων ὀπίσσω, θυμὸς ἄτολμος ἐών.

But among mortals the one is deprived of success by empty boasting, so another, too much distrustful of his strength, fails to secure the honours that rightfully belong to him, being dragged backward by a spirit deficient in daring.

SEEDS OF LINEAL WORTH APPEAR AT INTERVALS.

Nem. xi. 48.

'Αρχαῖαι δ' ἀρεταὶ
ἀμφέρουτ' ἀλλασσόμεναι γενεαῖς ἀνδρῶν σθένος.
'Εν σχερῷ δ' οὔτ' ὧν μέλαιναι καρπὸν ἔδωκαν ἄρουραι·
δένδρεά τ' οὐκ ἐθέλει πάσαις ἐτέων περιόδοις
ἄνθος εὐῶδες φέρειν πλούτῳ ἴσον,
ἀλλ' ἐν ἀμείβοντι. Καὶ
θνατὸν οὕτω σθένος ἄγει
μοῖρα. Τὸ δ' ἐκ Διὸς ἀνθρώποις σαφὲς οὐχ ἕπεται
τέκμαρ. 'Αλλ' ἔμπαν μεγαλανορίαις ἐμβαίνομεν,
ἔργα τε πολλὰ μενοι-
νῶντες. Δέδεται γὰρ ἀναιδεῖ
ἐλπίδι γυῖα· προμα-
θείας δ' ἀπόκεινται ῥοαί.
Κερδέων δὲ χρὴ μέτρον θηρευέμεν.
'Απροσίκτων δ' ἐρώτων ὀξύτεραι μανίαι.

The brave deeds of their ancestors are reproduced in men, alternating in generations. Lands of black loam do not continuously give forth their produce, nor will trees bear a rich perfume on every returning season, but only in turns. And thus, likewise, is the human race led on by fate, and the signs that men get from Zeus are not clear. Yet withal we enter upon proud schemes, and eagerly attempt many enterprizes, for we are led on by insatiate hopes, while the currents of events lie far beyond our knowledge.

Custom.

Frag. Schol. Nem. ix. 35.

Νόμος ὁ πάντων βασιλεὺς θνατῶν τε καὶ ἀθανάτων
ἄγει δικαιῶν τὸ βιαιότατον ὑπερτάτᾳ χειρί.

Custom is the sovereign of mortals and of gods ; with its powerful hand it regulates things the most violent.

"Sufficient unto the Day is the Evil Thereof."

Isthon. viii. 26.

Τὸ δὲ πρὸ ποδὸς ἄρειον αἰεὶ
χρῆμα πᾶν. Δόλιος γὰρ αἰὼν
ἐπ' ἀνδράσι κρέμαται,
ἑλίσσων βιότου πόρον.
'Ιατὰ δ' ἔστι βροτοῖς
σύν γ' ἐλευθερίᾳ
καὶ τά. Χρὴ δ' ἀγαθὰν
ἐλπίδ' ἀνδρὶ μέλειν.

That which is present it is best at all times to look to ; for an
age of calamities hangs over men, making the path of life to be
winding ; and yet even these evils are able to be amended, if men
enjoy but freedom. A man ought to indulge in good hopes.

PLATO.

BORN B.C. 428—DIED B.C. 347.

PLATO, the celebrated philosopher of Athens, is said to have been
the son of Ariston and Perictione, or Potone. His paternal family
boasted of being descended from Codrus, and his maternal ancestors traced their descent from Solon. He received instruction
from the most distinguished masters of his time in grammar,
music, and gymnastics ; but he attached himself, in his twentieth
year, to Socrates, and from that time was devoted to philosophy.
Towards the close of his life he thanked God that he had been
made a contemporary of Socrates. On the death of Socrates, he
betook himself to Eucleides, at Megara ; and through his eager-
ness for knowledge, he was induced to visit Egypt, Sicily, and the
Greek colonies of Lower Italy.

During his residence in Sicily he became acquainted with the elder Dionysius; but soon quarrelled with that tyrant. On his return to Athens, he began to teach in the gymnasium of the Academy, and its shady avenues near the city. His occupation as a teacher was twice interrupted by journeys to Sicily. He is said to have died while writing, in his eighty-first, or, according to others, in the eighty-fourth year of his age.

THE WISDOM OF THE WORLD OF NO VALUE.

Apolog. Socr. 9.

Τὸ δὲ κινδυνεύει, ὦ ἄνδρες, τῷ ὄντι ὁ θεὸς σοφὸς εἶναι, καὶ ἐν τῷ χρησμῷ τούτῳ τοῦτο λέγειν, ὅτι ἡ ἀνθρωπίνη σοφία ὀλίγου τινὸς ἀξία ἐστὶ καὶ οὐδενός.

The God, O men, seems to me to be really wise; and by His oracle to mean this, that the wisdom of this world is foolishness, and of none effect.

See 1 Cor. i. 19, 20, 25.

OBEY GOD RATHER THAN MAN.

Apolog. Socr. 17.

Εἰ οὖν με, ὅπερ εἶπον, ἐπὶ τούτοις ἀφίοιτε, εἴποιμ' ἂν ὑμῖν ὅτι ἐγὼ ὑμᾶς, ὦ ἄνδρες Ἀθηναῖοι, ἀσπάζομαι μὲν καὶ φιλῶ, πείσομαι δὲ μᾶλλον τῷ θεῷ ἢ ὑμῖν, καὶ ἕωσπερ ἂν ἐμπνέω καὶ οἷός τε ὦ, οὐ μὴ παύσωμαι φιλοσοφῶν καὶ ὑμῖν παρακελευόμενός τε καὶ ἐνδεικνύμενος ὅτῳ ἂν ἀεὶ ἐντυγχάνω ὑμῶν.

If you were to offer, as I said, to dismiss me on such conditions, I would exclaim, O Athenians! I regard you with the utmost respect and affection, but I shall obey God rather than you; and, as long as I have life, and am able, I shall not cease devoting my-self to the pursuit of wisdom, and warning every one of you whom I happen to meet.

See Acts iv. 19, 20; v. 29.

TAKE CARE OF THE SOUL RATHER THAN OF THE BODY.

Apolog. Socr. 17.

Οὐδὲν γὰρ ἄλλο πράττων ἐγὼ περιέρχομαι ἢ πείθων ὑμῶν καὶ νεωτέρους καὶ πρεσβυτέρους μήτε σωμάτων ἐπιμελεῖσθαι μήτε χρημάτων πρότερον μηδὲ οὕτω σφόδρα ὡς τῆς ψυχῆς, ὅπως ὡς ἀρίστη ἔσται, λέγων ὅτι οὐκ ἐκ χρημάτων ἀρετὴ γίγνεται, ἀλλ' ἐξ ἀρετῆς χρήματα καὶ τἆλλα ἀγαθὰ τοῖς ἀνθρώποις ἅπαντα καὶ ἰδίᾳ καὶ δημοσίᾳ.

For I go about doing nothing else than preaching to young and old among you that it is not the duty of man to take care of the body, and of riches, so much as to look after the soul, how it may be made into the most perfect state ; telling you that virtue is not acquired from riches, but men derive riches, and every other blessing, private and public, from virtue.

See Matt. vi. 31.

FEAR NOT THEM THAT KILL THE BODY.
Apolog. Socr. 18.

Ἐμὲ μὲν γὰρ οὐδὲν ἂν βλάψειεν οὔτε Μέλητος οὔτε Ἄνυτος· οὐδὲ γὰρ ἂν δύναιτο· οὐ γὰρ οἴομαι θεμιτὸν εἶναι ἀμείνονι ἀνδρὶ ὑπὸ χείρονος βλάπτεσθαι.

For neither Meletus nor Anytus can injure me. It is not in their power ; for I do not think that it is possible for a better man to be injured by a worse.

See Matt. x. 28.

A JUDGE IS BOUND TO DECIDE WITH JUSTICE.
Apolog. Socr. 24.

Οὐ γὰρ ἐπὶ τούτῳ κάθηται ὁ δικαστής, ἐπὶ τῷ καταχαρίζεσθαι τὰ δίκαια, ἀλλ' ἐπὶ τῷ κρίνειν ταῦτα· καὶ ὀμώμοκεν οὐ χαριεῖσθαι οἷς ἂν δοκῇ αὐτῷ, ἀλλὰ δικάσειν κατὰ τοὺς νόμους.

For a judge sits on the judgment-seat, not to administer laws by favour, but to decide with fairness ; and he has taken an oath that he will not gratify his friends, but determine with a strict regard to law.

WHAT IS DEATH ?
Apolog. Socr. 32.

Ἐννοήσωμεν δὲ καὶ τῇδε, ὡς πολλὴ ἐλπίς ἐστιν ἀγαθὸν αὐτὸ εἶναι. Δυοῖν γὰρ θάτερόν ἐστι τὸ τεθνάναι· ἢ γὰρ οἷον μηδὲν εἶναι μηδ' αἴσθησιν μηδεμίαν μηδενὸς ἔχειν τὸν τεθνεῶτα, ἢ κατὰ τὰ λεγόμενα μεταβολή τις τυγχάνει οὖσα καὶ μετοίκησις τῇ ψυχῇ τοῦ τόπου τοῦ ἐνθένδε εἰς ἄλλον τόπον. Καὶ εἴ γε μηδεμία αἴσθησίς ἐστιν, ἀλλ' οἷον ὕπνος, ἐπειδάν τις καθεύδων μηδ' ὄναρ μηδὲν ὁρᾷ, θαυμάσιον κέρδος ἂν εἴη ὁ θάνατος. Ἐγὼ γὰρ ἂν οἶμαι, εἴ τινα ἐκλεξάμενον δέοι ταύτην τὴν νύκτα, ἐν ᾗ οὕτω κατέδαρθεν, ὥστε μηδ' ὄναρ ἰδεῖν, καὶ τὰς ἄλλας νύκτας τε καὶ ἡμέρας τὰς τοῦ βίου τοῦ ἑαυτοῦ ἀντιπαραθέντα ταύτῃ τῇ νυκτὶ δέοι σκεψάμενον εἰπεῖν, πόσας ἄμεινον καὶ ἥδιον ἡμέρας καὶ νύκτας ταύτης τῆς νυκτὸς βεβίωκεν ἐν τῷ ἑαυτοῦ βίῳ, οἶμαι ἂν μὴ ὅτι ἰδιώτην τινά, ἀλλὰ τὸν μέγαν βασιλέα εὐαριθμήτους ἂν εὑρεῖν αὐτὸν ταύτας πρὸς τὰς ἄλλας ἡμέρας καὶ νύκτας. Εἰ οὖν τοιοῦτον ὁ θάνατός ἐστι, κέρδος ἔγωγε λέγω· καὶ γὰρ οὐδὲν πλείων ὁ πᾶς χρόνος φαίνεται οὕτω δὴ εἶναι

ἢ μία νύξ. Εἰ δ' αὖ οἷον ἀποδημῆσαί ἐστιν ὁ θάνατος ἐνθένδε εἰς
ἄλλον τόπον, καὶ ἀληθῆ ἐστὶ τὰ λεγόμενα, ὡς ἄρα ἐκεῖ εἰσὶν ἅπαντες
οἱ τεθνεῶτες, τί μεῖζον ἀγαθὸν τούτου εἴη ἄν, ὦ ἄνδρες δικασταί ;

Besides, we may conclude that there is great hope that death is
a blessing. For death is one of two things, either the dead may
be nothing and have no feeling, or, as some say, there is a certain
change and transference of the soul from one place to another.
Well, then, if there be no feeling, but it be like sleep, when the
sleeper has no dream, death would surely be a wonderful gain.
For I should think, if any one having picked out a night on
which he had slept so soundly that he had no dream, and having
compared all the nights and days of his life with this night,
should be asked to consider and say how many days and nights
he had lived better and more pleasantly than this night during
his whole life, I should think that not only a private person, but
even the great king himself, would find them easy to number in
comparison with other days and nights. If, then, death be a
thing of this kind, I call it gain, for thus all futurity appears to
be nothing more than one night. If, on the other hand, death be
a removal hence to another place, and what is said be true, that
all the dead are there, what greater blessing can there be than
this, ye judges ?

RETURN NOT EVIL FOR EVIL.
Crit. 10.

Οὐδὲ ἀδικούμενον ἄρα ἀνταδικεῖν, ὡς οἱ πολλοὶ οἴονται, ἐπειδή γε
οὐδαμῶς δεῖ ἀδικεῖν.

Neither ought a man to return evil for evil, as many think ;
since at no time ought we to do an injury to our neighbours.

See Rom. xii 19 ; 1 Thess. v. 15.

"FROM WHENCE COME WARS AND FIGHTINGS AMONG YOU ?"
Phæd. 11.

Καὶ γὰρ πολέμους καὶ στάσεις καὶ μάχας οὐδὲν ἄλλο παρέχει ἢ τὸ
σῶμα καὶ αἱ τούτου ἐπιθυμίαι.

For nothing else but the body and its desires cause wars, seditions, and fightings.

See James iv. 1.

THE SPIRIT AT WAR WITH THE FLESH.
Phæd. 11.

Ἕως ἂν τὸ σῶμα ἔχωμεν καὶ ξυμπεφυρμένη ᾖ ἡμῶν ἡ ψυχὴ μετ
τοῦ τοιούτου κακοῦ, οὐ μή ποτε κτησώμεθα ἱκανῶς οὗ ἐπιθυμοῦμεν.

As long as we are encumbered with the body, and our soul is polluted with such an evil, we shall never be able sufficiently to obtain what we desire.

So Matthew (xxvi. 41)—" The spirit indeed is willing, but the flesh is weak."

WISDOM IS THE RIGHT COIN.
Phæd. 13.

'Εκεῖνο μόνον τὸ νόμισμα ὀρθόν, ἀνθ' οὗ δεῖ ἅπαντα ταῦτα καταλλάττεσθαι, φρόνησις, καὶ τούτου μὲν πάντα καὶ μετὰ τούτου ὠνούμενά τε καὶ πιπρασκόμενα τῷ ὄντι ᾖ καὶ ἀνδρεία καὶ σωφροσύνη καὶ δικαιοσύνη καὶ ξυλλήβδην ἀληθὴς ἀρετὴ μετὰ φρονήσεως.

That alone—I mean wisdom—is the true and unalloyed coin, for which we ought to exchange all these things; for this, and with this, everything is in reality bought and sold—fortitude, temperance, and justice; and, in a word, true virtue subsists with wisdom.

See Matt. xiii. 45 ; Prov. xvi. 16.

THE SOUL.
Phæd. 29.

'Η δὲ ψυχὴ ἄρα, τὸ ἀειδές, τὸ εἰς τοιοῦτον τόπον ἕτερον οἰχόμενον γενναῖον καὶ καθαρὸν καὶ ἀειδῆ, εἰς "Αιδου ὡς ἀληθῶς, παρὰ τὸν ἀγαθὸν καὶ φρόνιμον θεόν, οἶ, ἂν θεὸς ἐθέλῃ, αὐτίκα καὶ τῇ ἐμῇ ψυχῇ ἰτέον, αὕτη δὲ δὴ ἡμῖν ἡ τοιαύτη καὶ οὕτω πεφυκυῖα ἀπαλλαττομένη τοῦ σώματος εὐθὺς διαπεφύσηται καὶ ἀπόλωλεν, ὥς φασιν οἱ πολλοὶ ἄνθρωποι ; πολλοῦ γε δεῖ, ὦ φίλε Κέβης τε καὶ Σιμμία, ἀλλὰ πολλῷ μᾶλλον ὧδε ἔχει· ἐὰν μὲν καθαρὰ ἀπαλλάττηται, μηδὲν τοῦ σώματος ξυνεφέλκουσα, ἅτε οὐδὲν κοινωνοῦσα αὐτῷ ἐν τῷ βίῳ ἑκοῦσα εἶναι, ἀλλὰ φεύγουσα αὐτὸ καὶ συνηθροισμένη αὐτὴ εἰς αὑτήν, ἅτε μελετῶσα ἀεὶ τοῦτο—τοῦτο δὲ οὐδὲν ἄλλο ἐστὶν ἢ ὀρθῶς φιλοσοφοῦσα καὶ τῷ ὄντι τεθνάναι μελετῶσα ῥᾳδίως· ἢ οὐ τοῦτ' ἂν εἴη μελέτη θανάτου ;

Is it possible, then, that the soul, which is invisible, and proceeding to another place, spotless, pure, and invisible (and, therefore, truly called Hades—*i.e.* invisible), to dwell with the good and wise God (where, if God so wills it, my soul must immediately go),—can this soul of ours, I say, being such and of such an essence, when it is separated from the body, be at once dissipated and utterly destroyed, as many men say? It is impossible to think so, beloved Cebes and Simmias; but it is much rather thus—if it is severed in a state of purity, carrying with it none of the pollutions of the body, inasmuch as it did not willingly unite with the body in this present life, but fled from it, and gathered itself within itself, as always meditating this—would this be anything else than studying philosophy in a proper spirit, and pondering how one might die easily? would not this be a meditation on death?

So 1 John (iii. 2)—" Beloved, it doth not yet appear what we shall be : but we know that, when He shall appear, we shall be like Him ; for we shall see Him as He is."

See (Lat.) Soul.

TRANSMIGRATION OF SOULS.

Phæd. 31.

Οἷον τοὺς μὲν γαστριμαργίας τε καὶ ὕβρεις καὶ φιλοποσίας μεμελητηκότας καὶ μὴ διευλαβημένους εἰς τὰ τῶν ὄνων γένη καὶ τῶν τοιούτων θηρίων εἰκὸς ἐνδύεσθαι. Τοὺς δέ γε ἀδικίας τε καὶ τυραννίδας καὶ ἁρπαγὰς προτετιμηκότας εἰς τὰ τῶν λύκων τε καὶ ἱεράκων καὶ ἰκτίνων γένη.

For example, those who have given themselves up to gluttony, sensuality, and drunkenness, and have put no restraint on their passions, will assume the form of asses, and such like beasts. And those who have preferred to lead a life of injustice, tyranny, and rapine, will put on the appearance of wolves, hawks, and kites.

CAUSE OF MISANTHROPY.

Phæd. 39.

Ἥ τε γὰρ μισανθρωπία ἐνδύεται ἐκ τοῦ σφόδρα τινὶ πιστεῦσαι ἄνευ τέχνης, καὶ ἡγήσασθαι παντάπασί γε ἀληθῆ εἶναι καὶ ὑγιῆ καὶ πιστὸν τὸν ἄνθρωπον, ἔπειτα ὀλίγον ὕστερον εὑρεῖν τοῦτον πονηρόν τε καὶ ἄπιστον καὶ αὖθις ἕτερον· καὶ ὅταν τοῦτο πολλάκις πάθῃ τις, καὶ ὑπὸ τούτων μάλιστα οὓς ἂν ἡγήσαιτο οἰκειοτάτους τε καὶ ἑταιροτάτους, τελευτῶν δὴ θαμὰ προσκρούων μισεῖ τε πάντας καὶ ἡγεῖται οὐδενὸς οὐδὲν ὑγιὲς εἶναι τὸ παράπαν.

For misanthropy arises from a man trusting another without having a sufficient knowledge of his character, and, thinking him to be truthful, sincere, and honourable, finds a little afterwards that he is wicked, faithless; and then he meets with another of the same character. When a man experiences this often, and, more particularly, from those whom he considered his most dear and best friends,—at last, having frequently made a slip, he hates the whole world, and thinks that there is nothing sound at all in any of them.

PUNISHMENT OF THE WICKED.

Phæd. 62.

Ἐπειδὰν δὲ φερόμενοι γένωνται κατὰ τὴν λίμνην τὴν Ἀχερουσιάδα, ἐνταῦθα βοῶσί τε καὶ καλοῦσιν, οἱ μὲν οὓς ἀπέκτειναν, οἱ δὲ οὒς ὕβρισαν, καλέσαντες δ᾽ ἱκετεύουσι καὶ δέονται ἐᾶσαι σφᾶς ἐκβῆναι εἰς τὴν λίμνην καὶ δέξασθαι.

But when, being borne along, they arrive at the Acherusian lake, there they call upon and entreat, some those whom they slew, others those whom they injured, entreating them, they implore and humbly pray that they would allow them to go into the lake and receive them.

So Luke (xvi. 23)—" And in hell he lifted up his eyes, being in torments, and seeth Abraham afar off, and Lazarus in his bosom. And he cried and said, Father Abraham, have mercy on me, and send Lazarus, that he may dip the tip of his finger in water, and cool my tongue ; for I am tormented in this flame."

The Body the Grave of the Soul.
Cratyl. 17.

Καὶ γὰρ σῆμά τινές φάσιν αὐτὸ εἶναι τῆς ψυχῆς, ὡς τεθαμμένης ἐν τῷ νῦν παρόντι.

For some say that the body is the tomb of the soul, as being buried at the present time.

See Romans vii 24.

Wisdom.
Sympos. 3.

Εὖ ἂν ἔχοι, φάναι, ὦ Ἀγάθων, εἰ τοιοῦτον εἴη ἡ σοφία, ὥστ᾽ ἐκ τοῦ πληρεστέρου εἰς τὸν κενώτερον ῥεῖν ἡμῶν, ἐὰν ἁπτώμεθα ἀλλήλων, ὥσπερ τὸ ἐν ταῖς κύλιξιν ὕδωρ τὸ διὰ τοῦ ἐρίου ῥέον ἐκ τῆς πληρεστέρας εἰς τὴν κενωτέραν.

It would be well, Agatho (said Socràtes), if wisdom were of that nature that it would flow from the person who was filled with it to the one who was empty, when we touched each other, like the water in two cups, which will flow through a flock of wool from the fuller into the emptier, until both are equal.

Drunkenness.
Sympos. 4.

Ἐμοὶ γὰρ δὴ τοῦτό γε οἶμαι κατάδηλον γεγονέναι ἐκ τῆς ἰατρικῆς, ὅτι χαλεπὸν τοῖς ἀνθρώποις ἡ μέθη ἐστί· καὶ οὔτε αὐτὸς ἑκὼν εἶναι πόρρω ἐθελήσαιμι ἂν πιεῖν οὔτε ἄλλῳ συμβουλεύσαιμι, ἄλλως τε καὶ κραιπαλῶντα ἔτι ἐκ τῆς προτεραίας.

For from my knowledge of medicine, it has become very clear to me that drunkenness is a bad thing to men, and I would neither myself be willing to drink far on nor advise any one else to do so, especially if they were suffering from a surfeit of the night before.

To Die for Another.
Sympos. 6.

Ὁ ἔφη Ὅμηρος, μένος ἐμπνεῦσαι ἐνίοις τῶν ἡρώων τὸν θεόν, τοῦτο ὁ Ἔρως τοῖς ἐρῶσι παρέχει γιγνόμενον πα' αὐτοῦ.

Καὶ μὴν ὑπεραποθνήσκειν γε μόνοι ἐθέλουσιν οἱ ἐρῶντες, οὐ μόνον ὅτι ἄνδρες, ἀλλὰ καὶ αἱ γυναῖκες.

As to what Homer said, that a god breathed strength into some heroes, Love furnishes this, produced from himself to all lovers.
Moreover, to die for another lovers alone are ready, not only men, but also women.

See Rom. v. 7.

Men of Sense contrasted with the Multitude.
Sympos. 17.

Ὅτι νοῦν ἔχοντι ὀλίγοι ἔμφρονες πολλῶν ἀφρόνων φοβερώτεροι.

For to a man of any mind a few persons of sense are more awful than a multitude of fools.

Love makes a Man to be a Poet.
Sympos. 19.

Πᾶς γοῦν ποιητὴς γίγνεται, κἂν ἄμουσος ᾖ τὸ πρίν, οὗ ἂν Ἔρως ἅψηται.

Each becomes a poet when Love touches him, though he was not musical before.

Shakespeare ("As You Like It," act ii., sc. 7) speaks of a lover—
"With his woful ballad, made to his mistress' eyebrow."

The Effect of Love.
Sympos. 19.

Ὅτι οὗτός ἐστιν ὁ ποιῶν
εἰρήνην μὲν ἐν ἀνθρώποις, πελάγει δὲ γαλήνην
νηνεμίαν ἀνέμων, κοίτῃ δ' ὕπνον νηκηδῆ.
Οὗτος δὲ ἡμᾶς ἀλλοτριότητος μὲν κενοῖ, οἰκειότητος δὲ πληροῖ, τὰς τοιάσδε ξυνόδους μετ' ἀλλήλων πάσας τιθεὶς ξυνιέναι, ἐν ἑορταῖς, ἐν χοροῖς, ἐν θυσίαις γιγνόμενος ἡγεμών· πραότητα μὲν πορίζων, ἀγριότητα δ' ἐξορίζων· φιλόδωρος εὐμενείας, ἄδωρος δυσμενείας· ἵλεως ἀγαθοῖς, θεατὸς σοφοῖς, ἀγαστὸς θεοῖς· ζηλωτὸς ἀμοίροις, κτητὸς εὐμοίροις· τρυφῆς, ἁβρότητος, χλιδῆς, χαρίτων, ἱμέρου, πόθου πατήρ· ἐπιμελὴς ἀγαθῶν, ἀμελὴς κακῶν· ἐν πόνῳ, ἐν φόβῳ, ἐν πόθῳ, ἐν λόγῳ κυβερνήτης, ἐπιβάτης, παραστάτης τε καὶ σωτὴρ ἄριστος, ξυμπάντων τε θεῶν καὶ ἀνθρώπων κόσμος, ἡγεμὼν κάλλισ

τος καὶ ἄριστος, ᾧ χρὴ ἕπεσθαι πάντα ἄνδρα ἐφυμνοῦντα καλῶς
καλῆς ᾠδῆς μετέχοντα, ἣν ᾄδει θέλγων πάντων θεῶν τε καὶ ἀνθρώπων νόημα.

For it is Love that causes peace among men, a calm on the sea,
a lulling of the winds, sweet sleep on joyless beds. It is he who
takes from us the feeling of enmity, and fills us with those of
friendship; who establishes friendly meetings, being the leader in
festivals, dances, and sacrifices, giving mildness and driving away
harshness; the beneficent bestower of goodwill, the non-giver of
enmity; gracious to the good, looked up to by the wise, admired by the gods; envied by those who have no lot in life,
possessed by those who have; the parent of luxury, of tender-
ness, of elegance, of grace, of desire, and regret; careful of the
good, regardless of the bad; in labour, in fear, in wishes, and in
speech, the pilot, the defender, the bystander and best saviour;
of gods and men, taken altogether, the ornament; a leader the
most beautiful and best, in whose train it becomes every man to
follow, hymning well his praise, and bearing a part in that sweet
song which he sings himself, when soothing the mind of every
god and man.

See 1 Corinthians xiii.

"If thy Right Hand Offend thee Cut it off."

Sympos. 24.

Ἐπεὶ αὐτῶν γε καὶ πόδας καὶ χεῖρας ἐθέλουσιν ἀποτέμνεσθαι οἱ
ἄνθρωποι, ἐὰν αὐτοῖς δοκῇ τὰ ἑαυτῶν πονηρὰ εἶναι. Οὐ γὰρ τὸ
ἑαυτῶν, οἶμαι, ἕκαστοι ἀσπάζονται, εἰ μὴ εἴ τις τὸ μὲν ἀγαθὸν
οἰκεῖον καλεῖ καὶ ἑαυτοῦ, τὸ δὲ κακὸν ἀλλότριον· ὡς οὐδέν γε ἄλλο
ἐστὶν οὗ ἐρῶσιν ἄνθρωποι, ἢ τοῦ ἀγαθοῦ.

Since men are willing to have their feet and hands cut off, if
their own limbs seem to them to be an evil; nor do they cherish
and embrace that which may belong to themselves merely because
it is their own : unless, indeed, any one should choose to say that
what is good is attached to his own nature, and is his own, while
that which is evil is foreign and accidental ; since there is nothing
else of which men are in love but good alone.

See Matt. xviii. 8.

Virtue is from God.

Menon. 42.

Ἀρετὴ ἂν εἴη οὔτε φύσει οὔτε διδακτόν, ἀλλὰ θείᾳ μοίρᾳ.

The virtue that is in us comes not from nature, nor is it taught,
but is put in us by the Divinity.

So 2 Corinthians (iii. 5)—"Not that we are sufficient of ourselves to think
anything as of ourselves ; but our sufficiency is of God."

The Atheist.
Theæt. 12.

Εἰσὶ δὲ οὗτοι οἱ οὐδὲν ἄλλο οἰόμενοι εἶναι ἢ οὗ ἂν δύνωνται ἀπρὶξ τοῖν χεροῖν λαβέσθαι.

Those are profane who think that nothing else exists except what they can grasp with their hands.

So Psalm (xiv. 1)—"The fool hath said his heart, There is no God. They are corrupt; they have done abominable works; there is none that doeth good."

The Philosopher.
Theæt. 24.

Εὖ δὲ ἢ κακῶς τις γέγονεν ἐν πόλει, ἢ τί τῳ κακόν ἐστιν ἐκ προγόνων γεγονὸς ἢ πρὸς ἀνδρῶν ἢ γυναικῶν, μᾶλλον αὐτὸν λέληθεν ἢ οἱ τῆς θαλάττης λεγόμενοι χόες. Καὶ ταῦτα πάντ' οὐδ' ὅτι οὐκ οἶδεν, οἶδεν· οὐδὲ γὰρ αὑτῶν ἀπέχεται τοῦ εὐδοκιμεῖν χάριν. ἀλλὰ τῷ ὄντι τὸ σῶμα μόνον ἐν τῇ πόλει κεῖται αὐτοῦ καὶ ἐπιδημεῖ, ἡ δὲ διάνοια, ταῦτα πάντα ἡγησαμένη σμικρὰ καὶ οὐδέν, ἀτιμάσασα πανταχῇ φέρεται κατὰ Πίνδαρον, τά τε γᾶς ὑπένερθε καὶ τὰ ἐπίπεδα γεωμετροῦσα, οὐρανοῦ τε ὕπερ ἀστρονομοῦσα, καὶ πᾶσαν πάντη φύσιν ἐρευνωμένη τῶν ὄντων ἑκάστου ὅλου, εἰς τῶν ἐγγὺς οὐδὲν αὐτὴν συγκαθιεῖσα.

Whether a man dwelling in the city is nobly or ignobly born, whether some unfortunate event has taken place to one of his ancestors, man or woman, is equally unknown to him as the number of measures of water in the sea, as the proverb goes. And he is not aware of his own ignorance; nor does he keep aloof from such things from mere vanity, but, in reality, his body only dwells in the city and sojourns there, while his mind, regarding all such things as trivial, and of no real moment, despising them, is carried about everywhere, as Pindar says, measuring things under the earth and upon its surface, raising his eyes to the stars in heaven, and examining into the nature of everything in the whole universe, never stooping to anything near at hand.

Folly of Pride of Birth.
Theæt. 24.

Τὰ δὲ δὴ γένη ὑμνούντων, ὡς γενναῖός τις ἑπτὰ πάππους πλουσίους ἔχων ἀποφῆναι, παντάπασιν ἀμβλὺ καὶ ἐπὶ σμικρὸν ὁρώντων ἡγεῖται τὸν ἔπαινον, ὑπὸ ἀπαιδευσίας οὐ δυναμένων εἰς τὸ πᾶν ἀεὶ βλέπειν οὐδὲ λογίζεσθαι ὅτι πάππων καὶ προγόνων μυριάδες ἑκάστῳ γεγόνασιν ἀναρίθμητοι, ἐν αἷς πλούσιοι καὶ πτωχοὶ καὶ βασιλεῖς καὶ δοῦλοι βάρβαροί τε καὶ Ἕλληνες πολλάκις μυρίοι γεγόνασιν ὁτῳοῦν.

And when they praise nobleness of birth,—how some great man is able to show seven rich ancestors,—he thinks that such praise can only proceed from the stupid, and from men who look merely at trifles ; in fact, from those who, through ignorance, are not able to take a comprehensive view of the question, nor to perceive that every man has countless myriads of ancestors and progenitors, amongst whom there must have been myriads of rich and poor, kings and slaves, barbarians and Greeks.

Evil.
Theæt. 25.

'Αλλ' οὔτ' ἀπολέσθαι τὰ κακὰ δυνατόν, ὦ Θεόδωρε· ὑπεναντίον γάρ τι τῷ ἀγαθῷ ἀεὶ εἶναι ἀνάγκη· οὔτ' ἐν θεοῖς αὐτὰ ἱδρύσθαι, τὴν δὲ θνητὴν φύσιν καὶ τόνδε τὸν τόπον περιπολεῖ ἐξ ἀνάγκης. Διὸ καὶ πειρᾶσθαι χρὴ ἐνθένδε ἐκεῖσε φεύγειν ὅ τι τάχιστα. Φυγὴ δὲ ὁμοίωσις θεῷ κατὰ τὸ δυνατόν· ὁμοίωσις δὲ δίκαιον καὶ ὅσιον μετὰ φρονήσεως γενέσθαι.

It is not possible, Theodorus, to get rid of evil altogether ; for there must always be something opposite to good : nor can it be placed among the gods, but must of necessity circulate round this mortal nature and world of ours. Wherefore we ought to fly hence as soon as possible to that upper region ; but this flight is our resembling the Divinity as much as we are able, and this resemblance is that we should be just, and holy, and wise.

So John (iii. 6)—"That which is born of the flesh is flesh."
See Matt. v. 48 ; xviii. 7 ; John xvii. 21.

God and Man.
Theæt. 25.

Θεὸς οὐδαμῇ οὐδαμῶς ἄδικος, ἀλλ' ὡς οἶόν τε δικαιότατος, καὶ οὐκ ἔστιν αὐτῷ ὁμοιότερον οὐδὲν ἢ ὃς ἂν ἡμῶν αὖ γένηται ὅ τι δικαιότατος. Περὶ τούτου καὶ ἡ ὡς ἀληθῶς δεινότης ἀνδρὸς καὶ οὐδεμία τε καὶ ἀνανδρία.

God is in nowise in the least unjust, but is as just as possible ; and there is no one more like to Him than the man among us who has become as just as possible. It is on this that the real excellence of a man depends, and his nothingness and worthlessness.

So Psalm (xi. 7)—"For the righteous Lord loveth righteousness."

"Who shall Deliver Me from the Body of this Death ?"
Phædr. 30.

'Ολόκληρα δὲ καὶ ἁπλᾶ καὶ ἀτρεμῆ καὶ εὐδαίμονα φάσματα μυού-

μενοί τε καὶ ἐποπτεύοντες ἐν αὐγῇ καθαρᾷ, καθαροὶ ὄντες καὶ ἀσή-
μαντοι τούτου, ὃ νῦν σῶμα περιφέροντες ὀνομάζομεν, ὀστρέου τρόπον
δεδεσμευμένοι.

Being initiated, and beholding perfect, simple, and happy visions
in the pure light—being ourselves pure, and, as yet, unclothed
with this, which, carrying about us, we call the body, to which
we are bound as an oyster to its shell.

See Rom. vii. 24.

Every Good Gift is from Above.
Euthyphron, 18.

Φράσον δέ μοι, τίς ἡ ὠφέλεια τοῖς θεοῖς τυγχάνει οὖσα ἀπὸ τῶν
δώρων ὧν παρ' ἡμῶν λαμβάνουσιν; ἃ μὲν γὰρ διδόασι, παντὶ δῆλον·
οὐδὲν γὰρ ἡμῖν ἐστὶν ἀγαθὸν ὅ τι ἂν μὴ ἐκεῖνοι δῶσιν· ἃ δὲ παρ'
ἡμῶν λαμβάνουσι, τί ὠφελοῦνται; ἢ τοσοῦτον αὐτῶν πλεονεκτοῦμεν
κατὰ τὴν ἐμπορίαν, ὥστε πάντα τἀγαθὰ παρ' αὐτῶν λαμβάνομεν,
ἐκεῖνοι δὲ παρ' ἡμῶν οὐδέν.

Tell me, therefore, what benefits the gods derive from the gifts
they receive from us ; for the advantage derived from what they
bestow is evident to every one ; for there is no perfect gift which
they do not bestow ; but how are they benefited by what they get
from us? Have we so much advantage in this traffic, that we receive everything good from them, and they nothing from us?

See James i. 17.

Experience.
Gorg. 2.

Ὦ Χαιρεφῶν, πολλαὶ τέχναι ἐν ἀνθρώποις εἰσὶν ἐκ τῶν ἐμπειριῶν
ἐμπείρως εὑρημέναι· ἐμπειρία μὲν γὰρ ποιεῖ τὸν αἰῶνα ἡμῶν πορεύεσθαι κατὰ τέχνην, ἀπειρία δὲ κατὰ τύχην.

Chærephon, there are many arts among men, the knowledge of
which is acquired bit by bit by experience. For it is experience
that causes our life to move forward by the skill we acquire, while
want of experience subjects us to the effects of chance.

See (Lat.) Experience.

Best Things are Health, Beauty, and Riches.
Gorg. 7.

Οἶμαι σὲ ἀκηκοέναι ἐν τοῖς συμποσίοις ᾀδόντων ἀνθρώπων τοῦτο
τὸ σκολιόν, ἐν ᾧ καταριθμοῦνται ᾀδοντες, ὅτι ὑγιαίνειν μὲν ἄριστόν
ἐστι, τὸ δὲ δεύτερον καλὸν γενέσθαι, τρίτον δέ, ὥς φησιν ὁ ποιητὴς
τοῦ σκολιοῦ, τὸ πλουτεῖν ἀδόλως.

I think you must have heard at banquets men singing that distich, in which the singers run over the various blessings of life, —how the best is health, the second is beauty, and the third, as the author of the song says, is to be rich with innocence.

PUNISHMENT.
Gorg. 34.

Σωφρονίζει γάρ που καὶ δικαιοτέρους ποιεῖ καὶ ἰατρικὴ γίγνεται πονηρίας ἡ δίκη.

Punishment brings wisdom, makes men more just, and is the healing art of wickedness.

So Hebrews (xii. 5)—" My son, despise not thou the chastening of the Lord, nor faint when thou art rebuked of .Iim."

THE ADVANTAGE OF CHASTISEMENT.
Gorg. 81.

Εἰσὶ δὲ οἱ μὲν ὠφελούμενοί τε καὶ δίκην διδόντες ὑπὸ θεῶν τε καὶ ἀνθρώπων οὗτοι, οἳ ἂν ἰάσιμα ἁμαρτήματα ἁμάρτωσιν· ὅμως δὲ δι' ἀλγηδόνων καὶ ὀδυνῶν γίγνεται αὐτοῖς ἡ ὠφέλεια καὶ ἐνθάδε καὶ ἐν "Αιδου· οὐ γὰρ οἷόν τε ἄλλως ἀδικίας ἀπαλλάττεσθαι.

Those who derive advantage, suffering punishment both from gods and men, are such as have been guilty of offences that can be cured ; yet it is through pain and torments that advantage is derived both here and in Hades ; for injustice cannot be got rid of in any other way.

So Psalm (ciii. 3)—" Who forgiveth all thine iniquities ; who healeth all thy diseases."

TO BE, AND NOT TO SEEM GOOD.
Gorg. 83.

'Ανδρὶ μελετητέον οὐ τὸ δοκεῖν εἶναι ἀγαθον ἀλλὰ τὸ εἶναι, καὶ ἰδίᾳ καὶ δημοσίᾳ.

Not merely to appear good ought man to care, but to be so both privately and publicly.

So Matthew (xxiii. 28)—" Within ye are full of hypocrisy and iniquity."

GOOD SENSE CANNOT BE TAUGHT.
Protag. 10.

'Επειδὰν δέ τι περὶ τῆς πόλεως διοικήσεως δέῃ βουλεύσασθαι, συμβουλεύει αὐτοῖς ἀνιστάμενος περὶ τούτων ὁμοίως μὲν τέκτων, ὁμοίως δὲ χαλκεύς, σκυτοτόμος, ἔμπορος, ναύκληρος, πλούσιος, πένης, γενναῖος, ἀγεννής, καὶ τούτοις οὐδεὶς τοῦτο ἐπιπλήττει ὥσπερ τοῖς πρότερον, ὅτι οὐδαμόθεν μαθών, οὐδὲ ὄντος διδασκάλου οὐδενὸς αὐτῷ, ἔπειτα συμβουλεύειν ἐπιχειρεῖ· δῆλον γάρ, ὅτι οὐχ ἡγοῦνται διδακτὸν εἶναι.

But when the affairs of the city are the subject of discussion, any one rises up and gives his opinion on such matters, whether he be a builder, a brazier, a shoemaker, a merchant, a ship's captain, rich or poor, noble or ignoble, and no one makes objection to them as to the former, that without having received instruction, or having been the pupil of any one, they yet attempt to give advice, for it is evident that they think this cannot be taught.

Fools.
Protag. 31.

Τῶν γὰρ ἠλιθίων ἀπείρων γενέθλα.

The race of fools is not to be counted.

We ought to Listen to our Elders.
Republ. i. 1, 2.

Καὶ μήν, ἦν δ' ἐγώ, ὦ Κέφαλε, χαίρω γε διαλεγόμενος τοῖς σφόδρα πρεσβύταις δοκεῖ γάρ μοι χρῆναι παρ' αὐτῶν πυνθάνεσθαι, ὥσπερ τινὰ ὁδὸν προεληλυθότων, ἣν καὶ ἡμᾶς ἴσως δεήσει πορεύεσθαι, ποία τίς ἐστι, τραχεῖα καὶ χαλεπή, ἢ ῥᾳδία καὶ εὔπορος.

As for me, Cephalus, it gives me great pleasure to converse with those who are far advanced in years; for I feel that I ought to learn from them, as from men who have proceeded before me on that road along which we must perhaps travel, what is the nature of the road, whether it is rough and difficult, or easy and level.

See (Lat.) Old age.

Men are Fond of the Riches Accumulated by Themselves.
Republ. i. 4.

Ὥσπερ γὰρ οἱ ποιηταὶ τὰ αὑτῶν ποιήματα καὶ οἱ πατέρες τοὺς παῖδας ἀγαπῶσι, ταύτῃ τε δὴ καὶ οἱ χρηματισάμενοι περὶ τὰ χρήματα σπουδάζουσιν ὡς ἔργον ἑαυτῶν, καὶ κατὰ τὴν χρείαν, ᾗπερ οἱ ἄλλοι.

For as poets are fond of their own poems, and parents of their children, so also those who have made their own fortune are delighted with their wealth, as the workmanship of their own hands, not looking merely at its utility, as others are apt to regard it.

APPROACH OF DEATH CAUSES MAN TO REFLECT.

Republ. i. 5.

Εὖ γὰρ ἴσθι, ἔφη, ὦ Σώκρατες, ὅτι, ἐπειδάν τις ἐγγὺς ᾖ τοῦ οἴεσθαι τελευτήσειν, εἰσέρχεται αὐτῷ δέος καὶ φροντὶς περὶ ὧν ἔμπροσθεν οὐκ εἰσήει. Οἵ τε γὰρ λεγόμενοι μῦθοι περὶ τῶν ἐν Ἅιδου, ὡς τὸν ἐνθάδε ἀδικήσαντα δεῖ ἐκεῖ διδόναι δίκην, καταγελώμενοι τέως, τότε δὴ στρέφουσιν αὐτοῦ τὴν ψυχὴν μὴ ἀληθεῖς ὦσι· καὶ αὐτὸς ἤτοι ὑπὸ τῆς τοῦ γήρως ἀσθενείας ἢ καὶ ὥσπερ ἤδη ἐγγυτέρω ὢν τῶν ἐκεῖ μᾶλλόν τι καθορᾷ αὐτά. Ὑποψίας δ' οὖν καὶ δείματος μεστὸς γίγνεται καὶ ἀναλογίζεται ἤδη καὶ σκοπεῖ, εἴ τινά τι ἠδίκηκεν. Ὁ μὲν οὖν εὑρίσκων ἑαυτοῦ ἐν τῷ βίῳ πολλὰ ἀδικήματα καὶ ἐκ τῶν ὕπνων, ὥσπερ οἱ παῖδες, θαμὰ ἐγειρόμενος δειμαίνει καὶ ζῇ μετὰ κακῆς ἐλπίδος· τῷ δὲ μηδὲν ἑαυτῷ ἄδικον ξυνειδότι ἡδεῖα ἐλπὶς ἀεὶ πάρεστι καὶ ἀγαθὴ γηροτρόφος, ὡς καὶ Πίνδαρος λέγει.

For be assured of this, Socrates, that when a man imagines that he is approaching the close of his life, fearful thoughts enter his mind, and anxiety about things which never occurred to him before. For the stories told us respecting the regions below,— how the man who has acted unjustly here must there dree his punishment, though he may have laughed at them hitherto, now torment his spirit, lest they should, after all, be true. And the man, either from the weakness incident to old age, or because they are seen closer to him, looks at them with more attention. Then he becomes full of suspicions and dread, ponders and considers in what he has done any one wrong. Finding in his life many wicked and base deeds, and waking up from his sleep, like a child, he is overwhelmed with terror, and lives on with sad thoughts of the future. But to the man who is conscious of no wicked deed, there is sweet and pleasant hope, the solace of old age, as Pindar says.

See (Lat.) Death.

HATE NOT YOUR ENEMY.

Republ. i. 9.

Εἰ ἄρα τὰ ὀφειλόμενα ἑκάστῳ ἀποδιδόναι φησί τις δίκαιον εἶναι, τοῦτο δὲ δὴ νοεῖ αὐτῷ, τοῖς μὲν ἐχθροῖς βλάβην ὀφείλεσθαι παρὰ τοῦ δικαίου ἀνδρός, τοῖς δὲ φίλοις ὠφέλειαν, οὐκ ἦν σοφὸς ὁ ταῦτα εἰπών· οὐ γὰρ ἀληθῆ ἔλεγεν· οὐδαμοῦ γὰρ δίκαιον οὐδένα ἡμῖν ἐφάνη ὃν βλάπτειν.

If, then, any man says that it is right to give every one his due, and therefore thinks within his own mind that injury is due from a just man to his enemies, but kindness to his friends, he was not wise who said so, for he spoke not the truth ; for in no case has it appeared to be just to injure any one.

See Matt. v. 43.

The Good are Happy.
Republ. i. 24.

'Αλλὰ μὴν ὅ γε εὖ ζῶν μακάριός τε καὶ εὐδαίμων, ὁ δὲ μὴ τάναντία.

Surely, then, he who lives well is both blessed and happy, and he who does not the opposite.

So James (i. 25)—"This man shall be blessed in his deed."

God shows Mercy to the Children of the Righteous.
Republ. ii. 6.

Οἱ δ' ἔτι τούτων μακροτέρους ἀποτείνουσι μισθοὺς παρὰ θεῶν· παῖδας γὰρ παίδων φασὶ καὶ γένος κατόπισθεν λείπεσθαι τοῦ ὁσίου καὶ εὐόρκου.

Some, however, extend still further than these the rewards of the gods : for they say that children's children, and a future generation of the holy and pious, are left behind them.

See Deut. v. 10.

Impostors who Deceive Mankind.
Republ. ii. 7.

'Αγύρται δὲ καὶ μάντεις ἐπὶ πλουσίων θύρας ἰόντες πείθουσιν ὡς ἔστι παρὰ σφίσι δύναμις ἐκ θεῶν ποριζομένη θυσίαις τε καὶ ἐπῳδαῖς, εἴτε τι ἀδίκημά του γέγονεν αὐτοῦ ἢ προγόνων, ἀκεῖσθαι μεθ' ἡδονῶν τε καὶ ἑορτῶν, ἐάν τέ τινα ἐχθρὸν πημῆναι ἐθέλῃ, μετὰ σμικρῶν δαπανῶν ὁμοίως δίκαιον ἀδίκῳ βλάψειν, ἐπαγωγαῖς τισὶ καὶ καταδέσμοις τοὺς θεούς, ὥς φασι, πείθοντές σφισιν ὑπηρετεῖν.

Itinerant mountebanks and priests, hanging about the doors of the rich, are able to persuade the foolish that they possess a power, conferred on them by the gods, of atoning, by means of sacrifices and spells, in the midst of pleasures and revellings, for crimes committed by themselves or forefathers; and if they wish to crush an enemy, they may, at small expense, oppress the just equally with the unjust; while they are able, as they say, to persuade the gods, by coaxing and magic charms, to aid them in their objects.

See (Lat.) Impostors.

Division of Labour Recommended.
Republ. ii. 11.

'Εκ δὴ τούτων κλείω τε ἔκαστα γίγνεται καὶ κάλλιον καὶ ῥᾷον, ὅταν εἷς ἓν κατὰ φύσιν καὶ ἐν καιρῷ, σχολὴν τῶν ἄλλων ἄγων, πράττῃ.

From these things it follows that more will be accomplished, and better, and with more ease, if each individual does one thing, according to the bent of his genius, at the proper time, being engaged in no other pursuit.

How the Young ought to be Educated.

Republ. ii. 17.

Πολλοῦ δεῖ γιγαντομαχίας τε μυθολογητέον αὐτοῖς καὶ ποικιλτέον, καὶ ἄλλας ἔχθρας πολλὰς καὶ παντοδαπὰς θεῶν τε καὶ ἡρώων πρὸς συγγενεῖς τε καὶ οἰκείους αὐτων· ἀλλ᾿ εἴ πως μέλλομεν πείσεν, ὡς οὐδεὶς πώποτε πολίτης ἕτερος ἑτέρῳ ἀπήχθετο οὐδ᾿ ἔστι τοῦτο ὅσιον, τοιαῦτα μᾶλλον πρὸς τὰ παιδία εὐθὺς καὶ γέρουσι καὶ γραυσὶ καὶ πρεσβυτέροις γιγνομένοις, καὶ τοὺς ποιητὰς ἐγγὺς τούτων ἀναγκαστέον λογοποιεῖν.

Much less must we tell legends, in highly ornamental language, about the battles of giants, and many other and various bickerings of gods and heroes with their relatives and intimate friends ; but if we expect to persuade them that no one ought, on any pretext, to hate his neighbour, and that it is impious to do so, such principles are rather to be impressed upon them in their boyhood by old men and women, and those advanced in years ; and the poets ought to be compelled to write with such views before their eyes.

God not the Author of Evil.

Republ. ii. 18.

Ἀγαθὸς ὁ θεός—καὶ τῶν μὲν ἀγαθῶν οὐδένα ἄλλον αἰτιατέον, τῶν δὲ κακῶν ἀλλ᾿ ἄττα δεῖ ζητεῖν τὰ αἴτια, ἀλλ᾿ οὐ τὸν θεόν.

God is good—and no other must be assigned as the cause of our blessings ; whereas of our sorrows we must seek some other cause, and not God.

See James i. 17.

The Wicked Punished for their Good.

Republ. ii. 19.

Ἀλλ᾿ εἰ μὲν ὅτι ἐδεήθησαν κολάσεως λέγοιεν, ὡς ἄθλιοι οἱ κακοί, διδόντες δὲ δίκην ὠφελοῦντο ὑπὸ τοῦ θεοῦ, ἐατέον.

If they should say that the impious, as wretched, require chastisement, and, being punished, receive benefit from God, such assertion must be allowed to pass.

See Job v. 17 ; Prov. iii. 11

CHILDREN SHOULD NOT BE FRIGHTENED BY FEARFUL STORIES.

Republ. ii. 20.

Μηδ' αὖ ὑπὸ τούτων ἀναπειθόμεναι αἱ μητέρες τὰ παιδία ἐκδει-
ματούντων, λέγουσαι τοὺς μύθους κακῶς, ὡς ἄρα θεοί τινες περιέρ-
χονται νύκτωρ πολλοῖς ξένοις καὶ παντοδαποῖς ἰνδαλλόμενοι, ἵνα μὴ
ἅμα μὲν εἰς θεοὺς βλασφημῶσιν, ἅμα δὲ τοὺς παῖδας ἀπεργάζωνται
δειλοτέρους.

Nor let mothers, persuaded by them, frighten their children,
telling them foolish stories, how certain gods go about by night,
assuming the appearance of many and various strangers, lest they
should be both speaking insultingly of the gods, and at the same
time be making their own children cowards.

CHARACTER OF GOD.

Republ. ii. 21.

Κομιδῇ ἄρα ὁ θεὸς ἁπλοῦν καὶ ἀληθὲς ἔν τε ἔργῳ καὶ ἐν λόγῳ,
καὶ οὔτε αὐτὸς μεθίσταται οὔτε ἄλλους ἐξαπατᾷ, οὔτε κατὰ λόγους
οὔτε κατὰ σημείων πομπάς, οὔθ' ὕπαρ οὔτ' ὄναρ.

Ay, and more than that, God is simple and true in word and
deed, never changes, never deceives any one by words, or by the
suggestion of visions either by day or by night.

See Mal. iii. 6; James i. 17.

OVER-ATTENTION TO HEALTH.

Republ. iii. 15.

Τὸ δὲ δὴ μέγιστον, ὅτι καὶ πρὸς μαθήσεις ἁπτιναοσοῦν καὶ ἐννοήσεις
τε καὶ μελέτας πρὸς ἑαυτὸν χαλεπή, κεφαλῆς τινας αἰεὶ διατάσεις
καὶ ἰλίγγους ὑποπτεύουσα καὶ αἰτιωμένη ἐκ φιλοσοφίας ἐγγίγνεσθαι,
ὥστε, ὅπῃ ταύτῃ ἀρετὴ ἀσκεῖται καὶ δοκιμάζεται, πάντῃ ἐμπόδιος·
κάμνειν γὰρ οἴεσθαι ποιεῖ ἀεὶ καὶ ὠδίνοντα μήποτε λήγειν περὶ τοῦ
σώματος.

But what is more particularly to be remarked is that this attention to health is a hindrance to learning of any kind, to invention,
and to diligent study, as we are always feeling suspicious shoot-
ings and swimmings of the head, and blaming our learned studies
as the cause ; so that it is a great stumbling-block when virtuous
objects are aimed at and pursued, for it makes us always think
ourselves ill, and never to cease feeling pain in our body.

ALL MEN ARE BRETHREN, BUT SOME ARE OF FINER CLAY

Republ. iii. 21.

Ἐστὲ μὲν γὰρ δὴ πάντες οἱ ἐν τῇ πόλε ἀδελφοί, ὡς φήσομεν πρὸς

N

αὐτοὺς μυθολογοῦντες, ἀλλ' ὁ θεὸς πλάττων, ὅσοι μὲν ὑμῶν ἱκανοὶ
ἄρχειν, χρυσὸν ἐν τῇ γενέσει ξυνέμιξεν αὐτοῖς, διὸ τιμιώτατοί εἰσιν·
ὅσοι δ' ἐπίκουροι, ἄργυρον· σίδηρον δὲ καὶ χαλκὸν τοῖς τε γεωργοῖς
καὶ τοῖς ἄλλοις δημιουργοῖς. Ἅτε οὖν ξυγγενεῖς ὄντες πάντες τὸ μὲν
πολὺ ὁμοίους ἂν ὑμῖν αὐτοῖς γεννῷτε, ἔστι δ' ὅτε ἐκ χρυσοῦ γεννηθείη
ἂν ἀργυροῦν καὶ ἐξ ἀργυροῦ χρυσοῦν ἔκγονον καὶ τἆλλα πάντα οὕτως
ἐξ ἀλλήλων.

For all you in the state are undoubtedly brethren (as we shall
say, speaking in parables); but God, who made you, has mixed
gold in the composition of as many as He found able to be
governors of men; wherefore they are deemed the most honourable. In such as are merely assistants, He put silver; in husbandmen and other craftsmen, iron and copper. Since, then, they
are all related to each other, you will, in general, beget children like
to yourselves. Sometimes silver would be generated out of gold;
and from silver sometimes there might spring a golden race; and
in this way they are all generated from one another.

See Ezek. xxii. 18.

Excellent Things are Rare.
Republ. iv. 11.

Ἴσως γάρ, ὦ Σώκρατες, τὸ λεγόμενον ἀληθές, ὅτι χαλεπὰ τὰ
καλά.

For, Socrates, perhaps the common proverb is true, that excellent things are rare.

See (Lat.) Excellence rare.

Virtue.
Republ. iv. 18.

Ἀρετὴ μὲν ἄρα, ὑγίειά τε τις ἂν εἴη καὶ κάλλος καὶ εὐεξία ψυχῆς.

Virtue is a kind of health, beauty, and good habit of the soul.
So Titus (i. 13)—" That they may be sound in the faith."

Sin.
Republ. iv. 18.

Κακία δὲ νόσος τε καὶ αἶσχος καὶ ἀσθένεια.

Sin is disease, deformity, and weakness.
So John (viii. 34)—" Whosoever committeth sin is the servant of sin;"
and 2 Corinthians (iii. 17)—" Where the Spirit of the Lord is, there is
liberty."

To be Driven into a Corner.
Republ. vi. 3.

Καὶ ὥσπερ ὑπὸ τῶν πεττεύειν δεινῶν οἱ μὴ τελευτῶντες ἀποκλείονται καὶ οὐκ ἔχουσιν ὅ τι φέρωσιν, οὕτω καὶ σφεῖς τελευτῶντες ἀποκλείεσθαι, καὶ οὐκ ἔχειν ὅ τι λέγωσιν ὑπὸ πεττείας αὖ ταύτης τινὸς ἑτέρας, οὐκ ἐν ψήφοις ἀλλ᾿ ἐν λόγοις.

And as those who play at talus with the skilful, if they themselves know little of the game, are at last driven into a corner and cannot move a piece, so also your hearers have nothing to say, being driven into a corner at this different kind of play, not with the dice, but your reasonings.

The Good Man in an Evil World.
Republ. vi. 10.

Ταῦτα πάντα λογισμῷ λαβὼν ἡσυχίαν ἔχων καὶ τὰ αὑτοῦ πράττων, οἷον ἐν χειμῶνι κονιορτοῦ καὶ ζάλης ὑπὸ πνεύματος φερομένου ὑπὸ τειχίον ἀποστάς, ὁρῶν τοὺς ἄλλους καταπιμπλαμένους ἀνομίας ἀγαπᾷ, εἴ πῃ αὐτὸς καθαρὸς ἀδικίας τε καὶ ἀνοσίων ἔργων τόν τε ἐνθάδε βίον βιώσεται καὶ τὴν ἀπαλλαγὴν αὑτοῦ μετὰ καλῆς ἐλπίδος ἵλεώς τε καὶ εὐμενὴς ἀπαλλάξεται.

Taking all these matters quietly into consideration, and minding his own business, like a man taking refuge under a wall in a storm of dust and spray carried forward by the wind, the good man, seeing his neighbours overwhelmed by lawless proceedings, is delighted if he may in any way lead a life here below free from injustice and unholy deeds, taking his departure from this life with good hopes, cheerfully, and in joyous spirits.

The Good Man.
Republ. vi. 12.

Ἄνδρα δὲ ἀρετῇ παρισωμένον καὶ ὡμοιωμένον μέχρι τοῦ δυνατοῦ τελέως ἔργῳ τε καὶ λόγῳ;

And as regards the man, who is, as completely as possible, squared and made consistent with virtue in word and deed?

Description of the Nature of Man in this World, as Confined in a Dark Cave.
Republ. vii. 1.

Μετὰ ταῦτα δή, εἶπον, ἀπείκασον τοιούτῳ πάθει τὴν ἡμετέραν φύσιν παιδείας τε πέρι καὶ ἀπαιδευσίας. Ἰδὲ γὰρ ἀνθρώπους οἷον ἐν

N 2

καταγείῳ οἰκήσει σπηλαιώ δεῖ, ἀναπεπταμένην πρὸς τὸ φῶς τὴν
εἴσοδον ἐχούσῃ μακρὰν παρ' ἅπαν τὸ σπήλαιον, ἐν ταύτῃ ἐκ παίδων
ὄντας ἐν δεσμοῖς καὶ τὰ σκέλη καὶ τοὺς αὐχένας, ὥστε μένειν τε αὐτοῦ εἴς τε τὸ πρόσθεν μόνον ὁρᾶν, κύκλῳ δὲ τὰς κεφαλὰς ὑπὸ τοῦ
δεσμοῦ ἀδυνάτους περιάγειν, φῶς δὲ αὐτοῖς πυρὸς ἄνωθεν καὶ πόρρω-
θεν καόμενον ὄπισθεν αὐτῶν, μεταξὺ δὲ τοῦ πυρὸς καὶ τῶν δεσμωτῶν
ἐπάνω ὁδόν, παρ' ἣν ἰδὲ τειχίον παρῳκοδομημένον, ὥσπερ τοῖς θαυ-
ματοποιοῖς πρὸ τῶν ἀνθρώπων πρόκειται τὰ παραφράγματα, ὑπὲρ
ὧν τὰ θαύματα δεικνύασιν.

After these things, said I, compare our nature, as to education,
or the want of it, to a state somewhat like the following : for
behold, as it were, men in an underground, grotto-like dwelling,
having the doors opening towards the light, and extended the
whole length of the cavern ; in it see men immured from their
childhood, with their legs and necks loaded with chains, so that,
remaining ever there, they can only direct their eyes forward,
being unable to turn their necks round by reason of their chains ;
then suppose the light they receive to arise from a fire burning
above, afar off, and behind, while there is a road above between
the fire and those in chains, along which you may see a little wall
built, very much like the raised platforms of conjurors in front of
the audience, on which they exhibit their tricks.

Boys are not to be Forced to Learning.

Republ. vii. 16.

Μὴ τοίνυν βίᾳ, εἶπον, ὦ ἄριστε, τοὺς παῖδας ἐν τοῖς μαθήμασιν
ἀλλὰ παίζοντας τρέφε, ἵνα καὶ μᾶλλον οἷός τ' ῇς καθορᾶν ἐφ' ὃ
ἕκαστος πέφυκεν.

Do not, then, said I, my best of friends, train boys to learning
by force and harshness ; but direct them to it by what amuses
their minds, so that you may be the better able to discover with
accuracy the peculiar bent of the genius of each.

A Drone in the State.

Republ. viii. 7.

Ἦν δὲ οὐδὲν ἄλλο ἢ ἀναλωτής. Βούλει οὖν, ἦν δ' ἐγώ, φῶμεν
αὐτόν, ὡς ἐν κηρίῳ κηφὴν ἐγγίγνεται, σμήνους νόσημα, οὕτω καὶ
τὸν τοιοῦτον ἐν οἰκίᾳ κηφῆνα ἐγγίγνεσθαι, νόσημα πόλεως ; Πάνυ
μὲν οὖν, ἔφη, ὦ Σώκρατες. Οὐκοῦν, ὦ Ἀδείμαντε, τοὺς μὲν πτηνοὺς
κηφῆνας πάντας ἀκέντρους ὁ θεὸς πεποίηκε, τοὺς δὲ πεζοὺς τούτους
ἐνίους μὲν αὐτῶν ἀκέντρους, ἐνίους δὲ δεινὰ κέντρα ἔχοντας ; καὶ ἐκ
μὲν τῶν ἀκέντρων πτωχοὶ πρὸς τὸ γῆρας τελευτῶσιν, ἐκ δὲ τῶν
κεκεντρωμένων πάντες ὅσοι κέκληνται κακοῦργοι.

He was nothing else but a consumer of the fruits of the earth. Dost thou then, said I, mean that we should call such a person as this, as we do a drone in a bee-hive, the annoyance of the hive, a mere drone in his house, and the cause of ailment in the state? Quite so, Socrates, he replied. And has not God, Adimantus, made all the winged drones without any sting—and those that have feet, some without stings, and some with dreadful stings? And do not those without stings continue poor to old age? whereas those that have stings are those that we called mischievous.

A Democracy.
Republ. viii. 10.

Δημοκρατία δή, οἶμαι, γίγνεται, ὅταν οἱ πένητες νικήσαντες τοὺς μὲν ἀποκτείνωσι τῶν ἑτέρων, τοὺς δὲ ἐκβάλωσι, τοῖς δὲ λοιποῖς ἐξ ἴσου μεταδῶσι πολιτείας τε καὶ ἀρχῶν [καὶ ὡς τὸ πολὺ ἀπὸ κλήρων αἱ ἀρχαὶ ἐν αὐτῇ γίγνονται].

This, then, is a democracy, in my opinion, when the poor, getting the upper hand in the state, kill some and banish others, sharing equally among the remaining citizens the magistracies and high offices, which are usually divided among them by lot.

Overbearing Character of a Democracy.
Republ. viii. 14.

῞Οταν, οἶμαι, δημοκρατουμένη πόλις ἐλευθερίας διψήσασα κακῶν οἰνοχόων προστατούντων τύχῃ, καὶ πορρωτέρω τοῦ δέοντος ἀκράτου αὐτῆς μεθυσθῇ, τοὺς ἄρχοντας δή, ἂν μὴ πάνυ πρᾶοι ὦσι καὶ πολλὴν παρέχωσι τὴν ἐλευθερίαν, κολάζει αἰτιωμένη ὡς μιαρούς τε καὶ ὀλιγαρχικούς.

When a state under democratic rule, thirsting after liberty, chances to have evil cupbearers appointed, and gets thoroughly drunk with an undiluted draught of it, then it punishes even its rulers, unless they be poor, mean-spirited beings, who grant them every licence, accusing them as oligarchs, and corrupt.

Like Mistress like Dog.
Republ. viii. 14.

Αἱ τε κύνες κατὰ τὴν παροιμίαν οἷαίπερ αἱ δέσποιναι γίγνονταί.

As the proverb goes, dogs are like to their mistresses.

Excess Causes Reaction.
Republ. viii. 15.

Καὶ τῷ ὄντι τὸ ἄγαν τι ποιεῖν μεγάλην φιλεῖ εἰς τοὐναντίον μεταβολὴν ἀνταποδιδόναι, ἐν ὥραις τε καὶ ἐν φυτοῖς καὶ ἐν σώμασι, καὶ δὴ καὶ ἐν πολιτείαις οὐχ ἥκιστα.

For it is a fact that to do anything in excess usually causes re-action, and produces a change in the opposite direction, whether it be in the seasons, or in plants, or in animal bodies; but this is still more the case in forms of government.

THE WEALTHY.

Republ. viii. 15.

Πλούσιοι δή, οἶμαι, οἱ τοιοῦτοι καλοῦνται κηφήνων βοτάνη.

Such wealthy people, I think, are called the pasture of the drones.

FEW MEN HEROES TO THEIR VALETS.

Republ. ix. 4.

Εἰ οὖν οἰοίμην δεῖν ἐκείνου πάντας ἡμᾶς ἀκούειν, τοῦ δυνατοῦ μὲν κρῖναι, ξυνῳκηκότος δὲ ἐν τῷ αὐτῷ καὶ παραγεγονότος ἔν τε ταῖς κατ᾽ οἰκίαν πράξεσιν, ὡς πρὸς ἑκάστους τοὺς οἰκείους ἔχει, ἐν οἷς μάλιστα γυμνὸς ἂν ὀφθείη τῆς τραγικῆς σκευῆς, καὶ ἐν αὖ τοῖς δημοσίοις κινδύνοις, καὶ ταῦτα πάντα ἰδόντα κελεύοιμεν ἐξαγγέλλειν, πῶς ἔχει εὐδαιμονίας καὶ ἀθλιότητος ὁ τύραννος πρὸς τοὺς ἄλλους ;

If, then, I thought that we should all listen to the man, who having dwelt in the same house with him, and joining in his domestic transactions, is able to judge how he acts towards each of his domestics, on which occasions a man especially appears stripped of his actor's finery ; and so also in public dangers we would order him who has observed all this to declare how the tyrant stands as regards happiness and misery in comparison with others.

THE CHARACTER OF THE LARGER NUMBER OF MANKIND.

Republ. ix. 10.

Οἱ ἄρα φρονήσεως καὶ ἀρετῆς ἄπειροι, εὐωχίαις δὲ καὶ τοῖς τοιού-τοις ἀεὶ ξυνόντες, κάτω, ὡς ἔοικε, καὶ μέχρι πάλιν πρὸς τὸ μεταξὺ φέρονταί τε καὶ ταύτῃ πλανῶνται διὰ βίου, ὑπερβάντες δὲ τοῦτο πρὸς τὸ ἀληθῶς ἄνω οὔτε ἀνέβλεψαν πώποτε οὔτε ἠνέχθησαν, οὐδὲ τοῦ ὄντος τῷ ὄντι ἐπληρώθησαν, οὐδὲ βεβαίου τε καὶ καθαρᾶς ἡδονῆς ἐγεύσαντο, ἀλλὰ βοσκημάτων δίκην κάτω ἀεὶ βλέποντες καὶ κεκυ-φότες εἰς γῆν καὶ εἰς τραπέζας βόσκονται χορταζόμενοι καὶ ὀχεύοντες, καὶ ἕνεκα τῆς τούτων πλεονεξίας λακτίζοντες καὶ κυρίττοντες ἀλλή-λους σιδηροῖς κέρασί τε καὶ ὁπλαῖς ἀποκτιννύασι δι᾽ ἀπληστίαν.

Those, then, who have no knowledge of wisdom and virtue, but spend their lives in banquetings and things of that nature, are carried downwards, as it appears, and back to the middle space, there wandering all their lives ; wherefore, never getting beyond this, they do not raise their eyes nor direct their steps to the true upper regions, nor do they ever really fill themselves with real being, nor yet have they ever tasted solid and unadulterated pleasure ; but always looking downwards, like brutes, bending to the earth and their dinner-tables, they wallow in the feeding-trough and in sensuality ; and, from their wish to obtain such pleasures, they kick and butt at one another, as with iron horns and hoofs, perishing from their very inability to be satisfied.

"What, if a Man Gain the Whole World ?"

Republ. ix. 12.

Ἔστιν οὖν ὅτῳ λυσιτελεῖ χρυσίον λαμβάνειν ἀδίκως, εἴπερ τοιόνδε τι γίγνεται, λαμβάνων τὸ χρυσίον ἅμα καταδουλοῦται τὸ βέλτιστον ἑαυτοῦ τῷ μοχθηροτάτῳ.

Is there anyone, whom it avails to take gold unjustly, if some such thing as the following happens ; if, while he is taking the money, he is at the same time subjecting the best part of his nature to the worst?

See Matt. xvi. 26.

All Things Work Together for Good to the Just.

Republ. x. 12

Οὕτως ἄρα ὑποληπτέον περὶ τοῦ δικαίου ἀνδρός, ἐάν τ' ἐν πενίᾳ γίγνηται ἐάν τ' ἐν νόσοις ἢ τινι ἄλλῳ τῶν δοκούντων κακῶν, ὡς τούτῳ ταῦτα εἰς ἀγαθόν τι τελευτήσει ζῶντι ἢ καὶ ἀποθανόντι. Οὐ γὰρ δὴ ὑπό γε θεῶν ποτε ἀμελεῖται, ὃς ἂν προθυμεῖσθαι ἐθέλῃ δίκαιος γίνεσθαι καὶ ἐπιτηδεύων ἀρετὴν εἰς ὅσον δυνατὸν ἀνθρώπῳ ὁμοιοῦσθαι θεῷ.

We must thus think of the just man, that, if he fall into poverty or disease, or any other of these seeming evils, all these things work together for good to him, either alive or dead. For the man is never neglected by the gods, whosoever exerts himself to the utmost to become just, and to practise virtue, so far as it is possible for a man to resemble God.

See Matt. v. 48 ; John xvii. 21 ; Rom. viii. 28.

All Run, but One Receiveth the Prize.

Republ. x. 12.

Τὰ μὲν δὴ παρὰ θεῶν τοιαῦτ' ἂν εἴη νικητήρια τῷ δικαίῳ. Τί δέ, παρ' ἀνθρώπων; οὐχ οἱ μὲν δεινοί τε καὶ ἄδικοι δρῶσιν ὅπερ οἱ

δρομῆς, ὅσοι ἂν θέωσιν εὖ ἀπο τῶν κάτω, ἀπὸ δὲ τῶν ἄνω μή ; τὸ
μὲν πρῶτον ὀξέως ἀποπηδῶσι, τελευτῶντες δὲ καταγέλαστοι γίγνονται, τὰ ὦτα ἐπὶ τῶν ὤμων ἔχοντες καὶ ἀστεφάνωται ἀποτρέχοντες·
οἱ δὲ τῇ ἀληθείᾳ δρομικοὶ εἰς τέλος ἐλθόντες τά τε ἄθλα λαμβάνουσι
καὶ στεφανοῦνται.

Such are the prizes which the just man receives from the gods.
What do they receive from men? Do not cunning and unjust
men do the same thing as those racers who run well at the beginning, but not so at the end? For at first they leap briskly;
but at last they become ridiculous, and, having their ears on their
neck, they run off without any reward. But such as are true
racers, coming to the goal, they both receive the prize, and are
crowned.

See 1 Cor. ix. 24.

THE JUDGMENT-DAY.

Republ. x. 13.

Ἀναβιοὺς δ' ἔλεγεν ἃ ἐκεῖ ἴδοι. Ἔφη δέ, ἐπειδὴ οὗ ἐκβῆναι τὴν
ψυχήν, πορεύεσθαι μετὰ πολλῶν, καὶ ἀφικνεῖσθαι σφᾶς εἰς τόπον
τινὰ δαιμόνιον, ἐν ᾧ τῆς τε γῆς δύ' εἶναι χάσματα ἐχομένω ἀλλή-
λοιν καὶ τοῦ οὐρανοῦ αὖ ἐν τῷ ἄνω ἄλλα καταντικρύ· δικαστὰς δὲ
μεταξὺ τούτων καθῆσθαι, οὕς, ἐπειδὴ διαδικάσειαν, τοὺς μὲν δικαίους
κελεύειν πορεύεσθαι τὴν εἰς δεξιάν τε καὶ ἄνω διὰ τοῦ οὐρανοῦ, σημεῖα
περιάψαντας τῶν δεδικασμένων ἐν τῷ πρόσθεν, τοὺς δὲ ἀδίκους τὴν
εἰς ἀριστεράν τε καὶ κάτω, ἔχοντας καὶ τούτους ἐν τῷ ὄπισθεν σημεῖα
πάντων ὧν ἔπραξαν. Ἑαυτοῦ δὲ προσελθόντος εἰπεῖν, ὅτι δέοι αὐτὸν
ἄγγελον ἀνθρώποις γενέσθαι τῶν ἐκεῖ καὶ διακελεύοιντό οἱ ἀκούειν τε
καὶ θεᾶσθαι πάντα τὰ ἐν τῷ τόπῳ. Ὁρᾶν δὴ ταύτῃ μὲν καθ' ἑκάτε-
ρον τὸ χάσμα τοῦ οὐρανοῦ τε καὶ τῆς γῆς ἀπιούσας τὰς ψυχάς, ἐπειδὴ
αὐταῖς δικασθείη, κατὰ δε τὼ ἑτέρω ἐκ μὲν τοῦ ἀνιέναι ἐκ τῆς γῆς
μεστὰς αὐχμοῦ τε καὶ κόνεως, ἐκ δὲ τοῦ ἑτέρου καταβαίνειν ἑτέρας
ἐκ τοῦ οὐρανοῦ καθαράς· καὶ τὰς ἀεὶ ἀφικνουμένας ὥσπερ ἐκ πολλῆς
πορείας φαίνεσθαι ἥκειν, καὶ ἀσμένας εἰς τὸν λειμῶνα ἀπιοῦσας οἷον
ἐν πανηγύρει κατασκηνᾶσθαι, καὶ ἀσπάζεσθαί τε ἀλλήλας ὅσαι γνώ-
ριμαι, καὶ πυνθάνεσθαι τάς τε ἐκ τῆς γῆς ἡκούσας παρὰ τῶν ἑτέρων
τὰ ἐκεῖ καὶ τὰς ἐκ τοῦ οὐρανοῦ τὰ παρ' ἐκείναις, διηγεῖσθαι δὲ ἀλλήλαις τὰς μὲν ὀδυρομένας τε καὶ κλαιούσας, ἀναμιμνησκομένας ὅσα τε
καὶ οἷα πάθοιεν καὶ ἴδοιεν ἐν τῇ ὑπὸ γῆς πορείᾳ—εἶναι δὲ τὴν πορείαν
χιλιέτη—τὰς δ' αὖ ἐκ τοῦ οὐρανοῦ εὐπαθείας διηγεῖσθαι καὶ θέας
ἀμηχάνους τὸ κάλλος. Τὰ μὲν οὖν πολλά, ὦ Γλαύκων, πολλοῦ
χρόνου διηγήσασθαι· τὸ δ' οὖν κεφάλαιον ἔφη τόδε εἶναι, ὅσα πω-
ποτέ τινα ἠδίκησαν καὶ ὅσους ἕκαστοι, ὑπὲρ ἁπάντων δίκην δεδω-
κέναι ἐν μέρει, ὑπὲρ ἑκάστου δεκάκις, τοῦτο δ' εἶναι κατὰ ἑκατον-
ταετηρίδα ἑκάστην, ὡς βίου ὄντος τοσούτου τοῦ ἀνθρωπίνου, ἵνα δεκα-
πλάσιον τὸ ἔκτισμα τοῦ ἀδικήματος ἐκτίνοιεν· καὶ οἷον εἴ τινες πολλῶν
θανάτων ἦσαν αἴτιοι, ἢ πόλεις προδόντες ἢ στρατόπεδα καὶ εἰς δου-

λεισς ἐμβεβληκ'τες, ἤ τινος ἄλλης κακουχίας μεταίτιοι, πάντων τού, ω δεκαπλασίας ἀλγηδόνας ὑπὲρ ἑκάστου κομίσαιντο, καὶ αὖ εἴ τινας ι:!εργεσίας εὐεργετηκότες καὶ δίκαιοι καὶ ὅσιοι γεγονότες εἶεν, κατὰ ταὐτὰ τὴν ἀξίαν κομίζοιντο.

Having come to life again, he told what he had seen in his deathlike state. He said that when his soul was separated from his body it proceeded with many others, and reached a certain hallowed spot, where were two chasms in the earth close to each other, and the same number in the heavens above opposite to them. Between them sat the judges. After they had given sentence, they ordered the just to go to the right upwards to heaven, fastening marks on the foreheads of those whose fate they had decided; and the unjust went to the left downwards, having behind an account of all which they had done. That the judges, having approached him, said that he must be a messenger to men, to give an account of the things which he had seen there, ordering him to see and hear all things in the place. And that he saw there souls departing, after they had been judged, through two openings, one in the heaven, and one in the earth. And from the other two openings he saw from the one souls ascending from the earth, covered with filth and dirt; and through the other he saw souls descending pure from heaven. And ever and anon, as they arrived, they seemed to come off a long journey, and with pleasure went to rest in a meadow, as in a public assembly. Then acquaintances saluted each other; and those from the earth asked news from above, and those from heaven inquired what was going on below. They told one another; the one party wailing and weeping when they called to mind what and how many things they had suffered and seen in their journey under the earth, (now the journey was for a thousand years;) and, on the other hand, those from heaven related their enjoyments, and sights of wondrous beauty. It would be tedious, Glaucon, to relate them all. The sum of all he said was this : whatever unjust acts they had committed, and whomsoever they had injured, for all these they atoned separately, tenfold for each, and it was in each at the rate of one hundred years, (as the life of a man was considered to be so long,) so that they might suffer tenfold punishment for their unjust deeds ; and if any one had been the cause of many deaths, either by betraying cities or camps, or enslaving men, or participating in any such wickedness, for all such things they should suffer tenfold pains ; and if, on the other hand, they had bestowed benefits on any, having been just and holy, they should be rewarded according to their deserts.

See Matt. xxv. 33 : xiii. 49.

No Man hath Seen God.

Tim. 5.

Τὸν μὲν οὖν ποιητὴν καὶ πατέρα τοῦδε τοῦ παντὸς εὑρεῖν τε ἔργον καὶ εὑρόντα εἰς πάντας ἀδύνατον λέγειν.

It is impossible to discover the Creator and Father of this universe, as well as His work, and when discovered to reveal Him to mankind at large.

See John i. 18.

God Created Man after His Own Image.

Tim. 10.

Ὡς δὲ κινηθὲν αὐτὸ καὶ ζῶν ἐνόησε ἀϊδίων θεῶν γεγονὸς ἄγαλμα ὁ γεννήσας πατήρ, ἠγάσθη τε καὶ εὐφρανθεὶς ἔτι δὴ μᾶλλον ὅμοιον, πρὸς τὸ παράδειγμα ἐπενόησεν ἀπεργάσασθαι.

When the Creator, the Father of all things, saw that this created image of the everlasting gods had both motion and life, He pronounced it to be good ; and, being delighted with the workmanship of His own hands, He proceeded to consider how He might make it still more to resemble its prototype.

See Gen. i. 31.

The Noblest Victory is to Conquer One's Self.

Leg. i. 3.

Τὸ νικᾶν αὐτὸν αὑτὸν πασῶν νικῶν πρώτη τε καὶ ἀρίστη, τὸ δὲ ἡττᾶσθαι αὐτὸν ὑφ᾽ ἑαυτοῦ πάντων αἴσχιστόν τε ἅμα καὶ κάκιστον. Ταῦτα γὰρ ὡς πολέμου ἐν ἑκάστοις ἡμῶν ὄντος πρὸς ἡμᾶς αὐτοὺς σημαίνει.

For a man to conquer himself is the first and noblest of all victories, whereas to be vanquished by himself is the basest and most shameful of all things. For such expressions show that there is a war in each of us against ourselves.

See Rom. vii. 15.

Passions of Man.

Leg. i. 13.

Περὶ δὴ τούτων διανοηθῶμεν οὑτωσί. Θαῦμα μὲν ἕκαστον ἡμῶν ἡγησώμεθα τῶν θεῶν ζῶον εἴτε ὡς παίγνιον ἐκείνων εἴτε ὡς σπουδῇ τινι ξυνεστηκός· οὐ γὰρ δὴ τοῦτό γε γιγνώσκομεν, τόδε δὲ ἴσμεν, ὅτι ταῦτα τὰ πάθη ἐν ἡμῖν οἷον νεῦρα ἢ μήρινθοί τινες ἐνοῦσαι σπῶσί τε ἡμᾶς καὶ ἀλλήλαις ἀνθέλκουσιν ἐναντίαι οὖσαι ἐπ᾽ ἐναντίας πράξεις, οὗ δὴ διωρισμένη ἀρετὴ καὶ κακία κεῖται· μιᾷ γάρ φησιν ὁ λόγος δεῖν τῶν ἕλξεων ξυνεπόμενον ἀεὶ καὶ μηδαμῇ ἀπολειπόμενον ἐκείνης ἀνθέλκειν τοῖς ἄλλοις νεύροις ἕκαστον, ταύτην δ᾽ εἶναι τὴν τοῦ λογισμοῦ ἀγωγὴν χρυσῆν καὶ ἱεράν, τῆς πόλεως κοινὸν νόμον ἐπικαλουμένην, ἄλλας δὲ σκληρὰς καὶ σιδηρᾶς, τὴν δὲ μαλακὴν ἅτε χρυσῆν οὖσαν καὶ μονοειδῆ τὰς δὲ ἄλλας παντοδαποῖς εἴδεσιν ὁμοίας.

Let us think of these things in this way ; let us imagine that each of us is a kind of animal, the wonder of the gods, either their plaything or made for some special purpose ; for as to this we know nothing, but this we do know, that these passions are part of our nature, pulling us like nerves or ropes and influencing us differently, drag us to contrary points, where virtue and vice sit apart from each other. For reason says that each person ought always to follow one of these pullings and never abandoning it, be drawn in the opposite direction by the other nerves, and that this is the golden and sacred leading of the reasoning power, which is called the common law of the state. Whereas the other pullings are hard and iron-like, while this is soft as being golden and uniform, but that the rest are like to every variety of form.

Man Twice a Child.

Leg. i. 14.

Οὐ μόνον ἄρ', ὡς ἔοικεν, ὁ γέρων δὶς παῖς γίγνοιτ' ἄν, ἀλλὰ καὶ ὁ μεθυσθείς.

Not only, as it seems, is the old man twice a child, but also the man who is drunk.

Wisdom and True Opinions.

Leg. ii. 1.

Φρόνησιν δὲ καὶ ἀληθεῖς δόξας βεβαίους, εὐτυχὲς ὅτῳ καὶ πρὸς τὸ γῆρας παρεγένετο· τέλεος δ' οὖν ἐστ' ἄνθρωπος ταῦτα καὶ τὰ ἐν τούτοις πάντα κεκτημένος ἀγαθά.

But as to wisdom and true opinions which are firmly held, happy the man, who can retain them to his latest day ; while he is perfect, who possesses these and all the good things that are contained in them.

Cicero (De Fin v. 21) says ; "Præclare enim Plato, Beatum, cui etiam in senectute contigerit, ut sapientiam verasque opiniones assequi possit."

Holidays Appointed for Man by the Gods.

Leg. ii. 1.

Θεοὶ δὲ οἰκτείραντες τὸ τῶν ἀνθρώπων ἐπίπονον πεφυκὸς γένος ἀναπαύλας τε αὐτοῖς τῶν πόνων ἐτάξαντο τὰς τῶν ἑορτῶν ἀμοιβὰς τοῖς θεοῖς.

The gods, feeling pity for the hard-worked race of men, have ordained, as a relaxation from their toils, that they should enjoy the returns of feast-days in honour of the gods.

Dancing.
Leg. ii. 4.

Ἀρ' οὖν οὐχ ἡμῶν οἱ μὲν νέοι αὐτοὶ χορεύειν ἕτοιμοι, τὸ δὲ τῶν πρεσβυτέρων ἡμῶν, ἐκείνους αὖ θεωροῦντες διάγειν ἡγούμεθα πρεπόντως, χαίροντες τῇ ἐκείνων παιδιᾷ τε καὶ ἑορτάσει, ἐπειδὴ τὸ παρ' ἡμῖν ἡμᾶς ἐλαφρὸν ἐκλείπει νῦν, ὃ ποθοῦντες καὶ ἀσπαζόμενοι τίθεμεν οὕτως ἀγῶνας τοῖς δυναμένοις ἡμᾶς ὅ τι μάλιστα εἰς τὴν νεότητα μνήμῃ ἐπεγείρειν ;

Are not, then, the young amongst us ready to dance? And as to the old of us, do we not think that we act properly in enjoying the sight, while we hail with delight their fun and merry-making after our activity has left us? Regretting this, and recollecting our fondness for such amusements, we establish games for those who are able in the highest degree to recall to our recollection the joyous days of our youth.

Use and Abuse of Wine.
Leg. ii. 8.

Ἀρ' οὐ νομοθετήσομεν πρῶτον μὲν τοὺς παῖδας μέχρι ἐτῶν ὀκτωκαίδεκα τὸ παράπαν οἴνου μὴ γεύεσθαι, διδάσκοντες ὡς οὐ χρὴ πῦρ ἐπὶ πῦρ ὀχετεύειν εἴς τε τὸ σῶμα καὶ τὴν ψυχήν, πρὶν ἐπὶ τοὺς πόνους ἐγχειρεῖν πορεύεσθαι, τὴν ἐμμανῆ εὐλαβούμενοι ἕξιν τῶν νέων· μετὰ δὲ τοῦτο οἴνου μὲν ἤδη γεύεσθαι τοῦ μετρίου μέχρι τριάκοντα ἐτῶν, μέθης δὲ καὶ πολυοινίας τὸ παράπαν τὸν νέον ἀπέχεσθαι· τετταράκοντα δὲ ἐπιβαίνοντα ἐτῶν ἐν τοῖς ξυσσιτίοις εὐωχηθέντα καλεῖν τούς τε ἄλλους θεοὺς καὶ δὴ καὶ Διόνυσον παρακαλεῖν εἰς τὴν τῶν πρεσβυτῶν τελετὴν ἅμα καὶ παιδιάν, ἣν τοῖς ἀνθρώποις ἐπίκουρον τῆς τοῦ γήρως αὐστηρότητος ἐδωρήσατο τὸν οἶνον φάρμακον, ὥστ' ἀνηβᾶν ἡμᾶς καὶ δυσθυμίας λήθην γίγνεσθαι, μαλακώτερόν τε ἐκ σκληροτέρου τὸ τῆς ψυχῆς ἦθος, καθάπερ εἰς πῦρ σίδηρον ἐντεθέντα, γιγνόμενον, καὶ οὕτως εὐπλαστότερον εἶναι ;

Shall we not, then, lay down a law, in the first place, that boys shall abstain altogether from wine till their eighteenth year, thereby teaching that it is wrong to add fire to fire, as through a funnel, pouring it into their body and soul before they proceed to the labours of life, thus exercising a caution as to the maddening habits of youth ; afterwards to taste, indeed, wine in moderation till thirty years of age, the young abstaining altogether from intoxication and excess in wine, whereas in reaching forty years of age, man may indulge freely in banquettings, call upon the other gods, and especially invite Dionysos to the mystic rites and sports of old men, for which he kindly bestowed wine upon men, as a remedy against the moroseness of old age, so that through this we might grow young again and that by a forgetfulness of heart-sinking, the habit of the soul might become soft instead of being hard, exactly as iron becomes, when placed in the fire and moulded thus more easily?

A Solitude Infinitely Terrible.

Leg. iii. 2.

Οὐκοῦν οὕτω δὴ λέγωμεν ἔχειν τότε, ὅτε ἐγένετο ἡ φθορά, τὰ περὶ τοὺς ἀνθρώπους πράγματα, μυρίαν μέν τινα φοβερὰν ἐρημίαν.

Let us, then, assert, that, when that destruction (the deluge) came upon the earth, the affairs of man had a solitude infinitely terrible.

Cowper thus refers to the horrors of solitude, when he feigns Alexander Selkirk to say :—

> " O solitude, where are the charms
> That sages have seen in thy face?
> Better live in the midst of alarms,
> Than reign in this horrible place."

Half More than Whole.

Leg. iii. 10.

᾽Αρ' οὐκ ἀγνοήσαντες τὸν ῾Ησίοδον ὀρθότατα λέγοντα ὡς τὸ ἥμισυ τοῦ παντὸς πολλάκις ἐστὶ πλέον ; [ὁπόταν ᾖ τὸ μὲν ὅλον λαμβάνειν ζημιῶδες, τὸ δ' ἥμισυ μέτριον, τότε τὸ μέτριον τοῦ ἀμέτρου πλέον ἡγήσατο, ἄμεινον ὂν χείρονος.]

Were they not, then, ignorant that Hesiod said, with great propriety, that "the half is often more than the whole?" For when to receive the whole brings us harm, while the half is a mark of moderation, then the smaller is of more value than what is immoderate, as it is better than the worse.

No Man is Ever a Legislator.

Leg. iv. 4.

᾽Εμελλον λέγειν, ὡς οὐδεὶς ποτε ἀνθρώπων οὐδὲν νομοθετεῖ, τύχαι δὲ καὶ ξυμφοραὶ παντοῖαι πίπτουσαι παντοίως νομοθετοῦσι τὰ πάντα ἡμῖν. ῍Η γὰρ πόλεμός τις βιασάμενος ἀνέτρεψε πολιτείας καὶ μετέβαλε νόμους, ἢ πενίας χαλεπῆς ἀπορία· πολλὰ δὲ καὶ νόσοι ἀναγκάζουσι καινοτομεῖν, λοιμῶν τε ἐμπιπτόντων καὶ χρόνον ἐπὶ πολὺν ἐνιαυτῶν πολλῶν πολλάκις ἀκαιρίαις.

I was on the point of saying that no man is ever a legislator ; it is fortune and a variety of accidents, that fall out in many ways, that are our legislators in every thing. For it may be a war that has by violence overturned the constitution and changed the laws of the state, or overwhelming poverty from want of means in the citizens. Many innovations too are brought about by diseases, when pestilences come upon states, and unfavourable seasons for a succession of years.

God, Justice, and the Wicked.

Leg. iv. 7.

Ἄνδρες, ὁ μὲν δὴ θεός, ὥσπερ καὶ ὁ παλαιὸς λόγος, ἀρχήν τε καὶ τελευτὴν καὶ μέσα τῶν ὄντων ἀπάντων ἔχων, εὐθείᾳ περαίνει κατὰ φύσιν περιπορευόμενος· τῷ δ᾽ ἀεὶ ξυνέπεται δίκη τῶν ἀπολειπομένων τοῦ θείου νόμου τιμωρός, ἧς ὁ μὲν εὐδαιμονήσειν μέλλων ἐχόμενος ξυνέπεται ταπεινὸς καὶ κεκοσμημένος, εἰ δέ τις ἐξαρθεὶς ὑπὸ μεγα- λαυχίας ἢ χρήμασιν ἐπαιρόμενος ἢ τιμαῖς ἢ καὶ σώματος εὐμορφίᾳ ἅμα νεότητι καὶ ἀνοίᾳ φλέγεται τὴν ψυχὴν μεθ᾽ ὕβρεως, ὡς οὔτ᾽ ἄρχοντος οὔτε τινὸς ἡγεμόνος δεόμενος, ἀλλὰ καὶ ἄλλοις ἱκανὸς ὢν ἡγεῖσθαι, καταλείπεται ἔρημος θεοῦ, καταλειφθεὶς δὲ καὶ ἔτι ἄλλους τοιούτους προσλαβὼν σκιρτᾷ ταράττων πάνθ᾽ ἅμα, καί πολλοῖς τισὶν ἔδοξεν εἶναι τίς.

Ye men, God, as the old proverb goes, having in His own being the beginning, end, and middle of all things, brings them to a just conclusion, proceeding, according to nature, in a circle.   Jus- tice always follows at His heels, as the punisher of those who have swerved from the Divine law ; and close upon her is the man who wishes to be happy, with downcast looks and well-ordered thoughts ; whereas if there be one who is puffed up with over- weening conceit, or proud on account of his riches or honours, or the beauty of his person, or who, it may be, is, through the thoughtless giddiness of youth, inflamed with insolence, thinking himself in need neither of ruler nor leader, but rather imagining himself fit to point out the right way to others, such a one is abandoned by the Deity to his own foolish devices.   Being thus left, and joining himself to others of the same silly nature, he swaggers, throwing everything into confusion—appearing to the vulgar to be somebody, when, in fact, he is a nobody.

So Revelations (i. 8)—"I am Alpha and Omega, the beginning and the ending, saith the Lord." See James iv. 6 ; 1 Peter v, 5.

The Unholy.

Leg. iv. 8.

Ἀκάθαρτος γὰρ τὴν ψυχὴν ὅ γε κακός, καθαρὸς δὲ ὁ ἐναντίος· παρὰ δὲ μιαροῦ δῶρα οὔτ᾽ ἀνδρ᾽ ἀγαθὸν οὔτε θεὸν ἔστι ποτέ τό γε ὀρθὸν δέχεσθαι. Μάτην οὖν περὶ θεοὺς ὁ πολύς ἐστι πόνος τοῖς ἀν- οσίοις, τοῖσι δὲ ὁσίοις ἐγκαιρότατος ἅπασι. Σκοπὸς μὲν οὖν ἡμῖν οὗτος, οὗ δεῖ στοχάζεσθαι· βέλη δὲ αὐτοῦ καὶ οἷον ἡ τοῖς βέλεσιν ἔφεσις τὰ ποῖ᾽ ἂν λεγόμενα ὀρθότατα φέροιτ᾽ ἄν.

For the wicked man is tainted in his soul, while the man of an opposite character is pure. To receive gifts from the impure is unjustifiable either in God or man. There is much vain labour to the impious in regard to the gods, but to all the pious it is quite right. Such, then, is the mark, at which we ought to aim. Whither, then, can be most directly carried, what are called the arrows of a man, and what is the shooting out by thought, as it were by arrows.

So Cicero (De Leg. ii. 16) says—" Donis impiis ne placare audeant deos, Platonem audiant, qui vetat dubitare, quâ sit mente futurus Deus, cum vir nemo bonus ab improbo se donari velit."

PARENTS ALWAYS TO BE TREATED KINDLY.

Leg. iv. 8.

Χρὴ πρὸς αὑτοῦ γονέας εὐφημίαν διαφερόντως, διότι κούφων καὶ πτηνῶν λόγων βαρυτάτη ζημία· πᾶσι γὰρ ἐπίσκοπος τοῖς περὶ τὰ τοιαῦτα ἐτάχθη Δίκης Νέμεσις ἄγγελος.

Through the whole course of life it is right to hold, and to have held in a pre-eminent degree, the kindest language towards our parents, because there is the heaviest punishments for light and winged words ; for Nemesis, the messenger of Justice, has been appointed to look after all men in such matters.

THE HUMAN RACE IS IMMORTAL.

Leg. iv. 11.

Γένος οὖν ἀνθρώπων ἐστί τι ξυμφυὲς τοῦ παντὸς χρόνου, ὃ διὰ τέλους αὐτῷ ξυνέπεται καὶ συνέψεται, τούτῳ τῷ τρόπῳ ἀθάνατον ὄν, τῷ παῖδας παίδων καταλειπόμενον ταὐτὸν καὶ ἓν ὂν ἀεὶ γενέσει τῆς ἀθανασίας μετειληφέναι.

The human race, then, is interlinked with all time, which follows, and will follow it to the end, being in this way immortal , inasmuch as leaving children's children, and being one and the same by generation, it partakes of immortality.

THE GREATEST PUNISHMENT FOR WICKEDNESS.

Leg. v. 1.

Ἔστι δ' ἡ μεγίστη τὸ ὁμοιοῦσθαι τοῖς οὖσι κακοῖς ἀνδράσιν.

The greatest punishment for evil conduct is the becoming like to bad men.

So Proverbs (xiii. 6)—" Wickedness overthroweth the sinner."

LEAVE MODESTY RATHER THAN GOLD TO CHILDREN.

Leg. v. 2.

Παισὶ δὲ αἰδῶ χρὴ πολλήν, οὐ χρυσὸν καταλείπειν.

It is proper to leave modesty rather than gold to children.

The Truthful.

Leg. v. 3.

'Αλήθεια δὴ πάντων μὲν ἀγαθῶν θεοῖς ἡγεῖται, πάντων δὲ ἀνθρώποις· ἧς ὁ γενήσεσθαι μέλλων μακάριός τε καὶ εὐδαίμων ἐξ ἀρχῆς εὐθὺς μέτοχος εἴη, ἵνα ὡς πλεῖστον χρόνον ἀληθὴς ὢν διαβιοῖ. Πιστὸς γάρ· ὁ δὲ ἄπιστος, ᾧ φίλον ψεῦδος ἑκούσιον· ὅτῳ δὲ ἀκούσιον, ἄνους. Ὧν οὐδέτερον ζηλωτόν· ἄφιλος γὰρ δὴ πᾶς ὅ τε ἄπιστος καὶ ἀμαθής, χρόνου δὲ προϊόντος γνωσθεὶς εἰς τὸ χαλεπὸν γῆρας ἐρημίαν αὑτῷ πᾶσαν κατεσκευάσατο ἐπὶ τέλει τοῦ βίου. ὥστε ζώντων καὶ μὴ ἑταίρων καὶ παίδων σχεδὸν ὁμοίως ὀρφανὸν αὑτῷ γενέσθαι τὸν βίον.

Truth is the source of every good to gods and men. He who expects to be blessed and fortunate in this world should be a partaker of it from the earliest moment of his life, that he may live as long as possible a person of truth ; for such a man is trustworthy. But that man is untrustworthy who loveth a lie in his heart ; and if it be told involuntary, and in mere wantonness, he is a fool. In neither case can they be envied ; for every knave and shallow dunce is without real friends. As time passes on to morose old age, he becomes known, and has prepared for himself at the end of his life a dreary solitude ; so that, whether his associates and children be alive or not, his life becomes nearly equally a state of isolation.

See (Lat.) Truth.

Self-love.

Leg. v. 4.

Τοῦτο δ' ἔστιν ὃ λέγουσιν ὡς φίλος αὑτῷ πᾶς ἄνθρωπος φύσει τ ἐστὶ καὶ ὀρθῶς ἔχει τὸ δεῖν εἶναι τοιοῦτον· τὸ δὲ ἀληθείᾳ γε πάντων ἁμαρτημάτων διὰ τὴν σφόδρα ἑαυτοῦ φιλίαν αἴτιον ἑκάστῳ γίγνεται ἑκάστοτε. Τυφλοῦται γὰρ περὶ τὸ φιλούμενον ὁ φιλῶν, ὥστε τὰ δίκαια καὶ τὰ ἀγαθὰ καὶ τὰ καλὰ κακῶς κρίνει, τὸ αὑτοῦ πρὸ τοῦ ἀληθοῦς ἀεὶ τιμᾶν δεῖν ἡγούμενος· οὔτε γὰρ ἑαυτὸν οὔτε τὰ ἑαυτοῦ χρὴ τόν γε μέγαν ἄνδρα ἐσόμενον στέργειν, ἀλλὰ τὰ δίκαια, ἐάν τε παρ' αὑτῷ ἐάν τε παρ' ἄλλῳ μᾶλλον πραττόμενα τυγχάνῃ.

This is what men say, that every man is naturally a lover of himself, and that it is right that it should be so. This is a mistake ; for, in fact, the cause of all the blunders committed by man arises from this excessive self-love. For the lover is blinded by the object loved ; so that he passes a wrong judgment on what is just, good, and beautiful, thinking that he ought always to honour what belongs to himself in preference to truth. For he who intends to be a great man ought to love neither himself nor his own things, but only what is just, whether it happens to be done by himself, or by another.

So 1 Timothy (vi. 10)—" The love of money is the root of all evil." See (Lat.) Self-love.

"Let Your Light so Shine Before Men."

Leg. v. 9.

Μεῖζον οὐδὲν πόλει ἀγαθὸν ἢ γνωρίμους αὐτοὺς αὑτοῖς εἶναι. ὅπου γὰρ μὴ φῶς ἀλλήλοις ἐστὶν ἀλλήλων ἐν τοῖς τρόποις ἀλλὰ σκότος, οὔτ᾽ ἂν τιμῆς τῆς ἀξίας ὀρθῶς τυγχάνοι· δεῖ δὴ πάντα ἄνδρα ἐν πρὸς ἐν τοῦτο σπεύδειν ἐν πάσαις πόλεσιν, ὅπως μήτε αὐτὸς κιβδηλός ποτε φανεῖται ὁτῳοῦν, ἁπλοῦς δὲ καὶ ἀληθὴς ἀεί.

For no greater good can be conferred on a state than that men should be intimate and well acquainted with each other's character. Since, where a light is not reflected from their good works in the face of each other, but where a moral darkness is around them, there we are sure to find that no one receives properly the honour due to his worth. It is meet, then, that every man should exert himself never to appear to any one to be of base metal, but always artless and true.

See John iii. 21 ; Matt. vi. 22, 23.

Even the Gods Cannot use Force Against Necessity.

Leg. v. 10.

Ἀνάγκην δὲ οὐδὲ θεὸς εἶναι λέγεται δυνατὸς βιάζεσθαι.

Even God is said to be unable to use force against necessity.

See Diog. Laërt. i. 77.

The Beginning is the Half of the Whole.

Leg. vi. 2.

Ἀρχὴ γὰρ λέγεται μὲν ἥμισυ παντὸς ἐν ταῖς παροιμίαις ἔργου, καὶ τό γε καλῶς ἄρξασθαι πάντες ἐγκωμιάζομεν ἑκάστοτε.

For according to the proverb, the beginning is half of the whole, and we all praise a good beginning.

A Man Must Have Been a Servant to Become a Good Master.

Leg. vi. 9.

Δεῖ δὴ πάντ᾽ ἄνδρα διανοεῖσθαι περὶ ἁπάντων ἀνθρώπων, ὡς ὁ μὴ δουλεύσας οὐδ᾽ ἂν δεσπότης γένοιτο ἄξιος ἐπαίνου, καὶ καλλωπίζεσθαι χρὴ τῷ καλῶς δουλεῦσαι μᾶλλον ἢ τῷ καλῶς ἄρξαι, πρῶτον μὲν τοῖς νόμοις, ὡς ταύτην τοῖς θεοῖς οὖσαν δουλείαν, ἔπειτα τοῖς πρεσβυτέροις.

It is proper for every one to consider, in the case of all men, that he who has not been a servant cannot become a praiseworthy master; and it is meet that we should plume ourselves rather on acting the part of a servant properly than that of the master, first, towards the laws (for in this way we are servants of the gods), and next, towards our elders.

IMPORTANCE OF EDUCATION.

Leg. vi. 12.

Ἄνθρωπος δέ, ὥς φαμεν, ἥμερον, ὅμως μὴν παιδείας μὲν ὀρθῆς τυχὸν καὶ φύσεως εὐτυχοῦς θειότατον ἡμερώτατόν τε ζῶον γίγνεσθαι φιλεῖ, μὴ ἱκανῶς δὲ ἢ μὴ καλῶς τραφὲν ἀγριώτατον ὁπόσα φύει γῆ. ὧν ἕνεκα οὐ δεύτερον οὐδὲ πάρεργον δεῖ τὴν παίδων τροφὴν τὸν νομοθέτην ἐᾶν γίγνεσθαι.

Now man, we say, is a tame, domesticated animal ; for when he receives a proper education, and happens to possess a good natural disposition, he usually becomes an animal most divine and tame ; but when he is not sufficiently nor properly trained, he is the most savage animal on the face of the earth. On this account a legislator ought to regard education neither as a secondary object, nor yet as a by-work.

EDUCATION OUGHT TO BE COMPULSORY.

Leg. vii. 11.

Οὐχ ὃν μὲν ἂν ὁ πατὴρ βούληται, φοιτῶντα, ὃν δ' ἂν μή, ἐῶντα τὰς παιδείας, ἀλλὰ τὸ λεγόμενον πάντ' ἄνδρα καὶ παῖδα κατὰ τὸ δυνατόν, ὡς τῆς πόλεως μᾶλλον ἢ τῶν γεννητόρων ὄντας, παιδευτέον ἐξ ἀνάγκης.

Not only the boy who comes to school at the will of his father, but he, too, who neglects his education from the fault of his father, as the saying is, every man and boy must be compelled to learn according to his ability, as they belong to the state rather than their parents.

A BOY DIFFICULT TO MANAGE.

Leg. vii. 14.

Ὁ δὲ παῖς πάντων θηρίων ἐστὶ δυσμεταχειριστότατον· ὅσῳ γὰρ μάλιστα ἔχει πηγὴν τοῦ φρονεῖν μήπω κατηρτυμένην, ἐπίβουλον καὶ δριμὺ καὶ ὑβριστότατον θηρίων γίγνεται· διὸ δὴ πολλοῖς αὐτὸ οἷον χαλινοῖς τισὶ δεῖ δεσμεύειν.

Now a boy is, of all wild beasts, the most difficult to manage ; for, in proportion as he has the fountain of his mental faculties not yet properly prepared, he becomes cunning and sharp, and the most insolent of wild beasts ; wherefore he must be bound, as it were, with many chains.

MUCH LEARNING BRINGS DANGER TO YOUTH.
Leg. vii. 15.

Κίνδυνόν φημι εἶναι φέρουσαν τοῖς παισὶ τὴν πολυμαθίαν.

Much learning, in my opinion, brings danger to youth. (This was the doctrine of Heracleitus.)

See Acts xxvi. 24.

GREAT LEARNING WITH AN IMPROPER EDUCATION IS A CALAMITY.
Leg. vii. 20.

Οὐδαμοῦ γὰρ δεινὸν οὐδὲ σφοδρὸν ἀπειρία τῶν πάντων οὐδὲ μέγιστον κακόν, ἀλλ᾽ ἡ πολυπειρία καὶ πολυμαθία μετὰ κακῆς ἀγωγῆς γίγνεται πολὺ τούτων μείζων ζημία.

For ignorance of all things is an evil neither terrible nor excessive, nor yet the greatest of all; but great cleverness and much learning, if they be accompanied by a bad training, is a much greater misfortune.

FISHERS OF MEN.
Leg. vii. 23.

Μηδ᾽ αὖ ἄγρας ἀνθρώπων κατὰ θάλατταν λῃστείας τε ἵμερος ἐπελθὼν ὑμῖν θηρευτὰς ὠμοὺς καὶ ἀνόμους ἀποτελοῖ.

May no desire ever seize you to catch men at sea, nor to rob them, making you cruel and lawless hunters.

See Luke v. 10 ; Jer. xvi. 16.

TIME IS MONEY.
Leg. viii. 3.

Τὴν μέν, ὑπ᾽ ἔραμιν πλαύτου πάντα χρόνον ἄσχολον ποιοῦντος τῶν ἄλλων ἐπιμελεῖσθαι πλὴν τῶν ἰδίων κτημάτων, ἐξ ὧν κρεμαμένη πᾶσα ψυχὴ πολίτου παντὸς οὐκ ἂν ποτε δύναιτο τῶν ἄλλων ἐπιμέλειαν ἴσχειν πλὴν τοῦ καθ᾽ ἡμέραν κέρδους.

One cause is that the love of money makes time without leisure for other things except the accumulation of private property, on which the soul of every citizen is hanging, and thus it can have no thought for anything but daily pecuniary gain.

A PROOF THAT THERE IS A GOD.
Leg. x. 1.

Πρῶτον μὲν γῆ καὶ ἥλιος ἄστρα τε [καὶ] τὰ ξύμπαντα καὶ τὰ τῶν ὡρῶν διακεκοσμημένα καλῶς οὕτως, ἐνιαυτοῖς τε καὶ μησὶ διειλημμένα· καὶ ὅτι πάντες Ἕλληνές τε καὶ βάρβαροι νομίζουσιν εἶναι θεούς.

In the first place, the earth, sun, and stars—all these, and the beautiful arrangement of the seasons, divided into years and months, prove that there is a God. Besides, both Greeks and barbarians believe that there are supreme beings.

See Rom. i. 20 ; Ps. xix. 1, 4.

No One has ever Died an Atheist.

Leg. x. 4.

Ὦ παῖ, νέος εἶ· προϊὼν δέ σε ὁ χρόνος ποιήσει πολλὰ ὧν νῦν δοξά-ζεις μεταβαλόντα ἐπὶ τἀναντία τίθεσθαι· περίμεινον οὖν εἰς τότε κριτὴς περὶ τῶν μεγίστων γίγνεσθαι. Μέγιστον δέ, ὃ νῦν οὐδὲν ἡγεῖ σύ, τὸ περὶ τοὺς θεοὺς ὀρθῶς διανοηθέντα ζῆν καλῶς ἢ μή. Πρῶτον δὲ περὶ αὐτῶν ἕν τι μέγα σοι μηνύων οὐκ ἄν ποτε φανείην ψευδής, τὸ τοιόνδε. Οὐ σὺ μόνος οὐδὲ οἱ σοὶ φίλοι πρῶτοι καὶ πρῶτον ταύτην δόξαν περὶ θεῶν ἔσχετε, γίγνονται δὲ ἀεὶ πλείους ἢ ἐλάττους ταύτην τὴν νόσον ἔχοντες· τόδε τοίνυν σοι παραγεγονὼς αὐτῶν πολλοῖσι φράζοιμ᾽ ἄν, τὸ μηδένα πώποτε λαβόντα ἐκ νέου ταύτην τὴν δόξαν περὶ θεῶν, ὡς οὔ εἰσί, διατελέσαι πρὸς γῆρας μείναντα ἐν ταύτῃ τῇ διανοήσει.

My child, thou art young ; but time, as it proceeds, will cause thee to change many of those opinions which thou now supportest, and induce thee to entertain the very opposite. Wait, then, till that time, that thou mayest be able properly to judge of matters of such great importance. Now, that which is of the highest moment, though thou thinkest it of no consequence at present, is that thou shouldst have correct notions of the gods, and thereby be able to direct thy course of life in a proper way. If I point out to thee, in the first place, one thing of the highest importance, I shall not appear to be telling a falsehood. Thou and thy friends are not the only parties, nor the first, who have maintained this opinion of the non-existence of the gods; for there have always been a larger or smaller number who have been labouring under this same disease. This, therefore, I shall tell thee respecting them, as I have had frequent intercourse with many of them, that not one ever, who has held such an opinion respecting the gods, has continued to old age to maintain it.

The Prosperity of the Wicked Leads to Doubts of the Justice of God.

Leg. x. 10.

Κακῶν δὲ ἀνθρώπων καὶ ἀδίκων τύχαι ἰδίᾳ καὶ δημοσίᾳ, ἀληθείᾳ μὲν οὐκ εὐδαίμονες, δόξαις δὲ εὐδαιμονιζόμεναι σφόδρα ἀλλ᾽ οὐκ ἐμμελῶς ἄγουσί σε πρὸς ἀσέβειαν, ἔν τε μούσαις οὐκ ὀρθῶς ὑμνούμεναι ἅμα καὶ ἐν παντοίοις λόγοις· ταράττει τὸ νῦν ἐν ἅπασι τούτοις, ἀγόμενος δὲ ὑπό τινος ἀλογίας ἅμα καὶ οὐ δυνάμενος δυσχεραίνειν θεοὺς εἰς τοῦτο νῦν τὸ πάθος ἐλήλυθας, ὥστ᾽ εἶναι μὲν δοκεῖν αὐτούς, τῶν δὲ ἀνθρωπίνων καταφρονεῖν καὶ ἀμελεῖν πραγμάτων.

But the prosperity of wicked and unjust men, both in public and in private life, who, though not leading a happy life in reality, are yet thought to do so in common opinion, being praised improperly in the works of poets, and all kinds of books, may lead thee—and I am not surprised at thy mistake—to a belief that the gods care nothing for the affairs of men. These matters disturb thee. Being led astray by foolish thoughts, and yet not being able to think ill of the gods, thou hast arrived at thy present state of mind, so as to think that the gods do indeed exist, but that they despise and neglect human affairs.

See Ps. lxiii. 2-13. Claudian. Ruf. i. 1-21.

WHERE YOUR HEART IS, THERE WILL BE YOUR TREASURE.

Leg. x. 12.

Ὅπη γάρ ἂν ἐπιθυμῇ καὶ ὁποῖός τις ὢν τὴν ψυχήν, ταύτῃ σχεδὸν ἑκάστοτε καὶ τοιοῦτος γίγνεται ἅπας ἡμῶν ὡς τὸ πολύ.

For whatever a man's desire is, and whatsoever he may be as to his soul, such every one becomes in a great measure.

See Matt. vi. 21.

THE OMNIPRESENCE OF GOD.

Leg. x. 12.

Ταύτης τῆς δίκης οὔτε σὺ μή ποτε οὔτε [εἰ] ἄλλος ἀτυχὴς γενόμενος ἐπεύξηται περιγενέσθαι θεῶν· οὐ γὰρ ἀμεληθήσει ποτὲ ὑπ' αὐτῆς· οὐχ οὕτω σμικρὸς ὢν δύσει κατὰ τὸ τῆς γῆς βάθος, οὐδ' ὑψηλὸς γενόμενος εἰς τὸν οὐρανὸν ἀναπτήσει, τίσεις δὲ αὐτῶν τὴν προσήκουσαν τιμωρίαν εἴτ' ἐνθάδε μένων εἴτε καὶ ἐν Ἅιδου διαπορευθεὶς εἴτε καὶ τούτων εἰς ἀγριώτερον ἔτι διακομισθεὶς τόπον.

But never must thou, nor any other, pray, having become unfortunate, to be superior to this judgment of the gods. For thou wilt never be neglected by it, not even though thou wert so small as to sink into the depths of the earth, nor so lofty as to ascend up into heaven ; but thou wilt suffer from them the proper punishment, whether thou remainest here, or go to Hades, or be carried to some place still more wild than these.

See Ps. cxxxix. 2-10 ; cxxxviii. 6-8.

LET NO ONE SPEAK EVIL OF HIS NEIGHBOUR.

Leg. xi. 13.

Μηδένα κακηγορείτω μηδείς.

Let no one speak evil of another.

See Titus iii 2.

LET THERE BE NO BEGGAR.

Leg. xi. 14.

Πτωχὸς μηδεὶς ἡμῖν ἐν τῇ πόλει γιγνέσθω.

Let there be no beggar in the state.

THE WICKED AND THE GOOD.

Philæb. 24.

Ψευδέσιν ἄρα ἡδοναῖς τὰ πολλὰ οἱ πονηροὶ χαίρουσιν, οἱ δ' ἀγαθοὶ τῶν ἀνθρώπων ἀληθέσιν. Εἰσὶ δὴ ψευδεῖς ἐν ταῖς τῶν ἀνθρώπων ψυχαῖς ἡδοναί, μεμιμημέναι μέντοι τὰς ἀληθεῖς ἐπὶ τὰ γελοιότερα.

The wicked generally take pleasure in false pleasures, but the good in the true : in the souls of men there are false pleasures, mimicking, however, in a very laughable way the true.

So John (viii 44)—"The devil is a liar and the father of it."

MATERIALISM.

Sophist. c. 33.

Οἱ μὲν εἰς γῆν ἐξ οὐρανοῦ καὶ τοῦ ἀοράτου πάντα ἕλκουσι, ταῖς χερσὶν ἀτεχνῶς ὡς πέτρας καὶ δρῦς περιλαμβάνοντες. Τῶν γὰρ τοιούτων ἐφαπτόμενοι πάντων διισχυρίζονται τοῦτο εἶναι μόνον ὃ παρέχει προσβολὴν καὶ ἐπαφήν τινα, ταὐτὸν σῶμα καὶ οὐσίαν ὁριζόμενοι.

Some of them draw down to earth all things from heaven and the unseen world, laying hold of them foolishly as if they were stones and oaks. For touching all such things as these they strenuously maintain that that alone exists, which affords impact and touch, defining body and existence to be the same.

Wisdom 2, Solomon xiii. 1, 2, 6-9.

TO FALL IN BATTLE IS HONOURABLE.

Menex. 2.

Καὶ μήν, ὦ Μενέξενε, πολλαχῇ κινδυνεύει καλὸν εἶναι τὸ ἐν πολέμῳ ἀποθνήσκειν.

And truly, Menexenus, it appears, on many accounts, to be an honourable thing to fall on the field of battle.

POWER OF ORATORY.

Menex. 2.

Οὕτως ἔναυλος ὁ λόγος τε καὶ ὁ φθόγγος παρὰ τοῦ λέγοντος ἐν

δύεται εἰς τὰ ὦτα, ὥστε μόγις τετάρτῃ ἢ πέμπτῃ ἡμέρᾳ ἀναμιμνή-
σκομαι ἐμαυτοῦ καὶ αἰσθάνομαι οὗ γῆς εἰμί, τέως δὲ οἶμαι μόνον οὐκ
ἐν μακάρων νήσοις οἰκεῖν.

So strongly does the speech and the tone of the orator ring in
my ears that scarcely, in the third or fourth day, do I recollect
myself, and perceive where on the earth I am; and, for a while, I
am willing to believe myself living in the Isles of the Blessed.

Milton, in Comus, says:—

"Who, as they say, would take the prison'd soul,
    And lap it in Elysium."

To Live with Dishonour Renders Life to be No Life.

Menex. 19.

Ἡγούμενοι τῷ τοὺς αὑτοῦ αἰσχύνοντι ἀβίωτον εἶναι, καὶ τῷ τοιούτῳ
οὔτε τινὰ ἀνθρώπων οὔτε θεῶν φίλον εἶναι οὔτ' ἐπὶ γῆς οὔθ' ὑπὸ γῆς
τελευτήσαντι.

Considering that to him who disgraces his family life is no life,
and that to such a person there is no one, of gods or of men, a
friend, neither while living upon earth, nor when dead under the
earth.

The Coward and the Knave.

Menex. 19.

Οὔτε γὰρ πλοῦτος κάλλος φέρει τῷ κεκτημένῳ μετ' ἀνανδρίας·
ἄλλῳ γὰρ ὁ τοιοῦτος πλουτεῖ καὶ οὐχ ἑαυτῷ· οὔτε σώματος κάλλος
καὶ ἰσχὺς δειλῷ καὶ κακῷ ξυνοικοῦντα πρέπονια φαίνεται ἀλλ' ἀπ-
ρεπῆ, καὶ ἐπιφανέστερον ποιεῖ τὸν ἔχοντα καὶ ἐκφαίνει τὴν δειλίαν.

Riches bring no honour to him who possesses it, if there is a
want of manly character; for such a one is rich for another, and
not for himself. Nor do beauty of person and strength of body,
if they be united with cowardice and knavery, appear becoming,
but the very opposite, making the possessor to be only more conspicuous, and to show forth his want of courage.

Pride of Ancestry.

Menex. 19.

Γνόντες ὅτι ἀνδρὶ οἰομένῳ τὶ εἶναι οὐκ ἔστιν αἴσχιον οὐδὲν ἢ παρέχειν ἑαυτὸν τιμώμενον μὴ δι' ἑαυτὸν ἀλλὰ διὰ δόξαν προγόνων. Εἶναι
μὲν γὰρ τιμὰς γονέων ἐκγόνοις καλὸς θησαυρὸς καὶ μεγαλοπρεπής.

Being well satisfied that, for a man who thinks himself to be somebody, there is nothing more disgraceful than to hold himself up as honoured, not on his own account, but for the sake of his forefathers, yet hereditary honours are a noble and splendid treasure to descendants.

See (Lat.) Deeds of ancestors.

DEPEND ON THYSELF.

Menex. 20.

῝Οτῳ γὰρ ἀνδρὶ εἰς ἑαυτὸν ἀνήρτηται πάντα τὰ πρός εὐδαιμονίαν φέροντα ἢ ἐγγὺς τούτου, καὶ μὴ ἐν ἄλλοις ἀνθρώποις αἰωρεῖται, ἐξ ὧν ἢ εὖ ἢ κακῶς πραξάντων πλανᾶσθαι ἠνάγκασται καὶ τὰ ἐκείνου, τούτῳ ἄριστα παρεσκεύασται ζῆν, οὗτός ἐστιν ὁ σώφρων καὶ οὗτος ὁ ἀνδρεῖος καὶ φρόνιμος.

For the man who makes everything that leads to happiness, or near to it, to depend upon himself, and not upon other men, on whose good or evil actions his own doings are compelled to hinge, —such a one, I say, has adopted the very best plan for living happily. This is the man of moderation; this is the man of a manly character, and of wisdom.

NOT WHAT A MAN WISHES, BUT WHAT HE CAN.

Hipp. Maj. 26.

Οὐχ οἷα βούλεταί τις, φασὶν ἄνθρωποι ἑκάστοτε παροιμιαζόμενοι, ἀλλ᾽ οἷα δύναται.

It is not what a man wishes, as men say, speaking proverbially, but what he can.

ORIGINAL BAD HABITS NOT TO BE GOT RID OF.

Alcibiad. i. 16.

Οὔκ ὦ ᾽γαθέ, ἀλλὰ πρὸς Μειδίαν σε δεῖ τὸν ὀρτυγοτρόφον ἀποβλέπειν καὶ ἄλλους τοιούτους, οἳ τὰ τῆς πόλεως πράττειν ἐπιχειροῦσιν, ἔτι τὴν ἀνδραποδώδη, φαῖεν ἂν αἱ γυναῖκες, τρίχα ἔχοντες ἐν τῇ ψυχῇ ὑπ᾽ ἀμουσίας καὶ οὔπω ἀποβεβληκότες, ἔτι δὲ βαρβαρίζοντες ἐληλύθασι κολακεύσοντες τὴν πόλιν, ἀλλ᾽ οὐκ ἄρξοντες.

My good friend, thou must not look to Midias, the quail-feeder, and others of that kidney, who affect to manage the affairs of the state, though they still have, as the women would say, the slave-cut of hair in their souls, from want of a gentlemanlike education; not yet having got rid of it. but still acting the part of barbarians, they have come to cajole and fawn upon the city, and not to rule it.

Noble Natures are Sprung from the Noble.

Alcibiad. i. 16.

Πότερον εἰκὸς ἀμείνους γίγνεσθαι φύσεις ἐν γενναίοις γένεσιν ἢ μή;

Whether or not is it probable that the nobler natures are sprung from noble races?

See Aristot. Polit. iii. 8.

Kind of Prayer to be Offered to God.

Alcibiad. ii. 5.

Λέγει δέ πως ὡδί·
Ζεῦ βασιλεῦ, τὰ μὲν ἐσθλά, φησί, καὶ εὐχομένοις καὶ ἀνεύκτοις
ἄμμι δίδου, τὰ δὲ δεινὰ καὶ εὐχομένοις ἀπαλέξειν κελεύει.

He says that we ought to pray thus : O Jupiter, our king, grant to us whatever is good, whether we pray for it or not ; but avert what is evil, even though we offer our prayers to obtain it.

Shakespeare ("Anthony and Cleopatra" act ii. sc. 1) says :—
"We, ignorant of ourselves,
Beg often our own harms, which the wise powers
Deny us for our good ; so find we profit,
By losing of our prayers."

Merrick (a Hymn No. ccxxv. in the Rev. W. Mercer's Church Psalter) says :—

"The good unasked in mercy grant ;
The ill, though asked, deny.

Jack of All Trades and Master of None.

Alcibiad. ii. 10.

Ὁ λέγει κατηγορῶν πού τινος, ὡς ἄρα πολλὰ μὲν ἠπίστατο ἔργα, κακῶς δέ, φησίν, ἠπίστατο πάντα.

Which he expresses, while he is bringing a charge against some one that—

"Trades many knew he ; but knew badly all."

God Not to be Gained Over by Gifts.

Alcibiad. ii. 13.

Οὐ γάρ, οἶμαι, τοιοῦτόν ἐστι τὸ τῶν θεῶν, ὥστε ὑπὸ δώρων παράγεσθαι οἷον κακὸν τοκιστήν.

For the Divine Nature, in my opinion, is not such as can be gained over by gifts, like a knavish usurer.

See (Lat.) The gods ; Isaiah i. 11, 16-18.

God from All Eternity.

Phædr. 24.

Ἀρχὴ δὲ ἀγένητον. ἐξ ἀρχῆς γὰρ ἀνάγκη πᾶν τὸ γιγνόμενον
γίγνεσθαι, αὐτὴν δὲ μηδ᾿ ἐξ ἑνός.

A beginning is uncreate : for every thing that is created must
necessarily be created from a beginning, but a beginning itself from
nothing whatever.

So Sirac (xxiv. 14).

What We Should Pray For.

Phædr. 64.

Ὦ φίλε Πάν τε καὶ ἄλλοι ὅσοι τῇ δέ θεοί, δοίητέ μοι καλῷ γενέσθαι
τἄνδοθεν· ἔξωθεν δ᾿ ὅσα ἔχω, τοῖς ἐντὸς εἶναί μοι φίλια.　πλούσιον
δὲ νομίζοιμι τὸν σοφόν· τὸ δὲ χρυσοῦ πλῆθος εἴη μοι ὅσον μήτε
φέρειν μήτε ἄγειν δύναιτ᾿ ἄλλος ἢ ὁ σώφρων. — Ἔτι ἄλλου του
δεόμεθα, ὦ Φαῖδρε; ἐμοὶ μὲν γὰρ μετρίως ηὖκται.

O beloved Pan, and ye other gods of this place, grant me to become beautiful in the inner man, and that whatever outward
things I may have may be at peace with these within.　May I
think the wise man to be rich, and may I have as much wealth as
a wise man can employ usefully and prudently.　Do we need anything else, Phædrus?　For myself I have prayed enough.

So Proverbs (xxx. 7)—"Two *things* have I required of thee ; deny me *them*
not before I die : Remove far from me vanity and lies ; give me neither
poverty nor riches ; feed me with food convenient for me : Lest I be full,
and deny *thee*, and say, Who *is* the Lord ? or lest I be poor, and steal, and
take the name of my God *in vain.*"

Divine Nature of Education.

Theag. 2.

Οὐ γὰρ ἔστι περὶ ὅτου θειοτέρου ἂν ἄνθρωπος βουλεύσαιτο, ἢ περὶ
παιδείας καὶ αὐτοῦ καὶ τῶν αὐτοῦ οἰκείων.

For there is nothing of a more divine nature about which a man
can consult than about the training of himself, and those who belong to him.

The Education of a Son.

Theag. 10.

Οὐ γὰρ οἶδα ὑπὲρ ὅτου ἄν τις νοῦν ἔχων μᾶλλον σπουδάζοι ὑπὲρ
υἱέος αὐτοῦ, ὅπως ὡς βέλτιστος ἔσται.

For I know not anything about which a man of sense ought to
feel more anxious than how his son may become the very best of
men.

ONLY A FEW BLESSED AND HAPPY.
Epin. c. 13.

Οὐ δυνατὸν ἀνθρώποις τελέως μακαρίοις τε καὶ εὐδαίμοσι γενέσθαι πλὴν ὀλίγων.

It is not possible for men to be perfectly blessed and happy, except a few.

So Matthew (vii. 14)—"Strait is the gate and narrow is the way which leadeth unto life, and few there be that find it."

PIETY TO THE GODS.
Epin. c. 11.

Μεῖζον μὲν γὰρ ἀρετῆς μηδεὶς ἡμᾶς ποτε πείθῃ τῆς εὐσεβείας εἶναι τῷ θνητῷ γένει.

Let no one ever attempt to persuade us that there is any part of virtue belonging to the race of men greater than piety to the gods.

So Genesis (iv. 7)—"If thou doest well, shalt thou not be accepted? and if thou doest not well, sin lieth at the door;" and 1 Timothy (iv. 8)—"Godliness is profitable unto all things, having the promise of the life that now is and of that which is to come."

DANGER OF EXCESSIVE LOVE OF FREEDOM.
Epistl. 8.

Τοῖς δὲ δὴ ἐλεύθερα διώκουσιν ἤθη καὶ φεύγουσι τὸν δούλειον ζυγὸν ὡς ὂν κακόν, εὐλαβεῖσθαι ξυμβουλεύοιμ᾽ ἂν μή ποτε ἀπληστίᾳ ἐλευθερίας ἀκαίρου, τινὸς εἰς τὸ τῶν προγόνων νόσημα ἐμπέσωσιν, ὃ διὰ τὴν ἄγαν ἀναρχίαν οἱ τότε ἔπαθον, ἀμέτρῳ ἐλευθερίας χρώμενοι ἔρωτι.

To those who are pursuing after free institutions, and flying from a servile yoke as an evil, I would take the liberty of giving this advice, that they be on their guard lest, from an immoderate love of ill-timed liberty, they fall into the disease with which their ancestors were afflicted, from excessive anarchy, abusing their measureless love of freedom.

See (Lat.) Liberty.

SLAVERY AND FREEDOM.
Epsitl. 8.

Δουλεία γὰρ καὶ ἐλευθερία ὑπερβάλλουσα μὲν ἑκατέρα πάγκακον, ἔμμετρος δὲ οὖσα πανάγαθον· μετρία δὲ ἡ θεῷ δουλεία, ἄμετρος δὲ ἡ τοῖς ἀνθρώποις· θεὸς δὲ ἀνθρώποις σώφροσι νόμος, ἄφροσι δὲ ἡδονή.

For slavery and freedom, if immoderate, are each of them an evil; if moderate, they are altogether a good. Moderate is the slavery to a god; but immoderate, to men. God is a law to the men of sense; but pleasure is a law to a fool.

FATHERLAND.
Epistl. 9.

'Αλλὰ κάκεῖνο, δεῖ σε ἐνθυμεῖσθαι, ὅτι ἕκαστος ἡμῶν οὐχ αὑτῷ μόνον γέγονεν, ἀλλὰ τῆς γενέσεως ἡμῶν τὸ μέν τι ἡ πατρὶς μερίζεται, τὸ δέ τι οἱ γεννήσαντες, τὸ δὲ οἱ λοιποὶ φίλοι.

But then you ought to consider that each of us is born not for himself only, but our country claims one part, our parents another, and our friends the remainder.

PHILOSOPHY.
Plat. ap. Diogen. Laert. iii. 1, 38.

Φιλοσοφία ὄρεξις τῆς θείας σοφίας.

Philosophy is a longing after heavenly wisdom.

So Psalm (xlii. 2)—"My soul thirsteth for God, for the living God: when shall I come and appear before God?" and Isaiah (lv. 6)—"Seek ye the Lord while He may be found; call ye upon Him while He is near."

PLUTARCHUS.

BORN ABOUT A. D. 50—DIED ABOUT A. D. 120.

PLUTARCH, one of the most celebrated writers of antiquity, was born at Chæroneia, in Bœotia. He was studying philosophy under Ammonius, at Delphi, at the time Nero was travelling through Greece, A.D. 66. His family was of distinction in his native place; and he was employed by his fellow-citizens to transact some public business for them at Rome, though it was late in life before he busied himself with Roman literature. He was lecturing at Rome in the reign of Domitian; but he spent the most of his life in his native city, where he discharged various magisterial offices, and had a priesthood. The work for which he is most distinguished is his "Parallel Lives of Forty-six Greeks and Romans."

VILLAINS.
Romul. 17.

'Αλλὰ κοινόν τι τοῦτο πάθος ἐστὶ πρὸς τοὺς πονηροὺς τοῖς δεομένοις αὐτῶν, ὥσπερ ἰοῦ καὶ χολῆς ἐνίων θηρίων δέονται· τὴν γὰρ χρείαν ὅτε λαμβάνουσιν, ἀγαπῶντες, ἐχθαίρουσι τὴν κακίαν.

When men avail themselves of the assistance of villains, they
regard them with the same feelings as they do venomous creatures
which they employ for their poison and gall. For, while they
make use of them, they show affection ; but, when their purpose
is accomplished, they detest their rascality.

THE PURE AND THE CARNAL-MINDED.
Romul. 28.

Αὔη γὰρ ψυχὴ [καὶ] ξηρὴ, ἀρίστη καθ' Ἡράκλειτον, ὥσπερ ἀσ-
τραπὴ νέφους, διαπταμένη τοῦ σώματος. Ἡ δὲ σώματι πεφυρμένη
καὶ περίπλεως σώματος, οἷον ἀναθυμίασις ἐμβριθὴς καὶ ὀμιχλώδης,
δυσέξαπτός ἐστι καὶ δυσανακόμιστος.

For, in the language of Heracleitus, the virtuous soul is pure
and unmixed light, springing from the body as a flash of lightning
darts from the cloud. But the soul that is carnal and immersed
in sense, like a heavy and dank vapour, can with difficulty be
kindled, and caused to raise its eyes heavenward.

So Romans—(viii. 7) "Because the carnal mind is enmity against God ;
for it is not subject to the law of God, neither indeed can be."

THE DUTY OF A PRINCE.
Thes. and Rom. 2.

Δεῖ γὰρ τὸν ἄρχοντα σώζειν πρῶτον αὐτὴν τὴν ἀρχήν· σώζεται δ'
οὐχ ἧττον ἀπεχομένη τοῦ μὴ προσήκοντος, ἢ περιεχομένη τοῦ προσήκοντος. Ὁ δ' ἐνδιδοὺς, ἢ ἐπιτείνων, οὐ μένει βασιλεὺς, οὐδὲ ἄρχων,
ἀλλ' ἢ δημαγωγὸς, ἢ δεσπότης γιγνόμενος, ἐμποιεῖ τὸ μισεῖν, ἢ καταφρονεῖν τοῖς ἀρχομένοις.

For it is the highest duty of a prince to maintain the government in its proper form ; and this may be accomplished not less
by abstaining from grasping into his hands powers that do not
belong to him; than by maintaining the authority which is his own.
Now he who surrenders his authority, and he who grasps a greater
power, does not continue a king or prince ; but degenerating
either into a demagogue or tyrant, causes his subjects to hate or
despise him.

ADVANTAGES OF A HOUSE OF PEERS.
Lycurg. 5.

Αἰωρουμένη γὰρ ἡ πολιτεία καὶ ἀποκλίνουσα νῦν μὲν ὡς τοὺς
βασιλεῖς ἐπὶ τυραννίδα, νῦν δέ ὡς τὸ πλῆθος ἐπὶ δημοκρατίαν, οἷον
ἕρμα τὴν τῶν γερόντων ἀρχὴν ἐν μέσῳ θεμένη καὶ ἰσορροπήσασα,
τὴν ἀσφαλεστάτην τάξιν ἔσχε καὶ κατάστασιν· ἀεὶ τῶν ὀκτὼ καὶ

εἴκοσι γερόντων τοῖς μὲν βασιλεῦσι προστιθεμένων, ὅσον ἀντιβῆναι πρὸς δημοκρατίαν, αὖθις δὲ ὑπὲρ τοῦ μὴ γενέσθαι τυραννίδα, τὸν δῆμον ἀναρρωννύντων.

For the constitution of the state before this time had been fluctuating, and inclining sometimes to despotism and sometimes to a pure democracy ; but the formation of a senate, an intermediate body, like ballast, gave it a just balance, and permanence to its institutions. For the twenty-eight senators supported the kings when the people made encroachments on their authority, and again sustained the just power of the commons when the kings attempted to make themselves absolute.

IMPORTANCE OF GOOD PRINCIPLES BEING INSTILLED INTO A PEOPLE.

Lycurg. 13.

Τὰ μὲν οὖν κυριώτατα καὶ μέγιστα πρὸς εὐδαιμονίαν πόλεως καὶ ἀρετὴν, ἐν τοῖς ἤθεσιν ᾤετο καὶ ταῖς ἀγωγαῖς τῶν πολιτῶν ἐγκατεστοιχειωμένα μένειν ἀκίνητα, καὶ βήβαια, ἔχοντα τὴν προαίρεσιν δεσμὸν ἰσχυρότερον τῆς ἀνάγκης, ἣν ἡ παίδευσις ἐμποιεῖ τοῖς νέοις, νομοθέτου διάθεσιν ἀπεργαζομένη περὶ ἕκαστον αὐτῶν.

Lycurgus thought that what tended most to secure the happiness and virtue of a people was the interweaving of right principles with their habits and training. These remained firm and steadfast when they were the result of the bent of the disposition, a tie stronger even than necessity ; and the habits instilled by education into youth would answer in each the purpose of a lawgiver.

OBEDIENCE OF A PEOPLE.

Lycurg. 30.

Οὐ γὰρ ἀκούειν ὑπομένουσι τῶν προστατεῖν μὴ δυναμένων. Ἀλλ' ἡ πειθαρχία μάθημα μέν ἐστιν ἄρχοντος. (Ἐμποιεῖ γὰρ ὁ καλῶς ἄγων, τὸ καλῶς ἔπεσθαι· καὶ καθάπερ ἱππικῆς τέχνης ἀποτέλεσμα, πρᾷον ἵππον καὶ πειθήνιον παρασχεῖν οὕτω βασιλικῆς ἐπιστήμης ἔργον, εὐπείθειαν ἐργάσασθαι.)

For it is certain that people will not continue obedient to those who know not how to command ; while it is the duty of a good governor to teach obedience. He who knows how to show the way well, is sure to be well followed ; and as it is by a knowledge of the act of horsemanship that a horse is rendered gentle and manageable, so it is by the skill and abilities of him who sits on the throne that the people become submissive and obedient.

GLORY ATTENDS ON THE NOBLE AFTER DEATH.

Num. 22.

Πᾶσι μὲν οὖν ἕπεται τοῖς δικαίοις καὶ ἀγαθοῖς ἀνδράσι μείζων ὧν
κατόπιν ὁ μετὰ τελευτὴν ἕπαινος, τοῦ φθόνου πολὺν χρόνον οὐκ
ἐπιζῶντος, ἐνίων δὲ καὶ προαποθνήσκοντος.

Glory attends on the just and noble. It increases after death ;
for envy does not long survive them, and sometimes has disappeared before their death.

WRITTEN LAWS BROKEN LIKE SPIDERS' WEBS.

Sol. 5.

Τὸν οὖν Ἀνάχαρσιν πυθόμενον καταγελᾶν τῆς πραγματείας τοῦ
Σόλωνος, οἰομένου γράμμασιν ἐφέξειν τὰς ἀδικίας καὶ πλεονεξίας τῶν
πολιτῶν, ἃ μηδὲν τῶν ἀραχνίων διαφέρειν, ἀλλ' ὡς ἐκεῖνα, τοὺς μὲν
ἀσθενεῖς λεπτοὺς καὶ τῶν ἀλισκομένων καθέξειν, ὑπὸ δὲ τῶν δυνατῶν
καὶ πλουσίων διαρραγήσεσθαι.

When Anacharsis heard what Solon was doing, he laughed at
the folly of thinking that he could restrain the unjust proceedings
and avarice of his citizens by written laws, which, he said, resembled in every way spiders' webs, and would, like them, catch
and hold only the poor and weak, while the rich and powerful
would easily break through them.

ABSOLUTE MONARCHY.

Sol. 14.

Καλὴν μὲν εἶναι τὴν τυραννίδα χωρίον, οὐκ ἔχειν δέ ἀπόβασιν.

Absolute monarchy is a fair field, but has no outlet.

NO ONE TO BE PRONOUNCED HAPPY BEFORE DEATH.

Sol. 27.

Τύχαις ὁρῶσα παντοδαπαῖς χρώμενον ἀεὶ τὸν βίον, οὐκ ἐᾷ τοῖς
παροῦσιν ἀγαθοῖς μέγα φρονεῖν, οὐδὲ θαυμάζειν ἀνδρὸς εὐτυχίαν
μεταβολῆς χρόνον ἔχουσαν. Ἔπεισι γὰρ ἑκάστῳ ποικίλον ἐξ ἀδήλου
τὸ μέλλον· ὦ δ' εἰς τέλος ὁ δαίμων ἔθετο τὴν εὐπραξίαν, τοῦτον
ἡμεῖς εὐδαίμονα νομίζομεν. Ὁ δὲ ζῶντος ἔτι κινδυνεύοντος ἐν τῷ
βίῳ μακαρισμός, ὥσπερ ἀγωνιζομένου κήρυγμα καὶ στέφανός, ἐστιν
ἀβέβαιας καὶ ἄκυρος.

There are many and various events in the life of man that do
not allow him to pride himself on present prosperity, nor to be
fascinated by that happiness which is so subject to change : for
futurity carries in its hidden bosom many vicissitudes for man.
The man who is blessed by heaven, to the last moment of his life

is pronounced by us to be happy; but the happiness of him who still lives, and is engaged in the conflicts of life, is uncertain and precarious, like that of the combatant ere the crown of victory is determined.

See (Lat.) No man blessed before death.

Man's Discourse like a Piece of Tapestry.

Themist. 29.

Ὁ δὲ Θεμιστοκλῆς ἀπεκρίνατο, τὸν λόγον ἐοικέναι τοῦ ἀνθρώποι τοῖς ποικίλοις στρώμασιν· ὡς γὰρ ἐκεῖνα, καὶ τοῦτον, ἐκτεινόμενον μὲν ἐπιδείκνυσθαι τὰ εἴδη, συστελλόμενον δὲ κρύπτειν καὶ διαφθείρειν. Ὅθεν αὐτῷ χρόνου δεῖν.

Themistocles replied, "That the conversation of a man resembled a piece of embroidered tapestry, which, when spread out, showed its figures, but, when it is folded up, they are hidden and lost; wherefore he requested time for consideration."

War has its Laws of Honour.

Camil. 10.

Ὡς χαλεπὸν μέν ἐστι πόλεμος, καὶ διὰ πολλῆς ἀδικίας καὶ βιαίων περαινόμενος ἔργων, εἰσὶ δὲ καὶ πολέμων ὅμως τινὲς νόμοι τοῖς ἀγαθοῖς ἀνδράσι, καὶ τὸ νικᾶν οὐχ οὕτω διωκτέον, ὥστε μὴ φεύγειν τὰς ἐκ κακῶν ἢ ἀσεβῶν ἔργων χάριτας, (ἀρετῇ γὰρ οἰκείᾳ τὸν μέγαν στρατηγὸν, οὐκ ἀλλοτρίᾳ θαρροῦντα κακίᾳ, χρῆναι στρατεύειν.)

War at best is a savage thing, and wades to its object through a sea of violence and injustice; yet there are certain laws connected with it to which men of honour will adhere. Nor must we be so bent upon victory as to try to gain it by acts of villany and baseness; for a great general ought to make use of his own skill and bravery, and not depend on the knavery of others.

See (Lat.) War.

That the Weak Must Obey the Strong, is a Law of Nature.

Camil. 17.

Τῷ πρεσβυτάτῳ τῶν νόμων ἀκολουθοῦντες, ὃς τῷ κρείττονι τὰ τῶν ἡττόνων δίδωσιν, ἀρχόμενος ἀπὸ τοῦ Θεοῦ, καὶ τελευτῶν εἰς τὰ θηρία. Καὶ γὰρ τούτοις ἐκ φύσεως ἔνεστι, τὸ ζητεῖν πλέον ἔχειν τὰ κρείττονα τῶν ὑποδεεστέρων.

Following the most ancient law of nature, which makes the weak obey the strong, beginning from God and ending with the irrational part of creation. For these are taught by nature to use the advantages which their strength gives them over the weak,

See (Lat.) Might makes right; The weakest goes to the wall.

CHARMED WITH THE WORK, WE DESPISE THE WORKMAN.

Pericl. 1.

Πολλάκις δὲ καὶ τοὐναντίον, χαίροντες τῷ ἔργῳ, τοῦ δημιουργοῦ καταφρονοῦμεν· ὡς ἐπὶ τῶν μύρων καὶ τῶν ἁλουργῶν, τούτοις μὲν ἡδόμεθα, τοὺς δὲ βαφεῖς καὶ μυρεψοὺς, ἀνελευθέρους ἡγούμεθα καὶ βαναύσους.

Often while we are delighted with the work, we regard the workman with contempt. Thus we are pleased with perfumes and purple, while dyers and perfumers are considered by us as low, vulgar mechanics.

THE BEAUTY OF GOODNESS.

Pericl. 2.

Τὸ γὰρ καλὸν ἐφ᾽ αὑτὸ πρακτικῶς κινεῖ, καὶ πρακτικὴν εὐθὺς ὁρμὴν ἐντίθησιν ἠθοποιοῦν οὐ τῇ μιμήσει τὸν θεατὴν, ἀλλὰ τῇ ἱστορίᾳ τοῦ ἔργου, τὴν προαίρεσιν παρεχόμενον.

For the beauty of goodness possesses a power of attraction, exciting in us a desire that our latter end may be the same as that of the righteous ; it exercises an influence over us not merely when the living example is before our eyes, but even the mere description of it is beneficial to our minds.

So Numbers (xxiii. 10)—"Let me die the death of the righteous, and let my last end be like his ! "

ANY WORK OF IMPORTANCE REQUIRES TIME AND LABOUR.

Pericl. 13.

Ἡ γὰρ ἐν τῷ ποιεῖν εὐχέρεια καὶ ταχύτης οὐκ ἐντίθησι βάρος ἔργῳ μόνιμον, οὐδὲ κάλλους ἀκρίβειαν· ὁ δ᾽ εἰς τὴν γένεσιν τῷ πόνῳ προδανεισθεὶς χρόνος, ἐν τῇ σωτηρίᾳ τοῦ γενομένου τὴν ἰσχὺν ἀποδίδωσιν.

For ease and quickness of execution are not fitted to give those enduring qualities that are necessary in a work for all time ; while, on the other hand, the time that is laid out on labour is amply repaid in the permanence it gives to the performance.

THE SPECULATIVE AND PRACTICAL PHILOSOPHER.

Pericl. 16.

Οὐ ταὐτὸν δ᾽ ἐστὶν, οἶμαι, θεωρητικοῦ φιλοσόφου καὶ πολιτικοῦ βίος, ἀλλ᾽ ὁ μὲν ἀνόργανον καὶ ἀπροσδεᾶ τῆς ἐκτὸς ὕλης ἐπὶ τοῖς καλοῖς κινεῖ τὴν διάνοιαν, τῷ δ᾽ εἰς ἀνθρωπείας χρείας ἀναμιγνύντι τὴν ἀρετὴν, ἔστιν οὗ γένοιτ᾽ ἂν οὐ τῶν ἀναγκαίων μόνον, ἀλλὰ καὶ τῶν καλῶν ὁ πλοῦτος.

O

In my opinion there is an essential distinction between the specu-
lative and practical philosophers; for while the former gives his
thoughts to scientific and metaphysical subjects, without reference
to what is material, the latter devotes the noble qualities of his
mind to the improvement of mankind, and to attain this object he
finds riches not only an excellent assistant, but really necessary.

To Err is Human.

Fab. Max. 13.

Ἄνδρες (ἔφη) συστρατιῶται, τὸ μὲν ἁμαρτεῖν μηδὲν ἐν πράγμασι
μεγάλοις, μεῖζον, ἢ κατ' ἄνθρωπόν ἐστι· τὸ δ' ἁμαρτόντα χρήσασθαι
τοῖς πταίσμασι διδάγμασι πρὸς τὸ λοιπὸν, ἀνδρὸς ἀγαθοῦ καὶ νοῦν
ἔχοντος.

Fellow-soldiers, to commit no blunders in the execution of mighty
transactions, is beyond the power of man; but the wise and good
learn from their errors and indiscretion wisdom for the future.

See (Lat.) To err is human.

God Loves a Cheerful Giver.

Fab. Max. 18.

Καὶ γὰρ τὸ θεῖον ἥδεσθαι τιμώμενον ὑπὸ τῶν εὐτυχούντων.

The worship most acceptable to God comes from a cheerful and
thankful heart.

So 2 Corinthians (ix. 7)—"For God loveth a cheerful giver."

How the Minds of Men ought to be Softened.

Fab. Max. 20.

Δεινὸν γὰρ ἡγεῖτο, τοὺς μὲν ἱππικοὺς καὶ κυνηγετικούς, ἐπιμελείᾳ
καὶ συνηθείᾳ καὶ τροφῇ μᾶλλον, ἢ μάστιγι καὶ κλοιοῖς τὴν χαλεπό-
τητα τῶν ζώων καὶ τὸ θυμούμενον καὶ τὸ δυσκολαῖνον ἐξαιρεῖν· τὸν δ'
ἀνθρώπων ἄρχοντα μὴ τὸ πλεῖστον ἐν χάριτι καὶ πρᾳότητι τῆς
ἐπανορθώσεως τίθεσθαι, σκληρότερον δὲ προσφέρεσθαι καὶ βιαιότε-
ρον, ἥπερ οἱ γεωργοῦντες ἐρινεοῖς καὶ ἀχράσι καὶ κοτίνοις προσφέ-
ρονται, τὰ μὲν εἰς ἐλαίας, τὰ δ' εἰς ἀπίους, τὰ δ' εἰς συκᾶς ἐξημε-
ροῦντες καὶ τιθασσεύοντες.

For he thought it shameful that, while those who breed horses
and dogs subdue their stubborn tempers, and bring into subjection
their fierce spirits, by watchfulness, kind treatment, and good feed-
ing, rather than by whipping and confinement, he who has the com-

mand of men should not depend chiefly on gentleness and kindness in amending their faults, acting, in fact, in a more stringent and harsh manner than even gardeners do to wild fig-trees, wild pears and olives, whose nature they change and soften by cultivation, thereby obtaining excellent and agreeable fruit.

ADVANTAGES OF A LIBERAL EDUCATION.

Coriol. 1.

Οὐδὲν γὰρ ἄλλο Μουσῶν εὐμενείας ἀπολαύουσιν ἄνθρωποι τοσοῦτον, ὅσον ἐξημερῶσαι τὴν φύσιν ὑπὸ λόγου καὶ παιδείας, τῷ λόγῳ δεξαμένην τὸ μέτριον, καὶ τὸ ἄγαν ἀποβαλοῦσαν.

Men derive no greater advantage from a liberal education than that it tends to soften and polish their nature, by improving their reasoning faculties and training their habits, thus producing an evenness of temper and banishing all extremes.

A PEOPLE RUINED BY INDULGENCE.

Coriol. 14.

Οὐ γὰρ κακῶς ἔοικεν εἰπεῖν ὁ εἰπὼν, ὅτι πρῶτος κατέλυσε τὸν δῆμον ὁ πρῶτος ἐστιάσας καὶ δεκάσας.

It was a shrewd saying, whoever said it, "That the man who first brought ruin on the Roman people was he who pampered them by largesses and amusements."

THE ANGRY MAN.

Coriol. 21.

ᾟ καὶ δοκεῖ δραστικὸς ὁ θυμούμενος, ὡς θερμὸς ὁ πυρέττων, οἷον ἐν σφυγμῷ καὶ διατάσει καὶ ὄγκῳ γενομένης τῆς ψυχῆς.

Hence the angry man is full of activity, in the same way as the man in a fever is hot, the mind glowing, and being in a high state of excitement.

THE ANGRY MAN INSISTS ON THE GRATIFICATION OF HIS DESIRES BY THE SACRIFICE OF HIS LIFE.

Coriol. 22.

Θυμῷ μάχεσθαι χαλεπόν· ὃ γὰρ ἂν θέλῃ, ψυχῆς ὠνεῖται.

Heracleitus says—

"Stern wrath, how strong thy sway! Though life 's the forfeit. Thy purpose must be gained."

MEN NEGLECTFUL OF RELIGIOUS WORSHIP.

Coriol. 25.

Ὡς τὰ πλεῖστα τῶν ἀνθρωπίνων ἀναγκαίῳ τινὶ τρόπῳ καὶ διὰ βίας περαινόμενα.

Being aware that man's attention to religious worship is only to be attained by a kind of violence and compulsion.

THE ASSISTANCE OF GOD TO MAN IS A MORAL INFLUENCE, NOT DESTROYING FREE-WILL.

Coriol. 32.

Ἐν δὲ ταῖς ἀτόποις καὶ παραβόλοις πράξεσι καὶ φορᾶς τινος ἐνθουσιώδους καὶ παραστάσεως δεομέναις, οὐκ ἀναιροῦντα ποιεῖ τὸν θεὸν, ἀλλὰ κινοῦντα τὴν προαίρεσιν· οὐδ' ὁρμὰς ἐνεργαζόμενον, ἀλλὰ φαντασίας ὁρμῶν ἀγωγούς· αἷς οὐδὲ ποιεῖ τὴν πρᾶξιν ἀκούσιον, ἀλλὰ τῷ ἑκουσίῳ δίδωσιν ἀρχὴν, καὶ τὸ θαρρεῖν καὶ τὸ ἐλπίζειν προστίθησιν. Ἢ γὰρ ἀπαλλακτέον ὅλως τὰ θεῖα πάσης αἰτίας καὶ ἀρχῆς τῶν καθ' ἡμᾶς, ἢ τίς ἂν ἄλλος εἴη τρόπος, ᾧ βοηθοῦσιν ἀνθρώποις καὶ συνεργοῦσιν; οὐ τὸ σῶμα δήπου πλάττοντες ἡμῶν, οὐδὲ τὰς χεῖρας, εἰς ἃ δεῖ, μετατιθέντες αὐτοὶ καὶ τοὺς πόδας, ἀλλὰ τῆς ψυχῆς τὸ πρακτικὸν καὶ προαιρετικὸν ἀρχαῖς τισι καὶ φαντασίαις καὶ ἐπινοίαις ἐγείροντες, ἢ τοὐναντίον, ἀποστρέφοντες καὶ ἱστάντες.

In surprising and startling actions, where the supernatural and the assistance of the Divinity may be required, Homer does not introduce the Supreme Being as taking away the freedom of the will, but merely as influencing it. The Divine Power is not represented as causing the resolution, but only thoughts and ideas which naturally lead to the resolution. In this way the act cannot be called altogether involuntary, since God is the moving cause to the voluntary, and thus gives confidence and good hope. For we must either banish entirely the Supreme Being from all causality and influence over our actions, or what other way is there in which He can assist and co-operate with men? for it is impossible to suppose that He fashions our corporeal organs, or directs the motions of our hands and feet, to accomplish what He intends ; but it is by suggesting certain motives, and predisposing the mind, that He excites the active powers of the will, or restrains them.

MIRACULOUS APPEARANCES NOT ALTOGETHER TO BE REJECTED.

Coriol. 38.

Ἰδίοντα μὲν γὰρ ἀγάλματα φανῆναι καὶ δακρυρροοῦντα, καί τινας θιέντα νοτίδας αἱματώδεις, οὐκ ἀδύνατόν ἐστι. Καὶ γὰρ ξύλα καὶ

λίθοι πολλάκις μὲν εὐρῶτα συνάγουσι γόνιμον ὑγρότητος, πολλὰς δὲ
χροιὰς ἀνιᾶσιν ἐξ ἑαυτῶν, καὶ δέχονται βαφὰς ἐκ τοῦ περιέχοντος·
οἷς ἔνια σημαίνειν τὸ δαιμόνιον, οὐδὲν ἂν δόξειε κωλύειν. Δυνατὸν
δὲ καὶ μυγμῷ καὶ στεναγμῷ ψόφον ὅμοιον ἐκβάλλειν ἀγάλματα,
κατὰ ῥῆξιν, ἢ διάστασιν μορίων βιαιοτέραν ἐν βάθει γενομένην· ἔναρ-
θρον δὲ φωνὴν, καὶ διάλεκτον οὕτω σαφῆ καὶ περιττὴν καὶ ἀρτίστομον,
ἐν ἀψύχῳ γενέσθαι παντάπασιν ἀμήχανον. Οὐ μὴν ἀλλὰ τοῖς ὑπ᾽
εὐνοίας καὶ φιλίας πρὸς τὸν θεὸν ἄγαν ἐμπαθῶς ἔχουσι, καὶ μηδὲν
ἀθετεῖν, μηδ᾽ ἀναίνεσθαι τῶν τοιούτων δυναμένοις, μέγα πρὸς πίστιν
ἐστὶ τὸ θαυμάσιον καὶ μὴ καθ᾽ ἡμᾶς τῆς τοῦ θεοῦ δυνάμεως. Οὐδὲν
γὰρ οὐδαμῶς ἀνθρωπίνῳ προσέοικεν, οὔτε φύσιν, οὔτε τέχνην, οὔτ᾽
ἰσχὺν· οὔτ᾽ εἴ τι ποιεῖ τῶν ἡμῖν ἀποιήτων, καὶ μηχανᾶται τῶν ἀμηχάνων, παράλογόν ἐστιν· ἀλλὰ μᾶλλον ἐν πᾶσι διαφέρων, πολὺ
μάλιστα τοῖς ἔργοις ἀνόμοιός ἐστι καὶ παρηλλαγμένος. Ἀλλὰ τῶν
μὲν θείων τὰ πολλὰ, καθ᾽ Ἡράκλειτον, ἀπιστίῃ διαφυγγάνει μὴ
γινώσκεσθαι.

Indeed, we shall not deny that sweating statues and weeping
images, and some even emitting drops of blood, may have existed;
for wood and stone often contract a mouldiness and mildew that
gives out moisture, not only exhibiting many different colours
themselves, but receiving a variety of tints from the circumam-
bient air. Yet, with all this, there is no reason why the Supreme
Being should not avail Himself of these signs to predict future
events. It is also very possible that a sound resembling a sigh or
a groan might come from a statue by the disruption or violent
separation of some of the interior parts; but it is quite beyond
the bounds of possibility to imagine that an inanimate thing can
give forth an articulate voice, or a clear, full, and perfect expression. As for those persons who are possessed with such a strong
sense of religion that they cannot reject anything of this kind,
they found their faith on the wonderful and incomprehensible
power of God, for there is no kind of resemblance between Him
and a human being, either in His nature, His wisdom, His power,
or His operations. If, therefore, He performs something which
we cannot effect, or executes what with us is impossible, there is
nothing in this contradictory to reason, since, though He far ex-
cels us in everything, yet the dissimilitude and distance between
Him and us appears most of all in the works that He has wrought.

Insult Worse to Bear than Wrong.

Timol. 32.

Οὕτως ὑπὸ λόγων μᾶλλον, ἢ πράξεων πονηρῶν, ἀνιᾶσθαι πεφύκασιν οἱ πολλοί· χαλεπώτερον γὰρ ὕβριν, ἢ βλάβην φέρουσι.

Thus the greater proportion of mankind are more sensitive to
contemptuous language than unjust acts; for they can less easily
bear insult than wrong.

RELIGION.

Paul. Æmil. 3.

Φιλοσόφοι, ὅσοι τὴν εὐσέβειαν ὡρίσαντο θεραπείας θεῶν ἐπιστήμην εἶναι.

There are some philosophers, who define religion to be the science of worshipping the gods.

So Cicero (De Invent. II. 25)—"Religio est, quæ superioris cujusdam naturæ, quam divinam vocant, curam cæremoniamque offert."

NO ONE VERY WICKED AT ONCE.

Paul. Æmil. 3.

Οὐδεὶς γὰρ ἐξ ἀρχῆς εὐθὺς μεγάλῳ παρανομήματι κινεῖ πολιτείαν, ἀλλὰ καὶ τὴν τῶν μειζόνων φρουρὰν καταλύουσιν οἱ προϊέμενοι τὴν ἐν τοῖς μικροῖς ἀκρίβειαν.

For no one ever began his attempts to shake a government by an enormous crime; but those who wink at small offences are withdrawing their attention from weightier matters.

So Psalm (lxix. 27)—"Add iniquity unto their iniquity."

INCOMPATIBILITY OF TEMPER IN MARRIED LIFE.

Paul. Æmil. 5.

Τῷ γὰρ ὄντι μεγάλαι μὲν ἁμαρτίαι ἀναπεπταμέναι γυναῖκας ἀνδρῶν ἄλλας [οὐκ] ἀπήλλαξαν· ταῖς δ', ἔκ τινος ἀηδίας, καὶ δυσαρμοστίας ἤθῶν, μικρὰ καὶ πυκνὰ προσκρούματα, λανθάνοντα τοὺς ἄλλους, ἀπεργάζεται τὰς ἀνηκέστους ἐν ταῖς συμβιώσεσιν ἀλλοτριότητας.

For, in general, women are divorced for glaring and notable faults; yet sometimes, also, a peevish disposition, an uncomplying temper, small but constant bickerings, though unknown to the world, cause incurable distastes in married life.

THE MINGLED LOT OF HUMAN LIFE.

Paul. Æmil. 24.

Πλὴν εἴ τι δαιμόνιον ἄρα τῶν μεγάλων καὶ ὑπερόγκων εἴληχεν εὐτυχιῶν ἀπαρύτειν, καὶ μιγνύναι τὸν ἀνθρώπινον βίον, ὅπως μηδενὶ κακῶν ἄκρατος εἴη καὶ καθαρός, ἀλλὰ, καθ' Ὅμηρον, ἄριστα δοκῶσι πράττειν, οἷς αἱ τύχαι τροπὴν ἐπ' ἀμφότερα τῶν πραγμάτων ἔχουσιν.

But perhaps there is some superior Being, whose business it is to throw a shade over every noble and eminent action, and to make such a mingled yarn of good and ill together in our life, that it may never be entirely free from calamity; but those, as Homer says, may consider themselves happy to whom fortune gives an equal share of good and evil.

Difference between True Bravery and a Disregard of Life.

Pelop. 1.

Κάτων ὁ πρεσβύτατος, πρός τινας ἐπαινοῦντας ἄνθρωπον ἀλογίστως παράβολον καὶ τολμηρὸν ἐν τοῖς πολεμικοῖς, διαφέρειν ἔφη τοῦ πολλοῦ τινα τὴν ἀρετὴν ἀξίαν τὸ μὴ πολλοῦ ἄξιον τὸ ζῆν νομίζειν.

Cato the elder, when somebody was praising a man for his foolhardy bravery, said "that there was an essential difference between a really brave man and one who had merely a contempt for life."

The Strong ought to Govern the Weak.

Pelop. 24.

Ὁ γὰρ πρῶτος, ὡς ἔοικε, καὶ κυριώτατος νόμος τῷ σώζεσθαι δεομένῳ τὸν σώζειν δυνάμενον ἄρχοντα κατὰ φύσιν ἀποδίδωσι.

The first and supreme law, that of nature herself, is for those who wish to be protected to assume as governor him who is most able to protect.

See (Lat.) Might makes right.

The Consolation of Envy.

Pelop. 25.

Κοινήν τινα τοῦ φθόνου παραμυθίαν ἔχοντος, ἂν ὧν αὐτοὶ μὴ δύνωνται βελτίους φανῆναι, τούτους ἀμωσγέπως ἐτέρων ἀποδείξωσι κακίους.

It is the usual consolation of the envious, if they cannot maintain their superiority, to represent those by whom they are surpassed as inferior to some one else.

Reverence of Gods brings Blessing.

Marcell. 4.

Οὕτω πάντα τὰ πράγματα Ῥωμαίοις εἰς τὸν θεὸν ἀνήγετο· μαντειῶν δὲ καὶ πατρίων ὑπεροψίαν οὐδ᾽ ἐπὶ ταῖς μεγίσταις εὐπραξίαις ἀπεδέχοντο, μεῖζον ἡγούμενοι πρὸς σωτηρίαν πόλεως, τὸ θαυμάζειν τὰ θεῖα τοὺς ἄρχοντας, ἢ τὸ κρατεῖν τῶν πολεμίων.

By the Romans the success of everything was ascribed to the gods, nor did they permit even in their greatest prosperity any neglect of the forms of divination and other sacred usages, regarding it as of much greater importance for the preservation of the state that their generals should show respect to the gods than that they should be victorious over their enemies.

So Sirach (i. 13)—" Whoso feareth the Lord, it shall go well with him at the last, and he shall find favour in the day of his death."

WHY MEN REVERENCE GOD.

Aristid. 6.

Ζηλοῦν μὲν αὐτοὺς καὶ μακαρίζειν ἐοίκασι κατὰ τὸ ἄφθαρτον καὶ αἴδιον.

Men admire the gods, and think them happy, because of their freedom from death and corruption.

So Daniel (iv. 34)—" I blessed the Most High, and I praised and honoured Him that liveth for ever, whose dominion is an everlasting dominion, and His kingdom is from generation to generation."

WHAT ONE DOES NOT NEED IS DEAR AT A PENNY.

Marc. Cat. 4.

῞Ολως δὲ μηδὲν εὔωνον εἶναι τῶν περιττῶν, ἀλλ᾽ οὗ τις οὐ δεῖται, κἂν ἀσσαρίου πιπράσκηται, πολλοῦ νομίζειν. Κτᾶσθαι δὲ τὰ σπειρόμενα καὶ νεμόμενα μᾶλλον, ἢ τὰ ῥαινόμενα καὶ σαιρόμενα.

He regarded nothing to be cheap that was superfluous, for what one does not need is dear at a penny ; and it was better to possess fields, where the plough goes and cattle feed, than fine gardens that require much watering and sweeping.

GOODNESS AND JUSTICE.

Marc. Cat. 5.

Καίτοι τὴν χρηστότητα τῆς δικαιοσύνης πλατύτερον τόπον ὁρῶμεν ἐπιλαμβάνουσαν. Νόμῳ μὲν γὰρ καὶ τῷ δικαίῳ πρὸς ἀνθρώπους μόνον χρῆσθαι πεφύκαμεν· πρὸς εὐεργεσίας δὲ καὶ χάριτας ἔστιν ὅτε καὶ μέχρι τῶν ἀλόγων ζώων, ὥσπερ ἐκ πηγῆς πλουσίας, ἀπορρεῖ τῆς ἡμερότητος.

But goodness has a wider range than justice ; for we are bound by nature to observe the dictates of law and equity in our dealings with men, while the feelings of kindness and benevolence overflow, as from a gushing fountain, from the breast of the tender-hearted to creatures of every species.

KINDNESS SHOULD BE SHOWN TO EVERY LIVING CREATURE.

Marc. Cat. 5.

Οὐ γὰρ, ὡς ὑποδήμασιν, ἢ σκεύεσι, τοῖς ψυχὴν ἔχουσι χρηστέον, κοπέντα καὶ κατατριβέντα ταῖς ὑπηρεσίαις ἀπορριπτοῦντας, ἀλλ᾽ εἰ

διὰ μηδὲν ἄλλο, μελέτης ἕνεκα τοῦ φιλανθρώπου, προεθιστέον ἑαυτὸν
ἐν τούτοις πρᾷον εἶναι καὶ μείλιχον. ᾿Εγὼ μὲν οὖν οὐδὲ βοῦν ἂν
ἐργάτην διὰ γῆρας ἀποδοίμην, μή τι γε πρεσβύτερον ἄνθρωπον, ἐκ
χώρας συντρόφου καὶ διαίτης συνήθους, ὥσπερ ἐκ πατρίδος, μεθιστά-
μενον ἀντὶ κερμάτων μικρῶν, ἄχρηστόν γε τοῖς ὠνουμένοις, ὥσπερ
τοῖς πιπράσκουσι, γεγενημένον.

For we should certainly not treat living creatures as old shoes
or household goods, which, if they are worn out by long use, we
cast away as useless ; and if it were for no other reason than to
cultivate a kind and loving disposition to mankind, we should be
merciful to other creatures. For my own part, I should never
think of selling an old ox which had laboured in my service, much
less would I be willing to remove an old slave, who had grown
grey in my service, from his accustomed dwelling and diet ; for to
him, poor man! it would be as bad as banishment, being of as
little use to the buyer as to the seller.

THE BELLY HAS NO EARS.

Marc. Cat. 8.

Χαλεπὸν μέν ἐστιν, ὦ πολῖται, πρὸς γαστέρα λέγειν ὦτα οὐκ
ἔχουσαν.

It is difficult to speak to the belly, because it has no ears.

STRIKING A WIFE.

Marc. Cat. 20.

Τὸν δὲ τύπτοντα γαμετὴν, ἢ παῖδα, τοῖς ἁγιωτάτοις ἔλεγεν ἱεροῖς
προσφέρειν τὰς χεῖρας.

He used to say that the man who struck his wife or his son laid
hands on what was most sacred.

So Ephesians (v. 33)—"Let every one of you in particular so love his wife
even as himself; and the wife see that she reverence her husband."

WHEN POVERTY IS DISHONOURABLE.

Aristid. and Cat. 4.

Πενία γὰρ αἰσχρὸν οὐδαμοῦ μὲν δι᾿ αὐτὴν, ἀλλ᾿ ὅπου δεῖγμα
ῥᾳθυμίας ἐστὶν, ἀκρασίας, πολυτελείας, ἀλογιστίας.

For poverty is not dishonourable in itself, but only when it
arises from idleness, intemperance, extravagance, and folly.

See (Lat.) Poverty.

JUSTICE VERY UNCOMMON.
Xamin. 11.

Ἦν δ' ἄρα σπάνιον μὲν ἀνδρεία καὶ φρόνησις ἐν ἀνθρώποις, σπανιώτατον δὲ τῶν ἄλλων ἀγαθῶν ὁ δίκαιος.

Among men, valour and prudence are seldom met with, and of all human excellences justice is still more uncommon.
So Genesis (xvii. 32)—"And Abraham said, Peradventure ten shall be found there. And the Lord said, I will not destroy it for ten's sake."

FAMILIARITY BREEDS CONTEMPT.
C. Mar. 16.

Ἡγεῖτο γὰρ πολλὰ μὲν ἐπιψεύδεσθαι τῶν οὐ προσόντων τὴν καινότητα τοῖς φοβεροῖς· ἐν δὲ τῇ συνηθείᾳ, καὶ τὰ φύσει δεινὰ τὴν ἔκπληξιν ἀποβάλλειν.

For he considered that novelty causes the imagination to add much to objects of terror, while things really fearful lose their effect by familiarity.

See (Lat.) Familiarity.

GOOD AND EVIL ACTIONS.
C. Mar. 29.

Τὸ κακόν τι πρᾶξαι, φαῦλον εἴη· τὸ δὲ καλὸν μὲν, ἀκινδύνως δὲ, κοινόν· ἴδιον δ' ἀνδρὸς ἀγαθοῦ τὸ μετὰ κινδύνων τὰ καλὰ πράσσειν.

To do an evil action is base ; to do a good action, without incurring danger, is common enough ; but it is the part of a good man to do great and noble deeds, though he risks everything.

CUSTOMS DEPENDING ON NATIONAL INSTITUTIONS.
Lysand. 17.

'Αλλὰ καὶ πολλῷ τάχιον ἀπὸ τῶν κοινῶν ἐπιτηδευμάτων ἐπιρρέουσιν οἱ ἐθισμοὶ τοῖς ἰδιωτικοῖς βίοις, ἢ τὰ καθ' ἕκαστον ὀλισθήματα καὶ πάθη τὰς πόλεις ἀναπίμπλησι πραγμάτων πονηρῶν. Τῷ γὰρ ὅλῳ συνδιαστρέφεσθαι τὰ μέρη μᾶλλον. ὅταν ἐνδῷ πρὸς τὸ χεῖρον, εἰκός· αἱ δ' ἀπὸ μέρους εἰς ὅλον ἁμαρτίαι πολλὰς ἐνστάσεις καὶ βοηθείας ἀπὸ τῶν ὑγιαινόντων ἔχουσιν.

But it is evident that customs, which depend on national institutions, must more speedily make an impression on the habits and lives of the mass of a community, than the profligacy and vices of individuals have the power of corrupting a whole nation. For wh+n the whole is diseased, the parts cannot escape ; whereas. if the disorder is only in some particular part, it may be amended by those who have not yet caught the infection.

How Far a Painter ought to Represent Blemishes.
Cim. 2.

῞Ωσπερ γὰρ τοὺς τὰ καλὰ καὶ πολλὴν ἔχοντα χάριν εἴδη ζωγρα-φοῦντ**ι**, ἂν προσῇ τι μικρὸν αὐτοῖς δυσχερές, ἀξιοῦμεν μήτε παρα-λιπεῖν τοῦτο τελέως, μήτ᾽ ἐξακριβοῦν, (τὸ μὲν γὰρ αἰσχρὰν, τὸ δ᾽ ἀνομοία**ν** παρέχεται τὴν ὄψιν.)

For as in the case of painters who have undertaken to give us a beautiful and graceful figure, which may have some slight blemishes, we do not wish them to pass over such blemishes altogether, nor yet to mark them too prominently. The one would spoil the beauty, and the other destroy the likeness of the picture.

Results of Prosperity and Adversity.
Lucull. 2.

Οὐδὲν γὰρ ἀνθρώπου δυσαρκτότερον, εὖ πράσσειν δοκοῦντος· οὐδ᾽ αὖ πάλιν δεκτικώτερον ἐπιστασίας, συσταλέντος ὑπὸ τῆς τύχης.

For there is nothing more difficult to direct than a man on whom fortune smiles ; nothing more easily managed, when the clouds of adversity overwhelm him.

Word-Catchers.
Nic. 1.

Ἐμοὶ δ᾽ ὅλως μὲν ἡ περὶ λέξιν ἄμιλλα καὶ ζηλοτυπία πρὸς ἑτέρους, μικροπρεπὲς φαίνεται καὶ σοφιστικόν· ἂν δὲ πρὸς τὰ ἀμίμητα γίγ-νηται, καὶ τελέως ἀναίσθητον.

For my own part, I cannot help saying that I think all envy and jealousy respecting the style of expression which others employ betrays littleness of mind, and is the characteristic of a sophist ; and when a spirit of envy leads a man to try to rival what is inimitable, it is perfectly ridiculous.

Peace and War.
Nic. 9.

Ἡδέως δὲ μεμνημένοι τοῦ εἰπόντος, ὅτι τοὺς ἐν εἰρήνῃ καθεύδοντος οὐ σάλπιγγες, ἀλλ᾽ ἀλεκτρυόνες ἀφυπνίζουσι.

They recollect with pleasure the saying, "That it was not the sound of the trumpet, but the crowing of the cock, that awoke sleepers in time of peace."

LOVE OF BRICK AND MORTAR.
N. Crass. 2.

Ἀλλ' ἔλεγε τοὺς φιλοικοδόλους αὐτοὺς ὑφ' ἑαυτῶν καταλύεσθαι, χωρὶς ἀνταγωνιστῶν.

He used to say, "That those who were found of building would soon ruin themselves without the assistance of enemies."

POLITICAL ECONOMY.
N. Crass. 2.

Τὴν γὰρ οἰκονομικὴν, ἐν ἀψύχοις χρηματιστικὴν οὖσαν, ἐν ἀνθρώποις πολιτικὴν γιγνομένην ὁρῶμεν.

For we observe that political economy, when it refers merely to inanimate objects, is employed for the paltry purposes of gain; but when it treats of human beings, it rises to a higher branch of the laws of nature.

BETTER TO ERR ON THE SIDE OF RELIGION, BY ADHERING TO RECEIVED OPINIONS.
Nic. and Crass. 5.

Ἐπιεικέστερον δὲ αὐτῆς τοῦ παρανόμου καὶ αὐθάδους, τὸ μετὰ δόξης παλαιᾶς καὶ συνήθους δι' εὐλάβειαν ἁμαρτανόμενον.

It is more fitting to err on the side of religion from a regard to ancient and received opinions, than to err through obstinacy and presumption.

RECURRENCE OF THE SAME EVENTS.
Sert. 1.

Θαυμαστὸν μὲν ἴσως οὐκ ἔστιν, ἐν ἀπείρῳ τῷ χρόνῳ τῆς τύχης ἄλλοτε ἄλλως ῥεούσης, ἐπὶ ταὐτὰ συμπτώματα πολλάκις καταφέρεσθαι τὸ αὐτόματον. Εἴτε γὰρ οὐκ ἔστι τῶν ὑποκειμένων ὡρισμένον τὸ πλῆθος, ἄφθονον ἔχει τῆς τῶν ἀποτελουμένων ὁμοιότητος χορηγὸν ἡ τύχη τὴν τῆς ὕλης εὐπορίαν· εἴτ' ἔκ τινων ὡρισμένων ἀριθμῷ ἐμπλέκεται τὰ πράγματα, πολλάκις ἀνάγκη ταὐτὰ γίνεσθαι διὰ τῶν αὐτῶν περαινόμενα.

It is not at all surprising that Fortune, being ever changeable, should, in the course of numberless ages, often hit on events perfectly similar. For if there be no limit to the number of events that happen, Fortune can have no difficulty in furnishing herself with parallels in this abundance of matter ; whereas, if their number be limited, there must necessarily be a return of the same occurrences when the whole cycle has been gone through.

True Honour.

Sert. 5.

Τῆς πίστεως μηδενὶ λογισμῷ χώραν διδούσης.

True honour leaves no room for hesitation and doubt.

Time Destroys the Strongest Thing.

Sert. 16.

Ἄμαχον γὰρ τὸ ἐνδελεχὲς, ᾧ πᾶσαν ἐπιὼν ὁ χρόνος αἱρεῖ καὶ κατεργάζεται δύναμιν, εὐμενὴς ὢν σύμμαχος τοῖς δεχομένοις λογισμῷ τὸν καιρὸν αὐτοῦ, τοῖς δ' ἀκαίρως ἐπειγομένοις πολεμιώτατος.

In fact, perseverance is all-powerful ; by it time, in its advances, undermines and is able to destroy the strongest things on earth ; being the best friend and ally to those who use properly the opportunities that it presents, and the worst enemy to those who are rushing into action before it summons them.

See (Lat.) Time.

Different Conduct of Men in Prosperity and Adversity.

Eum. 4.

Τὸ μὲν οὖν εὐτυχεῖν καὶ τοὺς φύσει μικροὺς συνεπικουφίζει τοῖς φρονήμασιν, ὥστε φαίνεσθαί τι μέγεθος περὶ αὐτοὺς καὶ ὄγκον, ἐκ πραγμάτων ὑπερεχόντων ἀποβλεπομένους. Ὁ δὲ ἀληθῶς μεγαλόφρων καὶ βέβαιος, ἐν τοῖς σφάλμασι μᾶλλον καὶ ταῖς δυσημερίαις ἀναφέρων, γίνεται κατάδηλος.

Prosperity inspires an elevation of mind even in the mean-spirited, so that they show a certain degree of high-mindedness and chivalry in the lofty position in which fortune has placed them ; but the man who possesses real fortitude and magnanimity will show it by the dignity of his behaviour under losses, and in the most adverse fortune.

Man neither Savage nor Unsocial by Nature.

Pomp. 28.

'Εννοήσας οὖν, ὅτι φύσει μέν ἄνθρωπος οὔτε γέγονεν, οὔτ' ἐστίν, ἀνήμερον ζῷον, οὐδ' ἄμικτον, ἀλλ' ἐξίσταται, τῇ κακίᾳ παρὰ φύσιν χρώμενος, ἔθεσι δὲ καὶ τόπων καὶ βίων μεταβολαῖς ἐξημεροῦται, καὶ θηρία, διαίτης κοινωνοῦντα πρᾳοτέρας, ἐκδύεται τὸ ἄγριον καὶ χαλεπόν.

Being convinced that man is neither by birth nor by disposition a savage, nor of unsocial habits, but only becomes so by indulging in vices contrary to his nature; yet even in this case, he may be improved by change of abode, and by a different mode of life, as beasts, that are naturally wild, lay aside their fury when they have been properly trained.

The Noble-minded adds Dignity to Every Act.

Pomp. 73.

Φεῦ τοῖσι γενναίοισιν ὡς ἅπαν καλόν.

The generous mind adds dignity
To every act, and nothing misbecomes it.

Dead Men do not Bite.

Pomp. 78.

Νεκρὸς οὐ δάκνει.

Dead men do not bite.

A Straw shows how the Wind Sets.

Alexand. 1.

Οὔτε ταῖς ἐπιφανεστάταις πράξεσι πάντως ἔνεστι δήλωσις ἀρετῆς, ἢ κακίας, ἀλλὰ πρᾶγμα βραχὺ πολλάκις καὶ ῥῆμα, καὶ παιδιά τις, ἔμφασιν ἤθους ἐποίησε μᾶλλον, ἢ μάχαι μυριόνεκροι, καὶ παρατάξεις αἱ μέγισται, καὶ πολιορκίαι πόλεων.

Nor is it always in the most distinguished actions that a man's worth or malicious temper may be most easily discovered; but very often an action of small note, a short expression, or a jest, shall point out a man's real character more clearly than the greatest sieges or the most important battles.

RELIGION AND SUPERSTITION.

Alexand. 75.

Οὕτως ἄρα δεινὸν μὲν ἀπιστία πρὸς τὰ θεῖα, καὶ καταφρόνησις αὐτῶν· δεινὴ δ' αὖθις ἡ δεισιδαιμονία.

So true it is that, though disbelief in religion and contempt of things divine be a great evil, yet superstition is a still greater.

See (Lat.) How God is to be worshipped.

THE GOOD MAN IN ADVERSITY.

Phoc. 1.

Τοσοῦτον δέ τῇ τύχῃ δοτέον, ἀντιταττομένῃ πρὸς τοὺς ἀγαθοὺς ἄνδρας, ἰσχύειν, ὅσον, ἀντὶ τῆς ἀξίας τιμῆς καὶ χάριτος ἐνίοις ψόγους πονηροὺς καὶ διαβολὰς ἐπιφέρουσαν, τὴν πίστιν ἀσθενεστέραν ποιεῖν τῆς ἀρετῆς.

When the good and upright are depressed by Fortune, the only real power she exercises over them is that she brings unjust aspersions and slanders upon their character, instead of the honour and esteem in which they ought to be held ; and in this way she diminishes the trust which tho world ought to have in their virtue.

A PEOPLE IN ADVERSE CIRCUMSTANCES.

Phoc. 2.

Καίτοι δοκοῦσιν οἱ δῆμοι μᾶλλον εἰς τοὺς ἀγαθοὺς ἐξυβρίζειν, ὅταν εὐτυχῶσιν, ὑπὸ πραγμάτων μεγάλων καὶ δυνάμεως ἐπαιρόμενοι· συμβαίνει δὲ τοὐναντίον. Ἀεὶ γὰρ αἱ συμφοραὶ πικρὰ μὲν τὰ ἤθη καὶ μικρόλυπα καὶ ἀκροσφαλῆ πρὸς ὀργὰς ποιοῦσι, δύσκολον δὲ τὴν ἀκοὴν καὶ τραχεῖαν, ὑπὸ παντὸς λόγου καὶ ῥήματος τόνον ἔχοντος ἐνοχλουμένην· ὁ δ' ἐπιτιμῶν τοῖς ἐξαμαρτανομένοις ἐξονειδίζειν τὰ δυστυχήματα δοκεῖ, καὶ καταφρονεῖν ὁ παρρησιαζόμενος. Καὶ καθάπερ τὸ μέλι λυπεῖ τὰ τετρωμένα καὶ ἡλκωμένα μέρη τοῦ σώματος, οὕτως πολλάκις οἱ ἀληθινοὶ καὶ νοῦν ἔχοντες λόγοι δάκνουσι καὶ παροξύνουσι τοὺς κακῶς πράττοντας, ἐὰν μὴ προσηνεῖς ὦσι καὶ συνείκοντες.

It is believed by some that when the affairs of a state are prosperous, the people, elated by their power and success, treat good ministers with the greater insolence ; but this is a mistake. For misfortunes always irritate their tempers and annoy them ; they take fire at trifles, and cannot bear to hear the smallest reproach. He who reproves their faults seems to make them the cause of their own misfortunes, and spirited language is regarded as an insult. And as honey causes wounds and ulcerated sores to smart, so it often happens that expostulation, however full of sense and truth it may be, provokes and alienates those in distress, unless gentleness and tact be shown in its application.

A People in Adversity.

Phoc. 2.

Καὶ γὰρ ὄμμα φλεγμαῖνον ἥδιστα τοῖς σκιεροῖς καὶ ἀλαμπέσιν ἐνδιατρίβει χρώμασι, τὰ δ᾽ αὐγὴν ἔχοντα καὶ φῶς ἀποστρέφεται· καὶ πόλις ἐν τύχαις ἀβουλήτοις γενομένη ψοφοδεὲς καὶ τρυφερόν ἐστι δι᾽ ἀσθένειαν ἀνέχεσθαι παῤῥησίας, ὅτε μάλιστα δεῖται, τῶν πραγμάτων ἀναφορὰν ἁμαρτήματος οὐκ ἐχόντων. Διὸ πάντη σφαλερὸν ἡ τοιαύτη πολιτεία. Συναπόλλυσι γὰρ τὸν πρὸς χάριν λέγοντα, καὶ προαπόλλυσι τὸν μὴ χαριζόμενον.

An eye in a state of inflammation avoids all bright and glaring colours, and loves to rest on what is dark and shady. In the same way a state, when fortune frowns, becomes timid and fearful, not being able to bear the voice of truth, though it is, above all things, necessary and salutary. Wherefore, it is no easy task to govern such a people ; for, if the man who tells them the truth falls the first victim, he who flatters them at last perishes with them.

The Word of the Good is Weighty.

Phoc. 5.

Ἐπεὶ καὶ ῥῆμα καὶ νεῦμα μόνον ἀνδρὸς ἀγαθοῦ μυρίοις ἐνθυμήμασι καὶ περιόδοις ἀντίῤῥοπον ἔχει πίστιν.

Since a mere word or a simple nod from the good and virtuous possesses more weight than the prepared speeches of other men.

See (Lat.) A Tumult.

Different Characters in the Same Man.

Phoc. 10.

Ἔστι δ᾽, οἶμαι, χαλεπόν, οὐ μὴν ἀδύνατον, ὥσπερ οἶνον, καὶ ἄνθρωπον τὸν αὐτὸν ἡδὺν ἅμα καὶ αὐστηρὸν εἶναι· καθάπερ ἕτεροι πάλιν, φαινόμενοι γλυκεῖς, ἀηδέστατοι τοῖς χρωμένοις εἰσὶ καὶ βλαβερώτατοι.

It is indeed difficult, but, I believe, not impossible, for the same man to be rough and gentle, as some wines are both sweet and sour ; and then again, some men, who have all the appearance of a gentle and kind manner, are worrying and unbearable by those who have to do with them.

What is gained with Labour is kept longest.

Cat. Min. 1.

Ὁ δὴ καὶ πέφυκεν ἄλλως, τοὺς μὲν εὐφυεῖς ἀναληπτικοὺς μᾶλλον εἶναι, μνημονικοὺς δὲ, τοὺς μετὰ πόνου καὶ πραγματείας παραδεχομένους. Γίνεται γὰρ οἷον ἔγκαυμα τῆς ψυχῆς τῶν μαθημάτων ἕκαστον.

It is usually the case that those who have sharp and ready wits possess weak memories, while that which is acquired with labour and perseverance is always retained longest ; for every hard-gained acquisition of knowledge is a sort of annealing upon the mind.

A Man requires to be Beloved as well as Esteemed if he is to have Influence over Others.

Cat. Min. 9.

Ἀρετῆς γὰρ ἀληθινὸς οὐκ ἐγγίνεται ζῆλος, ἢ δι' ἄκρας τοῦ παραδιδόντος εὐνοίας καὶ τιμῆς. Οἱ δ' ἄνευ τοῦ φιλεῖν ἐπαινοῦντες τοὺς ἀγαθοὺς, αἰδοῦνται μὲν τὴν δόξαν αὐτῶν, οὐ θαυμάζουσι δὲ τὴν ἀρετὴν, οὐδὲ μιμοῦνται.

There is no real desire to imitate virtue, except the person who sets the example be beloved as well as esteemed. Those who praise the good without loving them, only pay respect to their name, admiring their virtuous life without caring to follow their example.

The Honest Statesman.

Agis. 2.

Ὁ μὲν γὰρ ἀπηκριβωμένως καὶ τελείως ἀγαθὸς οὐδ' ἂν ὅλως δόξης δέοιτο, πλὴν ὅση πάροδον ἐπὶ τὰς πράξεις διὰ τοῦ πιστεύεσθαι δίδωσι.

The honest and upright statesman pays no regard to the popular voice except with this view, that the confidence it procures him may facilitate his designs, and crown them with success.

The Best not without Imperfections.

Cleom. 16.

Οἰκτείροντες δὲ τῆς ἀνθρωπίνης φύσεως τὴν ἀσθένειαν, εἰ μηδ' ἐν ἤθεσιν οὕτως ἀξιολόγοις καὶ διαφόροις πρὸς ἀρετὴν ἐκφέρειν δύναται τὸ καλὸν ἀνεμέσητον.

Pitying the weakness of human nature, which, not even in dispositions that are best formed to virtue, can produce excellence without some taint of imperfection.

So Seneca (Controv. iv. 25)—"Nemo pæne sine vitio est."

Money the Sinews of Business.

Cleom. 27.

'Αλλ' ὁ πρῶτος τὰ χρήματα νεῦρα τῶν πραγμάτων προσειπών, εἰς τὰ τοῦ πολέμου πράγματα μάλιστα βλέψας τοῦτ' εἰπεῖν ἔοικε.

He who first called money the sinews of business seems more particularly to have had regard to the affairs of war.

See (Lat.) Money the sinews of war.

Character of Weak Men.

Cleom. 33.

Τῆς ἀσθενείας ἐπιτεινούσης τὴν δειλίαν, καὶ, καθάπερ εἴωθεν ἐν τῷ μηδὲν φρονεῖν, τοῦ πάντα δεδοικέναι καὶ πᾶσιν ἀπιστεῖν ἀσφαλεστάτου δοκοῦντος εἶναι.

His weakness increased his timidity, as is common with men of weak understandings, and he began to place his safety in jealousy and suspicion.

The Sacrifice of Time.

Anton. 28.

Τὸ πολυτελέστατον, ὡς 'Αντιφῶν εἶπεν, ἀνάλωμα, τὸν χρόνον.

Antiphon said that the sacrifice of time was the most costly of all sacrifices.

Our Fortune depends on our own Exertions.

Demosth. 1.

Τὴν δ' ἀρετὴν, ὥσπερ ἰσχυρὸν καὶ διαρκὲς φυτὸν, ἐν ἅπαντι ῥιζοῦσθαι τόπῳ, φύσεώς τε χρηστῆς καὶ φιλοπόνου ψυχῆς ἐπιλαμβανομένην. "Οθεν οὐδ' ἡμεῖς, εἰ τοῦ φρονεῖν, ὡς δεῖ, καὶ βιοῦν ἐλλείπομεν, τοῦτο τῇ σμικρότητι τῆς πατρίδος, ἀλλ' αὑτοῖς δικαίως ἀναθήσομεν.

But virtue, like a strong and hardy plant, takes root in any place where it finds an ingenuous nature, and a mind that loves labour. Wherefore, if we do not reach that high position which

we desire, we ought not to ascribe it to the obscurity of the place
where we were born, but to our own little selves.

See (Lat.) The Upright.

Know Thyself.

Demosth. 3.

'Αλλὰ γὰρ ἴσως, εἰ παντὸς ἦν τὸ Γνῶθι Σαυτὸν ἔχειν πρόχειρον,
οὐκ ἂν ἐδόκει πρόσταγμα θεῖον εἶναι.

But perhaps the precept " Know thyself " would not be considered
divine, if every man could easily reduce it to practice.

No Beast more Savage than Man.

Cicer. 46.

Οὐδὲν ἀνθρώπου θηρίον ἐστὶν ἀγριώτερον, ἐξουσίαν πάθει προσλα-
βόντος.

There is no beast more savage than man, when he is possessed of
power equal to his passion.

Power tests a Man's Character.

Demosth. and Cicer. 3.

Ὁ δὲ δοκεῖ μάλιστα καὶ λέγεται τρόπον ἀνδρὸς ἐπιδεικνύναι καὶ
βασανίζειν, ἐξουσία καὶ ἀρχή, πᾶν πάθος κινοῦσα, καὶ πᾶσαν ἀπο-
καλύπτουσα κακίαν.

It is an observation no less just than common, that there is no
stronger test of a man's real character than power and authority,
exciting, as they do, every passion, and discovering every latent
vice.

Popular Government.

Dion. 53.

'Επενόει δὲ, τὴν μὲν ἄκρατον δημοκρατίαν, ὡς οὐ πολιτείαν, ἀλλὰ
παντοπώλιον οὖσαν πολιτειῶν, κατὰ τὸν Πλάτωνα, κολούειν.

His intention was to keep the democracy within bounds, which
cannot be properly called a government, but, as Plato terms it, a
warehouse of governments.

The Vain and Conceited.

Arat. 1.

Φιλαύτου γὰρ ἀνδρὸς, οὐ φιλοκάλου, παντὸς ἀεὶ βέλτιστον αὐτὸ
ἡγεῖσθαι.

It is the admirer of himself, and not the admirer of virtue, that thinks himself superior to others.

CAUSE OF MISFORTUNES IN A FAMILY.
De Lib. Educ. c. 2.

Ὅταν δὲ κρηπὶς μὴ καταβληθῇ γένους
Ὀρθῶς, ἀνάγκη δυστυχεῖν τοὺς ἐκγόνους.

Unless the foundations of a family be properly prepared and laid, those who are sprung from it must necessarily be unfortunate.

THE EVIL DEEDS OF PARENTS WEIGH DOWN THE CHILDREN.
De Lib. Educ. c. 2.

Δουλοῖ γὰρ ἄνδρα, κἂν θρασύσπλαγχνός τις ᾖ,
Ὅταν συνειδῇ πατρὸς ἢ μητρὸς κακά.

There is no one, however high-spirited he may be, that does not quail when he thinks of the evil-deeds of his parents.

NATURE, LEARNING, AND TRAINING.
De Lib. Educ. c. 4.

Ἡ μὲν γὰρ φύσις ἄνευ μαθήσεως, τυφλόν· ἡ δὲ μάθησις δίχα φύσεως ἐλλιπές· ἡ δὲ ἄσκησις χωρὶς ἀμφοῖν, ἀτελές. Ὥσπερ δὲ ἐπὶ τῆς γεωργίας, πρῶτον μὲν ἀγαθὴν ὑπάρξαι δεῖ τὴν γῆν, εἶτα δὲ φυτουργὸν, ἐπιστήμονα, εἶτα τὰ σπέρματα σπουδαῖα· τὸν αὐτὸν τρόπον γῇ μὲν ἔοικεν ἡ φύσις, γεωργῷ δὲ ὁ παιδεύων, σπέρματι δὲ αἱ τῶν λόγων ὑποθῆκαι καὶ τὰ παραγγέλματα.

Nature without learning is like a blind man; learning without nature is like the maimed; practice without both these is incomplete. As in agriculture a good soil is first sought for, then a skilful husbandman, and then good seed; in the same way nature corresponds to the soil,; the teacher to the husbandman; precepts and instruction to the seed.

MOTHERS OUGHT TO SUCKLE THEIR OWN CHILDREN.
De Lib. Educ. c. 5.

Δεῖ δὲ, ὡς ἐγὼ ἂν φαίην, αὐτὰς τὰς μητέρας τὰ τέκνα τρέφειν, καὶ τούτοις ὑπέχειν τοὺς μαστούς. Συμπαθέστερόν τε γὰρ θρέψουσι, καὶ διὰ πλείονος ἐπιμελείας, ὡς ἂν ἔνδοθεν, καὶ, τὸ δὴ λεγόμενον ἐξ ὀνύχων ἁπαλῶν ἀγαπῶσαι τὰ τέκνα. Αἱ τίτθαι δὲ καὶ αἱ τροφοὶ

τὴν εὔνοιαν ὑποβολιμαίαν καὶ παρέγγραπτον ἔχουσιν, ἅτε μισθοῦ
φιλοῦσαι.

In my opinion mothers ought to bring up and suckle their own
children ; for they bring them up with greater affection and with
greater anxiety, as loving them from the heart, and, so to speak,
every inch of them. But the love of a nurse is spurious and coun-
terfeit, as loving them only for hire.

TEACHERS MUST BE OF BLAMELESS LIVES.

De Lib. Educ. c. 7.

Διδασκάλους γὰρ ζητητέον τοῖς τέκνοις, οἵ καὶ τοῖς βίοις εἰσὶν ἀδιά-
βλητοι, καὶ τοῖς τρόποις ἀνεπίληπτοι, καὶ ταῖς ἐμπειρίαις ἄριστοι.
Πηγὴ γὰρ καὶ ρίζα καλοκαγαθίας, τὸ νομίμου τυχεῖν παιδέιας. Καὶ
καθάπερ τὰς χάρακας οἱ γεωργοὶ τοῖς φυτοῖς παρατιθέασι, οὕτως οἱ
νόμιμοι τῶν διδασκάλων, ἐπιμελεῖς τὰς ὑπο θήκας καὶ παραινέσεις
παραπηγνύουσι τοῖς νέοις, ἵν᾽ ὀρθὰ τούτων βλαστάνοι τὰ ἤθη.

Teachers ought to be sought who are of blameless lives, not
liable to be found fault with, and distinguished for learning ; for
the source and root of a virtuous and honourable life is to be
found in good training. And as husbandmen underprop plants,
so good teachers, by their precepts and training, support the young,
that their morals may spring up in a right and proper way.

THE EYE OF THE MASTER FATTENS THE HORSE.

De Lib. Educ. c. 13.

Κἀνταῦθα δὴ τὸ ρηθὲν ὑπὸ τοῦ ἱπποκόμου, χάριεν, ὡς οὐδὲν οὕτω
πιαίνει τὸν ἵππον ὡς βασιλέως ὀφθαλμός.

In this place we may very properly insert the saying of the
groom, who maintained that there was nothing which served to
fatten a horse so much as the eye of its master.

TO FIND FAULT WITH A SPEECH IS EASY.

De Rect. Rat. Audiendi, c. 5.

Τὸ μὲν γὰρ ἀντειπεῖν οὐ χαλεπὸν, ἀλλὰ καὶ πάνυ ῥᾴδιον, εἰρημένῳ
λόγῳ· τὸ δ᾽ ἕτερον ἀντανάστῆσαι βελτίονα, παντάπασιν ἐργῶδες.

For to find fault with a speech is not difficult—nay, it is very
easy ; but to put anything better in its place is a work of great
labour.

THE TALKATIVE.

De Garrulitate, c. 1.

Οἱ δ' ἀδόλεσχοι, οὐδενὸς ἀκούουσιν· ἀεὶ γὰρ λαλοῦσιν· καὶ τοῦτο ἔχει πρῶτον κακὸν ἡ ἀσιγησία τὴν ἀνηκοΐαν.

The talkative listen to no one, for they are ever speaking. And the first evil that attends those who know not to be silent is, that they hear nothing.

MAN.

De Exilio, c. 5

Ὁ γὰρ ἄνθρωπος, φυτὸν οὐκ ἔγγειον οὐδὲ ἀκίνητον, ἀλλ' οὐράνιον ἐστιν, ὥσπερ ἐκ ῥίζης τὸ σῶμα τῆς κεφαλῆς ὀρθὸν ἱστώσης, πρὸς τὸν οὐρανὸν ἀνεστραμμένον.

For man is a plant, not fixed in the earth, nor immovable, but heavenly, whose head, rising as it were from a root upwards, is turned towards heaven.

GOD.

De Isid. et Osir. 9.

Ἐγώ εἰμι πᾶν τὸ γεγονὸς καὶ ὂν καὶ ἐσόμενον.

I am all that was, is, and will be.

So Psalm (cii 27)—"But thou art the same, and thy years shall have no end."

POLYBIUS.

BORN PROBABLY ABOUT B.C. 204.—DIED B.C. 122.

POLYBIUS, a celebrated Greek historian, was the son of Lycortas, a native of Megalopolis, in Arcadia, who succeeded Philopœmen in the chief direction of the Achæan League. His character was formed under the eye of Philopœmen ; and at the funeral of that general he carried the urn which contained his ashes, B.C. 182. In the war which arose between the Romans and Perseus, king of

Macedon, the opinion of Polybius and his father Lycortas was, that the Achæans should observe a strict neutrality ; but they were overruled, and the Achæans were implicated in the ruin of Perseus. The Romans demanded a thousand of the principal citizens as hostages, and among these was Polybius, who was allowed to remain in Rome, where he resided for sixteen years, from B.C. 167 to B.C. 151. He became the intimate friend and instructor of Scipio the younger, at that time only eighteen years of age. At last, through the influence of Scipio and Cato, the Senate was prevailed upon to allow the Achæan exiles to return to their country. His principal work was entitled "General History," though it refers more particularly to a space of fifty-three years, from B.C. 220 to B.C. 168, from the commencement of the second Punic war, where the historian Timœus and Aratus of Sicyon had stopped, to the defeat of Perseus, king of Macedon, by the Romans.

KNOWLEDGE OF PAST EVENTS.

i. 1.

Διὰ τὸ μηδεμίαν ἑτοιμοτέραν εἶναι τοῖς ἀνθρώποις διόρθωσιν, τῆς τῶν προγεγενημένων πράξεων ἐπιστήμης.

Since the knowledge of what has gone before affords the best instruction for the direction and guidance of human life.

HISTORY.

i. 1.

Φάσκοντες, ἀληθινωτάτην μὲν εἶναι παιδείαν καὶ γυμνασίαν πρὸς τὰς πολιτικὰς πράξεις, τὴν ἐκ τῆς ἱστορίας μάθησιν· ἐναργεστάτην δὲ καὶ μόνην διδάσκαλον τοῦ δύνασθαι τὰς τῆς τύχης μεταβολὰς γενναίως ὑποφέρειν, τὴν τῶν ἀλλοτρίων περιπετειῶν ὑπόμνησιν.

History furnishes the only proper discipline to educate and train the minds of those who wish to take part in public affairs ; and the unfortunate events which it hands down for our instruction contain the wisest and most convincing lessons for enabling us to bear our own calamities with dignity and courage.

TRUTHFULNESS OF THE HISTORIAN.

i. 14.

Καὶ γὰρ φιλόφιλον δεῖ εἶναι τὸν ἀγαθὸν ἄνδρα, καὶ φιλόπατριν, καὶ συμμισεῖν τοῖς φίλοις τοὺς ἐχθρούς, καὶ συναγαπᾶν τοὺς φίλους.

Ὅταν δὲ τὸ ἱστορίας ἦθος ἀναλαμβάνῃ τις, ἐπιλαθέσθαι χρὴ πάντων τῶν τοιούτων· καὶ πολλάκις μὲν εὐλογεῖν καὶ κοσμεῖν τοῖς μεγίστοις ἐπαίνοις τοὺς ἐχθρούς, ὅταν αἱ πράξεις ἀπαιτῶσι τοῦτο· πολλάκις δὲ ἐλέγχειν καὶ ψέγειν ἐπονειδίστως τοὺς ἀναγκαιοτάτους, ὅταν αἱ τῶν ἐπιτηδευμάτων ἁμαρτίαι τοῦθ᾽ ὑποδεικνύωσιν. Ὥσπερ γὰρ ζώου τῶν ὄψεων ἀφαιρεθεισῶν, ἀχρειοῦται τὸ ὅλον· οὕτως ἐξ ἱστορίας ἀναιρεθείσης τῆς ἀληθείας, τὸ καταλειπόμενον αὐτῆς ἀνωφελὲς γίγνεται διήγημα. Διόπερ οὔτε τῶν φίλων κατηγορεῖν, οὔτε τοὺς ἐχθροὺς ἐπαινεῖν ὀκνητέον· οὔτε δὲ τοὺς αὐτοὺς ποτὲ μὲν ψέγειν, ποτὲ δὲ ἐγκωμιάζειν εὐλαβητέον· ἐπειδὴ τοὺς ἐν πράγμασιν ἀναστρεφομένους οὔτ᾽ εὐστοχεῖν ἀεὶ δυνατόν, οὔθ᾽ ἁμαρτάνειν συνεχῶς εἰκός. Ἀποστάντες οὖν τῶν πραττόντων, αὐτοῖς τοῖς πραττομένοις ἐφαρμοστέον τὰς πρεπούσας ἀποφάσεις καὶ διαλήψεις ἐν τοῖς ὑπομνήμασιν.

It is right for a good man to love his friends and his country, and to hate the enemies of both. But when a man takes upon him to write history, he must throw aside all such feelings, and be prepared, on many occasions, to extol even an enemy, when his conduct deserves applause ; nor should he hesitate to censure his dearest and most esteemed friends, whenever their deeds call for condemnation. For as an animal, if it be deprived of sight, is wholly useless ; so if we eliminate truth from history, what remains will be nothing but an idle tale. Now, if we pay a proper regard to truth, we shall not hesitate to stigmatise our friends on some occasions, and to praise our enemies ; but it may even be necessary to commend and condemn the same persons, as different circumstances may require ; since it is not to be supposed that those who are engaged in great transactions shall always be pursuing false or mistaken views ; nor yet is it probable that their conduct can at all times be free from error. A historian, therefore, in all that he relates, should take care to be guided in his judgment by the genuine and real circumstances of every action, without reference to those who may have been engaged in it.

See (Lat.) History.

WISE COUNSEL IS BETTER THAN STRENGTH.

i. 35.

Καὶ μὴν τὸ παρ᾽ Εὐριπίδῃ πάλαι καλῶς εἰρῆσθαι δοκοῦν, ὡς Ἓν σοφὸν βούλευμα τὰς πολλὰς χεῖρας νικᾷ, τότε δι᾽ αὐτῶν τῶν ἔργων ἔλαβε τὴν πίστιν.

We may also remark, in this event, the truth of that saying of Euripides, "that one wise counsel is better than the strength of many."

See (Lat.) Mind is the man.

Two Sources from which Man may derive Advantage.

i. 35.

Δυοῖν γὰρ ὄντων τρόπων πᾶσιν ἀνθρώποις τῆς ἐπὶ τὸ βέλτιον μεταθέσεως· τοῦ τε διὰ τῶν ἰδίων συμπτωμάτων, καὶ τοῦ διὰ τῶν ἀλλοτρίων· ἐναργέστερον μὲν εἶναι συμβαίνει τὸν διὰ τῶν οἰκείων περιπετειῶν, ἀβλαβέστερον δὲ τὸν διὰ τῶν ἀλλοτρίων. Διὸ τὸν μὲν οὐδέποθ᾽ ἑκουσίως αἱρετέον, ἐπεὶ μετὰ μεγάλων πόνων καὶ κινδύνων ποιεῖ τὴν διόρθωσιν· τὸν δὲ ἀεὶ θηρευτέον, ἐπεὶ χωρὶς βλάβης ἐστὶ συνιδεῖν ἐν αὐτῷ τὸ βέλτιον. Ἐξ ὧν συνιδόντι, καλλίστην παιδείαν ἡγητέον πρὸς ἀληθινὸν βίον τὴν ἐκ τῆς πραγματικῆς ἱστορίας περιγιγνομένην ἐμπειρίαν. Μόνη γὰρ αὕτη χωρὶς βλάβης, ἐπὶ παντὸς καιροῦ καὶ περιστάσεως, κριτὰς ἀληθινοὺς ἀποτελεῖ τοῦ βελτίονος.

For as there are only two sources from which any real advantage can be reaped —our own misfortunes, and those that have befallen others—and as the former of these, though it may be the more beneficial, is, at all events, more painful and annoying, it will always be the part of wisdom to prefer the latter, which will alone enable us to all times to perceive what is fit and useful without incurring hazard or anxiety. Hence may be seen the real value of history, which teaches us how we may direct our life, in every event that may happen, upon the truest and most approved models, without being exposed to the dangers and annoyances of other men.

Important Services excite Ill-will.

i. 36.

Αἱ γὰρ ἐπιφανεῖς καὶ παράδοξοι πράξεις, βαρεῖς μὲν ιοὺς φθόνους, ὀξείας δὲ τὰς διαβολὰς γεννῶσιν· ἃς οἱ μὲν ἐγχώριοι διά τε τὰς συγγενείας καὶ τὸ τῶν φίλων πλῆθος οἷοί τ᾽ ἂν εἶεν φέρειν· οἱ δὲ ξένοι ταχέως ἐφ᾽ ἑκατέρων ι ούτων ἡττῶνται, καὶ κινδυνεύουσι.

Great and illustrious deeds are very apt to excite feelings of ill-will and spite, which, though a native of the country, if he be supported by a host of friends and relations, may perhaps be able to get the better of, yet forcigners generally sink under such attacks, and are ruined by them.

Art of a Good General.

i. 62.

Τοῦ γὰρ αὐτοῦ νομιστέον εἶναι ἡγεμόνος, τὸ δύνασθαι βλέπειν τόν τε τοῦ νικᾷν. Ὁμοίως δὲ καὶ τὸν τοῦ λείπεσθαι καιρόν.

For the part of a consummate general is not only to see the way leading to victory, but also when he must give up all hopes of victory.

See (Lat.) Qualities of a general.

CHARACTER OF MERCENARIES.

i. 67.

Καρχηδόνιοι γὰρ ἀεὶ χρώμενοι ποικίλαις καὶ μισθοφορικαῖς δυνάμεσι, πρὸς μὲν τὸ μὴ ταχέως συμφρονήσαντας ἀπειθεῖν, μηδὲ δυσκαταπλήκτους εἶναι τοῖς ἡγουμένοις, ὀρθῶς στοχάζονται, ποιοῦντες ἐκ πολλῶν γενῶν τὴν δύναμιν· πρὸς δὲ τὸ, γενομένης ὀργῆς ἢ διαβολῆς ἢ στάσεως, διδάξαι καὶ πραῧναι καὶ μεταθεῖναι τοὺς ἠγνοηκότας, ὁλοσχερῶς ἀστοχοῦσιν. Οὐ γὰρ οἷον ἀνθρωπίνῃ χρῆσθαι κακίᾳ συμβαίνει τὰς τοιαύτας δυνάμεις, ὅταν ἅπαξ εἰς ὀργὴν καὶ διαβολὴν ἐμπέσωσι πρός τινας· ἀλλ' ἀποθηριοῦσθαι τὸ τελευταῖον, καὶ παραστατικὴν λαμβάνειν διάθεσιν.

The Carthaginians were in the habit of forming their armies of mercenaries drawn together from different countries ; if they did so for the purpose of preventing conspiracies, and of making the soldiers more completely under the control of their generals, they may seem perhaps, in this respect, not to have acted foolishly, for troops of this sort cannot easily unite together in factious counsels. But when we take another view of the question, the wisdom of the proceeding may be doubted, if we consider the difficulty there is to instruct, soften, and subdue the minds of an army so brought together when rage has seized them, and when hatred and resentment have taken root among them, and sedition is actually begun. In such circumstances, they are no longer men, but beasts of prey. Their fury cannot be restricted within the ordinary bounds of human wickedness or violence, but breaks out into deeds the most terrible and monstrous that are to be found in nature.

CIVIL WAR.

i. 71.

Διὸ καὶ τότε σαφῶς ἔγνωσαν, ἡλίκην ἔχει διαφορὰν ξενικὸς καὶ διαπόντιος πόλεμος, ἐμφυλίου στάσεως καὶ ταραχῆς.

Now were they thoroughly convinced that civil dissensions were much more to be dreaded than a war carried on in a foreign country against a foreign enemy.

MINDS OF MEN LIABLE TO MALIGNANT DISEASES.

i. 81.

Διόπερ εἰς ταῦτα βλέπων, οὐκ ἄν τις εἰπεῖν ὀκνήσειεν, ὡς οὐ μόνον τὰ σώματα τῶν ἀνθρώπων, καί τινα τῶν ἐν αὐτοῖς γεννωμένων ἑλκῶν καὶ φυμάτων ἀποθηριοῦσθαι συμβαίνει, καὶ τελέως ἀβοήθητα γίγνεσθαι· πολὺ δὲ μάλιστα τὰς ψυχάς. Ἐπί τε γὰρ τῶν ἑλκῶν, ἐὰν μὲν θεραπείαν τοῖς τοιούτοις προσάγῃ τις, ὑπ' αὐτῆς ἐνίοτε ταύτης ἐρε-

θιξόμενα, θᾶττον ποιεῖται τὴν νομήν· ἐὰν δὲ πάλιν ἀφῇ, κατὰ τὴν
ἐξ αὐτῶν φύσιν φθείροντα τὸ συνεχὲς, οὐκ ἴσχει παῦλαν, ἕως ἂν
ἀφανίσῃ τὸ ὑποκείμενον. Ταῖς τε ψυχαῖς παραπλησίως τοιαῦται πολλάκις ἐπιφύονται μελανίαι καὶ σηπεδόνες, ὥστε μηδὲν ἀσεβέστερον
ἀνθρώπου μηδὲ ὠμότερον ἀποτελεῖσθαι τῶν ζώων. Οἷς ἐὰν μὲν συγγνώμην τινὰ προσάγῃς καὶ φιλανθρωπίαν, ἐπιβουλὴν καὶ παραλογισ-
μὸν ἡγούμενοι τὸ συμβαῖνον, ἀπιστότεροι καὶ δυσμενέστεροι γίγνονται
πρὸς τοὺς φιλανθρωποῦντας. Ἐὰν δὲ ἀντιτιμωρῇ. διαμιλλώμενοι τοῖς
θυμοῖς, οὐκ ἔστι τὶ τῶν ἀπειρημένων ἢ δεινῶν, ὁποῖον οὐκ ἀναδέχονται,
σὺν καλῷ τιθέμενοι τὴν τοιαύτην τόλμαν· τέλος δ᾽ ἀποθηριωθέντες,
ἐξέστησαν τῆς ἀνθρωπίνης φύσεως. Τῆς δὲ διαθέσεως ἀρχηγὸν μὲν
καὶ μεγίστην μερίδα νομιστέον, ἔθη μοχθηρὰ καὶ τροφήν ἐκ παίδων
κακήν· συνεργὰ δὲ καὶ πλείω, μέγιστα δὲ τῶν συνεργῶν, τὰς ἀεὶ τῶν
προεστώτων ὕβρεις καὶ πλεονεξίας.

Whoever meditates on these horrible cruelties will not fail to be
satisfied that not only are the bodies of men attacked by corrupt
and ulcerous humours, which cannot easily be got rid of, but that
the minds of men are equally subject to strange disorders. In the
case of ulcerated sores, the very medicines which you apply often
only tend to irritate and inflame, quickening the progress of the
disease ; yet, on the other hand, if the disease be neglected and left
to its own course, it infects all the neighbouring parts, and proceeds till the whole body becomes unsound. So it is with the
mind ; when certain dark and malignant passions get possession of
it, they render men more savage than the beasts themselves. To
men in this state, if you show mercy and kindness, suspecting it to
be fraud and artifice, they become more suspicious than before, and
regard you with still stronger feelings of aversion. But if you
oppose their furious proceedings, there is no crime too horrible for
them to perpetrate. They exult and glory in their impieties, and
by degrees get rid of every feeling and affection that embellish
human nature. There is no doubt but that these disorders chiefly
arise from a bad education and evil communications, though there
are many other causes which may sometimes assist to bring them
on, among which none is so likely to be effectual as the insolent
conduct and rapacity of public governors.

BALANCE OF POWER IN THE WORLD.

i. 83.

Οὐδὲ τηλικαύτην οὐδενὶ συγκατασκευάζειν δυναστείαν, πρὸς ἣν
οὐδὲ περὶ τῶν ὁμολογουμένων ἐξέσται δικαίων ἀμφισβητεῖν.

Nor ought we ever to allow any growing power to acquire such
a degree of strength as to be able to tear from us, without resistance, our natural, undisputed rights.

Do not Calculate on the Future.

ii. 4.

Αἰτωλοὶ δὲ, τῇ παραδόξῳ χρησάμενοι συμφορᾷ, πάντας ἐδίδαξαν μηδέ ποτε βουλεύεσθαι περὶ τοῦ μέλλοντος, ὡς ἤδη γεγονότος· μηδὲ προκατελπίζειν βεβαιουμένους ὑπὲρ ὧν ἀκμὴν ἐνδεχόμενόν ἐστιν ἄλλως γενέσθαι· νέμειν δὲ μερίδα τῷ παραδόξῳ, πανταχῇ μὲν, ἀνθρώπους ὄντας, μάλιστα δ' ἐν τοῖς πολεμικοῖς.

A circumstance which happened to the Ætolians ought to convince us that we ought not to speculate on the future as if it were already past, nor build expectations on events which may eventually turn out very differently from what they seemed at first to promise; but in all human affairs, and especially in those that relate to war, to leave always some room to fortune and to accidents which cannot be foreseen.

See (Lat.) The Future.

Calamities arising from Fortune and Ourselves contrasted.

ii. 7.

Τὸ μὲν γὰρ, ἀνθρώπους ὄντας, παραλόγως περιπεσεῖν τινι τῶν δεινῶν, οὐ τῶν παθόντων, τῆς τύχης δὲ, καὶ τῶν πραξάντων, ἐστὶν ἔγκλημα. Τὸ δ' ἀκρίτως καὶ προφανῶς περιβαλεῖν αὑτοὺς ταῖς μεγίσταις συμφοραῖς, ὁμολογούμενόν ἐστι τῶν πασχόντων ἁμάρτημα. Διὸ καὶ τοῖς μὲν ἐκ τύχης πταίουσιν, ἔλεος ἔπεται μετὰ συγγνώμης, καὶ ἐπικουρία· τοῖς δὲ διὰ τὴν αὑτῶν ἀβουλίαν, ὄνειδος καὶ ἐπιτίμησις συνεξακολουθεῖ παρὰ τοῖς εὖ φρονοῦσιν.

For when man falls into any of those calamities to which human nature is subject, and which could not be guarded against by any care or foresight, the fault is justly attributed to fortune, or some enemy; but when our troubles arise from our foolish and indiscreet conduct, the blame can be imputed only to ourselves. And as unmerited misfortune usually excites the pity of mankind, while it induces them to participate in and aid us in our distresses; so, on the other hand, a clear and evident folly calls for the censure and reproaches of all who regard it in a proper light.

See (Lat.) Misfortunes that are undeserved.

A Roman Citizen.

ii. 8.

Εἶπε γὰρ, ὅτι Ῥωμαίοις μὲν, ὦ Τεῦτα, κάλλιστον ἔθος ἐστι, τὰ κατ' ἰδίαν ἀδικήματα κοινῇ μεταπορεύεσθαι, καὶ βοηθεῖν τοῖς ἀδικουμένοις.

But among the Romans, O queen, it is one of their noblest customs to demand public reparation for private wrongs, and at all times to insist on redress for the injuries done to their subjects.

See (Lat.) Roman Citizen.

CHARACTER OF THE GAULS.

ii. 35.

Κατὰ δὲ τὰς ἐπιβολὰς καὶ τὴν ἀκρισίαν τοῦ κατὰ μέρος χειρισμοῦ, τελέως εὐκαταφρόνητος· διὰ τὸ μὴ τὸ πλεῖον, ἀλλὰ συλλήβδην ἅπαν τὸ γιγνόμενον ὑπὸ τῶν Γαλατῶν, θυμῷ μᾶλλον ἢ λογισμῷ βραβεύεσθαι.

For the Gauls, I do not say frequently, but even in everything, they attempt, are carried forward headlong by their passions, and never listen to the dictates of reason.

See (Lat.) Gauls.

NOTHING WITHOUT A CAUSE.

ii. 38.

Χωρὶς γὰρ ταύτης, οὔτε τῶν κατὰ λόγον, οὔτε τῶν παρὰ λόγον εἶναι δοκούντων οὐδὲν οἷόν τε συντελεσθῆναι.

For nothing happens without a cause, not even among those events which seem to be most fortuitous.

See (Lat.) Predestination.

FEELINGS OF KINGS.

ii. 47.

Τοὺς δὲ βασιλεῖς σαφῶς εἰδὼς, φύσει μὲν οὐδένα νομίζοντας οὔτε ἐχθρὸν οὔτε φίλον, ταῖς δὲ τοῦ συμφέροντος ψήφοις ἀεὶ μετροῦντας τὰς ἔχθρας καὶ τὰς φιλίας.

But he recollected, also, that kings entertain feelings neither of enmity nor friendship towards any, but are in both guided solely by what they consider to be their interest.

WRITERS OF HISTORY AND TRAGEDY CONTRASTED.

ii. 56.

Τὸ δὲ τῆς ἱστορίας οἰκεῖον ἅμα καὶ χρήσιμον ἐξεταζέσθω. Δεῖ τοιγαροῦν οὐκ ἐκπλήττειν τὸν συγγραφέα, τερατευόμενον διὰ τῆς ἱστορίας τοὺς ἐντυγχάνοντας, οὐδὲ τοὺς ἐνδεχομένους λόγους ζητεῖν, καὶ τὰ παρεπόμενα τοῖς ὑποκειμένοις ἐξαριθμεῖσθαι, καθάπερ οἱ

τραγῳδιογράφοι· τῶν δὲ πραχθέντων καὶ ῥηθέντων κατ' ἀλήθειαι
αὐτῶν μνημονεύειν πάμπαν, ἂν πάνυ μέτρια τυγχάνωσιν ὄντα. Τὸ
γὰρ τέλος ἱστορίας καὶ τραγῳδίας, οὐ ταὐτὸν, ἀλλὰ τοὐναντίον. Ἐκεῖ
μὲν γὰρ δεῖ διὰ τῶν πιθανωτάτων λόγων ἐκπλῆξαι καὶ ψυχαγωγῆσαι
κατὰ τὸ παρὸν τοὺς ἀκούοντας· ἐνθάδε δὲ διὰ τῶν ἀληθινῶν ἔργων
καὶ λόγων εἰς πάντα τὸν χρόνον διδάξαι καὶ πεῖσαι τοὺς φιλομα-
θοῦντας. Ἐπειδήπερ ἐν ἐκείνοις μὲν ἡγεῖται τὸ πιθανὸν, κἂν ᾖ ψεῦδος,
διὰ τὴν ἀπάτην τῶν θεωμένων· ἐν δὲ τούτοις τἀληθὲς, διὰ τὴν ὠφέλειαν τῶν φιλομαθούντων.

Consider, then, the peculiar character of history, and what is its
proper aim. A historian ought not to try, like the writers of
tragedy, to astonish and terrify the reader by extraordinary occurrences, nor yet ought he to draw on his imagination for speeches
that might have been delivered. nor events that might have
happened ; but he should be satisfied to give a simple narrative of
the speeches actually delivered, and of the events as they occurred,
even though they may contain nothing noble or exciting. But the
object and scope of tragedy are altogether different from those of
history. It is the business of the latter to strike and fascinate the
minds of the audience who are listening by such representations
as are barely possible ; whereas history professes to deliver lessons,
from which all ages may derive improvement, by giving a true and
accurate account of the speeches and events as they actually took
place. In the one, therefore, the probable, though untrue, may
be sufficient to guide us to the end in view, which is the delight
and amusement of the audience ; but the other addresses itself to
a nobler object—the instruction and improvement of the human
race, and must have truth as its basis.·

Some End in all Human Actions proposed.

iii. 4.

Οὐ γὰρ δὴ τοῦτ' εἶναι τέλος ὑποληπτέον ἐν πράγμασιν, οὔτε τοῖς
ἡγουμένοις, οὔτε τοῖς ἀποφαινομένοις ὑπὲρ τούτων, τὸ νικῆσαι καὶ
ποιήσασθαι πάντας ὑφ' ἑαυτούς. Οὔτε γὰρ πολεμεῖ τοῖς πέλας οὐδεὶς
νοῦν ἔχων, ἕνεκεν αὐτοῦ τοῦ καταγωνίσασθαι τοὺς ἀντιταττομένους·
οὔτε πλεῖ τὰ πελάγη, χάριν τοῦ περαιωθῆναι μόνον· καὶ μὴν οὐδὲ
τὰς ἐμπειρίας καὶ τέχνας αὐτῆς ἕνεκα τῆς ἐπιστήμης ἀναλαμβάνει.
Πάντες δὲ πράττουσι πάντα, χάριν τῶν ἐπιγιγνομένων τοῖς ἔργοις
ἡδέων, ἢ καλῶν, ἢ συμφερόντων.

For certainly, it ought never to be imagined, either by the rulers
of states, or by those who are going to give an account of their
transactions, that the main object of war is victory, and putting
others in subjection to us. No wise man ever makes war merely
for the sake of showing his superiority over his neighbours, nor
navigates the sea for the sole purpose of passing from place to
place. Nor does he practise an art or science merely to acquire

a knowledge of it. In all human actions there is always some end
in view, either of pleasure, or honour, or advantage, as the result
of our labours.

DIFFERENCE BETWEEN THE CAUSE AND BEGINNING OF AN ACT.

iii. 6.

'Αλλ' ἔστιν ἀνθρώπων τὰ τοιαῦτα, μὴ διειληφότων, ἀρχὴ τί διαφέρει καὶ πόσον διέστηκεν αἰτίας καὶ προφάσεως, καὶ διότι τὰ μέν
ἐστι πρῶτα τῶν ἁπάντων, ἡ δ' ἀρχὴ τελευταῖον τῶν εἰρημένων.
'Εγὼ δὲ παντὸς ἀρχὰς μὲν εἶναι φημί, τὰς πρώτας ἐπιβολὰς καὶ
πράξεις τῶν ἤδη κεκριμένων· αἰτίας δὲ, τὰς προκαθηγουμένας τῶν
κρίσεων καὶ διαλήψεων· λέγω δ' ἐπινοίας καὶ διαθέσεις καὶ τοὺς περὶ
ταῦτα συλλογισμοὺς, καὶ δι' ὧν ἐπὶ τὸ κρῖναί τι καὶ προθέσθαι παρα-
γιγνόμεθα.

These misconceptions arise from our forgetting that there is a
difference between the beginning of a war and its cause and pretext, and that the latter of these are always in order antecedent
to the former. To speak correctly, the beginning is the first step
towards the execution of any project, after it has been resolved
on; but the cause is to be sought previous to the resolution. In
fact, it is something that first puts the idea into our heads, and
that inclines us, after mature deliberation, to carry it into execution.

A STATESMAN.

iii. 7.

Τί γάρ ὄφελος ἰατροῦ κάμνουσιν ἀγνοοῦντος τὰς αἰτίας τῶν περὶ
τὰ σώματα διαθέσεων; τί δ' ἀνδρὸς πραγματικοῦ, μὴ δυναμένου
οὕτω φυλακτέον συλλογίζεσθαι, πῶς καὶ διὰ τί καὶ πόθεν ἔκαστα
τῶν πραγμάτων τὰς ἀφορμὰς εἴληφεν; οὔτε γὰρ ἐκεῖνον εἰκὸς
οὐδέποτε δεόντως στήσασθαι τὰς τῶν σωμάτων θεραπείας· οὔτε τὸν
πραγματικὸν οὐδὲν οἷόν τε κατὰ τρόπον χειρίσαι τῶν προσπιπτόντων,
ἄνευ τῆς τῶν προειρημένων ἐπιγνώσεως. Διόπερ οὐδὲν οὕτω φυλακτέον καὶ ζητητέον, ὡς τὰς αἰτίας ἐκάστου τῶν συμβαινόντων.
'Επειδὴ φύεται μὲν ἐκ τῶν τυχόντων πολλάκις τὰ μέγιστα τῶν
πραγμάτων, ἰᾶσθαι δὲ ῥᾷστόν ἐστι παντὸς τὰς πρώτας ἐπιβολὰς καὶ
διαλήψεις.

For a statesman who is ignorant of the way in which events
have originated, and who cannot tell from what circumstances
they have arisen, may be compared to a physician who fails to make
himself acquainted with the causes of those diseases which he is
called in to cure. They are both equally useless and worthless;

for the latter cannot be supposed to be acquainted with the proper means of restoring the body to health, nor can the former be likely to discover the remedies necessary to get the better of the evils that are incident to states. For matters of the greatest importance often take their rise from the most trifling incidents ; and it is easier to resist the beginnings of evils than to stop them when they have made considerable progress.

HYPOCRISY OF MEN.

iii. 31.

Πρὸς μὲν γὰρ τὸ παρὸν ἀεί πως ἁρμοζόμενοι, καὶ συνυποκρινόμενοι, τοιαῦτα καὶ λέγουσι καὶ πράττουσι πάντες, ὥστε δυσθεώρητον εἶναι τὴν ἑκάστου προαίρεσιν, καὶ λίαν ἐν πολλοῖς ἐπισκοτεῖσθαι τὴν ἀλήθειαν.

For all those with whom we live are like actors on a stage, they assume whatever dress and appearance may suit their present purpose, and they speak and act in strict keeping with this character. In this way we find it difficult to get at their real sentiments, or to bring into clear day the truth which they have hid in a cloud of darkness.

So Shakespeare ("As You Like It," act ii., sc. 1)—
"All the world 's a stage,
And all the men and women merely players."

See (Lat.) Hypocrisy.

A MAN OF CONCEIT.

iii. 80.

Τὸν δὲ Φλαμίνιον ὀχλοκόπον μὲν καὶ δημαγωγὸν εἶναι τέλειον, πρὸς ἀληθινῶν δὲ καὶ πολεμικῶν πραγμάτων χειρισμὸν οὐκ εὐφυῆ, πρὸς δὲ τούτοις καταπεπιστευκέναι τοῖς σφετέροις πράγμασι.

Flaminius was well-suited to gain the affections of the populace, and very desirous to stand high in their favour ; but he was destitute of all those peculiar talents that are necessary for the conducting of war and actual business, though he entertained a high opinion of his own abilities.

See (Lat.) Self-love.

A GENERAL OUGHT TO EXAMINE THE CHARACTER OF HIS OPPONENT.

iii. 81.

Ὡς εἴ τις οἴεται κυριώτερόν τι μέρος εἶναι στρατηγίας, τοῦ γνῶναι τὴν προαίρεσιν καὶ φύσιν τοῦ τῶν ἐναντίων ἡγεμόνος, ἀγνοεῖ καὶ τετύφωται.

For every one must confess that there is no greater proof of the abilities of a general than to investigate, with the utmost care, into the character and natural abilities of his opponent.

MEN ASSIMILATED TO THE CLIMATE IN WHICH THEY LIVE.

iv. 21.

Θεωροῦντες δὲ τὴν τῶν ἠθῶν αὐστηρίαν, ἥτις αὐτοῖς παρέπεται διὰ τὴν τοῦ περιέχοντος ψυχρότητα καὶ στυγνότητα τὴν κατὰ τὸ πλεῖστον ἐν τοῖς τόποις ὑπάρχουσαν, ᾧ συνεξομοιοῦσθαι πεφύκαμεν πάντες ἄνθρωποι κατ᾽ ἀνάγκην. οὐ γὰρ δι᾽ ἄλλην, διὰ δὲ ταύτην τὴν αἰτίαν κατὰ τὰς ἐθνικὰς καὶ τὰς ὁλοσχερεῖς διαστάσεις πλεῖστον ἀλλήλων διαφέρομεν ἤθεσί τε καὶ μορφαῖς καὶ χρώμασιν, ἔτι δὲ τῶν ἐπιτηδευμάτων τοῖς πλείστοις.

Looking at their morose and austere manners, which are the necessary consequence of the cold and harsh climate that over-hangs the whole of their province, for men are very much in disposition and feelings according to the nature of the country which they inhabit ; nor can we attribute it to any other reason than that in the various nations of the world, so far removed from each other, we find so vast a difference in features, complexion, and customs.

EVERY INJURY IS NOT TO BE SUBMITTED TO.

iv. 31.

Ἐγὼ γὰρ, φοβερὸν μὲν εἶναι, φημί, τὸ πολεμεῖν, οὐ μὴν οὕτω γε φοβερόν, ὥστε πᾶν ὑπομένειν χάριν τοῦ μὴ προσδέξασθαι πόλεμον. Ἐπεὶ τί καὶ θρασύνομεν τὴν ἰσηγορίαν καὶ παρρησίαν καὶ τὸ τῆς ἐλευθερίας ὄνομα πάντες, εἰ μηδέν ἔσται προυργιαίτερον τῆς εἰρήνης ;

For it is my opinion that war is no doubt much to be dreaded, but still not to such a degree that we should be willing to submit to every kind of insult rather than engage in it. For why should we value so highly equality of government, liberty of speech, and the glorious name of freedom, if nothing is to be preferred to peace?

PEACE NOT TO BE PREFERRED TO EVERYTHING.

iv. 31.

Οὐδὲ Πίνδαρον, τὸν συναποφηνάμενον αὐτοῖς ἄγειν τὴν ἡσυχίαν, διὰ τῶνδε τῶν ποιημάτων·

"Τὸ κοινόν τις ἀστῶν ἐν εὐδίᾳ τιθεὶς
ἐρευνασάτω μεγαλάνορος ἡσυχίας
τὸ φαιδρὸν φάος."

P

δόξας γὰρ παραυτίκα πιθανῶς εἰρηκέναι, μετ᾽ οὐ πολὺ πάντων αἰσχίστην εὑρέθη καὶ βλαβερωτάτην πεποιημένος ἀπόφασιν. Εἰρήνη γὰρ μετὰ μὲν τοῦ δικαίου, καὶ πρέποντος, κάλλιστόν ἐστι κτῆμα καὶ λυσιτελέστατον· μετὰ δὲ κακίας ἢ δουλείας ἐπονειδίστου, πάντων αἴσχιστον καὶ βλαβερώτατον.

Nor can we approve of what Pindar recommends to his fellow-citizens, when he advises them to place all their happiness in peaceful repose, or, as he expresses it in his poetical language—

"In the radiant splendours of majestic Peace;"

for this plausible and specious advice was found in the end to be not less dishonourable than destructive of the best interests of their country. In short, peace is the greatest of all blessings, if it leaves us in the possession of our honours and lawful rights; but if it is attended with the loss of our national independence, and places a blot on our escutcheon, there is nothing more truly pernicious or fatal to our true interests.

See (Lat.) Peace.

RASH PROJECTS.
iv. 34.

Καί μοι δοκεῖ τοῦτ᾽ ἀληθὲς εἶναι, διότι Πολλάκις τὸ τολμᾶν περιττὸν εἰς ἄνοιαν καὶ εἰς τὸ μηδὲν καταντᾶν εἴωθεν.

So true it is, that to engage in reckless and desperate enterprises is most frequently the way to reduce men eventually to utter helplessness, and an inability to make resistance.

See (Lat.) Rashness.

WHAT THINGS ARE ALLOWABLE IN WAR.
v. 11.

Τὸ μὲν γὰρ παραιρεῖσθαι τῶν πολεμίων καὶ καταφθείρειν φρούρια λιμένας, πόλεις, ἄνδρας, ναῦς, καρποὺς, τἄλλα τὰ τούτοις παραπλήσια, δι᾽ ὧν μὲν ὑπεναντίους ἀσθενεστέρους ἄν τις ποιήσαι, τὰ δὲ σφέτερα πράγματα καὶ τὰς ἐπιβολὰς δυναμικωτέρας· ταῦτα μὲν ἀναγκάζουσιν οἱ τοῦ πολέμου νόμοι καὶ τὰ τούτου δίκαια δρᾶν. Τὸ δὲ, μήτε τοῖς ἰδίοις πράγμασιν ἐπικουρίαν μέλλοντα μηδ᾽ ἥντιν᾽ οὖν παρασκευάζειν, μήτε τοῖς ἐχθροῖς ἐλάττωσιν πρός γε τὸν ἐνεστῶτα πόλεμον, ἐκ περιττοῦ καὶ ναοὺς, ἅμα δὲ τούτοις ἀνδριάντας, καὶ πᾶσαν δὴ τὴν τοιαύτην κατασκευήν, λυμαίνεσθαι· πῶς οὐκ ἂν εἴποι τις εἶναι τρόπου καὶ θυμοῦ λυττῶντος ἔργον; Οὐ γὰρ ἐπ᾽ ἀπωλείᾳ δεῖ καὶ ἀφανισμῷ τοῖς ἀγνοήσασι πολεμεῖν τοὺς ἀγαθοὺς ἄνδρας, ἀλλ᾽ ἐπὶ διορθώσει καὶ μεταθέσει τῶν ἡμαρτημένων· οὐδὲ συναναιρεῖν τὰ μηδὲν ἀδικοῦντα τοῖς ἠδικηκόσι, ἀλλὰ συσσώζειν μᾶλλον καὶ συνεξαιρεῖσθαι τοῖς ἀναιτίοις τοὺς δοκοῦντας ἀδικεῖν. Τυράννου μὲν γὰρ ἔργον ἐστὶ, τὸ, κακῶς ποιοῦντα, τῷ φόβῳ δεσπόζειν ἀκουσίων, μισούμενον, καὶ μισοῦντα τοὺς ὑποταττομένους· βασιλέως δὲ, τὸ, πάντας εὖ ποιοῦντα.

διὰ τὴν εὐεργεσίαν καὶ φιλανθρωπίαν ἀγαπώμενον, ἑκόντων ἡγεῖσθαι
καὶ προστατεῖν.

For the laws of war force us to appropriate to ourselves what
belongs to our enemy, to destroy their forts and cities, their ships
and harbours, the fruits of their country, with the inhabitants, for
the purpose of weakening them, and adding strength to ourselves.
Yet when men proceed to wreak their fury on senseless objects,
whose destruction will neither be of advantage to themselves, nor
in the slightest degree disable their opponent from carrying on
the war, especially if they burn the temples of the gods, destroy
their statues, and waste their ornamental furniture, what else can
we say of such proceedings, except that they are the acts of men
devoid of all feelings of propriety, and infected by frenzy? For
it is in no way the object of war, at least among men who have
just notions of their duty, to annihilate and utterly subvert those
from whom they may have received provocation, but only to induce
them to amend that in which they have acted amiss—not to involve the innocent and guilty in one common ruin, but rather to
save them both. We may also observe, that it is the act of a
tyrant only, who hates, and is hated by, his subjects, to exact by
force and terror a reluctant and unwilling obedience; while a
king, distinguished for his kindness and forbearance, gains the
affections of his subjects, who learn to look upon him as their
friend and benefactor, and to submit with cheerfulness to his commands.

See (Lat.) War

Conquer Enemies by Generosity.

v. 12.

Καὶ μὴν τό γε νικῆσαι τοὺς πολεμίους καλοκαγαθίᾳ καὶ τοῖς δικαίοις,
οὐκ ἐλάττω, μείζω δὲ παρέχεται χρείαν τῶν ἐν τοῖς ὅπλοις κατορθω-
μάτων. Οἷς μὲν γὰρ δι᾽ ἀνάγκην, οἷς δὲ κατὰ προαίρεσιν, εἴκουσιν οἱ
λειφθέντες. Καὶ τὰ μὲν μετὰ μεγάλων ἐλαττωμάτων ποιεῖται τὴν
διόρθωσιν· τὰ δὲ χωρὶς βλάβης πρὸς τὸ βέλτιον μεταιτίθησι τοὺς
ἁμαρτάνοντας. Τὸ δὲ μέγιστον, ἐν οἷς μὲν τὸ πλεῖστόν ἐστι τῆς
πράξεως τῶν ὑποταττομένων· ἐν οἷς δ᾽ αὐτοτελὴς ἡ νίκη γίγνεται τῶν
ἡγουμένων.

When we conquer our enemies by kind treatment, and by acts
of justice, we are more likely to secure their obedience than by a
victory in the field of battle. For in the one case they yield to
necessity ; in the other, it is their own free choice. Besides, how
often is the victory dearly bought, while the conquest of an
enemy by affection may be brought about without expense or loss !
And what ought to be particularly observed is, that subjects have
a right to claim a large share in the success that has been obtained
by arms, whereas the prince alone reaps all the glory of a victory
which is gained by kind treatment.

See (Lat.) Affection ; Fear.

Fate of Courtiers.

v. 26.

Βραχεῖς γὰρ δὴ πάνυ καιροὶ πάντας μὲν ἀνθρώπους· ὡς ἐπίπαν
ὑψοῦσι καὶ πάλιν ταπεινοῦσι· μάλιστα δὲ τοὺς ἐν τοῖς βασιλείοις.
Ὄντως γάρ εἰσιν οὗτοι παραπλήσιοι ταῖς ἐπὶ τῶν ἀβακίων ψήφοις.
Ἐκεῖναί τε γὰρ κατὰ τὴν τοῦ ψηφίζοντος βούλησιν, ἄρτι χαλκοῦν, καὶ
παραυτίκα τάλαντον ἰσχουσιν· οἵ τε περὶ τὰς αὐλὰς κατὰ τὸ τοῦ
βασιλέως νεῦμα μακάριοι, καὶ παρὰ πόδας ἐλεεινοὶ γίγνονται.

For the rapidity with which men, in all the various positions of
life, rise and fall is very marked; but this is chiefly seen in those
who are attached to the court of kings. For as the counters
which are employed in calculation assume their particular value at
the will of the man who casts up the account,—sometimes representing a talent, sometimes a farthing,—so courtiers are rich and
prosperous, wretched and in poverty, at the nod of their prince.

See (Lat.) The Court.

A Work Begun is Half Done.

v. 32.

Οἱ μὲν γὰρ ἀρχαῖοι τὴν ἀρχὴν ἥμισυ τοῦ παντὸς εἶναι φάσκοντες,
μεγίστην παρῄνουν ποιεῖσθαι σπουδὴν ἐν ἑκάστοις ὑπὲρ τοῦ καλῶς
ἄρξασθαι.

For when the ancients said that a work begun was half done,
they meant that we ought to take the utmost pains in every undertaking to make a good beginning.

Execution, and not Words.

v. 33.

Τούτου δ' ἐστὶν αἴτιον, ὅτι τὸ μὲν τῷ λόγῳ τῶν μεγίστων ἔργων
ἀντιποιήσασθαι, τελείως ἐστὶ ῥᾴδιον· τὸ δὲ τοῖς πράγμασιν ἐφικέ-
σθαι τινὸς τῶν καλῶν, οὐκ εὐμαρές. Διὸ καὶ τὸ μὲν ἐν μέσῳ κεῖται,
καὶ πᾶσι κοινόν, ὡς ἔπος εἰπεῖν, τοῖς μόνον τολμᾶν δυναμένοις ὑπάρ-
χει· τὸ δὲ καὶ λίαν ἐστι σπάνιον, καὶ σπανίοις συνεξέδραμε κατὰ
τὸν βίον.

For the truth is, that as nothing is more easy than to bind one's
self by words to enter on the most daring enterprises, so there is
nothing more difficult than to bring them to a successful result.
For the former only requires that a man should have sufficient
confidence; while success depends on qualities which few possess,
and is very rarely reached in life.

Effects of Penury.

v. 93.

Διόπερ ἦν ἀμφισβητήσεως, φιλοτιμίας, ὀργῆς τῆς ἐν ἀλλήλοις,
πάντα πλήρη. Τοῦτο γὰρ δὴ φιλεῖ γίγνεσθαι, καὶ περὶ τὰ κοινὰ

πράγματα, καὶ περὶ τοὺς κατ᾽ ἰδίαν βίους, ὅταν ἐλλίπωσιν αἱ χορη-
γίαι τὰς ἑκάστων ἐπιβολάς.

Wherefore, there arose disputes, jealousy, and heart-burnings—
a state of things which generally takes place, not only in great
empires, but among private individuals, when they are depressed
by poverty, and are without the means of carrying their designs
into effect.

See (Lat.) Poverty.

BEST FORM OF GOVERNMENT.

vi. 3.

Δῆλον γὰρ, ὡς ἀρίστην μὲν ἡγητέον πολιτείαν τὴν ἐκ πάντων τῶν
προειρημένων ἰδιωμάτων συνεστῶσαν.

For that form of government is, no doubt, to be considered the
best which is composed of all the three now mentioned—namely,
royalty, aristocracy, and democracy.

THE USUAL END OF A DEMOCRATICAL GOVERNMENT.

vi. 9.

Συνειθισμένον γὰρ τὸ πλῆθος ἐσθίειν τὰ ἀλλότρια, καὶ τὰς ἐλπίδας
ἔχειν τοῦ ζῆν ἐπὶ τοῖς τῶν πέλας, ὅταν λάβῃ προστάτην μεγαλό-
φρονα καὶ τολμηρὸν, ἐκκλειόμενον δὲ διὰ πενίαν τῶν ἐν τῇ πολιτείᾳ
τιμίων· τότε δὴ χειροκρατίαν ἀποτελεῖ. Καὶ τότε συναθροιζόμενοι
ποιεῖ σφαγὰς, φυγὰς, γῆς ἀναδασμούς· ἕως ἂν, ἀποτεθηριωμένον,
πάλιν εὕρῃ δεσπότην καὶ μόναρχον.

For when the people are accustomed to gain their livelihood
without labour, and to live at the expense of others, and when at
that moment some bold and enterprising leader makes his appearance, who has been prevented from taking part in public affairs
by his poverty, it is then that we see a beautiful example of the
character of the multitude: they run together in tumultuous assem-
blies, and commit all kinds of violence, ending in assassinations,
banishments, and seizure of private property, till, being brought
at last to a state of savage anarchy, they once more find a master,
and submit themselves to arbitrary sway.

See (Lat.) Equality of Democracies ; Revolutionary madness.

HOW EACH FORM OF GOVERNMENT DEGENERATES.

vi. 10.

Καθάπερ γὰρ σιδήρῳ μὲν ἰὸς, ξύλοις δὲ θρῖπες καὶ τερηδόνες συμ-
φυεῖς εἰσι λῦμαι, δι᾽ ὧν, κἂν πάσας τὰς ἔξωθεν διαφύγωσι βλάβας,
ὑπ᾽ αὐτῶν φθείρονται τῶν συγγενομένων· τὸν αὐτὸν τρόπον καὶ τῶν
πολιτειῶν συγγίγνεται κατὰ φύσιν ἑκάστῃ καὶ παρέπεταί τις κακία·
βασιλείᾳ μὲν ὁ μοναρχικὸς λεγόμενος τρόπος, ἀριστοκρατίᾳ δὲ ὁ τῆς
ὀλιγαρχίας, δημοκρατίᾳ δὲ ὁ θηριώδης καὶ χειροκρατικός.

For as rust is the canker of iron, and worms destroy wood, and as these substances, even though they may escape a violent end, at last fall a prey to the decay that is, as it were, natural to them ; in the same manner, likewise, in every kind of government there is a particular vice inherent in it, which is attached to its very nature, and which brings it to a close. Thus royalty degenerates into tyranny, aristocracy into oligarchy, and democracy into savage violence and anarchy.

See (Lat.) Changes of Government ; (Fr.) Governments, how they degenerate.

Religion used to terrify the Vulgar.

vi. 55.

'Επεὶ δὲ πᾶν πλῆθός ἐστιν ἐλαφρὸν καὶ πλῆρες ἐπιθυμιῶν παρανόμων, ὀργῆς ἀλόγου, θυμοῦ βιαίου· λείπεται, τοῖς ἀδήλοις φόβοις καὶ τῇ τοιαύτῃ τραγῳδίᾳ τὰ πλήθη συνέχειν. Διόπερ οἱ παλαιοὶ δοκοῦσί μοι τὰς περὶ θεῶν ἐννοίας, καὶ τὰς ὑπὲρ τῶν ἐν ᾅδου διαλήψεις οὐκ εἰκῇ, καὶ ὡς ἔτυχεν, εἰς τὰ πλήθη παρεισαγαγεῖν· πολὺ δὲ μᾶλλον οἱ νῦν εἰκῇ καὶ ἀλόγως ἐκβάλλειν αὐτά.

But since the great mass of a people are fickle and inconstant, full of unruly desires, passionate, and reckless of consequences, there is no other way left to curb them than by filling them with horrible imaginings, and by the pageantry of terrifying myths. The ancients, therefore, did not, in my opinion, act unwisely, nor without sufficient reason, when they implanted such notions of the gods, and a belief in punishments in another world ; but those of the present day are much rather to be accused of folly, who try to extirpate all such opinions.

See (Lat.) Superstition.

Government of the Multitude is the Greatest of all Evils.

vi. 57.

"Οταν γὰρ, πολλοὺς καὶ μεγάλους κινδύνους διωσαμένη πολιτεία, μετὰ ταῦτα εἰς ὑπεροχὴν καὶ δυναστείαν ἀδήριτον ἀφίκηται· φανερὸν, ὡς, εἰσοικιζομένης εἰς αὐτὴν ἐπὶ πολὺ τῆς εὐδαιμονίας, συμβαίνει, τοὺς μὲν βίους γίγνεσθαι πολυτελεστέρους, τοὺς δ' ἄνδρας φιλονεικοτέρους τοῦ δέοντος περί τε τὰς ἀρχὰς, καὶ τὰς ἄλλας ἐπιβολάς. Ὧν προβαινόντων ἐπὶ πλέον, ἄρξει μὲν τῆς ἐπὶ τὸ χεῖρον μεταβολῆς ἡ φιλαρχία, καὶ τὸ τῆς ἀδοξίας ὄνειδος· πρὸς δὲ τούτοις ἡ περὶ τοὺς βίους ἀλαζονεία καὶ πολυτέλεια. Λήψεται δὲ τὴν ἐπιγραφὴν τῆς μεταβολῆς ὁ δῆμος, ὅταν ὑφ' ὧν μὲν ἀδικεῖσθαι δόξῃ διὰ τὴν πλεονεξίαν, ὑφ' ὧν δὲ χαυνωθῇ κολακευόμενος διὰ τὴν φιλαρχίαν. Τότε γὰρ ἐξοργισθεὶς, καὶ θυμῷ πάντα βουλευόμενος, οὐκ ἔτι θελήσει πειθαρχεῖν, οὐδ' ἴσοι

ἔχειν τοῖς προεστῶσιν, ἀλλὰ πᾶν καὶ τὸ πλεῖστον αὐτός. Οὗ γενομένου, τῶν μὲν ὀνομάτων τὸ κάλλιστον ἡ πολιτεία μεταλήψεται, τὴν
ἐλευθερίαν καὶ δημοκρατίαν· τῶν δὲ πραγμάτων τὸ χείριστον, τὴν
ὀχλοκρατίαν.

For when a state, after having gone through many and great
dangers, reaches to the highest pinnacle of power, and reigns with
undisputed sway, it cannot be otherwise than that luxury and
expensive habits should be developed, and that men should indulge
in ambitious projects, and be desirous to acquire the high dignities
of state. And as these evils are apt to increase, the appetite for
power grows on what it feeds upon, and men feel ashamed that
any of their fellow-citizens should in any way surpass them.
Hence arise all those vices which are the natural result of luxury
and overbearing arrogance. Then the people step in and give the
finishing stroke to the change in the form of government, finding
themselves oppressed by the grasping nature of some, and their
vanity flattered by the ambitious views of others. For, fired with
rage, and giving full play to their evil passions, they are no longer
willing to submit to control, and to share with their rulers the
administration of affairs, but insist on having everything subject
to their authority. The invariable result of such a state of things is,
that the government indeed assumes the noblest of all names, that
of a free and popular state, but becomes, in truth, the most
execrable of all—the dominion of the mob.

See (Lat.) Democracy ; Avarice and Luxury.

SECRECY RECOMMENDED.

ix. 13.

Ἔστι δ' ἀρχὴ μὲν τῶν προειρημένων τὸ σιγᾶν, καὶ μήτε διὰ
χαρὰν, παραδόξου προφαινομένης ἐλπίδος, μήτε διὰ φόβον, μήτε διὰ
συνήθειαν, μήτε διὰ φιλοστοργίαν, μεταδιδόναι μηδενὶ τῶν ἐκτός·
αὐτοῖς δὲ κοινωνοῦσθαι τούτοις, ὧν χωρὶς οὐχ οἷόν τε τὸ προτεθὲν ἐπὶ
τέλος ἀγαγεῖν, καὶ τούτοις μὴ πρότερον, ἀλλ' ὅταν ὁ τῆς ἑκάστου
χρείας καιρὸς ἐπαναγκάζῃ. Χρὴ δὲ σιγᾶν μὴ μόνον τῇ γλώττῃ, πολὺ
δὲ μᾶλλον τῇ ψυχῇ. Πολλοὶ γὰρ ἤδη, κρύψαντες τοὺς λόγους, ποτὲ
μὲν δι αὐτῆς τῆς ἐπιφάσεως, ποτὲ δὲ καὶ διὰ τῶν πραττομένων, φανε-
ρὰς ἐποίησαν τὰς ἑαυτῶν ἐπινοίας.

Now of all the precautions that have been mentioned, the first
that the general of an army ought to attend to is secrecy. He
ought to take care that his designs be not disclosed by his countenance betraying the joyful expectation of success, or the sadness
of defeat, nor yet by feelings of friendship or affection for those
around him. He should communicate his intention to none except
to those without whose assistance his plans cannot be carried into
execution, and not even to them till the time when their services
are required make it necessary that they should be made acquainted

with them. Nor should the tongue only be silent, but still more must the mind itself be on its guard ; for it has often happened that many, who have a strict watch over their tongue, have betrayed their intentions by some external signs, and sometimes by their actions.

See (Lat.) Great counsels betrayed by the countenance ; Qualities of a general.

FAVOURITES OF FORTUNE.

x. 2.

Οἱ μὲν οὖν ἄλλοι πάντες αὐτὸν ἐπιτυχῆ τινα, καὶ τὸ πλεῖον ἀεὶ παραλόγως καὶ ταὐτομάτῳ κατορθοῦντα τὰς ἐπιβολὰς παρεισάγουσι· νομίζοντες, ὡσανεὶ θειοτέρους εἶναι καὶ θαυμαστοτέρους τοὺς τοιούτους ἄνδρας τῶν κατὰ λόγον ἐν ἑκάστοις πραττόντων· ἀγνοοῦντες, ὅτι τὸ μὲν ἐπαινετὸν, τὸ δὲ μακαριστὸν εἶναι συμβαίνει τῶν πρειρημένων. Καὶ τὸ μὲν κοινόν ἐστι καὶ τοῖς τυχοῦσι, τὸ δ᾽ ἐπαινετὸν μόνον ἴδιον ὑπάρχει τῶν εὐλογίστων καὶ φρένας ἐχόντων ἀνδρῶν, οὓς καὶ θειοτάτους εἶναι καὶ προσφιλεστάτους τοῖς θεοῖς νομιστέον.

These writers, then, have all agreed in representing Scipio as one of those favourites of fortune who bring all their schemes to a happy end by a random thought, and, according to all appearance, by running counter to all the rules of reason. They regard such men as more immediately under the inspiration of Heaven, and more deserving of our admiration, than those who carry out their plans in strict consonance with rational principles, forgetting all the while that in the one case men truly merit praise, while in the other all that can be said of them is that they are fortunate. The most vulgar and commonplace of men may be fortunate, but the other are distinguished for their high mental qualities. These are the men who approach nearest to the Divine Being, and are in highest favour with the gods.

DIVINE IMPULSE.

x. 5.

Οἱ γὰρ μὴ δυνάμενοι τοὺς καιρούς, μηδὲ τὰς αἰτίας καὶ διαθέσεις ἑκάστων ἀκριβῶς συνθεωρεῖν, ἢ διὰ φαυλότητα φύσεως, ἢ δι᾽ ἀπειρίαν καὶ ῥαθυμίαν, εἰς θεοὺς καὶ τύχας ἀναφέρουσι τὰς αἰτίας τῶν δι᾽ ἀγχίνοιαν ἐκ λογισμοῦ καὶ προνοίας ἐπιτελουμένων.

For those who are unable, either from lack of mental capacity, or imperfect knowledge, or indolent habits, to discern clearly the right time for action, the causes and probable course of events, are very apt to attribute to the gods and fortune what is after all the result of sound sense and the proper use of our rational faculties.

MANY KNOW TO CONQUER, FEW TO USE THEIR VICTORY WITH ADVANTAGE.

x. 36.

Μεγάλου γὰρ ὄντος, ὡς πλεονάκις ἡμῖν εἴρηται, τοῦ κατορθοῦν ἐν πράγμασι, καὶ περιγίγνεσθαι τῶν ἐχθρῶν ἐν ταῖς ἐπιβολαῖς· πολλῷ μείζονος ἐμπειρίας προσδεῖται καὶ φυλακῆς, τὸ καλῶς χρήσασθαι τοῖς κατορθώμασι. Διὸ καὶ πολλαπλασίους ἂν εὕροι τις τοὺς ἐπὶ προτερημάτων γεγονότας, τῶν καλῶς τοῖς προτερήμασι κεχρημένων.

For as we have often observed, it is no doubt a great thing to be successful in our undertakings, and to defeat our enemy in the field of battle; but it is a proof of greater wisdom, and requires more skill, to make a good use of victory. For many know how to conquer; few are able to use their conquest aright.

POWER OF A MAN IN HIGH AUTHORITY.

xi. 10.

Οὕτως εἷς λόγος, εὐκαίρως ῥηθεὶς ὑπ' ἀνδρὸς ἀξιοπίστου, πολλάκις οὐ μόνον ἀποτρέπει τῶν χειρίστων, ἀλλὰ καὶ παρορμᾷ πρὸς τὰ κάλλιστα τοὺς ἀνθρώπους. Ὅταν δὲ καὶ τὸν ἴδιον βίον ἀκόλουθον εἰσφέρηται τοῖς εἰρημένοις ὁ παρακαλῶν, ἀνάγκη λαμβάνειν τὴν πρώτην πίστιν τὴν παραίνεσιν.

Thus an admonition, when it comes at the proper moment, from the lips of a man who enjoys the respect of the world, is often able not only to deter men from the commission of crime, but leads them into the right path. For when the life of a speaker is known to be in unison with his words, it is impossible that his advice should not have the greatest weight.

See (Lat.) A Tumult.

CHARACTER OF THE MULTITUDE.

xi. 29.

Ταῦτα δ' ἐστὶ, διότι πᾶς ὄχλος εὐπαραλόγιστος ὑπάρχει, καὶ πρὸς πᾶν εὐάγωγος. Ὅθεν αἰεὶ τὸ παραπλήσιον πάθος συμβαίνει περί τε τοὺς ὄχλους καὶ τὴν θάλατταν. Καθάπερ γὰρ κἀκείνης ἡ μὲν ἰδία φύσις ἐστὶν ἀβλαβὴς τοῖς χρωμένοις καὶ στάσιμος, ὅταν δ' εἰς αὐτὴν ἐμπέσῃ τὰ πνεύματα βίᾳ, τοιαύτη φαίνεται τοῖς χρωμένοις, οἷοί τινες ἂν ὦσιν οἱ κυκλοῦντες αὐτὴν ἄνεμοι· τὸν αὐτὸν τρόπον καὶ τὸ πλῆθος ἀεὶ καὶ φαίνεται καὶ γίγνεται πρὸς τοὺς χρωμένους, οἵους ἂν ἔχοι προστάτας καὶ συμβούλους.

The multitude is easily led astray, is moved in every direction by the smallest force, so that the agitations of the mob and the sea have a wonderful resemblance to each other. For as the latter is in its nature calm, and exhibits no appearance of danger to the

P 3

eye till some violent hurricane agitates its surface, when it becomes fierce as the winds themselves ; in the same way the multitude is swayed and guided in its actions according to the temper and character of its leaders and advisers.

See (Lat.) Multitude.

AVARICE.

xiii. 2.

Καθάπερ ἐπὶ τῶν ὑδροπικῶν οὐδέποτε ποιεῖ παῦλαν οὐδὲ κόρον ἡ τῶν ἔξωθεν ὑγρῶν παράθεσις, ἐὰν μὴ τὴν ἐν αὐτῷ τῷ σώματι διάθεσιν ὑγιάσῃ τις · τὸν αὐτὸν τρόπον οὐδὲ τὴν πρὸς τὸ πλεῖον ἐπιθυμίαν οἷόν τε κορέσαι, μὴ οὐ τὴν ἐν τῇ ψυχῇ κακίαν λόγῳ τινὶ διορθωσάμενον.

As in the case of those who are afflicted with dropsy, no external application is able to take away or allay the thirst, unless some internal change has been produced by proper remedies ; in the same way, also the desire of gain can never be satiated unless the vicious inclinations of the mind have been got rid of by reason.

See (Lat.) Avarice.

FORCE OF TRUTH.

xiii. 5.

Καὶ μοι δοκεῖ μεγίστην θεὸν τοῖς ἀνθρώποις ἡ φύσις ἀποδεῖξαι τὴν Ἀλήθειαν, καὶ μεγίστην αὐτῇ προσθεῖναι δύναμιν. Πάντων γοῦν αὐτὴν καταγωνιζομένων, ἐνίοτε δὲ καὶ πασῶν τῶν πιθανοτήτων μετὰ τοῦ ψεύδους ταττομένων · οὐκ οἶδ' ὅπως αὐτὴ δι' αὐτῆς εἰς τὰς ψυχὰς εἰσδύεται τῶν ἀνθρώπων · καὶ ποτὲ μὲν παραχρῆμα δείκνυσι τὴν αὐτῆς δύναμιν, ποτὲ δὲ πολὺν χρόνον ἐπισκοτισθεῖσα, τέλος αὐτὴ δι' ἑαυτῆς ἐπικρατεῖ, καὶ καταγωνίζεται τὸ ψεῦδος.

For my own part I am fully persuaded that the most powerful goddess, and one that rules mankind with the most authoritative sway, is Truth. For though she is resisted by all, and ofttimes has drawn up against her the plausibilities of falsehood in the subtlest forms, she triumphs over all opposition. I know not how it is that she, by her own unadorned charms, forces herself into the heart of man. At times her power is instantly felt ; at other times, though obscured for a while, she at last bursts forth in meridian splendour. and conquers by her innate force the falsehood with which she has been oppressed.

See (Lat.) Truth.

WANT OF PERSEVERANCE IN MAN.

xiv. 28.

Ταῦτα μὲν οὖν προήχθην εἰπεῖν, διὰ τὸ. τινὰς μὲν πρὸς τῷ τέρματι, καθάπερ οἱ κακοι τῶν σταδιέων, ἐγκαταλιπεῖν τὰς ἑαυ. ὧν προθέσεις, τινὰς δ' ἐν τούτῳ μάλιστα νικᾶν τοὺς ἀντιπάλους.

For some men, like unskilful jockeys, give up their designs when they have almost reached the goal ; while others, on the contrary, obtain a victory over their opponents, by exerting, at the last moment, more vigorous efforts than before.

SELF-ACCUSING CONSCIENCE.
xviii. 26.

Οὐδεὶς γὰρ οὕτως οὐδὲ μάρτυς ἐστὶ φοβερὸς, οὔτε κατήγορος δεινὸς, ὡς ἡ σύνεσις ἡ ἐγκατοικοῦσα ταῖς ἑκάστων ψυχαῖς.

There is no witness so terrible, no accuser so powerful, as conscience, that dwells in the breast of each.

See (Lat.) Conscience.

POSIDIPPUS.

FLOURISHED B.C. 289.

POSIDIPPUS, son of Cyniscus of Cassandreia, in Macedon, was one of the chief writers of the New Comedy, and began to exhibit three years after the death of Menander, B.C. 289. According to Suidas, he wrote forty plays.

AN EASY DEATH.
Fr. Com. Gr. p. 1144.

Ὧν τοῖς θεοῖς ἄνθρωπος εὔχεται τυχεῖν τῆς εὐθανασίας κρεῖττον οὐδὲν εὔχεται.

Of the things which man prays to obtain from the gods, he prays for nothing more fervently than an easy hour of death.

SORROW WITH MANY FEET.
Fr. Com. Gr. p. 1144.

Οὕτω τι πολύπουν ἐστὶν ἡ λύπη κακόν.

Sorrow is an evil with many feet.

DIFFICULT TO ESCAPE SORROW.
Fr. Com. Gr. p. 1144.

Ἔργον γε λύπην ἐκφυγεῖν, ἡ δ᾽ ἡμέρα ἀεί τι καινὸν εἰς τὸ φροντίζειν φέρει.

It is a difficult matter to escape sorrow ; every day brings some new cause of anxiety.

ACQUAINTANCES AND FRIENDS.

Fr. Com. Gr. p. 1148.

Διὰ τὴν τέχνην μὲν γνωρίμους ἐκτησάμην
πολλούς, διὰ τὸν τρόπον δὲ τοὺς πλείστους φίλους.

By my skill I have got many acquaintances, but by my manners very many friends.

SOPHOCLES.

BORN B.C. 495—DIED B.C. 406.

SOPHOCLES, the celebrated tragic poet, was a native of the Attic village of Colonus ; born five years before the battle of Marathon, about thirty years younger than Æschylus, and fifteen years older than Euripides. His father's name was Sophilus or Sophillus ; but what was his condition in life is a matter of which we have no certain knowledge. At all events, the young Sophocles received an education not inferior to that of the sons of the most distinguished citizens of Athens. His first appearance as a dramatist took place in B.C. 468, when he gained the first prize in competition with the veteran Æschylus ; and from that time Sophocles held the supremacy of the Athenian stage. Family dissensions troubled his last years. One of his sons summoned his father before the magistrates, on the charge that his mind was affected by old age. As his only reply, Sophocles answered, "If I am Sophocles, I am not beside myself ; and if I am beside myself, I am not Sophocles." He then read from the magnificent *parodos* to his unpublished play, " Œdipus at Colonus," beginning—

" Εὔιππου, ξένε, τᾶσδε φώρας,"

and when he had finished, the judges dismissed the case, and rebuked the ungrateful prosecutor. The poet was allowed to pass the remainder of his days in peace. He died at the extreme age of ninety.

DOING GOOD SHOULD BE THE TASK OF MAN.

Œd. Tyr. 314.

Ἄνδρα δ' ὠφελεῖν ἀφ' ὧν
ἔχοι τε καὶ δύναιτο κάλλιστος πόνων

For a man to exert his power in doing good so far as he can is a most glorious task.

The Honest contrasted with the Base.

Œd. Tyr. 609.

Οὐ γὰρ δίκαιον οὔτε τοὺς κακοὺς μάτην
χρηστοὺς νομίζειν οὔτε τοὺς χρηστοὺς κακούς.
φίλον γὰρ ἐσθλὸν ἐκβαλεῖν ἴσον λέγω
καὶ τὸν παρ' αὐτῷ βίοτον, ὃν πλεῖστον φιλεῖ.
ἀλλ' ἐν χρόνῳ γνώσῃ ταδ' ἀσφαλῶς· ἐπεὶ
χρόνος δίκαιον ἄνδρα δείκνυσιν μόνος·
κακὸν δὲ κἂν ἐν ἡμέρᾳ γνοίης μιᾷ.

For it is not just lightly to deem the wicked good or the good wicked.   He that throws a faithful friend away, I call as bad as if he threw his life away, which is most dear to him.   But in time thou wilt know all this; for time alone shows the honest man; the base thou mightest discover even in one day.

Quick Decision is Unsafe.

Œd. Tyr. 617.

Φρονεῖν γὰρ οἱ ταχεῖς οὐκ ἀσφαλεῖς.

Quick resolves are oft unsafe.

The Wise gather Wisdom from the Past.

Œd. Tyr. 916.

Ἔννους τὰ καινὰ τοῖς πάλαι τεκμαίρεται.

The wise form right judgment of the present from what is past.

The Aged.

Œd. Tyr. 961.

Σμικρὰ παλαιὰ σώματ' εὐνάζει ῥοπή.

A trifling bend of the scale sends aged frames to rest.

Man controlled by Fate.

Œd. Tyr. 977.

Τί δ' ἂν φοβοῖτ' ἄνθρωπος, ᾧ τὰ τῆς τύχης
κρατεῖ, πρόνοια δ' ἐστὶν οὐδενὸς σαφής;
εἰκῇ κράτιστον ζῆν, ὅπως δύναιτό τις.

For why should man fear, whom the decrees of fate control, while there is no sure foresight of aught? 'Twere best to live at random, even as one could.

LIFE AN AIRY DREAM.

Œd. Tyr. 1184.

'Ιὼ γενεαὶ βροτῶν,
ὡς ὑμᾶς ἴσα καὶ [τὸ] μηδὲν ζώσας ἐναριθμῶ.
τίς γάρ, τίς ἀνὴρ πλέον
τὰς εὐδαιμονίας φέρει
ἢ τοσοῦτον ὅσον δοκεῖν
καὶ δόξαντ' ἀποκλῖναι;

Ye race of mortals, how I deem your life as nothing but an airy dream! For this is the only happiness granted to man, to fancy that he has it, and so fancying to see the glittering vision melt away.

Grotius has translated the passage with great elegance :—

" Hæc est sola beatitas Humano generi data,
Quam quis, dum putat, accipit, amittitque putando."

NO ONE TO BE PRONOUNCED HAPPY BEFORE DEATH.

Œd. Tyr. 1528.

Ὥστε θνητὸν ὄντ' ἐκείνην τὴν τελευταίαν ἰδεῖν
ἡμέραν ἐπισκοποῦντα μηδέν' ὀλβίζειν, πρὶν ἂν
τέρμα τοῦ βίου περάσῃ μηδὲν ἀλγεινὸν παθών.

Wherefore since thou art looking out, as being mortal, for thy last day, call no man happy, before he has passed the boundary of life, having suffered nothing evil.

Lord Byron says—

"The first dark day of nothingness,
The last of danger and distress."

GOD SEES THE RIGHTEOUS AND THE WICKED.

Œd. Col. 278.

Ἡγεῖσθε δὲ
βλέπειν μὲν αὐτοὺς πρὸς τὸν εὐσεβῆ βροτῶν,
βλέπειν δὲ πρὸς τοὺς δυσσεβεῖς, φυγὴν δέ του
μήπω γενέσθαι φωτὸς ἀνοσίου βροτῶν.

Believe that the gods behold the righteous and also the wicked, nor has any impious man ever escaped their eye.

So Jeremiah (xxxii. 19)—" For Thine eyes are open upon all the ways of the sons of men : to give every one according to his ways, and according to the fruit of his doings."

A Good Man is his own Friend.

Œd. Col. 309.

Τίς γὰρ ἐσθλὸς οὐχ αὑτῷ φίλος;

For what good man is not his own friend?

The Psalmist (xlix. 18) says—"As long as thou doest good to thyself, men will speak well of thee."

Toiling for a Parent.

Œd. Col. 508.

Τοῖς τεκοῦσι γὰρ
οὐδ' εἰ πονῇ τις, δεῖ πόνου μνήμην ἔχειν.

For if any one toil for a parent, it is not fitting to bear remembrance of the toil.

We know not what a Day may bring forth.

Œd. Col. 566.

'Επεὶ
ἔξοιδ' ἀνὴρ ὤν, χὤτι τῆς ἐς αὔριον
οὐδὲν πλέον μοι σοῦ μέτεστιν ἡμέρας.

For I know that being a man I have no more power to rule the events of to-morrow than thou.

See (Lat.) To-morrow; Prov. xxvii. 1.

To lay my Bones among ye.

Œd. Col. 576.

Δώσων ἱκάνω τοὐμὸν ἄθλιον δέμας
σοὶ δῶρον, οὐ σπουδαῖον εἰς ὄψιν· τὰ δὲ
κέρδη παρ' αὐτοῦ κρείσσον' ἢ μορφὴ καλή.

I come to bestow on you as a gift, this my wretched body, not goodly to the sight, but the advantages to be gained from it are of greater consequence than a fair form.

Shakespeare ("Henry VIII." act iv., sc. 2) says—

"O father abbot,
An old man, broken with the storms of state,
Is come to lay his weary bones among ye;
Give him a little earth for charity."

Time changes Everything.

Œd. Col. 607.

Ὦ φίλτατ' Αἰγέως παῖ, μόνοις οὐ γίγνεται
θεοῖσι γῆρας οὐδὲ κατθανεῖν ποτε,

τὰ δ' ἄλλα συγχεῖ πάνθ' ὁ παγκρατὴς χρόνος.
φθίνει μὲν ἰσχὺς γῆς, φθίνει δὲ σώματος,
θνήσκει δὲ πίστις, βλαστάνει δ' ἀπιστία,
καὶ πνεῦμα ταὐτὸν οὔποτ' οὔτ' ἐν ἀνδράσιν
φίλοις βέβηκεν οὔτε πρὸς πόλιν πόλει.
τοῖς μὲν γὰρ ἤδη, τοῖς δ' ἐν ὑστέρῳ χρόνῳ
τὰ τερπνὰ πικρὰ γίγνεται καὖθις φίλα.

O dearest son of Ægeus, to the gods alone is given exemption
from old age and death ; but the all-powerful hand of time
crumbles everything else to dust. The vigour of the earth, the
vigour of the body wastes away ; faith dies and perfidy springs up
afresh ; the gale does not always blow the same to friends among
men, nor to state towards state. For what is grateful now becomes
hateful, to some at once, to others in distant time ; and then
delights again.

So 1 Timothy (vi. 16)—"Who only hath immortality, dwelling in the
light which no man can approach unto."

Where the Cause is Just, the Weak conquers the Strong.

Œd. Col. 880.

Τοῖς τοι δικαίοις χὠ βραχὺς νικᾷ μέγαν.

In a just cause, the weak subdue the strong.

The Dead feel no Grief.

Œd. Col. 945.

Θυμοῦ γὰρ οὐδὲν γῆράς ἐστιν ἄλλο πλὴν
θανεῖν· θανόντων δ' οὐδὲν ἄλγος ἅπτεται.

For rage is not abated but by death ; the dead feel no grief.

The Hunter taken in his own Toils.

Œd. Col. 1025.

Γνῶθι δ' ὡς ἔχων ἔχῃ,
καί σ' εἷλε θηρῶνθ' ἡ τύχη· τὰ γὰρ δόλῳ
τῷ μὴ δικαίῳ κτήματ' οὐχὶ σώζεται.

And know that thou art seized, as thou hast seized ; fortune
takes the hunter in his own toils ; for things got by fraud and injustice abide not.

Small Circumstances often Important.

Œd. Col. 1152.

Σμικρὸς μὲν εἰπεῖν, ἄξιος δὲ θαυμάσαι.
πρᾶγος δ' ἀτίζειν οὐδὲν ἄνθρωπον χρεών.

Things of trifling appearance are often pregnant with high import ; a prudent man neglects no circumstance.

Never to be Born, or Early Death, is Best.

Œd. Col. 1225.

Μὴ φῦναι τὸν ἄπαντα νικᾷ λόγον· τὸ
δ', ἐπεὶ φανῇ,
βῆναι κεῖθεν ὅθεν περ ἥκει
πολὺ δεύτερον ὡς τάχιστα.
ὡς εὖτ ἂν τὸ νέον παρῇ
κούφας ἀφροσύνας φέρον,
ταῖς πλάγχθη πολύμοχθος ἔξω, τίς ὄδ
καμάτων ἔνι ;
φόνοι, στάσεις, ἔρις, μάχαι
καὶ φθόνος· τό τε κατάμεμπτον
ἐπιλέλογχε
πύματον ἀκρατὲς ἀπροσόμιλον
γῆρας ἄφιλον, ἵνα πρόπαντα
κακὰ κακῶν ξυνοικεῖ.

Not to be born is best of all ; and if one has seen the light, to go back to the place whence he came, as quickly as possible, is by far the next best. For when youth comes, leading a train of idle follies, he is surrounded by many sorrows. What suffering is not there? Murders, seditions, strife, fightings, and envy ; and loathsome old age is last scene of all—powerless, unsocial, friendless, when all ills, worst of ills, dwell together.

Mercy.

Œd. Col. 1267.

'Αλλ' ἔστι γὰρ καὶ Ζηνὶ σύνθακος θρόνων
αἰδὼς ἐπ' ἔργοις πᾶσι.

Over every work is Mercy joint assessor to Jove on his throne.

High Office tries a Man.

Antig. 175.

Ἀμήχανον δὲ παντὸς ἀνδρὸς ἐκμαθεῖν

ψυχήν τε καὶ φρόνημα καὶ γνώμην, πρὶν ἂν
ἀρχαῖς τε καὶ νόμοισιν ἐντριβὴς φανῇ.

It is impossible to penetrate the secret thoughts, quality, and judgment of man till he is put to proof by high office and administration of the laws.

REWARDS OFT LEAD TO RUIN.

Antig. 221.

'Αλλ' ὑπ' ἐλπίδων
ἄνδρας τὸ κέρδος πολλάκις διώλεσεν.

But gain has oft with treacherous hopes led men to ruin.

GOLD.

Antig. 295.

Οὐδὲν γὰρ ἀνθρώποισιν οἷον ἄργυρος
κακὸν νόμισμ' ἔβλαστε. τοῦτο καὶ πόλεις
πορθεῖ, τόδ' ἄνδρας ἐξανίστησιν δόμων·
τόδ' ἐκδιδάσκει καὶ παραλλάσσει φρένας
χρηστὰς πρὸς αἰσχρὰ πράγμαθ' ἵστασθαι βροτῶν·
πανουργίας δ' ἔδειξεν ἀνθρώποις ἔχειν
καὶ παντὸς ἔργου δυσσέβειαν εἰδέναι.

For never did such evil institution as money spring up to mortals : it lays waste cities, it drives men far from their homes to roam : it seduces and corrupts the honest mind, turning its virtuous thoughts to deeds of baseness : it has taught men villany and how to perform all impious works.

See (Lat.) Gold.

UNJUST GAIN.

Antig. 313.

'Εκ τῶν γὰρ αἰσχρῶν λημμάτων τοὺς
ἀτωμένους ἴδοις ἂν ἢ σεσωσμένους.

For by unjust gains thou wilt see more sink in ruin than triumph in success.

MAN THE CHIEF OF NATURE'S WORKS.

Antig. 334.

Πολλὰ τὰ δεινὰ κοὐδὲν ἀνθρώπου δεινότερον πέλει·
τοῦτο καὶ πολιοῦ πέραν πόντου χειμερίῳ νότῳ

χωρεῖ, περιβρυχίοισιν
περῶν ὑπ' οἴδμασιν,
θεῶν τε τὰν ὑπερτάταν, γᾶν
ἄφθιτον, ἀκαμάταν ἀποτρύεται,
ἰλλομένων ἀροτῶν ἔτος εἰς ἔτος, ἱππείῳ γένει πολεύων.

Κουφονόων τε φῦλον ὀρνίθων ἀμφιβαλὼν ἄγει
καὶ θηρῶν ἀγρίων ἔθνη, πόντου τ' εἰναλίαν φύσιν
σπείραισι δικτυοκλώστοις,
περιφραδὴς ἀνήρ·
κρατεῖ δὲ μηχαναῖς ἀγραύλου
θηρὸς ὀρεσσιβάτα, λασιαύχενά θ'
ἵππον ἔξεται ἀμφίλοφον ζυγὸν οὔρειόν τ' ἀκμῆτα ταῦρον.

Καὶ φθέγμα καὶ ἀνεμόεν φρόνημα καὶ ἀστυνόμους
ὀργὰς ἐδιδάξατο καὶ δυσαύλων
πάγων αἴθρια καὶ
δύσομβρα φεύγειν βέλη,
παντοπόρος,
ἄπορος ἐπ' οὐδὲν ἔρχεται
τὸ μέλλον· Ἄιδα μόνον
φεῦξιν οὐκ ἐπάξεται·
νόσων δ' ἀμηχάνων
φυγὰς ξυμπέφρασται.

Σοφόν τι τὸ μηχανόεν τέχνας ὑπὲρ ἐλπίδ' ἔχων
ποτὲ μὲν κακόν, ἄλλοτ' ἐπ' ἐσθλὸν ἕρπει,
νόμους παρείρων χθονὸς
θεῶν τ' ἔνορκον δίκαν
ὑψίπολις·
ἄπολις ὅτῳ τὸ μὴ καλὸν
ξύνεστι τόλμας χάριν.
μήτ' ἐμοὶ παρέστιος
γένοιτο μήτ' ἴσον
φρονῶν ὃς τάδ' ἔρδει.

Many wonderful things appear in nature but nothing more wonderful than man : he sails even through the foaming deep with the wintry south-wind's blast, passing over the roaring billows; he furrows undecaying Earth, supreme of divinities immortal, as seed-times return from year to year, turning up the soil with the horse's aid ; ensnaring the feathered tribes that skim the air, he takes them as his prey, and the savage beasts and all the finny race of the deep with line-woven nets, he, all-inventive man ; he tames by his skill the tenants of the fields, the mountain-ranging herds ; he brings under the neck-encircling yoke the shaggy-maned horse and the reluctant mountain-bull. He hath taught himself language and winged thought, and the customs of civic law, and to escape the cold and stormy arrows of comfortless frosts ; with plans for all things, planless in nothing, meets he the future. But from death alone he finds no refuge, though he has devised remedies against racking diseases. Having a wonderful

skill beyond all belief he descends now to evil and again ascends
to virtue ; observing the laws of the land and the plighted justice
of heaven, he rises high in the state ; an outcast is he who is dishonourable and audacious ; may he, who acts thus, not dwell with
me nor rank among my friends.

The Unwritten Laws of the Gods.

Antig. 453.

Οὐδὲ σθένειν τοσοῦτον ᾠόμην τὰ σὰ
κηρύγμαθ, ὥστ᾽ ἄγραπτα κἀσφαλῆ θεῶν
νόμιμα δύνασθαι θνητὸν ὄνθ᾽ ὑπερδραμεῖν.
οὐ γάρ τι νῦν γε κἀχθές, ἀλλ᾽ ἀεί ποτε
ζῇ ταῦτα, κοὐδεὶς οἶδεν ἐξ ὅτου ᾽φάνη.

Nor did I deem thy edicts of such force that, mortal as thou
art, thou hast the power to overthrow the firm and unwritten laws
of the gods. For these are not of to-day nor yesterday, but they
live through all ages, and none knows whence they spring.

See (Lat.) Law.

Stern Spirits.

Antig. 473.

Ἀλλ᾽ ἴσθι τοι τὰ σκλήρ᾽ ἄγαν φρονήματα
πίπτειν μάλιστα, καὶ τὸν ἐγκρατέστατον
σίδηρον ὀπτὸν ἐκ πυρὸς περισκελῆ
θραυσθέντα καὶ ῥαγέντα πλεῖστ᾽ ἂν εἰσίδοις.
σμικρῷ χαλινῷ δ᾽ οἶδα τοὺς θυμουμένους
ἵππους καταρτυθέντας· οὐ γὰρ ἐκπέλει
φρονεῖν μέγ᾽ ὅστις δοῦλός ἐστι τῶν πέλας.

But know in truth that spirits too stern bend most easily ; and
thou wilt most frequently see the hardest steel forged in the fire
till brittle, shivered, and broken ; and I have known the most
spirited horses brought into obedience by a small bit ; for no one
ought to be proud who is the slave of others.

Kings.

Antig. 506.

Ἀλλ᾽ ἡ τυραννὶς πολλά τ᾽ ἄλλ᾽ εὐδαιμονεῖ
κἄξεστιν αὐτῇ δρᾶν λέγειν θ᾽ ἃ βούλεται.

Kings are happy in many other things and in this, that they
can do and say whatever they please.

The Wretched.

Antig. 563.

Οὐ γάρ ποτ᾽, ὦναξ, οὐδ᾽ ὃς ἂν βλάστῃ μένει
νοῦς τοῖς κακῶς πράσσουσιν, ἀλλ᾽ ἐξίσταται.

For never does the original vigour of the mind remain to the
unfortunate but it is changed.

The Power of God.

Antig. 605.

Τεάν, Ζεῦ, δύνασιν τίς ἀνδρῶν ὑπερβασία κατάσχοι,
τὰν οὔθ᾽ ὕπνος αἱρεῖ ποθ᾽ ὁ πανταγήρως
οὔτ᾽ ἀκάματοι θεῶν
μῆνες, ἀγήρῳ δὲ χρόνῳ δυνάστας
κατέχεις Ὀλύμπου
μαρμαρόεσσαν αἴγλαν.
τό τ᾽ ἔπειτα καὶ τὸ μέλλον
καὶ τὸ πρὶν ἐπαρκέσει
νόμος ὅδ᾽· οὐδὲν ἕρπει
θνατῶν βιότῳ πάμπολύ γ᾽ ἐκτὸς ἄτας.

O Jove, shall man with presumptuous pride control thy power?
whom neither enfeebling sleep ever seizes nor the months of the
gods that roll on, unconcious of toil: through unwasting time,
glorious in might, thou dwellest in heaven's resplendent light.
But this law, ordained in ages past, is now, and will be for ever, "in
all the life of mortals evil in every state her franchise claims."

Hope.

Antig. 615.

Ἁ γὰρ δὴ πολύπλαγκτος ἐλπὶς πολλοῖς μὲν ὄνησις ἀνδρῶν,
πολλοῖς δ᾽ ἀπάτα κουφονόων ἐρώτων·
εἰδότι δ᾽ οὐδὲν ἕρπει,
πρὶν πυρὶ θερμῷ πόδα τις προσαύσῃ.
σοφίᾳ γὰρ ἔκ του
κλεινὸν ἔπος πέφανται,
τὸ κακὸν δοκεῖν ποτ᾽ ἐσθλὸν
τῷδ᾽ ἔμμεν, ὅτῳ φρένας
θεὸς ἄγει πρὸς ἄταν·
πράσσει δ᾽ ὀλιγοστὸν χρόνον ἐκτὸς ἄτας.

For hope with flattering dreams is the delight of many, and
throws a deceitful illusion over man's light desires; ruin creeps
on him unawares before he treads on the treacherous fires. With
wisdom some one has uttered an illustrious saying : "that evil is

deemed to be good by him whose mind God leads to misery, but that he (God) practises this a short time without destroying such an one.'

ANARCHY AND ORDER.

Antig. 672.

'Αναρχίας δὲ μεῖζον οὐκ ἔστιν κακόν,
αὕτη πόλεις ὅλλυσιν, ἥδ' ἀναστάτους
οἴκους τίθησιν· ἥδε σὺν μάχῃ δορὸς
τροπὰς καταρρήγνυσι· τῶν δ' ὀρθουμένων
σώζει τὰ πολλὰ σώμαθ' ἡ πειθαρχία·
οὕτως ἀμυντέ' ἐστὶ τοῖς κοσμουμένοις,
κοὔτοι γυναικὸς οὐδαμῶς ἡσσητέα.
κρεῖσσον γὰρ, εἴπερ δεῖ, πρὸς ἀνδρὸς ἐκπεσεῖν
κοὐκ ἂν γυναικῶν ἥσσονες καλοίμεθ' ἄν.

There is no greater ill than anarchy ; it destroys cities, lays houses in ruins, and, in the contest of the spear, breaks the ranks ; but discipline saves those who obey command ; therefore we ought to aid those who govern and never yield to a woman ; for better, if we must fall, to fall by men than that we should be declared subject to woman.

WISDOM.

Antig. 683.

Πάτερ, θεοὶ φύουσιν ἀνθρώποις φρένας,
πάντων ὅσ' ἐστὶ χρημάτων ὑπέρτατον.

Father, the gods implant wisdom in men, which is the noblest of all treasures.

A FATHER'S GLORY.

Antig. 704.

Τί γὰρ πατρὸς θάλλοντος εὐκλείας τέκνοις
ἄγαλμα μεῖζον, ἢ τί πρὸς παίδων πατρί ;

What greater ornament is there to a son than a father's glory, or what to a father than a son's honourable conduct?
See (Lat.) Virtuous example of father.

SELF-CONCEIT.

Antig. 707.

Ὅστις γὰρ αὐτὸς ἢ φρονεῖν μόνος δοκεῖ,

ἢ γλῶσσαν, ἣν οὐκ ἄλλος, ἢ ψυχὴν ἔχειν,
οὗτοι διαπτυχθέντες ὤφθησαν κενοί.
ἀλλ' ἄνδρα, κεἴ τις ᾖ σοφός, τὸ μανθάνειν
πόλλ' αἰσχρὸν οὐδὲν καὶ τὸ μὴ τείνειν ἄγαν.
ὁρᾷς παρὰ ῥείθροισι χειμάρροις ὅσα
δένδρων ὑπείκει, κλῶνας ὡς ἐκσώζεται,
τὰ δ' ἀντιτείνοντ' αὐτόπρεμν' ἀπόλλυται.
αὕτως δὲ ναὸς ὅστις ἐγκρατῆ πόδα
τείνας ὑπείκει μηδέν, ὑπτίοις κάτω
στρέψας τὸ λοιπὸν σέλμασιν ναυτίλλεται.

For whoever thinks that he alone has wisdom or power of speech or judgment such as no other has, such men, when they are known, are found to be empty-brained. But it is no disgrace for even the wise to learn and not obstinately to resist conviction. Thou seest how the trees that bend by the wintry torrents preserve their boughs, while those that resist the blast fall uprooted. And so too the pilot who swells his sails without relaxing upsets his bark and floats with benches turned upside down.

DESPOTISM.

Antig. 737.

Πόλις γὰρ οὐκ ἔσθ' ἥτις ἀνδρός ἐσθ' ἑνός.

That is not a commonwealth where one man lords it with despotic sway.

LOVE.

Antig. 781.

Ἔρως ἀνίκατε μάχαν,
Ἔρως, ὃς ἐν κτήμασι πίπτεις,
ὃς ἐν μαλακαῖς παρειαῖς
νεάνιδος ἐννυχεύεις,
φοιτᾷς δ' ὑπερπόντιος ἔν τ' ἀγρονόμοις αὐλαῖς·
καί σ' οὔτ' ἀθανάτων φύξιμος οὐδεὶς
οὔθ' ἀμερίων ἐπ' ἀνθρώπων, ὁ δ' ἔχων μέμηνεν.

Σὺ καὶ δικαίων ἀδίκους
φρένας παρασπᾷς ἐπὶ λώβᾳ·
σὺ καὶ τόδε νεῖκος ἀνδρῶν
ξύναιμον ἔχεις ταράξας·
νικᾷ δ' ἐναργὴς βλεφάρων ἵμερος εὐλέκτρου
νύμφας, τῶν μεγάλων πάρεδρος ἐν ἀρχαῖς
θεσμῶν· ἄμαχος γὰρ ἐμπαίζει θεὸς Ἀφροδίτα.

O Love! resistless in thy might, thou who triumphest even over gold, making thy couch on youth's soft cheek, who roamest over the deep and in the rural cots—thee none of the immortals shall escape nor any of men, the creatures of a day, but all who feel thee feel madness in their hearts. Thou drawest aside the minds of the virtuous to unjust acts; thou hast raised this storm in hearts by blood allied; desire, lighted up from the eyes of the beauteous bride, gains the victory and sits beside the mighty laws of heaven, for Venus wantons without control.

Scott in his "Lay of the Last Minstrel" (cant. iii. 2) says—

> "In peace, Love tunes the shepherd's reed;
> In war, he mounts the warrior's steed;
> In halls, in gay attire is seen;
> In hamlets, dances on the green.
> Love rules the court, the camp, the grove,
> And men below, and saints above;
> For love is heaven and heaven is love."

To Err is Human.

Antig. 1023.

Ἀνθρώποισι γὰρ
τοῖς πᾶσι κοινόν ἐστι τοὐξαμαρτάνειν·
ἐπεὶ δ' ἁμάρτῃ, κεῖνος οὐκέτ' ἔστ' ἀνὴρ
ἄβουλος οὐδ' ἄνολβος, ὅστις ἐς κακὸν
πεσὼν ἀκῆται μηδ' ἀκίνητος πέλῃ.
αὐθαδία τοι σκαιότητ' ὀφλισκάνει.

To all of mortals to err is common; but having erred, that man is not unblessed nor unadvised who, having fallen into error, heals the wound, nor perseveres unmoved. It is the obdurate mind that incurs the imputation of folly.

See (Lat.) To err.

Instruction.

Antig. 1031.

Τὸ μανθάνειν δ'
ἥδιστον εὖ λέγοντος, εἰ κέρδος λέγοι.

Most pleasant is instruction when it comes from one who speaks wisely, and with it comes advantage.

The Impious.

Antig. 1103.

Συντέμνουσι γὰρ
θεῶν ποδώκεις τοὺς κακόφρονας βλάβαι.

For the swift-footed vengeance of heaven cuts short the impious.

THE LAWS.

Antig. 1113.

Δέδοικα γὰρ μὴ τοὺς καθεστῶτας νόμους
ἄριστον ᾖ σώζοντα τὸν βίον τελεῖν.

For I fear that to preserve the established laws through life is man's wisest part.

MAN'S LIFE UNCERTAIN.

Antig. 1155.

Οὐκ ἔσθ' ὁποῖον στάντ' ἂν ἀνθρώπου βίον
οὔτ' αἰνέσαιμ' ἂν οὔτε μεμψαίμην ποτέ.
τύχη γὰρ ὀρθοῖ καὶ τύχη καταρρέπει
τὸν εὐτυχοῦντα τόν τε δυστυχοῦντ' ἀεί·
καὶ μάντις οὐδεὶς τῶν καθεστώτων βροτοῖς.

It is not possible that I should praise or dispraise the life of man, whatever be its state ; for Fortune ever raises and casts down the happy and unhappy, and no man oan divine the fates to come.

JOYS OF LIFE.

Antig. 1165.

Τὰς γὰρ ἡδονὰς
ὅταν προδῶσιν ἄνδρες, οὐ τίθημ' ἐγὼ
ζῆν τοῦτον, ἀλλ' ἔμψυχον ἡγοῦμαι νεκρόν.
πλούτει τε γὰρ κατ' οἶκον, εἰ βούλει, μέγα,
καὶ ζῆ τύραννον σχῆμ' ἔχων, ἐὰν δ' ἀπῇ
τούτων τὸ χαίρειν, τἄλλ' ἐγὼ καπνοῦ σκιᾶς
οὐκ ἂν πριαίμην ἀνδρὶ πρὸς τὴν ἡδονήν.

For when man knows no more the joys of life I do not consider him to live, but look upon him as the living dead. Nay, let his house be stored with riches, if thou pleasest, and let him be attended with a monarch's pomp, yet, if heart-felt joys be absent, all the rest I would not purchase with the shadow of smoke when compared with real pleasures.

A CLAMOROUS SORROW.

Antig. 1251.

Ἐμοὶ δ' οὖν ἥ τ' ἄγαν σιγὴ βαρὺ
δοκεῖ προσεῖναι, χἠ μάτην πολλὴ βοή.

To me so deep a silence portends some dread event, a clamorous sorrow wastes itself in sound.

See (Lat.) Grief.

SILENCE.

Antig. 1254.

Καὶ τῆς ἄγαν γάρ ἐστί που σιγῆς βάρος.

There is something grievous in too great a silence.

CALAMITIES.

Antig. 1327.

Βράχιστα γὰρ κράτιστα τὰν ποσὶν κακά.

Calamities, present to the view, though slight, are poignant.

WISDOM LEADS TO HAPPINESS.

Antig. 1347.

Πολλῷ τὸ φρονεῖν εὐδαιμονίας
πρῶτον ὑπάρχει· χρὴ δὲ τά γ' εἰς θεοὺς
μηδὲν ἀσεπτεῖν· μεγάλοι δὲ λόγοι
μεγάλας πληγὰς τῶν ὑπεραύχων
ἀποτίσαντες
γήρᾳ τὸ φρονεῖν ἐδίδαξαν.

By far the best guide to happiness is wisdom, but irreverence to the gods is unbecoming; the mighty vaunts of pride, paying the penalty of severe affliction, have taught old age, thus humbled, to be wise.

NO MAN BLESSED BEFORE DEATH.

Trachin. 1.

Λόγος μέν ἐστ' ἀρχαῖος ἀνθρώπων φανείς,
ὡς οὐκ ἂν αἰῶν' ἐκμάθοις βροτῶν, πρὶν ἂν
θάνῃ τις, οὔτ' εἰ χρηστὸς οὔτ' εἴ τῳ κακός.

There is an ancient saying, famed among men, that thou canst not judge fully of the life of men, till death hath closed the scene, whether it should be called blest or wretched.

See (Lat.) No man blessed.

Constant Change in the Affairs of Life.

Trachin. 131.

Μένει γὰρ οὔτ' αἰόλα νὺξ βροτοῖσιν οὔτε κῆρες
οὔτε πλοῦτος, ἀλλ' ἄφαρ βέβακε, τῷ δ' ἐπέρχεται
χαίρειν τε καὶ στέρεσθαι.

For spangled night does not always spread its shade for mortals,
nor do sorrows and wealth remain for aye, but are quickly gone;
joy and grief succeed each other.

A Young Woman's Life.

Trachin. 144.

Τὸ γὰρ νεάζον ἐν τοιοῖσδε βόσκεται
χώροισιν αὑτοῦ, καί νιν οὐ θάλπος θεοῦ,
οὐδ' ὄμβρος, οὐδὲ πνευμάτων οὐδὲν κλονεῖ,
ἀλλ' ἡδοναῖς ἄμοχθον ἐξαίρει βίον
ἐς τοῦθ', ἕως τις ἀντὶ παρθένου γυνὴ
κληθῇ, λάβῃ τ' ἐν νυκτὶ φροντίδων μέρος
ἤτοι πρὸς ἀνδρὸς ἢ τέκνων φοβουμένη.

Youth feeds on its own flowery pastures, where neither the
scorching heat of heaven nor showers nor any gale disturb it, but
in pleasures it builds up a life that knows no trouble, till the
name of virgin is lost in that of wife, then receiving her share of
sorrows in the hours of night, anxious for her husband or children.

Imagination.

Trachin. 425.

Ταὐτὸ δ' οὐχὶ γίγνεται
δόκησιν εἰπεῖν κἀξακριβῶσαι λόγον.

It is not the same thing to speak on mere imagination and to
affirm a statement as certain.

Speak the Whole Truth.

Trachin. 453.

Ἀλλ' εἰπὲ πᾶν τἀληθές· ὡς ἐλευθέρῳ,
ψευδεῖ καλεῖσθαι, κὴρ πρόσεστίν οὐ καλή.

But speak the whole truth; since for a freeman to be called a
liar is a disgraceful stain on his character.

Anger.

Trachin. 727.

'Αλλ' ἀμφὶ τοῖς σφαλεῖσι μὴ 'ξ ἑκουσίας
ὀργὴ πέπειρα.

To those who err in judgment not in will we should be gentle
in our anger.

Uncertainty of Life.

Trachin. 943.

"Ωστ' εἴ τις δύο
ἢ καὶ πλέους τις ἡμέρας λογίζεται,
μάταιός ἐστιν· οὐ γάρ ἐσθ' ἥ γ' αὔριον,
πρὶν εὖ πάθῃ τις τὴν παροῦσαν ἡμέραν.

So that if man should make account of two days or of more,
he is a fool; for to-morrow is not till he has passed the present
day without misfortune.

See (Lat.) Uncertainty of life.

The Dead.

Trachin. 1171.

Κἀδόκουν πράξειν καλῶς.
τὸ δ' ἦν ἄρ' οὐδὲν ἄλλο πλὴν θανεῖν ἐμέ.
τοῖς γὰρ θανοῦσι μόχθος οὐ προσγίγνεται.

I fondly thought of happier days, whilst it denoted nothing
else but my death. To the dead there are no toils.

To deride our Enemies.

Ajax, 79.

Οὔκουν γέλως ἥδιστος εἰς ἐχθροὺς γελᾶν;

Is that not the most grateful laugh that we indulge against our
enemies?

The Modest and the Arrogant.

Ajax, 127.

Τοιαῦτα τοίνυν εἰσορῶν ὑπέρκοπον
μηδέν ποτ' εἴπῃς αὐτὸς εἰς θεοὺς ἔπος,
μηδ' ὄγκον ἄρῃ μηδέν', εἴ τινος πλέον

ἢ χειρὶ βρίθεις ἢ μακροῦ πλούτου βάθει.
ὡς ἡμέρα κλίνει τε κἀνάγει πάλιν
ἅπαντα τἀνθρώπεια· τοὺς δὲ σώφρονας
θεοὶ φιλοῦσι καὶ στυγοῦσι τοὺς κακούς.

Seeing that it is so, utter no vain vaunt against the gods nor
swell with pride if thou excellest any one in valour or in thy stores
of wealth, since a day sinks all human things in darkness and
again restores them to light : the gods love the sober-minded and
abhor the impious.

THE NOBLE ARE ENVIED.

Ajax, 154.

Τῶν γὰρ μεγάλων ψυχῶν ἰεὶς
οὐκ ἂν ἁμάρτοι· κατὰ δ' ἂν τις ἐμοῦ
τοιαῦτα λέγων οὐκ ἂν πείθοι.
πρὸς γὰρ τὸν ἔχονθ' ὁ φθόνος ἔρπει.

For he who launches his bolt against noble persons could not
miss ; but if any were to bring this charge against me he would
not be believed : for envy crawls towards the wealthy.

Shakespeare ("Henry VIII.," act i. sc. 2) says—
"If I am traduced by tongues, which neither know
My faculties nor person, yet will be
The chronicles of my doing—let me say,
'Tis but the fate of place."

See (Lat.) Vice in high places.

OUR OWN ILLS.

Ajax, 260.

Τὸ γὰρ εἰσλεύσσειν οἰκεῖα πάθη,
μηδενὸς ἄλλου παραπράξαντος,
μεγάλας ὀδύνας ὑποτείνει.

For to view ills all our own, where no associate shares the deed,
racks the heart with deep pangs.

See (Lat.) Others' misfortunes

WOMEN.

Ajax, 293.

Γύναι, γυναιξὶ κόσμον ἡ σιγὴ φέρει.

To women silence gives their proper grace.

GOD ASSIGNS EVERY EVENT.

Ajax, 383.

Ξὺν τῷ θεῷ πᾶς καὶ γελᾷ κὠδύρεται.

Each, as the god assigns, or laughs or weeps.

NOTHING IN LIFE CAN GIVE ME JOY.

Ajax, 394.

Ἰὼ
σκότος, ἐμὸν φάος,
ἔρεβος ὦ φαεννότατον, ὡς ἐμοί,
ἕλεσθ᾽ ἕλεσθέ μ᾽ οἰκήτορα,
ἕλεσθέ μ᾽· οὔτε γὰρ θεῶν γένος
οὔθ᾽ ἁμερίων ἔτ᾽ ἄξιος
βλέπειν τίν᾽ εἰς ὄνησιν ἀνθρώπων.

O darkness, now my light, O Erebus, now sole brightness to me, take me, oh ! take me, a wretch no longer worthy to behold the gods or men, creatures of a day : me they nought avail.
Shakespeare ("King John," act iii., sc. 4) says—
  " There 's nothing in the world can make me joy :
  Life is as tedious as a twice-told tale
  Vexing the dull ear of a drowsy man ;
  And bitter shame hath spoil'd the world's sweet taste,
  That it yields nought but shame and bitterness."

POWER OF THE GODS.

Ajax, 455.

Εἰ δέ τις θεῶν
βλάπτοι, φύγοι τἂν χὠ κακὸς τὸν κρείσσονα.

If a god foil him, even the dastard shall escape the brave man's vengeance.

THE UNHAPPY.

Ajax, 473.

Αἰσχρὸν γὰρ ἄνδρα τοῦ μακροῦ χρῄζειν βίου,
κακοῖσιν ὅστις μηδὲν ἐξαλλάσσεται.
τί γὰρ παρ᾽ ἦμαρ ἡμέρα τέρπειν ἔχει
προσθεῖσα κἀναθεῖσα τοῦ γε κατθανεῖν ;
οὐκ ἂν πριαίμην οὐδενὸς λόγου βροτόν,
ὅστις κεναῖσιν ἐλπίσιν θερμαίνεται.

ἀλλ' ἢ καλῶς ζῆν, ἢ καλῶς τεθνηκέναι
τὸν εὐγενῆ χρή.

For it is base to wish for length of life when there is no hope of
a change of ills. What pleasure can day alternating with day
present, when it does nothing but either add or take away from
the necessity of dying? I would not buy at any price the man
who deludes himself with vain hopes. No, to live with glory or
with glory die, this is the brave man's part.

GRATITUDE.

Ajax, 520.

'Ανδρί τοι χρεὼν
μνήμην προσεῖναι, τερπνὸν εἴ τί που πάθῃ.
χάρις χάριν γάρ ἐστιν ἡ τίκτουσ' ἀεί·
ὅτου δ' ἀπορρεῖ μνῆστις εὖ πεπονθότος,
οὐκ ἂν γένοιτ' ἔθ' οὗτος εὐγενὴς ἀνήρ.

It becomes a man, if he hath received aught grateful to his
mind, to bear it in remembrance ; it is kindness that gives birth
to kindness ; when recollection of a benefit melts from the thought,
that man could never have been of generous birth.

THE THOUGHTLESSNESS OF CHILDHOOD.

Ajax, 553.

'Εν τῷ φρονεῖν γὰρ μηδὲν ἥδιστος βίος.

The sweetest life
Consists in feeling nothing.

Gray says—

" Ah ! how regardless of their doom
The little victims play !
No sense have they of ills to come,
No care beyond to-day."

ULCERED WOUNDS.

Ajax, 580.

Οὐ πρὸς ἰατροῦ σοφοῦ
θρηνεῖν ἐπῳδὰς πρὸς τομῶντι πήματι.

For it is not the part of the skilful physician to scream a mystic
charm when the sore requires the knife.

The Gifts of Enemies.

Ajax, 664.

'Αλλ' ἔστ' ἀληθὴς ἡ βροτῶν παροιμία,
ἐχθρῶν ἄδωρα δῶρα κοὐκ ὀνήσιμα.

No, true is the popular adage : "The gifts of enemies are no gifts and fraught with mischief."

See (Lat.) Gifts of enemies.

The Weaker gives way to the Stronger.

Ajax, 669.

Καὶ γὰρ τὰ δεινὰ καὶ τὰ καρτερώτατα
τιμαῖς ὑπείκει· τοῦτο μὲν νιφοστιβεῖς
χειμῶνες ἐκχωροῦσιν εὐκάρπῳ θέρει·
ἐξίσταται δὲ νυκτὸς αἰανῆς κύκλος
τῇ λευκοπώλῳ φέγγος ἡμέρᾳ φλέγειν·
δεινῶν τ' ἄημα πνευμάτων ἐκοίμισε
στένοντα πόντον· ἐν δ' ὁ παγκρατὴς ὕπνος
λύει πεδήσας, οὐδ' ἀεὶ λαβὼν ἔχει.

For all that is terrible and all that is mighty gives way to higher power ; for this reason the snow-faced winters yield place to summer with its beauteous fruits, and the dark circle of the night retires that the day with his white steeds may flame forth in orient light ; the fury of the fierce blasts lulls and leaves a calm on the tempestuous deep : nay, even all-subduing sleep unbinds his chain nor always holds us captive.

Shakespeare ("Troilus and Cressida," act 1., sc. 3) says—
 "The heavens themselves, the planets, and this centre
 Observe degree, priority, and place,
 Insisture, course, proportion, season, form.
 Office, and custom, in all line of order."

So to hate as to be again a Friend.

Ajax, 678.

'Εγὼ δ', ἐπίσταμαι γὰρ ἀρτίως ὅτι
ὅ τ' ἐχθρὸς ἡμῖν ἐς τοσόνδ' ἐχθραντέος
ὡς καὶ φιλήσων αὖθις, ἔς τε τὸν φίλον
τοσαῦθ' ὑπουργῶν ὠφελεῖν βουλήσομαι,
ὡς αἰὲν οὐ μενοῦντα. τοῖς πολλοῖσι γὰρ
βροτῶν ἄπιστός ἐσθ' ἑταιρείας λιμήν.

For this wisdom I have learned, that our enemy is only to be so far hated by us as one who, perchance, may again be our friend, and that I should so far wish to aid my friend as if he were not

always to remain so ; for the haven of friendship is not always secure to the majority of mankind.

See (Lat.) As if to love.

PRIDE.

Ajax, 758.

Τὰ γὰρ περισσὰ κἀνόνητα σώματα
πίπτειν βαρείαις πρὸς θεῶν δυσπραξίαις
ἔφασχ᾽ ὁ μάντις, ὅστις ἀνθρώπου φύσιν
βλαστὼν ἔπειτα μὴ κατ᾽ ἄνθρωπον φρονῇ

For the seer declared that unwieldy and senseless strength is
wont to sink in ruin, crushed by the offended gods, when man of
mortal birth aspires with pride beyond a mortal.

See (Lat.) Righteous rewarded by the gods.

THE IMPOTENT OF MIND.

Ajax, 964.

Οἱ γὰρ κακοὶ γνώμαισι τἀγαθὸν χεροῖν
ἔχοντες οὐκ ἴσασι, πρίν τις ἐκβάλῃ.

For the impotent of mind, while they hold in their hands a
treasure, know it not till it be snatched from them.

Shakespeare ("Much Ado about Nothing," act iv., sc. 1) says—

"For it so falls out,
That what we have we prize not to the worth
Whiles we enjoy it ; but being lacked and lost,
Why then we rack the value, then we find
The virtue that possession would not show us
Whiles it was ours."

GOD DOES EVERYTHING FOR MANKIND.

Ajax, 1036.

Ἐγὼ μὲν οὖν καὶ ταῦτα καὶ τὰ πάντ᾽ ἀεὶ
φάσκοιμ᾽ ἂν ἀνθρώποισι μηχανᾶν θεούς.

I then would say that the gods devised both this and everything
else always for mankind.

So Psalms (cxlv. 15)— "The eyes of all wait upon Thee ; and Thou givest
them their meat in due season."

A SEDITIOUS ARMY.

Ajax, 1071.

Καίτοι κακοῦ πρὸς ἀνδρὸς ἄνδρα δημότην
μηδὲν δικαιοῦν τῶν ἐφεστώτων κλύειν.

Q

Οὐ γάρ ποτ᾽ οὔτ᾽ ἂν ἐν πόλει νόμοι καλῶς
φέροιντ᾽ ἄν, ἔνθα μὴ καθεστήκοι δέος,
οὔτ᾽ ἂν στρατός γε σωφρόνως ἄρχοιτ᾽ ἔτι
μηδὲν φόβου πρόβλημα μηδ᾽ αἰδοῦς ἔχων.

And indeed it is the mark of a bad man when he that is now raised above the common rank scorns to obey his rulers. For in a state never can laws be well enforced where fear does not support their establishment, nor could an army be ruled submissively, if it were not awed by fear and reverence of their chiefs.

IN A JUST CAUSE WE MAY ASSUME CONFIDENCE.

Ajax, 1125.

Ξὺν τῷ δικαίῳ γὰρ μέγ᾽ ἔξεστιν φρονεῖν.

When the cause is just,
An honest pride may be indulged.

Shakespeare ("Henry VI." part ii., act iii , sc. 2) says—
"Thrice is he armed that hath his quarrel just ;
And he but naked, though locked up in steel.
Whose conscience with injustice is corrupted."

A BOASTER.

Ajax, 1142.

Ἤδη ποτ᾽ εἶδον ἄνδρ᾽ ἐγὼ γλώσσῃ θρασὺν
ναύτας ἐφορμήσαντα χειμῶνος τὸ πλεῖν,
ᾧ φθέγμ᾽ ἂν οὐκ ἂν εὗρες, ἡνίκ᾽ ἐν κακῷ
χειμῶνος εἴχετ᾽, ἀλλ᾽ ὑφ᾽ εἵματος κρυφεὶς
πατεῖν παρεῖχε τῷ θέλοντι ναυτίλων.

Not long ago I saw a man of doughty tongue urging his crew to sail while a storm threatened, whose voice thou couldst not hear when he was surrounded by the tempest; but, wrapt in his cloak, he suffered every sailor's foot at will to trample on him.

SUNIUM'S MARBLED STEEP.

Ajax, 1217.

Γενοίμαν ἵν᾽ ὑλᾶεν ἔπεστι πόντου
πρόβλημ᾽ ἁλίκλυστον, ἄκραν
ὑπὸ πλάκα Σουνίου,
τὰς ἱερὰς ὅπως
προσείποιμεν Ἀθάνας.

Oh ! could I be where the woody foreland, washed by the wave,
beetles o'er the main, beneath Sunium's lofty plain, that I might
accost the sacred Athens.

Byron says—

> " Place me on Sunium's marbled steep,
> Where nothing save the waves and I
> May hear our mutual murmurs weep,—
> There, swanlike, let me sing and die."

THE PRUDENT MIND PREVAILS.

Ajax, 1250.

Οὐ γὰρ οἱ πλατεῖς
οὐδ' εὐρύνωτοι φῶτες ἀσφαλέστατοι,
ἀλλ' οἱ φρονοῦντες εὖ κρατοῦσι πανταχοῦ.
Μέγας δὲ πλευρὰ βοῦς ὑπὸ σμικρᾶς ὅμως
μάστιγος ὀρθὸς εἰς ὁδὸν πορεύεται.
Καὶ σοὶ προσέρπον τοῦτ' ἐγὼ τὸ φάρμακον
ὁρῶ τάχ', εἰ μὴ νοῦν κατακτήσῃ τινά·
ὃς ἀνδρὸς οὐκέτ' ὄντος, ἀλλ' ἤδη σκιᾶς,
θαρσῶν ὑβρίζεις κἀξελευθεροστομεῖς.

For 'tis not the high-built frame, the massy-structured limb,
that yield most protection , no, the man of prudent mind everywhere prevails. The ox, though vast his bulk, is taught the
straight road by a small whip. And thee, I see, this discipline will
soon reach, if thy mind acquire not prudence, thou who art confident in insolence, and in tongue unbridled—no more a man, but a
mere shadow.

Shakespeare (" Troilus and Cressida," act i., sc. 3) says—

> " So that the rain, that batters down the wall,
> For the great swing and rudeness of his poise,
> They place before the hand that made the engine;
> Or those that with the fineness of their souls,
> By reason guide his execution."

See (Lat.) Mind is the man.

THE DEAD.

Ajax, 1344.

Ἄνδρα δ' οὐ δίκαιον, εἰ θάνοι,
βλάπτειν τὸν ἐσθλόν, οὐδ' ἐὰν μισῶν κυρῇς.

It is unjust to wrong the brave man when he is dead, though
hated by thee.

POWER OF GOD IRRESISTIBLE.

Electr. 696.

Ὅταν δέ τις θεῶν
βλάπτῃ, δύναιτ' ἂν οὐδ' ἂν ἰσχύων φυγεῖν.

When God afflicts him, not even a strong man can escape.
So Isaiah (xxiii. 11)—"The Lord hath given a commandment to destroy the strongholds thereof."

GOD KNOWS EVEN THE THOUGHTS OF MAN.

Electr. 657.

Τὰ δ' ἄλλα πάντα καὶ σιωπώσης ἐμοῦ
ἐπαξιῶ σε δαίμον' ὄντ' ἐξειδέναι.

I deem that, being God, thou knowest all things, though I be silent.
So John (ii. 25)—"For He knew what was in man."

TO DIE IS NOT THE GREATEST OF EVILS.

Electr. 1007.

Οὐ γὰρ θανεῖν ἔχθιστον, ἀλλ' ὅταν θανεῖν
χρῄζων τις εἶτα μηδὲ τοῦτ' ἔχῃ λαβεῖν.

For death is not the most dreadful ill, but when we wish to die, and have not death within our power.
See Job iii. 21 ; Rev. ix. 6.   Dante iii. 46.

LET THEM LAUGH THAT WIN.

Electr. 1299.

Ὅταν γὰρ εὐτυχήσωμεν, τότε
χαίρειν παρέσται καὶ γελᾶν ἐλευθέρως.

For when we shall have succeeded, then will be our time to rejoice and freely laugh.

THE BASE AND THE GENEROUS.

Philoc. 446.

Ἐπεὶ οὐδέν πω κακόν γ' ἀπώλετο,
ἀλλ' εὖ περιστέλλουσιν αὐτὰ δαίμονες,
καί πως τὰ μὲν πανοῦργα καὶ παλιντριβῆ
χαίρουσ' ἀναστρέφοντες ἐξ "Αιδου, τὰ δὲ
δίκαια καὶ τὰ χρήστ' ἀποστέλλουσ' ἀεί.
ποῦ χρὴ τίθεσθαι ταῦτα, ποῦ δ' αἰνεῖν, ὅταν
τὰ θεῖ' ἐπαινῶν τοὺς θεοὺς εὕρω κακούς ;

Since never at any time hath the base perished, but of such the gods take special care, delighting to snatch the crafty and the guileful from Hades, whereas they are always sinking the just and upright in ruin. How shall we account for these things, or how approve them? When I find the gods unjust, how can I praise their heavenly governance?

THE WORSE PREVAIL.

Philoc. 456.

Ὅπου γ᾽ ὁ χείρων τἀγαθοῦ μεῖζον σθένει,
κἀποφθίνει τὰ χρηστὰ, χὠ δειλὸς κρατεῖ,
τούτους ἐγὼ τοὺς ἄνδρας οὐ στέρξω ποτέ.

Where the worse has greater power than the good, and all that is good is on the wane, and the coward prevails, such never will I hold dear.

GRATITUDE.

Philoc. 672.

Ὅστις γὰρ εὖ δρᾶν εὖ παθὼν ἐπίσταται,
παντὸς γένοιτ᾽ ἂν κτήματος κρείσσων φίλος.

For whoever knows to requite a favour, must be a friend above all price.

"THERE IS A TIDE IN THE AFFAIRS OF MEN."

Philoc. 837.

Καιρός τοι πάντων γνώμαν ἴσχων
πολὺ παρὰ πόδα κράτος ἄρνυται.

Opportunity, be assured, possessing the power over all things, acquires much power in its course.

MISERIES.

Philoc. 1316.

Ἀνθρώποισι τὰς μὲν ἐκ θεῶν
τύχας δοθείσας ἔστ᾽ ἀναγκαῖον φέρειν·
ὅσοι δ᾽ ἐκουσίοισιν ἔγκεινται βλάβαις,
ὥσπερ σύ, τούτοις οὔτε συγγνώμην ἔχειν
δίκαιόν ἐστιν οὔτ᾽ ἐποικτείρειν τινά.

For the ills inflicted on men by the gods they must sustain, but those involved in voluntary miseries, as thou art, on these it is not just for any one to bestow either pardon or pity.

Base Deeds.

Philoc. 1360.

Οἷς γὰρ ἡ γνώμη κακῶν
μήτηρ γένηται, τἄλλα παιδεύει κακούς.

For the mind that, like a parent, gives birth to base deeds, trains up everything else to become base.

Piety.

Philoc. 1443.

Οὐ γὰρ εὐσέβεια συνθνήσκει βροτοῖς,
[κἂν ζῶσι κἂν θάνωσιν, οὐκ ἀπόλλυται.]

For piety dies not with man; live they or die they, it perishes not.

Man cannot escape the Vengeance of God.

Frag. ex Stob.

Θεοῦ δὲ πληγὴν οὐχ ὑπερπηδᾷ βροτός.

Man cannot escape the vengeance of God.

Vengeance.

Frag. ex Stob.

Τὸ χρύσεον δὲ τῆς Δίκης
δέδορκεν ὄμμα, τὸν δ' ἄδικον ἀμείβεται.

The bright eye of Vengeance sees and punishes the wicked.

Vengeance.

Frag. ex Stob.

Εἰ δειν' ἔδρασας δεινὰ καὶ παθεῖν σε δεῖ,
δίκης γὰρ ἐξέλαμψε νῦν ὅσιον φάος.

If thou hast committed iniquity, thou must expect to suffer, for Vengeance with its sacred light shines upon thee.

Time.

Frag. ex Stob.

Πρὸς ταῦτα κρύπτε μηδὲν, ὡς ὁ πάνθ' ὁρῶν
καὶ πάντ' ἀκούων πάντ' ἀναπτύσσει χρόνος.

Therefore, conceal nothing; for Time, that sees and hears all things, discovers everything.

One Good Turn asks another.

Frag. Inc.

Χάρις χάριν τίκτει.

Grace begets grace.

SOSICRATES.

Sosicrates, a comic poet, whose time is unknown.

The Beam in our own Eye.

Fr. Com. Gr. p. 1182.

Αγαθοὶ δὲ τὸ κακόν ἐσμεν ἐφ' ἑτέρων ἰδεῖν,
αὑτοὶ δ ὅταν ποιῶμεν ον γινώσκομεν.

We are quick to spy the evil conduct of others; but when we ourselves do the same, we are not aware of it.

THEOCRITUS.

FLOURISHED ABOUT B.C. 272.

Theocritus, the most famous of all the pastoral poets, a native of Syracuse, was the son of Praxagoras and Philinna. He was the contemporary of Aratus, Callimachus, and Nicander. He celebrates the younger Hiero; but his great patron was Ptolemy Philadelphus, king of Egypt, of whom he speaks in terms of high commendation. Of his personal history we know nothing further. He was the creator of bucolic poetry as a branch of Greek, and, through imitators such as Virgil, of Roman literature. His pas-

torals have furnished models for all succeeding poets, and are
remarkable for their simplicity—very often elegant, but sometimes
approaching to rudeness. Thirty Idyls bear his name; but it may
be doubted whether they were all produced by the same poet.

THE SWEET MURMURING OF THE WOODS.

Idyl, i. 1.

'Αδύ τι τὸ ψιθύρισμα καὶ ἁ πίτυς, αἰπόλε, τήνα,
"Α ποτὶ ταῖς παγαῖσι μελίσδεται· ἁδὺ δὲ καὶ τὺ
Τυρίσδες.

Sweet is the music, O goat-herd, of yon whispering pine to the
fountains, and sweetly, too, is thine, breathed from thy pipe.

Pope (Past. iv. 80) says—
  "In some still evening, when the whispering breeze
  Pants on the leaves, and dies among the trees."

And again, in the same Pastoral—
  "Thyrsis, the music of that murmuring spring
  Is not so mournful as the strains you sing."

  Virgil (Eclog. viii. 22) speaks of the "pinus loquentes"—the "whispering pines."

THE MURMURING OF THE BROOKLET.

Idyl, i. 7.

"Αδιον, ὦ ποιμάν, τὸ τεὸν μέλος ἢ τὸ καταχὲς
Τῆν' ἀπὸ τᾶς πέτρας καταλείβεται ὑψόθεν ὕδωρ.

Sweeter, good shepherd, thy song than yonder gliding down of
waters from the rock above.

Thus Virgil (Eclog. v. 83)—
  "Nec percussa juvant fluctu tam litora, nec quæ
  Saxosas inter decurrunt flumina valles."

  "Nor am I so much charmed by the music of the waves beat back from
the shore, nor of the streamlets as they rush along the rocky valleys."

So, too, Pope (Past. iv.)—
  "Nor rivers winding through the vales below,
  So sweetly warble, or so sweetly flow."

THE WISH OF A LOVER.

Idyl, iii. 12.

Αἴθε γενοίμαν
Ἁ βομβεῦσα μέλισσα, καὶ ἐς τεὸν ἄντρον ἱκοίμαν,
Τὸν κισσὸν διαδὺς, καὶ τὰν πτέριν, ᾇ τὺ πυκάσδη.
Νῦν ἔγνων τὸν Ἔρωτα· βαρὺς θεός.

Would that I were a humming bee, and could fly to thy cave, creeping through the ivy and the fern, with which thou art covered in. Now I know Cupid a powerful god.

This is like the passage in Psalms (lv. 6)—" Oh that I had wings like a dove! for then would I fly away, and be at rest."

And Pope (Past. iii. 88) says—

" I know thee, Love ; on foreign mountains bred,
 Wolves gave thee suck, and savage tigers bred."

FORTUNE CHANGES.

Idyl, iv. 41.

Θαρσεῖν χρὴ, φίλε βάττε· τάχ᾽ αὔριον ἔσσετ᾽ ἄμεινον,
Ἐλπίδες ἐν ζωοῖσιν· ἀνέλπιστοι δὲ θανόντες.
Χὼ Ζεὺς ἄλλοκα μὲν πέλει αἴθριος, ἄλλοκα δ᾽ ὕει.

Courage, my friend Battus, to-morrow perhaps will be more favourable ; while there is life there is hope, the dead alone are without hope. Jove shines brightly one day, and the next showers down rain.

See (Lat.) Hope.

INJURIES FROM THOSE TO WHOM THOU HAST BEEN KIND.

Idyl, v. 37.

Ἴδ᾽ ἁ χάρις ἐς τὶ ποθ᾽ ἔρπει,
Θρέψαι καὶ λυκιδεῖς, θρέψαι κύνας, ὥς τυ φάγωντι.

See the result of my favours ! It is like rearing wolf-whelps or dogs—to rend you for your pains.

So Matthew (vii. 6) says—" Neither cast ye your pearls before swine, lest they trample them under their feet, and turn again and rend you."

A SYLVAN SCENE.

Idyl, v. 45.

Οὐχ ἐρψῶ τηνέι· τούτῳ δρύες, ὧδε κύπειρος,
Ὧδε καλὸν βομβεῦντι ποτὶ σμάνεσσι μέλισσαι·
Ἔνθ᾽ ὕδατος ψυχρῶ κρᾶναι δύο· ταὶ δ᾽ ἐπὶ δένδρων
Ὄρνιχες λαλαγεῦντι· καὶ ἁ σκιὰ οὐδὲν ὁμοία
Τᾷ παρὰ τίν· βάλλει δὲ καὶ ἁ πίτυς ὑψόθε κώνους.

I shall not go thither ; here are oaks, here is the galingale, here bees hum sweetly around their hives ; here are two springs of coolest water, here birds warble on the trees, nor is there any shade equal to that beside thee, and the pine showers its cones from on high.

It may be compared with the celebrated passage in Shakespeare (" Merchant of Venice," act v., sc. 1)—

Q 3

> " How sweet the moonlight sleeps upon this bank !
> Here will we sit, and let the sounds of music
> Creep in our ears ; soft stillness and the night
> Become the touches of sweet harmony.
> Sit, Jessica. Look how the floor of heaven
> Is thick inlaid with patines of bright gold."

THE DOG OF POLYPHEMUS.

Idyl, vi. 6.

Βάλλει τοι, Πολύφαμε, τὸ ποίμνιον ἁ Γαλάτεια
μάλοισιν, δυσέρωτα τὸν αἰπόλον ἄνδρα καλεῦσα·
καὶ τύ νιν οὐ ποθόρησθα τάλαν, τάλαν, ἀλλὰ κάθησαι
ἁδέα συρίσδων. Πάλιν ἅδ᾽ ἴδε, τὰν κύνα βάλλει,
ἅ τοι τᾶν ὀΐων ἕπεται σκόπος· ἁ δὲ βαῦσδει
εἰς ἅλα δερκομένα· τὰ δέ νιν καλὰ κύματα φαίνει
ἅσυχα καχλάζοντος ἐπ᾽ αἰγιαλοῖο θέοισαν.
Φράζεο μὴ τᾶς παιδὸς ἐπὶ κνάμαισιν ὀρούσῃ
ἐξ ἁλὸς ἐρχομένας, κατὰ δὲ χρόα καλὸν ἀμύξῃ.
Ἀ δὲ καὶ αὐτόθε τοι διαθρύπτεται, ὡς ἀπ᾽ ἀκάνθας
ταὶ καπυραὶ χαῖται, τὸ καλὸν θέρος ἁνίκα φρύττει·
καὶ φεύγει φιλέοντα, καὶ οὐ φιλέοντα διώκει.
Καὶ τὸν ἀπὸ γραμμᾶς κινεῖ λίθον· ἦ γὰρ ἔρωτι
πολλάκις, ὦ Πολύφαμε, τὰ μὴ καλὰ καλὰ πέφανται

Polyphemus! the shepherdess Galatea pelts thy flock with apples,
calling thee a rude clown, insensible to love ; and thou lookest not
at her, pining in wretchedness, wretchedness, but sittest playing
sweet strains on thy pipe. See, again she is pelting thy dog,
which follows to watch thy sheep. He barks, looking towards
the sea ; the beauteous waves soft murmuring show him running to
and fro along the beach. Take heed lest he leap not on her, coming
fresh from the sea-wave, and tear her fair flesh. But the soft
morning comes and goes, like the dry thistle-down when summer
glows. She pursues him who flies her, flies her pursuer, and moves
the landmarks of love's boundaries. For, Polyphemus, what is not
lovely often seems lovely to the lover.

Virgil (Eclog. iii. 64) says—
> " Malo me Galatea petit, lasciva puella."

" Galatea, the wanton girl, pelts me with apples."

The coquettishness of woman is well expressed by Terence.

See (Lat.) Woman full of opposition.

THE MID-DAY HEAT.

Idyl, vii. 21.

Σιμιχίδα, πᾷ δὴ τὺ μεσαμέριον πόδας ἕλκεις,
ἁνίκα δὴ καὶ σαῦρος ἐφ᾽ αἱμασιαῖσι καθεύδει,
οὐδ᾽ ἐπιτυμβίδιοι κορυδαλλίδες ἠλαίνονται.

Simichidas! whither, pray, hurriest thou at this mid-day time,
when even the lizard is sleeping by the dry-stone wall, nor do the
crested larks wander about?

Tennyson, in his "Œnone," says—
" Now the noonday quiet holds the hill ;
The grasshopper is silent in the grass ;
The lizard, with his shadow on the stone,
Rests like a shadow, and the cicala sleeps."

Virgil (Eclog. ii. 9) says—
" Nunc virides etiam occultant spineta lacertos."
" Even now the green lizards hide themselves in the hedges."

The Delights of Summer.

Idyl, vii. 135.

Πολλαὶ δ' ἄμμιν ὕπερθε κατὰ κρατὸς δονέοντο
Αἴγειροι πτελέαι τε· τὸ δ' ἐγγύθεν ἱερὸν ὕδωρ
Νυμφᾶν ἐξ ἄντροιο κατειβόμενον κελάρυσδε.
Τοὶ δὲ ποτὶ σκιεραῖς ὀροδαμνίσιν αἰθαλιῶνες
Τέττιγες λαλαγεῦντες ἔχον πόνον· ἁ δ' ὀλολυγὼν
Τηλόθεν ἐν πυκινῇσι βάτων τρύζεσκεν ἀκάνθαις.
Ἀειδον κόρυδοι καὶ ἀκανθίδες, ἔστενε τρυγών.
Πωτῶντο ξουθαὶ περὶ πίδακας ἀμφὶ μέλισσαι.
Πάντ' ὦσδεν θέρεος μάλα πίονος, ὦσδε δ' ὀπώρης.
Ὄχναι μὲν πὰρ ποσσί, παρὰ πλευρῇσι δὲ μάλα
Δαψιλέως ἄμμιν ἐκυλίνδετο· τοὶ δ' ἐκέχυντο
Ὅρπακες βραβύλοισι καταβρίθοντες ἔρασδε.

And from aloft, overhead, were waving to and fro poplars and
elms ; and near by, a sacred stream kept murmuring, as it flowed
from a cavern of the nymphs ; and the bright cicalas on the
shady branches kept laboriously chirping ; while, in the distance,
amidst the thick thorn bushes, the thrush was warbling. Tufted
larks and goldfinches were singing ; the turtledove was cooing ;
tawny bees were humming round about the fountains ; everything
was redolent of golden summer, and redolent of fruit time.
Pears, indeed, at our feet, and by our sides, apples were rolling
for us in abundance ; and the boughs hung plentifully, weighed
down to the ground, with damsons.

See (Lat.) Country pleasures

Joy at the Approach of a Beloved.

Idyl, viii. 41.

Παντᾷ ἔαρ, παντᾷ δὲ νομοί, παντᾷ δὲ γάλακτος
Οὔθατα πλήθουσιν, καὶ τὰ νέα τρέφεται,
Ἔνθ' ἁ καλὰ παῖς ἐπινίσσεται· αἰ δ' ἂν ἀφέρπῃ,
Χὠ ποιμὰν ξηρὸς τηνόθι, χαὶ βοτάναι.

Everywhere it is spring, everywhere are pastures, and everywhere milkful udders are swelling, and the lambkins are suckled at the approach of my fair maiden ; but should she depart, both shepherd and herbage are withered there.

Virgil (Eclog. vii. 59) speaks much in the same way—
"Phyllidis adventu nostræ nemus omne virebit ;
Jupiter et læto descendet plurimus imbri."

"At the approach of our Phyllis the whole grove will put forth its leaves, and the æther will send down an abundant shower that gives joy to the fields."

And again (55)—
"Omnia nunc rident ; at si formosus Alexis
Montibus his abeat, videas et flumina sicca "

" All things now smile ; but if the fair Alexis depart from these mouutains, thou wouldst see even the rivers dry up."

Pope (Past. i. 69) says— .
" All nature mourns, the skies relent in showers,
Hushed are the birds, and closed the drooping flowers ;
If Delia smile, the flowers begin to spring,
The skies to brighten, and the birds to sing."

THE SONG OF THE BELOVED.

Idyl, viii. 81.

Ἀδύ τι τὸ στόμα τοι, καὶ ἐφίμερος, ὦ Δάφνι, φωνά·
Κρέσσον μελπομένω τεῦ ἀκουέμεν ἢ μέλι λείχεν.

Sweet is thy mouth, and sweetest tones awake from thy lips, Daphnis. I would rather hear thee sing than suck the honeycomb.

Plautus (Casin. ii. 8, 21) says—
" Ut, quia te tango, mel mihi videor lingere ! "

" How I seem to sip honey because I touch thee ! "

This idea is found in the Song of Solomon (iv. 11)—" Thy lips, O my spouse, drop as the honeycomb ; honey and milk are under thy tongue."

" BIRDS OF A FEATHER FLOCK TOGETHER."

Idyl, ix. 31.

Τέττιξ μὲν τέττιγι φίλος, μύρμακι δὲ μύρμαξ,
Ἴρηκες δ' ἴρηξιν· ἐμὶν δ' ἁ Μῶσα καὶ ᾠδά
Τᾶς μοι πᾶς εἴη πλεῖος δόμος· οὔτε γὰρ ὕπνος,
Οὔτ' ἔαρ ἐξαπίνας γλυκερώτερον, οὔτε μελίσσαις
Ἄνθεα, ὅσσον ἐμὶν Μῶσαι φίλαι.

Cicala is dear to cicala, ant loves ant, hawks hawk ; but me the muse and song enchant. Of this may my house be full ; for neither sleep nor spring suddenly appearing is more sweet, nor flowers to bees, than the presence of the Muses to me.

So Ecclesiasticus (xiii. 6) we find—" All flesh consorteth according to kind, and a man will cleave to his like ; the birds will return to their like."

And Pope—
> " Not bubbling fountains to the thirsty swain,
> Not balmy sleep to labourers faint with pain,
> Not showers to larks, or sunshine to the bee,
> Are half so charming as thy sight to me."

REAPERS.

Idyl, x. 50.

Ἄρχεσθαι δ' ἀμῶντες, ἐγειρομένῳ κορυδαλλῷ,
Καὶ λήγειν, εὔδοντος· ἐλινῦσαι δὲ τὸ καῦμα.

Up with the lark to reap, and cease when it goes to sleep ; rest yourself at mid-day.

Milton (L'Allegro l. 41) says—
> " To hear the lark begin his flight,
> And startle, singing, the dull night,
> From his watchtower in the skies,
> Till the dappled dawn doth rise."

SIMILITUDES.

Idyl, xii. 3.

Ὅσσον ἔαρ χειμῶνος, ὅσον μῆλον βραβύλοιο
Ἥδιον, ὅσσον ὄϊς σφετέρης λασιωτέρη ἀρνός,
Ὅσσον παρθενικὴ προφέρει τριγάμοιο γυναικός,
Ὅσσον ἐλαφροτέρη μόσχου νεβρός, ὅσσον ἀηδὼν
Συμπάντων λιγύφωνος ἀοιδοτάτη πετεηνῶν·
Τόσσον ἔμ' εὔφρηνας σὺ φανείς· σκιερὴν δ' ὑπὸ φηγὸν
Ἡελίου φρύγοντος ὁδοιπόρος ἔδραμον ὥς τις.

As much as spring is more delightful than winter, as much as the apple than the sloe, as much as the sheep is more woolly than its lambkin, as much as a virgin is better than a thrice-wed dame, as much as a fawn is nimbler than a calf, as much as a nightingale surpasses in song all feathered kind, so much does thy longed-for presence cheer my mind ; to thee I hasten as the travellers to the shady beech, when the fierce sun blazes.

Pope (Past. iii. 43) says—
> " Not bubbling fountains to the thirsty swain,
> Not balmy sleep to labourers faint with pain,
> Not showers to larks, nor sunshine to the bee,
> Are half so charming as thy sight to me."

Drummond of Hawthornden says—
> " Cool shades to pilgrims, whom hot glances burn,
> Are not so pleasing as thy safe return."

USE OF WEALTH TO THE WISE.

Idyl, xvi. 22.

Δαιμόνιοι, τί δὲ κέρδος ὁ μυρίος ἔνδοθι χρυσὸς
Κείμενος ; οὐχ ἅδε πλούτου φρονέουσιν ὄνασις·

Ἀλλὰ.τὸ μὲν ψυχᾷ, τὸ δὲ καὶ τινι δοῦναι ἀοιδῶν·
Πολλοὺς δ' εὖ ἔρξαι παῶν, πολλοὺς δὲ καὶ ἄλλων
Ἀνθρώπων· αἰεὶ δὲ θεοῖς ἐπιβώμια ῥέζειν·
Μηδὲ ξεινοδόκον κάκον ἔμμεναι, ἀλλὰ τραπέζᾳ
Μειλίξαντ' ἀποπέμψαι, ἐπὰν ἐθέλῃτι νέεσθαι·
Μουσάων δὲ μάλιστα τίειν ἱερούς ὑποφήτας
Ὄφρα ἀκλεῆς μύρηαι ἐπὶ ψυχρῷ Ἀχέροντος.

Fools! what boots the gold hid within doors in untold heaps?
Not so the truly wise employ their wealth ; some give part to
their own enjoyment, some to the bard should be assigned, part
should be employed to do good to our kinsmen and others of mankind, and even to offer sacrifices to the gods ; not to be a bad host,
guests should be welcome to come and go whenever they choose,
but chiefly to honour the sacred interpreters of the Muses, that
you may live to fame when life is done.

THE AVARICIOUS.

Idyl, xvi. 60.

Ἀλλ' ἴσος γὰρ ὁ μόχθος, ἐπ' ἀόνι κύματα μετρεῖν,
Ὄσσ' ἄνεμος χέρσονδε μετὰ γλαυκᾶς ἁλὸς ὠθεῖ,
Ἢ ὕδατι νίζειν θολεράν ἰοειδεῖ πλίνθον,
Καὶ φιλοκερδείᾳ βεβλαμμένον ἄνδρα παρελθεῖν.
Χαιρέτω ὅστις τοῖος· ἀνήριθμος δὲ οἱ εἴη
Αργυρος· αἰεὶ δὲ πλεόνων ἔχοι ἵμερος αὐτόν.
Αὐτὰρ ἐγὼν τιμάν τε καὶ ἀνθρώπων φιλότητα
Πολλῶν ἡμιόνων τε καὶ ἵππων πρόσθεν ἑλοίμαν.

It would be as great a toil to count the waves upon the shore,
when the wind drives them to land along the surface of the green
sea, or to wash the dirty brick clean with violet-coloured water, as
to overreach the man who is a slave to avarice. Away with such
an one! let him have silver without end, yet always let the desire
of a greater store possess him. But I should prefer the respect
and esteem of men to myriads of mules and horses.
The idea in Jeremiah (xiii. 23) is somewhat similar—" Can the Ethiopian
change his skin, or the leopard his spots ? "

JOYS OF PEACE.

Idyl, xvi. 90.

Αγροὺς δ' ἐργάζοιντο τεθαλότας· αἴ τ' ἀνάριθμοι
Μήλων χιλιάδες βοτάναις διαπιανθεῖσαι
Ἀν πεδίον βληχοῖντο, βόες δ' ἀγελαδὸν ἐς αὖλιν
Ερχόμεναι σκνιπαῖον ἐπισπεύδοιεν ὁδίταν·
Νειοὶ δ' ἐκπόνεοιντο ποτὶ σπόρον, ἁνίκα τέττιξ,

Ποιμένας ἐνδίους πεφυλαγμένος, ἔνδοθ, δένδρων
'Αχεῖ ἐν ἀκρεμόνεσσιν· ἀράχνια δ' εἰς ὁπλ' ἀράχναι
Λεπτὰ διαστήσαιντο, βοᾶς δ' ἔτι μηδ' ὄνομ' εἴη.

And, oh! that they might till rich fields, and that unnumbered
sheep and fat might bleat cheerily through the plains, and that
oxen coming in herds to the stalls should urge on the traveller by
twilight. And oh! that the fallow lands might be broken up for
sowing, when the cicala, sitting on his tree, watches the shepherd
in the open day, and chirps on the topmost spray; that spiders
may draw their fine webs over martial arms, and not even the
name of the battle-cry be heard.

Virgil (Eclog. ii. 21) says—
   "Mille meæ Siculis errant in montibus agnæ."
"A thousand of my lambs wander on the Sicilian mountains."

In Psalms (lxv. 13) we find—"The pastures are clothed with flocks; the
valleys also are covered with corn; they shout for joy, they also sing;" and
(cxliv. 13)—" That our garners may be full, affording all manner of store;
that our sheep may bring forth thousands and ten thousands in our
streets." It is like to Isaiah (ii. 4)—"Nation shall not lift sword against
nation, neither shall they learn war any more."

"WHY HOP YE SO, YE HIGH HILLS?"
Idyl, xvii. 64.

Κόως δ' ὀλόλυξεν ἰδοῖσα,
Φᾶ δε, καθαπτομένα βρέφεος χείρεσσι φίλαισιν.

And Cos, when she beheld him, broke forth with jubilant
rapture, and said, touching the infant with fondling hands.

This resembles the idea in Psalms (cxiv. 4)—"The mountains skipped like
rams, and the little hills like lambs."

JOY BREAKING FORTH IN DANCING.
Idyl, xviii. 7.

'Αειδον δ' ἄρα πᾶσαι ἐς ἓν μέλος ἐγκροτέοισαι
Ποσσὶ περιπλέκτοις, περὶ δ' ἴαχε δῶμ' ὑμεναίῳ.

And they began to sing, all beating time with cadence with
many twinkling feet, and the house was ringing round with
hymenean hymn.

In Gray's "Progress of Poesy" we find —
   "Thee the voice, the dance, obey,
   Tempered to thy warbled lay,
   O'er Idalia's velvet green
   The rosy-crowned Loves are seen
      On Cytherea's day,
   With antic sports, and blue-eyed pleasures,
   Frisking light in frolic measures;
   Now pursuing, now retreating,
      Now in circling troops they meet;
   To brisk notes in cadence beating,
      Glance their many twinkling feet."

Contrast of Morn and Night.

Idyl, xviii. 26.

'Ἀὼς ἀντέλλοισα καλὸν διέφαινε πρόσωπον,
Πότνια νὺξ ἅτε, λευκὸν ἔαρ χειμῶνος ἀνέντος,
*Ὧδε καὶ ἁ χρυσέα *Ελενα διεφαίνετ' ἐν ἁμῖν.

As rising morn shows its fair countenance against the dusky night,—as the clear spring, when winter's gloom is gone,—so also the golden Helen was wont to shine out amongst us.

So in Solomon's Song (vi. 10) we find—"Who is she that looketh forth as the morning, fair as the moon, clear as the sun, and terrible as an army with banners ? "

In Campbell's " Gertrude of Wyoming " we have—

" A boy   .   .   .   .   .   .
Led by his dusky guide, like morning brought by night."

And again in Solomon's Song (ii. 11)—" For lo, the winter is past, the rain is over and gone."

" Love that 's in Her E'e."

Idyl, xviii. 37.

'Ὡς 'Ελένα, τὰς πάντες ἐπ' ὄμμασιν ἵμεροι ἐντί.

As Helen, in whose eyes the light of love lies.

Burns says—

" The kind love that 's in her e'e."

A Loving Pair.

Idyl, xviii. 54.

Εὑδετ' ἐς ἀλλάλων στέρνον φιλότητα πνέοντες
Καὶ πόθον. *Εγρεσθαι δὲ πρὸς ἀῶ μὴ 'πιλάθησθε.

Sleep on, happy pair, breathing into each other's bosom love and desire, and forget not to rise towards morning.

In Solomon's Song (viii. 3) we have—" His left hand should be under my head, and his right hand should embrace me. I charge you, O daughters of Jerusalem, that ye stir not up nor awake my love, until he pleases."

My Lips drop as the Honeycomb.

Idyl, xx. 26.

'Εκ στομάτων δὲ
*Ερρεέ μοι φωνὰ γλυκερωτέρα ἢ μελικήρω.

From my lips flowed tones more sweet than from a honeycomb.

In Solomon's Song (iv. 11) we find—" Thy lips, O my spouse, drop as the honeycomb ; honey and milk are under thy tongue."

NECESSITY THE MOTHER OF INVENTION.

Idyl, xxi. 1.

Ἁ πενία, Διόφαντε, μόνα τὰς τέχνας ἐγείρει·
Αὐτὰ τῶ μόχθοιο διδάσκαλος· οὐδὲ γὰρ εὕδειν
Ἀνδράσιν ἐργατίναισι κακαὶ παρέχοντι μέριμναι.
Κἂν ὀλίγον νυκτός τις ἐπιψαύσῃσι, τὸν ὕπνον
Αἰφνίδιον θορυβεῦσιν ἐφιστάμεναι μελιδῶναι.

Need alone, Diophantus, imparts the knowledge of arts, and is
the mistress of labour, for corroding cares take everything from
toiling man, and if soft slumbers refresh his eyelids during the
night, suddenly some anxiety stealing in disturbs him.

See (**Lat.**) Industry ; The belly.

DREAMS.

Idyl, xxi. 44.

Καὶ γὰρ ἐν ὕπνοις
Πᾶσα κύων ἄρτως μαντεύεται· ἰχθύα κῆγών.

For in sleep every dog dreams of food, and I, a fisherman, of
fish.

SYLVAN SCENE.

Idyl, xxii. 36.

Παντοίην δ' ἐν ὄρει θηεύμενοι ἄγριον ὕλην,
Εὗρον ἀένναον κράναν ὑπὸ λισσάδι πέτρῃ
Ὕδατι πεπληθυῖαν ἀκηράτῳ· αἱ δ' ὑπένερθεν
Λάλλαι κρυστάλλῳ ἠδ' ἀργύρῳ ἐνδάλλοντο
Ἐκ βυθοῦ· ὑψηλαὶ δ' ἐπεφύκεσαν ἀγχόθι πεῦκαι
Λεῦκαί τε πλάτανοί τε καὶ ἀκρόκομοι κυπάρισσοι,
Ἄνθεά τ' εὐώδη, λασίαις φίλα ἔργα μελίσσαις,
Ὅσσ' ἔαρος λήγοντος ἐπιβρύει ἂν λειμῶνας.

They spying on a mountain a wild wood of various kinds of
trees, found under a smooth rock a perennial spring, filled with
clear water, and the pebbles below shone like crystal or silver from
the depths ; near the spot had grown tall pines, poplars, plane
trees, cypresses with leafy tops, and odorous flowers, pleasant
work for hairy bees, flowers as many as bloom in the meads when
spring is ending.

Virgil (Æn. i. 164) seems to have copied this—

"Tum silvis scena coruscis
Desuper horrentique atrum nemus imminet umbrâ ;
Fronte sub adversâ scopulis pendentibus antrum ;
Intus aquæ dulces, vivoque sedilia saxo
Nympharum domus."

"Then a canopy of woods chequered with light and shade and gloomy grove, overhangs with awful shade ; under the opposite precipitous cliff is a cave in the overhanging rocks ; within is a spring of fresh water and seats of natural rock, the abode of the Nymphs."

The Despised Lover's Resolution.

Idyl, xxiii. 22.

'Αλλὰ βαδίζω
Ἔνθα τύ μευ κατέκρινας· ὅπη λόγος ἦμεν ἀταρπὸν
Ξυνάν, τοῖσιν ἐρῶσι τὸ φάρμακον, ἔνθα τὸ λᾶθος.
'Αλλὰ καὶ ἢν ὅλου αὐτὸ λαβὼν ποτὶ χεῖλος ἀμέλξω,
Οὐδέ κε τὼς σβέσσω τὸν ἐμὸν πόθον.

Now I go whither thou hast sentenced me, whither, 'tis said, the road is common, where oblivion is the remedy for those that love. But could I drink it all, not even thus could I slake my passionate longing.

Virgil (Æn. vi. 714) says—
"Lethæi ad fluminis undam,
Securos latices et longa oblivia potant."

"They drink at the waters of Lethe cups that relieve from care, and causing deep oblivion."

And Song of Solomon (viii. 6) says—"Love is strong as death ; jealousy is cruel as the grave ; the coals thereof are coals of fire, which hath a most vehement flame. Many waters cannot quench love, neither can the floods drown it."

Beauty fades.

Idyl, xxiii. 28.

Καὶ τὸ ῥόδον καλόν ἐστι, καὶ ὁ χρόνος αὐτὸ μαραίνει·
Καὶ τὸ ἴον καλὸν ἐστιν ἐν εἴαρι καὶ ταχὺ γηρᾷ·
Λευκὸν τὸ κρίνον ἐστι, μαραίνεται ἀνίκα πίπτει·
'Α δὲ χιὼν λευκὰ καὶ τάκεται ἀνίκα παχθῆ·
Καὶ κάλλος καλὸν ἐστι τὸ παιδικὸν ἀλλ' ὀλίγον ζῇ.

The rose is beauteous, but time causes it to fade ; the violet is fair in spring, and quickly grows out of date ; the lily is white, fading when it droops ; the snow is white, melting at the very time when it is congealed, and beautiful is the bloom of youth, but it lasts only for a short time.

See (Lat.) Passage of time.

The Ills of Life must be borne.

Idyl, xxiv. 70.

Οὐκ ἔστιν ἀλύξαι
'Ανθρώποις ὅ, τι μοῖρα κατὰ κλωστῆρος ἐπείγει.

Those ills which fate determines, man must bear.

"The Wolf shall dwell with the Lamb."

Idyl, xxiv. 84.

Ἔσται δὴ τοῦτ᾽ ἆμαρ, ὁπανίκα νεβρὸν ἐν εὐνᾷ
Καρχαρόδων σίνεσθαι ἰδὼν λύκος οὐκ ἐθελήσει.

In truth the day will come when the sharp-toothed wolf, having
seen the kid in his lair, shall not wish to harm it.

This is very much the same as in Isaiah (xi. 6)—"The wolf also shall
dwell with the lamb, and the leopard shall lie down with the kid ; and the
calf, and the young lion, and the fatling together ; and a little child shall
lead them."

Man stands in Need of Man.

Idyl, xxv. 50.

Ἄλλου δ᾽ ἄλλον ἔθηκε θεός γ᾽ ἐπιδεύεα φωτῶν.

For Heaven's eternal wisdom has decreed
That man of man should ever stand in need.

Love gives Value even to Small Gifts.

Idyl, xxviii. 25.

Ἦ μεγάλα χάρις
Δώρῳ ξὺν ὀλίγῳ· πάντα δὲ τιμᾶντα τὰ πὰρ φίλων.

For love the smallest gift commends ;
All things are valued by our friends.

See (Lat.) Gifts we like, when we prize the giver.

Wine and Truth.

Idyl, xxix. 1.

Οἶνος, ὦ φίλε παῖ, λέγεται, καὶ ἀλάθεα.

Wine, dear youth, and truth is the proverb.

See (Lat.) Wine and its advantages.

THEOGNIS.

BORN ABOUT B.C. 570.—DIED ABOUT B.C. 490.

THEOGNIS, a native of Megara, of whose personal history little is
known, except that he belonged to the Oligarchical party in the

state, and shared its fate. He was a noble by birth, and all his sympathies were with the nobles. In one of the revolutions there was a division of the property of the nobles, in which he lost his all.

LIVE WITH THE GOOD.

Eleg. 35.

Ἐσθλῶν μὲν γὰρ ἀπ' ἐσθλὰ μαθήσεαι· ἢν δὲ κακοῖσιν
Συμμίσγῃς, ἀπολεῖς καὶ τὸν ἐόντα νόον.

From the good thou shalt learn good, but if thou associate with the bad, thou wilt lose even the sense thou possessest.

SPEAK UNRESERVEDLY TO FEW.

Eleg. 73.

Πρῆξιν μηδὲ φίλοισιν ὅμως ἀνακοινέο πᾶσιν,
Παῦροί τοι πολλῶν πιστὸν ἔχουσι νόον.

Communicate not to all friends alike thy affairs ; few out of a number have a trusty mind.

So Shakespeare ("Henry VIII." act ii. sc. 1)—
  " Where you are liberal of your loves and counsels,
  Be sure you be not loose ; for those you make friends
  And give your hearts to, when they once perceive
  The least rub in your fortunes, fall away
  Like water from ye."

THE HYPOCRITE.

Eleg. 87.

Μή μ' ἔπεσιν μὲν στέργε, νόον δ' ἔχε καὶ φρένας ἄλλῃ,
Εἴ με φιλεῖς καί σοι πιστὸς ἔνεστι νόος.

Delude me not with empty phrase, having your mind and heart elsewhere, if thou lovest me, and there be in thee a faithful mind.

So Psalm (xxviii. 3)—" Which speak peace to their neighbour, but mischief is in their hearts ;" (lxii. 4)—" They bless with their mouth, but they curse inwardly."

KINDNESS TO THOSE OF LOW DEGREE.

Eleg. 105.

Δειλοὺς εὖ ἔρδοντι ματαιοτάτη χάρις ἐστίν·
Ἴσον καὶ σπείρειν πόντον ἁλὸς πολιῆς.
Οὔτε γὰρ ἂν πόντον σπείρων βαθὺ λήϊον ἀμῷς,
Οὔτε κακοὺς εὖ δρῶν εὖ πάλιν ἀντιλάβοις.

Ἄπληστον γὰρ ἔχουσι κακοὶ νόον, ἢν δ᾽ ἐν ἁμάρτῃς,
Τῶν πρόσθεν πάντων ἐκκέχυται φιλότης.
Οἱ δ᾽ ἀγαθοὶ τὸ μέγιστον ἐπαυρίσκουσι παθόντες,
Μνῆμα δ᾽ ἔχουσ᾽ ἀγαθῶν καὶ χάριν ἐξοπίσω.

It is the vainest task to bestow kindness on men of low degree,
the same as to sow the hoary-foaming sea : since neither by sowing
the deep with scattered grain, wouldst thou reap a rich crop, nor
by doing kindness to the mean, wouldst thou be repaid. For the
mean have an insatiate spirit ; if thou refusest a request, gratitude for all former favours vanishes. While gallant hearts enjoy
in the highest degree kindnesses, retaining the memory of good
deeds and gratitude in after times.

So Shakespeare ("Timon of Athens," act iii. sc. 1)—
" Thou disease of a friend, and not himself !
Has friendship such a faint and milky heart,
It turns in less than two nights? This slave,
Unto his honour has my lord's meat in him."

TRENCHER-FRIENDS.

Eleg. 115.

Πολλοί τοι πόσιος καὶ βρώσιός εἰσιν ἑταῖροι,
᾽Εν δὲ σπουδαίῳ πρήγματι παυρότεροι.
Κιβδήλου δ᾽ ἀνδρὸς γνῶναι χαλεπώτερον οὐδὲν,
Κύρν᾽, οὐδ᾽ εὐλαβὶης ἐστὶ περὶ πλέονος,
Χρυσοῦ κιβδήλοιο καὶ ἀργύρου ἀνσχετὸς ἄτη,
Κύρνε, καὶ ἐξευρεῖν ῥάδιον ἀνδρὶ σοφῷ.
Εἰ δὲ φίλου νόος ἀνδρὸς ἐνὶ στήθεσσι λελήθῃ
Ψυδρὸς ἐὼν, δόλιον δ᾽ ἐν φρεσὶν ἦτορ ἔχῃ,
Τοῦτο θεὸς κιβδηλότατον ποίησε βροτοῖσιν,
Καὶ γνῶναι πάντων τοῦτ᾽ ἀνιηρότατον.
Οὐ γὰρ ἐν εἰδείης ἀνδρὸς νόον οὔτε γυναικός,
Πρὶν πειρηθείης ὥσπερ ὑποζυγίου.

Many are trencher-friends, few adhere to thee in matters
of difficulty. Nothing is harder than to detect a soul of base alloy,
O Cyrnus, and nothing of more value than caution. The loss of
alloyed gold and silver may be borne ; it is easy for a shrewd
intellect to discover its real quality ; but if a friend's heart be
secretly untrue, and a treacherous heart be within him, this is the
falsest thing that God has made for man, and this is hardest of all
to discover. For thou canst not know man's mind, nor woman's
either, before thou hast proved it, like as of a beast of burden.

So Shakespeare ("Timon," act iii. sc. 6)—
" Live loath'd, and long,
Most smiling, smooth, detested parasites ;
You fools of fortune, trencher-friends, time's flies."

See (Lat., Fr.) Summer friends ; Friends.

VAIN THOUGHTS OF MEN.

Eleg. 141.

Ἄνθρωποι δὲ μάταια νομίζομεν, εἰδότες οὐδέν·
Θεοὶ δὲ κατὰ σφέτερον πάντα τελοῦσι νόον.

We men have vain thoughts, knowing nothing; while the gods accomplish all things after their own mind.

So Psalm (xciv. 11)—"The Lord knoweth the thoughts of man, that they are vanity;" (xxxix. 6)—"Man walketh in a vain show."

A LITTLE GOTTEN HONESTLY.

Eleg. 145.

Βούλεο δ' εὐσεβέων ὀλίγοις σὺν χρήμασι οἰκεῖν
Ἢ πλουτεῖν ἀδίκως χρήματα πασάμενος,
Ἐν δὲ δικαιοσύνῃ συλλήβδην πᾶσ' ἀρετή 'στιν,
Πᾶς δέ τ' ἀνὴρ ἀγαθὸς Κύρνε δίκαιος ἐών.
Χρήματα μὲν δαίμων καὶ παγκάκῳ ἀνδρὶ δίδωσι,
Κύρν'· ἀρετῆς δ' ὀλίγοις ἀνδράσι μοῖρ' ἕπεται.

Prefer to live piously on small means than to be rich on what has been gotten unjustly. Every virtue is included in the idea of justice, as every just man is good. Fortune gives wealth indeed to the worst of men, but virtue is found in few.

So Proverbs (xv. 16)—"Better is little with the fear of the Lord than great treasure and trouble therewith;" and Psalm (xxxvii. 14)—"A little that a righteous man hath is better than the riches of many wicked."

A BEGGAR ON HORSEBACK.

Eleg. 153.

Τίκτει τοι κόρος ὕβριν, ὅταν κακῷ ὄλβος ἔπηται
Ἀνθρώπῳ, καὶ ὅτῳ μὴ νόος ἄρτιος ᾖ.

Wealth nurses insolence, when it comes to a man of paltry spirit, and whose mind is not sound.

So Shakespeare ("Henry VI.," part ii. act ii. sc. 4)—
"Beggars mounted run their horse to death."

"BOAST NOT THYSELF OF TO-MORROW."

Eleg. 159.

Οἶδε γὰρ οὐδεὶς
Ἀνθρώπων ὅ,τι νὺξ χἠμέρη ἀνδρὶ τελεῖ.

For no man knows what a night or a day may bring forth.

So Proverbs (xxvii. 1)—"Boast not thyself to-morrow; for thou knowest not what a day may bring forth."

See (Lat.) Uncertainty of life.

LUST OF RICHES.

Eleg. 227.

Πλούτου δ' οὐδὲν τέρμα πεφασμένον ἀνθρώποισιν·
Οἳ γὰρ νῦν ἡμῶν πλεῖστον ἔχουσι νόον,
Διπλάσιον σπεύδουσι. τίς ἂν κορέσειεν ἅπαντας ;
Χρήματά τοι θνητοῖς γίγνεται ἀφροσύνη.

There is no limit to riches among men ; for those of us who have most, strive after twice as much. Who could satisfy all? Riches truly to mortals become folly.

So Ecclesiastes (v. 10)—" He that loveth silver shall not be satisfied with silver ; nor he that loveth abundance with increase ;" and Psalm (xxxix. 6) —" Surely they are disquieted in vain ; he heapeth up riches, and knoweth not who shall gather them."

THE LION.

Eleg. 293.

Οὐδὲ λέων αἰεὶ κρέα δαίνυται, ἀλλὰ μιν ἔμπης
Καὶ κρατερόν περ ἐόνθ' αἱρεῖ ἀμηχανίη.

The lion does not always feast on flesh, but, strong though he be, anxiety for food seizes him.

So Psalm (civ. 21)—" The young lions roar after their prey, and seek their meat from God."

"THE RACE IS NOT TO THE SWIFT."

Eleg. 329.

Καὶ βραδὺς εὔβουλος εἷλεν ταχὺν ἄνδρα διώκων,
Κύρνε, σὺν ἰθείῃ θεῶν δίκῃ ἀθανάτων.

Even the slow man, if possessed of wisdom, has overtaken the swift in the pursuit, with the aid of the straightforward justice of the immortal gods.

So Ecclesiastes (ix. 11)—" I returned and saw under the sun that the race is not to the swift, nor the battle to the strong."

RESTRAIN THY TONGUE.

Eleg. 365.

Ἴσχε νόον, γλώσσῃ δὲ τὸ μείλιχον αἰὲν ἐπέστω·
Δειλῶν τοι τελέθει καρδίη ὀξυτέρη.

Restrain thyself; let honeyed words ever attend thy tongue; the heart indeed of men of low degree is more sharp than is right.

So Proverbs (xiii. 3)—" He that keepeth his mouth keepeth his life ;" (xxxi. 6)—" In her tongue is the law of kindness ;" and Shakespeare (" Hamlet," act i. sc. 3)—
" Give thy thoughts no tongue, nor any unproportioned thought his act."

The Righteous and Wicked treated equally.

Eleg. 377.

Πῶς δή σευ Κρονίδη τολμᾷ νόος ἄνδρας ἀλιτρούς
'Εν ταὐτῇ μοίρῃ τόν τε δίκαιον ἔχειν,
῍Ην τ' ἐπὶ σωφροσύνην τρεφθῇ νόος, ἥν τε πρὸς ὕβριν
'Ανθρώπων ἀδίκοις ἔργμασι πειθομένων ;

How, pray, son of Saturn, canst thou reconcile it to thy sense
of right and wrong to treat the wicked and the good in the same
way, whether thou turnest thy attention to the wise or whether
to the insolence of men, who yield to unjust deeds ?

So Psalm (lxxiii. 3-5, 11-12)—" For I was envious at the foolish, when I saw
the prosperity of the wicked. For there are no bands in their death ; but their
strength is firm   They are not in trouble as other men ; neither are they
plagued like other men.   And they say, How doth God know ? and is there
knowledge in the Most High ?   Behold, these are the ungodly, who prosper
in the world ; they increase in riches."

Judicial Blindness.

Eleg. 405.

Καὶ οἱ ἔθηκε δοκεῖν, ἃ μὲν ᾖ κακά, ταῦτ' ἀγάθ' εἶναι
Εὐμαρέως, ἃ δ' ἂν ᾖ χρήσιμα, ταῦτα κακά.

Fortune is wont to make him regard easily what is bad to be
good and what is good to be bad.

So Isaiah (v. 20)—" Woe unto them that call evil good, and good evil;
that put darkness for light, and light for darkness ; that put bitter for sweet,
and sweet for bitter ! "

"Keep the Door of my Lips."

Eleg. 421.

Πολλοῖς ἀνθρώπων γλώσσῃ θύραι οὐκ ἐπίκεινται
'Αρμόδιαι, καί σφιν πόλλ' ἀμέλητα μέλει.

Many men have not well-fitting doors on their tongues, and they
care for many things, which it would be better to leave alone.

So Psalm (cxli. 3)—" Set a watch, O Lord, before my mouth ; keep the
door of my lips."

Better not to be Born.

Eleg. 425.

Πάντων μὲν μὴ φῦναι ἐπιχθονίοισιν ἄριστον
Μηδ' ἐσιδεῖν αὐγὰς ὀξέος ἠελίου,
Φύντα δ' ὅπως ὤκιστα πύλας 'Αΐδαο περῆσαι
Καὶ κεῖσθαι πολλὴν γῆν ἐπαμησάμενον.

Of all things, it is best for men not to be born, nor to see the rays of the bright sun ; the next best is speedily to die and lie beneath a load of earth.

See (Lat.) Better not to be born.

"Grapes of Thorns."
Eleg. 537.

Οὔτε γὰρ ἐκ σκίλλης ῥόδα φύεται οὐδ' ὑάκινθος,
Οὔτε ποτ' ἐκ δούλης τέκνον ἐλευθέριον.

For neither roses nor the hyacinth spring from the squill, no, nor ever a high-spirited child from a bond-woman.

So Matthew (vii. 16)—"Do men gather grapes of thorns or figs of thistles?" and Horace (Od. iv. 4, 31)—

"Nec imbellem feroces
Progenerant aquilæ columbam."
"Nor do fierce eagles produce the timorous dove."

Riches not carried to the Grave.
Eleg. 725.

Τὰ γὰρ περιώσια πάντα
Χρήματ' ἔχων οὐδεὶς ἔρχεται εἰς ᾿Αΐδεω,
Οὐδ' ἂν ἄποινα διδοὺς θάνατον φύγοι οὐδὲ βαρείας
Νούσους οὐδὲ κακὸν γῆρας ἐπερχόμενον.

For no one descends to Hades with his immense wealth, nor can he by paying ransom escape death, or heavy diseases, or wretched old age creeping upon him.

So Psalm (xlix. 17)—"For when he dieth he shall carry nothing away ; his glory shall not descend after him."

See (Lat.) Life of man.

The Prosperity of the Ungodly.
Eleg. 749.

᾿Ανὴρ ἄδικος καὶ ἀτάσθαλος, οὔτε τευ ἀνδρὸς
Οὔτε τευ ἀθανάτων μῆνιν ἀλευόμενος,
῾Υβρίζῃ πλούτῳ κεκορημένος, οἱ δὲ δίκαιοι
Τρύχωνται χαλεπῇ τειρόμενοι πενίῃ ;

Should a wicked and infatuated wretch, who cares for neither God nor man, be glutted with wealth, while the good are destroyed, ground down by pinching poverty ?

So Psalm (lxxiii. 3-5, 11-12)—"For I was envious at the foolish, when I saw the prosperity of the wicked. For there are no bands in their death ; but their strength is firm. They are not in trouble as other men ; neither are they plagued like other men. And they say, How doth God know ? and is there knowledge in the Most High ? Behold, these are the ungodly, who prosper in the world ; they increase in riches."

Youth passes quickly.

Eleg. 985.

Αἶψα γὰρ ὥστε νόημα παρέρχεται ἀγλαὸς ἥβη·
Οὐδ' ἵππων ὁρμὴ γίγνεται ὠκυτέρη.

For bright youth passes quickly as thought, nor is the speed of coursers fleeter.

"The Godly Man ceaseth."

Eleg. 1139.

Ὅρκοι δ' οὐκέτι πιστοὶ ἐν ἀνθρώποισι δίκαιοι,
Οὐδὲ θεοὺς οὐδεὶς ἅζεται ἀθανάτους.
Εὐσεβέων δ' ἀνδρῶν γένος ἔφθιτο, οὐδὲ θέμιστας
Οὐκέτι γιγνώσκουσ' οὐδὲ μὲν εὐσεβίας.

Just oaths are no longer in existence among men, neither does any one reverence the immortal gods. The race of godly men has vanished, nor do they any longer know laws ; no, nor holy lives.
So Psalm (xii. 1)—"Help, Lord ; for the godly man ceaseth ; for the faithful fail from among the children of men."

"Weep with Them that Weep."

Eleg. 1217.

Μή ποτε πὰρ κλαίοντα καθεζόμενοι γελάσωμεν,
Τοῖς αὐτῶν ἀγαθοῖς Κύρν' ἐπιτερπόμενοι.

Never let us sit down and laugh beside those who weep, O Cyrnus, taking pleasure in our own advantages.
So Romans (xii. 15)—"Rejoice with them that do rejoice, and weep with them that weep."

THUCYDIDES.

BORN B.C. 471—WAS ALIVE B.C. 403.

THUCYDIDES, the celebrated historian of Athens, was the son of Olorus and Hegesipyle, through whom he claimed kindred with the family of Miltiades, the conqueror of Marathon. He is supposed to have been a pupil of Antiphon, of Rhamnus, and of Anaxagoras. At all events, as he was living in the centre of

Greek civilisation, he would, no doubt, receive all the advantages which Athens, then in the acme of its intellectual fame, was able to bestow. We have no trustworthy evidence that he distinguished himself as an orator; but he was in command of a small squadron at Thasos, on his way to the relief of Amphipolis, B.C. 424, then besieged by the Lacedæmonians. He arrived too late at the scene of action; and, in consequence of this failure, he became an exile, probably to avoid a severer punishment. He lived twenty years in exile, and returned to Athens about the time when Thrasybulus freed Athens. He is said to have been assassinated a short time after his return. The subject of his great work is the Peloponnesian war, which lasted from B.C. 431 to B.C. 404.

A Possession for all Times.

i. 22.

Κτῆμά τε ἐς ἀεὶ μᾶλλον ἢ ἀγώνισμα ἐς τὸ παραχρῆμα ἀκούειν ξύγκειται.

My history is presented to the public as a possession for all times, and not merely as a rhetorical display to catch the applause of my contemporaries.

The Best Security of Power.

i. 42.

Τὸ γὰρ μὴ ἀδικεῖν τοὺς ὁμοίους ἐχυρωτέρα δύναμις ἢ τῷ αὐτίκα φανερῷ ἐπαρθέντας διὰ κινδύνων τὸ πλέον ἔχειν.

For power is more firmly secured by treating our equals with justice than if, elated by present prosperity, we attempt to enlarge it at every risk.

See (Lat.) How a kingdom ought to be governed.

Expostulation with Friends.

i. 69.

Αἰτία μὲν γὰρ φίλων ἀνδρῶν ἐστιν ἁμαρτανόντων, κατηγορία δὲ ἐχθρῶν ἀδικησάντων.

Expostulation is just towards friends who have failed in their duty; accusation is to be used against enemies guilty of injustice.

Acts of Injustice, and Acts of Violence.

i. 77.

'Αδικούμενοί τε, ὡς ἔοικεν, οἱ ἄνθρωποι μᾶλλον ὀργίζονται ἢ βιαζό-
μενοι· τὸ μὲν γὰρ ἀπὸ τοῦ ἴσου δοκεῖ πλεονεκτεῖσθαι, τὸ δ' ἀπὸ τοῦ
κρείσσονος καταναγκάζεσθαι.

Mankind, as it seems, are more apt to resent acts of injustice
than acts of violence. Those that are inflicted by equals are regarded as the result of a grasping and rapacious disposition ; those
coming from superiors are submitted to as a matter of necessity.

The Present is Grievous to Subjects.

i. 77.

Τὸ παρὸν γὰρ ἀεὶ βαρὺ τοῖς ὑπηκόοις.

The present is always burdensome to subjects.

The Success of War depends very much on Money.

i. 83.

Καὶ ἔστιν ὁ πόλεμος οὐχ ὅπλων τὸ πλέον, ἀλλὰ δαπάνης, δι' ἣν τὰ
ὅπλα ὠφελεῖ, ἄλλως τε καὶ ἠπειρώταις πρὸς θαλασσίους.

The success of war is not so much dependent on arms, as on the
possession of money, by means of which arms are rendered serviceable, and more particularly so when a military power is fighting
with a naval.

See (Lat,) Money the sinews of war.

War sometimes is to be Preferred to Peace.

i. 120.

'Ανδρῶν γὰρ σωφρόνων μέν ἐστιν, εἰ μὴ ἀδικοῖντο, ἡσυχάζειν,
ἀγαθῶν δὲ ἀδικουμένους ἐκ μὲν εἰρήνης πολεμεῖν, εὖ δὲ παρασχὸν ἐκ
πολέμου πάλιν ξυμβῆναι, καὶ μήτε τῇ κατὰ πόλεμον εὐτυχίᾳ ἐπαίρεσθαι μήτε τῷ ἡσυχίῳ τῆς εἰρήνης ἡδόμενον ἀδικεῖσθαι.

It is, indeed, the part of the wise, so long as they are not injured,
to be lovers of peace. But it is the part of the brave, if they are
injured, to give up the enjoyments of peace, that they may enter
upon war ; and, as soon as they are successful, to be ready to
sheathe their swords. Thus, they ought never to allow themselves
to be too much elated by military success, nor yet to be so fond of
peace as to submit to insult.

See (Lat.) War only to be made to secure peace.

DIFFERENCE OF RESULTS IN PLANS.

i. 120.

Πολλὰ γὰρ κακῶς γνωσθέντα ἀβουλοτέρων τῶν ἐναντίων τυχόντωι
κατωρθώθη, καὶ ἔτι πλέω ἃ καλῶς δοκοῦντα βουλευθῆναι ἐς τοὐναντίον αἰσχρῶς περιέστη· ἐνθυμεῖται γὰρ οὐδεὶς ὁμοίᾳ τῇ πίστει καὶ ἔργῳ
ἐπεξέρχεται, ἀλλὰ μετ᾽ ἀσφαλείας μὲν δοξάζομεν, μετὰ δέους δὲ ἐν
τῷ ἔργῳ ἐλλείπομεν.

For many enterprises, that have been badly planned, have come
to a successful issue, from the thoughtless imprudence of those
against whom they were directed ; and a still greater number, that
have appeared to be entering on the path of victory, have come to
a disastrous end. This arises from the very different spirit with
which we devise a scheme, and put it into execution. In council,
we consult in the utmost security ; in execution, we fail from
being surrounded with dangers.

THE POOR MORE WILLING TO GIVE THE SERVICES OF THEIR
BODIES THAN THEIR MONEY.

i. 141.

Αἱ δὲ περιουσίαι τοὺς πολέμους μᾶλλον ἢ αἱ βίαιοι ἐσφοραὶ ἀνέ-
χουσι. Σώμασί τε ἑτοιμότεροι οἱ αὐτουργοὶ τῶν ἀνθρώπων ἢ χρήμασι
πολεμεῖν, τὸ μὲν πιστὸν ἔχοντες ἐκ τῶν κινδύνων κἂν περιγενέσθαι,
τὸ δὲ οὐ βέβαιον μὴ οὐ προαναλώσειν, ἄλλως τε κἂν παρὰ δόξαν,
ὅπερ εἰκός, ὁ πόλεμος αὐτοῖς μηκύνηται.

Accumulated wealth is a far surer support of war than forced
contributions from unwilling citizens. The poor, who gain their
livelihood by the sweat of their brow, are more willing to give the
services of their body in defence of their country, than to contribute from their contracted means. The former, though at some
risk, they think it possible may survive the crisis ; while the latter,
they are certain, will be gone for ever, especially if the war should
be protracted beyond expectations—a very likely event.

HOW MARITIME SUPREMACY IS TO BE ATTAINED.

i. 142.

Τὸ δὲ ναυτικὸν τέχνης ἐστίν, ὥσπερ καὶ ἄλλο τι, καὶ οὐκ ἐνδέχεται,
ὅταν τύχῃ, ἐκ παρέργου μελετᾶσθαι, ἀλλὰ μᾶλλον μηδὲν ἐκείνῳ
πάρεργον ἄλλο γίγνεσθαι.

Seamanship, and a knowledge of maritime affairs, is as much a
science as any other art. It cannot be learned by snatches, nor
can a knowledge of it be acquired except by a persisting and uninterrupted devotion to its study.

Uncertainty of War.

ii. 11.

Ἄδηλα γὰρ τὰ τῶν πολέμων καὶ ἐξ ὀλίγου τὰ πολλὰ καὶ δι' ὀργῆς αἱ ἐπιχειρήσεις γίγνονται· πολλάκις τε τὸ ἔλασσον πλῆθος δεδιὸς ἄμεινον ἠμύνατο τοὺς πλέονας διὰ τὸ καταφρονοῦντας ἀπαρασκεύους γενέσθαι. Χρὴ δὲ ἀεὶ ἐν τῇ πολεμίᾳ τῇ μὲν γνώμῃ θαρσαλέους στρατεύειν, τῷ δὲ ἔργῳ δεδιότας παρασκευάζεσθαι. οὕτω γὰρ πρός τε τὸ ἐπιέναι τοῖς ἐναντίοις εὐψυχότατοι ἂν εἶεν, πρός τε τὸ ἐπιχειρεῖσθαι ἀσφαλέστατοι.

For the events of war are ever changing, and fierce attacks are frequently made by small numbers with great fury. Often, too, an inferior body, by cautious measures, have defeated a superior force, whom contempt of their opponent had led to neglect proper precautions. In an enemy's country it is always the duty of soldiers to have their minds girt up for action, and, looking around with circumspection, to have their arms ready to resist. Thus they will find themselves best able to rush forward to the attack, and least likely to suffer from the attacks of their opponents.

See (Lat.) War.

Discipline.

ii. 11.

Κάλλιστον γὰρ τόδε καὶ ἀσφαλέστατον πολλοὺς ὄντας ἑνὶ κόσμῳ χρωμένους φαίνεσθαι.

The noblest sight, and surest defence for a numerous army, is to observe strict discipline and undeviating obedience to their officers.

Envy.

ii. 35.

Μέχρι γὰρ τοῦδε ἀνεκτοὶ οἱ ἔπαινοί εἰσι περὶ ἑτέρων λεγόμενοι, ἐς ὅσον ἂν καὶ αὐτὸς ἕκαστος οἴηται ἱκανὸς εἶναι δρᾶσαί τι ὧν ἤκουσε· τῷ δ' ὑπερβάλλοντι αὐτῶν φθονοῦντες ἤδη καὶ ἀπιστοῦσιν.

For the praises bestowed upon others are only to be endured so long as men imagine that they are able to perform the actions which they hear others to have done ; they envy whatever they consider to be beyond their power, and are unwilling to believe in its truth.

Equality.

ii. 37.

Χρώμεθα γὰρ πολιτείᾳ οὐ ζηλούσῃ τοὺς τῶν πέλας νόμους, παράδειγμα δὲ μᾶλλον αὐτοὶ ὄντες τινὶ ἢ μιμούμενοι ἑτέρους, καὶ ὄνομα

μὲν διὰ τὸ μὴ ἐς ὀλίγους ἀλλ' ἐς πλείονας οἰκεῖν δημοκρατία κέκλη-
ται, μέτεστι δὲ κατὰ μὲν τοὺς νόμους πρὸς τὰ ἴδια διάφορα πᾶσι τὸ
ἴσον, κατὰ δὲ τὴν ἀξίωσιν, ὡς ἕκαστος ἕν τῳ εὐδοκιμεῖ, οὐκ ἀπὸ μέρους τὸ πλεῖον ἐς τὰ κοινὰ ἢ ἀπ' ἀρετῆς προτιμᾶται, οὐδ' αὖ κατὰ
πενίαν, ἔχων δέ τι ἀγαθὸν δρᾶσαι τὴν πόλιν, ἀξιώματος ἀφανείᾳ
κεκώλυται. 'Ελευθέρως δὲ τά τε πρὸς τὸ κοινὸν πολιτεύομεν καὶ ἐς
τὴν πρὸς ἀλλήλους τῶν καθ' ἡμέραν ἐπιτηδευμάτων ὑποψίαν, οὐ δι'
ὀργῆς τὸν πέλας, εἰ καθ' ἡδονήν τι δρᾷ, ἔχοντες, οὐδὲ ἀζημίους μέν,
λυπηρὰς δὲ τῇ ὄψει ἀχθηδόνας προστιθέμενοι. 'Ανεπαχθῶς δὲ τὰ
ἴδια προσομιλοῦντες τὰ δημόσια διὰ δέος μάλιστα οὐ παρανομοῦμεν,
τῶν τε ἀεὶ ἐν ἀρχῇ ὄντων ἀκροάσει καὶ τῶν νόμων, καὶ μάλιστα
αὐτῶν ὅσοι τε ἐπ' ὠφελίᾳ τῶν ἀδικουμένων κεῖνται καὶ ὅσοι ἄγραφοι
ὄντες αἰσχύνην ὁμολογουμένην φέρουσι.
Καὶ μὴν καὶ τῶν πόνων πλείστας ἀναπαύλας τῇ γνώμῃ ἐπορισά-
μεθα, ἀγῶσι μέν γε καὶ θυσίαις διετησίοις νομίζοντες, ἰδίαις δὲ κατα-
σκευαῖς εὐπρεπέσιν, ὧν καθ' ἡμέραν ἡ τέρψις τὸ λυπηρὸν ἐκπλήσσει.
ἐπεισέρχεται δὲ διὰ μέγεθος τῆς πόλεως ἐκ πάσης γῆς τὰ πάντα,
καὶ ξυμβαίνει ἡμῖν μηδὲν οἰκειοτέρᾳ τῇ ἀπολαύσει τὰ αὐτοῦ ἀγαθὰ
γιγνόμενα καρποῦσθαι ἢ καὶ τὰ τῶν ἄλλων ἀνθρώπων.

For we possess a form of government of such excellence, that it
gives us no reason to envy the laws of our neighbours. We often
serve as a pattern to others ; but we have never found it necessary
to follow their example. It is called a popular government, because its object is not to favour the interests of the few, but of
the greater number. In private disputes we are all equal in the
eye of the law ; and, in regard to the honours of the state, we rise
according to merit, and not because we belong to a particular
class. Though we are poor, if we are able to serve our country by
our talents, obscurity of birth is no obstacle. We carry on public
affairs with gentlemanly feeling, having no unworthy suspicions
of each other in the daily affairs of life, nor indulging in angry
passion towards our neighbour for pursuing his own course, nor
yet putting on that look of displeasure, which pains, though it can
do nothing more. Conversing with the kindliest feeling towards
each other in private society, above all things we avoid to break
the enactments of the state, reverencing the magistrates, and obeying the laws—those more particularly that have been enacted for
the protection of the injured, as well as those which, though they
are unwritten, bring sure disgrace on the transgressors. In addition to all this, in order that our minds might unbend occasionally
from the dull routine of business, we have appointed numerous
games and sacred festivals throughout the year, performed with a
certain solemn pomp and elegance, so that the charms of such
daily sights may drive away melancholy. The grandeur of this
city causes the produce of the whole world to be imported into
it, so that we enjoy not only the delicacies peculiar to our own
country, but also those that come from other lands.

CHARACTER OF BRITISH NATION FORESHADOWED.

ii. 39.

Διαφέρομεν δὲ καὶ ταῖς τῶν πολεμικῶν μελέταις τῶν ἐναντίων τοῖσδε. Τήν τε γὰρ πόλιν κοινὴν παρέχομεν καὶ οὐκ ἔστιν ὅτε ξενηλασίαις ἀπείργομέν τινα ἢ μαθήματος ἢ θεάματος, ὃ μὴ κρυφθὲν ἄν τις τῶν πολεμίων ἰδὼν ὠφεληθείη, πιστεύοντες οὐ ταῖς παρασκευαῖς τὸ πλέον καὶ ἀπάταις ἢ τῷ ἀφ' ἡμῶν αὐτῶν ἐς τὰ ἔργα εὐψύχῳ· καὶ ἐν ταῖς παιδείαις οἱ μὲν ἐπιπόνῳ ἀσκήσει εὐθὺς νέοι ὄντες τὸ ἀνδρεῖον μετέρχονται, ἡμεῖς δὲ ἀνειμένως διαιτώμενοι οὐδὲν ἧσσον ἐπὶ τοὺς ἰσοπαλεῖς κινδύνους χωροῦμεν.

In military tactics we feel superior to our opponents; for we throw open our state to all who choose to resort to it ; nor do we ever drive any stranger from our shores who comes for instruction, or from curiosity, making no concealment of anything, lest our enemies should derive some benefit. We trust not so much to being thoroughly prepared, or to cunning devices, as to our own innate courage. In training, there are some people who are, from their youth, inured by laborious exercise to submit to toil ; but we, leading an easy and luxurious life, are ready at any moment to face dangers with the same recklessness as they.

POVERTY.

ii. 40.

Καὶ τὸ πένεσθαι οὐχ ὁμολογεῖν τινι αἰσχρόν, ἀλλὰ μὴ διαφεύγειν ἔργῳ αἴσχιον.

An avowal of poverty is a disgrace to no man ; to make no effort to escape from it is indeed disgraceful.

See (Lat.) Poverty.

THE BRITISH NATION FORESHADOWED IN THE ATHENIAN.

ii. 40.

Μόνοι γὰρ τόν τε μηδὲν τῶνδε μετέχοντα οὐκ ἀπράγμονα, ἀλλ' ἀχρεῖον νομίζομεν, καὶ αὐτοὶ ἤτοι κρίνομέν γε ἢ ἐνθυμούμεθα ὀρθῶς τὰ πράγματα, οὐ τοὺς λόγους τοῖς ἔργοις βλάβην ἡγούμενοι, ἀλλὰ μὴ προδιδαχθῆναι μᾶλλον λόγῳ πρότερον ἢ ἐπὶ ἃ δεῖ ἔργῳ ἐλθεῖν. Διαφερόντως γὰρ δὴ καὶ τόδε ἔχομεν ὥστε τολμᾶν τε οἱ αὐτοὶ μάλιστα καὶ περὶ ὧν ἐπιχειρήσομεν ἐκλογίζεσθαι· ὃ τοῖς ἄλλοις—ἀμαθία μὲν θράσος, λογισμὸς δὲ ὄκνον φέρει. Κράτιστοι δ' ἂν τὴν ψυχὴν δικαίως κριθεῖεν οἱ τά τε δεινὰ καὶ ἡδέα σαφέστατα γιγνώσκοντες καὶ διὰ ταῦτα μὴ ἀποτρεπόμενοι ἐκ τῶν κινδύνων.

For we are the only people who think him that does not take part in public affairs to be not merely lazy, but good for nothing.

Besides, we pass the soundest judgments, and have an intuitive knowledge of what is likely to happen; never considering that discussion of a subject stands in the way of its execution, but rather that we suffer from not having duly examined the question before we proceed to carry it out. It is in this that we show our distinguishing excellence—that we are bold as lions in the hour of action, and yet can calmly deliberate on the expediency of our measures. The courage of others is the consequence of ignorance; caution makes them cowards. But those, undoubtedly, must be regarded to be the bravest who, having the most acute perception of the sufferings of war and the sweets of peace, are yet not in the least prevented from facing danger.

ADVERSITY.

ii. 43.

Οὐ γὰρ οἱ κακοπραγοῦντες δικαιότερον ἀφειδοῖεν ἂν τοῦ βίου, οἷς ἐλπὶς οὐκ ἔστ᾽ ἀγαθοῦ, ἀλλ᾽ οἷς ἡ ἐναντία μεταβολὴ ἐν τῷ ζῆν ἔτι κινδυνεύεται καὶ ἐν οἷς μάλιστα μεγάλα τὰ διαφέροντα, ἤν τι πταίσωσιν. Ἀλγεινοτέρα γὰρ ἀνδρί γε φρόνημα ἔχοντι ἡ [ἐν τῷ] μετὰ τοῦ μαλακισθῆναι κάκωσις ἢ ὁ μετὰ ῥώμης καὶ κοινῆς ἐλπίδος ἅμα γιγνόμενος ἀναίσθητος θάνατος.

For it is not those who are reduced to misery, and who have no hopes of bettering their fortunes, that ought to be ready to shed their blood in defence of their country; but much more those who, if they live long enough, will find a change from their present prosperity difficult to be borne, and to whom adversity, therefore, is a serious calamity. For hard times, after a life of luxurious ease, are felt more keenly by a man of spirit than death, which leaves us without feeling; so that the stroke is met with fortitude, and reaches us in the midst of public prosperity.

PRUDENT MEASURES.

ii. 62.

Αὔχημα μὲν γὰρ καὶ ἀπὸ ἀμαθίας εὐτυχοῦς καὶ δειλῷ τινι ἐγγίγνεται, καταφρόνησις δὲ ὃς ἂν καὶ γνώμῃ πιστεύῃ τῶν ἐναντίων προέχειν, ὃ ἡμῖν ὑπάρχει. Καὶ τὴν τόλμαν ἀπὸ τῆς ὁμοίας τύχης ἡ ξύνεσις ἐκ τοῦ ὑπέρφρονος ἐχυρωτέραν παρέχεται, ἐλπίδι τε ἧσσον πιστεύει, ἧς ἐν τῷ ἀπόρῳ ἡ ἰσχύς, γνώμῃ δὲ ἀπὸ τῶν ὑπαρχόντων, ἧς βεβαιοτέρα ἡ πρόνοια.

For boasting and bravado may exist in the breast even of the coward, if he is successful through a mere lucky hit; but a just contempt of an enemy can alone arise in those who feel that they are superior to their opponent by the prudence of their measures, as is the case with us. And even when the parties are pretty equally matched in other respects, the very consciousness of this superiority in prudence gives an additional stimulus to courage ; and the man who is in difficulties trusts less to hopes, which may deceive him, than to a wise judgment, the foresight of which enables him to guard against disappointments.

See (Lat.) **Prudence.**

Evils inflicted by Heaven.

ii. 64.

Φέρειν τε χρὴ τά τε δαιμόνια ἀναγκαίως τά τε ἀπὸ τῶν πολεμίων ἀνδρείως.

The evils inflicted by Heaven ought to be borne with patient resignation, and the evils inflicted by enemies with manly fortitude,

Men of Merit subject to Envy.

ii. 64.

Τὸ δὲ μισεῖσθαι καὶ λυπηροὺς εἶναι ἐν τῷ παρόντι πᾶσι μὲν ὑπῆρξε δὴ ὅσοι ἕτεροι ἑτέρων ἠξίωσαν ἄρχειν· ὅστις δ᾽ ἐπὶ μεγίστοις τὸ ἐπίφθονον λαμβάνει, ὀρθῶς βουλεύεται. Μῖσος γὰρ οὐκ ἐπὶ πολὺ ἀντέχει, ἡ δὲ παραυτίκα τε λαμπρότης καὶ ἐς τὸ ἔπειτα δόξα ἀείμνηστος καταλείπεται.

To be an object of hatred and aversion to their contemporaries has been the usual fate of all those whose merit has raised them above the common level. The man who submits to the shafts of envy for the sake of noble objects, pursues a judicious course for his own lasting fame. Hatred dies with its object, while merit soon breaks forth in full splendour, and his glory is handed down to posterity in never-dying strains.

See (Lat.) **Envy.**

The Duller Part of Mankind.

iii. 37.

Οἵ τε φαυλότεροι τῶν ἀνθρώπων πρὸς τοὺς ξυνετωτέρους ὡς ἐπὶ τ πλεῖον ἄμεινον οἰκοῦσι τὰς πόλεις. Οἱ μὲν γὰρ τῶν τε νόμων σο φώτεροι βούλονται φαίνεσθαι τῶν τε ἀεὶ λεγομένων ἐς τὸ κοινὸ. περιγίγνεσθαι, ὡς ἐν ἄλλοις μείζοσιν οὐκ ἂν δηλώσαντες τὴν γνώμην καὶ ἐκ τοῦ τοιούτου τὰ πολλὰ σφάλλουσι τὰς πόλεις· οἱ δ᾽ ἀπιστοῦν τες τῇ ἐξ ἑαυτῶν ξυνέσει ἀμαθέστεροι μὲν τῶν νόμων ἀξιοῦσιν εἶναι ἀδυνατώτεροι δὲ τοῦ καλῶς εἰπόντος μέμψασθαι λόγον, κριταὶ δ ὄντες ἀπὸ τοῦ ἴσου μᾶλλον ἢ ἀγωνισταὶ ὀρθοῦνται τὰ πλείω.

The duller part of mankind, in general, hold the reins of government with a steadier hand than your men of wit and vivacity. The latter are anxious to appear wiser than the laws. In every discussion about the public good they look merely to victory, as if they would have no other opportunity to show off their superior talents. In this way they are very apt to destroy the proper balance of the constitution. The former, who have no confidence in their own abilities, are quite willing to confess that they are not above the laws of their country, though they are unable to cope with the specious statements of the showy orator. Therefore, they are abler administrators of public affairs ; because they are good judges of what is equitable, though inferior in debate.

THE EFFECT OF PROSPERITY.

iii. 39.

Εἴωθε δὲ τῶν πόλεων αἶς ἂν μάλιστα καὶ δι' ἐλαχίστου ἀπροσδόκητος εὐπραξία ἔλθῃ, ἐς ὕβριν τρέπειν· τὰ δὲ πολλὰ κατὰ λόγον τοῖς ἀνθρώποις εὐτυχοῦντα ἀσφαλέστερα ἢ παρὰ δόξαν· καὶ κακοπραγίαν, ὡς εἰπεῖν, ῥᾷον ἀπωθοῦνται ἢ εὐδαιμονίαν διασώζονται.

It is the usual result of a sudden and unexpected gleam of prosperity on a people, that it makes them vainglorious and arrogant. Good fortune, attained as a consequence of judicious measures, is more likely to last than what bursts upon us at once. And, to conclude, men are much more dexterous in warding off adversity than in preserving prosperity.

See (Lat.) Results of prosperity.

PECULIAR TEMPER OF MAN.

iii. 39.

Πέφυκε γὰρ καὶ ἄλλως ἄνθρωπος τὸ μὲν θεραπεῦον ὑπερφρονεῖν, τὸ δὲ μὴ ὑπεῖκον θαυμάξειν.

For so remarkably perverse is the nature of man, that he despises whoever courts him, and admires whoever will not bend before him.

ALL MEN ARE SINNERS.

iii. 45.

Πεφύκασί τε ἅπαντες καὶ ἰδίᾳ καὶ δημοσίᾳ ἁμαρτάνειν, καὶ οὐκ ἔστι νόμος ὅστις ἀπείρξει τούτου, ἐπεὶ διεξεληλύθασί γε διὰ πασῶν τῶν ζημιῶν οἱ ἄνθρωποι προστιθέντες, εἴ πως ἧσσον ἀδικοῖντο ὑπὸ τῶν κακούργων.

The whole of mankind, whether individuals or communities, are by nature liable to sin ; and there is no law that can ever prevent this, since men have had recourse to all kinds of punishment without effect, adding to their severity, if by any means they might restrain the outrages of the wicked.

The Incentives of Hope and Love.

iii. 45.

"Η τε ἐλπὶς καὶ ὁ ἔρως ἐπὶ παντί, ὁ μὲν ἡγούμενος, ἡ δ' ἐφεπομένη,
καὶ ὁ μὲν τὴν ἐπιβολὴν ἐκφροντίζων, ἡ δὲ τὴν εὐπορίαν τῆς τύχης
ὑποτιθεῖσα πλεῖστα βλάπτουσι, καὶ ὄντα ἀφανῆ κρείσσω ἐστὶ τῶν
ὁρωμένων δεινῶν. Καὶ ἡ τύχη ἐπ' αὐτοῖς οὐδὲν ἔλασσον ξυμβάλλεται
ἐς τὸ ἐπαίρειν· ἀδοκήτως γὰρ ἔστιν ὅτε παρισταμένη καὶ ἐκ τῶν ὑποδεεστέρων κινδυνεύειν τινὰ προάγει καὶ οὐχ ἧσσον τὰς πόλεις, ὅσῳ
περὶ τῶν μεγίστων, ἐλευθερίας ἢ ἄλλων ἀρχῆς, καὶ μετὰ πάντων
ἕκαστος ἀλογίστως ἐπὶ πλέον τι αὐτὸν ἐδόξασεν.

The greatest stimuli in every undertaking are hope and ambition ; the one points the way, the other follows closely on its
heels ; the one devises the mode in which it may be accomplished,
the other suggests the aid to be got from Fortune. These two
principles are the cause of all our evils ; and, though unseen, are
much stronger than the terror which wasteth by noonday. And
then, in addition to these, Fortune herself is active in urging men
to the encountering of dangers ; for, presenting herself suddenly
before them, she incites even the faint-hearted to make an effort.
And, above all, this is the case with communities, which contend
for matters of great concernment, such as liberty, or the dominion
over others. In the general ardour each individual feels himself
roused to put forth his strength to the utmost.

See (Lat.) Results of ambition.

Contrast of Times of Peace and War.

iii. 82.

'Εν μὲν γὰρ εἰρήνῃ καὶ ἀγαθοῖς πράγμασιν αἵ τε πόλεις καὶ οἱ
ἰδιῶται ἀμείνους τὰς γνώμας ἔχουσι διὰ τὸ μὴ ἐς ἀκουσίους ἀνάγκας
πίπτειν· ὁ δὲ πόλεμος ὑφελὼν τὴν εὐπορίαν τοῦ καθ' ἡμέραν βίαιος
διδάσκαλος καὶ πρὸς τὰ παρόντα τὰς ὀργὰς τῶν πολλῶν ὁμοιοῖ.

In the piping times of peace and prosperity, communities, as
well as individuals, have their feelings as well as nature less excited, because they are not under the compulsion of stern neces-
sities. Whereas war, which strips them of their daily food, is a
rough teacher, and renders their passions in accordance with their
present condition.

See (Lat.) Peace and war.

Words Lose their Significance.

iii. 82.

Καὶ τὴν εἰωθυῖαν ἀξίωσιν τῶν ὀνομάτων ἐς τὰ ἔργα ἀντήλλαξαν τῇ
δικαιώσει. Τόλμα μὲν γὰρ ἀλόγιστος ἀνδρία φιλέταιρος ἐνομίσθη,
μέλλησις δὲ προμηθὴς δειλία εὐπρεπής, τὸ δὲ σῶφρον τοῦ ἀνάνδρου

πρόσχημα, καὶ τὸ πρὸς ἅπαν ξυνετὸν ἐπὶ πᾶν ἀργόν· τὸ δ᾽ ἐμπλήκ-
τως ὀξὺ ἀνδρὸς μοίρᾳ προσετέθη, ἀσφαλίᾳ δὲ τὸ ἐπιβουλεύσασθαι
ἀποτροπῆς πρόφασις εὔλογος. Καὶ ὁ μὲν χαλεπαίνων πιστὸς ἀεί, ϛ
δ᾽ ἀντιλέγων αὐτῷ ὕποπτος. Ἐπιβουλεύσας δέ τις τυχὼν ξυνετὸς καὶ
ὑπονοήσας ἔτι δεινότερος· προβουλεύσας δὲ ὅπως μηδὲν αὐτῶν δεήσει,
τῆς τε ἑταιρίας διαλυτὴς καὶ τοὺς ἐναντίους ἐκπεπληγμένος. Ἁπλῶς
δὲ ὁ φθάσας τὸν μέλλοντα κακόν τι δρᾶν ἐπῃνεῖτο, καὶ ὁ ἐπικελεύσας
τὸν μὴ διανοούμενον.

They changed the common signification of words at their pleasure, and distorted them, in order to palliate their actions. For
what was once thought senseless audacity began to be esteemed
contempt of danger in defence of a friend ; prudent caution to be
plausible cowardice ; bashfulness to be the pretext for sloth ; and
the being wary in everything as only another word for laziness.
A hot, fiery temper was looked upon as the exhibition of a manly
character ; circumspect and calm deliberation to be a specious pretext for intended knavery. He who was subject to gusts of passion
was always considered trustworthy ; who presumed to contradict
was ever the object of suspicion. He who succeeded in a roguish
scheme was wise, but he who anticipated it in others was still a
more able genius ; but he whose foresight enabled him to be above
all such proceedings was looked upon as one who put an end to
friendship, and was awed by his enemies. In short, the highest
praise was considered to be due to him who forestalled his neighbour in doing mischief, or who egged on another to it.

VILLAINS.

iii. 82.

Ῥᾷον δ᾽ οἱ πολλοὶ κακοῦργοι ὄντες δεξιοὶ κέκληνται ἢ ἀμαθεῖς
ἀγαθοί, καὶ τῷ μὲν αἰσχύνονται, ἐπὶ δὲ τῷ ἀγάλλονται.

The number of villains is large in this world ; and they are more
successful in acquiring a name for adroitness than their dupes are
for goodness. The latter cannot refrain from blushing ; the former
rejoice in their iniquities.

PRECEDENTS.

iii. 84.

Ἀξιοῦσί τε τοὺς κοινοὺς περὶ τῶν τοιούτων οἱ ἄνθρωποι νόμους, ἀφ᾽
ὧν ἅπασιν ἐλπὶς ὑπόκειται σφαλεῖσι κἂν αὐτοὺς διασώζεσθαι, ἐν
ἄλλων τιμωρίαις προκαταλύειν καὶ μὴ ὑπολείπεσθαι, εἴ ποτε ἄρα τις
κινδυνεύσας τινὸς δεήσεται αὐτῶν.

Men are foolish enough, in their desire for vengeance, to make
precedents against themselves by infringing those laws which are
the common protection of mankind, and from which alone they
can expect aid if they fall into difficulties.

See (Lat.) Precedents.

Make Allowance for Chance in Everything.

iv. 18.

Σωφρόνων δὲ ἀνδρῶν οἵτινες τἀγαθὰ ἐς ἀμφίβολον ἀσφαλῶς ἔθεντο (καὶ ταῖς ξυμφοραῖς οἱ αὐτοὶ εὐξυνετώτερον ἂν προσφέροιντο,) τόν τε πόλεμον νομίσωσι μὴ καθ᾽ ὅσον ἄν τις αὐτοῦ μέρος βούληται μεταχειρίζειν, τούτῳ ξυνεῖναι, ἀλλ᾽ ὡς ἂν αἱ τύχαι αὐτῶν ἡγήσωνται· καὶ ἐλάχιστ᾽ ἂν οἱ τοιοῦτοι πταίοντες διὰ τὸ μὴ τῷ ὀρθουμένῳ αὐτοῦ πιστεύοντες ἐπαίρεσθαι ἐν τῷ εὐτυχεῖν ἂν μάλιστα καταλύοιντο.

It is the part of the wise, in their estimates of success, to make due allowance for the effects of chance. These men will be more likely to bear the frowns of Fortune with equanimity ; and will be prepared to think that war does not invariably take the direction which we wish to give it, but that to which Fortune leads us. And men of this character have little chance of failing in their schemes, or of having the pedestal of their fortune thrown down, because they are too much puffed up by present appearances.

Calamities of War.

iv. 59.

Καὶ περὶ μὲν τοῦ πολεμεῖν ὡς χαλεπὸν τί ἄν τις πᾶν τὸ ἐνὸν ἐκλέγων ἐν εἰδόσι μακρηγοροίη ; οὐδεὶς γὰρ οὔτε ἀμαθίᾳ ἀναγκάζεται αὐτὸ δρᾶν, οὔτε φόβῳ, ἢν οἴηταί τι πλέον σχήσειν, ἀποτρέπεται. Ξυμβαίνει δὲ τοῖς μὲν τὰ κέρδη μείζω φαίνεσθαι τῶν δεινῶν, οἱ δὲ τοὺς κινδύνους ἐθέλουσιν ὑφίστασθαι πρὸ τοῦ αὐτίκα τι ἐλασσοῦσθαι· αὐτὰ δὲ ταῦτα εἰ μὴ ἐν καιρῷ τύχοιεν ἑκάτεροι πράσσοντες, αἱ παραινέσεις τῶν ξυναλλαγῶν ὠφέλιμοι.

And, in regard to the calamities of war, what need is there to relate, in minute detail, all that happens in the ears of men who have only too much experience of them ? No one ever plunges headlong into these from ignorance of what will follow ; nor yet, when they expect to gratify their ambitious views, are they ever deterred by fear. In the latter case, the expectations of what is to be gained are thought to overbalance the dangers that are likely to accrue ; and the former prefer to undergo any danger than to suffer diminution of their present possessions. If neither party seem likely to carry out their views, then exhortations to mutual ᵥreement seem highly proper.

Revenge not Certain.

iv. 62.

Τιμωρία γὰρ οὐκ εὐτυχεῖ δικαίως, ὅτι καὶ ἀδικεῖται· οὐδὲ ἰσχὺς βέβαιον, διότι καὶ εὔελπι. Τὸ δὲ ἀστάθμητον τοῦ μέλλοντος ὡς ἐπὶ πλεῖστον κρατεῖ, πάντων τε σφαλερώτατον ὂν ὅμως καὶ χρησιμώτα-

τον φαίνεται· ἐξ ἴσου γὰρ δεδιότες προμηθίᾳ μᾶλλον ἐπ᾽ ἀλλήλους ἐρχό-
μεθα.

Vengeance does not necessarily follow because a man has sustained an injury ; nor is power sure of its end because it is full of
sanguine expectations. Fortune hangs up, in general, her un-
steady balance, which, while little dependence can be placed upon
it, yet gives us most useful hints. For, as we have thus a wholesome dread of each other, we advance to the contest with thoughtful premeditation.

MIGHT MAKES RIGHT.

iv. 86.

᾽Απάτῃ γὰρ εὐπρεπεῖ αἴσχιον τοῖς γε ἐν ἀξιώματι πλεονεκτῆσαι ἢ
βίᾳ ἐμφανεῖ· τὸ μὲν γὰρ ἰσχύος δικαιώσει, ἢν ἡ τύχη ἔδωκεν, ἐπέρχεται, τὸ δὲ γνώμης ἀδίκου ἐπιβουλῇ.

For it is more disgraceful for men in high office to improve their
private fortune by specious fraud than by open violence. Might
makes right in the one case ; while, in the other, man throws over
his proceedings the cloak of despicable cunning.

See (Lat.) Might makes right.

HOW A STATE CAN PRESERVE ITSELF FREE.

iv. 92.

Πρός τε γὰρ τοὺς ἀστυγείτονας πᾶσι τὸ ἀντίπαλον καὶ ἐλεύθερον
καθίσταται.

For it is a maxim allowed, that no state can possibly preserve
itself free, unless it be a match for neighbouring powers.

THE SANGUINE NATURE OF HOPE.

iv. 108.

Εἰωθότες οἱ ἄνθρωποι οὗ μὲν ἐπιθυμοῦσιν ἐλπίδι ἀπερισκέπτῳ διδόναι, ὃ δὲ μὴ προσίενται λογισμῷ αὐτοκράτορι διωθεῖσθαι.

It is the usual way of mankind blindly to indulge in sanguine
hopes of gaining a favourite object, and to throw aside with despotic scorn whatever has the appearance of running counter to
their wishes.

HOPE.

v. 103.

᾽Ελπὶς δέ, κινδύνῳ παραμύθιον οὖσα, τοὺς μὲν ἀπὸ περιουσίας
χρωμένους αὐτῇ, κἂν βλάψῃ, οὐ καθεῖλε· τοῖς δ᾽ ἐς ἅπαν τὸ ὑπάρχον

ἀναρριπτοῦσι (δάπανος γὰρ φύσει) ἅμα τε γιγνώσκεται σφαλέντων
καὶ ἐν ὅτῳ ἔτι φυλάξεταί τις αὐτὴν γνωρισθεῖσαν οὐκ ἐλλείπει.

Hope, a solace in dangerous emergencies, is not always fatal to
those who indulge in its flattering tales, if they are in a position
to bear a disappointment. By those, however, who place their
all on the hazard of a cast, its delusions (for hope is extravagant
in its nature) are then only known by experience, when it is no
longer possible to guard against its snares.

Men have Recourse to Divinations in Calamity.

v. 103.

Μηδὲ ὁμοιωθῆναι τοῖς πολλοῖς, οἷς παρὸν ἀνθρωπείως ἔτι σώζεσθαι,
ἐπειδὰν πιεζομένους αὐτοὺς ἐπιλίπωσιν αἱ φανεραὶ ἐλπίδες, ἐπὶ τὰς
ἀφανεῖς καθίστανται, μαντικήν τε καὶ χρησμοὺς καὶ ὅσα τοιαῦτα μετ'
ἐλπίδων λυμαίνεται.

Be not like the mob of mankind, who, though they might be
saved by human exertions, as soon as faint hopes of safety are
visible, have recourse to others of a darker cast, — to necromancy,
fortune-tellers, and such foolish courses as hope suggests to draw
them on to destruction.

Dishonour.

v. 111.

Οὐ γὰρ δὴ ἐπί γε τὴν ἐν τοῖς αἰσχροῖς καὶ προὔπτοις κινδύνοις
πλεῖστα διαφθείρουσαν ἀνθρώπους αἰσχύνην τρέψεσθε. Πολλοῖς γὰρ
προορωμένοις ἔτι ἐς οἷα φέρονται τὸ αἰσχρὸν καλούμενον ὀνόματος
ἐπαγωγοῦ δυνάμει ἐπεσπάσατο. ἡσσηθεῖσι τοῦ ῥήματος, ἔργῳ ξυμφοραῖς ἀνηκέστοις ἑκόντας περιπεσεῖν καὶ αἰσχύνην αἰσχίω μετὰ
ἀνοίας ἢ τύχης προσλαβεῖν.

For you will be no longer controlled by that sense of shame
which leads men to ruin when dishonour stares them in the face,
and danger presses them from behind. For many, though they
see plainly enough into what evils they are going to plunge, yet,
to avoid the imputation of dishonour, — so powerful is the force of
one bewitching sound!—feel themselves obliged to yield to a
course of which their better reason may disapprove, and rush
wilfully into irremediable calamities, and incur a more shameful
weight of dishonour through their own mad obstinacy than Fortune
would have awarded them.

Men who maintain themselves in Credit.

v. 111.

Οἵτινες τοῖς μὲν ἴσοις μὴ εἴκουσι, τοῖς δὲ κρείσσοσι καλῶς προσφέ-
·ονται, πρὸς δὲ τοὺς ἥσσους μέτριοί εἰσι, πλεῖστ' ἂν ὀρθοῖντο.

For those are the men to maintain themselves with credit in the world, who never suffer their equals to insult them, who show proper respect to their superiors, and act with thoughtful kindness to their inferiors.

See Rom. xiii. 1; Eph. vi. 9.

EVERYTHING UNKNOWN IS MAGNIFIED.

vi. 11.

Τὰ γὰρ διὰ πλείστου πάντες ἴσμεν θαυμαζόμενα καὶ τὰ πεῖραν ἥκιστα τῆς δόξης δόντα.

For we all know that things placed at the greatest distance from us, as well as those whose character we have never known by experience, are most apt to excite our admiration.

See (Lat.) The unknown.

SUCCESS.

vi. 13.

Γνόντας ὅτι ἐπιθυμίᾳ μὲν ἐλάχιστα κατορθοῦνται, προνοίᾳ δὲ πλεῖστα.

You are convinced by experience that very few things are brought to a successful issue by impetuous desire, but most by calm and prudent forethought.

MONEY THE SINEWS OF WAR.

vi. 34.

Χρυσὸν γὰρ καὶ ἄργυρον πλεῖστον κέκτηνται, ὅθεν ὅ τε πόλεμος καὶ τἆλλα εὐπορεῖ.

For they are possessed of plenty of money, by means of which war and every other human enterprise are easily brought to a successful end.

See (Lat.) Money the sinews of war.

THE ASSAILANT IS MOST TO BE DREADED.

vi. 34.

Τῶν δ' ἀνθρώπων πρὸς τὰ λεγόμενα καὶ αἱ γνῶμαι ἵστανται, καὶ τοὺς προεπιχειροῦντας ἢ τοῖς γε ἐπιχειροῦσι προδηλοῦντας ὅτι ἀμυνοῦνται μᾶλλον πεφόβηνται, ἰσοκινδύνους ἡγούμενοι.

The opinions of men depend very much on rumours; and they have a greater dread of an enemy who proclaims himself ready to begin the attack, than of one who merely professes his intention to defend himself against assaults, as they think that there will be then only an equality of danger.

See (Lat.) The assailant.

R 3

The Government of an Oligarchy and Democracy.

vi. 39.

Φήσει τις δημοκρατίαν οὔτε ξυνετὸν οὔτ' ἴσον εἶναι, τοὺς δ' ἔχοντας τὰ χρήματα καὶ ἄρχειν ἄριστα βελτίστους. 'Εγὼ δέ φημι πρῶτα μὲν δῆμον ξύμπαν ὠνομάσθαι, ὀλιγαρχίαν δὲ μέρος, ἔπειτα φύλακας μὲν ἀρίστους εἶναι χρημάτων τοὺς πλουσίους, βουλεῦσαι δ' ἂν βέλτιστα τοὺς ξυνετούς, κρῖναι δ' ἂν ἀκούσαντας ἄριστα τοὺς πολλούς, καὶ ταῦτα ὁμοίως καὶ κατὰ τὰ μέρη καὶ ξύμπαντα ἐν δημοκρατίᾳ ἰσομοιρεῖν. 'Ολιγαρχία δὲ τῶν μὲν κινδύνων τοῖς πολλοῖς μεταδίδωσι, τῶν δ' ὠφελίμων οὐ πλεονεκτεῖ μόνον, ἀλλὰ καὶ ξύμπαν ἀφελομένη ἔχει.

It may, perhaps, be said that a democracy is a form of government repugnant to the dictates of wisdom and justice ; that those who are the wealthiest are more likely to conduct public affairs successfully. To this I answer, in the first place, that by the word people is meant a whole community, including every individual; whereas an oligarchy is only a small portion of the people : in the next place, that the wealthy are, no doubt, the best guardians of the public treasure, and that men of prudence and forethought are the best advisers in public matters ; but the people in the mass are, after listening to a discussion, the best judges of measures. And that these different ranks of citizens are thus, in a democracy, able, both as a part and as a whole, to enjoy an equality of privilege. But, on the other hand, an oligarchy compels the great mass of the people to share in the dangers of the state, while it not only monopolises most of the advantages, but actually takes to itself everything on which it can lay its hand.

Danger in Multitude of Counsellors.

vi. 72.

Μέγα δὲ βλάψαι καὶ τὸ πλῆθος τῶν στρατηγῶν καὶ τὴν πολυαρχίαν.

A multitude of generals and many counsellors are very injurious.

Revenge is Sweet.

vii. 68.

"Αμα δὲ ἐχθροὺς ἀμύνασθαι ἐκγενησόμενον ἡμῖν καὶ τὸ λεγόμενόν που ἥδιστον εἶναι.

Nay more, we have the best opportunity of revenging ourselves on a detested enemy, which, according to the proverb, is the most pleasant thing in the world.

TIMOCLES.

FLOURISHED ABOUT B.C. 340.

TIMOCLES, an Athenian comic poet of the middle comedy, who flourished about B.C. 340. Suidas gives the titles of nineteen dramas.

POVERTY.

Fr. Com. Gr. p. 808.

Πολλοὺς γὰρ ἐνίοθ᾽ ἡ πενία βιάζεται
ἀνάξι᾽ αὐτῶν ἔργα παρὰ φύσιν ποιεῖν.

For poverty sometimes forces many to do, contrary to their natural disposition, things unworthy of them.

TYRTŒUS.

FLOURISHED ABOUT B.C. 660.

TYRTŒUS, son of Archembrotus, is said to have been by birth an Athenian, but became a citizen of Lacedæmon. There is a story that he was a lame schoolmaster, of low family and reputation, whom the Athenians, when applied to by the Lacedæmonians, in accordance with the oracle, purposely sent as the most inefficient leader they could select; but it turned out that his poetry achieved that victory which his physical condition seemed to forbid his aspiring.

TO DIE FOR ONE'S COUNTRY.

ii. 7, 1.

Τεθνάμεναι γὰρ καλὸν ἐπὶ προμάχοισι πεσόντο
ἄνδρ᾽ ἀγαθὸν περὶ ᾗ πατρίδι μαρνάμενον.

It is honourable for a brave man to die, having fallen in front of the ranks, fighting for his fatherland.

See (Lat.) To die for country.

COWARDICE.

ii. 8, 15.

Οὐδεὶς ἄν ποτε ταῦτα λέγων ἀνύσειεν ἕκαστα,
ὅσσ' ἦν αἰσχρὰ πάθῃ, γίγνεται ἀνδρὶ κακά.

It is not in the force of words to paint the varied ills which befall a man if he has been actuated by cowardice.

THE BRAVE MAN.

ii. 9, 13.

Ἦδ' ἀρετή, τόδ' ἄεθλον ἐν ἀνθρώποισι ἄριστον
κάλλιστόν τε φέρειν γίγνεται ἀνδρὶ νέῳ·
Ξυνὸν δ' ἐσθλὸν τοῦτο πόληί τε παντί τε δήμῳ,
ὅστις ἀνὴρ διαβὰς ἐν προμάχοισι μένῃ
Νωλεμέως, αἰσχρᾶς δὲ φυγῆς ἐπὶ πάγχυ λαθῆται
ψυχὴν καὶ θυμὸν τλήμονα παρθέμενος
Θαρσύνῃ δ' ἔπεσεν τὸν πλησίου ἄνδρα παρεστώς·
οὗτός ἀνὴρ ἀγαθὸς γίγνεται ἐν πολέμῳ.

This is virtue—this the noblest meed among men, and the best for a young man to carry off—this is a common good to a city and all its people, namely, whoever, standing firm, is foremost of the embattled train, and is altogether forgetful of base flight, when he has staked his life and firm spirit, but has the courage to die beside his neighbours. Such a man is a brave warrior.

THE DEATH OF THE BRAVE.

ii. 9, 23.

Αὐτὸς δ' ἐν προμάχοισι πεσὼν φίλον ὤλεσε θυμὸν
ἄστυ τε καὶ λαοὺς καὶ πατέρ' ἐνκλείσας,
Πολλὰ διὰ στέρνοιο καὶ ἀσπίδος ὀμφαλοέσσης
καὶ διὰ θώρηκος πρόσθεν ἐληλαμένος·
Τὸν δ' ὀλοφύρονται μὲν ὁμῶς νέοι ἠδὲ γέροντες,
ἀργαλέῳ τε πόθῳ πᾶσα κέκηδε πόλις·
Καὶ τύμβος καὶ παῖδες ἐν ἀνθρώποις ἀρίσημοι
καὶ παίδων παῖδες καὶ γένος ἐξοπίσω.
Οὐδέ ποτε κλέος ἐσθλὸν ἀπόλλυται οὐδ' ὄνομ' αὐτοῦ,
ἀλλ' ὑπὸ γῆς περ ἐὼν γίγνεται ἀθάνατος·
Ὄντιν' ἀριστεύοντα μένοντά τε μαρνάμενόν τε
γῆς περὶ καὶ παίδων θοῦρος Ἄρης ὀλέσῃ.

He, having fallen amidst the foremost, loses his life, bringing glory to his city, people, and father, pierced in many places through breast and bossed shield, and through his armour in front. Young and old alike lament him with sad regret. His tomb and children are famed among men,—childrens' children, and his whole descendants after him. Never does his fair fame or name perish ; but though he be under the ground, he becomes immortal. Whoever acting nobly, fighting for country and children, impetuous Ares shall have destroyed.

XENOPHON.

BORN PROBABLY BEFORE B.C. 444—WAS ALIVE B.C. 357.

XENOPHON, the illustrious commander, historian, and philosopher, was the son of Gryllus, an Athenian. He was the pupil of Socrates, and made rapid progress in that moral wisdom for which his master was so eminent. He joined the army of Cyrus the younger, in his expedition against his brother Artaxerxes Mnemon, king of Persia ; and when that enterprise proved unfortunate, he took command of the Greek troops, and assisted, by his prudence and skill, in bringing them safely back to Greece. When Socrates was put to death, B.C. 399, we find that Xenophon was shortly after obliged to leave Athens, and took refuge, with his family, at Scillus, under the protection of the Lacedæmonians. Here he spent twenty years in exile, hunting, writing, and entertaining his friends. After this long residence, he was compelled by the Eleans to leave Scillus, and is said to have retired to Corinth. Of the historical works of Xenophon, the "Anabasis," or the History of the Expedition of the Younger Cyrus, and of the Retreat of the Greeks who formed part of his army, has immortalised his name.

THE GODS OMNISCIENT.

Memorab. i. 1.

Σωκράτης δὲ πάντα μὲν ἡγεῖτο θεοὺς εἰδέναι, τά τε λεγόμενα καὶ πραττόμενα, καὶ τὰ σιγῇ βουλευόμενα, πανταχοῦ δὲ παρεῖναι καὶ σημαίνειν τοῖς ἀνθρώποις περὶ τῶν ἀνθρωπείων πάντων.

Socrates thought that the gods knew all things, both what is said, what is done, and what is meditated in silence, are everywhere present, and give warnings to men of everything human.

So 1 John (iii. 20)—"God is greater than our heart, and knoweth all things."

See (Lat.) God hears and sees.

Evil Communications.

Memorab. i. 2.

Διὸ καὶ τοὺς υἱεῖς οἱ πατέρες, κἂν ὦσι σώφρονες, εἴργουσιν ὅμως ἀπὸ τῶν πονηρῶν ἀνθρώπων, ὡς τὴν μὲν τῶν χρηστῶν ὁμιλίαν ἄσκησιν οὖσαν τῆς ἀρετῆς, τὴν δέ τῶν πονηρῶν, κατάλυσιν. Μαρτυρεῖ δὲ καὶ τῶν ποιητῶν ὅ, τε λέγων,

Ἐσθλῶν μὲν γὰρ ἄπ' ἐσθλὰ διδάξεαι· ἢν δὲ κακοῖσι
Συμμιχθῆς, ἀπολεῖς καὶ τὸν ἐόντα νόον καὶ ὁ λέγων,
Αὐτὰρ ἀνὴρ ἀγαθὸς, τοτὲ μὲν κακὸς, ἄλλοτε δ' ἐσθλός.

Wherefore fathers keep their sons, even though they be virtuous, from the society of the wicked, as they consider association with the virtuous as likely to incline them to virtue, and with the wicked as sure to prove its destruction.

The truth of this is borne witness to by one of the poets (Theognis v. 35) — "From every good man thou wilt learn what is good ; but if thou associatest with the wicked, thou wilt lose the sense that is in thee." And another poet says—"A good man is at one time good, and at another bad."

God knows best what is Good for Man.

Memorab. i. 3.

Καὶ εὔχετο δὲ πρὸς τοὺς θεοὺς ἀπλῶς τἀγαθὰ διδόναι, ὡς τοὺς θεοὺς κάλλιστα εἰδότας, ὁποῖα ἀγαθά ἐστι· τοὺς δὲ εὐχομένους χρυσίον, ἢ ἀργύριον, ἢ τυραννίδα, ἢ ἄλλο τι τῶν τοιούτων, οὐδὲν διάφορον ἐνόμιζεν εὔχεσθαι, ἢ εἰ κυβείαν, ἢ μάχην, ἢ ἄλλο τι εὔχοιντο τῶν φανερῶς ἀδήλων, ὅπως ἀποβήσοιτο.

Socrates prayed to the gods simply that they would give him what was good, inasmuch as the gods knew best what things are good for man. Those who prayed for gold, or silver, or high power, or anything of that kind, he regarded as doing the same as if they prayed that they might play at dice, or fight, or anything of that kind, of which the result was dependent on chance.

So Matt. (vi. 7)—"But when ye pray, use not vain repetitions, as the heathen do ; for they think that they shall be heard for their much speaking."

"The Poor Widow's Mite."

Memorab. i. 3.

Θυσίας δὲ θύων μικρὰς ἀπὸ μικρῶν, οὐδὲν ἡγεῖτο μειοῦσθαι τῶν ἀπὸ πολλῶν καὶ μεγάλων πολλὰ καὶ μεγάλα θυόντων. Οὔτε γὰρ τοῖς θεοῖς ἔφη καλῶς ἔχειν, εἰ ταῖς μεγάλαις θυσίαις μᾶλλον, ἢ ταῖς μικραῖς ἔχαιρον.

When Socrates presented small sacrifices from his small means, he considered that he was not at all inferior in merit to those who offered many and great sacrifices from ample and abundant means ;

for he said that it was not becoming for the gods to delight in large rather than in small sacrifices.

Who are most Respectful to the Gods.

Memorab. i. 4.

Οὐχ᾽ ὁρᾷς, ὅτι τὰ πολυχρονιώτατα καὶ σοφώτατα τῶν ἀνθρωπίνων, πόλεις καὶ ἔθνη, θεοσεβέστατά ἐστιν, καὶ αἱ φρονιμώταται ἡλικίαι, θεῶν ἐπιμελέσταται;

Dost thou not see that the oldest and wisest of human communities and cities and nations show most respect to the gods, and that the wisest age of man is most careful of the worship of the gods?

God Omnipresent and Omniscient.

Memorab. i. 4.

Τὸ θεῖον, ὅτι τοσοῦτον καὶ τοιοῦτόν ἐστιν, ὥσθ᾽ ἅμα πάντα ὁρᾷν, καὶ πάντα ἀκούειν, καὶ πανταχοῦ παρεῖναι, καὶ ἅμα πάντων ἐπιμελεῖσθαι.

The Divinity is so great, and of such a character, that He both sees and hears all things, is everywhere present, and attends to all things at once.

So Psalms (cii. 25)—"Of old hast Thou laid the foundation of the earth; and the heavens are the work of Thy hands. They shall perish, but Thou shalt en lure; yea, all of them shall wax old like a garment; as a vesture shalt Thou change them, and they shall be changed. But Thou art the same, and Thy years shall have no end."

The Best Sauce.

Memorab. i. 6.

Οὐκ οἶθσα, ὅτι ὁ μὲν ἥδιστα ἐσθίων, ἥκιστα ὄψου δεῖται, ὁ δὲ ἥδιστα πίνων, ἥκιστα τοῦ μὴ παρόντος ἐπιθυμεῖ ποτοῦ;

Dost thou not know that he who eats with most pleasure is he who least requires sauce, and that he who drinks with the greatest pleasure is he who least desires other drink than that which he has?

Divine Nature is Perfection.

Memorab. i. 6.

Ἐγὼ δὲ νομίζω τὸ μὲν μηδενὸς δέεσθαι θεῖον εἶναι, τὸ δὲ ὡς ἐλαχίστων, ἐγγυτάτω τοῦ θείου· καὶ τὸ μὲν θεῖον, κράτιστον, τὸ δὲ ἐγγυτάτω τοῦ θείου, ἐγγυτάτω τοῦ κρατίστου.

I think to want nothing is to resemble the gods, and to want as little as possible is to make the nearest approach to the gods; that the Divine nature is perfection, and that to be nearest to the Divine nature is to be nearest to perfection.

So Psalms (l. 9)—"I will take no bullock out of thy house, nor he-goats out of thy folds : for every beast of the forest is mine, and the cattle upon a thousand hills."

HONOUR GOD.

Memorab. ii. 1.

Εἴτε τοὺς θεοὺς ἵλεως εἶναί σοι βούλει, θεραπευτέον τοὺς θεούς.

If thou wishest the gods to be propitious to thee, thou must honour the gods.

So Psalms (cxv. 18)—"The Lord is nigh unto all them that call upon Him, that all that call upon Him in truth."

GOD GRANTS NOTHING WITHOUT LABOUR.

Memorab. ii. 1.

Τῶν γὰρ ὄντως ἀγαθῶν καὶ καλῶν οὐδὲν ἄνευ πόνου καὶ ἐπιμελείας θεοὶ διδόασιν ἀνθρώποις.

The gods give nothing really good and beautiful without labour and diligence.

So Genesis (iii. 19)—"In the sweat of thy face shalt thou eat bread."

See Lat.) All must labour.

WHAT BENEFITS CHILDREN RECEIVE FROM THEIR PARENTS.

Memorab. ii. 2.

Τίνας οὖν, ἔφη, ὑπὸ τίνων εὕροιμεν ἂν μείζονα εὐεργετημένους ἢ παῖδας ὑπὸ γονέων; οὓς οἱ γονεῖς ἐκ μὲν οὐκ ὄντων ἐποίησαν εἶναι, τοσαῦτα δὲ καλὰ ἰδεῖν καὶ τοσούτων ἀγαθῶν μετασχεῖν, ὅσα οἱ θεοὶ παρέχουσι τοῖς ἀνθρώποις· ἃ δὴ καὶ οὕτως ἡμῖν δοκεῖ παντὸς ἄξια εἶναι, ὥστε πάντες τὸ καταλιπεῖν αὐτὰ πάντων μάλιστα φεύγομεν.

Whom then, said Socrates, can we find receiving greater advantages from any persons than from their parents ? Children, whom their parents have brought from non-existence into existence, to behold so many beautiful objects, and to partake of so many blessings which are granted by the gods to men : blessings which appear to us so inestimable that we shrink in the highest degree from abandoning them.

The Low-Minded and the Honourable.

Memorab. ii. 3.

Τὰ μὲν γὰρ πονηρὰ ἀνθρώπια οὐκ ἂν ἄλλως μᾶλλον ἕλοις, ἢ εἰ διδοίης τι· τοὺς δὲ καλοὺς κἀγαθοὺς ἀνθρώπους προσφιλῶς χρώμενος μάλιστ᾽ ἂν κατεργάσαιο.

The low-minded thou canst not gain otherwise than by giving them something; whereas the honourable and the good thou mayest best attract by treating them in a kindly manner.

We are Members of One Body to assist Each Other.

Memorab. ii. 3.

Νῦν μὲν γὰρ οὕτως, ἔφη, διάκεισθε, ὥσπερ, εἰ τὼ χεῖρε, ἃς ὁ θεὸς ἐπὶ τὸ συλλαμβάνειν ἀλλήλαιν ἐποίησεν, ἀφεμένω τούτου τράποιντο πρὸς τὸ διακωλύειν ἀλλήλω· οὐκ ἂν πολλὴ ἀμαθία εἴη καὶ κακοδαιμονία, τοῖς ἐπ᾽ ὠφελείᾳ πεποιημένοις ἐπὶ βλάβῃ χρῆσθαι;

At present, Socrates said, you are in the same state as if the two hands, which the gods have made to assist each other, should neglect their duty, and begin to impede each other. Would it not be a great folly and misfortune to use for our hurt what was intended for our benefit?

The Qualifications of a General.

Memorab. iii. 1.

Ἀλλὰ μὴν, ἔφη ὁ Σωκράτης, τοῦτό γε πολλοστὸν μέρος ἐστὶ στρατηγίας. Καὶ γὰρ παρασκευαστικὸν τῶν εἰς τὸν πόλεμον τὸν στρατηγὸν εἶναι χρὴ, καὶ ποριστικὸν τῶν ἐπιτηδείων τοῖς στρατιώταις, καὶ μηχανικὸν, καὶ ἐργαστικὸν, καὶ ἐπιμελῆ, καὶ καρτερικὸν, καὶ ἀγχίνουν, καὶ φιλόφρονά τε καὶ ὠμὸν, καὶ ἁπλοῦν τε καὶ ἐπίβουλον, καὶ φυλακτικόν τε καὶ κλέπτην, καὶ προετικὸν, καὶ ἅρπαγα, καὶ φιλόδωρον, καὶ πλεονέκτην, καὶ ἀσφαλῆ, καὶ ἐπιθετικὸν, καὶ ἄλλα πολλὰ καὶ φύσει, καὶ ἐπιστήμῃ δεῖ τὸν εὖ στρατηγήσοντα ἔχειν.

But, said Socrates, this is much the best part of the qualifications of a general: for a general must be skilful in preparing what is necessary for war, furnishing provisions for his soldiers ; a man of mechanical contrivance and activity, careful, persevering, sagacious, affectionate, and, at the same time, severe ; open, yet crafty ; careful of his own, yet ready to steal from others ; profuse, yet rapacious ; lavish of presents, yet eager to acquire money ; cautious, yet enterprising,—and many other qualities, both natural and acquired, which he who would fill the office of general well, must possess.

Best Men most Pious before God.

Memorab. iii. 9.

Καὶ ἀρίστους δὲ καὶ θεοφιλεστάτους.

Socrates said that the best men were the most observant of the worship of the gods.

So Joshua (xxiv. 15)—" As for me and my house, we will serve the Lord."

The Looks and Gestures show the Character.

Memorab. iii. 10.

'Αλλὰ μὴν καὶ τὸ μεγαλοπρεπές τε καὶ ἐλευθέριον, καὶ τὸ ταπεινόν τε καὶ ἀνελεύθερον, καὶ τό σωφρονητικόν τε καὶ φρόνιμον, καὶ τὸ ὑβριστικόν τε καὶ ἀπειρόκαλον καὶ διὰ τοῦ προσώπου καὶ διὰ τῶν σχημάτων, καὶ ἑστώτων καὶ κινουμένων ἀνθρώπων διαφαίνει.

Surely, also, nobleness and generosity of disposition, lowness of mind and illiberality, modesty and intelligence, insolence and stupidity, are shown both in the countenance and gestures of men, whether they are standing or moving.

God shows Himself by His Works.

Memorab. iv. 3.

Καὶ ὁ τὸν ὅλον κόσμον συντάττων τε καὶ συνέχων, ἐν ᾧ πάντα καλὰ καὶ ἀγαθά ἐστι, καὶ ἀεὶ μὲν χρωμένοις ἀτριβῆ τε, καὶ ὑγιᾶ, καὶ ἀγήρατον παρέχων, θᾶττον δὲ νοήματος ἀναμαρτήτως ὑπηρετοῦντα, οὗτος τὰ μέγιστα μὲν πράττων ὁρᾶται, τάδε δὲ οἰκονομῶν ἀόρατος ἡμῖν ἐστιν.

He who arranges and holds together the whole universe, in which are all things beautiful and good, and who preserves it always unimpaired, undisordered, and undecaying, obeying His will swifter than thought, and without irregularity, is Himself manifested only in the performance of His mighty works, but is invisible to us while He is regulating them.

The Soul of Man.

Memorab. iv. 3.

Καὶ ἀνθρώπου γε ψυχὴ, εἴπερ τι καὶ ἄλλο τῶν ἀνθρωπίνων, τοῦ θείου μετέχει.

The soul of man is part of the Divinity, if there be any part of man really so.

So Romans (v. 5)—" Because the love of God is shed abroad in our hearts by the Holy Ghost, which is given unto us."

ALL MEN HAVE WORSHIPPED GOD FROM THE BEGINNING OF THE WORLD.

Memorab. iv. 4.

Παρὰ πᾶσιν ἀνθρώποις πρῶτον νομίζεται τοὺς θεοὺς σέβειν.

It is believed that the gods have been worshipped by all men from the very beginning.

See (Lat.) God, no nation, &c.

HONOUR THE GODS ACCORDING TO YOUR MEANS.

Memorab. iv. 3.

Χρὴ οὖν μηδέν ἐλλείποντα κατὰ δύναμιν τιμᾶν τοὺς θεοὺς, θαρρεῖν τε καὶ ἐλπίζειν τὰ μέγιστα ἀγαθά. Οὐ γὰρ παρ' ἄλλων γ' ἄν τις μείζω ἐλπίζων σωφρονοίη, ἢ παρὰ τῶν τὰ μέγιστα ὠφελεῖν δυναμένων.

It becomes the man who fails in no ways to honour the gods to the best of his means, to be of good courage, hoping for the greatest blessings ; for no one can with reason hope for greater blessings from others than from those who are able to benefit him most.

So Psalms (xxxii. 10)—" He that trusteth in the Lord, mercy shall encompass him about."

THE OMNIPRESENCE OF GOD.

Anab. ii. 5.

Τὸν γὰρ θεῶν πόλεμον οὐκ οἶδα οὔτ' ἀπὸ ποίον ἂν τάχους φεύγων τὶς ἀποφύγοι, οὔτ' εἰς ποῖον ἂν σκότος ἀποδραίη, οὔθ ὅπως ἂν εἰς ἐχυρὸν χωρίον ἀποσταίη. Πάντη γὰρ πάντα τοῖς θεοις ὕποχα, καὶ πανταχῆ πάντων ἴσον οἱ θεοὶ κρατοῦσι.

The fury of the gods I know not how any man may escape by flight, nor in what darkness he could hide himself, nor in what strong place he could take refuge. For all things are everywhere subject to the control of the gods, and they rule in the armies of heaven as among the inhabitants of the earth.

See Psalm cxxxix. 7.

RULERS ARE NECESSARY.

Anab. iii. 1.

Ἄνευ γὰρ ἀρχόντων οὐδὲν ἂν οὔτε καλὸν οὔτε ἀγάθον γένοιτο, ὡς μὲν συνελόντι εἰπεῖν, οὐδαμοῦ· ἐν δὲ δὴ τοῖς πολεμικοῖς παντά πασιν.

For without rulers and directors nothing honourable or useful can be accomplished, to sum up in one word, anywhere ; but chiefly of all in the affairs of war.

The Brave live where the Coward dies in Battle.

Anab. iii. 1.

'Εντεθύμημαι δ' ἔγωγε, ὦ ἄνδρες, καὶ τοῦτο, ὅτι, ὁπόσοι μὲν μασ-
τεύουσι ζῆν ἐκ παντὸς τρόπου ἐν τοῖς πολεμικοῖς, οὗτοι κακῶς τε καὶ
αἰσχρῶς ὡς ἐπιτοπολὺ ἀποθνήσκουσιν· ὁπόσοι δὲ τὸν μὲν θάνατον
ἔγνωσαν πᾶσι κοινὸν εἶναι καὶ ἀναγκαῖον ἀνθρώποις, περὶ δὲ τοῦ καλῶς ἀποθνήσκειν ἀγωνίζονται, τούτους ὁρῶ μᾶλλόν πως εἰς τὸ γῆρας
ἀφικνουμένους, καὶ, ἕως ἂν ζῶσιν, εὐδαιμονέστερον διάγοντας.

For I have always observed this, fellow-soldiers, that those who
use every means to save their lives in war generally meet with a
base and disgraceful death ; whereas those who feel that death is
the common and allotted fate of all men, I often see to reach old
age, and while they live they enjoy a happy life.

Praise is the Sweetest of all Sounds.

Hier. i. 15.

Ἥδιστον ἄκουσμα ἔπαινος.

The sweetest of all sounds is praise.

See (Lat.) Man fond of praise.

Impossible to do all Things well.

Cyrop. viii. 2, 5.

Ἀδύνατον οὖν πολλὰ τεχνώμενον ἄνθρωπον πάντα καλῶς ποιεῖν.

It is impossible for a man attempting many things to do them
all well.

ADDENDA.

GOD IS SELF-SUFFICIENT.

Aristot. Ethic. ad. Eudem. vii. 12.

Δῆλον ὡς οὐδενὸς προσδεόμενος ὁ θεός.

It is evident that God stands in need of nothing.

So Psalms (l. 9, 10)—"I will take no bullock out of thy house, . . . for every beast of the forest is mine."

GOD IS OUR FATHER AND CREATOR.

Diogen. Laert. vii. 1, 147.

Εἶναι δὲ τὸν μὲν δημιουργὸν τῶν ὅλων καὶ ὥσπερ πατέρα πάντων, κοινῶς τε, καὶ τὸ μέρος αὐτοῦ τὸ διῆκον διὰ πάντων.

God is the Creator of the universe, and also the Father of all things, in common with all, and a part of Him penetrating all things.

CHAOS.

Diogen. Laert. Prœm. iii. 4.

Ἦν ποτέ τοι χρόνος οὗτος ἐν ᾧ ἅμα πάντ' ἐπεφύκει.

There was once a time when all things were huddled together.

So Genesis (i. 1)—"In the beginning God created the heaven and the earth."

GRANDEUR OF THE WORLD.

Diogen. Laert. i. 35.

Κάλλιστον, ὁ κόσμος· ποίημα γὰρ θεοῦ.

The world is perfectly beautiful, for it is a work of God.

Good Spirits.

Orpheus.

Σῷ δὲ θρόνῳ πυρόεντι παρεστᾶσιν πολύμοχθοι
ἄγγελοι, οἷσι μέμηλε, βροτοῖς ὡς πάντα τελεῖται.

Round thy fiery throne stand labour-loving angels, whose business it is that all things be accomplished for men.

So Revelation (v. 11)—" And I beheld, and I heard the voice of many
angels round about the throne."

Evil Spirits.

Plutarch. de Orac. iv. 16.

Εἰσὶ γὰρ ὡς ἐν ἀνθρώποις, καὶ ἐν δαίμοσιν ἀρετῆς διαφοραί.

As among men, so also among spirits there are differences of
goodness.

So 1 Peter (iii. 22)—" Angels and authorities and powers being made
subject unto Him."

Evil Spirits.

Orpheus.

Δαίμονες ὃν φρίσσουσι θεῶν τε δέδοικεν ὅμιλος.

(God) whom the devils fear, and the multitude of gods regard
with awe.

So James (ii. 19)—"Thou believest that there is one God, thou doest
well ; the devils also believe and tremble."

The Way to the Grave.

Diogen. Laert. 287.

Εὔκολον τὴν εἰς ᾅδου ὁδόν· καταμύοντας γοῦν ἀπιέναι.

The way to the world below is easy, for men go to it with shut
eyes.

So 1 Samuel (xx. 3)—"There is but a step between thee and death."

"Cast your Care upon God."

Stobæ. Anthol. iii. 312.

Πάντα προστίθει θεοῖσι· πολλάκις μὲν ἐκ κακῶν
ἄνδρας ὀρθοῦσιν μελαίνῃ κειμένους ἐπὶ χθονί.
Πολλάκις δ᾿ ἀνατρέπουσι καὶ μάλ᾿ εὖ βεβηκότας.

Cast all thy care upon the gods : they often raise men from misfortunes, who are lying on the dark earth ; and again, often overthrow those who are enjoying the height of prosperity.

So 1 Peter (v. 7)—"Casting all your care upon Him ; for He careth for you."

ETERNAL FIRE.

Plutarch. de Andiend. Poët. 17.

Ἄϊδου τινὲς ἀνοίγονται πύλαι βαθεῖαι καὶ ποταμοὶ πυρὸς ὁμοῦ.

Deep doors open towards hell, and rivers of fire are seen.

So Matthew (xxv. 41)—"Depart from me, ye cursed, into everlasting fire, prepared for the devil and his angels."

THE WICKED.

Diogen. Laert. viii. c. i. 31.

Τὰς ἀκαθάρτους ψυχὰς δεῖσθαι ἐν ἀρρήκτοις δεσμοῖς ὑπὸ Ἐρινύων.

The impure souls are bound by the Furies in chains that cannot be broken.

So Matthew (xxii. 13)—"Bind him hand and foot, and take him away, and cast him into outer darkness."

WHO INJURES THEE ?

Plutarch. de Cons. ad. Apoll. III. c. xxx. 1, p. 117, A.

Θεὸς δέ σοι πῆμ' οὐδὲν ἀλλ' αὐτὸς σὺ σοί.

It is not God that injures thee, but thou thyself.

So Deuteronomy (iv. 31)—"God will not forsake thee, neither destroy thee."

GOD IS ETERNAL.

Plutarch. de Iside. et Osir. c. ix., p. 11, 354, C.

Ἐγώ εἰμι πᾶν τὸ γεγονὸς καὶ ὄν, καὶ ἐσόμενον.

"I am all that was, and is, and will be." This was an inscription on a temple at Saïs.

So Revelation (i. 8)—"The Lord which is, and which was, and which is to come, the Almighty."

GOD EVERYWHERE PRESENT.

Plutarch. de Superst. c. iv. p. 166. D.

Ὁ τὴν τῶν θεῶν ἀρχὴν ὡς τυραννίδα φοβούμενος σκυθρωπὴν καὶ ἀπαραίτητον, ποῦ μεταστῇ, ποῦ φύγῃ,

ποίαν γῆν ἄθεον εὕρῃ, ποίαν θάλασσαν; εἰς τί καταδὺς
τοῦ κόσμου μέρος καὶ ἀποκρύψας σεαυτὸν, ὦ ταλαίπωρε,
πιστεύσεις, ὅτι τὸν θεὸν ἀποπέφευγας ;

He who fears the government of the gods as being gloomy and inexorable, whither will he go, whither will he flee? What land or what sea will he find without God? Into what part of the earth wilt thou descend and hide thyself, O unhappy wretch! where thou canst escape from God?

So Psalms (cxxxix. 7-10)—"Whither shall I go from Thy Spirit? or whither shall I flee from Thy presence? If I ascend up into heaven, Thou art there: if I make my bed in hell, behold, Thou art there. If I take the wings of the morning, and dwell in the uttermost parts of the sea; even there shall Thy hand lead me, and Thy right hand shall hold me."

God is All-wise.

Stobæ. Anthol. xi. 279.

Ἀεὶ τὰ πάντα διοικεῖ τε ὁ θεὸς καὶ ζώει αὐτὸς ἐν αὐτῷ κεκτημένος τὴν σοφίαν.

God always directs all things and lives in Himself since He is Wisdom itself.

So Romans (xvi. 27)—"To God, only wise, be glory."

God is Holy.

Stobæ. Serm. i. 13.

Διαφέρει δέ θεὸς ἀνθρώπου ἀγαθοῦ, ὅτι θεὸς μὲν εἰλικρινῆ καὶ διυλισμένην ἔχει τὴν ἀρετὴν ἀπὸ παντὸς τοῦ θνητοῦ πάθεος.

God differs from the good man this much, that God is Virtue pure and uncorrupted, free from all human weakness.

So Revelation (xv. 4)—"For Thou only art holy."

God.

Stobæ. Eclog. Phys. i. 94.

Θεός ἐστι νόος καὶ ψυχὰ καὶ τὸ ἀγεμονικὸν τῷ σώματος κόσμῳ. Ὁ θεὸς αὐτὸς οὔτε ὁρατὸς οὔτε αἰσθητὸς ἀλλὰ λόγῳ μόνον καὶ νόῳ θεωρητός. Τὰ δ᾽ ἔργα αὐτῷ καὶ πράξεις ἐναργέες τε καὶ αἰσθηταί ἐστι πάντεσιν ἀνθρώποις.

God is Mind and Spirit, and the Ruler of the whole mass of the universe. God can neither be seen nor perceived by any sense, but is only comprehended by words and the mind's eye. But His works and what He does are evident, and perceived by all men.

So 1 Corinthians (ii. 11, 14)—"Even so the things of God knoweth no man, but the Spirit of God. But the natural man receiveth not the things of the Spirit of God. Neither can he know them, because they are spiritually discerned."

Dionysius Cato says—

"Si Deus ut animus, nobis ut carmina dicunt,
Hic tibi præcipue purâ sit mente colendus."

"If God be a Spirit, as our poets say, He is to be specially worshipped with a pure mind."

So John (iv. 24)—"God is a Spirit : and they that worship Him must worship Him in spirit and in truth."

A Thousand Years as one Day.

Plutarch. de Ser. Num. Vind. c. ix., p. 554.

Τοῖς γε θεοῖς πᾶν ἀνθρωπίνου βίου διάστημα, τὸ μηδέν ἐστι· καὶ τὸ νῦν, ἀλλὰ μὴ πρὸ ἐτῶν τριάκοντα, τοιοῦτόν ἐστιν οἷον τὸ δείλης, ἀλλὰ μὴ πρωΐ, στρεβλοῦν ἢ κρεμαννύναι τὸν πονηρόν.

To the gods the whole span of a man's life is as nothing; the same as if a culprit is tortured or hung in the evening, and not in the morning.

So Psalms (xc. 4)—"For a thousand years in Thy sight are but as yesterday when it is past, and as a watch in the night."

Heaven our Fatherland.

Diogen. Laert. xi. 2, 7.

Πρὸς τὸν εἰπόντα, Οὐδέν σοι μέλει τῆς πατρίδος ; Εὐφήμει, ἔφη, ἐμοὶ γὰρ καὶ σφόδρα μέλει τῆς πατρίδος, δείξας τὸν οὐρανόν.

To one who said to Anaxagoras, "Hast thou no regard for thy fatherland?" "Softly," said he, "I have great regard for my fatherland," pointing to heaven.

So John (xiv. 2)—"In my Father's house are many mansions : if it were not so, I would have told you. I go to prepare a place for you."

The Release of the Soul.

Plutarch. de Iside. et Osir.

Ὅταν δὲ ἀπολυθεῖσαι αἱ ψυχαὶ μεταστῶσιν εἰς τὸ ἀειδὲς καὶ ἀόρατον καὶ ἀπαθὲς καὶ ἁγνόν, αὐταῖς ἡγεμών ἐστι καὶ βασιλεὺς ὁ θεὸς, ἐξηρτημέναις ἀπ' αὐτοῦ καὶ θεωμέναις ἀπλήστως καὶ ποθούσαις τὸ μὴ φατὸν μηδὲ ῥητὸν ἀνθρώποις κάλλος.

When the souls set free go to the unseen, invisible, unfelt, and pure region, God is their Leader and King, as they depend upon Him, looking on Him without ever being satisfied, and striving after a beauty which cannot be expressed or described.

So Psalms (xxxvi. 9)—"In Thy light shall we see light."

Punishment of the Wicked.

Lucian. Jov. Confut. iv. 261.

Οὐ γὰρ οἶσθα, ἡλίκας μετὰ τὸν βίον οἱ πονηροὶ τὰς κολάσεις
ὑπομένουσιν, ἢ ἐν ὅσῃ οἱ χρηστοὶ εὐδαιμονίᾳ διατρίβουσιν;

Dost thou not know what punishment awaits the wicked after
this life, and in what happiness the good live?

So Matthew (xxv. 46)—"And these shall go away into everlasting punishment · but the righteous into life eternal."

Friends and Enemies.

Diogen. Laert. i. 6, 91.

Τὸν φίλον δεῖ εὐεργετεῖν, ὅπως ἢ μᾶλλον φίλος, τὸν δὲ ἐχθρὸν
φ\ον ποιεῖν.

We must treat our friend kindly, that he may be still more a
f end, but make our enemy our friend.

So Romans (xii. 20)—"Therefore, if thine enemy hunger, feed him; if he
thirst, give him drink: for in so doing thou shalt heap coals of fire on his
head."

Voiceless Law.

Æschyl. Fragm. (Stobæ. Ecl. Phys. vii.)

Ὁρᾷς δίκην ἄναυδον οὐχ ὁρωμένην
εὕδοντι καὶ στείχοντι καὶ ˙καθημένῳ,
ἑξῆς δ᾿ ὁπάζει δόχμιον, ἄλλοθ᾿ ὕστερον.
Οὐδ᾿ ἐγκαλύπτει νὺξ κακῶς εἰργασμένα˙
ὅτι δ᾿ ἂν ποιῇς δεινόν, νόμιζ᾿ ὁρᾶν τινα.

Thou seest voiceless Law, which is not seen by thee while thou
sleepest, walkest, and sittest, but which accompanies thee now
sideways, now behind. For the darkness of night does not conceal thy evil deeds, but whatsoever crime thou hast committed,
doubt not some one has seen it.

The Mighty Power of God.

Æschyl. Fragm. (Stobæ. Ecl. Phys. vii.)

Ὦ Ζεῦ, πάτερ Ζεῦ, σὸν μὲν οὐρανοῦ κράτος˙
σὺ δ᾿ ἔργ᾿ ἐπουρανίων τε κἀνθρώπων ὁρᾷς
λεωργὰ κἀθέμιστα˙ σοὶ δὲ θηρίων
ὕβρις τε καὶ δίκη μέλει.

O Jupiter! father Jupiter! thine is the mighty power of heaven; thou lookest on the villanous and lawless acts of the celestials

and of men; it belongs to thee to watch the violence of, and pass sentence on, the deeds of savage beasts.

A Prosperous Fool.

Æschyl. Fragm. (Stobæ. Ethic. iv.)

Ἢ βαρὺ φόρημ' ἄνθρωπος εὐτυχῶν ἄφρων.

A senseless fool in prosperity is certainly a heavy burden.

So Proverbs (xxx. 22)—"A fool, when he is filled with meat."

The Results of Indulgence in Wine.

Æschyl. Fragm. (Stobæ. Ethic. xviii.)

Κάτοπτρον εἴδους χαλκός ἐστ', οἶνος δὲ νοῦ.

Bronze is the mirror to reflect the face, wine to reflect the mind.

One God.

Orpheus.

Εἶς ἐστ' αὐτογενής, ἑνὸς ἔκγονα πάντα τέτυκται,
οὐδέ τις ἐσθ' ἕτερος χωρὶς μεγαλοῦ βασιλῆος.

There is one self-existent Being; everything that is generated is produced by Him alone, and there is no one that rules except the Almighty King.

So Ephesians (iv. 6)—"One God and Father of all, who is above all, and through all, and in you all."

Holiness to the Lord.

Clem. Alex. Strom. v. 551.

Αγνὸν χρὴ νηοῖο θυώδεος ἐντὸς ἰόντα
ἔμμεναι· ἀγνείη δ' ἔστι φρονεῖν ὅσια.

"He who enters within the precincts of the temple full of incense, ought to be holy: holiness is to have holy thoughts." This is the inscription on the Temple at Epidaurus.

So Genesis (xxviii. 17)—"How dreadful is this place! this is none other but the house of God, and this is the gate of heaven."

Curse not your Enemy.

Diogen. Laert. i. 4, 4.

Φίλον μὴ λέγειν κακῶς, ἀλλὰ μηδὲ ἐχθρόν.

Speak not ill of your friend, and curse not your enemy.

So Matthew (v. 44)—"But I say unto you, Love your enemies, bless them that curse you, do good to them that hate you, and pray for them which despitefully use you, and persecute you."

Men know not the Truth.

Lucian. Jov. Confut. iv. 246.

Ἄνθρωποι ὄντες ἀγνοοῦσι τὸ ἀληθές.

As they are men, they know not the truth.

So Ephesians (iv. 18)—"Having the understanding darkened, . . . because of the blindness of their heart."

God seen by None.

Orpheus.

Οὐδέ τις αὐτὸν
εἰσορᾷ θνητῶν, αὐτὸς δέ γε πάντας ὁρᾶται.

No mortal sees God, but He sees all.

So Exodus (xx. 21)—"But Moses drew near unto the thick darkness where God was."

We should Strive after God.

Plato. Leg. iv. 716.

Φύσει εἶναι θεὸν πάσης σπουδῆς ἄξιον.

By nature God is worthy of every pains to be acquainted with.

So Colossians (iii. 2)—"Set your affections on things above, not on things on the earth."

Law of God.

Diogen. Laert. cxi. 51.

Δικαιοσύνην θεοῦ νόμον ὑπελάμβανεν.—Νόμου διαιρέσεις δύο· ὁ μὲν γὰρ αὐτοῦ, γεγραμμένος· ὁ δὲ, ἄγραφος·—ὁ κατὰ ἔθη γενόμενος, οὗτος ἄγραφος καλεῖται.

He (Plato) regarded justice as God's law. There are two divisions of law, the one written, the other unwritten: the one arising from nature and habit is called unwritten.

This is referred to by Seneca (Controv. 1)—

"Jura non scripta, sed omnibus scriptis certiora."

"Laws not written, but more certain in their influence than laws that are written."

So Romans (ii. 14, 15)—"For when the Gentiles, which have not the law.

do by nature the things contained in the law, these, having not the law, are a law unto themselves : which show the work of the law written in their hearts, their conscience also bearing witness, and their thoughts the meanwhile accusing or else excusing one another."

Conscience is a God.

Poet. Gnom. 139, *ed. Weig.*

Βροτοῖς ἅπασιν ἡ συνείδησις θεός.

Conscience is a god to all men.

Seneca (Ep. 41), says much to the same effect :—

" Sacer intra nos spiritus sedet, malorum bonorumque nostrorum observator et custos ; hic prout a nobis tractatus est, ita nos ipse tractat."

" There is a sacred spirit seated within us, the observer and guardian of what is good and bad to us ; he, according as he is treated by us, so he treats us."

So Romans (ix. 1)—" I lie not, my conscience also bearing me witness in the Holy Ghost."

Words.

Æschyl. Fragm. (Stobæ. Ethic. xx.)

Ὀργῆς ματαίας εἰσὶν αἴτιοι λόγοι.

Words are the cause of senseless wrath.

So Proverbs (xv. 1)—" A soft answer turneth away wrath ; but grievous words stir up anger."

Oaths.

Æschyl. Fragm. (Stobæ. Ethic. xxvii.)

Οὐκ ἀνδρὸς ὅρκοι πίστις, ἀλλ' ὅρκων ἀνήρ.

Oaths are not the cause why a man is believed, but the character of the man is the cause why the oath is believed.

The Distressed.

Æschyl. Fragm. (Stobæ. Ethic. xxix.)

Φιλεῖ δὲ τῷ κάμνοντι συσπεύδειν θεός.

God loves to assist those in distress.

So Psalms (xlvi. 1)—"God is our refuge and strength, a very present help in trouble."

The Wicked in Prosperity.

Æschyl. Fragm. (Stobæ. Ethic. xlv.)

Κακοὶ γὰρ εὖ πράσσοντες οὐκ ἀνάσχετοι.

The wicked in prosperity are not to be borne.

So Psalms (x. 2)—"The wicked in his pride doth persecute the poor ; let them be taken in the devices that they have imagined."

The Race of Man.

Æschyl. Fragm. (Stobæ. Ethic. xcviii.)

Τὸ γὰρ βρότειον σπέρμ' ἐφήμερα φρονεῖ,
καὶ πιστὸν οὐδὲν μᾶλλον ἢ κάπνου σκία.

For the race of man has thoughts that last merely for a day, and are no more real than the shadow of smoke.

So Psalms (cii. 3)—"For my days are consumed like smoke, and my bones are burned as an hearth."

Fortune.

Æschyl. Fragm. (Stobæ. Phys. x.)

Τύχα μερόπων ἀρχὰ καὶ τερμα !
  τὺ καὶ σοφίας τιμὰν
  βροτέοις ἐπέθηκας ἔργοις·
καὶ τὸ καλὸν πλέον ἢ κακὸν ἐκ *σέθεν.*
  "Α τε χάρις λάμπει
περὶ σὰν πτέρυγα χρύσεον·
καὶ τὸ τεᾷ πλάστιγγι δοθὲν
  μακαριστότατον τελέθει.
Σὺ δ' ἀμαχανίας πόρον εἶδες ἐν ἄλγεσι,
καὶ λαμπρὸν φάος ἄγαγες ἐν σκότῳ,
  προφερέστατα θεῶν.

Fortune, thou beginning and end of mortals! it is thou that bestowest the glory of wisdom on human works ; and the good more than the bad spring from thee. Beauty and grace shine around thy golden wing ; and whatever is weighed by thy scales is most blessed. In the midst of distresses thou pointest the way out of difficulties ; thou sheddest a bright light in darkness, thou most excellent of divinities.

Man dies only at his Fated Moment.

Æschyl. Fragm. (Euseb. Præp. Evang. xiii.)

'Αλλ' οὔτε πολλὰ τρώματ' ἐν στέρνοις λαβὼν
θνήσκει τις, εἰ μὴ τέρμα συντρέχοι βίου·
οὔτ' ἐν στέγῃ τις ἥμενος παρ' ἑστίᾳ
φεύγει τι μᾶλλον τὸν πεπρωμένον μόρον.

But neither does any one, however many wounds he may have received, die, unless he has run his allotted term of life ; nor does any man, though he sits quietly by the fireside under his own roof, escape the more his fated doom.

So Job (vii. 1)—"Is there not an appointed time to man upon earth ? are not his days also like the days of an hireling ?"

Hatred of Death not just.

Æschyl. Fragm. (Plutarch. de Consol.)

Ὡς οὐ δικαίως θάνατον ἔχθουσιν βροτοί,
ὅσπερ μέγ᾽ ἐστ᾽ ἴαμα τῶν πολλῶν κακῶν.

Men do not with justice hate death, which is a mighty remedy for many woes.

The Industrious.

Æschyl. Fragm. (Clemens. Alex. Strom. iv)

Τῷ πονοῦντι δ᾽ ἐκ θεῶν
ὀφείλεται, τέκνωμα τοῦ πόνου, κλέυς.

Glory, begotten of labour, is a debt owed by the gods to the man who works laboriously.

So Proverbs (xiii. 11)—"He that gathereth by labour shall increase."

Power and Justice.

Æschyl. Fragm. (Schol. in Homer. ap. Valcken.)

Ὅπου γὰρ ἰσχὺς συζυγοῦσι καὶ δίκη,
πόια ξυνωρὶς τῆσδε καρτερώτερα ;

When power and justice unite, what stronger pair is there than this?

Death to be preferred to a Life of Wickedness.

Æschyl. Fragm. (Stobæ. ed Grot. Ti. cxxii.)

Ζωῆς πονηρᾶς θάνατος εὐπορώτερος,
τὸ μὴ γενέσθαι δ᾽ ἐστὶν ἢ πεφυκέναι
κρεῖσσον κακῶς πράσσοντα.

Death is more desirable than a wicked life. And not to be born is better than to lead a disgraceful life.

Death spurns Gifts.

Æschyl. Fragm. (Stobæ. Ethic. cxvii.)

Μόνος θεῶν γὰρ Θάνατος οὐ δώρων ἐρᾷ,
οὔτ᾽ ἄν τι θύων, οὔτ᾽ ἐπισπένδων λάβοις·
οὐ βωμός ἐστιν, οὐδὲ παιωνίζεται.
μόνου δὲ Πειθὼ δαιμόνων ἀποστατεῖ.

Death alone of the gods cares not for gifts, nor wilt thou accept
sacrifices nor libations.   No altar is erected to thee. nor is any
hymn sung to thy praise.   Persuasion stands aloof from thee alone
of the gods.

Death the Physician.

Æschyl. Fragm. (Stobæ. Ethic. cxxi.)

*Ὦ θάνατε παιὰν, μή μ᾽ ἀτιμάσῃς μολεῖν·
μόνος γὰρ εἶ σὺ τῶν ἀνηκέστων κακῶν
ἰατρός· ἄλγος δ᾽ οὐδὲν ἅπτεται νεκρῶν.

O thou saviour Death ! do not despise me coming to thee, for
thou alone art the physician of incurable woes ; no sorrow reaches
the dead.

See (Lat.) Death, a reprieve ; close of all pains.

Justice watches over the Dead.

Æschyl. Fragm. (Stobæ. Ethic. cxxvi.)

Καὶ τοὺς θανόντας εἰ θέλεις ἐνεργετεῖν,
ἢ γοῦν κακουργεῖν, ἀμφιδεξίως ἔχει,
οἷς μήτε χαίρειν μήτε λυπεῖσθαι πάρα.
ἡμῶν γε μέντοι Νέμεσις ἐσθ᾽ ὑπερτέρα,
καὶ τοῦ θανόντος ἡ δίκη πράσσει κότον.

If thou wishest to do good or ill to the dead, thou hast in both
ways those who have neither joy nor sorrow ; yet recollect that
there is an avenging goddess superior to us, and Justice feels a
jealousy over the character of the dead.

Anger.

Fr. Stobæus Floril. xxii. 2.

Πολλάκις ἀνθρώπων ὀργὴ νόον ἐξεκάλυψε
κρυπτόμενον, μανίης πουλὺ χερειότερον.

Anger often has revealed the concealed thoughts of men much
more effectually than madness.

Force without Prudence.

Fr. Stobæus Floril. li. 17.

Πρὸς σοφίᾳ μὲν ἔχειν τόλμαν μάλα σύμφορόν ἐστιν,
χωρὶς δὲ βλαβερὴ καὶ κακότητα φέρει.

Force attended by wisdom is very advantageous, but ruinous apart; it brings calamity.

See (Lat.) The violent.

Children.

Fr. Eveni ex Plut. Morall. xi. 497, A.

Ἢ δέος ἢ λύπη παῖς πατρὶ πάντα χρόνον.

A child is either a cause of fear or grief during the whole of life.

Inexorable Necessity.

Fr. Philetæ ex Stobœ. Eclog. v. 4, 156, *Heeren.*

Ἰσχυρὰ γὰρ ἐπικρατεῖ ἀνδρὸς ἀνάγκη,
ἢ ῥ᾽ οὐδ᾽ ἀθανάτους ὑποδείδιεν, οἵ τ᾽ ἐν Ὀλύμπῳ
ἔκτοσθεν χαλεπῶν ἀχέων οἴκους ἐκάμοντο.

For inexorable necessity has power over man; it has no dread of the immortals, who have houses in Olympus away from sad grief.

See (Lat.) Necessity.

Speak not Ill of the Dead.

Fr. Archilochi ex Stobœ. Floril. cxxv. 5.

Οὐ γὰρ ἐσθλὰ κατθανοῦσι κερτομέειν ἐπ᾽ ἀνδράσιν.

For it is not good to jeer at the dead.

Old Age.

Fr. Herodis ex Stobœ. Floril. cxvi. 21.

Ἐπὴν τὸν ἑξηκοστὸν ἥλιον κάμψῃς,
Ὦ Γρύλλε, Γρύλλε, θνῆσκε καὶ τέφρη γίγνευ·
ὡς τυφλὸς οὐκέκεινα τοῦ βίου καμπτηρ·
ἤδη γὰρ αὐγὴ τῆς ζωῆς ἀπήμβλυνται.

S

When thou hast got past the sixtieth sun, O Gryllus! die and become ashes : how dark is the angle of life after that! for now the light of life is dimmed.

The Way to Hades.

Fr. Simonidis ex Stobœ. Floril. cxx. 9.

Εὔθυμος ὢν ἔρεσσε τὴν ἐπ' Ἄϊδος
ἀταρπὸν ἕρπων· οὐ γάρ ἐστι δύσβατος
οὐδὲ σκαληνὸς οὐδ' ἐνίπλειος πλάνης,
ἰθεῖα δὴ μάλιστα καὶ κατακλινὴς
ἅπασα, κἠκ μεμυκότων ὁδεύεται.

Being of good cheer, proceed creeping along the road to Hades : for it is not of difficult passage nor uneven, nor full of windings, but all very straight and down-hill, and can be gone along with shut eyes.

The Two Pleasantest Days in regard to Woman.

Fr. Hipponactis ex Stobœ. Floril. lxviii. 8.

Δύ' ἡμέραι γυναικὸς εἰσὶν ἥδισται,
ὅταν γαμῇ τις κἀκφέρῃ τεθνηκυῖαν.

The two pleasantest days of a woman are her marriage day and the day of her funeral.

How we Live.

Fr. Simonidis ex Stobœ. Floril. cxxi. 1.

Πολλὸς γὰρ ἄμμιν εἰς τὸ τεθνάναι χρόνος, ζῶμεν δ' ἀριθμῷ παῦρα κακῶς ἔτεα.

For there is plenty of time to die, but we lead a bad life for a few years.

Life of Men here Below.

Fr. Simonidis ex Plut. Morall. xi. 107, B.

Ἀνθρώπων ὀλίγον μὲν κάρτος, ἄπρηκτοι δὲ μεληδόνες,
αἰῶνι δὲ παύρῳ πόνος ἀμφὶ πόνῳ·
ὁ δ' ἄφυκτος ἐπικρέμαται θάνατος·
κείνου γὰρ ἴσον λάχον
μέρος οἵ τ' ἀγαθοὶ ὅστις τε κακός.

The vigour of man is but for a day, and his sorrows are incurable. Labour upon labour comes for a few short years ; unavoidable death is impending ; for the good and the bad have got an equal share of it.

OLD AGE.

Fr. Anacreontis ex Stobæ. Floril. cxviii. 13.

Πολιοὶ μὲν ἡμῖν ἤδη κρόταφοι κάρη τε λευκόν,
χαρίεσσα δ' οὐκέτ' ἤβη πάρα, γηράλεοι δ' ὀδόντες,
γλυκεροῦ δ' οὐκέτι πολλὸς βιότου χρόνος λέλειπται.
Διὰ ταῦτ' ἀνασταλύζω θαμὰ Τάρταρον δεδοικώς.
Ἀΐδεω γὰρ ἐστι δεινὸς μυχὸς, ἀργαλέη δ' ἐς αὐτὸν
κάθοδος· καὶ γὰρ ἑτοιμον καταβάντι μὴ ἀναβῆναι.

Now we have grey temples and a white head; no longer is graceful youth present, but decayed teeth; no longer is there remaining much time of pleasant life. Therefore, often do I drop the tear, dreading Tartarus. The gulf of Hades is terrific, and the way to it painful, for it is not for man, once down, to re-ascend.

NO ONE ALWAYS HAPPY.

Fr. Bacchylidis ex Stobæ. Floril. xcviii. 27.

Θνατοῖσι μὴ φῦναι φέριστον
μηδ' ἀελίου προσιδεῖν φέγγος·
ὄλβιος δ' οὐδεὶς βροτῶν πάντα χρόνον.

It is best for mortals not to be born, nor to see the light of the sun. No one is fortunate all his life.

MARRIED LIFE *v.* BACHELORHOOD.

Fr. Susario ex Stobæ. Flor. lxix. 2.

Ἀκούετε λεῴ· Σουσαρίων λέγει τάδε,
υἱὸς Φιλίνου Μεγαρόθεν Τριποδίσκιος·
κακὸν γυναῖκες, ἀλλ' ὅμως, ὦ δημόται,
οὐκ ἔστιν οἰκεῖν οἰκίαν ἄνευ κακοῦ.
Καὶ γὰρ τὸ γῆμαι καὶ τὸ μὴ γῆμαι κακόν.

Hear, ye people! Susario, son of Philinus, of the village of Tripodiscus, in Megaris, says this —"Women are an evil; but yet, O fellow-citizens! we cannot conduct our household affairs without this evil. For to marry and not to marry is equally an evil.

OLD AGE.

Fr. Com. Gr. p. 129. (*Pharecrates.*)

Ὦ γῆρας, ὡς ἐπαχθὲς ἀνθρώποισιν εἶ
καὶ πανταχῆ λυπηρόν, οὐ καθ' ἓν μόνον.

’Εν ᾧ γὰρ οὐδὲν δυνάμεθ’ οὐδ’ ἰσχύομεν,
σὺ τηνικαῦθ’ ἡμᾶς προδιδάσκεις εὖ φρονεῖν.

O old age! how burdensome and grievous everywhere art thou!
only not in one thing; for when we fail in strength and power,
thou teachest us at that time to use our understanding with wisdom.

The Dregs of Life are like Vinegar.

Fr. (Antiphanes) Com. Gr. p. 570.

Σφόδρ’ ἐστὶν ἡμῶν ὁ βίος οἴνῳ προσφερής·
ὅταν ᾖ τὸ λοιπὸν μικρόν, ὄξος γίνεται.
Πρὸς γὰρ τὸ γῆρας ὥσπερ ἐργαστήριον
ἅπαντα τἀνθρώπεια προσφοιτᾷ κακά.

Our life has great resemblance to wine; when little of it remains, it becomes vinegar: for all human ills proceed to old age
as to a workshop.

“Riches take unto Themselves Wings.”

Fr. (Alexis) Com. Gr. p. 764.

Τῶν γὰρ ἀγαθῶν τὸν πλοῦτον ὕστατον τίθει·
ἀβεβαιότατον γάρ ἐστιν ὧν κεκτήμεθα.
Τὰ δ’ ἄλλ’ ἐπιεικῶς τοῖς ἔχουσι παραμένει.

Regard riches as the last of the good things of this life, for they
are the least certain of the things we possess: other things remain
with those who possess them in a moderate degree.

Woman difficult to be Guarded.

Fr. (Alexis) Com. Gr. p. 765.

Οὐκ ἔστιν οὔτε τεῖχος οὔτε χρήματα,
οὐδ’ ἄλλο δυσφύλακτον οὐδὲν ὡς γυνή.

Neither walls nor goods nor anything is more difficult to be
guarded than woman.

Pleasure.

Fr. (Alexis) Com. Gr. p. 765.

Φεῦγ’ ἡδονὴν φέρουσαν ὕστερον βλάβην.

Fly pleasure, which at last brings loss.

POVERTY.

Fr. (*Timocles*) *Com. Gr.* p. 808.

Πολλοὺς γὰρ ἐνίοθ᾽ ἡ πενία βιάζεται
ἀνάξι᾽ αὑτῶν ἔργα παρὰ φύσιν ποιεῖν.

Poverty sometimes forces many to do acts unworthy of them.
contrary to their natural disposition.

OLD AGE AND MARRIAGE.

Fr. Com. Gr. p. 1248.

Παραπλήσιον πρᾶγμ᾽ ἐστὶ γῆρας καὶ γάμος.
Τυχεῖν γὰρ αὐτῶν ἀμφοτέρων σπουδάζομεν,
ὅταν δὲ τύχωμεν ὕστερον λυπούμεθα.

Old age and marriage have a great resemblance to each other,
for we are in a hurry to obtain both ; and when we have obtained
them, then we are grieved.

BRAVE MEN THE BEST BULWARK OF A CITY.

Fr. (*Alcœus*) *Poet. Ecloq.* p. 268.

Οὐ λίθοι
τειχέων εὖ δεδομαμένοι,
ἀλλ᾽ ἄνδρες πόλιος πύργος ἀρήϊοι.

It is not stones of a city, well built in, but brave men, that are
the bulwark of a city.

HISTORY IS PHILOSOPHY TEACHING BY EXAMPLES.

Dionysius, Ars Rhet. c. xi. s. 2, p. 212. (*Tauchnitz.*)

Τοῦτο καὶ Θουκυδίδης ἔοικε λέγειν περὶ ἱστορίας λέγων· ὅτι καὶ
ἱστορία φιλοσοφία ἐστὶν ἐκ παραδειγμάτων.

Thucydides (i. 22, 4) too seems to say this, when speaking in regard to history, that history is philosophy teaching by examples.

TO-MORROW.

Fr. (*Simonides*) *ex Stobœ. Flor.* cv. 52.

Ανθρωπος ἐὼν μή ποτε εἴπῃς ὅ τι γίγνεται αὔριον,
μηδ᾽ ἄνδρα ἰδὼν ὄλβιον, ὅσσον χρόνον ἔσσεται.
Ὠκεῖα γὰρ οὐδὲ τανυπτερύγον μυίας
οὕτως ἀ μετάστασις.

Being mortal, thou canst not tell what will be to-morrow, nor
when thou seest a man happy, how long he will be so, for not so
swift is the flight of the wide-winged fly.

THE COWARD.

Fr. (Simonides) ex Stobœ. Floril. cxviii. 6.

'Ο δ' αὖ θάνατος κίχε καὶ τὸν φυγόμαχον.

Death overtakes even the coward.

See Hor. Od. iii. 2, 14.

THE ADVANTAGE OF SILENCE.

Fr. (Simonides) Poet. Eleg. p. 398.

Ἔστι καὶ σιγᾶς ἀκίνδυνον γέρας.

The reward of silence, too, is attended by no danger.

See Hor. Od. iii. 2, 25.

TIME IS THE TOUCHSTONE OF EVERYTHING.

Fr. (Simonides) ex Stob. Eclog. i. 9, 15.

Οὐκ ἐστὶν μείζων βάσανος χρόνου οὐδενὸς ἔργου,
ὃς καὶ ὑπὸ στέρνοις ἀνδρὸς ἔδειξε νόον.

There is no greater touchstone of every deed than time, which
shows the mind of man in his breast.

HEALTH.

Fr. (Ariphron) Athen. xv. 702, A.

Ὑγίεια, πρεσβίστα μακάρων, μετὰ σεῦ ναίοιμι τὸ λειπόμενον
βιοτᾶς, σὺ δέ μοι πρόφρων σύνοικος εἴης·
εἰ γάρ τις ἢ πλούτου χάρις ἢ τεκέων,
ἢ τᾶς ἰσοδαίμονος ἀνθρώποις βασιληΐδος ἀρχᾶς,
ἢ πόθων, οὓς κρυφίοις Ἀφροδίτας ἄρκυσιν θηρεύομεν,
ἢ εἴ τις ἄλλα θεόθεν ἀνθρώποισι τέρψις ἢ πονων ἀμπνοὰ
   πέφανται
μετὰ σεῖο, μάκαιρ' Ὑγίεια,
τέθαλε πάντα καὶ λάμπει χαρίτων ἔαρ·
σέθεν δὲ χωρὶς οὔτις εὐδαίμων ἔφυ.

Health! thou most august of the blessed goddesses, with thee
may I spend the remainder of my life, mayest thou benignly dwell
with me; for if there be any pleasure to be derived from riches,

or children, or royal power making men equal to the gods, or longing desire, which we hunt after with the secret nets of Venus, or if there be any other delight bestowed on men by the gods, or respite from pains, with thee, blessed Health, all these flourish and beam effulgent like the spring arising from the Graces ; without thee no one is happy.

ONE GOD WITH VARIOUS NAMES.

Aristot. de Mundo v. init.

Εἶς ὢν πολυώνυμός ἐστι κατονομαζόμενος τοῖς πάθεσι πᾶσιν, ἅπερ αὐτὸς νεοχμεῖ.

Though He be one Being, God has many names, being called according to the variety of outward conditions of things, which He is always changing.

So 1 Corinthians (viii. 4)—" There is none other God but one."

ONLY ONE GOD.

Plutarch. de Iside. et Osir. c. 67.

Ἑνὸς λόγου τοῦ πάντα κοσμοῦντος καὶ μιᾶς προνοίας ἐπιτροπευούσης καὶ δυνάμεων ὑπουργῶν ἐπὶ πάντα τεταγμένων ἕτεραι παρ' ἑτέροις κατὰ νόμους γεγόνασι τιμαὶ καὶ προσηγορίαι.

To the one Mind that arranges the whole universe, and one Providence set over all, and to the helping Powers that are or dained to all, different honours and names are given by different people through legal enactments.

So Psalms (xlvi. 10)—"I will be exalted among the heathen, I will be exalted in the earth "

See (Lat.) God and nature the same.

FALSE SWEARING.

Plut. Lys. 8.

Ὁ ὅρκῳ παρακρουόμενος τὸν μὲν ἐχθρὸν ὁμολογεῖ δεδιέναι, τοῦ δὲ θεοῦ καταφρονεῖν.

He who deceives by an oath, acknowledges that he fears his enemy, but despises God.

So Matthew (v. 33)—"Thou shalt not forswear thyself, but shalt perform unto the Lord thine oaths."

Rest from Work.

Plut. Num. 36.

'Εν ταῖς προπομπαῖς καὶ ὅλως τῶν ἱερέων ταῖς πομπαῖς προηγοῦντο κήρυκες ἀνὰ τὴν πόλιν ἐλινύειν κελεύοντες καὶ τὰ ἔργα καταπαύοντες.

In all kinds of attendance and of escorting the priests' heralds went before throughout the city, ordering men to keep the festival and to cease from work.

So Exodus (xxiii. 12)—"Six days shalt thou do thy work, and on the seventh day thou shalt rest."

Men are Bad through Ignorance of what is Good.

Plut. Artax. c. 28.

Βούλονται δ' οἱ πλεῖστοι τὰ φαῦλα δι' ἀπειρίαν τῶν καλῶν καὶ ἄγνοιαν.

Most men are wicked, because they have never known or tried the enjoyment of virtuous conduct.

So Ephesians (iv. 18)—"Having the understanding darkened, being alienated from the life of God through the ignorance that is in them, because of the blindness of their hearts."

Bad Men are Slaves.

Plut. Lat. Min. c. 67.

Δούλους εἶναι τοὺς φαύλους ἅπαντας.

All bad men are slaves.

So John (viii. 34)—"Whosoever committeth sin is the servant of sin;" and 2 Corinthians (iii. 17)—"Where the Spirit of the Lord is, there is liberty."

Evil Counsel.

Plut. Artax. c. 28.

Ταχεῖα πειθὼ τῶν κακῶν ὁδοιπορεῖ.

Evil counsel is swift in its march.

So Romans (xvi. 18)—"By good words and fair speeches deceive the hearts of the simple;" and Wisdom of Solomon (iv. 12)—"For the bewitching of naughtiness doth obscure things that are honest."

God is slow in Punishing.

Solon. Ὑποθῆκαι, l. 25.

Τοιαύτη Ζηνὸς πέλεται τίσις, οὐδ' ἐφ' ἑκάστῳ
ὥσπερ θνητὸς ἀνὴρ γίγνεται ὀξύχολος·
αἰεὶ δ' οὔτι λέληθε διαμπερές, ὅστις ἀλιτρόν
θυμὸν ἔχῃ· πάντως δ' ἐς τέλος ἐξεφάνη.
Ἀλλ' ὁ μὲν αὐτίκ' ἔτισεν, ὁ δ' ὕστερον· εἰ δὲ φύγωσιν
αὐτοὶ μηδὲ θεῶν μοῖρ' ἐπιοῦσα κίχῃ,
ἤλυθε πάντως αὖθις· ἀναίτια ἔργα τίνουσιν
ἢ παῖδες τούτων ἢ γένος ἐξοπίσω.

Such is the way that God punishes, not on every occasion as a mortal man, who is quick in temper. Whoever commits transgression is not altogether forgotten, but in every case is found out at last. He punishes one immediately, another at a later period ; if they escape, and approaching fate does not come hastily upon them, it comes in every case at last : either their children or their distant posterity suffer for their deeds, though themselves guiltless.

So Sirach (v. 5)—"Say not, I have sinned, and what harm hath happened to me ? for the Lord is long-suffering, He will in no way let thee go."

What is Good in thee is of God.

Diogen. Laert. i. 5, 88.

Οἱ πλεῖστοι κακοί· ὅ, τι ἂν ἀγαθὸν πράττῃς, εἰς θεοὺς ἀνάπεμπε.

Most men are bad ; whatever good thing thou doest, ascribe to God.

So Philippians (ii. 13)—"For it is God which worketh in you, both to will and to do of His good pleasure ;" and Sirach (vi. 37)—"Let thy mind meditate continually on God's commandments: He shall establish thine heart, and give thee wisdom at thine own desire."

God is a Spirit.

Stobæ. Eclog. Phys. i. 98.

Τοιαύτα φύσις θεῷ οὔτε ἐκ δύο συνήρμοσται, ψυχᾶς καὶ σώματος· ἃ γὰρ διόλω ἐντὶ ψυχά· οὔτ' ἐναντίων τινῶν· τὰ γὰρ ἐναντία καὶ κρατεῖν καὶ κρατεῖσθαι πέφυκεν.

This divine nature is not compounded of two, spirit and body, for it is wholly spirit ; nor is it of things opposed, for things that are opposed are formed by nature to rule and to be ruled.

God is Omniscient.

Lucian. Epigr. iv. 571.

'Ανθρώπους μὲν ἴσως λήσεις ἄτοπόν τι ποιήσας,
οὐ λήσεις δὲ θεοὺς οὐδέ λογιζόμενος.

When thou committest a sin, thou mayest perhaps conceal it from men, but thou wilt not conceal it from God, however much thou strivest.

So Wisdom of Solomon (i. 6)—"For God is a true beholder of man's heart."

God deprives of his Reason him whom He wishes to Destroy.

Stobæ. Serm. II. de Malitia.

Θεὸς μεν αἰτίαν φύει βροτοῖς,
Ὅταν κακῶσαι δῶμα παμπήδην θέλῃ.

God originates a cause to men, when He wishes utterly to destroy a family.

In the story to'ᴅ by the Christian Broker ("Arabian Nights") we have—
"When God willeth an event to befall a man, who is endowed with reason,
and hearing, and sight,
He deafeneth his ears, and blindeth his heart, and draweth his reason
from him as a hair,
Till, having fulfilled His purpose against him, He restoreth him his reason
that he may be admonished."

ENGLISH INDEX.

T

INDEX

OF

PASSAGES FROM THE HOLY SCRIPTURES ILLUSTRATED IN THIS WORK.

THE END.